The New St. Martin's Handbook

The New St. Martin's Handbook

Andrea Lunsford
THE OHIO STATE UNIVERSITY

Robert Connors
UNIVERSITY OF NEW HAMPSHIRE

With a section for multilingual writers by
Franklin E. Horowitz
TEACHERS COLLEGE, COLUMBIA UNIVERSITY

BEDFORD / ST. MARTIN'S
BOSTON / NEW YORK

For Bedford / St. Martin's

Publisher: Marilyn Moller
Developmental Editor: John Elliott
Production Editor: Diana M. Puglisi
Production Supervisor: Joe Ford
Marketing Manager: Karen Melton
Editorial Assistant: Eva Peck
Art Director: Lucy Krikorian
Text and Cover Design: Anna George
Copy Editor: Judith Green Voss
Indexer: Riofrancos and Co. Indexes
Composition: Monotype Composition Co., Inc.
Printing and Binding: R. R. Donnelley & Sons Co.

President: Charles H. Christensen
Editorial Director: Joan E. Feinberg
Editor in Chief: Nancy Perry
Director of Editing, Design, and Production: Marcia Cohen
Managing Editor: Erica T. Appel

Library of Congress Catalog Card Number: 98-84406

First edition, 1989. Second edition, 1992. Third edition, 1995.

Manufactured in the United States of America.

4 3 2 1 0 9
f e d

For information, write: Bedford / St. Martin's, 75 Arlington Street, Boston, MA 02116 (617-426-7440)

ISBN: 0-312-25117-3 (hardcover)
0-312-25101-7 (paperback)

Acknowledgments

Gwendolyn Brooks. "We Real Cool" from *Blacks* by Gwendolyn Brooks. Copyright ©1991 by Gwendolyn Brooks. (Chicago, IL: Third World Press, 1991). Reprinted with the permission of the author.

(Acknowledgments and copyrights are continued at the back of the book on pages 792–793, which constitute an extension of the copyright page.)

Preface

These are high times for teachers and students of writing. New genres emerge almost daily, online and off. Our vocabulary is changing and growing before our very eyes, our spelling and even our capitalization along with it. Stylistic elements long beyond an ordinary writer's grasp – varied fonts and type sizes, color, boxes, icons, sidebars, graphics, even sound – now call out for our experimentation. In a time of such challenging possibilities, what's a poor handbook author to do? In our case, the answer seemed clear: we needed to take on the challenges posed by the new technologies and to provide answers to the many new questions students are now asking.

The New St. Martin's Handbook is the result. In it, we've pursued two major goals. First of all, we've taken advantage of some of the new stylistic elements ourselves to make this book easier to navigate and to use. Second, we have added crucial new material about writing, reading, researching, and collaborating online.

Easy to use, easy to understand

An appealing new size and format. We've made the *Handbook* shorter and wider, with a more colorful and more modern design that makes the book much easier to use. Key reference information – correction codes, most cross-references, URLs, multilingual notes – is out in the margins and thus easy to find on the page.

Boxed editing tips. All handbooks provide rules, but *The New St. Martin's Handbook* goes the extra step by providing tips that help students apply those rules to their own writing. Printed on pale green stripes for easy reference, these editing tips appear on the second page of most chapters and elsewhere in the book as well.

Attention to everyday language. Many chapters open with brief vignettes of language in everyday use, linking the material in the handbook (and the classroom) to students' lives beyond the classroom. And everyday language pervades the book, giving students clear, straightforward answers they can easily understand.

A guide to editing the most common errors. The Introduction serves as a "crisis control center" for writers, providing guidelines for recognizing, understanding, and editing the most common errors. Screened pale orange for easy reference and with cross-references into the rest of the book, this section works nicely as a brief handbook within the larger handbook.

Hand-edited examples. Most examples are now shown hand-edited, allowing students to see the error and its revision at a glance. Black pointers and boldface type make these examples easy to spot on the page.

A user-friendly index. Even the index is especially easy to use, listing everyday words (such as *that* or *which*) as well as grammatical terms (such as *relative pronoun*), so that students can find information even if they don't know grammatical terminology.

Crucial new advice about writing online

A new research study of online writing habits. Like its previous editions, *The New St. Martin's Handbook* is informed by new research into student writing. Through a nationwide survey of teachers and students, we tried to determine how and when students work online, what problems they most often encounter, and what questions they have about online writing and research.

FAQs about online writing and research. Where do you break a URL when it won't fit on one line? How important are grammatical conventions in email and other online writing? How do online audiences differ from print audiences? Answers to these and other frequently asked questions about online work can be found on the orange pages at the beginning of each part of this book.

Annotated URLs throughout. Because so much information is now available on the Web, we've added URLs referring students to sites especially useful to writers. These URLs can be found in the margins throughout the book and also in a directory on pp. 735 – 751. All Web sites listed here can be accessed through links on *The New St. Martin's Handbook*'s own Web site, <www.bedfordstmartins.com/nsmhandbook>.

A full section on using the new media. While earlier editions focused primarily on the medium of print, *The New St. Martin's Handbook* includes a full section on using various media – oral, print, and electronic. Chapter 50 offers guidance on preparing and giving oral presentations. Chapter 51 provides advice about various kinds of graphics and print or online documents students may be asked to produce, and Chapter 52 offers guidance in using hypertext, PowerPoint, and other forms of multimedia.

A completely revised research section with guidance in new forms of online research as well as in library and field research. New technologies have forever changed the face of research, and much of the research students now do takes place online. While continuing to help students understand how to use print and field research and offering guidelines for synthesizing and interpreting sources and data, our research section now also offers specific guidelines for finding electronic resources and using and evaluating them critically and carefully. In addition, we include up-to-date guidelines for citing and documenting sources in MLA, APA, CBE, and Chicago styles.

Other highlights

For all the dramatic changes resulting from electronic forms of communication, student writers still work to understand and to enter academic discourse – and to think about the audiences, purposes, and rhetorical situations their writing addresses. Online or off, students carry out research, collaborate, and work to draft, design, edit, and proofread their work. *The New St. Martin's Handbook* continues to provide helpful, up-to-date advice in all these areas.

Attention to writing, not just to correctness. Our ongoing research and experience convince us that students need extensive practice in writing, and in writing that is compelling and powerful. Like all composition handbooks, this book provides guidance in checking and revising for correctness. Unlike most others, however, it also pays attention to rhetorically effective writing throughout the book, including the chapters dealing with grammar and mechanics. The chapter on adjectives and adverbs (Chapter 12), for instance, asks students to focus not only on how to use adjectives and adverbs correctly – but also on the more compelling question of why and in what circumstances to use them at all. The end punctuation chapter (Chapter 32) provides rules for using periods, question marks, and exclamation points, and, in addition, asks students to try revising a piece of their own writing for sentence variety using declarative, interrogatory, and exclamatory structures. In other words, we present grammar and mechanics as tools to use for a writing purpose, not simply to use "correctly."

Attention to rhetorical situations. Since writing always responds in some ways to its context – including audiences, purposes, and other texts – we put special emphasis on the importance of understanding rhetorical situations that student writers encounter. Beginning with Chapter 2, we urge students to think critically and imaginatively about what they want to do in writing, whom they want to reach, and how they want to do so. This emphasis on rhetorical choice is present throughout the text, as we show students over and over again how to go about making particular choices (which word to use, what example to choose for particular situations).

Two other chapters put special focus on rhetorical situations. Chapter 29, "Considering Others: Building Common Ground," rests on two major assumptions: that writers will wish to address readers whose backgrounds, values, and perspectives will vary widely and will also be different from their own; and that language offers a primary means of both respecting and bridging such differences. Based on Kenneth Burke's theories of identification and division in language use, this chapter asks students to take a close look at how the words they use can help them include – or exclude – their readers. Chapter 28, "Considering Language Variety," discusses standard, regional, ethnic, and occupational varieties of English, showing students how different varieties of English (and of other languages as well) can be used appropriately and effectively, not only outside of school but also in their academic writing. This chapter helps students "shift language gears" as needed between the contexts of community, workplace, and school.

Systematic attention to reading. Because we see writing and reading as inextricably linked (and particularly so in online environments), we include reading instruction throughout. Not only do we offer extensive guidance to help students read observantly and critically – whether evaluating a draft, an argument, a paragraph, or an online source – but we also present reading as one more tool that can help improve writing and research skills. The first chapter offers explicit guidelines for reading, as do the chapters on research, on the disciplines, on literature, and on using and evaluating sources.

Attention to critical thinking throughout. Beginning with the Introduction, "Thinking Critically about Your Writing," this book focuses on critical thinking in almost every chapter. The Introduction provides a framework to help students approach their writing with a critical eye, including guidelines to help them check for the most common errors. This framework continues through subsequent chapters, with editing guidelines to help students think about and revise their drafts along with end-of-chapter activities that ask them to think critically about issues in the chapter and to apply what they learn to their own writing

Attention to the needs of multilingual writers. Franklin Horowitz of Teachers College, Columbia University, provides coverage of grammatical and rhetorical issues of concern to multilingual writers in Part 11 of *The New St. Martin's Handbook.* In addition, marginal notes throughout the book offer advice on topics where multilingual writers need extra help, in language-specific terms whenever possible.

Attention to the needs of basic writers. Several features of this text are especially appropriate for basic writers. The focus on reading not only provides instruction and practice in critical reading but also offers practice drawing conclusions and inferences from reading – practice that is valuable for basic writers. In addition, the focus on their own writing helps basic writers to make crucial links between their first-year writing courses and other academic and professional writing they might do. Finally, the use of actual student sentences and essays throughout the book and the emphasis on everyday uses of language invite students – and especially basic writing students – to link the language of this handbook and the classrooms it is used in with their lives beyond the classroom.

Informed by research into student writing

From the beginning, *The St. Martin's Handbook* has always been informed by our own research into student writing. In fact, we first began work on *The St. Martin's Handbook* in 1983, when we realized that most college handbooks were based on research on student writing conducted fifty years earlier. Our own historical studies had convinced us that student writing and what teachers think of as "good" writing change over time, and so we began by gathering a nationwide sample of over 21,000 marked student essays and carefully analyzed a scientifically stratified sample of those to identify the twenty surface errors most characteristic of contemporary student writing. One of the most intriguing discoveries was how many of these errors related in some way to visual memory – wrong words, wrong or missing verb endings, missing or misplaced possessive apostrophes, even the *its/it's* confusion – which suggests that students today are less familiar with visual aspects of print-based writing than students once were. One effect of an oral, electronic culture seems to be that students do not automatically bring with them the visual knowledge of writing conventions that textwise writers possess and use effortlessly.

This problem of visualization was most pronounced in terms of spelling errors, which occurred – by a factor of 300 percent – more frequently than any other error, and so we next undertook a second research study examining all the spelling errors in our sample of student essays. Out of this study came our own list of the words student writers misspell most frequently, as well as the discovery that most of these words are homonyms. These findings further suggest that the visual aspect of spelling is particularly important. In a world of secondary orality, we need to find ways to help students visualize their language.

Since our original research revealed that many errors are governed not so much by hard-and-fast rules as by large-scale rhetorical decisions, we turned back to the 21,000 essays in a third study, looking this time at content and organization. Again, we got some provocative results. We found, for instance, that these aspects of the composing process are as important to readers today as they were over two thousand years ago: the use of good reasons, proof, evidence, and examples – the rhetorical tools of invention – elicited the most consistent commentary from teachers, followed by commentary on the ways in which such materials were arranged and organized. These findings strongly suggest that readers are interested in the *what* as well as the *how* of student writing. More specifically, they suggest that student writers need to become conversant with traditional methods of analysis and patterns of development not simply to demonstrate that they can recognize the difference between classification and division, for example, but rather to gain the understanding and assent of their readers.

Good research, of course, always generates new research questions that beg to be pursued. As we approached the third edition, we found ourselves wondering, "How are we doing here?" Were we providing the guidance that student writers need? Next, then, we turned to the students using *The St. Martin's Handbook,* aiming to find out how students actually use our book and what we could do to make it more useful. Their astute judgments and suggestions and their complex realization that good writing means more than just following rules led us, in the third edition, to add a chapter on oral presentations (95 percent of our student respondents asked for help here); to develop a special section providing help for multilingual writers; to provide guidelines for using varieties of English (and other languages) in academic writing; and to offer more help with using and documenting electronic sources.

However, even as the third edition went to press reflecting all we had learned from over a decade of ongoing research, we already had our sights set on what we needed to do next. Our student respondents had convinced us that the increased availability of home computers, access to the Internet, and the advent of something called the World Wide Web (which was a very, very new electronic space back in 1992) would have a swift and major impact on student writing. Thus for *The New St. Martin's Handbook* we again conducted a nationwide survey, this time of 2,500 students and 53 teachers, about their computer-based and online work.

This study confirmed our intuitions that almost all students (95 percent) are doing most of their work on a computer, with all the challenges that entails. In addition, we found that most students (71 percent) have experimented with using the Web – and that those who have not want to do so. Most important, students voiced a number of concerns and questions about how to get online and how to work effectively once there. In their questions, they often seemed to be straining for language to describe writing situations that were new and unfamiliar. Our attempts to address these concerns appear throughout this edition in the FAQs.

Looking back over fifteen years of research gives us a renewed sense of the dramatic changes that have taken place in the writing that students do. We began our research with a historical understanding that writing conventions and notions of "correctness" change over time. Our ongoing investigations have only emphasized this linguistic fact of life: in 1985, we were counting conventional "errors" in student essays that were largely typewritten (some were even handwritten); today, students work in virtual or paperless environments where what counts as error is daily called into question. Formerly simple choices – about what words to capitalize, for example – are now much more complex, as some new words include internal capitalization (*HotJava,* for example) and some online writers eschew capitalization altogether.

This complexity makes even more important the clear message we have always tried to send about the role of "correctness" in standard academic English. Without oversimplification, our goal now as always is to help student writers make effective choices.

Throughout, *The New St. Martin's Handbook* seeks to serve students as a ready reference that will help them make appropriate grammatical and rhetorical choices. Beyond this immediate goal, we hope to guide students in understanding and experiencing for themselves the multiple ways in which truly good writing always means more than just following the rules. Truly good writing, we believe, means applying those rules in specific rhetorical situations for specific purposes and with specific audiences in ways that will bring readers and writers, teachers and students, to spirited conversation as well as to mutual understanding and respect.

A wide array of ancillaries

Several useful resources accompany *The New St. Martin's Handbook.* All are available free of charge to instructors. The *Workbook* is available for students to purchase.

TEACHING RESOURCES

Instructor's Notes
by Andrea Lunsford and Cheryl Glenn

The New St. Martin's Guide to Teaching Writing,
by Robert Connors and Cheryl Glenn

Assigning, Responding, Evaluating: A Writing Teacher's Guide, Third Edition
by Edward M. White

The St. Martin's Sourcebook for Writing Tutors
by Christina Murphy and Steve Sherwood

The St. Martin's Manual for Writing in the Disciplines
by Richard Bullock

STUDENT RESOURCES

The New St. Martin's Workbook
by Lex Runciman

The New St. Martin's Pocket Guide to Research and Documentation

Preparing for the CLAST

Preparing for the TASP

ELECTRONIC RESOURCES

The New St. Martin's Handbook Online
An HTML version of the complete handbook, including Internet links and interactive exercises

The New St. Martin's Handbook Web Site
http://www.bedfordstmartins.com
/nsmhandbook

Acknowledgments

The New St. Martin's Handbook remains a collaborative effort in the best and richest sense of the word. As always, we are enormously indebted to Marilyn Moller, whose efforts as publisher on this edition – as on all others – have been quite simply invaluable. For this edition, we have also had the extraordinary gift of John Elliott's astute, attentive (and, we are tempted to say, "truly awesome") editing: The marks of his painstakingly careful work are everywhere present – and greatly appreciated. Diana Puglisi has managed the entire handbook from manuscript to bound book with skill and grace – and together with Joe Ford has made an enormously complex project run smoothly. In many matters large and small, Eva Peck has provided valuable assistance. For the wonderful new cover and interior design, we are indebted to Anna George. We are fortunate indeed to have had Karen Melton as our marketing manager; in our experience, she sets the standard. And as always, we are grateful to the entire SASMP sales force; they are the *best.*

The New St. Martin's Handbook is for the first time available in an imaginative and highly interactive HTML version. For his extraordinary work in creating this electronic version, we thank John Sisson.

From its inception, this text has had the benefit of meticulous and insightful reviews of Franklin Horowitz, Teachers College of Columbia University – and, starting with the last edition, Frank has contributed a superb section for multilingual writers. Special thanks also go to colleagues Richard Bullock, Mike Hennessy, Christina Murphy, Marcia Muth, Lex Runciman, Steve Sherwood, and Ed White, who contributed uncommonly innovative books to accompany the handbook, and to Cheryl Glenn for her outstanding work on the *Instructor's Notes* and *The St. Martin's Guide to Teaching Writing.* And finally, we thank friend and colleague Nick Carbone, whose extensive and detailed reviews of all new material relating to online writing have been, for us, the *sine qua non.* Thanks also to Nick for the up-to-date and helpful URLs and annotations found throughout the margins of the text.

As always, we feel extremely fortunate to have had the contributions of very fine student writers, whose work appears throughout this text: Kelly Barr, Laura Brannon, Leah Clendening, Tisha Clevinger, Kristin Convery, Mike Dangler, Amy Dierst, Sean Finnerty, Jennifer Georgia, Jennifer Gerkin, Jeff Loew, Patricia Medley, Leslie Shaffer, Zakiyyah Shabazz, and Tamara Washington. For this edition, we are especially grateful to Shannan Palma, whose imaginative essay on movie heroes appears in Chapter 44. In addition, we are grateful to the many instructors who generously shared their assignments with us: Karen Burke LeFevre and Kenneth Connor of Rensselaer Polytechnic Institute; Richard Shiels, Ray Jazerinak, Lori Mathis, and Louis Ulman of the Ohio State University; Keith Walters of the University of Texas; and Tom Bredehoft of the University of Northern Colorado.

For *The New St. Martin's Handbook,* we have been blessed with a group of very special reviewers. Their incisive comments, queries, criticisms, and suggestions have improved this book immeasurably: Alan Ainsworth, Houston Community College Central; J. Robert Baker, Fairmont State College; Valerie Balester, Texas A & M University; Dennis Baron, University of Illinois at Urbana-Champaign; Anne Beaufort, American University; Sue Beebe, Southwest Texas State University; Charles Boyd, Genesee Community College; Santi Buscemi, Middlesex County College; Nick Carbone, Marlboro College; Paul Chambers, Sonoma State University; Sandra Clark, Anderson University; Elizabeth Curtin, Salisbury State University; Michel de Benedictis, Miami Dade Community College; Raymond Dumont, University of Massachusetts, Dartmouth; Ray Foster, Scottsdale Community College; Laurie George, University of Washington; Barbara Goldstein, Hillsborough Community College; Gordon Grant, Baylor University; Wilford Griffin, Norfolk State University; Kay Harkins, Point Loma Nazarene College; Michael Hennessy, Southwest Texas State University; Don Hettinga, Calvin College; Dave Hogsette, Long Island Institute of Technology; Maurice Hunt, Baylor University; Peggy B. Jolly, University of Alabama at Birmingham; Wayne Keene, University of

Tennessee at Martin; Lynn Kennedy, Darton College; Steven D. Krause, Southern Oregon State College; Kitty Locker, Ohio State University; Quentin Martin, Loyola University; Patrick McMahon, Tallahassee Community College; Jaime Armin Mejia, Southwest Texas State University; Marshall Myers, Eastern Kentucky University; Amoena Norcross, Tri-County Technical College; Annie S. Perkins, Norfolk State University; William Provost, University of Georgia; Jan Zlotnik Schmidt, State University of New York at New Paltz; Dorothy H. Schnare, Berea College; J. W. Schouten, Solano College; David Teague, Dutchess Community College; Audrey Wick, University of Texas at Arlington; Sallie Wolf, Arapahoe Community College; and Linda Woodson, University of Texas at San Antonio.

We are grateful to the thousands of students who responded so thoughtfully to our survey about online writing. Their names are far too numerous to list here, but we would like to thank the instructors who distributed surveys to their students and offered their own thoughtful and helpful advice: James Allen, College of Du Page; Ellen Arl, University of South Carolina at Sumter; Jay Atkinson, University of Massachusetts, Lowell; Evelyn Beck; Sue Belles; S. K. Benson; Randall A. Clack, Elizabeth City State University; Ben Davis Jr.; Ruth Fischer, George Mason University; Beverly Furlow; Stephanie Garcia; Yohma Gray, DePaul University; Russell Greinke, Central Missouri State University; G. Grunow, Henry Ford Community College; Sandra Hall, Corning Community College; Kay Harkins, Point Loma Nazarene College; Mike Harsh, Hagerstown Junior College; Anne Hawkes, Charleston Southern University; Don Hettinga, Calvin College; Diane Hyer, Truett-McConnell College; Mary B. Joseph; Linda A. Julian, Furman University; Pamela Katzir, Florida International University; Lynn Kennedy, Darton College; William King, Western State College; Noel J. Kinnamon, Mars Hill College; Penne Laubenthal, Athens State College; Kitty Locker, Ohio State University; Elaine Marshall, Barton College; John F. Minter, Truman College; Stephen R. Mohr, Heidelberg College; Michael Montgomery, Life College; Donald M. Moser, Johnson C. Smith University; Kathleen Nickerson, St. Clair County Community College; Linda O'Kane, University of Illinois at Chicago; Erin Page; Janet T. Palmer; Gosia Pasternak-McMurry, West Valley College; Mildred Pate, Georgia Southern University; Kathy Patterson; Laurine Paule, Southeastern Community College; Helen Pyke, Southern Adventist University; Mike Ritchie, Ohio State University; Michael I. Roehm, American University; Sarah Sloane, University of Puget Sound; Louise Taylor, Meredith College; Melanie Thomas; Cloe M. Vincent; Janice R. Walker, University of South Florida; Denise Weeks, Nebu State University; Lynn West, Spokane Community College; George Whitaker, Florence-Palington Technical College; Barbara Williamson, Brevard Community College; and Laura E. Yowell, Hutchinson Community College.

Finally, we wish to offer very special thanks to the extraordinary community of teacher-researchers at the Breadloaf School of English, whose responses to this text have helped to shape and refine its goals. More special thanks go to Ohio State colleagues Melissa Goldthwaite, Jeff Loew, Jennifer Cognard-Black, and Jennifer Phegley, whose good-natured help tracking down sources, identifying readings, and looking for examples has been just what we needed – every time. Thanks are likewise extended to Jim Fredal, who provided very helpful information on speaking and writing. And to our very special friends, Keith Walters, Beverly Moss, Cheryl Glenn, and – always – Lisa Ede, we are continually grateful.

We could go on and on in praise of the support and help we have received, for we are fortunate (beyond our wildest dreams, as our mentor Edward P. J. Corbett would say) to be part of a unique scholarly community, one characterized by compassion as well as passionate commitment to students and to learning. We remain grateful to be among you.

Andrea Lunsford
Robert Connors

A Note to Students

Our goal in writing *The New St. Martin's Handbook* has been to produce a book that will help you become competent and compelling writers, a book that you can use easily throughout – and beyond – your college years.

The introductory chapter of this book, "Thinking Critically about Your Writing," is our attempt to provide a tool for analyzing your use of the writing patterns and strategies most college students need to practice. The introduction – and indeed, the entire book – offers a critical thinking program for building on strengths and eliminating weaknesses in your own writing.

Throughout this text, we thus ask that you become accustomed to carefully analyzing your own prose. In most chapters, we will not only provide explanations and opportunities for practice but also ask you to apply the principles presented directly to your own writing. If you follow our directions, they will guide you in becoming a systematic self-critic – and a more effective writer. And since writing and reading in many ways go hand in hand, many chapters will also offer you a chance to read with an eye for various logical or stylistic or conventional aspects of writing, often in the work of some of the finest writers in English. Sometimes you will be asked to try to imitate their sentences. As your writing improves, so will your reading.

Chapters 1 – 6 will guide you through the process of expository and argumentative essays – from your first choice of a topic to your final typed essay. Chapters 7 – 39 provide thorough discussion of writing conventions – grammar, word choice, punctuation, and mechanics. These chapters provide examples and practice to guide you in mastering such conventions and in learning to use them appropriately and effectively.

Next come chapters that will help you carry out and use research in your writing and examine the writing of your chosen discipline. Then come chapters that focus on different kinds of media: making oral presentations, designing print documents, and using hypertext and multimedia. Finally, there is a section for multilingual writers.

How to use *The New St. Martin's Handbook*

This book has been designed to be as easy as possible to use. Depending on what information or advice you're looking for, you may want to consult any or all of the following:

- **Tables of Contents.** If you know what general topic you're looking for (such as using commas), the **Brief Contents** on the inside front cover will lead you to the chapter where you'll find that topic. If you're looking for a specific kind of information within a general topic (such as using commas in a series), the detailed **Contents** on the inside back cover or the even more detailed **Contents** following this introduction can lead you to this information.
- **Index.** The index lists everything covered in the book. It's especially useful for finding specific words you need help with (such as *that* or *which*) but don't know the exact technical term for (*relative pronouns*).
- **Information about Online Writing.** If you have questions specific to working online, from how to indicate italics to how to evaluate Web sites as sources for a research paper, you'll find answers on the FAQ pages in each section of the book. A directory to all these questions appears on page 794.
- **Common Errors.** On pages I-12 – I-27 are an explanation and examples of twenty of the most common surface errors in the writing of U.S. college students, with references to pages in the book where you can find additional help in revising those errors.
- **Revising and Editing Guidelines.** On the second page of most chapters, and elsewhere as well in some chapters, are brief guidelines for revising and editing your writing that focus on the issues covered in that chapter (such as paragraphs or sentence fragments).
- **Documentation Guidelines.** For information on documenting sources, see the directories for MLA (p. 517), APA (p. 565), CBE (p. 588) and Chicago (p. 602) styles.
- **Glossaries.** The **Glossary of Usage** (p. 726) gives help with troublesome words (such as *accept* and *except*); the **Glossary of Grammatical and Computer Terms** (p. 713) gives definitions of these kinds of terms (such as *clause* and *listserv*).

- **World Wide Web Sources.** In the margins of the text are addresses and brief descriptions of many World Wide Web sites that offer more information or interesting insights about issues under discussion in the text. There is also a Directory of Web Sites on pp. 735 – 751.
- **Multilingual Issues.** Chapters 53 – 56 cover some of the most common and most important problems that speakers of other languages face in understanding and using English. In addition, throughout the book advice on specific issues appears in the margins under the heading "For Multilingual Writers"; a list of these marginal discussions is on page 795.

A tutorial on using *The New St. Martin's Handbook*

For this book to serve you well, you need to get to know it — to know what's inside and how to find it. The following tutorial is designed to help you familiarize yourself with *The New St. Martin's Handbook;* the answers are on p. xix – xx.

Starting with the table of contents

1. Where will you find advice on revising a draft?
2. Where will you find quick information on checking verbs for *-s* and *-es* endings? On checking subject-verb agreement in general?
3. Where will you find guidelines on documenting Internet sources?
4. Is there any help in the handbook for multilingual students, including those who speak English as a second language?

For planning and drafting

5. It's the first week of class, and you are at work on your first essay. Where in the handbook can you find general guidelines on planning and drafting an essay?
6. Assigned to write an essay that argues a claim, you've been warned to be very careful about using any personal narratives as support for your argument. Does the handbook offer any advice about how to use narrative appropriately in college writing?
7. In an essay arguing for "equal pay for equal work" addressed to members of your writing class, you want to avoid any language that stereotypes members of any group. Where in the handbook can you find advice about using considerate rather than hurtful language?
8. You've been assigned to give an oral presentation. Where does the handbook offer advice on writing and giving oral presentations? How did you find this information?

For editing

9. As you edit a final draft, you stop at the following sentence: *Winning may be the name of the game but it isn't a name I care for very much.* You can't decide whether to put a comma before *but.* What does the handbook recommend that you do? How and where do you find this answer?
10. You speak several languages, and you still confuse the prepositions *in* and *on.* Where in the handbook can you find help?
11. Does the word *none* take a singular or plural verb form? You can't decide. Where in the handbook can you find a quick answer to this question? How did you find the answer?
12. Your teacher has written *ref* next to this sentence: *Transmitting video signals by satellite is a way of overcoming the problem of scarce airwaves and limiting how they are used.* Where do you look in the handbook for help responding to your teacher's comment?

For doing research

13. You've found some Web sites related to your topic, but you aren't sure how reliable they are. Where can you find help in evaluating them?
14. Should you quote, paraphrase, or summarize? Are there any guidelines in the handbook to help you decide? How do you find these guidelines?
15. You're required to use something called *APA* style in a psychology paper. Where in the handbook can you find this information?
16. Using *MLA* style, how do you document information obtained from a CD-ROM source?

For all your college courses

17. A take-home exam in political science asks you to compare Marx's and Lenin's theories of revolution. You've never before written a political science paper, and so you're not sure how to proceed. Do you need to cite sources – and if so, do they need to be primary? Do political science papers follow any set format?
18. You need to write an abstract as part of a biology report. Is there a model in the handbook?
19. For a literature course, you're writing an essay interpreting a poem by Emily Dickinson. Where can you find help in the handbook?
20. A report you're working on must include both tables and figures. You aren't sure of the difference, nor do you know how to set them up. Where in the handbook can you get help?

We hope that this book will prove to be a useful reference. But in the long run, a book can be only a guide. You are the one who will put such guidance into practice, as you work to become a precise, powerful, and persuasive writer. Why not get started on achieving that goal right now?

Andrea Lunsford
Robert Connors

ANSWERS TO THE TUTORIAL

1. Chapter 4.
2. Chapter 9, on using verbs, includes quick-reference guidelines on editing *-s* and *-es* verb endings. Chapter 10 covers subject-verb agreement.
3. Chapter 44 is on documenting sources, including Internet sources, in MLA style; Chapters 45 – 47 are on documenting sources in APA, CBE, and Chicago styles, respectively.
4. Part 11 includes four chapters (53 – 56) that cover language issues of special interest to students who speak languages in addition to English. Page 795 has a quick reference chart that refers you to all the materials in the handbook for multilingual writers.
5. Chapter 3 offers guidelines on exploring, planning, and drafting.
6. Looking up "narrative" in the index leads you to a discussion of using narrative to support an argument in 5e, with guidelines on checking your own use of narrative on p. 77.
7. Looking up "audience" in the index leads you to 2h, about focusing on your audience, and to Chapter 29, on considering others and building common ground.
8. A look at the table of contents leads you to Chapter 50, on making oral presentations.
9. Looking up *"but"* in the index leads to 30b, which explains that a comma usually precedes a coordinating conjunction such as *but* when it joins two independent clauses in a compound sentence. You could also get to this section by turning directly to Chapter 30, on using commas, and looking for examples of how to use commas in similar sentences.
10. The table of contents tells you that Chapter 55 covers prepositions; 55a includes a set of strategies for using prepositions idiomatically, including several examples of sentences using *in* and *on*.
11. Looking up *"none"* in the index leads to 10e, where you learn that *none* can be singular or plural, depending on the noun it refers to: *none of the cake was eaten; none of the cakes were eaten.*
12. *Ref* is a revision symbol commonly used by instructors. A list of revision symbols appears on page 797 of the handbook. Consulting this list tells you that *ref* refers to unclear pronoun reference and that this subject is discussed in Chapter 13.
13. Skimming the table of contents leads you to Chapter 42, on using sources, and in particular to 42a3 on evaluating online sources and to 42b on reading sources with a critical eye.

14. Consulting the index under "quoting," "paraphrasing," or "summarizing" leads you to guidelines in 42c on deciding whether to quote, paraphrase, or summarize.
15. The table of contents tells you that Chapter 45 includes a section on APA documentation, with guidelines and a student essay that uses APA style.
16. The table of contents leads to Chapter 44, which provides a full discussion of MLA documentation conventions. It also lists a directory to MLA style, which leads you to section 44c5 on documenting electronic sources.
17. Scanning the table of contents leads you to Part 9, which covers academic writing in general, and to Chapter 48, which includes sections on understanding the vocabulary, style, use of evidence, and conventional formats in different disciplines.
18. Consulting the index under "biology," you see that Chapter 46, on CBE documentation, contains an excerpt from a biology paper. Turning to 46c, you find an example of an abstract in the excerpt.
19. A glance at the table of contents leads you to Chapter 49, on writing about literature. Section 49a provides guidelines for reading a literary work and an example of a student's annotations of a poem. Section 49b includes a glossary of literary terms, and section 49d includes a student's essay interpreting a novel. Checking the index under "poetry," you will find a poem by Emily Dickinson at the end of Chapter 36.
20. Looking up "tables" or "figures" in the index leads you to 51d, on using visuals, with examples and guidelines on constructing tables and figures.

Contents

The ▭ symbol marks quick-reference guidelines.

Thinking Critically about Your Writing

What do Bill Clinton, Oprah Winfrey, and Phil Jackson all have in common? For one thing, all three must find ways to manage enormous amounts of information if they are to stay on top of their fields – to leave a lasting political legacy, maintain a top Nielsen rating, or win an NBA championship. Their commonalities go further, however, for these public figures are all known to be very quick on their mental feet. Each is able to grasp complex organizational structures and problems quickly, to hold a great deal of information in their heads, and to see patterns in ways that help them succeed. In short, we might say they are all very good at **critical thinking,** that quality most often identified as necessary not only to economic success but also to personal fulfillment in an age as complex as ours.

As a college student, you share with Clinton, Winfrey, and Jackson a need for critical-thinking skills. Throughout your college years, you too will be called on to absorb and analyze vast amounts of information across a broad range of fields and to identify and pursue a course of study that will in some ways define your future, one that can launch you on a path of lifetime learning, work, and personal fulfillment. One way to make the most of these college years is to consciously strive to improve your critical-thinking abilities, to be one of those who can look at a body of diffuse and often conflicting information and identify where a problem lies, one who can cut through reams of red tape to get to the heart of a matter. Your writing course is in many ways a foundation course in critical thinking, providing guidance and practice in figuring out what you think about particular topics and issues, in articulating your thoughts, and in then convincing others that your ideas are worthy of consideration.

Thinking Critically about Your Writing

Every chapter in *The New St. Martin's Handbook* offers guidance and practice to help you think critically about your writing. Most chapters include editing guidelines to help you check and revise – that is, to think about – your drafts. (See the guidelines for editing verbs, for example, on p. 173.) And most chapters also conclude with guided practice in critical thinking to help you think hard about issues raised in the chapter. Usually this practice is in two parts – first, asking you to read critically a passage written by someone else, then, leading you to think critically about your own writing. (See "Thinking Critically about Verbs," for example, on p. 190.)

In addition, you will find explicit guidance in building critical-thinking skills in the following chapters:

- **Chapter 1** calls attention to the ways talking, listening, reading, and writing all work together to foster strong critical thinking and offers specific guidelines for listening and reading critically.
- **Chapter 2** guides you in thinking critically about rhetorical situations, including those you encounter online, while **Chapter 29** helps you to think hard about the language you use and how it can build common ground with others.
- **Chapter 4** provides extensive guidelines for reviewing texts, your own as well as those of others.
- **Chapter 5** takes you through the process of developing a critical stance on an issue and analyzing and arguing for that stance. The chapter includes a sample student essay and practical guidelines to help you analyze arguments using two different systems of argument.
- **Chapter 27** includes advice about analyzing denotative and connotative meanings of words for the agendas or biases they may reveal.
- **Chapter 28** calls attention to the many varieties of English and guides you in thinking about the ways you can use some of these varieties in your college writing.
- **Chapter 42** provides concrete guidelines to help you think critically about any sources you read as a researcher, including online sources, and about how to move from those sources to your own ideas.
- **Chapter 48** guides you in thinking critically in all the disciplines across the curriculum – to consider and recognize their expectations, conventions, and constraints.
- **Chapter 49** provides guidelines for reading literature with a critical eye.

- **Chapter 50** helps you prepare for critical thinking on your feet, giving oral presentations.
- **Chapter 51** helps you think critically about how you design documents and use visual effects, while **Chapter 52** asks you to examine the potential of multimedia for your writing.

What we mean by critical thinking, then, is pretty straightforward: it calls for stepping back from your own work and taking a good, hard, close look at it, getting down to the fine details as well as examining the big picture of how well your writing works to achieve your purposes. But critical thinking only begins with this close-up look; as a critical thinker, you can use the information you gain by examining your writing very closely to draw conclusions about how to make your writing better and more effective.

Almost every chapter in *The New St. Martin's Handbook* asks you to reflect on and articulate what you have learned from that chapter and to apply those lessons to your own writing. As you work through this book and use it as a reference, then, you will be practicing critical thinking at almost every turn. Eventually, this way of thinking critically – of stopping to identify what you are doing and trying to make these analyses as systematic and effective as possible – will become habitual. In the meantime, you can speed that process along by analyzing your own writing through a writing inventory.

Taking a writing inventory

What is a writing inventory? How can taking one help you develop critical-thinking abilities? The word *inventory* comes from a Latin word meaning "find," and in reference to writing, taking inventory carries the familiar meaning of taking stock – finding items in your stock of writing and cataloging those items – much as you might take inventory of your CDs or as a store manager might take inventory of items on hand. But taking inventory also carries another sense of "find," one we more often associate with the words *invent* and *invention.* In this sense, taking inventory means to discover new things about your writing and to use your discoveries to articulate its strengths and weaknesses as well as to build a plan for improvement.

This dual sense of taking inventory runs throughout *The New St. Martin's Handbook,* asking you to think critically and analytically about your own writing. How might you identify those features of your writing most important for such an inventory? In analyzing a representative sample of twenty thousand essays from first- and second-year writing courses in U.S. colleges, we found that the features that readers of essays most often comment on fall into three categories:

1. broad content issues
2. organization and presentation
3. surface errors

These research findings suggest that you can benefit from organizing an inventory of your own writing according to these three major categories. Following are some guidelines for doing so:

TAKING A WRITING INVENTORY

1. If you are using this chapter in a writing course, assemble copies of the first two or three pieces of writing you do, making sure to select pieces to which either your instructor or other students have responded.
2. Read through this writing, adding your own comments about its strengths and weaknesses.
3. Examine the instructor and peer comments very carefully, and compare them with your own comments.
4. Group all the comments into the categories discussed in this chapter – broad content issues, organization and presentation, and surface errors.
5. Make an inventory of your own strengths and weaknesses in each category.
6. Identify the appropriate sections of this book for more detailed help in areas where you need it.
7. Make up a priority list of three or four particular problems you have identified, and write out a plan for eliminating them.
8. Note at least two strengths you want to build on in your writing.

Keeping a writing log

One very good way to keep track of your writing strengths and weaknesses is by establishing a **writing log,** a notebook or folder in which you can record observations and comments about your writing – from instructors, other students, or yourself. This book will offer you frequent opportunities to make entries in a writing log, beginning with this chapter. As you take inventory of some of your writing, you will be gathering information about how readers respond to various features of it – broad content issues, organization and presentation, and surface errors. This information can serve as the data for an opening entry in your writing log. Here is an example of one such entry, made by Tamara Washington, an undergraduate at Ohio State University.

ENTRY 1 WRITING INVENTORY

I've taken a first look at the essay I wrote on the second day of class, one my response group and the instructor read. Here's what I've found so far:

	Strengths	**Weaknesses**
Broad content issues	lots of good examples	some examples unclear to some readers
Organization, presentation	great title! (Everyone loved it.)	paragraphs too short to make my points (Two are only one sentence long.)
Surface errors	semicolons used correctly – I was worried about this!	one unintentional sentence fragment, an *its/it's* mistake (!) (See p. 380, and *never* make this mistake again!!)

ASSESSING BROAD CONTENT ISSUES

As a writer, you are in some ways like the conductor of an orchestra or the supervisor of a large construction job: you must orchestrate all the elements of your writing into a persuasive performance, assemble all the ideas, words, evidence, and so on into one coherent structure. Doing so calls on you to attend carefully to several big questions: What is the purpose of your writing? To whom is it addressed? What points does it make? Does it fully develop, support, or prove those points?

Our research indicates that readers comment most often on the following broad content issues in student writing:

1. use of supporting evidence
2. use of sources
3. achievement of purpose
4. attention to audience
5. overall impression

Use of supporting evidence

According to Aristotle, an effective speaker needs to do two basic things: make a claim and prove it. Readers expect that a piece of writing will make one or more points clearly and illustrate or support those points with ample evidence – good reasons, examples, or other details. Effective use of such evidence helps readers understand a point, makes abstract concepts concrete, and offers "proof" that what you are saying is sensible and worthy of attention. In fact, this element is the one readers in our research commented on *most often,* accounting for 56 percent of all comments we analyzed. These readers tended to make statements like these:

This point is underdeveloped.

I like the way you back this claim up.

The details here don't really help me see your point.

I'm not convinced – what's your authority?

The three reasons you offer are very persuasive.

Good examples.

For a brief discussion of the use of good reasons, see 5d; of examples and details, see 5g–j. For more on providing such support in paragraphs, see 6e.

Use of sources

One special kind of supporting evidence for your points comes from source materials. Choosing possible sources, evaluating them, and using the results of your research effectively in your writing not only supports your claim but also builds your credibility as a writer, demonstrating that you understand what others have to say about a topic and that you are fully informed about varying perspectives on the topic. But finding enough sources, judging their usefulness, and deciding when to quote, when to summarize, and when to paraphrase – and then doing so accurately and effectively – are skills that take considerable practice, ones you should develop throughout your college writing career. You can begin sharpening those skills now by taking a close look at how well you use sources in your writing. The readers whose responses we studied commented regularly on use of sources. Here are some of their remarks:

Your list of sources is extraordinarily thorough – impressive reading!

Only two sources? You need at least several more.

Who said this?

Nice use of Sagan's main argument!

One of the clearest paraphrases I've seen of this crucial passage.

Your summary leaves out three of the writer's main points.

Your summary is just repetition – it doesn't add anything new.

This quotation beautifully sums up your argument.

Why do you quote at such length here? Why not paraphrase?

You cite only sources that support your claim – citing one or two with differing views would help show me you've considered other opinions.

For more discussion of choosing, reading, and evaluating sources, see 42a and b; of quoting, paraphrasing, and summarizing, see 42c; and of incorporating source materials in your text, see 43d.

Achievement of purpose

Purposes for writing vary widely – from asking for an appointment for a job interview to sending greetings or condolences to summarizing information for a test to tracing the causes of World War II for an essay. In college writing, your primary purpose will often be directly related to the assignment you receive. As a result, you need to pay careful attention to what an assignment asks you to do, noting particularly any key terms in the assignment such as *analyze* or *argue* or *define* or *summarize.* Such words are important in meeting the requirements of the assignment, staying on the subject, and thus achieving your purpose.

Readers' responses often reveal how well you have achieved your primary purpose. Here are some comments concerning purpose:

Why are you telling us all this?

What is the issue here, and what is your stand on it?

What is your purpose here? What do you want to happen as a result of your argument?

You simply give a plot summary here, one that does little to analyze character development.

Your writing will profit from some time spent identifying the purposes of several pieces of writing you have done and thinking about how well you achieved those purposes.

For guidelines on considering purposes, see 2d.

Attention to audience

Most college writing is addressed to instructors and other students, though you may sometimes write to another audience – a political figure, a prospective employer, a campus administrator. The most effective writing is that which is sensitive to readers' backgrounds, values, and needs. Such writing, for example, takes time to define terms readers may not know, to provide necessary background information, to consider readers' perspectives on and feelings about a topic. Here are some reader comments on audience:

This doesn't sound like something written for fourth-graders.

Careful you don't talk down to your readers.

You've left me behind here. I can't follow.

Your level of diction is perfect for relating to the Board of Trustees.

I'm really enjoying reading this!

Don't assume everyone shares your opinion about this issue.

For guidelines on considering your audience, see 2h and 29b.

Overall impression

When friends or instructors read your writing, they may often give you information about the overall impression it makes, perhaps noting how it seems to be improving or how you may be lapsing into bad habits. As a writer, you need to make such comments as concrete as you can by trying to determine, for instance, exactly what has caused some improvement or weakness in your writing. Setting up a conference with the instructor is one way to explore these general responses. Before doing so, however, carry out your own analysis of what the comments mean, and then find out what your instructor thinks.

In the sample of twenty thousand essays we examined, readers tended to give their overall impression most often in a note at the very beginning or the very end of an essay, saying things like the following:

I was looking for more critical analysis from you, and I've found it!

Much improved over your last essay.

Your grasp of the material here is truly impressive.

What happened here? I can't understand your point in this essay.

I know you can do a much better job of summarizing than this shows.

For more specific ways of assessing the overall impression your writing creates, see the final exercises in most chapters of this book. Each of these exercises is set up to help you take inventory of your use of the topics in the chapter.

EXERCISE I.1

Begin your writing inventory by recording the results of a careful look at broad content issues in at least one piece of your own writing. (1) First, list all comments your instructors and classmates have made about your use of supporting evidence, use of sources, achievement of purpose, attention to audience, and overall progress. If you find other large-scale issues referred to, include them in your list. (2) Then look over your writing with your own critical eye, using the guidelines in this introduction to evaluate your handling of broad content elements. (3) After examining the lists, summarize your major areas of strength and those areas in which you need to improve. (4) If you are keeping a writing log, enter this inventory there.

ASSESSING ORGANIZATION AND PRESENTATION

The most important or brilliant points in the world may have little effect on readers if they are presented in a way that makes them hard to recognize, read, or follow. Indeed, research for this book confirms that readers depend on writers to organize and present their material – sections, paragraphs, sentences, arguments, details, source citations – in ways that aid understanding. After use of supporting evidence, the features of student writing most often commented on had to do with organizational issues. In addition to clear and logical organization of information, readers appreciate careful formatting and documentation of sources. Although you can't always "tell a book by its cover," our research suggests that the "cover" of your writing – its physical format – can offer an important aid to readers and help establish your credibility as a conscientious writer. Careful attention to the conventions of source documentation can produce the same result. Here are those organizational and presentational features most often commented on in the student writing we examined:

1. overall organization
2. sentence structure and style
3. paragraph structure
4. format
5. documentation

Overall organization

Readers expect a writer to provide organizational patterns and signals that will help them follow the thread of what the writer is trying to say. Sometimes such cues are simple. If you are giving directions, for example, you might give chronological cues (first you do A, then B, and so on), and if you are describing a place, you might give spatial cues (at the north end is A, in the center is B, and so on). But complex issues often call for complex organizational patterns, so you might need to signal readers that you are moving from one problem to several possible solutions, for example, or that you are moving through a series of comparisons and contrasts. Readers responded in the following ways to organizational features:

I'm confused here – what does this point have to do with the one before it?

Your most important point is buried here in the middle. Why not move it up front?

Organization here is chronological rather than topical; as a result, you write synopsis, not analysis.

How did we get here? You need a transition.

Very clear, logical essay. A joy to read.

I'm lost: this sentence seems totally out of place.

You need to reorganize the three details: son, friend, then *you*.

For more discussion of overall organization, see 4e and 5j. For more on organizational methods of development, see 3d; on transitional signals that aid organization, see 6d; and on ways of linking paragraphs, see 6h.

Sentence structure and style

Effective sentences form the links in a chain of writing, guiding readers in ways that aid reading and understanding. If you have never taken a close look at how your sentences work (or don't work) to help organize your writing and guide readers, a little time and effort now will provide an overview. How long do your sentences tend to be? Do you use strings of short sentences that make the reader work to fill in the connections between them? Do any long sentences confuse the reader or wander off the topic? How do your sentences open? How do you link them logically? Here are some comments the readers in our research made about sentences:

The pacing of your sentences here really keeps me reading – excellent variation of length and type.

Combine sentences to make the logical connection explicit here.

Your use of questions helps clarify this complex issue.

This is not effective word order for a closing sentence – I've forgotten your main point.

These sentences all begin with nouns – the result is a kind of dull clip-clop, clip-clop, clip-clop.

Too many short, simple sentences here. This reads like a grocery list rather than an explanation of a complex issue.

This sentence goes on forever – how about dividing it up?

For guidelines on editing sentences, see p. 138. For detailed discussion of sentence types, see 7d; of sentence effectiveness, see Chapter 19; and of sentence variation, see Chapter 22.

Paragraph structure

Just as overall organization can help readers follow the thread of thought in a piece of writing, so too can paragraph structure. You may tend to paragraph by feel, so to speak, without spending much time thinking about structure. In fact, the time to examine your paragraphs should generally be *after* you have completed a draft. Begin by studying any readers' comments that refer to your paragraphs. Here are some of the kinds of comments you might find:

The sentences in this paragraph don't follow in a logical order.

Why the one- and two-sentence paragraphs? Elaborate!

Your introductory paragraph immediately gets my attention and gives an overview of the essay – good!

I can't follow the information in this paragraph.

This paragraph is not unified around one main idea.

Very effective ordering of details in this paragraph.

This paragraph skips around two or three points. It has enough ideas for three paragraphs.

For guidelines on editing paragraphs, see 6h. For detailed information on paragraph development in general, see Chapter 6.

Format

Readers depend on the format of a piece of writing to make their job as pleasant and efficient as possible. Therefore, you need to pay very close attention to how your materials are physically presented and to the visual effect they create. Because format guidelines vary widely, part of your job as a writer is always to make certain you know what format is most appropriate for a particular course or assignment.

In the research conducted for this book, readers made the following kinds of comments about format:

You need a title, one that really works to get across your meaning.

This tiny single-spaced type is almost impossible to read.

The table of contents here is very clear and helpful.

Number pages – these were not in the right order!

Your headings and subheadings helped me follow this report.

Never turn in a computer-printed essay without separating the pages and tearing off the tractor holes.

For a more thorough discussion of format, see Chapter 51.

Documentation

Any writing that uses source materials requires careful documentation – parenthetical citations, endnotes, footnotes, lists of works cited, bibliographies – to guide readers to your sources and let them know you have carried out accurate research. A close look at your writing may reveal that you have learned certain documentation rules – listing an author's last name first, for instance – but that you don't understand others at all. Here are some readers' comments that focus on documentation:

I checked my copy of *Emma* and this quotation's not on the page you list.

Footnote numbers should come at the *end* of quotations.

What are you paraphrasing here? Your introduction merely drops readers into the middle of things. *Introduce the material paraphrased.*

What are you summarizing here? Where do these ideas come from?

I can't tell where this quotation ends.

Keep your parenthetical citations as simple as possible – see 44a.

Why aren't works listed in alphabetical order?

This is *not correct* MLA citation style. Check your book!

What is the date of this publication?

For more information on documenting sources in MLA style, see Chapter 44; in APA style, see Chapter 45; in CBE style, see Chapter 46; in Chicago style, see Chapter 47.

EXERCISE I.2

Continue your writing inventory by analyzing at least one piece of your writing in regard to the five features of organization and presentation just described. (1) Chart your instructor's comments, and consider asking a classmate whose opinions you value to comment on your use of these features. (2) Then add your own observations about your use of these features. (3) On the basis of these analyses, summarize what you take to be your major areas of strength as well as those areas in which you need to improve. (4) If you are keeping a writing log (see pp. I-4 and I-5), enter the results of your analysis there.

LEARNING FROM YOUR SURFACE ERRORS

Whereas readers may notice your handling of broad content issues and your organization and presentation either because these provide stepping stones for following your meaning or because they create stumbling blocks to such understanding, your spelling, grammar, punctuation, word choice, and other small-scale matters will seldom draw attention unless they look wrong. Because such surface errors disrupt communication between writers and readers, they are an important source of information about your writing.

What can we tell you about the kinds of surface errors you are likely to find in your writing and the responses they elicit from readers? Our study of student writing reveals, first of all, that – even with spell checkers — spelling errors are *by far the most common,* by a factor of more than three to one. Second, readers are not disturbed by all surface errors, nor do instructors always mark all of them. In fact, whether your instructor comments on an error in any particular assignment will depend on his or her judgment about how serious and distracting it is and what you should be dealing with at the time. Finally, not all surface errors are even consistently viewed as errors. In fact, some of the patterns identified in our research are considered errors by some instructors but stylistic options by others.

For a list of the words most often misspelled, see Chapter 24.

Although many people may tend to think of "correctness" as absolute, based on hard and fast, unchanging "rules," instructors and students know better. We know that there are "rules," all right, but that the rules change all the time. "Is it okay to use *I* in essays for this class?" asks one student. "My high school teacher wouldn't let us." "Will more than one comma error flunk an essay?" asks another. These questions show that rules clearly exist, but they also suggest that these rules are always shifting and thus constantly need to be explored.

Our research shows some of the shifts that have occurred in the last century alone. Mechanical and grammatical questions that no longer concern most people used to be perceived as extremely important. In the late nineteenth century, for instance, instructors at Harvard said that the most serious writing problem their students had was an inability to distinguish between the proper uses of *shall* and *will.* Similarly, split infinitives seemed to many instructors of the 1950s a very serious problem, but at least since the starship *Enterprise* set out "to boldly go" where no one has gone before, split infinitives have wrinkled fewer brows.

These examples of shifting standards do not mean that there is no such thing as "correctness" in writing — only that *correctness always depends on some context.* Correctness is not so much a question of absolute right or wrong as it is a question of the way the choices a writer makes are perceived by readers. The world judges us by our control of the conventions we have agreed to use, and we all know it. As Robert Frost once said of poetry, trying to write without honoring the conventions and agreed-upon rules is like playing tennis without a net.

A major assumption this book makes is that you want to understand and control not only the broad content issues and organizational features of writing but the surface conventions of academic writing as well. Since you already know the vast majority of these conventions, the most efficient way to proceed is to focus on those that are still unfamiliar or puzzling. Achieving this practical focus means identifying, analyzing, and overcoming patterns of surface error in your writing.

Why not decide right now to take charge of your own writing by charting and learning from your errors? This effort need not mean becoming obsessed with errors to the exclusion of everything else in your writing. Perfectly correct writing is, after all, a limited and limiting goal. You want to aim for a perfectly persuasive and enlightening piece of writing – that also happens to be correct.

To aid you in producing writing that is conventionally correct, we have identified the twenty most common error patterns (other than misspelling) among U.S. college students in the late 1980s. Here they are, listed in the order of occurrence:

THE TWENTY MOST COMMON ERRORS

1. missing comma after an introductory element
2. vague pronoun reference
3. missing comma in a compound sentence
4. wrong word
5. missing comma(s) with a nonrestrictive element
6. wrong or missing verb ending
7. wrong or missing preposition
8. comma splice
9. missing or misplaced possessive apostrophe
10. unnecessary shift in tense
11. unnecessary shift in pronoun
12. sentence fragment
13. wrong tense or verb form
14. lack of agreement between subject and verb
15. missing comma in a series
16. lack of agreement between pronoun and antecedent
17. unnecessary comma(s) with a restrictive element
18. fused sentence
19. misplaced or dangling modifier
20. *its/it's* confusion

Statistically, these twenty are the errors most likely to cause you trouble. A brief explanation and examples of each one are given in this chapter, and each error pattern is cross-referenced to at least one place elsewhere in this book where you can find more detail or additional examples.

1 Missing comma after an introductory element

When a sentence opens with an introductory word, phrase, or clause, readers usually need a small pause between the introductory element and the main part of the sentence. Such a pause is most often signaled by a comma.

- ▶ **Frankly, we were baffled by the committee's decision.**
- ▶ **In fact, the Philippines consists of more than eight thousand islands.**
- ▶ **To tell the truth, I never have liked the Mets.**
- ▶ **Because of its isolation in a rural area surrounded by mountains, Crawford Notch doesn't get many visitors.**
- ▶ **Though I gave detailed advice for revising, his draft became only worse.**

Short introductory elements do not always need a comma. The test is whether the element seems to need a pause after it. The following sentence, for example, would at first be misunderstood if it did not have a comma — readers would think the introductory phrase was *In German nouns,* rather than *In German.* The best advice is that you will rarely be wrong to add a comma after an introductory element.

For more on commas and introductory elements, see 7c, 22b, and 30a.

- ▶ **In German, nouns are always capitalized.**

2 Vague pronoun reference

A pronoun like *he, she, it, they, this, that,* or *which* should usually refer clearly to a specific word (or words) elsewhere in the sentence or in a previous sentence. When readers cannot tell for sure whom or what the pronoun refers to, the reference is said to be vague. There are two common kinds of vague pronoun reference. The first occurs when there is more than one word that the pronoun might refer to; the second, when the reference is to a word that is implied but not explicitly stated.

POSSIBLE REFERENCE TO MORE THAN ONE WORD

the latter

▶ **Before Mary Grace physically and verbally assaulted Mrs. Turpin, ~~she~~ was a judgmental woman who created her own ranking system of people.**

REFERENCE IMPLIED BUT NOT STATED

▶ **The troopers burned an Indian camp as a result of the earlier attack.**
destruction of the camp
This ^ was the cause of the war.

such an assertion

▶ **They believe that a zygote, an egg at the moment of fertilization, is as deserving of protection as the born human being, but ~~it~~ cannot be proven scientifically.**

For guidelines on editing for clear pronoun reference, see p. 214. For more on pronoun reference, see Chapter 13.

3 Missing comma in a compound sentence

A compound sentence is made up of two (or more) parts that could each function as an independent sentence. If there are only two parts, they may be linked by either a semicolon or a coordinating conjunction (*and, but, so, yet, nor, or, for*). When a conjunction is used, a comma should usually be placed before it to indicate a pause between the two thoughts.

▶ **The words "I do" may sound simple, but they mean a complex commitment for life.**

▶ **We wish dreamily upon a star, and then we look down to see that we have stepped in the mud.**

For further discussion and examples of commas in compound sentences, see 7d1 and 30b.

In *very* short sentences, this use of the comma is optional if the sentence can be easily understood without it. The following sentence, for example, would be misunderstood if it did not have a comma – readers would think at first that Meredith was wearing her feet. The best advice is to use the comma before the coordinating conjunction because it will always be correct.

▶ **Meredith wore jeans, and her feet were bare.**

4 Wrong word

"Wrong word" errors range from simple lack of proofreading, like using *should* for *would,* to mistakes in basic word meaning, like using *prevaricate* when you mean *procrastinate,* to mistakes in shades of meaning, like using *sedate* when you mean *sedentary.* Many errors marked "wrong word" are *homonyms,* words that are pronounced alike but spelled differently, like *their* and *there.*

For guidelines on checking a draft for wrong words, see 27b. For additional, more detailed information about choosing the right word for your meaning, see Chapter 27.

▶ **A knowledge of computers is ~~inherent~~** *assumed* **in his office.**

▶ **Mark noticed the ~~stench~~** *fragrance* **of roses as he entered the room.**

▶ ***Paradise Lost* contains many ~~illusions~~** *allusions* **to classical mythology.**

5 Missing comma(s) with a nonrestrictive element

A nonrestrictive element is a word, phrase, or clause that gives additional information about the preceding part of the sentence but does not restrict or limit the meaning of that part. A nonrestrictive element is not essential to the sentence; it can be deleted without changing the sentence's basic meaning. As an indication that it is not essential, it is always set off from the rest of the sentence with a comma before it and, if it is in the middle of the sentence, after it as well.

For additional explanation and examples of commas with nonrestrictive elements, see 30c.

▶ **Marina, who was the president of the club, was first to speak.**

▶ **Louis was forced to call a session of the Estates General, which had not met for 175 years.**

▶ **The bottom of the pond was covered with soft brown clay, a natural base for a good swimming hole.**

6 Wrong or missing verb ending

The verb endings *-s* (or *-es*) and *-ed* (or *-d*) are important markers in standard academic English. It is easy to forget these endings in writing because they are not always pronounced clearly when spoken. In addition, some varieties of English do not use these endings in the same way as standard academic English.

▶ **Eliot ~~use~~ *uses* feline imagery throughout the poem.**

▶ **I runs a mile every morning before breakfast.**

▶ **The United States ~~drop~~ *dropped* two atomic bombs on Japan in 1945.**

▶ **Nobody ~~imagine~~ *imagined* he would actually become president.**

An *-s* (or *-es*) ending must be added to present-tense indicative verbs whose subjects are singular nouns; *he, she,* and *it;* and most indefinite pronouns (such as *anyone, each, everybody, nobody, nothing, someone*). The ending is not added to verbs whose subjects are plural nouns; *I, you, we,* and *they;* and indefinite pronouns that have a plural meaning (such as *both* and *few*). The past-tense and past-participle forms of most verbs must end in *-ed* (or *-d*).

For guidelines on editing for verb endings, see pp. 174 and 176. For more on verb endings, see Chapter 9 and 10a.

7 Wrong or missing preposition

Many words in English are regularly used with a particular preposition to express a particular meaning; for example, throwing a ball *to* someone is different from throwing a ball *at* someone. The first ball is thrown to be caught; the second, to hurt someone. Using the wrong preposition in such expressions is a common error. Because most prepositions are so short and are not stressed or pronounced clearly in speech, they are also often accidentally left out of writing.

▶ **The bus committee is trying to set a schedule that will meet the needs of most people who rely ~~in~~** *on* **public transportation.**

▶ **Nixon compared the United States ~~with~~** *to* **a "pitiful, helpless giant."**

▶ **Finally, she refused to comply ~~to~~** *with* **army regulations.**

▶ **In his moral blindness, Gloucester is similar ~~with~~** *to* **Lear.**

▶ **Hilary is absolutely enamored ~~with~~** *of* **Barbie.**

For guidelines on using prepositions, see 55a. For additional information about choosing the correct preposition, see 7b6.

8 Comma splice

A comma splice occurs when two (or sometimes more) clauses that could each stand alone as a sentence are written with only a comma between them. Such clauses must be either clearly separated by a punctuation mark stronger than a comma — a period or semicolon — or clearly connected with a word such as *and* or *although,* or else the ideas they state should be combined into one clause.

For guidelines on editing for comma splices, see p. 224. For additional information about ways to avoid or revise comma splices, see Chapter 15.

▶ **Westward migration had passed Wyoming by~~,~~***;* **even the discovery of gold in nearby Montana failed to attract settlers.**

▶ **I was strongly attracted to her,** *for* **she had special qualities.**

▶ *Having* **~~They always had~~ roast beef for Thanksgiving~~,~~ ~~this~~ was a family tradition.**

9 Missing or misplaced possessive apostrophe

To show that one thing belongs to another, either an apostrophe and an *-s* or an apostrophe alone is added to the word representing the thing that possesses the other. An apostrophe and *-s* are used for singular nouns (words that refer to one thing, such as *leader* or *Chicago*); for indefinite pronouns (words like *anybody, everyone, nobody, somebody*); and for plural nouns (words referring to more than one thing) that do not end in *-s,* such as *men* and *women*. For plural nouns ending in *-s,* such as *creatures* or *fathers,* only the apostrophe is used.

▶ **Overambitious parents can be very harmful to a ~~childs~~ *child's* well-being.**

▶ **Ron Guidry was once one of the ~~Yankee's~~ *Yankees'* most electrifying pitchers.**

For guidelines on editing for possessive apostrophes, see p. 329. For more detailed information on possessive apostrophes, see 33a.

10 Unnecessary shift in tense

An unnecessary shift in tense occurs when the verbs in a sentence or passage shift for no reason from one time period to another, such as from past to present or from present to future. Such tense shifts confuse the reader, who must guess which tense is the right one.

▶ **Lucy was watching the great blue heron take off when she ~~slips~~ *slipped* and ~~falls~~ *fell* into the swamp.**

▶ **Each team of detectives is assigned to three or four cases at a time. They ~~will~~ investigate only those leads that seem most promising.**

For guidelines on editing for confusing shifts in tense, see 14a. For more on using verb tenses in sequence, see 9g.

11 Unnecessary shift in pronoun

An unnecessary pronoun shift occurs when a writer who has been using one kind of pronoun to refer to someone or something shifts to another for no reason. The most common shift in pronoun is from *one* to *you* or *I*. This shift often results from an attempt at a more formal level of diction, which is hard to maintain when it is not completely natural.

▶ **When one first sees a painting by Georgia O'Keeffe, ~~you are~~ *one is* impressed by a sense of power and stillness.**

▶ **If we had known about the ozone layer, ~~you~~ *we* could have banned aerosol sprays years ago.**

For more discussion of unnecessary pronoun shifts, see 14d.

12 Sentence fragment

A sentence fragment is a part of a sentence that is written as if it were a whole sentence, with a capital letter at the beginning and a period, question mark, or exclamation point at the end. A fragment lacks one or both of the two essential parts of a sentence, a subject and a complete verb; or else it begins with a subordinating word, which means that it depends for its meaning on another sentence.

LACKING SUBJECT

▶ **Marie Antoinette spent huge sums of money on herself and her favorites.** *Her extravagance helped* **~~Helped~~ bring on the French Revolution.**

LACKING COMPLETE VERB

▶ **The old aluminum boat** *was* **sitting on its trailer.**

BEGINNING WITH SUBORDINATING WORD

▶ **We returned to the drugstore**~~.~~*, where* **~~Where~~ we waited for the rest of the gang.**

For guidelines on editing for sentence fragments, see p. 230. For more detailed information on sentence fragments, see Chapter 16.

13 Wrong tense or verb form

Errors that are marked as being the wrong tense or verb form include using a verb that does not indicate clearly that the action or condition it expresses is (or was or will be) completed – for example, using *walked* instead of *had walked* or *will go* instead of *will have gone.* In some dialects of English, the verbs *be* and *have* are used in ways that differ significantly from their use by most native speakers; these uses may also be labeled as the wrong verb form. Finally, many errors of this kind occur with verbs whose basic forms for showing past time or a completed action or condition do not follow the regular pattern, like *begin, began, begun* and *break, broke, broken.* Errors may occur when a writer confuses the second and third forms or treats these verbs as if they followed the regular pattern – for example, using *beginned* instead of *began* or *have broke* instead of *have broken.*

▶ **Ian was shocked to learn that Joe** *had* **died only the day before.**

For guidelines on editing verb tenses, see 9f. For more detailed information about verb tenses and forms, see 7b1 and Chapters 9 and 10.

▶ **The poet ~~be~~ *is* looking at a tree when she ~~have~~ *has* a sudden inspiration.**

▶ **Florence Griffith Joyner has ~~broke~~ *broken* many track records.**

▶ **The Greeks ~~builded~~ *built* a wooden horse that the Trojans ~~taked~~ *took* into the city.**

14 Lack of agreement between subject and verb

A subject and verb must agree, or match. In many cases, the verb must take a different form depending on whether the subject is singular (one) or plural (more than one): *The old man is angry and stamps into the house* but *The old men are angry and stamp into the house.* Lack of agreement between a subject and verb is often just a matter of leaving the *-s* ending off the verb out of carelessness and failure to proofread, or of using a dialect form that does not have this ending (see errors 6 and 13). Sometimes, however, it results from particular kinds of subjects or sentence constructions.

When other words come between a subject and verb, a writer may mistake the noun nearest to the verb for the verb's real subject. In the following sentence, for example, the subject is the singular *part,* not the plural *goals.*

▶ **A central part of my life goals ~~have~~ *has* been to go to law school.**

Other problems can arise from subjects made up of two or more parts joined by *and* or *or;* subjects like *committee* or *jury,* which can take either singular or plural verb forms depending on whether they are treated as a unit or as a group of individuals; and subjects like *mathematics* and *measles,* which look plural but are singular in meaning.

▶ **My brother and his friend Larry commute~~s~~ every day from Louisville.**

▶ **The committee ~~was~~ *were* taking all the responsibility themselves.**

▶ **Measles ~~have~~ *has* become much less common in the United States.**

Pronoun subjects cause problems for many writers. Most indefinite pronouns, such as *each, either, neither,* or *one,* take a singular verb. The relative pronouns *who, which,* or *that* take verbs that agree with the word the pronoun refers to.

▶ **Each of the items in these designs ~~coordinate~~ *coordinates* with the others.**

▶ **Johnson was one of the athletes who ~~was~~ *were* disqualified.**

Finally, some problems occur when writers make a verb agree with the word that follows or precedes it rather than with the grammatical subject. In the following sentences, for example, the subjects are *source* and *man,* not *parents* and *curtains.*

▶ **His only source of income ~~were~~ *was* his parents.**

▶ **Behind the curtains ~~stand~~ *stands* an elderly man producing the wizard's effects.**

For guidelines on editing for subject-verb agreement, see p. 192. For additional information about subject-verb agreement, see Chapter 10.

15 Missing comma in a series

A series consists of three or more parallel words, phrases, or clauses that appear consecutively in a sentence. Traditionally, all the items in a series are separated by commas. Many newspapers and magazines do not use a comma before the *and* or *or* between the last two items, and some instructors do not require it. Check your instructor's preference, and be consistent in either using or omitting this comma.

▶ **Sharks eat mostly squid, shrimp, crabs, and other fish.**

▶ **You must learn to talk to the earth, smell it, squeeze it in your hands.**

For more on parallel structures in a series, see 21a. For more on using commas in a series, see 30d.

16 Lack of agreement between pronoun and antecedent

Most pronouns (words like *I, it, you, him, her, this, themselves, someone, who, which*) are used to replace another word (or words) so that it does not have to be repeated. The word that the pronoun replaces or stands for is called its antecedent. Pronouns must agree with, or match, their antecedents in gender – for example, using *he* and *him* to replace *Abraham*

Lincoln and *she* and *her* to replace *Queen Elizabeth.* They must also agree with their antecedents in referring to either one person or thing (singular) or more than one (plural) – for example, using *it* to replace *a book* and *they* and *them* to replace *fifteen books.*

Most people have few problems with pronoun-antecedent agreement except with certain kinds of antecedents. These include words like *each, either, neither,* and *one,* which are singular and take singular pronouns; antecedents made up of two or more parts joined by *or* or *nor;* and antecedents like *audience* or *team,* which can be either singular or plural depending on whether they are considered a single unit or a group of individuals.

its
▶ **Every one of the puppies thrived in ~~their~~ ^ new home.**

her
▶ **Neither Jane nor Susan brought ~~their~~ ^ husband to the party.**

their
▶ **The team frequently changed ~~its~~ ^ positions to get varied experience.**

The other main kind of antecedent that causes problems is a singular antecedent (such as *each* or *an employee*) that could be either male or female. Rather than use masculine pronouns (*he, him,* and so on) with such an antecedent, a traditional rule that excludes or ignores females, a writer should use *he or she, him or her,* and so on, or else rewrite the sentence to make the antecedent and pronoun plural or to eliminate the pronoun.

or her
▶ **Every student must provide his ^ own uniform.**

All students *their* *uniforms.*
▶ **~~Every student~~ ^ must provide ~~his~~ ^ own ~~uniform.~~ ^**

a
▶ **Every student must provide ~~his own~~ ^ uniform.**

For guidelines on editing for pronoun-antecedent agreement, see p. 201. For additional information about pronoun-antecedent agreement, see Chapter 11.

17 Unnecessary comma(s) with a restrictive element

A restrictive element is a word, phrase, or clause that restricts or limits the meaning of the preceding part of the sentence; it is essential to the meaning of what precedes it and cannot be left out without changing the sentence's basic meaning. Because of this close relationship, it is *not* set off from the rest of the sentence with a comma or commas.

▶ **An arrangement, for orchestra, was made by Ravel.**

▶ **Several groups, opposed to the use of animals for cosmetics testing, picketed the laboratory.**

▶ **People, who wanted to preserve wilderness areas, opposed the plan to privatize national parks.**

▶ **The vice president succeeds, if and when the president dies or becomes incapacitated.**

▶ **Shakespeare's tragedy, *Othello*, deals with the dangers of jealousy.**

In the last example above, the appositive is essential to the meaning of the sentence because Shakespeare wrote more than one tragedy.

For additional information about restrictive phrases and clauses, see 30c and 30j.

18 Fused sentence

Fused sentences (sometimes called run-on sentences) are created when two or more groups of words that could each be written as an independent sentence are written without any punctuation between them. Such groups of words must be either divided into separate sentences, by using periods and capital letters, or joined in a way that shows their relationship, by either adding words and punctuation or by rewriting completely.

▶ **The current was swift ~~he~~ could not swim to shore.** [. He]

▶ **Klee's paintings seem simple they are very sophisticated.** [, but]

▶ **She doubted the value of meditation she decided to try it once.** [; nevertheless]

For guidelines on editing for fused sentences, see p. 224. For more information about ways to revise fused sentences, see Chapter 15.

19 Misplaced or dangling modifier

A misplaced modifier is a word, phrase, or clause that is not placed close enough to the word it describes or is related to. As a result, it seems to modify some other word, phrase, or clause, and readers can be confused or puzzled.

With binoculars, they
▶ **~~They~~ could see the eagles swooping and diving. ~~with binoculars.~~**

When he was ten years old, he
▶ **~~He~~ had decided he wanted to be a doctor. ~~when he was ten years old.~~**

slowly and precisely.
▶ **~~Slowly and precisely~~ I watched the teller count out the money.**

only
▶ **The architect ~~only~~ wanted to use pine paneling for decoration.**

T *rising over the trees.*
▶ **~~Rising over the trees,~~ the campers saw a bright red sun.**

A dangling modifier is a word, phrase, or elliptical clause (a clause from which words have been left out) that is not clearly related to any other word in the sentence. The word that it modifies exists in the writer's mind, but not on paper in the sentence. Such a modifier is called "dangling" because it hangs precariously from the beginning or end of the sentence, attached to nothing very solid.

you are
▶ **A doctor should check your eyes for glaucoma every year if over fifty.**

one sees
▶ **Looking down the stretch of sandy beach, people ~~are~~ lying face down trying to get a tan.**

M *that I, a white male college student,*
▶ **~~As a white male college student,~~ many people seem surprised ~~at my~~ support ~~for~~ affirmative action.**

For guidelines on editing misplaced and dangling modifiers, see p. 235. For additional information, see 17a and c.

20 *Its / It's* confusion

The word *its,* spelled without an apostrophe, is the possessive form of *it,* meaning "of it" or "belonging to it." The word *it's,* spelled with an apostrophe, is a shortened form of *it is* or *it has.* Even though with nouns an apostrophe often indicates a possessive form, the possessive form of a pronoun in this case is the one *without* the apostrophe.

▶ **The car is lying on it's side in the ditch.**

For guidelines on editing for misuse of its and it's, see 33b.

▶ It's a white 1986 Buick.

▶ It's been lying there for two days.

EXERCISE I.3

Continue your writing inventory by analyzing the surface errors (and strengths) in one piece of your writing. (1) Go through your writing, noting all comments, positive or critical, in such areas as spelling, grammar, punctuation, capitalization, and other issues like those discussed in the preceding section. (2) Then go through once more, using the guidelines on the twenty most common errors in this introduction, to add your own observations about strengths and areas that need improvement. (3) Finally, compile a list of both strengths and weaknesses, and decide which areas you plan to work on first. (4) If you are keeping a writing log, enter the results of your writing inventory there.

THINKING ABOUT WRITING AND WORKING ONLINE

As electronic forms of communication become more and more important to all our lives, writers find themselves doing more of their writing not only with computers but also online – on listservs and email, in chat rooms, and on the World Wide Web. To find out more about how student writers are participating in technological changes, we have conducted some basic research, asking college students across the country about the ways in which they are using electronic forms of communication both in and out of class.

In the spring of 1997, over 900 students responded to our call for information, along with the 53 instructors who were teaching the first-year writing classes the students were taking. And what these people told us confirmed many of our own intuitions: students are doing a large proportion of their writing with a computer, and they are increasingly using the Internet and the World Wide Web for a multitude of purposes. As might be expected, this increasing use of electronic communication carries a number of benefits as well as some serious challenges for student writers. These findings suggest that you need to think carefully and critically about the way you are using technology for your college work, especially writing, as well as for your personal goals.

Like students throughout the United States, you are probably now using a word-processing program for the great majority of your college work (94 percent of the students we surveyed reported doing so). Given the extremely widespread use of word-processing systems, we were surprised that students reported so much frustration in using them, noting persistent difficulties in saving, retrieving, printing, transferring, and designing documents. Our survey suggests, then, that you should take note of what student writers have told us about how to solve these difficulties and how to use word-processing systems most effectively and efficiently. Here are some of their suggestions:

- take time to learn your own system or the one you have access to at school. Many major problems in saving, retrieving, and printing documents – not to mention computer crashes, freeze-ups, and so on – could be avoided simply by spending a few hours working through the help menu or the tutorial that accompanies most word-processing software and making notes for future reference.
- remember to save work frequently – at least every twenty minutes (and note that you can set your computer to do this automatically).
- print out paper copies of each version or draft. Editing onscreen is inefficient and usually not very accurate – and hard on your eyes.
- Keep an extra copy of your project on a floppy disk, just in case you lose the copy on your hard drive.
- give each writing assignment or file a name, and save all related files in a folder for easiest retrieval. And remember that you need to instruct the computer which folder to save the file to.

In addition to these general guidelines, the students we surveyed reported taking advantage of the features word-processing and related systems offer for layout, design, and editing. More specifically, their responses suggest that you will be wise to

- take the time to learn the layout and design features of your word-processing system. For most college writing, you will want to use standard size 11- or 12-point type and easy-to-read fonts (such as New Times Roman). (See page 3.) In addition, you should learn how to insert bullets and other symbols (such as diacritical marks needed for certain words from other languages), to insert graphics, and to draw simple lines and boxes. Finally, learn to use your system's color capabilities, but use color judiciously, making sure that it clearly enhances your purpose; a garish, frenetically colored document will probably not be reader-friendly. (See 51a.)

- take full advantage of the spell checker on your word-processing system, since it will help you identify a good percentage of the problem words and misspellings in your text. Don't rely on the spell checker alone, however; it will not catch wrong words or homonyms, for instance. (See 24f.)
- use thesaurus programs and grammar- and style checkers with caution. You will be wise not to use a word offered by the thesaurus if you're not absolutely sure what it means, for instance. Grammar checkers not only miss many errors but also mistakenly label many perfectly acceptable sentences as erroneous. And remember that grammar checkers cannot make rhetorical choices: they won't know what your intended purpose is or who your audience is. Some of our student respondents pointed out that, as a result, the changes their programs suggest are often not helpful – and may even be highly inappropriate.
- avoid equating spell-checking and grammar-checking (which are part of editing and proofreading) with revision, which calls for looking at the overall effect your draft creates, for examining the organization, for assessing the use of evidence and examples and details, and for making substantial cuts, additions, or changes. (See Chapter 4.) In addition, remember that student writers report that trying to edit texts onscreen almost guarantees a flawed final product. You need to print out your text and see for yourself how the cutting and pasting, adding and substituting, and other changes have turned out.

Using the Internet and World Wide Web

Students across the United States are going online in ever-increasing numbers. Among the group we surveyed, 71 percent reported that they use the Internet and Web – and this percentage has almost certainly grown in the ensuing months. Of those not currently using the Internet and Web, many reported that they wanted either to gain access to these tools or to learn to use them; and many remarked on their need to do so as soon as possible. If you don't have such access or knowledge, then, our study suggests that you should move quickly to get it. Begin with your library, where you may be able to access programs specifically aimed at helping you learn to use the Net. Many colleges and universities have developed their own tutorials, usually based in the library, so check yours out soon.

For more advice on gaining access to the Internet and World Wide Web and learning to use them, see pages 430 – 434 and text sections 41f and g.

Working online for college assignments

Once you do have access and have learned the basics of using the Internet and Web, you will find – as our student respondents reported –

that these tools are useful for many, many different tasks. More specifically, students report using the Net and Web in four specific ways for college-related work.

- to gather information on an assigned topic
- to explore possible topics for an assignment
- to identify research related to assignments
- to find sources (people to interview, relevant web sites, and so on) to support arguments

Going online for other reasons

You may also find, as did many students in our survey, that you use the Net and Web for many reasons that go well beyond your college classes. For example, 25 percent of student respondents told us they use these tools for their own personal interest; 28 percent use them for entertainment; and over 6 percent use them for work-related interests or tasks. More specifically, here is a brief list of some of the many reasons students are now going online:

- to do personal and business-related banking
- to get shopping and product information
- to get schedules and other information about sports teams
- to find scholarship opportunities
- to do genealogical research
- to keep up with bands and the music scene, or the movie scene
- to find career opportunities and look for jobs
- to get travel and vacation information
- to get weather information
- to meet new people or to visit with people in other countries
- to play games and use other kinds of online entertainment
- to track stocks or keep up with the news on particular topics
- for the fun of browsing

Perhaps even more interesting, some students found that the information they turned up just surfing or having fun online wound up helping in a college writing assignment. Thus one point that our research strongly suggests is that – at least in terms of uses of technology – school and nonschool activities may be becoming more closely related, blending and merging with one another from time to time. In addition, working online has made research for everyday kinds of activities (comparing prices on products, for instance) easier than ever.

Searching the Internet and World Wide Web

For online work, and especially for research, students are using a number of search tools, from Yahoo! to WebCrawler to Hotbot. You are probably using these tools as well. If so, student respondents to our survey tell us that you need to pay particular attention to the following issues:

- take the time to learn the search logic of individual search engines, since they differ considerably. To find out what the logic of any particular engine is, go to the "help" button on the menu, and look for a discussion of how you need to enter terms to get the best results. (See 41e.)
- consider using a meta search engine, which will search a number of other engines for you. At <www.dogpile.com> for instance, you can search up to twenty-five engines – once you have learned to use the search syntax for dogpile!
- remember that the information you gather on the Internet and World Wide Web is only as accurate and reliable as its source. You must be careful, then, to evaluate online sources you wish to use (see 42a3 and pages 431 – 432) and then to cite these sources fully (see 42d). In addition, if you intend to post on the Web any work in which you use another source extensively, you need to ask for permission to reproduce that source. (See pages 432 – 433.)

Using email, listservs, and newsgroups

Over half of the students we surveyed (56 percent) reported using email regularly, and many of them said they also posted to listservs, newsgroups, or chat rooms. These new opportunities for communication offer wonderful ways to communicate with classmates and instructors, keep in touch with family and friends, make new friends, and gather and share information about topics of mutual interest. They also call for developing conventions about how to communicate most effectively. Here are some of the most common and most important issues students report facing in their day-to-day encounters with email and online postings.

- online writing often seems to invite very informal writing, perhaps full of slang and colloquialisms, abbreviations, and so on. But such informality is not always appropriate. As a writer, you should keep your purpose, your audience, and other elements of your rhetorical situation uppermost in mind as you decide what level of formality to use. (See 2i and pages 2 – 3, 212, 248, 286, and 350.)

- online writing raises many concerns about privacy. Remember that once you send an email message or a listserv posting, it is easily forwarded to anyone else and is easily printed out and distributed as well. (See 2i1.)
- much online writing is limited stylistically: no italics in email, for example, or no ability to do paragraph indentations. Some alternative conventions are currently in use, and you need to know them. (See pages 3 and 404.)
- online addresses and URLs (uniform resource locators) must be followed to the letter – or you won't be able to access a document, reach an intended email recipient, and so on. It pays to take time to learn how to "read" these addresses. (See page 136 and 41f1.)
- those you are communicating with may not have compatible software systems. As a result, it is best to check in advance to see how you should send an attached document (saved as rich-text file, for example, instead of as WordPerfect). And remember that pictures and graphics can take a very long time to download; be thoughtful of those you are sending messages to.
- Many students complained to us about receiving what feels like tons of online junk mail, strange chain letters and mass forwardings from unknown people, "spamming" (advertising online), even flaming and use of profanity. Don't contribute to the proliferation of online pollution. (See 2i3.)

Reading what these students and instructors had to say about writing and working online helped us to add important information throughout this book, particularly in the FAQ sections at the beginning of each part. But their responses also left us with an overwhelming impression of how swiftly changing the tools of electronic communication are, not to mention the conventions for using them. Our best advice, then, returns to a point we stress throughout *The New St. Martin's Handbook:* the importance of collaboration. Your best bet for keeping up with the many changes in electronic communication is to share information widely with your student and teacher colleagues; be ready and willing to learn with and from one another as well as from texts like this one that aim to help you out along the way.

CONSTRUCTING A WRITING PORTFOLIO

You may be most familiar with the term *portfolio* as it is used by artists who collect and display their work or by investors who build portfolios of investments. But another kind of portfolio – and one that makes for an ideal culmination of the process of thinking critically about your writing – is a writing portfolio, one that will show your writing abilities to best advantage. After you have thought carefully and critically about broad content issues related to your writing, about organization, presentation, and surface errors, and about ways to improve individual pieces of writing, you may well want to construct a writing portfolio (indeed, you may be assigned to do so for a course). And as more writing takes place online, you may want or need to create an online portfolio (often called a "Webfolio") that could contain multimedia hypertext. In any event, in constructing a portfolio you can best begin by considering the following issues:

Purpose and audience

What are the purposes for your portfolio: to fulfill course requirements? to show at a job interview? to collect examples of your writing to keep and reflect on throughout your life? Each of these purposes will lead you to make different decisions about what to include and how to arrange the portfolio. If you are fulfilling an assignment, your instructor may well specify what you need to include.

Who is your audience: your instructor? a prospective employer? a scholarship committee? an online community? What you choose to include will be affected by audience. If, for example, it is a writing instructor, you will need to demonstrate what you've learned; if it is a prospective employer, you may need to show what you can do.

Selections

How many entries will you include? Unless the portfolio is strictly for personal purposes and you wish to include everything you write in it, you should probably limit yourself to five to seven examples of your writing. Here and on the next page are some kinds of writing you might include in your portfolio:

- an academic essay demonstrating your ability to argue a claim or position
- an autobiographical essay of some kind, one that shows self-insight and that demonstrates your ability to paint vivid pictures with words
- a brief report, prepared for any class or community project
- a formal essay showing your ability to analyze and solve a problem
- your favorite piece of writing
- writing based on field, library, and online research
- a hypertext or other online document
- an example of a collaboratively written document, accompanied by a description of how the team worked and what you contributed

- an example of your best writing on an essay examination
- correspondence, such as a letter, a memo, a substantive email message or listserv posting, or a job application
- a résumé – either print or online

You should also include the assignments for this work. If your portfolio is for a writing course, you may be expected to include examples of your notes and early drafts, as well as of any response you got from other readers.

Introduction

Regardless of how many and what kinds of examples of your writing you choose to include, you need to include a written statement, perhaps in the form of a memo, that explains and reflects on your work. If you are building a Webfolio, the homepage should include an introduction to the site, an indication of the purpose of the Webfolio, and a clear set of links. In general, introductory statements should:

- *describe what is in the portfolio,* explaining briefly the purpose for each work
- *explain your choices:* how did you decide these pieces of writing represented your best work?
- *reflect on your strengths and abilities as a writer:* what have you learned about writing? what problems have you encountered, and how have you solved them?

Organization

For a print portfolio, prepare a table of contents, and number all pages. Label and date each piece of writing. Put a cover sheet on top with your name and the date; if the portfolio is for a class, include the course title and number and the instructor's name. Then assemble everything in a folder or create some special holder for your portfolio. For a Webfolio, make sure that all links are clearly indicated and that the relationship among links is clear. Also remember to include a "return to homepage" option with each link.

Response

Once you have assembled your portfolio, invite response to it from classmates, friends, instructors, or online audiences. To elicit the best response, you may want to pose specific questions (or for a class in which this text is being used, refer your respondents to the guidelines for reviewing a draft in 4c). Especially if you have assembled a Webfolio, be sure to include a way for readers to contact you, preferably by adding your email address as a link.

If you intend to use a print portfolio as part of a job search, you will want to print out clean copies after you receive any response and make necessary changes. And for a Webfolio, be sure to recheck each part of it carefully before inviting a prospective employer to visit your site, remembering that this kind of online editing is difficult but essential to making a good impression. Whether you decide on a print or an online portfolio, the time and effort you spend revising and editing will be very well spent.

PART 1

THE WRITING PROCESS

documentation

writing/editing

hypertext

message

www.bedfordstmartins.com/nsmhandbook

thinking & collaborating

FAQ ········→

?

FAQ: Writing Online

Online writing takes many forms, including EMAIL, LISTSERV, and NEWSGROUP POSTINGS, HOMEPAGES, HYPERTEXTS, MOOS, MUDS, and IRCS. Before you apply the following advice, be sure it is appropriate for the particular form you're using:

What online format conventions should you know?

- **Subject Lines.** In email and postings, make sure your SUBJECT LINE states your purpose as clearly and succinctly as possible.

  Subject: oops . . .

  This subject line may announce that you've made a mistake of some sort, but it gives no further clues to your purpose in writing. A much more helpful subject line would read:

  Subject: Sorry to miss the meeting 10/3/98

- **Replies.** In email, you may sometimes use the "reply" function to send a message back to someone about a subject that is entirely different from the one stated in the original subject line. In such cases, you should change the subject line. Suppose a colleague has written you under the subject of "trading work shifts." In your reply, if you are changing the subject to ask something about vacation days in 1998, change the subject line to read "Vacation days '98."
- **.Sig files.** Many writers conclude their online communications with a signature block (known as a .SIG FILE) that gives their name, title, address, phone and fax numbers, and so on. These signature files not only identify you but also establish your credentials and thus your authority. Keep your signature block concise:

  Beverly Moss, Director   moss.1@osu.edu
  University Writing Center   614-292-5607
  Ohio State University   614-292-7816 (FAX)

- **Brevity.** In general, keep online messages and postings as brief as possible. Because readers need to scroll to read online text, shorter is often better. Consider limiting your lines to 60–70 characters in order to avoid one- or two-word lines that sometimes occur when one system DOWNLOADS to another.
- **Shouting.** Typing words in all capital letters can seem like SHOUTING and can be very annoying to readers. (Remember, too, that using all lowercase letters can also be annoying.)
- **Graphics.** Before sending any graphics, check to see that the recipients will be able to download them.

http://www.owl@omni.cc.purdue.edu

The Purdue Online Writing Lab *provides handouts on writing-related issues as well as an extensive list of other useful resources on the Web.*

http://uwc.fac.utexas.edu/resource/index.html

The University of Texas Undergraduate Writing Center *offers resources on writing well in college, including handouts on specific issues such as revision, information on documentation and citation of sources, and links to other helpful sites.*

- **Type fonts.** For most academic and professional work, choose traditional fonts such as Courier, New Times Roman, or Arial in 11- or 12-point size. More exotic fonts such as *Bellevue* or **Chicago** are interesting but hard for many people to read.
- **MOOs and MUDs.** Learn from other participants what format conventions are in place.

What should you pay special attention to when you represent yourself online?

- **Introductions.** Include a brief introduction to any messages, especially if you are new to a group or aren't known to readers ("Hello from an interested participant in a recent workplace seminar at which you spoke. I am writing to . . ."). Doing so can help clarify the purpose of your message and thus encourage prompt response.
- **Flaming.** Sometimes writers say things online that they would never say in face-to-face communication. Be careful not to slip into the kind of inconsiderate language known as FLAMING.
- **Proofreading.** Unless you are part of a speedy MOO or MUD conversation, proofread and spell-check your messages before you send them. The higher the stakes of the message, especially if it's likely to be printed out, the more careful you should be about its accuracy.

How do online audiences differ from "print" audiences?

- **Privacy.** Remember that the INTERNET is public and that online readers can take quick action in regard to your messages and postings, printing them out or forwarding them with the click of a MOUSE. If privacy is a prerequisite for a message you want to send, think twice before emailing or posting it.
- **Tone.** Though informal online exchanges can seem a lot like talking, remember that closeness to others doesn't happen instantly, online or off. Write according to how well you really know your audience, as well as to the specific context. Your good friend may also be the company president; when you write to her about company business, you should use an appropriately businesslike tone.

How do you mark paragraphs online?

Long chunks of text are often difficult for readers to process, especially when no diversity of font, use of italics, or boldfacing is possible. If you can't indent your online paragraphs, break your text into block paragraphs, leaving an extra space between each one. You can also help readers by stating the most important information at the beginning of each paragraph.

http://www.missouri.edu/~writery

The University of Missouri's Online Writery *offers advice about writing via email as well as an open discussion list called The Writery Cafe.*

http://www.albion.com/netiquette/index.html

Netiquette Home Page *provides links to a Netiquette Quiz and an online version of Virginia Shea's* Netiquette, *with chapters on writing online, flaming, electronic style, and conventions guiding business and discussion-group netiquette.*

1 Writing, Reading, and Research

Chances are that you have been a writer, reader, and researcher since you were a small child. When you first began trying to write your name, for instance, you were also learning to read what you had written. You were, in addition, doing research — making observations, asking questions, proceeding by trial and error, and probably taking cues from the responses your newfound skills evoked from admiring relatives. You may recall doing some research on possible schools when you were applying to colleges, poring over catalogs (or Web sites) to decide which ones seemed promising before writing up your final applications. In fact, whether you've been aware of it or not, the processes of writing, reading, and researching have been closely interrelated throughout your life. ■

1a Considering the process of writing

No one can complete college without doing a lot of writing, but being able to write effectively is just as important after graduation. In fact, research shows that writing encourages and enhances certain kinds of learning and even that some kinds of complex thinking are extremely difficult to sustain without it. Writing, then, is not a mysterious artistic talent that only a lucky few are born with but an essential and powerful means of discovering what you know and communicating that knowledge to others.

Writers are people who create and explore observations and ideas on paper and care about their readers' responses. In order to write successfully, however, it helps to understand how the writing process works and how to develop a method that works for you. Looking carefully at the way you go about writing, at your processes of writing, should help you determine how to make the kinds of changes that will lead to better writing and greater intellectual rewards.

Although the mental activities that accompany the writing process are tremendously complex, we do know that writers always set and reset a series of goals as they write. These goals range from those as large as "try to make the reader laugh here" or "explain this concept" to those as small as "use a semicolon instead of a period here to make this section flow more smoothly." Researchers often describe the process of writing as **recursive,** meaning that its goals or parts are constantly flowing into and influencing one another, without any clear break among them. This shifting set of goals may focus one moment on deciding how to organize a paragraph and the next moment on using knowledge gained from that decision to revise the wording of a sentence.

In some ways, it is useful to think of the writing process as a series of activities. In *considering the rhetorical situation,* the writer thinks carefully about the purposes the writing is intended to accomplish, the persons to whom it is addressed, his or her own stance toward the topic, and the kind of genre and language best suited to these purposes and this audience. In *exploring, planning, and drafting,* the writer gathers information, develops a tentative thesis and organization, and writes an initial version of the piece. And in *revising, editing, formatting, and proofreading,* the writer improves the draft and polishes its language and appearance to their final form.

But the recursive nature of these activities means that they seldom if ever occur in a linear sequence, with one completed step rigidly following another. Rather, most writers move back and forth – considering the assignment, exploring the topic, thinking about audience, gathering more information, planning, drafting, revising, drafting another section, getting a new idea for formatting while revising again, planning a little more, focusing more sharply on audience, revising yet again, editing, and proofreading – until the writing process is complete.

www

http://www.spaceland.org/paradigm/whtfrms.htm

The Paradigm Online Writing Assistant *offers advice and prompts to help you through all stages of the writing process, from exploring a topic to revising a draft to documenting sources.*

1 Considering the rhetorical situation

In most of your college work, the writing process will begin with an assignment for a course, which becomes the context for your writing – your **rhetorical situation.** It is a good idea to think carefully about the assignment itself, making sure you understand what it is asking you to do and, if necessary, clarifying it with your instructor.

In addition to presenting yourself well and demonstrating your skill as a writer, you will want your writing to accomplish some **purpose** – to persuade your readers to take a certain action, to explain some event or phenomenon to them, and so on. And because specific purposes can be fulfilled only in relation to specific readers, you will want to think carefully about your **audience,** the particular readers you are addressing.

For a complete discussion of the rhetorical situation, see Chapter 2.

2 Exploring

Writing worth reading usually starts with a nagging question or puzzle or idea that calls for some exploration – thinking about what you already know, coming up with a working thesis, gathering information if necessary. Depending on the writing task, **exploring** can last a few minutes or several months. If you have to write a one-page essay in class about your family, you will probably jot down a few notes and start writing very quickly. If, on the other hand, you have six weeks to prepare a fifteen-page paper on U.S.-Japanese relations, you will need to do some research and explore the topic thoroughly before planning what you want to say.

For a complete discussion of exploring, see 3a.

3 Planning

Planning involves deciding how to organize your writing. Sometimes an organizational plan will occur to you at an early stage and help shape your thesis and direct any research you need to do. More often, perhaps, a plan will grow out of the thesis or your search for information. However your plan develops and however tentative it is, it will act as a guide as you produce a first draft. See 3d and 3e.

For a complete discussion of planning, see 3d and 3e.

4 Drafting

As one student put it, **drafting** is that point "where the rubber meets the road," the time when you try your ideas out in writing. As much as anything, drafting serves as a continuation of the process of exploration. No matter how thoroughly you may already have explored your topic, you will discover more about it while drafting. Sometimes these new insights will cause you to turn back – to change your organizational plan, to bring in more information, to approach the subject from a new angle, to rethink the way you appeal to your audience, or even to reconsider your purpose. Drafting, then, is *not* just putting your ideas down on paper. More often than not, it also involves coming up with new ideas.

Because writing an actual draft is just one part of this recursive process, experienced writers rarely try to make their writing come out perfectly the first time. The goal of drafting is not a final copy or even a version good enough to show anyone else. Smooth sentences, the ideal wording and the right punctuation can come later; in your first draft, just write until you run out of ideas to explore.

For a complete discussion of drafting, see 3f.

5 Revising

Revising means literally "seeing again." It means looking at your draft with a critical eye – seeing it anew and deciding if it accomplishes your original goals. You may have assumed before now that revising is simply a matter of correcting misspellings, inserting commas, and keying in the result. Although such tasks are important, true revision is something more. It means examining the draft to reassess the main ideas, the organization, the structure of paragraphs, the variety of sentences, the choice of words, the attitudes toward the topic and the audience, the thoroughness with which the topic is developed. It means polishing to achieve smooth phrasing and memorable prose. It may mean writing new sentences, moving paragraphs, eliminating sections, doing additional research, or even choosing a new topic and starting over.

For a complete discussion of revising, see 4a – g.

Getting responses from others

In addition to analyzing the draft yourself, you may want to get responses from other people. Most writing assumes an audience larger than the writer alone; and revising can be easier and more productive if you actually use such an audience, be it your friends, your classmates, your instructor, or members of online communities you belong to.

For guidelines on reviewing a draft and getting response from others, see 4c.

6 Editing, formatting, and proofreading

Editing involves making what you have written ready for the world, which means making it meet those conventions of written form known as correctness. Sentence structure, spelling, mechanics, punctuation – all should ordinarily meet conventional standards. Editing, too, may lead you to reconsider an idea, a paragraph, a transition, or an organizational pattern – and you may find yourself planning or drafting once again. While you edit, you also need to make final decisions about document design: What font will you use? Will you use color or other graphic devices? When all editing and **formatting** are complete and you have produced a final text, you then must spell-check and **proofread** to catch and correct any typographical errors.

For a complete discussion of editing and proofreading, see 4i and 4j.

7 Thinking critically about your own writing

You probably already have your own characteristic writing process, and one of the best ways to improve this process is to make the effort to analyze it from time to time. You can do this most systematically by keeping a **writing log,** a notebook in which you jot down your thoughts about a writing project while you are working on it or after you have completed it. Studying these notes will help you identify patterns of strength and weakness in your writing, and sharing the writing log with your instructor or your classmates may yield some helpful advice. For more on keeping a writing log and for a sample entry from one student's log, see p. I-4.

To get started thinking critically about your writing process, answer the following questions. If you keep a writing log, record your answers there.

Examining your own process of writing

1. How do you typically go about preparing for a writing assignment? Describe the steps you take – rereading the assignment, asking questions about it, talking to instructors or friends, jotting down ideas, gathering information, and so on. How far in advance of the due date do you usually begin work?
2. When and where do your best ideas often come to you?
3. Where do you usually write? Describe this place. Is it a good place to write? Why, or why not?
4. When you write, are you usually alone? Is there usually music, conversation, or other sounds in the background?
5. What materials do you use? pen or pencil, notepad, loose-leaf paper, index cards, typewriter, computer? What do you find most (and least) helpful about these materials?
6. What audience do most assignments ask you to address? the instructor? classmates? a wider audience? How much thought do you typically give to the audience as you work on the assignment?
7. What strategies do you typically use to explore a topic?
8. How do you usually go about writing a first draft? Do you finish it in one sitting, or do you prefer to take breaks?
9. How do you typically go about revising, and what do you think about most as you revise? Do you write out complete revised drafts or simply insert, delete, or move material? How many drafts or stages of revision do you usually go through? Why?
10. If you get stuck while writing, what do you usually do to get moving again?
11. What would you say is most efficient and most effective about your writing process? What is most enjoyable? What is least efficient and least effective? What is least enjoyable?
12. What specific steps could you take to improve your writing process?

EXERCISE 1.1

Take a few moments to remember all the writing you did when you were applying to college: the letters you wrote, the forms you completed, and so on. In a brief paragraph, describe this writing, and speculate on how it may have helped you be accepted by the college(s) that did accept you. Using the guidelines in 1a7, try to recall the process you followed.

1b Considering the process of reading

If you have ever read a book or seen a movie about Helen Keller, you will remember the electrifying moment when she first learns to "read," when she first realizes that the symbols traced in her palm contain meanings. And so it is with all readers, for all of us build imaginative worlds of meaning, "virtual realities," from words. Think of a time when you were reading along and suddenly realized that you were not getting any meaning, that you were just looking at marks on a page or a screen. Only when you went back and engaged those words actively were you really reading.

1 Reading to write

Reading is closely related to writing, if only because writers need to be able to read their own work with a careful eye. Indeed, one good way to improve your writing is by paying close attention to what you read, taking tips from writers you especially admire. In the words of William Faulkner, "Read, read, read. Read everything – trash, classics, good and bad, and see how they do it." Throughout this handbook, we will be examining the work of well-known writers to "see how they do it," to see what they do with the strategies and structures you yourself will be practicing.

In addition, most chapters include exercises asking you to read a passage with an eye for some element – adjectives, subordination, dashes, and so on. These exercises are designed to help you learn to use these elements in your own writing, to make it more accurate and more powerful.

www •

http://www.dartmouth.edu/admin/acskills/

The Dartmouth College Academic Skills Page *provides tips on reading (and on many other study skills). Click on Learning Strategies Guides.*

2 Reading with a critical eye

The writer Anatole Broyard once cautioned readers about the perils of "just walking through" a book. A good reader, he suggested, "stomps around" in a book – underlining passages, scribbling in the margin, noting any questions or comments. The following guidelines can help you do more than just "walk through" your reading: for more help on reading and evaluating online documents, see 42a3.

SOME GUIDELINES FOR CRITICAL READING

PREVIEWING

→ Determine your purpose for reading. Is it to gather information for an assignment? to determine whether a source will be useful for a research project? to study for a test? to prepare for class discussion?
→ Consider the title. What does it tell you about what is to come?
→ Think about what you already know about the subject. What opinions do you hold on this subject? What do you hope to learn?
→ What do you know about the author? What is the author's purpose? What expertise does he or she have in this subject? What biases might he or she have?
→ Look at how the text is structured. Are there subdivisions? Read over any headings. Skim the opening sentences of each paragraph.
→ Decide what you think the main point or theme of the text will be.

READING AND ANNOTATING

→ Identify key points, important terms, recurring images, and interesting ideas, either by underlining them or by making notes in the margin.
→ Mark places that are confusing or that you want to reread.
→ Note any statements that you disagree with or question and any counterevidence or counterarguments that occur to you.
→ Note any sources used in the text.

SUMMARIZING

→ Summarize the main points. Do they match your expectations? (42c3)
→ Jot down any ideas you want to remember, questions you want to raise, and ideas for how you may use this material.

ANALYZING

→ Identify evidence that supports the main argument or illustrates the main point, as well as any that seems to contradict it.

(continued on page 11)

(continued from page 10)

→ Decide whether the sources used are trustworthy.
→ Identify the writer's underlying assumptions about the subject as well as any biases revealed in the text. (42b)

TALKING WITH OTHERS

→ Compare your understanding of the text with that of some classmates.
→ Pinpoint any differences between your interpretation of main points and that of your classmates.
→ Take turns saying what is most memorable about the reading, what is most confusing or unclear, and what you would like to know more about.

REREADING

→ Reread quickly to be sure you have understood the reading, keeping in mind any alternative views offered by your classmates.
→ Identify the author's purpose. Was that purpose accomplished?
→ Determine whether all the questions you had during the first reading have been answered.

RESPONDING

→ Think about the reading as a whole. What did you like best about it? What puzzled or irritated you? Were your expectations met? If not, why not? What more would you like to know about the subject?
→ Note what you have learned about effective writing from this reading. If you keep a writing log, record your notes there.

EXERCISE 1.2

Following the guidelines in 1b2, read one of the assigned essays from your course text or the student essay in Chapter 4 or Chapter 5 of this book. Summarize the reading briefly, and note any thoughts you have about your critical reading process (in your writing log, if you keep one).

1c Doing research

The reading and writing you do in college are part of what we broadly think of as research: your own *re*-curring search, that is, your own ongoing search for knowledge. In fact, much of the work you do in college turns this sometimes informal search into various kinds of more formal research. An idea that comes to you over pizza, for example, may lead you to conduct a survey that in turn becomes an important piece of evidence in a research project for your sociology class.

Many of your writing assignments will require extensive or formal research. Even if you know the topic very well, your research will be an important tool for establishing credibility with your audience and thus gaining their confidence in you as a writer.

For a complete discussion of research, see Chapters 40 – 43.

1d Remembering the importance of talking and listening

For a number of reasons, the arts of language – reading, writing, speaking, and listening – are often treated separately in school. As printed or electronic text has taken on more and more importance in our society, reading and writing have come to take precedence over talking and listening in most formal education.

Recent developments in media and technology, however, have made it seem both impractical and unwise to draw strict boundaries among these arts. After all, as noted above, writers are always readers of their own texts; they may also hear their texts read aloud, and they may read or speak them aloud themselves. To take a familiar example, when we watch a presidential State of the Union Address, we appear to be listening. But we are also "reading" the president's presentation – his facial expressions, gestures, and body language. And if we go on to think about or otherwise interpret the address, then in some sense we may be said to be "writing" as well. Moreover, the president is almost always reading a carefully crafted written text and listening to the response of the live audience and perhaps even to electronic cues from his advisors in order to make minute changes in his delivery.

1 Talking to learn

www

http://www.wwcd.org/action/ampu/bray.html

In a short essay on the importance of talking and listening to sustain a civil and culturally diverse society, Rosemary Bray argues for the importance of shared stories and a kind ear.

In your college work, you will do plenty of talking and listening, and those activities will add immeasurably to the quality of your thinking and learning. Throughout, this text encourages you to talk over your work with others, to engage in collaborative learning. Talking in this way can help you in all of the following areas:

- making points you can use later
- explaining your ideas to others and getting immediate feedback

- working out problems with writing and other assignments
- putting what you learn into your own words
- warming up for writing or reading assignments

2 Listening to learn

The flip side of talking is listening, an art that is of tremendous importance to success in personal relationships as well as in college. You can maximize the value of listening if you use these tips:

- *Really* listen — consistently and attentively. Practicing this kind of concentration will yield surprisingly quick results.
- Try to listen purposefully. Concentrate on the big points and on what you most need to know.
- Ask questions that will yield answers worth listening to, that will help you get the information you need.
- Take notes. Try to repeat information in your own words.

3 Using spoken and written language appropriately

Writing is linked to talking in important ways, particularly if the speaker is a political leader or a talk-show host working on television or radio — or anyone using technologies that tend to blur distinctions between speech and writing (such as email). In spite of their close connection, however, mixing spoken and written forms is not always appropriate. In most college writing, stick primarily to written forms of standard academic English, inserting spoken forms to quote others, to capture the sounds and rhythms of speech, or to create other special effects. Even in making oral presentations, you will probably want to write out your presentation to make sure it is clear and accessible.

For a discussion of oral presentations, see Chapter 50.

EXERCISE 1.3

One good way to recognize differences in degree between spoken and written language is to record yourself and a friend in casual conversation for half an hour or so. Listen to the tape, choose a five-minute segment, and transcribe it word for word, trying to get down exactly what you said. You may have to invent some spellings to capture your speech accurately. Then choose a two-page sample of your writing that you think represents some of your best work. Compare the two samples, noting differences in the occasion or purpose for writing or speaking, in content, in sentence types, and in word choice. What differences can you note between your own speaking and writing?

For guidelines on taking notes while doing research, see 42c.

1e Taking notes

In much college work, good note-taking is a kind of survival skill; and learning how to take notes most effectively will add to your success as a critical reader, writer, and listener. Here are some guidelines to help you review your own note-taking processes.

- *Consider your purpose.* Are you taking down a quotation that you intend to use in an essay? recording key words and phrases in outline form during a lecture to use when you study for an exam? recording the major points in a reading assignment, using your own words, paraphrases, or summaries in preparation for a class discussion? noting your personal responses and reactions to something you are reading, looking for an idea you may turn into the beginning of an essay? Knowing your purpose in note-taking can help you decide exactly what you should write down.
- *Consider your own style.* Do you think best with pencil in hand, stopping often as you read to jot down an idea, or writing notes almost continuously as you listen to a lesson or lecture? Or does the act of writing distract you, so that you lose track of what you are reading or hearing? Thinking about these questions can help you decide whether you should take notes while reading and listening – or whether it is more effective for you to listen or read first and then take notes soon thereafter.
- If you are taking notes while reading or attending a lecture, *look for the major points, and note their relationships to one another.* When you want to recall information from a reading or a lecture, a series of random jottings is usually less helpful than a series of clearly related points.
- *Label your notes* so that you can remember where they came from. If you are taking notes in class, simply head the sheet of paper with the course title and date. If you are taking notes from a printed source, note the book's or the article's author, title, and place and date of publication. If you are taking notes from an online document, write down the precise electronic address as well as the date and time of your access. If you are taking personal notes, consider heading the page with a label reminding you of the purpose for the notes.

1f Benefiting from collaboration

The philosopher Hannah Arendt once remarked that "for excellence, the presence of others is always required." Nowhere is Arendt's observation more accurate than in the college community, where you can be part of a broad conversation that includes all the texts you read; all the writing you produce; all the talks you have with teachers, friends, classmates, and others (whether in person or electronically); all the observations and interviews you conduct; all the discussions and lectures you listen to. It is this broad conversation we have in mind when we stress the importance of collaboration to you as a student seeking to achieve excellence in college and throughout your life.

For this term at least, the most immediate and valuable of your collaborators may be the members of the class in which you are using this book. You can learn a great deal by talking over issues and comparing ideas with them and by using them as a first audience for your writing; for they will inevitably offer you new perspectives, new ways of seeing and knowing.

In online communication, the categories of "writer" and "reader" and "text" become dramatically fluid and permeable, as almost instantaneously readers can become writers and then readers again, and as texts refuse to stay put, modulating and evolving in dizzying and intriguing ways. Because of these possibilities, online communication is often deeply and richly collaborative, full of multiple voices and texts. But while computers allow for more and more varied kinds of collaboration, working with others always demands special care and attention. The following guidelines can help you work effectively with others, whether the collaboration takes place online or off:

www •

http://www.shout.net/~sigfried

The Collaborator *is a site where you can post work for response. Anyone with Web access can participate.*

SOME GUIDELINES FOR COLLABORATING WITH OTHERS

1. **Your instructor may well assign groups of students to work together in class or online. If not, remember that for face-to-face work, the smaller the group, the better your chances of finding meeting times in common. Consider setting up a group of between three and five members.**
2. **Think carefully about the purposes of your collaboration. Can these purposes be best accomplished by working face-to-face, online, or some combination of both?**
3. **Agree on a way to contact one another out of class, and set a regular time for meetings.**
4. **Set an agenda for each meeting. If, for instance, you need to work on introductions to an essay, agree to provide several versions for**

(continued on page 16)

(continued from page 15)

each member of the group to evaluate and respond to in advance, perhaps by email. If you intend to read and critique entire drafts, arrange to distribute copies to each member ahead of time. If you are assigned to do a *group* project or report, divide up the work fairly, and set up a time line to guide each person's work.

5. Use the meetings not only to discuss assignments but also to work together on difficult readings or problems – or to prepare for an examination. If an assignment is long, ask each member to explain one section to the others. If the group has trouble understanding something, ask your instructor for help.
6. Establish ground rules for your group work. The first might be that every member have an equal opportunity to contribute to the group. Consider assigning (and sharing) duties at each meeting: one person acts as general notetaker, for instance, and another keeps the discussion on the topic at hand. Remember the importance of courtesy; for online work, be especially cautious of *flaming* (see p. 3) or of making comments *offlist*.
7. Listen carefully to what each person says. If discussion lags or disagreements arise, try paraphrasing what each person has said to see if everyone is hearing the same things.
8. Decide on a means of resolving conflicts. Will the group work by majority rule? If so, all members must have an opportunity to state their positions fully before a vote is taken. Remember that creative and constructive conflict is desirable in group discussions: if everyone just agrees to go along, the result is usually a watered-down effort. The trick is to get a really spirited debate going, to listen to all perspectives, to argue out all possibilities – without being hostile. If a conflict does arise, take turns putting the point of contention in the words of each participant, and then look for some common ground that can serve to get the discussion going again.
9. Establish periodic times at which to assess the group's effectiveness, with all group members addressing the following questions: What has the group accomplished so far? What has it been most helpful with? What has it been least helpful with? What has each member contributed? What about the group is not working well? How can we make the group more effective?

(continued on page 17)

(continued from page 16)

10. If the group will be making a presentation, be sure you know exactly what the assignment calls for and exactly how much time you will have. Divide the preparatory work fairly, and complete it some days *before* the presentation, leaving time for at least two practice sessions. Then decide how each group member will contribute to the presentation, making sure that everyone has a role – especially if individual grades will be assigned. (See Chapter 50.)

11. If you are preparing a group-written document, consider dividing up the drafting duties among all group members. Then schedule at least two meetings to hammer out the draft *together,* working for clarity and consistency of tone as well as for strong organization and plenty of supporting detail. (If possible, these meetings should be face-to-face so that you can read the draft aloud.) When the final draft is ready, have every member proofread, and assign one member to make last-minute corrections.

12. For working collaboratively online, consider logistics, and establish clear duties for each participant. Share information on all electronic resources: What kinds of computers, printing capabilities, and access to email and the Internet do all participants have?

    → If necessary, identify an "expert" to create a distribution list and to teach others how to use email, how to attach files to email, how to save files in various formats, and how to join in real-time conferences. (See 2i.)

    → Choose an archivist who will be responsible for making frequent backups of all material generated in online communication, for archiving all materials, and for providing summaries of conversational strands to help keep everyone on track.

    → If you are preparing a group-written document or print text, choose an editor who will be responsible for formatting and other design issues.

    → Divide remaining duties as equally as possible.

2 Considering Rhetorical Situations

What do an engaging magazine article, a letter that leads to a correction in your Visa bill, and a successful proposal for a scientific research grant all have in common? Most likely, the writers of all three have analyzed their rhetorical situations astutely and then responded to them in appropriate ways. The rhetorical situation is made up of a number of important elements: the writing assignment (if any), the writer's purpose(s) and stance toward the topic, the audience for which the writing is intended, and the genre of writing and kind of language these elements seem to call for. And now electronic contexts bring many new rhetorical questions to consider. This chapter will get you started in thinking about these crucial elements of any writing situation. ■

2a Deciding to write

Because elements like purpose and audience are such important considerations in effective writing, you should start thinking about them at an early stage, as soon as you make the decision to write. In a general sense, of course, this decision is often made for you. Your editor sets a Tuesday deadline for your newspaper story; a professor announces that a research paper will be due next month; your employer asks for a full report on a complex issue before the next management meeting. But even in such situations, consciously *deciding to write* is important. Experienced writers report that making up their minds to begin a writing task represents a big step toward getting the job done.

2b Identifying a problem

When a topic is left open, many writers put off getting started because they can't think of or decide on the topic. Experienced writers say that the best way to choose a topic is literally to let the topic choose you. That is, the subjects that compel you – that puzzle, confuse, irritate, or in some way pose a problem for you – are likely to engage your interests and hence evoke your best writing.

You can begin to identify a problem by thinking through the following questions:

- What topics do you wish you knew more about?
- What topics are most likely to get you fired up?
- What about one of these topics is most confusing to you? most exciting? most irritating? most tantalizing?
- What person or group might this topic raise problems for?

EXERCISE 2.1

Think back to a recent writing assignment. What helped you finally decide to write? Once you had decided to write, what exactly did you do to get going? In a paragraph or two, describe your situation, and answer these questions. Then compare your description with those of two or three classmates.

2c Understanding writing assignments

Most on-the-job writing addresses specific purposes, audiences, and topics: a group of scientists produces a report on food additives for the federal government; an editorial assistant composes a memo for an editor, summarizing the problems in a new manuscript; a team of psychologists prepares video scripts intended to help companies deal with alcoholism among their employees. These writers all have one thing in common: specific goals. They know why, for whom, and about what they are writing.

College writing assignments, in contrast, may seem to appear out of the blue, with no specific purpose, audience, or topic. In extreme cases, they may be only one word long, as in a theater examination that consisted of the single word *Tragedy!* At the opposite extreme come assignments in the form of fully developed, very specific cases, often favored in business and engineering courses.

www •

http://www.cohums.ohio-state.edu/history/essayexm.htm

Tips on writing essay exams provide useful — and downloadable — test-taking strategies.

In between the one-word exam and the fully developed case, you may get assignments that specify purpose but not audience – to write an essay arguing for or against capital punishment, for example. Or you may be given an organizational pattern to use – to compare and contrast two of the novels you have read in a course – but no specific topic. Because comprehending an assignment accurately and fully is crucial to your success in responding to it, you should always make every effort to do so.

→ *What exactly does the assignment ask you to do?* Look for words like *analyze, classify, compare, contrast, describe, discuss, define, explain,* and *survey.* Remember that these words may differ in meaning among disciplines – *analyze* might mean one thing in literature, another in biology.

→ *What knowledge or information do you need?* Do you need to do any research? (3a and c)

→ *How can you limit – or broaden – the topic or assignment to make it more interesting?* Do you have interest in or knowledge about any particular aspect of the topic? Be sure to check with your instructor if you wish to redefine the assignment in any way.

→ *What problem(s) does the topic suggest to you?* How might the problem(s) give you an interesting angle on the topic?

→ *What are the assignment's specific requirements?* Consider genre, length, format, organization, and deadline. Being sure of such things will help you know the scope expected. Your instructor is not likely to expect extensive library research for a paper due in twenty-four hours, for example. If no length is designated, ask for some guidelines. (2e)

→ *What is your purpose as a writer?* Do you need to demonstrate knowledge of certain material? Do you mainly need to show your ability to express certain ideas clearly? (2d)

→ *Who is the audience for this writing?* Does the task imply that you will *assume* a particular readership besides your instructor? (2h)

In the next two chapters, we will follow the work of Jennifer Gerkin on an essay for her first-year English course at Ohio State University. Her class was given the assignment "Examine the effects of prejudice on your life, and discuss your efforts to deal with those effects."

Jennifer saw that the assignment was broad enough to allow her to focus on something that interested her, and she knew that the key word *examine* invited her to describe – and analyze – situations concerning prejudice in her life. Her instructor said to assume that he and members of the class would be the primary audience.

EXERCISE 2.2

The following assignment was given to an introductory psychology class: "Discuss in an essay the contributions of Jung and Freud to modern clinical psychology." What would you need to know about the assignment in order to respond successfully? Using the questions in 2c, analyze this assignment.

2d Deciding on your purposes

The writing of college essays, reports, and other assignments almost always involves multiple purposes. On one level, you are writing to establish your credibility with your instructor, to demonstrate that you are a careful thinker and an effective writer. On another level, though, you are writing to achieve goals of your own, to say as clearly and forcefully as possible what you think about a topic.

For example, if you are writing an essay about abortion, your purposes might be to inform your readers, to persuade them to support or oppose legalized abortion, or even to clarify in your own mind the medical information about abortion or the moral debate over it. If you are writing a profile of your eccentric grandfather, you might be trying to amuse your readers and to pay tribute to someone who has been important to you.

In ancient Rome, the great orator Cicero noted that a good speech generally fulfills one of three major purposes: to delight, to teach, or to move. Today, our purposes when we communicate with one another remain pretty much the same: we seek to *entertain* (delight), to *inform and explain* (teach), and to *persuade or convince* (move).

Most of the writing you do in college will address one or some of these purposes, and it is thus important for you to be able to recognize the overriding purpose of any piece of writing. If, for example, a history professor asks you to explain the events that led up to the 1964 Civil Rights Act (primary purpose: to explain) and you write an impassioned argument on the need for the act (primary purpose: to persuade), you have misunderstood the purpose of the assignment.

For most college writing, you should consider purpose in terms of the *assignment,* the *instructor's expectations,* and *your own goals.*

CONSIDERING PURPOSES

→ **_What is the primary purpose of the assignment_ — to entertain? to explain? to persuade? or some other purpose? What does this purpose suggest about the best ways to achieve it? If you are unclear about the primary purpose, have you talked with your instructor about it? Are there any secondary purposes to keep in mind?**

→ **_What are the instructor's purposes in giving this assignment_ — to make sure you have read certain materials? to determine whether you understand**

(continued on page 22)

(continued from page 21)

certain materials? to evaluate your thinking and writing abilities? to determine whether you can evaluate certain materials critically? How can you fulfill these expectations?

→ ***What are your goals in carrying out this assignment*** **— to meet the instructor's expectations? to learn as much as possible about a new topic? to communicate your ideas as clearly and forcefully as possible? How can you achieve these goals?**

As she considered the assignment, Jennifer Gerkin saw that her primary purpose was to explain the effects of prejudice on her life, but she recognized some other purposes as well. Because this essay was assigned early in the term, she wanted to get off to a good start; thus one of her purposes was to write as well as she could, to demonstrate her ability to her classmates and her instructor. In addition, she decided that she wanted to find out something new about herself and to use this knowledge to get her readers to think about themselves.

FOR MULTILINGUAL WRITERS

Bringing in Other Languages

Even when you write in English, you may want or need to include words, phrases, or whole passages in another language. If so, consider whether your readers will understand that language and whether you need to provide a translation, as in this example from John (Fire) Lame Deer's "Talking to the Owls and Butterflies":

Listen to the air. You can hear it, feel it, smell it, taste it. *Woniya waken* — the holy air — which renews all by its breath. *Woniya, woniya waken* — spirit, life, breath, renewal — it means all that.

In this instance, translation is necessary because the phrase Lame Deer is discussing has multiple meanings in English. (See 28f for details about how to provide translations in your text.)

EXERCISE 2.3

Choose one of the following assignments, and describe its various purposes. If your instructor chooses, this exercise may be done in small groups, with one member taking notes and reporting to the rest of the class.

1. Compare two book-length studies of Malcolm X.
2. Discuss the controversies surrounding the use of genetic engineering to change characteristics of unborn children.
3. Analyze the use of headlines in a group of twenty advertisements.
4. Describe a favorite spot in your hometown.
5. Explain the concept of virtual reality.

2e Considering genre

Most of the writing you do in college will fall into the broad genre of academic discourse. Thus you can benefit from considering what distinguishes academic discourse from other **genres,** or kinds, of writing, such as poetry, drama, fiction, business correspondence, or advertising copy, to name but a few examples. The **academic writing** you do most often will have the following characteristics:

- *standard academic English,* characterized by the conventional use of grammar, spelling, punctuation, and mechanics
- *reader-friendly organization,* which introduces and links ideas clearly so that readers can easily follow the text — or hypertext
- *a clearly stated claim supported by various kinds of information,* including examples, statistics, personal experiences, anecdotes, and authority
- *conventional academic formats,* among them lab reports, literature reviews, and research essays
- *a conventional and easy-to-read font size and typeface*

2f Considering language

Although most of your college writing will be done in standard academic English, some of it may demand that you use specialized occupational or professional varieties of English — those characteristic of medicine, say, or science or law or music. Similarly, you may wish to use regional or ethnic varieties of English to catch the sound of someone's spoken words. You may even need to use words from a language other than English — in quoting someone, perhaps, or in using certain technical terms. In considering your use of language, think about what languages and varieties of English will be most appropriate for reaching your audience and accomplishing your purposes.

For a discussion of using different varieties of English and other languages, see Chapter 28.

EXERCISE 2.4

Consider a writing assignment you are currently working on. What are its purposes in terms of the assignment, the instructor, and you, the writer? What genre, or kind of writing, does it call for?

2g Considering your rhetorical stance

"Where do you stand on that?" is a question often asked, particularly of those running for office or occupying positions of authority. But as writers, we must ask the question of ourselves as well. Thinking about where you stand on your topic, your **rhetorical stance,** will help you examine where your opinions come from and thus help you address the topic fully. And knowing your own stance well will help you see how it might differ from the stances held by members of your audience.

A student writing a proposal for increased services for people with disabilities, for instance, knew that having a brother with Down syndrome gave her an intense interest in this topic that her audience might not have. She would need to work hard, then, to get her audience to understand – and share – her stance.

EXAMINING YOUR RHETORICAL STANCE

- **→ What is your overall attitude toward the topic? approval? dislike? curiosity? indifference? How strong are your opinions?**
- **→ What social, political, religious, personal, or other influences have contributed to your attitude?**
- **→ How much do you know about the topic? What questions do you have about it?**
- **→ What interests you *most* about the topic? Why?**
- **→ What interests you *least* about it? Why?**
- **→ What seems important – or unimportant – about the topic?**
- **→ What preconceptions, if any, do you have about it?**
- **→ What do you expect to conclude about the topic?**

2h Focusing on your audience

We know that skilled writers consider their audiences carefully. In fact, one of the characteristic traits of a mature writer is the ability to write for a variety of audiences, using language, style, and evidence appropriate to particular readers. The key word here is *appropriate:* just as a funeral director would hardly greet a bereaved family with *Hi, there! What can I do for you?* neither would you be likely to sprinkle jokes through an analysis of child abuse written for a PTA. Why not? Because such behavior would be wildly inappropriate given the nature of your audience.

Although an instructor may serve as the primary audience for much of your college writing, you may sometimes find yourself writing for others: lab reports addressed to your class, business proposals addressed to a hypothetical manager, or information searches posted to an online audience. Every writer can benefit from thinking carefully about who the audience is, what the audience already knows or thinks, and what the audience needs and expects to find out.

→ What person or group do you most want to reach? your boss? other students? scientists? people already sympathetic to your views? people unsympathetic to your views? potential voters? an online group you belong to — or don't belong to?

→ How much do you know about your audience? In what ways may its members differ from you? from one another? Think in terms of education, geographical region, age, gender, occupation, social class, ethnic and cultural heritage, politics, religion, marital status, sexual orientation, and so on. (See Chapter 29.)

→ What assumptions can you make about your audience? What might they value? Think in terms of qualities such as brevity, originality, conformity, honesty, security, adventure, wit, seriousness, thrift, generosity, and so on. What goals and aspirations do they have?

→ What languages and varieties of English does your audience know and use? What special language, if any, will they expect you to use? (See Chapter 28.)

→ What is your audience's stance toward your topic? What are they likely to know about it? What preconceived views might they have?

→ What is your relationship to the audience? Is it student to instructor? friend to friend? subordinate to superior? superior to subordinate? citizen to community? something else?

→ What is your attitude toward the audience? Is it friendly? hostile? neutral? one of admiration? of impatience?

→ What attitudes will the audience expect you to hold? What attitudes might disturb or offend them?

→ What kind(s) of response(s) do you want to evoke?

In addition to her instructor, Jennifer Gerkin's audience included the members of her writing class. Thinking about her classmates, Jennifer saw that they were mostly her age; that they were almost all the same race, Caucasian; that they were all from the Midwest. But she was also sure that they had many differences, which she would learn about as they all worked together.

1 Addressing specific audiences

Thinking systematically about your audience can help you make decisions about a writing assignment. For example, it can help you decide what sort of organizational plan to follow (you might choose one that would be easiest for a particular audience to understand), what information to include or exclude, and even what specific words to use. If you are writing an article for a journal for nurses about a drug that prevents patients from developing infections from intravenous feeding tubes, you will not need to give much information about how such tubes work or to define many terms. But if you are writing about the same topic in a pamphlet for patients, you will have to give a great deal of background information and define (or avoid) technical terms.

EXERCISE 2.5

To experiment with how considerations of appropriateness for a particular audience affect what you write, describe one of your courses to three audiences: your best friend, your parents, and a group of high school students attending an open house at your college. Then describe the differences in content, organization, and wording that the differences in audience led you to make.

2 Appealing to your whole audience

All writers need to pay very careful attention to the ways in which their writing can either invite readers to participate as part of the audience or leave them out. Look at the following sentence:

> As every schoolchild knows, the world is losing its rain forests at the rate of one acre per second.

The writer here gives a clear message about who is — and who is not — part of the audience: if you don't know this fact or have reason to suspect it is not true, you are not invited to participate.

There are various ways you, as a writer, can help make readers feel they are part of your audience. Be especially careful with the pronouns you use, the assumptions you make, and the kinds of support you offer for your ideas.

Using appropriate pronouns

The pronouns you use can include or exclude readers. Study the following example:

> As Americans, we have an absolute constitutional right to bear arms.

The sentence implies that all of "us" Americans agree that "we" have the right to carry guns. But what if you are not in favor of this proposition?

Then this language is likely to make you feel even more antagonistic, because the writer is speaking for you in ways you don't like. As a writer, use *we* to include your readers only when those you are addressing really fall into the group you are implying.

Making no unfounded assumptions

Be careful about any assumptions you make about your readers and their views, especially in the use of language that may unintentionally exclude readers you want to include. Use words like *naturally* and *of course* carefully, for what seems natural to you – that English should be the official U.S. language, for instance, or that smoking should be outlawed – may not seem at all natural to some members of your audience. The best advice about any audience you wish to address is to take nothing about them for granted.

Offering appropriate evidence

The examples and other evidence you offer in support of your arguments can help draw in your readers. The student mentioned in 2g, for example, who was writing about services for people with disabilities, might ask readers who have no personal experience with the topic to imagine themselves in a wheelchair, trying to enter a building with steps but no ramp. She would be clearly inviting them to be part of her audience and would be helping them accept her ideas. On the other hand, inappropriate evidence can leave readers out. Complex statistical evidence might well appeal to public-policy planners but may bore or even irritate ordinary citizens.

For more about building common ground with an audience, see Chapter 29.

2i Considering online rhetorical situations

Before the advent of writing systems, the contexts for communication were always oral, what many now call "f2f" or face-to-face. Contexts for oral exchanges still vary widely (from an intimate dinner conversation, say, to a formal lecture), but written scripts have made these contexts ever more varied. Today, with the wide availability of personal computers, the possibilities for written communication can seem almost endless, as children in Alaskan villages exchange email with counterparts in Samoa or as teams of investigators around the world converse simultaneously online to solve a mutual problem.

SOME ONLINE CONTEXTS

- → **Internet** – the network that links computers worldwide, giving you access to the following options:
- → **World Wide Web** – in the words of *WiredStyle*, "an application running on top of the Internet" that is a "warehouse of information on almost every conceivable subject"
- → **email** – short for "electronic mail," a system for getting and sending messages
- → **listservs** – the software that allows you to join various online groups, including newsgroups, bulletin boards (BBSes), even class discussion groups that may be set up by your instructor
- → **synchronous communication systems** – such as IRCs (chat rooms), MOOs, and MUDs, that allow you to talk with others in **real time**, with messages delivered as they are typed

1 Understanding online contexts

The contexts for online communication are changing and multiplying daily. But what can we say about them as they currently exist?

First, *online contexts offer many new ways to get information and join conversations*. As a result, you will need to learn to manage large amounts of information and to sharpen your critical-thinking skills so that you are able to distinguish what is reliable, accurate, and useful to you.

Second, *online contexts are primarily public*. List managers, institutional officers, often anyone with technical know-how or even just access to your name, can retrieve past email you have sent. What may seem like a private email conversation is routinely archived and accessible, as was the case with messages one writer thought had been "trashed" but were later subpoenaed as part of a legal trial. Therefore you will need to consider whether you are willing to have what you are putting online become public knowledge.

Third, *online messages travel*. Just as you may clip a paragraph out of a message and send it on to a friend, so your online messages may be forwarded to others, downloaded, and disseminated. As a result, you have to consider how such traveling may affect the messages you send – and keep careful track of what you may be moving from one context to another. In the same way, you have to think carefully before you forward someone else's messages: do you think you have the writer's permission to do so?

Finally, *online writing is faster than other forms of written communication.* The flashing indicator onscreen, the ability of MOO and MUD participants to respond immediately to a message or of Web browsers to call up whole texts and images with the click of a mouse — all create sensations of speed and urgency in readers' minds, making them expect to be able to process and respond to messages quickly. Even lengthy messages may need to be clearer and more concise online than offline.

2 Considering specific online rhetorical issues

Online contexts create distinctive rhetorical situations that require careful thought and decisions by writers. What are some of the considerations you need to keep in mind?

Purposes

The purposes of online communication may vary widely — from getting or sharing information, to participating in a game in a virtual world, to asking for or giving help, to holding a conference. Let your purpose guide you in choosing an appropriate online context and audience(s) for your communication.

Persona

Consider whether the way you are representing yourself online is appropriate to your purpose, your subject, and your audience. The *persona* or identity you establish in email messages or listserv postings plays an important part in determining how effective they are. Remember that the immediacy of online communication can make audiences seem "up close and personal" when in fact they are distant from the writer both physically and emotionally. Think about your relationship to your online readers, and adopt a tone appropriate to that relationship.

www •

http://www.levity.com/julian/alamodem.html

"The Writer a la Modem" is an essay by Julian Dibbell about how going online helped him as a writer.

Responsibilities

As an online communicator, you stand behind the *accuracy and reliability* of information you send or post. Make sure you can take full responsibility for your messages and the effects they may have on others — especially if you are using a pseudonym. The *sources* you use need to be accounted for, especially if you are forwarding a message or a text you have found elsewhere on the Net. If the materials you want to use may be copyrighted, get permission to use them. (See pages 432 - 433.)

Logistics

Physical, financial, and other constraints may affect your ability to communicate online. Especially when readers may be paying for the messages they get from you, you will want to be as concise as possible. And if you have a deadline or other time constraints, or if you are working in a lab, you need to use your time efficiently: no game playing or aimless surfing!

Online formats and conventions

Subject lines should be clear, accurate, and straightforward (not "Help" but "Request for background reading on hypertext"). In addition, messages should be as concise and easy to read as possible; use *asterisks or numbers* to create lists and blank space to break up text. **Signature lines** (.sig files) at the ends of messages are also important: keep them straightforward and brief (no more than five lines). Finally, if you want to use **emoticons** (or *smileys*) such as :-) or :-o (for *smile* or *surprise*), make sure that they will be meaningful to your readers and add to the clarity and effectiveness of your message.

3 Considering issues of netiquette

Netiquette, the good manners of the digital world, calls for treating others online as you hope they will treat you. Here are some tips for being a good online citizen:

- Make it your business to *know and respect the rules or policies* set forth by the college or company whose online services you are using. In addition to not using computers for games or commercial purposes, these may include such matters as cleaning out files to free up disc space for others. In MOOs, listservs, and other group discussion formats, check the new-subscriber information or ask other participants for guidelines.
- *Avoid **flaming,*** or personal attacks. Try to put yourself in your readers' shoes; think about how they may interpret your message, and check to see that it won't be perceived as a flame. If you feel that you have been flamed, try not to respond in kind. Sometimes what you perceive as a flame was not intended as one. And even if it was, similar behavior on your part won't help improve communication.
- Whenever possible, *be a generous reader* of other people's communications, especially if they are hurried or part of real-time communication: no need to harp on every typo, for example.

- In general, *use capital and lowercase letters in the conventional way*. Using all capital letters comes across online as SHOUTING and is often irritating or even offensive to readers, and using all lowercase letters can make writing harder to read.
- If you are including part of an original message in a response or posting, *keep only the part that is related to your response* so that readers don't have to wade through a lot of irrelevant material. Avoid adding your response at the bottom of someone else's message or posting: doing so forces readers to scroll all the way through the original message(s) to get to your response.

THINKING CRITICALLY ABOUT PURPOSE AND AUDIENCE

Reading with an Eye for Purpose and Audience

Advertisements provide good examples of writing that is tailored carefully for specific audiences. Find two ads for the same product that appeal to different audiences. You might compare ads in a men's magazine to those in a women's magazine to see what differences there are in the messages and photography. Or you could look at products that seem to appeal to men (Marlboro cigarettes, perhaps) next to those that are marketed to women (such as Virginia Slims). What conclusions can you draw about ways of appealing to specific audiences?

Thinking about Your Own Attention to Purpose and Audience

Consider something you have written or are working on right now.

1. Can you state its purpose(s) clearly and succinctly? If not, what can you do to clarify its purpose(s)?
2. What other purposes for this piece of writing can you imagine? How would fulfilling some other purpose change the writing?
3. Can you tell from reading the piece who the intended audience is? If so, what in your text clearly relates to that audience? If not, what can you add that will strengthen your appeal to this audience?
4. What other audiences can you imagine? How would the writing change if you were to address a different audience?
5. Does your writing follow the conventions of standard academic discourse — and if not, how should you revise so it will?

If you are keeping a writing log, enter any conclusions you can make about purpose and audience in your own writing.

3 Exploring, Planning, and Drafting

The late Lewis Thomas, one of America's most celebrated essayists, began writing essays when he was invited to contribute a monthly column to the *New England Journal of Medicine*. A scientist and medical doctor, Thomas at first tried various methods of planning and organizing, including making meticulous outlines. Nothing seemed to work. After producing several "dreadful" essays, he shook off all attempts at detailed planning and just plunged right in, thinking about and developing his ideas by simply writing as fast as he could.

Like Thomas, you may do your best by diving right into your writing projects, exploring your topics as you draft. Or you may work more effectively by producing detailed blueprints before you ever begin drafting. There are many productive ways to go about exploring, planning, and drafting. This chapter takes a close look at some of the ways these activities work in practice. ■

3a Exploring a topic

The point is so simple that we often forget it: we write best about topics we know well. One of the most important parts of the entire writing process, therefore, is exploring your topic, surveying what you know about it and then determining what you need to find out about it. If you do not already have a system for exploring topics you wish to write about, this chapter's brief description of strategies may be very useful. The strategies include brainstorming, freewriting, looping, clustering, and questioning.

1 Brainstorming: talking with others

The most immediate way to begin exploring a topic is also the easiest and most familiar: *talk it over* with others. As you talk about your topic, you can hear your mind at work, articulating what you think about the topic and what you most need to know about it. You can also seek out those who know about your topic and talk with them, listening carefully and taking notes.

One excellent way to talk with others about your topic is in a brainstorming session. Used widely in business and industry, **brainstorming** means tossing out ideas – either in person or via computer – to discover new ways to approach a topic. If you don't have others to talk with, however, you can still easily brainstorm. All you need is a pen, pencil, or computer keyboard and some blank paper, and you are ready to carry out the following steps:

1. Set a time limit of five or ten minutes to write down in list form *every* word or phrase that comes to mind about your topic. Just put down key words and phrases, not sentences. No one has to understand the list but you. Don't worry about whether something will be useful or not. Just get it *all* down.
2. If nothing much seems to occur to you, try thinking the opposite. If you are trying, for instance, to think of reasons to reduce tuition at your college and are coming up blank, try concentrating on reasons to *increase* tuition. Once you start generating ideas in one direction, you can move back to exploring the other side of the topic.
3. When the time is up, stop and read over your list. If anything else comes to mind, add it to the list. Then reread the list, looking for patterns, clusters of interesting ideas, or one central idea.

2 Freewriting

Freewriting is a method of exploring a topic by writing about it – or whatever else it brings to mind – for a period of time *without stopping*. Here is the way to do it:

1. Set a time limit of no more than ten minutes. Begin by thinking about your topic, and then simply let your mind wander, writing down everything that occurs to you, in complete sentences as much as possible. Don't stop for anything; if necessary, write "I can't think of what to write next" over and over until something else occurs to you.
2. When the time is up, look at what you have written. You are sure to find much that is unusable, irrelevant, or nonsensical. But you may also find important insights and ideas.
3. If you are using a computer for freewriting, remember to save everything to a special file. You can then go back and reread, easily cutting and pasting sentences or even parts of paragraphs into a draft.

www •

http://www.dejanews.com/

Sometimes you can't find anyone who can talk with you about a topic. If so, try DejaNews, *a tool for searching Usenet discussion groups. Usenet groups cover thousands of topics.*

3 Looping

Looping is a form of directed freewriting that narrows or focuses a topic in five-minute stages, or loops. Here is how to do looping:

1. With your topic in mind, spend five minutes freewriting *without stopping*. This is your first loop.
2. Look back at what you have written. Find the strongest or most intriguing thought. This is your "center of gravity," which you should summarize in a single sentence; it will become the starting point of your next loop. If

you are using a computer, simply cut and paste, or copy, the sentence you have chosen to a new page – and continue with your looping.

3. Starting with the summary sentence from your first loop, spend another five minutes freewriting. Look for a center of gravity within this second piece of freewriting, which will form the basis of a third loop. Keep this process going until you discover a clear angle on your topic.

4 Clustering

Clustering is a way of generating ideas using a visual scheme or chart. It is especially useful for understanding the relationships among the parts of a broad topic and for developing subtopics. Clustering is done as follows:

1. Write down your topic in the middle of a blank piece of paper and circle it.
2. In a ring around the topic circle, write down what you see as the main parts of the topic. Circle each one, and draw a line from it to the topic.
3. Think of any ideas, examples, facts, or other details relating to each main part. Write each of these down near the appropriate part, circle it, and draw a line from it to the part.
4. Repeat this process with each new circle until you can't think of any more details. Some trails may dead-end, but you will still have various trains of thought to follow and many useful connections among ideas. (See 3a7.)

FOR MULTILINGUAL WRITERS

Using Your Native Language to Explore Ideas

For generating and exploring ideas – the work of much brainstorming, freewriting, and looping – you may be most successful at coming up with good ideas quickly and spontaneously if you work in your native language. Later in the process of writing, you can choose the best of these ideas and begin working with them in English.

5 Questioning

The strategies presented thus far for exploring topics are all informal and based on the freewheeling association of ideas. There are also more formal, structured strategies, which involve asking – and answering – questions. The following are several widely used sets of questions designed to help you explore your topic, either on your own or with one or two others.

Questions to describe a topic

Originally developed by Aristotle, the following questions can help you explore any topic by carefully and systematically describing it:

1. *What is it?* What are its characteristics, dimensions, features, and parts? What does it look like?
2. *What caused it?* What changes occurred to create your topic? How is it changing? How will it change? What part of the changing process is your topic involved with? What may your topic lead to in the future?

3. *What is it like or unlike?* What features differentiate your topic from others? What analogies does your topic support?
4. *What larger system is your topic a part of?* How does your topic relate to this system?
5. *What do people say about it?* What reactions does your topic arouse? What about the topic causes those reactions?

Questions to explain a topic

This is the well-known question set of *who, what, when, where, why,* and *how.* Widely used in news reporting, these questions are especially useful to help you explain a topic:

1. *Who* is doing it?
2. *What* is at issue?
3. *When* does it take place?
4. *Where* is it taking place?
5. *Why* does it occur?
6. *How* is it done?

Questions to persuade

When your purpose is to persuade or convince, the following questions, developed by philosopher Stephen Toulmin, can help you think analytically about your topic:

For more about Toulmin's system, see 5j2.

1. What *claim* are you making about your topic?
2. What *good reasons* support your claim?
3. What *underlying assumptions* support the reasons for your claim?
4. What *backup evidence* can you find for your claim?
5. What *refutations* of your claim can be made?
6. In what ways is or should your claim be *qualified*?

6 Trying other genres

One good way to get yourself thinking in a fresh, new way about a topic, to get a new angle or a different take on it, is to try translating your subject into a different genre, or kind of writing. If, for example, you have been assigned to write an essay on the Wife of Bath in *The Canterbury Tales,* why not try writing some rap lyrics that she might have come up with – or country blues? The idea is to jog your customary thinking patterns, to try seeing your subject from a new perspective and thus to find something new and compelling to say about it.

7 Looking at one student's exploratory work

Jennifer Gerkin, the student whose work we began following in Chapter 2, tried two strategies to explore her topic: brainstorming and clustering. Since she was already part of a peer group, she turned to members of the group to discuss the general topic the class was working on: the effects of prejudice on their lives. After the group brainstormed for half an hour, they made separate notes. Here are some of Jennifer's:

Some prejudice in everyone
Where does it come from?
Learned – we aren't born with it
Examples: against some races or other groups
against some ways of thinking
against some ways of dressing

Talking and brainstorming helped her get an idea of what she might have to say about prejudice. In order, then, to find out whether she really wanted to pursue this angle on her topic, she decided to try clustering. What she produced is shown below.

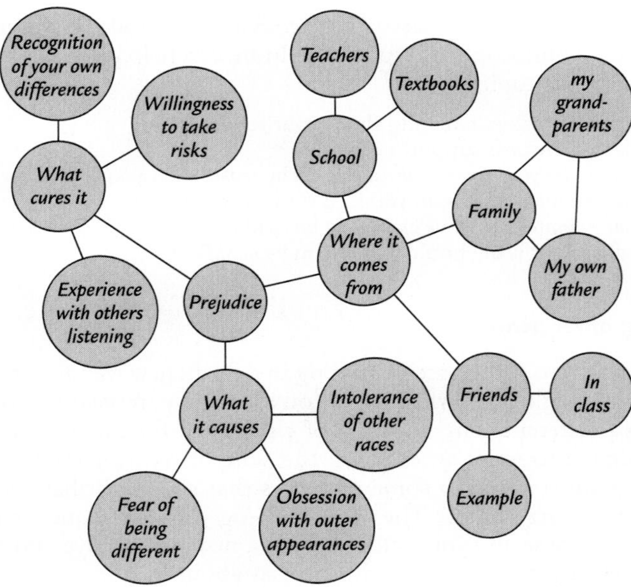

EXERCISE 3.1

Choose a topic that interests you, and explore it by using two of the strategies described in 3a. When you have generated some material, you might try comparing your results to those of other members of the class to see how effective or helpful each strategy was. If you have trouble choosing a topic, use one of the preliminary working theses in Exercise 3.2.

3b Establishing a working thesis

A **thesis** states the main idea of a piece of writing. Most kinds of college writing contain a thesis statement, often near the beginning, which functions as a promise to the readers, letting them know what will be discussed. You should establish a tentative **working thesis** early on in your writing process. Even though it will probably change as you write, a working thesis is important for two reasons: (1) it focuses your thinking, research, and investigation on a particular point about the topic and thus keeps you on track; and (2) it provides concrete questions to ask about purpose, audience, and your rhetorical stance (helping you see, for example, what you must do to design a thesis for a particular audience).

A working thesis should have two parts: a **topic** part, which states the topic, and a **comment** part, which makes an important point about the topic. Here is an example:

TOPIC: Recent studies of depression
COMMENT: suggest that it is much more closely related to physiology than scientists had previously thought.

A successful working thesis has three characteristics:

1. It is potentially *interesting* to your intended audience.
2. It is as *specific* as possible.
3. It limits the topic enough to make it *manageable*.

You can evaluate a working thesis by checking it against each of these criteria. The following example is for a working thesis on global warming:

PRELIMINARY WORKING THESIS

Theories about global warming are being debated around the world.

INTEREST The topic itself holds interest, but it seems to have no real comment attached to it. The thesis merely states a bare fact, and the only place to go from here is to more bare facts.

www•

http://www.hamilton.edu/academic/resource/wc/Intro_Thesis.html

Introductions and Thesis Statements, *by two students at Hamilton College, provides useful advice and samples from student papers in many disciplines. [Hint: to find more examples and tips, type* thesis statement *into any search engine.]*

SPECIFICITY The thesis is fairly clear but not specific. Who is debating these theories? What is at issue in this debate?

MANAGEABILITY The thesis is not manageable: it would require research on many countries and in many languages.

ASSESSMENT This thesis needs to be narrowed with the addition of a workable comment before it can be useful. Also, the field for investigation is too large and vague. This preliminary thesis can be narrowed into the following working thesis:

WORKING THESIS

Scientists from several countries have challenged global-warming theories and claimed that they are more propaganda than science.

Jennifer Gerkin produced this preliminary working thesis: "Prejudice is learned." Subjecting this thesis to the criteria of interest, specificity, and manageability, she decided that it was interesting but not very specific or manageable. After further discussion with her peer group and her instructor, she decided to focus on a specific kind of prejudice and to adopt this working thesis: "Obsession with appearances has been part of my life since the day I was labeled 'the smart one.'"

EXERCISE 3.2

Choose one of the following preliminary working theses, and after specifying an audience, evaluate the thesis in terms of interest, specificity, and manageability. Revise it as necessary to meet these criteria.

1. Drug abuse presents the United States with a big problem.
2. Abortion is a right.
3. Othello is a complex character whose greatest strength is, ironically, also his greatest weakness.
4. White-collar crime poses greater danger to the economy than street crime, even though the latter is more obvious.
5. An educated public is the key to a successful democracy.

EXERCISE 3.3

Using the topic you chose in Exercise 3.1, write a preliminary working thesis. Evaluate it in terms of interest, specificity, and manageability. Revise it as necessary to create a satisfactory working thesis.

3c Gathering information

Many of your writing assignments will call for some research at various stages of the writing process – early on, to help you understand or define your topic, or later on, to find additional examples in support of your thesis. But once you have defined a working thesis, consider what additional information you might need.

If you find it necessary to do research, you should probably begin with those resources closest at hand: your instructor, who can help you decide what kind of research to do, and your textbooks, which may include a bibliography or list of references. Basically, you can do three kinds of research: traditional **library research,** which includes books and periodicals you can access from your college library or through interlibrary loan; **online research,** which gives you access to both texts and people on the Internet and World Wide Web; and **field research,** which includes personal observation, interviews, surveys, and other means of gathering information directly.

For a detailed discussion of how to conduct all three kinds of research, see Chapter 41.

3d Organizing information

While you are finding information on your topic, you should be thinking about how you will group or organize that information so that it will be accessible and persuasive to your readers. At the simplest level, writers most often group information according to four principles:

1. **space** – *where* bits of information occur
2. **time** – *when* bits of information occur, usually chronologically
3. **logic** – *how* bits of information are related logically
4. **association** – *how* bits of information are related in terms of images, motifs, personal memories, and so on

1 Organizing information spatially

If the information you have gathered is *descriptive*, you may choose to organize it spatially. Using **spatial organization** allows the reader to "see" your information, to fix it in space. A report on a college library's accessibility to students in wheelchairs, for example, might describe the spaces in the library that are most often used and then evaluate their accessibility to a student in a wheelchair – one room or space or area at a time. In this case, the description might even be accompanied by a map.

For questions that help you describe a topic, see 3a5.

For examples of information organized spatially, see 6d1.

2 Organizing information chronologically

You are probably already very familiar with **chronological organization,** since it is the basic method used in stories, cookbooks, and instruction manuals. All of these kinds of writing group information according to when it occurs in some process or sequence of events. Reports of laboratory studies and certain kinds of experiments also use chronological order.

A student studying the availability of motorcycle parking in a campus lot ordered his information chronologically to show the times when motorcycles entered and exited the lot and thus identify peak periods of demand for parking spaces. If you choose to present information in a narrative, or story form, you will probably use chronological order. But reversing that order – starting in the middle or at the end and then using a flashback to the beginning – can also be effective.

Chronological order is especially useful in *explaining a process,* step by step by step. A biology report might require describing the process of circulation in a frog. An anthropology essay might include an explanation of the initiation rituals in a Native American culture.

3 Organizing information logically

In much of the writing you do in college, you will find it appropriate to organize information according to some set of logical relationships. The most commonly used **logical patterns** include *illustration, definition, division and classification, comparison and contrast, cause and effect, problem and solution,* and *narration.*

For examples of paragraphs organized according to these logical patterns, see 6e1.

Illustrating a point

Often much of the information you gather will serve as examples to **illustrate a point.** An essay discussing how one novelist influenced another might cite a number of examples from the second writer's books that echo themes, characters, or plots from the first writer's works. An appeal for donating money to the Red Cross might be organized in a series of examples of how donations are used. For maximum effect, arrange your examples in order of increasing importance.

Defining terms

Many topics can be developed by **definition:** by saying what something is – or is not – and perhaps by identifying the characteristics that distinguish it from things that are similar or in the same general category. A magazine article about poverty in the United States, for example, would have to define very carefully what level of income, assets, or other measure defines a person, family, or household as "poor." An essay about Pentecostalism for a religion class might develop the topic by explaining what characteristics separate Pentecostalism from related religious movements.

Dividing and classifying

Division means breaking a single topic into separate parts; **classification** means grouping many separate items of information about a topic according to their similarities. An essay about the recruiting policies of the U.S. military, for instance, might be organized by dividing the military into its different branches – army, air force, and so on – and then discussing how each branch recruits volunteers. If you were reading histories of the eighteenth century in preparation for writing an essay on women's roles in that time, you could begin to organize your notes by classifying them into categories: information related to women's education, women's occupations, women's legal status, and so on.

Comparing and contrasting

Comparison focuses on the similarities between two things, whereas **contrast** highlights their differences, but the two are often used together. Asked to read two chapters in a philosophy text (one on Plato and the other on Aristotle), to analyze the information, and to write a brief response, you might well organize the response by presenting all the information on Plato in one section and all on Aristotle in another (*block comparison*) or by alternating between Plato and Aristotle, looking at particular characteristics of each (*alternating comparison*).

Analyzing causes and effects

Cause-effect analysis either examines why something happens or happened by looking at its causes, or it looks at a set of conditions and explains what effects result or are likely to result from them. An environmental-impact study of the probable consequences of building a proposed dam, for instance, suggests moving from causes to effects. On the other hand, a newspaper article on the breakdown of authority in inner-city schools might be organized by tracing the effects of the breakdown back to their causes.

Considering problems and solutions

Moving from a **problem** to a **solution** is a natural and straightforward way of organizing certain kinds of information. The student studying motorcycle parking decided to organize his paper in just this way: he identified a problem (the need for more parking) and then offered two possible solutions. Many assignments in engineering, business, and economics call for a similar organizational strategy.

Narrating

Narration involves telling a story of some kind. You might, for example, choose to tell the story of your first day on campus as a way of illustrating some of the challenges new students face. Or you might tell the story of the conflict between President Clinton and Congress over the 1996 welfare-reform bill in order to explore the causes and effects of the bill's enactment. Narrating calls on the writer to set the story in a context readers can understand, providing any necessary background and descriptive details as well as chronological markers and transitions (*later that day, following,* and so on) to guide readers through the story.

4 Organizing information associationally

Many contemporary essays are organized through a series of **associations** that grow directly out of the writer's memory or experience. Henry Louis Gates Jr. uses such a method in an essay about his mother's kitchen beauty parlor. He opens with an evocation of vividly remembered smells, and that leads to a series of images related to washing, cutting, treating, and, especially, straightening hair. These sensory memories call up other associations for Gates: his own hair type, style, and process – and those of people he is interested in, such as Malcolm X, Sammy Davis Jr., and Nat King Cole. All of these associations come together for Gates, he says in his concluding paragraph, one day in "an Arab restaurant on the island of Zanzibar" as he suddenly catches the strains of a Nat King Cole song. As this example suggests, associational organization is most often used in personal narrative, where writers can use a chain of associations to render an experience vividly for readers.

5 Combining organizational patterns

In much of your writing, you will want to combine two or more organizational patterns. You might, for example, combine several passages of narration with vivid descriptive illustrations so as to make a striking comparison, as one student recently did in an essay about the dramatic differences between her life on her Native American reservation and her life as a teacher in a predominantly Anglo school. The possibilities for combining patterns have increased considerably with the advent of electronic forms of text production; such combinations may now include not only pictures but sound and other multimedia effects as well.

Jennifer Gerkin begins by narrating an important personal experience and then uses that story as a means of illustrating her tentative thesis – the problem that her excessive concern with appearances poses for her. She follows the narrative with several paragraphs that consider the effects of that problem, and she closes the essay by offering some possible solutions to the problem. Thus her essay, which is based on personal experience, combines the patterns of narration, cause-effect, and problem-solution.

EXERCISE 3.4

Using the topic you chose in Exercise 3.1, identify the most effective means of organizing your information. Write a brief paragraph explaining why you chose this particular method (or these methods) of organization.

EXERCISE 3.5

Identify which method or methods of organization you would recommend for students who are writing on the following topics, and explain why.

1. the need for a new undergraduate library
2. the autobiographical elements in Virginia Woolf's *To the Lighthouse*
3. why voting rates in U.S. elections are declining
4. education to prevent the spread of AIDS
5. the best contemporary rap artist or group

3e Writing out a plan

A writer who has organized information carefully is one who already has a plan for a draft, a plan that should then be written down. The student who wrote about the motorcycle-parking shortage organized all his data and developed the following plan. Notice that his plan calls for several organizational strategies within an overall problem-solution framework.

INTRODUCTION

give background on the problem (use *chronological order*)
give overview of the problem in detail (use *division*)
state purpose – to offer solutions

BODY

describe the current situation (use *narration*)
present proof of the problem in detail (use *illustration*)
present two possible solutions (use *comparison*)

CONCLUSION

recommend against first solution because of cost and space
recommend second solution, and summarize benefits of doing so

Preparing a formal outline

You may wish – or be required – to prepare a more formal outline, which allows you to see before drafting exactly how the parts of your essay will fit together. Most formal outlines follow a conventional format of numbered and lettered headings and subheadings, using Roman numerals, capital letters, Arabic numerals, and lowercase letters to show the levels of importance of the various ideas and their relationships. Each new level is indented to show its subordination to the preceding level. The following example shows the structure:

Thesis statement

I. First main topic
  A. First subordinate idea
    1. First supporting idea
    2. Second supporting idea
      a. First supporting detail
      b. Second supporting detail
    3. Third supporting idea
  B. Second subordinate idea
    1. First supporting idea
    2. Second supporting idea
II. Second main topic

Each level contains at least two parts, so there is no A without a B, no 1 without a 2. Comparable items are placed on the same level – all capital letters, for instance, or all Arabic numerals. Each level develops the idea before it – 1 and 2 under A, for example, include the points that develop, explain, or demonstrate A. Headings are stated in parallel form – either all sentences, or all grammatically parallel topics.

Formal outlining requires logical thought and careful evaluation of your ideas, and this is precisely why it is valuable. (A full-sentence outline will reveal the relationships between ideas – or the lack of relationships – most clearly; so if you want to give your organization the most rigorous test, try working it into a full-sentence outline.) Remember, however, that an outline is at best a means to an end, not an end in itself. Indeed, whatever form your plan takes, you may want or need to change it as you begin drafting.

For an example of a formal outline, see 44d.

EXERCISE 3.6

Write out a plan for an essay supporting the working thesis you developed for Exercise 3.3.

3f Producing a draft

Most of us are in some sense "producing a draft" the moment we begin thinking about a topic. At some point, however, we sit down with pen, typewriter, or computer to attempt an actual version of a draft.

1 Be flexible

No matter how good your planning, investigating, and organizing have been, chances are you will need to do more of them as you draft. This fact of life leads to the first principle of successful drafting: be flexible. If you see that your organizational plan is not working, do not hesitate to alter it. If some information now seems irrelevant, leave it out, even if you went to great lengths to obtain it. You may learn that your whole thesis must be reshaped or that your topic is too broad and should be narrowed.

2 Know your best writing situation

There may be almost as many ways to produce a successful draft as there are people to do it. Nevertheless, you can profit by learning as much as possible about what kind of situation is likely to help you produce your best writing. *Where* and *when* are you most comfortable and productive writing? *What conditions* do you prefer – complete quiet? music? Do you have any *rituals* that help – exercising beforehand? making a pot of coffee?

SOME GUIDELINES FOR DRAFTING

- → ***Have all your information close at hand and arranged according to your organizational plan.*** **Stopping to search for a piece of information can break your concentration or distract you.**
- → ***Try to write in stretches of at least twenty minutes.*** **Writing can provide momentum, and once you get going, the task becomes easier.**
- → ***Don't let small questions bog you down.*** **Just make a note of them or a tentative decision and move on.**
- → ***Remember that a first draft need not be perfect.*** **Concentrate on getting all your ideas down on paper, and don't worry about anything else.**
- → ***Stop writing at a place where you know exactly what will come next.*** **Doing this will help you start easily when you return to the draft.**

Here is Jennifer Gerkin's first draft:

Prejudice in My Life

"Your daughter is absolutely beautiful!" the woman gushed as she talked to my father. She was a friend of his from work, and had heard much about my sister Tracy and I, but had never met us before. I could tell that she was one of those blunt, elderly ladies, the type that pinches cheeks, because as soon as she finished appraising my sister, she turned to me with a deductive look in her eye. Her face said it all. Her beady brown eyes traveled slowly from my head to my toe as she sized me up and said rather condescendingly, "Oh, and she must be the smart one." I looked down at my toes as I rocked nervously back and forth. Then, looking at my sister I realized for the first time that she was very pretty, and I was, well, the smart one. 1

The incident, which occurred when I was six and my sister was seven, has changed me in many ways. Primar- 2 ily, as a result of the harsh appraisal my father's acquaintance gave me, I have always been very concerned about my appearance. Conceivably, a concern about my appearance can be beneficial, however, at times it is a bit of an obsession. I have become overly critical of my own appearance, but even more critical of the appearance of those around me. I instantly judge a person by the way he or she looks, a prejudice that includes everyone, not just minorities.

Certainly, there are many men and women who are obsessed with their appearance. Although my obsession over my own appearance has relaxed dramatically over the past few years, especially since I've been in college, it is still a problem that affects my life in many ways. I can remember exactly what I wore for every first day of school since eighth grade, or on any other important day of my life. Granted, this simply may mean that I have a good memory, but I can also remember what a majority of my friends wore on the first day of school, and describe each garment with amazing speed and accuracy, right down to the last accessory. 3

Similarly, I used to take two to two and a half hours to get ready for school, church, shopping, or simply to walk the dog. Fortunately, I have cut my "primping time" down and can now get ready in a thrifty half an hour. 4

My obsession with my appearance is something I can overcome, or at least control, but as I mentioned before, my critical eyes are always turned towards others. The minute I see someone, I assess them by their appearance. For example, if I see a person who is dressed shabbily, I instantly assume they are poor and unintelligent. If I see someone with fancy clothes and nice jewelry, I usually assume that they are rich and snobbish. For a more concrete example, on one of the first few days of class, a young man walked into my English class with a bandanna on his head and blue 5 lipstick on his lips. I immediately thought, "What a weirdo!" Later, after talking to this classmate, I found that he was a very interesting, intelligent member of society that I respect very much. I am ashamed that I judge people so hastily, and I try very hard to overcome my prejudice.

I include everyone in my hasty assessment of people by their appearance. So in a way, I guess I am extremely prejudiced. The only difference between my assessment of whites and of ethnic minorities is that the latter includes a few stereotypes, as well as "surface judgments." Hence, I have two hurdles to overcome; traditional stereotyping, and my own "personal stereotyping." 6

I have taken major steps to overcome my harsh judgment of people. Several years ago, I would have let the fact that a classmate had blue lipstick and a bandanna on deprive me of meeting an interesting individual. Now I never let my first judgement of people be the one that counts; I find out how the person really is inside. This has widened my horizons to include many people that I may have never had the pleasure to meet if I had maintained my original judgement. 7

I feel that many people are preoccupied with appearances. When we overcome this shallow perception of our brothers and sisters, prejudice will vanish. I am waiting anxiously for the important day when we will no longer judge each other according to what is on the outside, but for what is on the inside. And when this day finally arrives, I promise to all mankind that I will not remember what I was wearing. 8

EXERCISE 3.7

Write a draft of an essay from the plan you produced for Exercise 3.6.

3g Reflecting on your own writing process

Once you finish a draft, make a point of reflecting a bit on your own exploring, planning, and drafting and of noting your thoughts in your writing log if you are keeping one. Note down what went well, what gave you problems and why, what you would like to change or improve.

When Jennifer Gerkin reflected in this way, she discovered that brainstorming with her classmates and clustering had been the most fruitful methods for generating ideas and examples and that answering questions to explain the topic hadn't added much. She also recognized that she felt very comfortable with her classmates and her professor (her audience), which made writing about something personal relatively easy. In addition, she saw that she'd worked extra hard to make her essay interesting, wanting to impress an audience she liked and respected so much. The main weaknesses, she decided, were in grammar, punctuation, organization, and diction.

WRITING PROCESS
Reflecting on Your Own Writing Process

For a checklist of questions to use in reviewing your writing process, see 1a7.

THINKING CRITICALLY ABOUT YOUR OWN WRITING PROCESS

Using the following guidelines, reflect on the process you went through as you prepared for and wrote the draft of your essay for Exercise 3.7. Make your answers an entry in your writing log, if you are keeping one.

1. How did you arrive at your specific topic?
2. When did you first begin to think about the assignment?
3. What kinds of exploring or planning did you do?
4. How long did it take to complete your draft (including the time spent gathering information)?
5. Where did you write your draft? Briefly describe the setting.
6. How did awareness of your audience help shape your draft?
7. What have you learned from your draft about your own rhetorical stance on your topic?
8. What did you learn about your ideas for this topic by exploring, planning, and talking to others about it?
9. What do you see as the major strengths of your draft?
10. What do you see as the major weaknesses of your draft?
11. What would you like to change about your process of exploring, planning, and drafting?

4 Revising and Editing

Whether you are writing a wedding invitation, an English paper, or an email to a customer, you will want to make time to revise and edit. You may have thought of revising and editing as the same thing; after all, both involve changes in a draft. Noting the distinction between them, however, can help you become a more powerful and more efficient writer.

Revising involves re-envisioning your draft — taking a fresh look at how clearly your thesis is stated and how persuasively it is developed, how effective your organization is, how varied your sentences are, how appropriate your choice of words is. **Editing,** on the other hand, involves fine-tuning your prose, attending to details of grammar, usage, punctuation, and spelling. While revising and editing, you also need to format and proofread your writing carefully to make it completely ready for public presentation. ■

4a Getting distance before revising

The ancient Roman poet Horace advised aspiring writers to get distance from their work by putting it away for nine years. However impractical it sounds, Horace's advice holds a germ of truth: the more time you give yourself between the writing of a draft and its final revision, the more objectivity you will gain and the more options you will have as a writer. Even putting the draft away for a day or two will help clear your mind and give you some distance from your writing.

4b Rereading your draft

After giving yourself — and your draft — a rest before revising, review the draft by rereading it carefully for meaning, by recalling your purpose, and by considering your audience.

1 Rereading for meaning

Effective writers are almost always effective readers, particularly of their own writing. You can best begin revising, then, by rereading your draft carefully. For this reading, concentrate on your meaning and how clearly you have expressed it. If you see places where the meaning seems unclear, note them in the margin.

2 Remembering your purpose

After rereading, quickly note the main purpose of the piece of writing, and decide whether it matches your original purpose. You may want to go back to your original assignment to see exactly what it asks you to do. If the assignment asks you to propose a solution to a problem, make sure you have indeed set forth a well-supported solution rather than, for instance, an analysis of the problem.

For more about considering your rhetorical stance, see 2c and 2d.

3 Reconsidering your stance

Before or during the revision process, you can profit by taking time to look at your draft with one central question in mind: where are you coming from in this draft? That is, you should articulate the rhetorical stance you take in the draft and ask yourself what factors or influences have led you to that position. Early on in her revision process, Jennifer Gerkin noted that her draft seemed to take a somewhat defensive stance. After brainstorming with her group and talking with her instructor, she decided that some of her feeling of defensiveness came from her growing recognition of how she had become prejudiced in ways that she had never before thought about and that frankly she did not like. She then decided to try to incorporate this insight into her revision.

4 Considering your audience

How appropriate is the essay for your audience? Think carefully about how your audience's experiences and expectations may be different from yours. Will they be interested in and able to follow your discussion? Is the language formal or informal enough for these readers? Have you defined any terms they may not know? What objections might they raise?

For more about considering your audience, see 2h.

EXERCISE 4.1

Take twenty to thirty minutes to look critically at the draft you prepared for Exercise 3.7. Reread it carefully, check to see how well the purpose is accomplished, and consider how appropriate the draft is for the audience. Then write a paragraph about how you would go about revising it.

4c Collaborating with others: getting responses to a draft

In addition to your own critical appraisal, you may want to get responses from friends, classmates, or colleagues you have met in classes – or online. Remember that they probably won't want to hurt your feelings by criticizing your writing; you can help by convincing them that constructive criticism is what you need.

Ask readers to tell you in detail what they see, and then compare their reading to what you see. Be sure to pose questions that require more than yes/no answers. Merely asking, "Is my thesis clear?" will not tell you nearly so much as "Would you paraphrase my thesis so I can see if it's clear?"

The following are some questions for evaluating a draft. They can be used to respond to someone else's draft or one of your own. When you ask someone to evaluate your draft, be sure that person knows your assignment, intended audience, and major purposes.

FOR MULTILINGUAL WRITERS

Asking a Native Speaker to Review Your Draft

One good way to make sure that your writing is well developed and easy to follow is to have someone else read it. You might find it especially helpful to ask a native speaker to read over your draft and to point out any words or patterns that are unclear or not idiomatic.

REVIEWING A DRAFT

1. *The assignment.* Does the draft carry out the assignment? What could the writer do to better fulfill the assignment?
2. *The title and introduction.* Does the title tell the reader what the draft is about? Does it catch the reader's interest? How? What does the opening accomplish? How else might the writer begin? (4f1 and f2)
3. *The thesis and purpose.* Paraphrase the thesis as a promise: "In this paper I will . . ." Does the draft fulfill that promise? Why, or why not? Does it fulfill the writer's major purposes? (4b2 and 4d)
4. *The audience.* How does the draft capture the interest of and appeal to the intended audience? (4b4)
5. *The rhetorical stance.* Where does the writer stand on the issues involved in the topic? Is the writer an advocate or a critic? What words or phrases in the draft indicate the stance? Where does the writer's stance come from – that is, what influences have likely contributed to that stance? (4b3)
6. *The supporting points.* List the main points in order of presentation. Then number them in order of interest to you. Review them one by

(continued on page 53)

(continued from page 52)

one. Do any need to be explained more or less fully? Should any be eliminated? Do any seem confusing or boring? Do any make you want to know more? How well are the main points supported by evidence, examples, or details? (4d)

7. *The organization.* What kind of overall organizational plan is used – spatial, chronological, logical, or some other plan? Are the points presented in the most useful order? What, if anything, might be moved? Can you suggest ways to make connections between paragraphs clearer and easier to follow? (4e)
8. *The paragraphs.* Which paragraphs are clearest and most interesting to read, and why? Which ones are well developed? How are they developed? Which paragraphs need further development? What kind of information seems to be missing? (4g1)
9. *The sentences.* Choose the three sentences you consider the most interesting or the best written – stylistically effective, entertaining, or otherwise memorable. Then choose three sentences you see as weak – confusing, awkward, or uninspired. Are the sentences varied in length, structure, and openings? (4g2)
10. *The words.* Mark words that are particularly effective, that draw vivid pictures or provoke strong responses. Then mark words that are weak, vague, or unclear. Do any words need to be defined? Are the verbs active and vivid? Are any words potentially offensive, to the intended audience or to anyone else? (4g3)
11. *The tone.* What dominant impression does the draft create – serious, humorous, satiric, persuasive, passionately committed, highly objective? Mark specific places where the writer's voice comes through most clearly. Is the tone appropriate to the topic and the audience? Is it consistent throughout? If not, is there a reason for its being varied? (4g4)
12. *The conclusion.* Does the draft conclude in a memorable way, or does it seem to end abruptly or trail off into vagueness? If you like the conclusion, tell why. How else might it end? (4f3)
13. *Final thoughts.* What are the main strengths and weaknesses of the draft? What surprised you, and why? What was the single most important thing said? What do you want to know more about?

Following are some responses Jennifer Gerkin got from her classmates Tisha Clevinger, Chris Reeves, and Sean Finnerty:

1. *The assignment.* You do what we were asked to do: "Investigate the effect of prejudice on your life." (Clevinger)
2. *The introduction.* I like it. . . . It's a dramatic scene that catches the reader's interest. Also, it makes the reader feel for the author. (Clevinger) Another way to begin would be with your first encounter with the young man in the bandanna and then use a flashback to give the cause of your prejudice. (Finnerty)
3. *The thesis.* No apparent thesis statement. (Finnerty) "In this paper I will describe how this incident has caused me to be very critical of myself and those around me, solely on the basis of looks." The essay fulfills the thesis by showing specific examples to illustrate the point. (Clevinger)
4. *The audience.* Well, we are your audience, along with Professor Walters. You got my attention right away. . . . I didn't feel like you ever talked down to us. (Clevinger)
5. *The rhetorical stance.* You take a very strong stand against prejudice, especially your own. It's clear that you are mostly criticizing yourself. Does this change a little at the end, though? (Reeves)
6. *The supporting points.* (1) Original cause of obsession, (2) obsession over your own appearance, (3) obsession and judgment of others' appearances, (4) realization of the ramifications of such judgments, (5) benefits. All these points are necessary. Each was interesting, but I'd like to see the part about the classmate with blue lipstick developed more. (Reeves)
7. *The organization.* The essay is organized in a cause-effect analysis. You show what causes your obsession with appearance and its effect on you. This is a good way to organize. The transitions are smooth. (Reeves)
8. *The paragraphs.* Paragraphs 1 and 5 are the most interesting because you tell the reader about your own experiences; paragraphs 3 and 4 are a close second; 5 and 6 might be stronger combined as one paragraph. (Clevinger) Paragraph 1 is the clearest, but 3 and 4 are the most interesting to read; 3 begins awkwardly, however: how about saving the statement about how you relaxed your prejudice until 7, where it would fit in better? (Finnerty)
9. *The sentences.* Sentence 3 is very descriptive; I can picture the lady standing there. The last sentence is interesting and made me remember the essay. Sentence 29 could be reworded to read more smoothly. (Reeves)
10. *The words.* The words *beady, harsh appraisal, thrifty,* and *horizons* are effective; I had difficulty with *deductive*. How about looking for some other words for *appearance?* You use it excessively. (Clevinger) I like the descriptive words in the first paragraph, except for *deductive; primarily* might be unnecessary in paragraph 2; paragraph 3 would be better without *dramatically* (*relaxed some* sounds more genuine). (Finnerty)
11. *The tone.* Serious and objective. This tone is appropriate because prejudice is a serious topic, and it's important to try to be objective about oneself.

The last sentence is humorous in tone, which shows you are taking the topic seriously but taking yourself lightly. (Reeves)

12. *The conclusion.* The final sentence is memorable. (Clevinger, Reeves) Glad the paper ends humorously. (Clevinger) It could have ended by saying something about the woman in paragraph 1. (Reeves)
13. *Final thoughts.* The main strength of the paper is the way it keeps the reader's attention. (Finnerty)

As these responses demonstrate, different readers do not always agree on what is effective or ineffective. In addition, you may find that you simply do not agree with their advice. In examining responses to your writing, you can often proceed efficiently by looking first for areas of agreement ("everyone was confused by this sentence – I'd better revise it") or strong disagreement ("one person said my conclusion was 'perfect,' and someone else said it 'didn't conclude' – better look carefully at that paragraph again").

THE INSTRUCTOR'S RESPONSE

Jennifer Gerkin also got some advice from her instructor, Professor Keith Walters, in the form of marginal comments on her draft. Here are excerpts from these comments:

```
     The incident, which occurred when I was six and my       2
sister was seven, has changed me in many ways.  Primar-
ily, as a result of the harsh appraisal my father's
acquaintance gave me, I have always been very concerned
about my appearance.  Conceivably, a concern about my      ?
appearance can be beneficial; however, at times it is a
bit of an obsession.  I have become overly critical of my   comma splice
own appearance, but even more critical of the appearance
of those around me.  I instantly judge a person by the
way he or she looks, a prejudice that includes everyone,
not just minorities.
```

Such judgments are not a prejudice but a practice that may be a basis for prejudice.

for parallelism Similarly, I used to take two to two and a half 4
hours to get ready for school, church, shopping, or
simply ~~to~~ walk*ing* the dog. Fortunately, I have cut my
"primping time" down and can now get ready in a thrifty *good word choice!*
half an hour. *Why a 2-sentence paragraph?*

In addition, her instructor suggested that Jennifer reconsider how well her examples work and that she add more concrete detail to make it easier for readers to imagine the examples. Based on all the responses she received, she decided to (1) state her thesis more explicitly, (2) provide concrete examples of her own biases, and (3) reconsider individual word choice as well as her conclusion.

EXERCISE 4.2

Using the questions listed in 4c as a guide, analyze the draft you wrote for Exercise 3.7.

4d Evaluating the thesis and its support

Once you have received advice on your draft from all available sources and have studied the responses, reread the draft once more, paying special attention to your thesis and its support. Make sure your thesis sentence contains a clear statement of the *topic* that you will discuss and a *comment* explaining what is particularly significant or noteworthy about the topic. As you continue to read, ask yourself how each paragraph relates to or supports the thesis and how each sentence develops the paragraph topic. Such careful rereading can help eliminate irrelevant sections or details or identify sections needing further details or examples.

Be particularly careful to note what kinds of evidence, examples, or good reasons you offer in support of your major points. If some points need more elaboration, look back at your exploratory work and at suggestions from your readers. Jennifer Gerkin, for example, saw that one of her readers had asked for further development of paragraph 6, and so she added two examples. If necessary, take time to gather more information and do further exploration.

For more about exploring a topic and gathering information, see 3a and 3c.

EXERCISE 4.3

After rereading the draft you wrote for Exercise 3.7, evaluate the revised working thesis you produced for Exercise 3.3, and then evaluate its support in the draft. Identify points that need further support, and list those things you must do to provide that support.

4e Analyzing organization

One good way to check the organization of a draft is by outlining it. After numbering the paragraphs in the draft, read through each one, jotting down its main idea or topic. Then examine your list and ask yourself the following questions:

What organizational strategies are used? spatial? chronological? logical? associational? Are they used effectively? Why, or why not?

Do the main points clearly relate to the thesis and to one another? Are any of them irrelevant?

Can you identify any confusing leaps from point to point? Do you need to provide additional or stronger transitions?

Can you identify clear links between paragraphs and ideas? Do any others need to be added?

Have any important points been left out?

www •

http://www-english.tamu.edu/wcenter/journal.html

From the Texas A & M Writing Center *come questions to help you analyze an essay.*

EXERCISE 4.4

Draw up a brief outline of Jennifer Gerkin's first draft (in 3f), and evaluate its organization. Begin by answering the questions in 4e.

EXERCISE 4.5

Check the paragraph transitions in Jennifer Gerkin's first draft (in 3f). Did you find any that were weak or missing? If so, suggest at least two ways of strengthening them or adding some.

4f Reconsidering the title, introduction, and conclusion

First and last impressions count. In fact, readers remember the first and last parts of a piece of writing better than anything else. For this reason, it is wise to pay careful attention to three important elements – the title, the introduction, and the conclusion.

1 The title

A good title gives readers information, draws them into the piece of writing, and may even indicate the writer's view of the topic. The title of Jennifer Gerkin's draft, "Prejudice in My Life," was accurate enough but not vivid or intriguing. Following a discussion of this draft, she produced a new draft and titled it "The Smart One." This title piques readers' curiosity and leads up to the startling statement that ends paragraph 1, though it does not really let readers know the essay's topic.

2 The introduction

A good introduction accomplishes two important tasks: first, it draws readers into the piece of writing, and second, it presents the topic and makes some comment on it. It contains, in other words, a strong lead, or hook, to attract readers' interest and often an explicit thesis as well. One common kind of introduction opens with a general statement about the topic and then goes into more detail, leading up to a statement of the specific thesis at the end. A writer can also begin an introduction effectively with a *vivid statement* of the problem that led to the thesis or with an *intriguing quotation,* an *anecdote,* a *question,* or a *strong opinion.* The rest of the introduction then develops this beginning item into a more general or detailed presentation of the topic and the thesis.

For more discussion and examples of introductory paragraphs, see 6f1.

In many cases, especially when the writer begins with a quotation or an anecdote, the introduction consists of two paragraphs, the first providing the hook and the second, an explanation of its significance. Jennifer Gerkin followed this pattern in her introduction, whose first paragraph contains a very strong hook: a narrative anecdote from her childhood that immediately appeals to readers. The second paragraph then explains how this experience led to the obsession with appearance that is her topic. Although she considered the suggestion of one of her respondents that she open with paragraph 2 in order to make the topic clear immediately, she decided that the dramatic opening paragraph makes the introduction more effective.

3 The conclusion

A good conclusion leaves readers satisfied that a full discussion has taken place. Often a conclusion will begin with a restatement of the thesis and end with more general statements that grow out of it: this pattern reverses the common general-to-specific pattern of the introduction. Writers can also draw on a number of other ways to conclude effectively, including a *provocative question*, a *quotation*, a *vivid image*, a *call for action*, a *warning*.

Jennifer Gerkin's concluding paragraph clearly restates her thesis, and the final sentence packs just the punch she wants. But the first three sentences are general, and two of her respondents described them as "too idealistic" and "righteous and heavy." She decided to qualify her statements in the second sentence and thus make the conclusion more realistic.

For more discussion and examples of concluding paragraphs, see 6f2.

> When we overcome this shallow perception of our brothers and sisters, prejudice ~~will vanish.~~ ^ *may not disappear but will certainly diminish.*

EXERCISE 4.6

Review Jennifer Gerkin's draft in 3f, and compose an alternative conclusion, perhaps taking the advice of one of her respondents to "end by saying something about the woman in paragraph 1." Then write a paragraph commenting on the strengths and weaknesses of the conclusion she used.

4g Examining paragraphs, sentences, words, and tone

In addition to the large-scale task of examining the logic, organization, and development of their writing, effective writers look closely at the smaller elements: paragraphs, sentences, and words. Many writers, in fact, look forward to this part of revising because its results are often dramatic. Turning a bland sentence into a memorable one – or finding exactly the right word to express a thought – can yield great satisfaction and self-confidence.

1 Examining paragraphs

Paragraphing serves the reader by visually breaking up long expanses of writing and signaling a shift in focus. Readers expect a paragraph to develop an idea or a topic, a process that almost always demands several sentences or more. The following guidelines can help you evaluate your paragraphs as you revise:

For guidelines on paragraphing for readers, see 6a.

1. Look for the topic or main point of each paragraph, whether it is stated or implied. Then check to see that every sentence expands, supports, or otherwise relates to the topic.

2. Check to see how each paragraph is organized – spatially, chronologically, associationally, or by some logical relationship. Then determine whether the organization is appropriate to the topic of the paragraph and whether it is used fully to develop the paragraph. (See 6c and d.)
3. Count the number of sentences in each paragraph, noting paragraphs that have only a few. Do these paragraphs sufficiently develop the topic of the paragraph?

See also the guidelines for editing paragraphs at the beginning of Chapter 6.

In paragraph 4 of her draft, Jennifer Gerkin had only two sentences, and these actually illustrate a point made in paragraph 3. She decided, therefore, to combine the two paragraphs and elaborate on the first sentence in the original paragraph 4.

```
Similarly, I used to take two to two and a half hours
to get ready for school, church, shopping, or simply
walking the dog. ^ Fortunately, I have cut my "primping
time" down and can now get ready in a thrifty half an
hour.
```

For example, I might try on five different outfits (and five different shades of lipstick), none of which would satisfy my demanding eyes.

EXERCISE 4.7

Choose two other paragraphs in Jennifer Gerkin's draft in 3f, and evaluate them using the guidelines on pages 52 – 53. Write a brief paragraph in which you suggest ways to improve the development or organization of these paragraphs.

2 Examining sentences

See the guidelines for editing sentences at the beginning of Chapter 7.

As with life, variety is the spice of sentences. You can add variety to your sentences by looking closely at their length, structure, and opening patterns.

Varying sentence length

Too many short sentences, especially one after another, can sound like a series of blasts on a car horn – or like an elementary school textbook – whereas a steady stream of long sentences may tire or confuse readers. Most writers, then, aim for some variety of length.

For more about varying sentence length, see 22a.

In looking at paragraph 2, Jennifer Gerkin found that all of its five sentences were almost exactly the same length: nineteen, twenty-two, nineteen, twenty, and twenty words. In revising, she decided to shorten the second sentence and to extend the last one.

> The incident, which occurred when I was six and my sister was seven, has changed me in many ways. *One* ~~Primarily as a~~ result of *that* ~~the~~ harsh appraisal *has been an extreme concern for* ~~my father's acquaintance gave me, I have always been very concerned about~~ my appearance. Conceivably, a concern about my appearance can be beneficial; however, at times it is a bit of an obsession. I have become overly critical of my own appearance, but even more critical of the appearance of those around me. I instantly judge a person by the way he or she looks, a *practice that is the basis for prejudice and one that limits my appreciation of myself as well as of others.* ~~prejudice that includes everyone, not just minorities.~~

Varying sentence structure

The simple sentence is the most common kind of sentence in modern English, but using only simple sentences can be very dull. On the other hand, overusing compound sentences may result in a singsong or repetitive rhythm, and strings of complex sentences may sound, well, overly complex. It is best to vary your sentence structure.

For more about varying sentence structure, see 22c.

Varying sentence openings

Most sentences in English follow subject-predicate order and hence open with the subject of an independent clause, as does the sentence you are now reading. But opening too many sentences in a row this way results in a jerky, abrupt, or choppy rhythm. You can vary sentence openings by beginning with a dependent clause, a phrase, an adverb, a conjunctive adverb, or a coordinating conjunction.

For more about varying sentence openings, see 22b.

Jennifer Gerkin's opening paragraph provides vivid description and imaginative use of dialogue, but it can be improved by varying the sentence openings. Note how revising some of the openings improves the flow and makes the entire paragraph easier to read and more memorable.

> "Your daughter is absolutely beautiful!" the woman gushed as she talked to my father. ~~She was a~~ A friend of his from work, ~~and~~ she had heard much about my sister Tracy and I, but had never met us before. I could tell that she was one of those blunt, elderly ladies, the type that pinches cheeks, because as soon as she finished appraising my sister, she turned to me with a deductive look in her eye. Her face said it all. ~~Her b~~Beady brown eyes ~~traveled~~ traveling slowly from my head to my toe, ~~as~~ she sized me up and said rather condescendingly, "Oh, and she must be the smart one." I looked down at my toes as I rocked nervously back and forth. Then, looking at my sister I realized for the first time that she was very pretty, and I was, well, the smart one.

Checking for sentences opening with *it* and *there*

As you go over the sentences of your draft, look especially carefully at those beginning with *it* or *there* followed by a form of *be*. Sometimes such a construction can create a special emphasis, as in "It was a dark and stormy night." But such structures can also easily be overused or misused. You don't know what *it* means, for instance, unless the writer has already pointed out exactly what the word stands for. A more subtle problem with these openings, however, is that they may be used to avoid taking responsibility for a statement. Look at the following two sentences:

For more about sentences opening with it *and* there, *see 13c and 23a1.*

It is necessary to raise student fees.

The university must raise student fees.

The first sentence avoids responsibility by failing to tell us *who says* it is necessary.

EXERCISE 4.8

Here are two sentences from Jennifer Gerkin's draft that feature *it is* or *there are*. Make at least two revisions that eliminate these constructions.

1. Certainly, there are many men and women who are obsessed with their appearance.
2. Conceivably, a concern about my appearance can be beneficial; however, at times it is a bit of an obsession.

EXERCISE 4.9

Find a paragraph in your own writing that lacks variety in sentence length, sentence structure, or sentence openings. Then write a revised version.

3 Examining words

Even more than paragraphs and sentences, **word choice,** or diction, offers writers an opportunity to put their personal stamp on a piece of writing. The following questions should help you become aware of the kinds of words you most typically use:

1. Are the nouns primarily abstract and general or concrete and specific? Too many abstract and general nouns can create boring prose. To say that you bought a new car is much less memorable and interesting than to say you bought a new convertible or a new Nissan. (See 27c.)
2. Are there too many nouns in relation to the number of verbs? The *effect* of the *overuse* of *nouns* in *writing* is the *placing* of too much *strain* on the inadequate *number* of *verbs* and the resultant *prevention* of *movement* of the *thought*. In the preceding sentence, one tiny form of the verb *be* (*is*) has to drag along the entire weight of all those nouns. The result is a heavy, boring sentence. Why not say instead, *Overusing nouns places a big strain on the verbs and consequently slows down the prose*?
3. How many verbs are forms of *be*? If *be* verbs account for more than about a third of your total verbs, you are probably overusing them. (See Chapter 9.)

www •

http://www.emory.edu/ENGLISH/WC/diction.html

A short and wry essay on diction from Emory University's Writing Center offers good examples of how words can change meaning and tone (and a tongue-in-cheek look at the word diction *itself).*

4. Are verbs *active* wherever possible? Passive verbs are harder to read and remember than active ones. Although the passive voice has many uses (see Chapter 9), often your writing will be stronger and more energetic if you use active verbs.
5. Are your words *appropriate*? Check to be sure they are not too fancy – or too casual. (See Chapter 27.)

Jennifer Gerkin made a number of changes in diction on the basis of her classmates' responses, her instructor's comments, and her own critical analysis. In paragraph 1, for example, her use of *deductive* puzzled several people. After checking the dictionary, she decided she had chosen the wrong word and substituted *judgmental.* In addition, she replaced overly general words in several places, changing *looked* to *stared* in paragraph 1 and *fancy* to *stylish* and *nice* to *expensive* in paragraph 5. Finally, in the last sentence, she took her instructor's suggestion and substituted *humankind* for *mankind,* which many people object to as sexist.

4 Examining tone

Word choice is closely related to **tone,** the attitude toward the topic and the audience that the writer's language conveys. In examining the tone of your draft, you need to consider the nature of the topic, your own attitude toward it, and that of your intended audience. Check for connotations of words as well as for slang, jargon, emotional language, and the level of formality to see whether they create the tone you want to achieve (humorous, serious, impassioned, and so on) and whether that tone is an appropriate one, given your audience and topic.

For more about creating an appropriate tone, see Chapter 27.

Since Jennifer Gerkin's respondents and instructor praised her draft highly for its combination of humor, seriousness, and objectivity, she felt that her general tone needed no major changes. As mentioned earlier, however, she did revise her conclusion somewhat to tone down its excessive idealism and what one respondent called its "righteous and heavy" quality.

EXERCISE 4.10

Turn to 3f, and read Jennifer Gerkin's paragraphs 3, 4, and 5. Describe the tone you think she achieves. Does it seem appropriate to the audience she is writing to – her professor and classmates in a first-year college writing course – and to her topic? Assume these paragraphs are intended instead for a group of third-graders. What would you do to alter the tone for this audience?

4h Determining format

Before you produce a copy for final editing and proofreading, take the time to consider issues of format. Particularly if you are using a computer, you have many helpful formatting options. You can easily insert headings in a larger size type or in bold type, for instance. You can consider using a different font for examples. If you have a graphics program, you can include charts or other illustrations. Whatever your final decisions, now is the time to think carefully about the overall visual appearance of your final draft.

For more about designing documents, see Chapters 51 and 52.

4i Editing

Because readers expect, even demand, a final copy that is clean and correct in every way, you need to make time for thorough and careful editing. You can make editing somewhat systematic by keeping a personal checklist of the *patterns* of editing problems you find in your writing.

An editing inventory

To begin, list all the errors or corrections marked on the last piece of writing you did. Then note the context of the sentence in which each error appeared. Finally, try to derive a guideline to spot future errors of the same kind. You can broaden these guidelines as you begin to find patterns of errors, and you can then add to your inventory every time you write and edit a draft. Here is an example of such a checklist:

MARKED ERRORS	IN CONTEXT	LOOK FOR
spelling	*to* for *too*	*to* before adjectives and adverbs
fragment	starts with *when*	sentences beginning with *when*
missing comma	after *however*	sentences opening with *however*
missing apostrophe	*Michael's*	all names
missing apostrophe	*company's*	all possessive nouns
tense shift	*go* for *went*	use of present tense
spelling	*sacrifice*	*sacrafice*
missing comma	after *for example*	use of introductory elements

This writer has begun to isolate patterns, like her tendency to leave out apostrophes in possessives and commas after introductory elements.

Some errors, such as the use of wrong words and misspellings, may seem so unsystematic that you are unable to identify patterns in them. If spelling presents a special problem for you, try keeping a spelling checklist or using a spell checker on a computer program.

EXERCISE 4.11

Using several essays you have written, establish your own editing checklist based on the one shown in 4i.

4j Proofreading the final draft

As a writer, you need to make your final draft as free from error as possible. You can do so by taking time for one last, careful proofreading, which means reading to correct any typographical errors or other slips, such as inconsistencies in spelling and punctuation. To proofread most effectively, read through the copy aloud, making sure that punctuation marks are used correctly and consistently, that all sentences are complete, and that no words are left out. Then go through it again, this time reading backward so that you can focus on each word and its spelling.

You have already seen and read about a number of the revisions Jennifer Gerkin made in her first draft. On pages 67 – 69 is the edited and proofread version she turned in to her instructor. If you compare her final draft to her first draft, you will notice a number of additional changes made in editing and proofreading. For example, she corrected *I* to *me* in the second sentence, made the spelling of *judgment* consistent, made several pronouns singular in new paragraph 4 to agree with their antecedents, and deleted unnecessary commas. What other improvements can you spot?

EXERCISE 4.12

Using the guidelines in 4c, read the draft you wrote in Exercise 3.7 with an eye for revising. Try to do this at least a day after the time you finished the draft. List the things you need or want to address in your revision. At this point, you may want to exchange drafts with some classmates and share responses.

EXERCISE 4.13

Revise, edit, and proofread the draft you wrote for Exercise 3.7.

Jennifer Gerkin
Professor Walters
English 110
October 18, 1997

The Smart One

"Your daughter is absolutely beautiful!" the woman gushed to my father. A friend of his from work, she had heard much about my sister Tracy and me but had never met us before. I could tell that she was one of those blunt, elderly ladies, the type that pinches cheeks, because as soon as she finished appraising my sister, she turned to me with a judgmental look in her eye. Her face said it all. Beady brown eyes traveling slowly from my head to my toes, she sized me up and said rather condescendingly, "Oh, and she must be the smart one." I stared down at my toes and I rocked nervously back and forth. Then, looking at my sister, I realized for the first time that she was very pretty, and I was, well, the smart one. 1

This incident, which occurred when I was six and my sister was seven, has affected me in many ways. One result of that harsh appraisal has been an extreme concern for my appearance. Although some concern about how one looks can be beneficial, at times it has become a bit of an obsession with me. I have become not only overly critical of my own appearance but even more critical of the appearance of those around me. I instantly judge a person by the way he or she looks, a practice that is the basis of most kinds of prejudice and one that limits my appreciation of myself and of others. 2

Although many men and women are preoccupied with their appearance, my particular obsession has affected my life to an extent that now seems incredible to me. I can remember exactly what I have worn on the first day of school every year since eighth grade and on every other important day of my life. Often, I attempt to attribute these amazing recollections to the fact that I 3 have a good memory. However, additional evidence confirms that an obsession with appearance better accounts for my behavior. I can also recall what a majority of my friends wore on the first day of school and describe each garment with amazing speed and accuracy, right down to the last accessory, whereas I remember almost nothing about the day's events. Similarly, I used to take more than two hours to get ready for school, church, shopping, or even walking the dog. I would, for example, frantically try on five different outfits and five different shades of lipstick, none of which would satisfy my demanding eyes. Fortunately, since coming to college, I have cut down my "primping time" and can now get ready in a thrifty half hour.

My obsession with my own appearance is something I have managed to overcome or at least control, but it affects my relationships as well: my critical eyes are always turned toward others. The minute I see someone, I assess him or her on the basis of appearance. For example, if I see a person who is dressed shabbily, I instantly assume that she is poor and unintelligent. If I see someone with stylish clothes and expensive jewelry, I usually assume that he is rich and snobbish. More specifically, on one of the first few days of this quarter, a young man walked into my English class wearing a bandanna on his head and blue lipstick. I immediately thought, "What a weirdo!" Later, after talking to this classmate, I came to realize that he is a very interesting, intelligent person whom I respect very much. 4

I include everyone in my hasty assessment of people by their appearance. My assessment of minorities, however, includes a few traditional stereotypes in addition to "surface judgments" based on appearances. For example, when I see a woman wearing the traditional Muslim veil, I instantly assume she is meek and subservient to men; when I see an Amish family in a black horse-drawn buggy, I assume that their lives are 5 dull and emotionally repressed. Hence, I have two hurdles to overcome: traditional stereotyping and my own "personal stereotyping."

6 I am ashamed that I judge people so hastily, and I try very hard to overcome my prejudice because I realize it limits me. Several years ago, I would have let the fact that a classmate wore blue lipstick and a bandanna deprive me of meeting an interesting individual. Now, I try never to let my first judgment of people be the one that counts; I make the effort to find out how the person really is inside. I have widened my horizons to include many delightful people whom I might never have had the pleasure to meet had I maintained my original judgment.

7 I know, however, that many people in our society remain preoccupied with appearances. When this shallow perception of our brothers and sisters is overcome, prejudice may not disappear, but it will certainly diminish. Eagerly, I await the important day when we no longer judge each other according to what is on the outside but pay attention instead to what is on the inside. And when this day finally arrives, I promise all humankind that I will not remember what I--or anyone else--was wearing.

THINKING CRITICALLY ABOUT YOUR OWN REVISING PROCESS

1. How did you begin revising?
2. What kinds of comments on or responses to your draft did you have? How helpful were they, and why?
3. How long did revising take? How many drafts did you produce?
4. Were most of your revisions additions? deletions? replacements of one word, one example, and so on by another? transfers of material from one place to another?
5. What kinds of changes did you tend to make? in organization, paragraphs, sentence structure, wording, adding or deleting information?
6. What gave you the most trouble as you were revising?
7. What pleased you most? What would you most like to change about your process of revising, and how do you plan to go about doing so?

5 Thinking Critically: Constructing and Analyzing Arguments

How do we come to make up our minds about something? What causes us to give our assent to some ideas but not to others? And how do we seek — and sometimes gain — agreement from others?

These are questions that thinkers have pondered down through the ages, from Plato, Confucius, Mohammed, and the Apostle Paul to Joan of Arc, Mahatma Gandhi, and Nelson Mandela.

The need to explore such questions has never been more pressing than it is today, as language intended to persuade us — to gain our assent (and often our souls, our bank accounts, and our votes) — surrounds us more than ever before. In advertisements, news stories, textbooks, reports, and electronic media of all kinds, language competes for our attention and argues for our agreement. Since argument so pervades our lives, we need to be able to recognize and use it effectively — and to question our own arguments as well as those put forth by others. ■

5a Thinking critically

Although **critical thinking** may be given a number of fancy or complex definitions, it is essentially just the process by which we make sense of all the information around us. As such, critical thinking is a crucial component of argument, for it guides us in recognizing, formulating, and examining the arguments that are important to us. For the purposes of considering such arguments, several elements of critical thinking are especially important:

Taking a questioning stance. Rather than accepting your own ideas and beliefs as true, and rather than accepting what you read, see, and hear at face value, approach all ideas with a potentially critical eye.

Asking pertinent questions. Concentrate on asking questions that will get to the heart of the matter at hand. Whether you are thinking about ideas put forth by others or about those you yourself hold, you will want to ask the following kinds of questions:

- What is the writer's agenda?
- Why does he or she hold these ideas or beliefs? What larger social, economic, political, or other conditions may have influenced them?
- What does the writer want readers to do — and why?
- What reasons does the writer offer in support of his or her ideas? Are they good reasons?

- What sources does the writer rely on? How reliable are they? What agendas do these sources have?
- What objections might be made to the argument?
- What are the writer's underlying or unstated assumptions? Are they acceptable – and why, or why not?

Getting information. To help you decide whether to accept an argument, often you will need to find *more information* on the topic as well as *other perspectives.*

For a discussion of how to research a topic, see Chapters 41 and 42.

Interpreting and assessing information. No information that comes to us in language is neutral; all of it has a perspective, a "spin," if you will. Your job as a critical thinker is to identify the perspective and to *assess* it, examining its sources and finding out what you can about its context. Asking the kinds of pertinent questions suggested here will help you examine the interpretations and conclusions drawn by others.

Making and assessing your own arguments. The ultimate goal of all critical thinking is to construct your own ideas, reach your own conclusions. These, too, you must question and assess. The rest of this chapter will guide you in the art of making and assessing your own arguments.

5b Recognizing argument

In one important sense, all language use has an argumentative edge. When you greet friends warmly, you wish to convince them that you are genuinely glad to see them, that you value their presence. Even apparently objective news reporting has strong argumentative overtones. By putting a particular story on the front page, for example, a paper argues that this subject is more important than others; by using emotional language and focusing on certain details in reporting an event, a newscaster tries to persuade us to view the event in a particular way. What one reporter might call *a massive demonstration,* for example, another might call *a noisy protest,* and yet another, *an angry march.*

www

http://www.idbsu.edu/english/cguilfor/paradigm/argument.htm

This essay on argumentative essays features good definitions, examples, and charts — and links to many useful guidelines. Adapted from A Contemporary Rhetoric, *by Maxine Hairston.*

Jennifer Gerkin's primary purpose in her essay "The Smart One" (in 4j) is to explain the roots of her own prejudice. Yet her essay clearly has an argumentative edge: to persuade readers to guard against their own biases. This chapter will look at writing whose *primary* purpose is argument and, specifically, at ways to provide convincing support for a claim.

1 Understanding the purposes of argument

If all language is in some sense argumentative, then it goes almost without saying that the purposes of argument will vary widely. For many, many years, however, traditional notions of argumentation tended to highlight one purpose – winning. Although winning is still one important purpose of argumentation, studies of the argumentative strategies of people from groups historically excluded from public debate – including women and people of color – have demonstrated that it is by no means the only purpose of argument. Nor may it be the one you most often wish to use. For instance, if you are trying to decide whether to major in business or in chemistry, you may want to consider, or "argue," all sides of the issue. Your purpose is hardly to win out over someone else; instead, it is to understand your choices in order to make a wise decision.

To win or conquer

The most traditional purpose of academic argument, arguing to win is used in campus debating societies, in political debates, in trials, and often in business. The writer or speaker aims to control the audience, to present a position that prevails over or defeats the positions of others. Presidential debates and trials, for example, focus most often not on changing the opponent's mind but on defeating him or her in order to appeal to another party – the voting public, the judge, or the jury.

To convince

More often than not, out-and-out defeat of another is not only unrealistic but undesirable. Rather, the goal is *to convince* another person to change his or her mind about an issue. Doing so calls on a writer to provide reasons so compelling that the audience willingly agrees with the writer's conclusion. Such is the goal of Dr. Jack Kevorkian, who knows he cannot conquer or defeat those who oppose assisted suicide. Rather, Kevorkian realizes he must provide reasons compelling enough to change people's minds. And such would be your purpose if you were asked to prepare a report on the major causes of the Civil War: your job would be to convince your readers that you have identified the major causes.

www •

http://www.dartmouth.edu/alumni/almag/rhetoric1.html

"Why Americans Can't Argue," an online essay from Dartmouth's alumni magazine, explores the need for civil discussion and fair argument in public debate — with links to such key government sites as Congress and the White House.

To reach a decision or explore an issue

This purpose often calls on the writer to enter into conversation with others, to collaborate in seeking the best possible understanding of a problem, exploring all possible approaches and choosing the best alternative. Argument *to decide or explore* seeks not to conquer or control others or even to convince. Rather, it seeks a sharing of information and perspectives in order to make informed political, professional, and personal choices. This will be your purpose in many situations – from trying to decide which computer to buy to exploring with your family the best health care system for an elderly relative.

To meditate

Sometimes you will find yourself arguing primarily with yourself, and those arguments often take the form of intense meditations on a theme, or even of prayer. In such cases, you may be hoping to transform something in yourself or to reach peace of mind on a troubling subject. If you know a familiar mantra or prayer, for example, think of what it "argues" for and how it uses quiet meditation to help achieve that goal.

2 Checking whether a statement can be argued

In much of your work in college, you will be asked to take a position and argue for that position – whether to analyze a trend or explain a historical event or prove a mathematical equation. Such work will usually call for you to convince or decide and will therefore require you to make an arguable statement, to make a claim based on the statement, and finally to present good reasons in support of the claim.

An early step in the process of argument to convince or decide is to make a statement about a topic and then check to see that the statement can, in fact, be argued. An arguable statement should have three characteristics:

1. It should attempt to convince readers of something, change their minds about something, or urge them to do something – or explore a topic in order to make a wise decision.
2. It should address a problem for which no easily acceptable solution exists or ask a question to which no absolute answer exists.
3. It should present a position that readers might realistically have varying perspectives on.

EXERCISE 5.1

Using the three characteristics in 5b2, decide which of the following statements are arguable and which are not.

1. *Amistad* was the best movie of the last twenty years.
2. The climate of the earth is gradually getting warmer.
3. The United States must further reduce military spending in order to balance the budget.
4. Shakespeare died in 1616.
5. Marlowe really wrote the plays of Shakespeare.
6. Water boils at 212 degrees Fahrenheit.
7. Van Gogh's paintings are the work of a madman.
8. The incidence of breast cancer has risen in the last ten years.
9. Abortion denies the fetus's inherent right to life.
10. A fifty-five-mile-per-hour speed limit lowers accident rates.

5c Formulating an argumentative thesis

Once you have an arguable statement, you need to make a claim about it, one you will then ask readers to accept. For example, look at the following statement:

> The use of pesticides endangers the lives of farm workers.

For more on how to formulate a thesis, see 3b.

This statement is arguable because it aims to convince, it addresses an issue with no easily identifiable answer, and it can realistically be disputed.

Although it does make a kind of claim – that pesticides threaten lives – the claim is just a factual statement about *what is.* To develop a claim that can become the working thesis for an argument, you often need to direct this kind of statement toward some action; that is, your claim needs to move from *what is* to *what ought to be.*

STATEMENT ABOUT WHAT IS	Pesticides endanger the lives of farm workers.
CLAIM ABOUT WHAT OUGHT TO BE	Because pesticides endanger the lives of farm workers, their use should be banned.

This claim becomes your argumentative thesis. Like any working thesis, it contains two elements: a topic (the statement about what is), and a comment (the claim about what ought to be).

> TOPIC: Because pesticides endanger the lives of farm workers,
> COMMENT: their use should be banned.

Recognizing implied theses

In academic writing, you will often be making a claim that urges readers not to take action but to interpret something in a certain way, to see certain information as you see it. Doing so calls on you first to offer readers your interpretation as clearly as possible and then to support your interpretation in a way that will bring readers to share your view.

In such cases, the claim about what ought to be is usually implied rather than stated. For example, a history report making the claim that moral opposition to slavery was the major cause of the Civil War is in effect arguing that readers should view the Civil War in this light – that they should accept this particular interpretation of its cause – rather than seeing the cause as a constitutional struggle over states' rights or an economic conflict between northern industrialists and southern planters.

EXERCISE 5.2

Using two arguable statements from Exercise 5.1 or two that you create, formulate two working argumentative theses, identifying the topic and the comment of each one.

EXERCISE 5.3

Formulate an arguable statement, and create a working argumentative thesis, for two of the following general topics.

1. the Arab-Israeli conflict
2. mandatory testing of prison inmates for HIV
3. free access to computers for all students on campus
4. a new federal student-loan program
5. human cloning

5d Formulating good reasons

In his *Rhetoric,* Aristotle discusses the various ways one can argue a point. Torture, he notes, makes for a very convincing argument, but not one that reasonable people will resort to. In effecting real changes in minds and hearts, we need instead to rely on *good reasons* that establish our credibility, that appeal to logic, and that appeal to emotion.

5e Using narratives to support an argument

Because storytelling is universal, narratives can be very persuasive in helping readers understand and accept an argument. In arguing for increased funding for the homeless, for instance, you might include a brief narrative about a day in the life of a homeless person, to dramatize the issue and help readers *see* the need for more funding.

Stories drawn from your own experience can exert particular appeal to readers, for they not only help make your point in true-to-life, human terms but also establish your credibility by helping readers know you better and therefore identify with you more closely. In arguing for a stronger government campaign against smoking, President Clinton often draws on personal stories of his own family's experience with lung cancer. In much the same way, the writer bell hooks tells the story of her own experience with elitist educational institutions as a way of arguing for changes in those institutions.

If you include stories in an argument, make sure they are used not merely to add interest but rather to support your thesis. In general, do not rely solely on the power of stories to carry your argument, since readers usually expect writers to state and argue their reasons more directly and abstractly as well. An additional danger if you use only your own experiences is that you can seem focused too much on yourself (and perhaps not enough on your readers).

In writing the essay at the end of this chapter, Jennifer Georgia began by reflecting on her own experiences with her topic, choosing a major field of study. As a result, her first draft relied heavily on her own story about why she designed her own major. Readers liked hearing her story, but they told her that for her argument to be convincing, she needed to give other reasons as well. In revising, she thus condensed the story and used it as only one of a number of good reasons in support of her thesis.

FOR MULTILINGUAL WRITERS

COUNTING YOUR OWN EXPERIENCE

You may have learned that your own personal experience doesn't count in making academic arguments. If so, reconsider this advice, for showing an audience that you have personal experience with a topic can carry strong persuasive appeal with many English-speaking audiences. As with all evidence used in an argument, however, evidence based on your own experience must be pertinent to the topic, understandable to the audience, and clearly related to your purpose.

→ Does the narrative support your thesis?
→ Will the story's significance to the argument be clear to your readers?
→ Is the story one of several good reasons, or does it have to carry the main burden of the argument?

5f Establishing credibility

To make your argument convincing, you must first gain the respect and trust of your readers, or **establish your credibility** with them. The ancient Greeks called this particular kind of character appeal *ethos* and valued it highly. In general, writers can establish credibility in three ways:

1. by demonstrating knowledge about the topic at hand
2. by establishing common ground with the audience in the form of respect for their points of view and concern for their welfare
3. by demonstrating fairness and evenhandedness

1 Demonstrating knowledge

A writer can establish credibility first by establishing his or her credentials. You can, for instance, show that you have some personal experience with the subject, as Jennifer Georgia does in the opening of her essay in 5j3. In addition, if you show that you have thought about the subject carefully or researched it, you can establish a confident tone.

To determine whether you can effectively present yourself as knowledgeable enough to argue an issue, consider the following questions:

- Can you provide information about your topic from sources other than your own knowledge?
- What are the sources of your information?
- How reliable are your sources?
- Do any sources contradict each other? If so, can you account for or resolve the contradictions?
- If you have personal experience relating to the issue, would telling about this experience help support your claim?

These questions may help you see what other work you need to do to establish credibility. They may well show that you must do more research, check sources, resolve contradictions, refocus your working thesis, or even change your topic.

2 Establishing common ground

Many arguments between people or groups are doomed to end without resolution because the two sides occupy no common ground, no starting point of agreement. They are, to use an informal phrase, coming from completely different places. Such has often been the case, for example, in Arab-Israeli talks, in which the beginning positions of each party were so far apart that no resolution could be reached.

Lack of common ground also dooms many arguments closer to our everyday lives. If you and your roommate cannot agree on how often to clean your apartment, for instance, the difficulty may well be that your definition of a clean apartment conflicts radically with your roommate's. You may find, in fact, that you will not be able to resolve such issues until you can establish common definitions, ones that can turn futile quarrels into constructive arguments.

For more about establishing common ground, see Chapter 29.

Common ground is just as important in written arguments as it is in diplomatic negotiations or personal disputes. The following questions can help you find common ground in presenting an argument:

- What are the differing perspectives on this issue?
- What common ground can you find – aspects of the issue on which all sides agree?
- How can you express such common ground clearly to all sides?
- How can you discover – and consider – opinions on this issue that differ from your own?
- How can you use language – occupational, regional, or ethnic varieties of English, or languages other than English – to establish common ground with those you address?

If you turn to Jennifer Georgia's essay in 5j3, you will see that she attempts to establish common ground with her readers by relating her experience in focusing on a course of study to theirs.

3 Demonstrating fairness

In arguing a position, writers must demonstrate fairness toward opposing arguments. Audiences are more inclined to give credibility to writers who seem to be fairly considering and representing their opponents' views than to those who seem to be ignoring or distorting such views. To be an effective writer, you need to avoid such tactics and establish yourself as open-minded and evenhanded. The following questions can help you discover ways of doing so:

- How can you show that you are taking into account all significant points of view?
- How can you demonstrate that you understand and sympathize with points of view other than your own?
- What can you do to show that you have considered evidence carefully, even that which does not support your position?

4 Recognizing ethical fallacies

Some arguments focus not on establishing the credibility of the writer but on destroying the credibility of an opponent. At times, such attacks are justified: if a nominee for the Supreme Court has acted in unethical ways in law school, for example, that information is a legitimate argument against the nominee's confirmation. Many times, however, someone attacks a person's character in order to avoid dealing with the issue at hand. Be extremely careful about attacking an opponent's credibility, for doing so without justification can harm your own credibility. Such unjustified attacks are called **ethical fallacies.** They take two main forms: ad hominem charges and guilt by association.

Ad hominem (Latin for "to the man") charges directly attack someone's character rather than focusing on the issue at hand, suggesting that because something is "wrong" with this person, whatever he or she says must also be wrong.

> Patricia Ireland is just a hysterical feminist. We shouldn't listen to her views on abortion. [Labeling Ireland *hysterical* and linking that label with *feminist* focuses on Ireland's character rather than on her views on the issue at hand.]

Guilt by association attacks someone's credibility by linking that person with a person or activity the audience considers bad, suspicious, or untrustworthy.

> Senator Fleming does not deserve reelection; one of her assistants turned out to be involved with organized crime. [Is there any evidence that the senator knew about the organized-crime involvement?]

EXERCISE 5.4

Study carefully the following advertisement for a mutual fund, and then list the ways in which the copywriters demonstrate knowledge, establish common ground, and demonstrate fairness. Do you think they succeed or fail in establishing credibility?

EXERCISE 5.5

Using a working argumentative thesis you drafted for Exercise 5.2 or 5.3, write a paragraph or two describing how you would go about establishing your credibility in arguing that thesis.

5g Appealing to logic

While the character we present in writing always exerts a strong appeal (or lack of appeal) in an argument, our credibility alone cannot and should not carry the full burden of convincing readers. Indeed, many are inclined to view the **logic of the argument** — the reasoning behind it — as equally if not more important. This section will examine the most effective means of providing logical support for a written argument: examples and precedents, authority and testimony, and causes and effects.

1 Providing examples and precedents

Just as a picture can sometimes be worth a thousand words, so can a well-conceived **example** be extremely valuable in arguing a point. Examples are used most often to support generalizations or to bring abstractions to life. For instance, a *Newsweek* review of the movie *Star Trek IV* makes the general statement that the movie contains "nutty throwaway lines that take a minute to sink in" and then illustrates the generalization with this example:

> When the crew, flying the Klingon warship they inherited . . . , land in Golden Gate Park, they fan out to different corners of the city. . . . Kirk's parting command, spoken like a PTA mother at the county fair: "Everybody remember where we parked."

The generalization would mean little without the example.

Examples can also help us understand abstractions. *Famine,* for instance, may be difficult for us to think about in the abstract, but a graphic description of a drought-stricken community, its riverbed cracked and dry, its people listless, emaciated, and with stomachs bloated by hunger, speaks directly to our understanding.

Precedents are particular kinds of examples taken from the past. The most common use of precedent occurs in law, where an attorney may ask a judge to rule that a defendant was negligent, for example, because the Supreme Court upheld a ruling of negligence in an almost identical case ten years earlier. Precedent appears in everyday arguments as well. If, as part of a proposal for increased lighting in the library garage, you point out that the university has increased lighting in four similar garages in the past year, you are arguing on the basis of precedent.

In research writing, you usually must list your sources for any examples or precedents not based on your own knowledge.

For a discussion of acknowledging sources, see 42d.

The following questions can help you check any use of example and precedent:

- How representative are the examples?
- Are they sufficient in strength or number to lead to a generalization?
- In what ways do they support your point?
- How closely does the precedent relate to the point you're trying to make? Are the situations really similar?
- How timely is the precedent? (What would have been applicable in 1520 is not necessarily applicable today.)

2 Citing authority and testimony

Another way to support an argument logically is to cite an **authority.** In recent decades, the use of authority has figured prominently in the controversy over smoking. Since the U.S. surgeon general's 1963 announcement that smoking is hazardous to health, many Americans have quit smoking, largely convinced by the authority of the scientists offering the evidence.

But as with other strategies for building support for an argumentative claim, citing authorities demands careful consideration. Ask yourself the following questions to be sure you are using authorities effectively:

- Is the authority timely? (The argument that the United States should pursue a policy just because it was supported by Thomas Jefferson will probably fail because Jefferson's time was so radically different from ours.)
- Is the authority qualified to judge the topic at hand? (To cite a botanist in an essay on linguistics is not likely to strengthen your argument.)
- Is the authority likely to be known and respected by readers? (To cite an unfamiliar authority without some identification will lessen the impact of the evidence.)

Authorities are commonly cited in research writing, which often relies on the findings of other people. In addition, you may cite authorities in an assignment that asks you to review the literature of any field.

For a complete discussion of research, see Chapters 40 – 47.

Testimony – the evidence an authority presents in support of a claim – is a feature of much contemporary argument. If testimony is timely, accurate, representative, and provided by a respected authority, then it, like authority itself, can add powerful support to an argument. In an essay for a literature class, for example, you might argue that a new edition of a literary work will open up many new areas of interpretation. You could strengthen this argument by adding a quotation from the author's biographer, noting that the new edition carries out the author's intentions much more closely than the previous edition did.

In research writing, you should list your sources for authority and testimony not based on your own knowledge.

For a discussion of acknowledging sources, see 42d.

3 Establishing causes and effects

Showing that one event is the cause – or the effect – of another can sometimes help support an argument. To take an everyday example, suppose you are trying to explain, in a petition to change your grade in a course, why you were unable to take the final examination. In such a case, you would probably try to trace the **causes** of your failure to appear – the death of your grandmother followed by the theft of your car, perhaps – so that the committee reading the petition would consider anew the **effect** – your not taking the examination.

Tracing causes often lays the groundwork for an argument, particularly if the effect of the causes is one we would like to change. In an environmental science class, for example, a student may argue that a national law regulating smokestack emissions from utility plants is needed because (1) acid rain on the east coast originates from emissions at utility plants in the Midwest, (2) acid rain kills trees and other vegetation, (3) utility lobbyists have prevented midwestern states from passing strict laws controlling emissions from such plants, and (4) in the absence of such laws, acid rain will destroy most eastern forests by 2020. In this case, the first point is that the emissions cause acid rain; the second, that acid rain causes destruction in eastern forests; and the third, that states have not acted to break the cause-effect relationship established by the first two points. The fourth point ties all of the previous points together to provide an overall argument from effect: unless X, then Y.

In fact, a cause-effect relationship is often extremely difficult to establish. Scientists and politicians continue to disagree, for example, over the extent to which acid rain is responsible for the so-called dieback of many eastern forests. If we can show that X definitely causes Y, though, we will have a powerful argument at our disposal.

4 Using inductive and deductive reasoning

Traditionally, logical arguments are classified as using either inductive or deductive reasoning, both of which almost always work together. **Inductive reasoning,** most simply, is the process of making a generalization based on a number of specific instances. If you find you are ill on ten occasions after eating seafood, for example, you will likely draw the inductive generalization that seafood makes you ill. It may not be an absolute certainty that seafood was the culprit, but the *probability* lies in that direction.

Deductive reasoning, on the other hand, reaches a conclusion by assuming a general principle (known as a **major premise**) and then applying that principle to a specific case (the **minor premise**). In practice, this general principle is usually derived from induction. The inductive generalization *Seafood makes me ill,* for instance, could serve as the

FOR MULTILINGUAL WRITERS

BRINGING IN OTHER VOICES

Sometimes quoting authorities will prompt you to use language other than standard academic English, and in ways that support your own authority. For instance, if you're writing about political relations between Mexico and the United States, you might quote a leader of a Mexican American organization; using that person's *own words* — which may be partly or entirely in Spanish or a regional variety of English — can carry extra power, calling up a voice from a pertinent community. See Chapter 28 for advice about using varieties of English and other languages.

major premise for the deductive argument *Since all seafood makes me ill, the plate of it just put before me is certain to make me ill.*

Deductive arguments like these have traditionally been analyzed as **syllogisms,** three-part statements containing a major premise, a minor premise, and a conclusion.

MAJOR PREMISE	All people die.
MINOR PREMISE	I am a person.
CONCLUSION	I will die.

Syllogisms, however, are too rigid and absolute to serve in arguments about questions that have no absolute answers, and they often lack any appeal to an audience. From Aristotle came a simpler alternative, the **enthymeme,** which calls on the audience to supply the implied major premise. Consider the following example:

> This bridge is carrying twice as much traffic as it was built for, so we need to build a new bridge or restrict traffic on this one.

You can analyze this enthymeme by restating it in the form of two premises and a conclusion.

MAJOR PREMISE	Bridges should carry only the amount of traffic for which they were built.
MINOR PREMISE	This bridge carries twice the traffic for which it was built.
CONCLUSION	We need a new bridge or traffic restrictions on this one.

Note that the major premise is one the writer can count on an audience agreeing with or supplying: safety and common sense demand that bridges carry only the amount of traffic for which they are built. By thus inspiring audience participation, an enthymeme actually gets the audience to contribute to the argument.

Jennifer Gerkin's essay in 4j rests on an enthymeme whose implied major premise she assumes her readers will accept: "Prejudice is harmful to all of us." She goes on to demonstrate her own prejudice and to show how that prejudice has harmed her as well as others.

Whether it is expressed as a syllogism or an enthymeme, a deductive conclusion is only as strong as the premises on which it is based. The citizen who argues that *Ed is a crook and shouldn't be elected to public office* is arguing deductively, based on an implied major premise: *No crook should be elected to public office.* In this case, most people would agree with this major premise. So the issue in this argument rests on the minor premise — that Ed is a crook. Only if that premise can be proved satisfactorily are we likely to accept the deductive conclusion that Ed shouldn't be elected.

At other times, the unstated premise may be more problematic. The person who says, *Don't bother to ask for Jack's help with physics — he's a jock* is arguing deductively on the basis of an implied major premise: *Jocks don't know anything about physics.* In this case, careful listeners would demand proof of the unstated premise. Because bigoted or prejudiced statements often rest on this kind of reasoning, writers should be particularly alert to it.

For a discussion of stereotyping and prejudice in writing, see Chapter 29.

5 Recognizing logical fallacies

Although **logical fallacies** are usually defined as errors in formal reasoning, they can often work very effectively to convince audiences. Some readers will detect fallacious appeals, however — and may even reject an otherwise worthy argument that relies on them. Your time will be well spent, therefore, in learning to recognize these fallacies. Common logical fallacies include begging the question, *post hoc,* non sequitur, either-or, hasty generalization, and oversimplification.

Begging the question is a kind of circular argument that treats a question as if it has already been answered.

> That TV news provides accurate and reliable information was demonstrated conclusively on last week's *60 Minutes.* [This statement says in effect that television news is accurate and reliable because TV news says so.]

The ***post hoc*** **fallacy,** from the Latin *post hoc, ergo propter hoc,* which means "after this, therefore caused by this," assumes that just because B happened *after* A, it must have been *caused* by A.

> We should not rebuild the town docks because every time we do, a big hurricane comes along and damages them. [Does the reconstruction cause hurricanes?]

A **non sequitur** (Latin for "it does not follow") attempts to tie together two or more logically unrelated ideas as if they *were* related.

> If we can send a spacecraft to Mars, then we can discover a cure for cancer. [These are both scientific goals, but do they have anything else in common? What does achieving one have to do with achieving the other?]

The **either-or fallacy** asserts that a complex situation can have only two possible outcomes, one of which is necessary or preferable.

> If we do not build the new aqueduct, businesses in the tri-cities area will be forced to shut down because of lack of water. [What is the evidence for this claim? Do no other alternatives exist?]

www •

http://calvin.assiniboinec.mb.ca/user/downes/fall/

Stephen Downes's Guide to the Logical Fallacies *compiles definitions and examples of fallacies from philosophy, rhetoric, and logic texts, with an excellent reference list.*

A **hasty generalization** bases a conclusion on too little evidence or on bad or misunderstood evidence.

> I couldn't understand the lecture today, so I'm sure this course will be impossible. [How can the writer be so sure of this conclusion based on only *one* piece of evidence?]

Oversimplification of the relation between causes and effects is another fallacy based on careless reasoning.

> If we prohibit the sale of alcohol, we will get rid of drunkenness. [This claim oversimplifies the relation between laws and human behavior.]

EXERCISE 5.6

The following sentences contain deductive arguments based on implied major premises. Identify each of the implied premises.

1. Active euthanasia is morally acceptable when it promotes the best interests of everyone concerned and violates no one's rights.
2. Women soldiers should not serve in combat positions because doing so would expose them to a much higher risk of death.
3. Animals can't talk, so therefore they can't feel pain as humans do.

EXERCISE 5.7

Analyze the advertisement in Exercise 5.4 for the use of examples, narratives, and precedents; authority and testimony; causes and effects; induction and deduction; and logical fallacies.

EXERCISE 5.8

Using your working argumentative thesis from Exercise 5.2 or 5.3, write a paragraph describing the logical appeals you would use to support the thesis.

5h Appealing to emotion

Most successful arguments appeal to our hearts as well as to our minds. Thus, good writers supplement appeals to logic and reason with those designed to **enlist the emotional support** of their readers. This principle was vividly demonstrated a number of years ago, when we began hearing about famine in Africa. Facts and figures (logical appeals) convinced many that the famine was real and serious. What brought an outpouring of aid, however, was the arresting emotional power of photographs of children, at once skeletal and bloated, dying of starvation. Writers can gain similarly powerful effects with the careful use of stories – and with description, concrete language, and figurative language.

1 Using description and concrete language

Like photographs, vivid, detailed **description** can bring a moving immediacy to any argument. The student in 3d1 amassed plenty of facts and figures, including diagrams and maps, to illustrate the problem of wheelchair access to the library. But her first draft seemed lifeless in spite of all her information. She decided, therefore, to ask a friend who used a wheelchair to accompany her to the library – and she revised her proposal, opening it with a detailed description of that visit and its many frustrations for her friend.

Concrete language stands at the heart of effective description and hence helps build emotional appeal. Although the student in 3d1, for instance, could have said simply that her friend "had trouble entering the library," such a general statement would not appeal to readers' emotions by helping them imagine themselves in a similar position. Her actual version, full of concrete description, does so: "Maria inched her heavy wheelchair up the narrow, steep entrance ramp, her arms straining to pull up the last twenty feet, her face pinched with the sheer effort."

2 Using figurative language

Figurative language, or figures of speech, are crucial elements in painting a detailed and vivid picture. They do so by making striking comparisons between something you are writing about and something else that helps a reader visualize, identify with, or understand it.

For more about figurative language, see 27d.

Figures of speech include metaphors, similes, and analogies. **Metaphors** compare two things directly: *Richard the Lion-Hearted; old age is the evening of life.* **Similes** make comparisons using *like* or *as: Richard is as brave as a lion; old age is like the evening of life.* **Analogies** are extended metaphors or similes that compare an unfamiliar concept or process to a more familiar one to help the reader understand the unfamiliar concept.

> I see the Internet as a city struggling to be built, its laws only now being formulated, its notions of social order arising out of the needs of its citizens and the demands of their environment. Like any city, the Net has its charlatans and its thieves as well as its poets, engineers, and philosophers. . . . Our expe-

rience of the Internet will be determined by how we master its core competencies. They are the design principles that are shaping the electronic city.

– PAUL GILSTER, *Digital Literacy*

A student arguing for a more streamlined course-registration process may find good use for an analogy, saying that the current process makes students feel like laboratory rats in a maze. This analogy, which suggests manipulation, victims, and a clinical coldness, creates a vivid description and hence adds emotional appeal to the argument. For the analogy to work effectively, however, the student would have to show that the current registration process has a number of similarities to a laboratory maze, such as confused students wandering through complex bureaucratic channels and into dead ends.

3 Shaping your appeal to your audience

As with appeals to credibility and logic, appealing to emotions is effective only insofar as it moves your particular audience. A student arguing for increased lighting in campus parking garages, for instance, might consider the emotions such a discussion might raise (fear of attackers, anger at being subjected to such danger, compassion for victims of such attacks), decide which emotions the intended audience would be most responsive to, and then look for descriptive and figurative language to carry out such an appeal.

In a leaflet to be distributed on campus or an online notice to a student listserv, for example, the student might describe the scene in a dimly lit garage as a student parks her car and then has to walk to an exit alone down shadowy corridors. Parking in the garage might be compared to venturing into a dangerous jungle.

In a proposal to the university administration, on the other hand, the student might describe past attacks on students in campus garages and the negative publicity and criticism these provoked among students, parents, alumni, and other groups. For the administration, the student might compare the lighting in the garages to high-risk gambling, arguing that increased lighting would lower the odds of future attacks.

Notice that shaping your appeal to specific audiences calls on you to consider very carefully the language you use. The student arguing for better lighting in campus parking garages, for instance, would probably stick to standard academic English in a proposal to the university administration but might well want to use more informal language, even slang, in a leaflet written for students.

4 Recognizing emotional fallacies

Appeals to the emotions of an audience constitute a valid and necessary part of argument. Unfair or overblown emotional appeals, however, attempt to overcome readers' good judgment. Most common among these **emotional fallacies** are bandwagon appeal, flattery, in-crowd appeal, veiled threats, and false analogies. **Bandwagon appeal** suggests that a great movement is under way and the reader will be a fool or a traitor not to join it.

> Voters are flocking to candidate X by the millions, so you'd better cast your vote the right way. [Why should you jump on this bandwagon? Where is the evidence to support this claim?]

Flattery tries to persuade readers to do something by suggesting that they are thoughtful, intelligent, or perceptive enough to agree with the writer.

> We know you have the taste to recognize that an investment in an Art-Form ring will pay off in the future. [How will it pay off?]

In-crowd appeal, a special kind of flattery, invites readers to identify with an admired and select group.

> Want to know a secret that more and more of Middletown's successful young professionals are finding out about? It's Mountainbrook Manor, the condominiums that combine the best of the old with the best of the new. [Who are these "successful young professionals," and will you become one by moving to Mountainbrook Manor?]

Veiled threats try to frighten readers into agreement by hinting that they will suffer adverse consequences if they don't agree.

> If Public Service Electric Company does not get an immediate 15 percent rate increase, its services to you, its customers, may be seriously affected. [How serious is this possible effect? Is it legal or likely?]

False analogies make comparisons between two situations that are *not* alike in most or important respects.

> If the United States gets involved in a land war in the Middle East, it will turn out just like Vietnam. [Is there any point of analogy except that they are both wars? This example was written in 1988. The Persian Gulf War of 1991 demonstrates well the weaknesses of such analogies.]

EXERCISE 5.9

Make a list of the common human emotions that might be attached to the following topics, and suggest appropriate ways to appeal to those emotions in a specific audience you choose to address.

1. banning smoking on campus
2. assisted suicide
3. generating nuclear power
4. television evangelism
5. steroid use among athletes

EXERCISE 5.10

Jennifer Gerkin's essay in Chapter 4 argues that people shouldn't judge others on the basis of appearance. Reread the essay, underlining emotional appeals, including descriptive passages, concrete language, and figurative language.

EXERCISE 5.11

Read the following paragraph, and then write a paragraph evaluating its use of description and figurative language.

In 1973, all women in the United States became legally entitled to have abortions performed in hospitals by licensed physicians. Before they were legal, abortions were frequently performed by persons who bore more resemblance to butchers than they did to doctors. The all-too-common result was serious complications or death for the woman. Since 1989, states have been able to restrict where and when abortions are performed. Even if the 1973 Supreme Court decision is completely reversed, abortion will not end. Instead, women will again resort to illegal abortions, and there will be a return to the slaughterhouse. Since abortions are going to take place no matter what the law says, why not have them done safely and legally in hospitals instead of in basements, alleys, or dirty compartments in some killing shed? The decision to have an abortion is not an easy one to make, and I believe that a woman who makes it deserves to have her wish carried out in the very safest way possible. Critics of abortion stress the importance of the unborn child's life. At the very least, they should also take the woman's life and safety into consideration.

EXERCISE 5.12

Using a working argumentative thesis you formulated for Exercise 5.2 or 5.3, make a list of the emotional appeals most appropriate to your topic and audience. Then spend ten to fifteen minutes brainstorming, looking for descriptive and figurative language to carry out the appeals.

5i Using sources in an argument

In constructing a written argument, it is usually necessary – and often essential – to use sources. The key to persuading people to accept your argument is good reasons; and even if your assignment doesn't specify that you must consult outside sources, they are often the most effective way of finding and establishing these reasons. Sources can help you in a number of ways:

- to provide background information on your topic
- to demonstrate your knowledge of the topic to readers
- to cite authority and testimony in support of your thesis
- to find opinions that differ from your own, which can help you sharpen your thinking, qualify your thesis if necessary, and demonstrate fairness to opposing arguments

For a thorough discussion of finding, gathering, and evaluating sources, both off- and online, see Chapter 42.

5j Organizing an argument

Once you have assembled good reasons in support of an argumentative thesis, you must organize your material in order to present the argument convincingly. Although there is no ideal or universally favored organizational framework, you may find it useful to try one of the following ones.

1 The classical system

The classical system of argument was often followed by ancient Greek and Roman orators. The speaker began with an *introduction,* which stated the thesis and then gave the *background* information. Next came the different *lines of argument* and then the *consideration of opposing arguments.* A *conclusion* both summed up the argument and made a final appeal to the audience. You can adapt this format to written arguments as follows:

1. *Introduction*
   - gains readers' attention and interest
   - establishes your qualifications to write about your topic
   - establishes common ground with readers
   - demonstrates fairness
   - states or implies your thesis
2. *Background*
   - presents any necessary background information, including pertinent personal narrative
3. *Lines of argument*
   - present good reasons (including logical and emotional appeals) in support of your thesis
   - generally present reasons in order of importance
   - demonstrate ways your argument may be in readers' best interest
4. *Consideration of alternative arguments*
   - examines alternative points of view
   - notes advantages and disadvantages of alternative views
   - explains why one view is better than other(s)
5. *Conclusion*
   - may summarize the argument
   - elaborates on the implication of your thesis
   - makes clear what you want readers to think or do
   - makes a strong ethical or emotional appeal

2 The Toulmin system

Another useful system of argument was developed by philosopher Stephen Toulmin. In simplified form, it can help you organize an argumentative essay in this way:

1. Make your claim (a statement that is debatable or controversial).
2. Qualify your claim if necessary.
3. Present good reasons to support your claim.
4. Explain the warrant (underlying assumptions) that connects your claim and your reasons. If the warrant is controversial, provide backing for it.
5. Provide grounds to support your claim (facts, statistics, testimony, the use of other logical, ethical, or emotional appeals).
6. Acknowledge and respond to possible counterarguments.
7. Draw your conclusion.

Suppose you were writing an essay about the dangers of smoking and you want to claim that the federal government should ban smoking. You might then qualify this claim by suggesting that the ban be limited to all public places. As reasons in support of your claim, you might say that smoking causes serious diseases in smokers and that nonsmokers are endangered by others' smoke. A warrant (or underlying assumption) you might offer is the fact that the Constitution was established to "promote the general welfare" or that citizens are entitled to protection from harmful actions by others. Since some might debate these warrants, you might introduce as backing the logical claim that the United States is based on a political system that is supposed to serve the basic needs of its people, including their health. As grounds for your claim, you could then cite not only statistics about lung and heart disease and the incidence of deaths attributed to secondhand smoke but also facts about the several lawsuits won recently against large tobacco companies and about the bans on smoking already imposed by many public institutions and places of employment. You might quote the U.S. surgeon general as an authority on the subject, or President Clinton, whose experience with lung cancer in his family is related to his stand against tobacco use. One counterargument you could anticipate is that smokers have rights, too – and you could respond by reminding readers that you are suggesting a ban only in public places. Smokers would still be free to smoke in private. Finally, you could state your own conclusion in the strongest way possible.

3 A sample argumentative essay

Asked to write an argumentative essay on an issue of interest to her and addressed to her classmates, Jennifer Georgia decided to draw on her experience in designing her own program of study. She wanted to urge other students to think hard before choosing a course of study – and to consider designing their own. She used her own experience as well as several other good reasons to back up her argument. Her purposes for argument were twofold – to explore the advantages and disadvantages of prescribed programs of study, and to convince other students to examine their own programs critically and consider possible alternatives.

Her essay, which follows, is roughly organized according to the classical system and annotated to point out the various parts of her argument as well as her use of pertinent ethical, logical, and emotional appeals.

Major Problems

How do we decide on a course of study?* For me it was easy. When my college advisor asked me to choose my major, I said "No Problem," and unhesitatingly checked the box marked "English." After

Introduction gets readers' attention, presents background

all, I liked English in high school. I had even visited the English Department Web site.

Is this a good way to decide on a course of study? If not, how should we choose? One thing seems certain: we should not be encouraged to check off a box on a form. Instead, we ought first to think critically about what we want to learn--about the topics we wish to study and about the career and life path they will put us on. Then, and only then, should we choose our course of study.

Establishes common ground

Thesis

The decision about a major or other course of study is crucial because it determines both what we study and how we come to think about the world. The philosopher Kenneth Burke explains that we are inevitably affected not only by our experiences but also by the terminologies through which our perceptions of those experiences are filtered. Burke calls these filters "terministic screens" and says that they affect our perception, highlighting some aspects of an experience while obscuring others. Thus the terminologies (or languages) we use influence how we see the world and how we think about what we see.

Cites authority

Figurative language used to explain a point

Burke extends this concept of terministic screens to the various courses in a college curriculum, which he says are "in effect but so many different terminologies" (41). In other words, a program's curriculum brings with it certain frames of reference--terminologies--that affect the way we think about the world. In

Offers testimony

addition, of course, a curriculum filters out or deemphasizes various ideas or perspectives according to a program's agendas, thus potentially limiting our perception of the world. In pursuing particular courses of study, then, we are not just choosing an academic path; we are also choosing a frame of reference from which to see and think about the world. The engineering student learns to see the world from an engineer's perspective; the criminal justice student learns to see the world from a criminologist's perspective.

Establishes cause-effect relationship

Gives concrete examples

Once I declared my major, I began to see the world through an English major's eyes, which helped me to see certain things--and not to see others. I found the required courses--almost all in periods of English and U.S. literature--stimulating, but I was frustrated that my many other interests had no place in my program other than as electives or extracurricular activities. As I began to recognize art, architecture, music, language, and literature as interrelated forms of expression, I began to feel more and more closed in by my English program. I wanted a program that affirmed all these disciplines as points along a continuum of communicative acts rather than a program that focused exclusively on "literary" communication.

Tells about pertinent personal experience

Surely I am not the first student to feel constrained by prescribed courses. But such constraints are often necessary, as those favoring set requirements are quick to point out. Set course requirements are needed by colleges in order to

Demonstrates fairness, considers and notes advantages of alternative viewpoints

allocate funds and do other logistical planning. They are needed in certain fields to make sure practitioners have necessary skills--airplane mechanics, for example, have to work to certain specific codes to ensure the safety of air travel. And as the Undergraduate Studies in English at The Ohio State University: A Handbook points out, they can help guide students through undergraduate studies and toward specific fields (3).

Cites source in support of alternative viewpoints

If accepted unquestioningly, however, set requirements can hinder our ability to think critically and creatively. Indeed, they can often keep students from thinking about their course of study at all. And such uncritical acceptance seems especially dangerous at a time when, according to anthropologist Clifford Geertz, the boundaries between disciplines are breaking down (19). In addition, by tending to track students, set requirements often force us to take courses we're not interested in and keep us from others we are interested in. So while we come to college to gain the credentials associated with a certain program, we also come to explore our interests and realize our potential as well as to prepare for future jobs. Thus it is imperative to find a balance between the college's track and our own. The college experience is supposed to be a time to explore many paths, not to follow a totally fixed guidebook.

Deductive reasoning

Figurative language

In fact, the process of thinking about and choosing what we study can be an important exercise in critical thinking. In questioning the tracks offered by our

Appeals directly to audience

school, we students can shape our own development and assert our individuality.

It was through this sort of questioning that I discovered a loophole in the system at Ohio State--a program of personalized study called the Personal Study Program, or PSP. The PSP can offer a solution to the problems experienced by many undergraduates who, like me, seek greater flexibility. The PSP allows students not only to design individual programs but, more importantly, to become actively (and critically) involved in our own education. Drawing up a PSP is not an easy process, but the rewards to me by far outweigh the frustrations. The PSP has allowed me to realize my potential in a unique way, by pursuing the many connections between language study (in my case, English, French, and Italian) and speech, music, poetry, and architecture. I have established my own "terministic screens" rather than accepting screens imposed by others. The PSP isn't for everyone, of course. But the process of looking closely at a college program or major <u>should</u> be for everybody, if only to be aware of its limits and strengths.

Gives pertinent personal example

Establishes common ground

Such a step is in line with the educational philosophy of Ohio State University president Dr. E. Gordon Gee, who echoes Geertz by acknowledging that many of the boundaries that currently divide the university are "artificial." As Dr. Gee said in a recent address to the university senate, "I challenge you to think beyond collegiate boundaries. To think creatively. To bring to the decision

Cites authority

Offers testimony

process the flexibility and adaptability that we bring as scientists and scholars to our intellectual activity" (2). As Dr. Gee suggests, it is our critical skills and ability to think independently and creatively that will allow us to meet the ever-changing world around us and to adapt to the future. Through programs like the PSP, we can assert our independence from the institutional frameworks and afford ourselves new dimensions for critical thinking.

What's your major? Think about it. And then--you decide.

Closes with strong appeal

Note

*A special thanks to the students of Carrie Dirmeikis's English 110 class for their help in responding to this paper, and to Hakan Aytac for his insights.

Works Cited

Burke, Kenneth. Language as Symbolic Action: Essays on Life, Literature, and Method. Berkeley: U. of California, 1966. 44-62.

The English Major. The Ohio State University. 27 Nov. 1997 <http://www.cohums.ohio-state.edu/coh/student/majors/english.htm>.

Gee, E. Gordon. "Address to the University Senate." The Ohio State University. Columbus. 9 Oct. 1993.

Geertz, Clifford. Local Knowledge: Further Essays in Interpretive Anthropology. New York: Basic, 1983.

The Ohio State Department of English. _Undergraduate Studies in English at The Ohio State University: A Handbook._ Columbus: Ohio State Dept. of English, 1993.

EXERCISE 5.13

Using the classical or Toulmin system, draft an argument in support of one of the theses you formulated for Exercise 5.2 or 5.3.

5k Analyzing an argument

Here are some questions based on the classical system and the Toulmin system that can help you judge the effectiveness of an argument:

ANALYZING AN ARGUMENT WITH THE CLASSICAL SYSTEM

1. What is there to gain readers' interest? (5h)
2. How has the writer established qualifications to write about the topic – by showing personal experience with it? by citing authoritative sources? (5f1)
3. What in the introduction establishes common ground with readers? (5f2)
4. Is the thesis stated? If not, will readers be able to recognize it? Is it sufficiently focused? (5c)
5. What background information is given? Is it sufficient? (5f)
6. What reasons are given in support of the thesis – examples? precedents or authorities? testimony? cause-effect relationships? (5g)
7. How has the writer appealed to readers' emotions? (5h)
8. Are there any fallacies? (5f4, 5g5, and 5h4)
9. Is there attention to opposing points of view? Has the writer noted both their advantages and disadvantages? (5f3)
10. How does the essay conclude – by summarizing the argument? elaborating on its implications? making an emotional appeal? Has the writer made clear what readers should think or do? (5j)

1. What is the claim or thesis? (5c)
2. How is the claim qualified? (5c)
3. What good reasons support the claim? (5d)
4. What warrants or assumptions support these reasons? (5f)
5. What backs up the warrant? (5g)
6. What grounds support the claim – what facts, statistics, testimony, and so on? (5g2)
7. How are counterarguments acknowledged and responded to? (5f3)

EXERCISE 5.14

Using the categories in the Toulmin system described in 5j2 and the preceding questions, try analyzing the argument implicit in the advertisement for Working Assets in Exercise 5.4. Write out your analysis in a page or so.

THINKING CRITICALLY ABOUT ARGUMENTS

Reading with an Eye for Argument

In this brief opinion essay from *TV Guide,* Jeff Jarvis considers the Rush Limbaugh phenomenon by reviewing a television program (*Monty*) whose star is highly reminiscent of Limbaugh. What claim(s) does Jarvis make? What ethical, logical, and emotional appeals does he offer in support of his claim(s)? How convincing are these appeals?

> Rush Limbaugh is the phenom that will not shrink. Rush is huge in radio, TV, and books. Rush appeared with David Letterman the same night that Jay Leno had America's other frighteningly gigantic media monster, Howard Stern – and Rush won big. William Shatner played a Rush clone in a Columbo movie – quite an honor. And now Rush is the inspiration for a sitcom, making him even more of a laughingstock than he already is.
>
> Now hold on, Rush fans. Already I can see you filling your pens with poison and aiming them at me. Save it. I've admitted that I kind of enjoy the guy. But he *is* getting too big for his already big britches. He's relying on infantile, cheap, smug insults about liberals who are short or have speech impediments – in lieu of real arguments or actual thought. He needs a sitcom to cut him down to size.
>
> So here comes Henry Winkler as Monty, the conservative, ego-rich host of a TV show filled with nothing but his own caustic opinions and gags (like a find-a-blind-date-for-

Janet-Reno contest). He's a Rush, all right. But we get to go home with this Rush, to his wife (the smartly appealing Kate Burton), two sharp-witted sons, and one feminist, liberal, vegetarian almost-a-daughter-in-law (China Kantner). So far, the show favors scenes at home, where Monty sneers at his son for throwing away a Yale degree to become a cook. Or he learns to support his wife when she suffers an abuse he thought liberals made up: sexual harassment. Or he wars with Kantner, the female Meathead to Winkler's well-dressed Archie Bunker.

Problem is, I never imagined someone like Rush having a home or a home life. What's fascinating about him is that he seems to be the kind of guy who'd eat franks 'n' beans out of a can and sleep under velvet portraits of Ronald Reagan in a bomb shelter somewhere — yet he turns out to be smart, urbane, funny. *Monty* needs such irony. What it doesn't need is another stock sitcom family.

I wish *Monty* would spend more time in its show-within-a-show, where he lists the ugly names he's called — white trash, a Neanderthal, a blowhard, a pig — so he can shrug it all off and tell America "we have to stop being so sensitive." The guy has a point, yet even his own show ignores him and quickly moves on to a stale Clinton-at-McDonald's gag. How much more fun it would be — how much more of a challenge — if *Monty* could honestly ask whether, behind all the bluster and blather of Rush and his fellow media phenoms, there may actually be something worth listening to — or at least something worth arguing about.

– JEFF JARVIS, *"Monty"*

Thinking Critically about Your Own Arguments

Using the guidelines in 5k, analyze the argument in something you've recently written or in the draft you wrote for Exercise 5.13. Decide what you need to do to revise your argument, and write out a brief plan for your revision.

6 Constructing Paragraphs

The hero of the Rex Stout mysteries, Nero Wolfe, once solved a case by identifying the paragraph structure of a particular writer-murderer. A person's style of paragraphing, Wolfe claimed, serves even more reliably than fingerprints as a stamp of identity. Like Stout's character, you probably already have a characteristic way of paragraphing, one you can learn to understand and use to advantage.

In most academic writing, the sentences in a paragraph all revolve around one main idea. When a new idea comes up, a new paragraph begins. Within this broad general guideline, however, paragraph structure is highly flexible, allowing writers to create many different individual effects for various writing purposes. Especially in workplace and online writing, flexibility is paramount, as writers create paragraphs for particular purposes and settings. ■

6a Paragraphing for readers

Numerous studies indicate that most readers come to any piece of writing with certain expectations about conventional paragraphs:

- Paragraphs will begin and end with important information.
- The opening sentence will often let readers know what a paragraph is about.
- The middle of a paragraph will develop what the paragraph is about.
- The end of a paragraph may sum up the paragraph's contents, bringing the discussion of an idea to a close in anticipation of the paragraph that follows.
- A paragraph will "make sense" as a whole; its words and sentences will be clearly related.
- A paragraph will relate or "talk" to the paragraphs around it.

6b Constructing conventional paragraphs

Let us look now at the elements in a well-written paragraph – one that is easy for readers to understand and follow.

> I never knew anyone who'd grown up in Jackson without being afraid of Mrs. Calloway, our librarian. She ran the Library absolutely by herself, from the desk where she sat with her back to the books and facing the stairs, her dragon

1. What is the topic sentence of each paragraph? Is it stated or implied? If stated, where in the paragraph does it fall? Should it come at some other point? Would any paragraph be improved by deleting or adding a topic sentence? (6c1)
2. Which sentences, if any, do not relate in some way to the topic sentence? Is there any way to justify their inclusion? (6c2)
3. What is the most general sentence in each paragraph? If it is not the topic sentence, should it remain or be omitted? (6c2 and 6d1)
4. Is each paragraph organized in a way that is easy for readers to follow? By what means are sentences linked? Do any more links need to be added? Do any of the transitional expressions try to create links between ideas that do not really exist? (6d)
5. How completely does each paragraph develop its topic sentence? What methods of development are used? Are they effective? What other methods might be used? Does the paragraph need more material? (6e)
6. Does the first sentence in each paragraph let readers know what the paragraph is about? Does the last sentence in some way conclude that paragraph's discussion? If not, does it need to?
7. Are paragraphs varied in length? Does any paragraph seem too long or too short? Is there any point that might be given strong emphasis by a one-sentence paragraph? (6e2 and 6f3)
8. By what means are the paragraphs linked? Do more links need to be added? Do any of the transitional expressions try to create links between ideas that do not really exist? (6h)
9. How does the introductory paragraph catch readers' interest? How exactly does it open – with a quotation? an anecdote? a question? a strong statement? How else might it open? (6f1)
10. How does the last paragraph draw the essay to a conclusion? What lasting impression will it leave with readers? How exactly does it close – with a question? a quotation? a vivid image? a warning or a call for action? How else might it conclude? (6f2)

www •

http://aix1.uottawa.ca/academic/arts/writcent/hypergrammar/paragrph.html

Writing Paragraphs, a page providing an excellent overview and exercises, is part of the University of Ottawa's HyperGrammar *site, a wonderful resource in itself.*

> eye on the front door, where who knew what kind of person might come in from the public? SILENCE in big black letters was on signs tacked up everywhere. She herself spoke in her normally commanding voice; every word could be heard all over the Library above a steady seething sound coming from her electric fan; it was the only fan in the Library and stood on her desk, turned directly onto her streaming face.
>
> – EUDORA WELTY, *One Writer's Beginnings*

This paragraph begins with a general statement of the main idea: that everyone who grew up in Jackson feared Mrs. Calloway. All the other sentences then give specific details about why she inspired such fear. This example demonstrates the three qualities essential to most academic paragraphs: *unity, coherence,* and *development.* It focuses on one main idea (**unity**); its parts are clearly related (**coherence**); and its main idea is supported with specifics (**development**).

6c Making paragraphs unified: focusing on a main idea

Highly readable conventional paragraphs generally focus on one main idea. One good way to achieve such paragraph unity is to state the main idea clearly in one sentence and relate all the other sentences in the paragraph to that idea. The sentence that presents the main idea is called the **topic sentence.** Like the thesis for an essay, the topic sentence includes a topic and some comment on that topic. In the preceding paragraph by Eudora Welty, the topic sentence opens the paragraph. Its topic is Mrs. Calloway; its comment, that those who grew up in Jackson were afraid of her.

For a discussion of the thesis of an essay, see 3b.

1 Positioning a topic sentence

Although a topic sentence often appears at the beginning of a paragraph, it may appear anywhere in the paragraph – or it may not appear at all but, rather, be implied.

Topic sentence at the beginning

If you want readers to see your point immediately, open with the topic sentence. Such a strategy can be particularly useful in memos or in argumentative writing. The following paragraph opens with a clear topic sentence, on which subsequent sentences build:

For an example of a memo, see 51e; for a discussion of argumentative writing, see Chapter 5.

Our friendship was the source of much happiness and many memories. We danced and snapped our fingers simultaneously to the soul tunes of the Jacksons and Stevie Wonder. We sweated together in the sweltering summer sun, trying to win the championship for our softball team. I recall the taste of pepperoni and sausage pizza as we discussed the highlights of our team's victory. Once we even became attracted to the same young man, but luckily we were able to share his friendship.

Topic sentence at the end

When specific details lead up to a generalization, putting the topic sentence at the end of the paragraph makes sense. In the following paragraph about Alice Walker's "Everyday Use," the last sentence is a general statement that sums up and accounts for the specifics that have preceded it:

> During the visit, Dee takes the pictures, every one of them, including the one of the house that she used to live in and hate. She takes the churn top and dasher, both whittled out of a tree by one of Mama's uncles. She tries to take Grandma Dee's quilts. Mama and Maggie use these inherited items every day, not only appreciating their heritage but living it too. *Dee, on the other hand, wants these items only for decorative use, thus forsaking and ignoring their real heritage.*

Topic sentence at the beginning and end

Sometimes you will want to state a topic sentence at the beginning of a paragraph and then refer to it in a slightly different form at the end. Such an echo of the topic sentence adds emphasis, pointing up the importance you attach to the idea. In the following paragraph, the writer begins with a topic sentence announcing a problem:

> *Many of the difficulties we experience in relationships are caused by the unrealistic expectations we have of each other.* Think about it. Women are expected to feel comfortable doing most of the sacrificing. They are supposed to stay fine, firm, and forever twenty-two while doing double duty, in the home and in the workplace. The burden on men is no easier. They should be tall, handsome, and able to wine and dine the women. Many women go for the glitter and then expect these men to calm down once in a relationship and become faithful, sensitive, supportive, and loving. Let's face it. Both women and men have been unrealistic. *It's time we develop a new sensitivity toward each other and ask ourselves what it is we need from each other that is realistic and fair.*

The last sentence restates the topic sentence as a proposal for solving the problem. This approach is especially appropriate, for the essay goes on to specify how the problem might be solved.

Topic sentence implied but not stated

Occasionally a topic will be so obvious that no topic sentence is necessary at all. Here is an example of such a paragraph, from an essay about working as an airport cargo handler:

> In winter the warehouse is cold and damp. There is no heat. The large steel doors that line the warehouse walls stay open most of the day. In the cold months, wind, rain, and snow blow across the floor. In the summer the warehouse becomes an oven. Dust and sand from the runways mix with the toxic fumes of fork lifts, leaving a dry, stale taste in your mouth. The high windows above the doors are covered with a thick, black dirt that kills the sun. The men work in shadows with the constant roar of jet engines blowing dangerously in their ears.
>
> – PATRICK FENTON, "Confessions of a Working Stiff"

Here the implied topic sentence might be stated as *Working conditions in the warehouse are uncomfortable, dreary, and hazardous to one's health.* But the writer does not have to state this information explicitly because we can infer it easily from the examples and specific details he provides.

Though implied topic sentences are common, especially in descriptions, in some college writing they may be viewed as weaknesses.

EXERCISE 6.1

Choose an essay you have written, and identify the topic sentence of each paragraph, noting where in the paragraph the topic sentence appears and whether any topic sentence is implied rather than stated. Experiment with one paragraph, positioning its topic sentence in at least two different places. What difference does the change make? If you have any implied topic sentences, try stating them explicitly. Does the paragraph become easier to read?

2 Relating each sentence to the main idea

Whether the main idea of a paragraph is stated in a topic sentence or is implied, each sentence in the paragraph should contribute to the main idea. Look, for example, at the following paragraph, which opens an essay about African American music:

> When I was a teenager, there were two distinct streams of popular music: one was black, and the other was white. The former could only be heard way at the end of the radio dial, while white music dominated everywhere else. This separation was a fact of life, the equivalent of blacks sitting in the back of the bus and "whites only" signs below the Mason-Dixon line. Satchmo might grin for days on "The Ed Sullivan Show" and certain historians hold forth *ad nauseam* on the black contribution to American music, but the truth was that our worlds rarely twined.
>
> – Marcia Gillespie
> "They're Playing My Music, but Burying My Dreams"

The first sentence announces the topic (there were two streams of popular music: black and white). The second sentence relates the topic to the positions of black and white music on the radio dial, and the third sentence expands on this notion of musical separation by comparing it to the separate seats for blacks on buses and their exclusion from certain public places. The last sentence rephrases the topic sentence much more pointedly: though black music was heard regularly on television and people have written extensively on the black contribution to American music, the worlds of black and white music were separate. Each sentence clearly relates to the topic, and the paragraph as a whole is unified.

EXERCISE 6.2

Choose one of the following topic sentences, and spend some time exploring the topic (see 3a). Then write a paragraph that includes the topic sentence, making sure that each of the other sentences relates to it. Assume that the paragraph will be part of a letter you are writing to an acquaintance.

1. I found out quickly that college life was not quite what I had expected.
2. Being part of the "in crowd" used to be of utmost importance to me.
3. My work experience has taught me several important lessons.
4. Until recently, I never appreciated my parents fully.
5. I expect my college education to do more than assure me of a job.

EXERCISE 6.3

Choose an essay you have written recently, and examine the second, third, and fourth paragraphs. Does each have a topic sentence or strongly imply one? Do all the other sentences in the paragraph focus on its main idea? Would you now revise any of these paragraphs — and if so, how?

6d Making paragraphs coherent: fitting details together

A paragraph has coherence if its details fit together clearly in a way that readers can easily follow. You can achieve paragraph coherence by organizing ideas, by repeating key terms or phrases, and by using parallel structures and transitional devices.

1 Organizing ideas

If you take a five- or six-sentence paragraph and rearrange the sentences in random order, you will probably *not* create a new paragraph. Why not? Though the sentences will be connected to the same topic, the lack of any organizational relationship will result in incoherence. Clear organization of ideas goes a long way toward creating coherence. The following discussion will review some common means of organizing a paragraph – spatial order, chronological order, logical order, and associational order.

Using spatial order

Paragraphs organized in **spatial order** take a "tour," beginning at one point and moving, say, from near to far, left to right, north to south. Especially useful in descriptive paragraphs, spatial order allows a writer to direct readers' attention in an orderly way to various elements of something in physical space. A topic sentence may be unnecessary in such a paragraph because the paragraph's organization will be obvious to the reader. Sometimes, however, a topic sentence at the beginning of the paragraph helps set the scene. Note the movement from ceiling to walls to floor in the following paragraph:

> The professor's voice began to fade into the background as my eyes wandered around the classroom in the old administration building. The water-stained ceiling was cracked and peeling, and the splitting wooden beams played host to a variety of lead pipes and coils. My eyes followed these pipes down the walls and around corners until eventually I saw the electric outlets. I thought it strange that they were exposed, and not built in, until I realized that there probably had been no electricity when the building was built. Below the outlets the sunshine was falling in bright rays across the hardwood floor, and I noticed how smoothly the floor was worn. Time had taken its toll on this building.

Using chronological order

Paragraphs organized in **chronological order** arrange a series of events according to time, putting earliest events first, followed in sequence by later events, one at a time. Chronological order is used frequently in **narrative** paragraphs, which tell a story. They may not require a topic sentence if the main idea is obvious in the action. The following paragraph uses careful chronology to tell a story and build suspense so that we want to know what the last event will be. The phrases expressing time help build this suspense: *all of a sudden, three months, a year later,* and so on.

> The experience of Lloyd S., an Oregon businessperson, is one of the most convincing cases for taking vitamins. For his first forty years, Lloyd was healthy and robust. He owned a thriving nursery and loved to hike, fish, and camp. All of a sudden, he started feeling fatigued. A loss of appetite and weight soon followed, and in three months he was transformed from a ruddy, muscular man into a pallid, emaciated one. Lloyd had cancer of the pancreas. After he was given a prognosis of six months to live, his family and friends were devastated, but Lloyd was a fighter. When the conventional treatments of drugs and chemotherapy did not help, he turned to a holistic approach, which emphasized a change in diet and lifestyle – and large doses of vitamins. After a series of blood tests to discover every possible nutritional deficiency, Lloyd was given concentrated vitamin and mineral supplements to ensure maximum cell efficiency and growth so that his body could attempt to heal itself. At the end of six months, Lloyd not only was alive but also showed improvement. A year later he was free of cancer and began the long battle to regain his original vitality.

General topic

Specifics

Chronological order is also commonly used in **explaining a process** – that is, in describing how something happens or how something is done: first one step, then the next, and then the next. You are already familiar with process as a means of organizing information. After all, every set of directions, every recipe, every user's manual, presents a series of steps that makes up a process to be learned or followed. Here is an example:

> Before trying to play the flute, figure out how to put it together. The flute is divided into three parts: the mouthpiece, the main body, and the end piece. First remove the main body (the longest part) from the case, and set it down with the keys facing up and the openings away from you. Now pick up the mouthpiece (the piece with one hole), and attach it to the hole at the far left end of the main body by gently twisting it from side to side, in a manner similar to jiggling a door knob. Repeat the same process in attaching the end

piece to the other end of the main body, taking care not to twist or smash the keys. The keys on the end piece should be lined up with those on the main body.

In college writing, you will probably use process paragraphs less often to tell readers how to do something than to explain how a process occurs in general – for example, how a bill becomes law or how aerosol sprays destroy the ozone layer of the atmosphere.

Using logical order

Paragraphs organized in **logical order** arrange details to reflect certain logical relationships. Explanations and examples of some of these relationships – illustration, definition, division and classification, comparison and contrast, cause and effect, problems and solutions, narration, and reiteration – are given in 6e. Two other logical patterns commonly used in paragraphs are *general to specific* and *specific to general.*

Paragraphs organized in a **general-to-specific pattern** usually open with a topic sentence presenting a general or abstract idea and are followed by a number of more specific points designed to substantiate or prove or elaborate on the generalization.

GENERAL TO SPECIFIC

Specifics

General topic

One of the most tragic manifestations of the pressure black people feel to assimilate is expressed in the internalization of racist perspectives. I was shocked and saddened when I first heard black professors at Stanford downgrade and express contempt for black students, expecting us to do poorly, refusing to establish nurturing bonds. At every university I have attended as a student or worked at as a teacher, I have heard similar attitudes expressed with little or no understanding of factors that might prevent brilliant black students from performing to their full capability. Within universities, there are few educational and social spaces where students who wish to affirm positive ties to ethnicity – to blackness, to working-class backgrounds – can receive affirmation and support. Ideologically, the message is clear – assimilation is the way to gain acceptance and approval from those in power.

– BELL HOOKS, *Talking Back*

Paragraphs can also follow a **specific-to-general organization,** first providing a series of specific examples or details and then tying them together with a general conclusion.

SPECIFIC TO GENERAL

At 8:01 A.M. on Saturday morning, the bright images hawk cereal: Fruit Loops, Frosted Flakes, Captain Crunch. At 8:11, it's toy time, as squads of delighted children demonstrate the pleasures of owning Barbie, Ken, or GI Joe. By 8:22, Coca-Cola is quenching thirsts everywhere, and at 8:31, kids declare devotion to their Nikes, ensuring that every child tuned in will want a pair. And so goes Saturday morning children's programming: one part "program" (and that exclusively cartoons) to three parts advertising. "Children's television" today is simply a euphemism for one long, hard sell, an initiation rite designed to create more and more American consumers.

Specifics

General topic

Using associational order

Paragraphs that organize information associationally do so by means of a series of associations directly related to the writer's own experiences and memories. This chain of association often relies on a central image or sensory memory – a particular aroma, for instance, or visual pattern. In the following paragraph, Victor Villanueva uses a series of memories that are linked associationally to a central image of differences among children alone:

> Walking from Bartlett to John Lee's hand laundry, alone. Maybe aged four. From Bartlett to somewhere. Near the Myrtle Avenue el. Shortest person on street corners. The only one waiting for lights to turn green. No memory of anyone asking where his Mommy is. Just last week, 1992, Flagstaff, Arizona. A little three- or four-year-old child is wandering around a supermarket. A concerned woman bends over: "Did you lose your Mommy?" The same week, the same store, a little three- or four-year-old American Indian child is wandering, bawling loudly. People stop and stare. No one asks.
>
> – VICTOR VILLANUEVA, *Bootstraps,* p. 15

Note that the writer uses a series of sentence fragments to suggest the fragmented nature of his memories and their association with more recent experiences.

2 Repeating key words and phrases

A major means of building coherence in paragraphs is through **repetition.** Weaving in repeated references to key words and phrases not only links sentences but also alerts readers to the importance of those words or phrases in the larger piece of writing. Notice in the following example how the repetition of the key words *shop* (*shopping, shoppers, shops*), *market(s)*, *bargain(ing)*, *customers, buy, price, store,* and *item* helps hold the paragraph together:

> Over the centuries, *shopping* has changed in function as well as in style. Before the Industrial Revolution, most consumer goods were sold in open-air *markets, customers* who went into an actual *shop* were expected to *buy* something, and *shoppers* were always expected to *bargain* for the best possible *price.* In the nineteenth century, however, the development of the department *store* changed the relationship between buyers and sellers. Instead of visiting several *market* stalls or small *shops, customers* could now *buy* a variety of merchandise under the same roof; instead of feeling expected to *buy,* they were welcome just to look; and instead of *bargaining* with several merchants, they paid a fixed *price* for each *item.* In addition, they could return an *item* to the *store* and exchange it for a different one or get their money back. All of these changes helped transform *shopping* from serious requirement to psychological recreation.

EXERCISE 6.4

Read the following paragraph. Then identify the places where the author uses repetition of key words and phrases, and explain how they bring coherence to the paragraph.

> This is not to say that technology was an unadulterated plus in the '90s. The Information Superhighway was pretty much of a dud. Remember that? By the mid-'90s, just about everybody was hooked up to the vast international computer network, exchanging vast quantities of information at high speeds via modems and fiber-optic cable with everybody else. The problem, of course, was that even though the information was coming a lot faster, the vast majority of it, having originated with human beings, was still wrong. Eventually people realized that the Information Superhighway was essentially CB radio, but with more typing. By late in the decade millions of Americans had abandoned their computers and turned to the immensely popular new VirtuLib 2000, a $14,000 device that enables the user to experience, with uncanny realism, the sensation of reading a book.
>
> – DAVE BARRY, "The '90s"

3 Using parallel structures

Parallel structures — structures that are grammatically similar — are another effective way to bring coherence to a paragraph. They emphasize the connection between related ideas or events in different sentences. For example:

> William Faulkner's "Barn Burning" tells the story of a young boy trapped in a no-win situation. If he betrays his father, he loses his family. If he betrays justice, he becomes a fugitive. In trying to free himself from his trap, he does both.

In this paragraph, the writer skillfully uses the parallel structure *if he does x, he does y* in order to give the effect of a no-win situation. At the end of the paragraph, we are prepared for the last sentence in the parallel sequence: *In doing x, he does y.* As readers, we feel pulled along by the force of the parallel structures.

For more on using parallel structures, see Chapter 21.

4 Using transitional devices

Transitions are words and phrases that help bring coherence to a paragraph by signaling relationships between and among sentences. In acting as signposts, transitions such as *after all, for example, indeed, so,* and *thus* help readers follow the progression of one idea to the next within a paragraph. *Finally* indicates that a last point is at hand; *likewise,* that a similar point is about to be made; and so on. To get an idea of how important transitions can be for readers, try reading the following paragraph, from which all transitional devices have been removed:

A PARAGRAPH WITH NO TRANSITIONS

> In "The Fly," Katherine Mansfield tries to show us the "real" personality of "the boss" beneath his exterior. The fly helps her to portray this real self. The boss goes through a range of emotions and feelings. He expresses these feelings to a small but determined fly, whom the reader realizes he unconsciously relates to his son. The author basically splits up the story into three parts, with the boss's emotions and actions changing quite measurably. With old Woodifield, with himself, and with the fly, we see the boss's manipulativeness. Our understanding of him as a hard and cruel man grows.

We can, if we work at it, figure out the relationship of these ideas to one another, for this paragraph is essentially unified by one major idea. But the lack of transitions results in an abrupt, choppy rhythm that lurches from one idea to the next, dragging the confused reader behind. See how much easier the passage is to read and understand with transitions added.

THE SAME PARAGRAPH, WITH TRANSITIONS

In "The Fly," Katherine Mansfield tries to show us the "real" personality of "the boss" beneath his exterior. The fly *in the story's title* helps her to portray this real self. *In the course of the story,* the boss goes through a range of emotions. *At the end,* he *finally* expresses these feelings to a small but determined fly, whom the reader realizes he unconsciously relates to his son. *To accomplish her goal,* the author basically splits up the story into three parts, with the boss's emotions and actions changing measurably *throughout. First* with old Woodifield, *then* with himself, and *last* with the fly, we see the boss's manipulativeness. *With each part,* our understanding of him as a hard and cruel man grows.

For a discussion of using transitional devices to link paragraphs, see 6h.

Most of the transitional devices here point to movement in time, helping us follow the chronology of the story being discussed: *in the course of the story; at the end; finally; throughout; first; then; last.*

It is important to note that transitions can only clarify connections between thoughts; they cannot create connections. As a writer, you must choose transitions that fit your meaning – you should not expect a transition to provide meaning.

FOR MULTILINGUAL WRITERS

DISTINGUISHING AMONG TRANSITIONS

Distinguishing among very similar transitions can be difficult for multilingual writers. The difference between *however* and *nevertheless,* for example, is a subtle one: although each introduces statements that contrast with what comes before it, *nevertheless* emphasizes the contrast whereas *however* tones it down. To help make such fine distinctions, check the usage of transitions in English dictionaries such as *The American Heritage Dictionary of the English Language* or *The Oxford Advanced Learner's Dictionary,* which provide usage notes for easily confused words.

COMMONLY USED TRANSITIONS

TO SIGNAL SEQUENCE

again, also, and, and then, besides, finally, first . . . second . . . third, furthermore, last, moreover, next, still, too

TO SIGNAL TIME

after a few days, after a while, afterward, as long as, as soon as, at last, at that time, before, earlier, immediately, in the meantime, in the past, lately, later, meanwhile, now, presently, simultaneously, since, so far, soon, then, thereafter, until, when

TO SIGNAL COMPARISON

again, also, in the same way, likewise, once more, similarly

(continued on page 115)

(continued from page 114)

TO SIGNAL CONTRAST

although, but, despite, even though, however, in contrast, in spite of, instead, nevertheless, nonetheless, on the contrary, on the one hand . . . on the other hand, regardless, still, though, yet

TO SIGNAL EXAMPLES

after all, even, for example, for instance, indeed, in fact, of course, specifically, such as, the following example, to illustrate

TO SIGNAL CAUSE AND EFFECT

accordingly, as a result, because, consequently, for this purpose, hence, so, then, therefore, thereupon, thus, to this end

TO SIGNAL PLACE

above, adjacent to, below, beyond, closer to, elsewhere, far, farther on, here, near, nearby, opposite to, there, to the left, to the right

TO SIGNAL CONCESSION

although it is true that, granted that, I admit that, it may appear that, naturally, of course

TO SIGNAL SUMMARY, REPETITION, OR CONCLUSION

as a result, as has been noted, as I have said, as we have seen, as mentioned earlier, in any event, in conclusion, in other words, in short, on the whole, therefore, to summarize

EXERCISE 6.5

Identify the devices — repetition of key words or phrases, parallel structures, transitional expressions — that make the following paragraph coherent.

I must make two honest confessions to you, my Christian and Jewish brothers. First, I must confess that over the past few years I have been gravely disappointed with the white moderate. I have almost reached the regrettable conclusion that the Negro's great stumbling block on his stride toward freedom is not the White Citizen's Counciler or the Ku Klux Klanner, but the white moderate, who is more devoted to "order" than to justice; who prefers a negative peace which is the absence of tension to a positive peace which is the presence of justice; who constantly says, "I agree with you in the goal you seek, but I cannot agree with your methods of direct action"; who paternalistically believes he can set the timetable for another man's freedom; who lives by a mythical concept of time and who constantly advises the Negro to wait for a "more convenient season." Shallow understanding from people of good will is more frustrating than absolute misunderstanding from people of ill will. Lukewarm acceptance is much more bewildering than outright rejection.

– MARTIN LUTHER KING JR., "Letter from Birmingham Jail"

6e Developing paragraphs fully: providing details

In addition to being unified and coherent, a conventional paragraph should hold readers' interest and explore its topic fully, using whatever details, evidence, and examples are necessary. Without such **development,** a paragraph may seem lifeless and abstract.

Most good academic writing does two things: it presents generalized ideas and explanations, and it backs up these generalities with specifics. This balance, the shifting between general and specific, is especially important at the paragraph level. If a paragraph contains nothing but specific details, with no explanation of how they should be viewed as a whole, readers may have trouble following the writer's meaning. If, on the other hand, a paragraph contains only abstract ideas and general statements, readers may become bored or may fail to be convinced. Consider the following poorly developed paragraph:

A POORLY DEVELOPED PARAGRAPH

No such thing as "human nature" compels people to behave, think, or react in certain ways. Rather, from the time of our infancy to our death, we are constantly being taught, by the society that surrounds us, the customs, norms, and mores of our distinct culture. Everything in culture is learned, not genetically transmitted.

This paragraph is boring. Although its main idea is clear and its sentences hold together, it fails to gain our interest, hold our attention, or convince us because it lacks any concrete illustrations. Now look at the paragraph revised to include needed specifics.

THE SAME PARAGRAPH, REVISED

Imagine a child in Ecuador dancing to salsa music at a warm family gathering, while a child in the United States is decorating a Christmas tree with bright, shiny red ornaments. Both of these children are taking part in their country's cultures. It is not by instinct that one child knows how to dance to salsa music, nor is it by instinct that the other child knows how to decorate the tree. No such thing as "human nature" compels people to behave, think, or react in certain ways. Rather, from the time of our infancy to our death, we are constantly being taught by the society that surrounds us, the customs, norms, and mores of our distinct culture. A majority of people feel that the evil in human beings is "human nature." However, the Tasaday, a "Stone Age" tribe discovered not long ago in the Philippines, do not even have equivalents in their language for the words *hatred, competition, acquisitiveness, aggression,* and *greed.* Such examples suggest that everything in culture is learned, not genetically transmitted.

Though both paragraphs argue the same point, only the second one comes to life. It does so by bringing in specific details *from* life. We want to read this paragraph, for it appeals to our senses (a child dancing; bright, shiny red ornaments) and our curiosity (who are the Tasaday?).

Almost every paragraph can be improved by making sure that its general ideas rest on enough specific detail. You can, of course, add too many details, pushing examples at the reader when no more are needed. For every writer who has to chop back jungles of detail, however, there are five whose greatest task is to irrigate deserts of generality.

EXERCISE 6.6

Rewrite the following undeveloped paragraphs by adding concrete supporting details, examples, and reasons.

1. *The introduction to an essay tentatively titled "A Week on $12.80"*

   Nothing is more frustrating to a college student than being dead broke. Not having money for enough food or for the rent, much less for entertainment, is not much fun. And of course debts for tuition and books keep piling up. No, being broke is not to be recommended.

2. *The introduction to a humorous essay contrasting cats and dogs*

   Have you threatened your cat lately? If not, why not? Why not get a *real* pet — a dog? Dogs, after all, are better pets. Cats, on the other hand, are a menace to the environment.

1 Using logical patterns of development

The patterns shown in 3d for organizing essays can also serve as a means of developing paragraphs. These **logical patterns** include illustrating, defining, dividing and classifying, comparing and contrasting, exploring causes and effects, considering problems and solutions or questions and answers, narrating, and reiterating.

Illustrating

One of the most common ways of developing a paragraph is by **illustrating a point** with concrete examples or with good reasons.

A SINGLE EXAMPLE

The Indians made names for us children in their teasing way. Because our very busy mother kept my hair cut short, like my brothers', they called me Short Furred One, pointing to their hair and making the sign for short, the right hand with fingers pressed close together, held upward, back out, at the height intended. With me this was about two feet tall, the Indians laughing gently at my abashed face. I am told that I was given a pair of small moccasins that first time, to clear up my unhappiness at being picked out from the dusk behind the fire and my two unhappy shortcomings made conspicuous.

– Mari Sandoz, "The Go-Along Ones"

SEVERAL REASONS

But I did not want to shoot the elephant. I watched him beating his bunch of grass against his knees, with the preoccupied grandmotherly air that elephants have. It seemed to me that it would be murder to shoot him. At that age I was not squeamish about killing animals, but I had never shot an elephant and never wanted to. (Somehow it always seems worse to kill a large animal.) Besides, there was the beast's owner to be considered. Alive, the elephant was worth at least a hundred pounds; dead, he would only be worth the value of his tusks, five pounds, possibly. But I had got to act quickly. I turned to some experienced-looking Burmans who had been there when we arrived, and asked them how the elephant had been behaving. They all said the same thing: he took no notice of you if you left him alone, but he might charge if you went too close to him.

– George Orwell, "Shooting an Elephant"

Defining

You will often have occasion to develop an entire paragraph by **defining** a word or concept. Some college courses, particularly ones that deal with difficult abstractions, require writing that calls for this strategy. A philosophy exam, for instance, might require you to define concepts such as *truth* or *validity*. Often, however, you will find it necessary to combine definition with other methods of development. You may need to show examples or draw comparisons or divide a term you are defining into two parts. In the following paragraph, Tom Wolfe defines *pornoviolence,* a word he has coined, by contrasting it first with "accumulated slayings and bone crushings" and then with violence seen from the point of view of "the hero":

> It is not the accumulated slayings and bone crushings that make [this TV show into] pornoviolence, however. What makes pornoviolence is that in almost every case the camera angle, therefore the viewer, is with the gun, the fist, the rock. The pornography of violence has no point of view in the old sense that novels do. You do not live the action through the hero's eyes. You live with the aggressor, whoever he may be. One moment you are the hero. The next you are the villain. No matter whose side you may be on consciously, you are in fact with the muscle, and it is you who disintegrate all comers, villains, lawmen, women, anybody. On the rare occasions in which the gun is emptied into the camera – i.e., into your face – the effect is so startling that the pornography of violence all but loses its fantasy charm. There are not nearly so many masochists as sadists among those little devils whispering into one's ears.
>
> – TOM WOLFE, "Pornoviolence"

Dividing and classifying

Dividing breaks a single item into parts. **Classifying,** which is actually a form of dividing, groups many separate items according to their similarities. You could, for instance, develop a paragraph evaluating a history course by dividing the course into several segments – textbooks, lectures, assignments – and examining each one in turn. Or you could develop a paragraph giving an overview of history courses at your college by classifying, or grouping, the courses in a number of ways – by the time periods or geographic areas covered, by the kinds of assignments demanded, by the number of students enrolled, or by some other criterion.

DIVIDING

> We all listen to music according to our separate capacities. But, for the sake of analysis, the whole listening process may become clearer if we break it up into its component parts, so to speak. In a certain sense we all listen to music on three separate planes. For lack of a better terminology, one might name these: (1) the sensuous plane, (2) the expressive plane, (3) the sheerly musical plane. The only advantage to be gained from mechanically splitting up the listening process into these hypothetical planes is the clearer view to be had of the way in which we listen.
>
> – AARON COPLAND, *What to Listen for in Music*

CLASSIFYING

Two types of people are seduced by fad diets. Those who have always been overweight turn to them out of despair; they have tried everything, and yet nothing seems to work. The second group to succumb appear perfectly healthy but are baited by slogans such as "look good, feel good." These slogans prompt self-questioning and insecurity – do I really look good and feel good? – and as a direct result, many healthy people fall prey to fad diets. With both types of people, however, the problems surrounding such diets are numerous and dangerous. In fact, these diets provide neither intelligent nor effective answers to weight control.

Comparing and contrasting

You can develop some paragraphs easily and effectively by comparing and contrasting various aspects of the topic or by comparing and contrasting the topic with something else. **Comparing** things highlights their similarities; **contrasting** points to their differences. Whether used alone or together, comparing and contrasting both act to focus the topic at hand more clearly – we can better understand an unknown by comparing it to something we know well.

You can structure comparison-contrast paragraphs in two basic ways. One way is to present all the information about one item and then all the information about the other item (the **block method**). The other possibility is to switch back and forth between the two items, focusing on particular characteristics of each in turn (**alternating method**).

BLOCK METHOD

You could tell the veterans from the rookies by the way they were dressed. The knowledgeable ones had their heads covered by kerchiefs, so that if they were hired, tobacco dust wouldn't get in their hair; they had on clean dresses that by now were faded and shapeless, so that if they were hired they wouldn't get tobacco dust and grime on their best clothes. Those who were trying for the first time had their hair freshly done and wore attractive dresses; they wanted to make a good impression. But the dresses couldn't be seen at the distance that many were standing from the employment office, and they were crumpled in the crush. – MARY MEBANE, "Summer Job"

ALTERNATING METHOD

Malcolm X emphasized the use of violence in his movement and employed the biblical principle of "an eye for an eye and a tooth for a tooth."

King, on the other hand, felt that blacks should use nonviolent civil disobedience and employed the theme "turning the other cheek," which Malcolm X rejected as "beggarly" and "feeble." The philosophy of Malcolm X was one of revenge, and often it broke the unity of black Americans. More radical blacks supported him, while more conservative ones supported King. King thought that blacks should transcend their humanity. In contrast, Malcolm X thought they should embrace it and reserve their love for one another, regarding whites as "devils" and the "enemy." King's politics were those of a rainbow, but Malcolm X's rainbow was insistently one color – black. The distance between Martin Luther King Jr.'s thinking and Malcolm X's was the distance between growing up in the seminary and growing up on the streets, between the American dream and the American reality.

EXERCISE 6.7

Outline the preceding paragraph on Martin Luther King Jr. and Malcolm X, noting its alternating pattern. Then rewrite the paragraph using block organization: the first part of the paragraph devoted to King, the second to Malcolm X. Finally, write a brief paragraph analyzing the two paragraphs, explaining which seems more coherent and easier to follow and why.

Exploring causes and effects

Certain topics will require you to consider the process of **cause and effect,** and you can often develop paragraphs by detailing the causes of something or the effects that something brings about. A question on geology, for instance, may lead you to write a paragraph describing the major causes of soil erosion in the Midwest – or the effects of such erosion. The following paragraph discusses the effects of television on the American family:

> Television's contribution to family life has been an equivocal one. For while it has, indeed, kept the members of the family from dispersing, it has not served to bring them *together.* By its domination of the time families spend together, it destroys the special quality that distinguishes one family from another, a quality that depends to a great extent on what a family *does,* what special rituals, games, recurrent jokes, familiar songs, and shared activities it accumulates.
>
> – Marie Winn, *The Plug-in Drug: Television, Children, and the Family*

Considering problems and solutions or questions and answers

Paragraphs developed in the **problem-solution pattern** open with a statement of a problem, usually the topic sentence, and then offer a solution in the sentences that follow, as in this paragraph about an organization for women who travel around the United States in recreational vehicles, or RVs.

> RVing Women's rapid growth created a dilemma for its founding mothers. They could either quit traveling and rent an office, or get a bigger RV. So they traded in the Class C for a 34-foot fifth wheel (a trailer that is hitched to the bed of a pickup truck). Now, Lovern and Zoe have an office equipped with two computers, two printers, and a copy machine in their rig, where they handle the mail and newsletter comfortably. They also publish a directory and maintain a Phonelink service so members can find each other on the road, organize caravans, and plan excursions and outings. In addition, with help from members, they have organized eight gatherings around the country, with 16 more planned for the rest of 1992. It's beginning to look as if Zoe and Lovern's new pastime is turning into their second careers.
>
> – Marilyn Murphy, "Roam, Sweet Home"

Similar to the problem-solution pattern is the **question-and-answer pattern** of development, which does just what its name suggests: the first sentence poses a question, and the rest of the paragraph provides the answer. Beginning with a question provides a means of getting – and focusing – readers' attention.

Narrating

Narrating allows writers to provide personal or historical accounts in order to develop ideas. Narrative paragraphs are often arranged chronologically, sometimes with such variations on chronological order as flashbacks and flash-forwards. They sometimes include dialogue and may lead to a **climax,** which provides the point of the story being told. Here is one student's narrative paragraph that tells a personal story in order to support a point about the dangers of racing bicycles with flimsy alloy frames. This paragraph builds to a climax, saving the most extreme point (*He couldn't even walk*) for last. It also uses **description,** adding specific, concrete details to help the reader "see" the story: *catapulted onto Vermont pavement at fifty miles per hour,* for instance, or *My Italian racing bike was pretzeled.*

> People who have been exposed to the risk of dangerously designed bicycle frames have paid too high a price. I saw this danger myself in the 1984 Putney Race. A Stowe-Shimano graphite frame failed, and the rider was catapulted onto Vermont pavement at fifty miles per hour. The pack of riders behind him was so dense that most other racers crashed into a tangled, sliding heap. The aftermath: four hospitalizations. I got off with some stitches, a bad road rash, and severely pulled tendons. My Italian racing bike was pretzeled, and my racing was over for that summer. Others were not so lucky. An Olympic hopeful, Brian Stone of the Northstar team, woke up in a hospital bed to find that his cycling was over – and not just for that summer. His kneecap had been surgically removed. He couldn't even walk.

One form of narration **embeds a narrative,** often in the middle of a paragraph, to elaborate on a point or relate a personal experience that supports the point. In the following example, the writer embeds a narrative to explain how he got the idea for the essay:

> For the term essay in Ethnic Art, we were free to write on any relevant subject. Openness, however, can bring its own headaches. With so much to choose from, a guy can feel overwhelmed. Or so I thought – until I suddenly said, "Braids and dreads: that's it!" These are the words that popped into my head as I was driving to school recently, just when I was worrying about a subject for my art paper. I was inspired, I suppose, by friends, people around me, and perhaps the rap group Kriss Kross – all people who wear braided hair. My first thought was to write only about braids, but then I thought about people who wear their hair in a particular style of braids known as dreadlocks, like Bob Marley. As my brain kept churning, I asked myself, "What are the differences between the two hairstyles? What do these styles mean? Why are they 'in' right now?" In short, I was on my way to an exploration of what I claim is one form of ethnic art.

Reiterating

Reiterating, often used in oral as well as written discourse, is an organizational pattern you may recognize from political discourse or some styles of preaching. In this pattern, the writer states the main point of a paragraph and then reiterates it in a number of different ways, hammering home the point and often building in intensity as well. This strategy found particular power in a number of works by Martin Luther King Jr. In the following example, King reiterates the topic of the paragraph (we are on the move) five different ways, repeating the idea like a drumbeat throughout the paragraph, building to the climactic move *to the land of freedom:*

> We are on the move now. The burning of our churches will not deter us. We are on the move now. The bombing of our homes will not dissuade us. We are on the move now. The beating and killing of our clergymen and young people will not divert us. We are on the move now. The arrest and release of known murderers will not discourage us. We are on the move now. Like an idea whose time has come, not even the marching of mighty armies can halt us. We are moving to the land of freedom.
>
> – MARTIN LUTHER KING JR., "Our God Is Marching On"

Combining patterns

Most paragraphs combine methods of development. In the following paragraph, the writer divides a general topic (the accounting systems used by American companies) into two subtopics (the system used to summarize a company's overall financial state and the one used to measure internal transactions) and then develops the second subtopic through illustration (the assessment of costs for a delivery truck shared by two departments) and cause and effect (the system produces some disadvantages):

> Most American companies have basically two accounting systems. One system summarizes the overall financial state to inform stockholders, bankers, and other outsiders. That system is not of interest here. The other system, called the managerial or cost accounting system, exists for an entirely different reason. It measures in detail all of the particulars of transactions between departments, divisions, and key individuals in the organization, for the purpose of untangling the interdependencies between people. When, for example, two departments share one truck for deliveries, the cost accounting system charges each department for part of the cost of maintaining the truck and driver, so that at the end of the year, the performance of each department can be individually assessed, and the better department's manager can receive a larger raise. Of course, all of this information processing costs money, and furthermore may lead to arguments between the departments over whether the costs charged to each are fair.
>
> – WILLIAM OUCHI, "Japanese and American Workers: Two Casts of Mind"

EXERCISE 6.8

Choose two of the following topics or two others that interest you, and brainstorm or freewrite about each one for ten minutes (see 3a1 and 3a2). Then use the information you have produced to determine what method(s) of development would be most appropriate for each topic.

1. the pleasure a hobby has given you
2. Tupac Shakur's image and Will Smith's image
3. an average Saturday morning
4. why Monopoly is an appropriate metaphor for U.S. society
5. the best course you've ever taken

EXERCISE 6.9

Refer to the argument you drafted for Exercise 5.13, and study the ways you developed each paragraph. For one of the paragraphs, write a brief evaluation of its development. How would you expand or otherwise improve the development?

2 Determining paragraph length

Though writers must keep their readers' expectations in mind, paragraph length must be determined primarily by content and purpose. Paragraphs should develop an idea, create any desired effects (such as suspense or humor), and advance the piece of writing. Fulfilling these aims will sometimes call for short paragraphs, sometimes for long ones. For example, in an argumentative essay, you may put all your lines of argument or all your evidence into one long paragraph to create the impression of a solid, overwhelmingly convincing thesis. In a narrative about an exciting event, on the other hand, you may use a series of short paragraphs to create suspense, to keep the reader rushing to each new paragraph to find out what happened next.

Remember that a new paragraph often signals a pause in thought. Just as timing can make a crucial difference in telling a joke, so the pause signaled by a paragraph can lead readers to anticipate what is to follow or give them a moment to digest mentally the material presented in the previous paragraph.

Reasons to start a new paragraph

- to turn to a new idea
- to emphasize something (such as a point or an example)
- to change speakers (in dialogue)
- to lead readers to pause
- to break up lengthy text (often to take up a subtopic)
- to start the conclusion

EXERCISE 6.10

Examine the paragraph breaks in something you have written recently. Explain briefly in writing why you decided on each of the breaks. Would you change any of them now? If so, how and why?

6f Composing special-purpose paragraphs

Paragraphs serving specialized functions include opening paragraphs, concluding paragraphs, transitional paragraphs, and dialogue paragraphs.

1 Opening paragraphs

Even a good piece of writing may remain unread if it has a weak opening paragraph. In addition to announcing your topic (usually in a thesis statement), therefore, an introductory paragraph must engage readers' interest and focus their attention on what is to follow. At their best, introductory paragraphs serve as hors d'oeuvres, whetting the appetite for the following courses, or as the title sequences in a film, carefully setting the scene. Writers often leave the final drafting of the introduction until last because the focus of the piece may change during the process of writing.

One common kind of opening paragraph follows a general-to-specific pattern, ending with the thesis. In such an introduction, the writer opens with a general statement and then gets more and more specific, concluding with the most specific sentence in the paragraph – the thesis. The following paragraph illustrates such an opening:

> The United States has seen many changes in its economy during the last hundred years. Among these changes is the organization of workers. Unions were formed in the late nineteenth and early twentieth centuries to battle against long workdays and bad working conditions. It was not uncommon then for a worker to be required to work twelve or more hours a day, six days a week, in hazardous and often deadly conditions. The workers organized against their employers and won their battles. Today it is very uncommon to find such oppressive conditions in the workplace. Why, then, do unions still exist? When we examine many of the labor battles of recent years, we find that unions exist mostly as bargaining units through which workers can gain higher wages – at any cost.

General statement

Move to specificity

Thesis

In this paragraph, the opening sentence introduces a general subject, changes in the U.S. economy; subsequent sentences focus more specifically on unionization; and the last sentence presents the thesis, which the rest of the essay will develop. Other ways of opening an essay include quotations, anecdotes, questions, and opinions.

Opening with a quotation

There is a bumper sticker that reads, "Too bad ignorance isn't painful." I like that. But ignorance is. We just seldom attribute the pain to it or even recognize it when we see it. Take the postcard on my corkboard. It shows a young man in a very hip jacket smoking a cigarette. In the background is a high school with the American flag waving. The caption says, "Too cool for school. Yet too stupid for the real world." Out of the mouth of the young man is a bubble enclosing the words "Maybe I'll start a band." There could be a postcard showing a jock in a uniform saying, "I don't need school. I'm going to the NFL or NBA." Or one showing a young man or woman studying and a group of young people saying, "So you want to be white." Or something equally demeaning. We need to quit it. – NIKKI GIOVANNI, "Racism 101"

Opening with an anecdote

I first met Angela Carter at a dinner in honor of the Chilean writer José Donoso at the home of Liz Calder, who then published all of us. My first novel was soon to be published; it was the time of Angela's darkest novel, "The Passion of New Eve." And I was a great fan. Mr. Donoso arrived looking like a Hispanic Buffalo Bill, complete with silver goatee, fringed jacket and cowboy boots, and proceeded, as I saw it, to patronize Angela terribly. His apparent ignorance of her work provoked me into a long expostulation in which I informed him that the woman he was talking to was the most brilliant writer in England. Angela liked that. By the end of the evening, we liked each other, too. That was almost 18 years ago. She was the first great writer I ever met, and she was one of the best, most loyal, most truth-telling, most inspiring friends anyone could ever have. I cannot bear it that she is dead.

– SALMAN RUSHDIE, "Angela Carter"

Opening with a question

Why are Americans terrified of using nuclear power as a source of energy? People are misinformed, or not informed at all, about its benefits and safety. If Americans would take the time to learn about what nuclear power offers, their apprehension and fear might be transformed into hope.

Opening with a strong opinion

> Men need a men's movement about as much as women need chest hair. A brotherhood organized to counter feminists could be timely because – let's be honest – women are no more naturally inclined to equality and fairness than men are. They want power and dominion just as much as any group looking out for its own interests. Organizing to protect the welfare of males might make sense. Unfortunately, the current men's movement does not.
>
> – JOHN RUSZKIEWICZ, *The Presence of Others*

2 Concluding paragraphs

A good conclusion wraps up a piece of writing in a meaningful and memorable way. If a strong opening paragraph whets the appetite of readers or arouses their curiosity, a strong concluding paragraph satisfies them, allowing them to feel that their expectations have been met. A strong conclusion reminds readers of the thesis of the essay and leaves them feeling that they know a good deal more than they did when they began. The concluding paragraph provides the last opportunity for you to impress your message on your readers' minds and create desired effects. As such, it is well worth your time and effort.

One of the most common strategies for concluding uses the specific-to-general pattern, often beginning with a restatement of the thesis (but not a word-for-word repetition of it) and moving to several more general statements. The following paragraph moves in such a way, opening with a final point of contrast, specifying it in several sentences, and then ending with a much more general statement:

> Lastly, and perhaps greatest of all, there was the ability, at the end, to turn quickly from war to peace once the fighting was over. Out of the way these two men behaved at Appomattox came the possibility of a peace of reconciliation. It was a possibility not wholly realized, in the years to come, but which did, in the end, help the two sections to become one nation again . . . after a war whose bitterness might have seemed to make such a reunion wholly impossible. No part of either man's life became him more than the part he played in this brief meeting in the McLean house at Appomattox. Their behavior there put all succeeding generations of Americans in their debt. Two great Americans, Grant and Lee – very different, yet under everything very much alike. Their encounter at Appomattox was one of the great moments of American history.
>
> – BRUCE CATTON, "Grant and Lee: A Study in Contrasts"

Other effective strategies for concluding include questions, quotations, vivid images, calls for action, and warnings.

Concluding with a question

All so-called "permanent" antifreeze is basically the same. It is made from a liquid known as ethylene glycol, which has two amazing properties: It has a lower freezing point than water, and a higher boiling point than water. It does not break down (lose its properties), nor will it boil away. And every permanent antifreeze starts with it as a base. Also, just about every antifreeze has now got antileak ingredients, as well as antirust and anticorrosion ingredients. Now, let's suppose that, in formulating the product, one of the companies comes up with a solution that is pink in color, as opposed to all the others, which are blue. Presto – an exclusivity claim. "Nothing else looks like it, nothing else performs like it." Or how about, "Look at ours, and look at anyone else's. You can see the difference our exclusive formula makes." Granted, I'm exaggerating. But did I prove a point?

– PAUL STEVENS, "Weasel Words: God's Little Helpers"

Concluding with a quotation

Despite the celebrity that accrued to her and the air of awesomeness with which she was surrounded in her later years, Miss Keller retained an unaffected personality, certain that her optimistic attitude toward life was justified. "I believe that all through these dark and silent years God has been using my life for a purpose I do not know," she said. "But one day I shall understand and then I will be satisfied."

– ALDEN WHITMAN, "Helen Keller: June 27, 1880 – June 1, 1968"

Concluding with a vivid image

It is, in any case, finally you that I end up having to trust not to laugh, not to snicker. Even as you regard me in these lines, I try to imagine your face as you read. You who read "Aria," especially those of you with your theme-divining yellow felt pen poised in your hand, you for whom this essay is yet another "assignment," please do not forget that it is my life I am handing you in these pages – memories that are as personal for me as family photographs in an old cigar box.

– RICHARD RODRIGUEZ, from a postscript to "Aria"

Concluding with a call for action

It is now almost 40 years since the invention of nuclear weapons. We have not yet experienced a global thermonuclear war – although on more than one occasion we have come tremulously close. I do not think our luck can hold forever. Men and machines are fallible, as recent events remind us. Fools and madmen do exist, and sometimes rise to power. Concentrating always on the near future, we have ignored the long-term consequences of our actions. We have placed our civilization and our species in jeopardy.

Fortunately, it is not yet too late. We can safeguard the planetary civilization and the human family if we so choose. There is no more important or more urgent issue. – CARL SAGAN, "The Nuclear Winter"

Concluding with a warning

Because propaganda is so effective, it is important to track it down and understand how it is used. We may eventually agree with what the propagandist says because all propaganda isn't necessarily bad; some advertising, for instance, urges us not to drive drunk, to have regular dental checkups, to contribute to the United Way. Even so, we must be aware that propaganda is being used. Otherwise, we will have consented to handing over our independence, our decision-making ability, and our brains.

– ANN MCCLINTOCK, "Propaganda Techniques in Today's Advertising"

3 Transitional paragraphs

On some occasions, you may need to call your readers' attention very powerfully to a major transition between ideas. To do so, consider using an entire short paragraph to signal that transition, as in the following example from an essay on television addiction. The opening paragraphs of the essay characterize addiction in general, concluding with the paragraph about its destructive elements. The one-sentence paragraph that follows arrests our attention, announcing that these general characteristics will now be related to television viewing.

Finally a serious addiction is distinguished from a harmless pursuit of pleasure by its distinctly destructive elements. A heroin addict, for instance, leads a damaged life: his increasing need for heroin in increasing doses prevents him from working, from maintaining relationships, from developing in human ways. Similarly an alcoholic's life is narrowed and dehumanized by his dependence on alcohol.

Let us consider television viewing in the light of the conditions that define serious addictions.

– MARIE WINN, *The Plug-in Drug: Television, Children, and the Family*

4 Paragraphs to signal dialogue

Paragraphs of dialogue can add life to almost any sort of writing. The traditional way to set up dialogue in written form is simple: start a new paragraph each time the speaker changes, no matter how short each bit of conversation is. Here is an example:

> Whenever I brought a book to the job, I wrapped it in newspaper – a habit that was to persist for years in other cities and under other circumstances. But some of the white men pried into my packages when I was absent and they questioned me.
>
> "Boy, what are you reading those books for?"
>
> "Oh, I don't know, sir."
>
> "That's deep stuff you're reading, boy."
>
> "I'm just killing time, sir."
>
> "You'll addle your brains if you don't watch out."
>
> – Richard Wright, *Black Boy*

6g Composing paragraphs online

Email, listserv and newsgroup postings, hypertext – all have created particular demands for writers trying to create effective paragraphs. Both the limitations of electronic communication (such as lack of indentation in some email software) and the dizzying possibilities (such as ways to arrange hypertext) call for special creativity in writing paragraphs.

Paragraphing in messages and postings

Even without indentations, you can create paragraphs in online writing by skipping lines every time you shift topics or introduce a new idea. As with any text, remember that long, dense paragraphs – especially in the small fonts characteristic of email – make for hard reading. Here is an example of a student message that uses paragraphing to separate topics:

```
To:  lunsford.2@osu.edu
From:  Shannan Palma <palma.7@osu.edu>
Subject:  heroes essay
```

```
Dear Professor Lunsford,

I've been working on my essay about heroes and film this
past week and I've found a few new sources on the WWW
that sound interesting.  I've printed out hard copies
and will show them to you at our next meeting.

In the meanwhile, I've rewritten my conclusion (again)
and would appreciate it if you could read the new
version and let me know what you think.

Thanks,
Shannan
```

Because online readers expect to be able to understand messages quickly, you may also want to make a point of stating the main idea of a paragraph right at the beginning. Consider, also, whether some information would be faster and easier to read in list rather than paragraph form. But keep your purpose and audience in mind: if you have a reason for leading up to the main idea gradually, or if a list seems too informal for your intended reader, those considerations should determine your choices.

Paragraphing for Web pages and hypertext essays

www

http://info.med.yale.edu/caim/manual/pages/page_design.html

Advice on Web page design from the Yale C/AIM Web Style Guide, *one of the most comprehensive guides on Web design.*

Whereas email offers very limited options for highlighting texts, on the Web there are no holds barred: color, boldfacing, fonts of all kinds, and even pictures and sound are available to writers. In designing effective paragraphs for the Web, then, you will need to think very carefully about your purpose(s) for the page and the readers you expect to visit it.

As with any graphic design, you should design your Web paragraphs to guide the reader's eye easily around the page. For a home or introductory page, this principle may mean that you will use very few (perhaps no) paragraphs, opting for a strong title and an arresting image, followed by a simple list of links – perhaps with its own set of icons – that readers can click on to visit further pages. In these later pages, you are more likely to use traditional paragraphs, set up as blocks of text (per-

For an example of paragraphing on a Web page, see pp. 677–678.

haps in columns or other kinds of configurations on the page, such as surrounding three sides of an illustration). Remember that readers will be working with one screen at a time and that your paragraphs should be designed to break up long blocks of text and to ease readability.

6h Linking paragraphs

The same methods that you use to link sentences and create coherent paragraphs can be used to link paragraphs themselves so that a whole piece of writing flows smoothly and coherently. Some reference to the previous paragraph, either explicitly stated or merely implied, should occur in each paragraph after the introduction. As in linking sentences, you can create this reference by repeating or paraphrasing key words and terms and by using parallel structures and transitional expressions.

Repeating key words

In fact, human offspring remain *dependent on their parents* longer than the young of any other species.

Children are *dependent on their parents* or other adults not only for their physical survival but also for their initiation into the uniquely human knowledge that is collectively called culture. . . .

Using parallel structure

Kennedy made an effort to assure non-Catholics that he would respect the separation of church and state, and most of them did not seem to hold his religion against him in deciding how to vote. Since his election, *the church to which a candidate belongs* has become less important in presidential politics.

The region from which a candidate comes remains an important factor. . . .

Using transitional expressions

While the Indian, in the character of Tonto, was more positively portrayed in *The Lone Ranger,* such a portrayal was more the exception than the norm.

Moreover, despite this brief glimpse of an Indian as an ever loyal sidekick, Tonto was never accorded the same stature as the man with the white horse and silver bullets. . . .

EXERCISE 6.11

Look at the essay you drafted for Exercise 3.7 or the argument you drafted for Exercise 5.13, and identify the ways your paragraphs are linked together. Identify each use of repetition, parallel structures, and transitional expressions, and then evaluate how effectively you have joined the paragraphs.

THINKING CRITICALLY ABOUT PARAGRAPHS

Reading with an Eye for Paragraphs

Read something by a writer you admire. Find one or two paragraphs that impress you in some way, and analyze them, using the guidelines at the beginning of this chapter. Try to decide what makes them effective paragraphs.

Thinking about Your Own Use of Paragraphs

Examine two or three paragraphs you have written, using the guidelines at the beginning of this chapter, to evaluate the unity, coherence, and development of each one. Identify the topic of each paragraph, the topic sentence (if one is explicitly stated), any methods of development, and any means used to create coherence. Decide whether or not each paragraph successfully guides your readers, and explain your reasons. Then choose one paragraph, and revise it.

PART 2

SENTENCES: MAKING GRAMMATICAL CHOICES

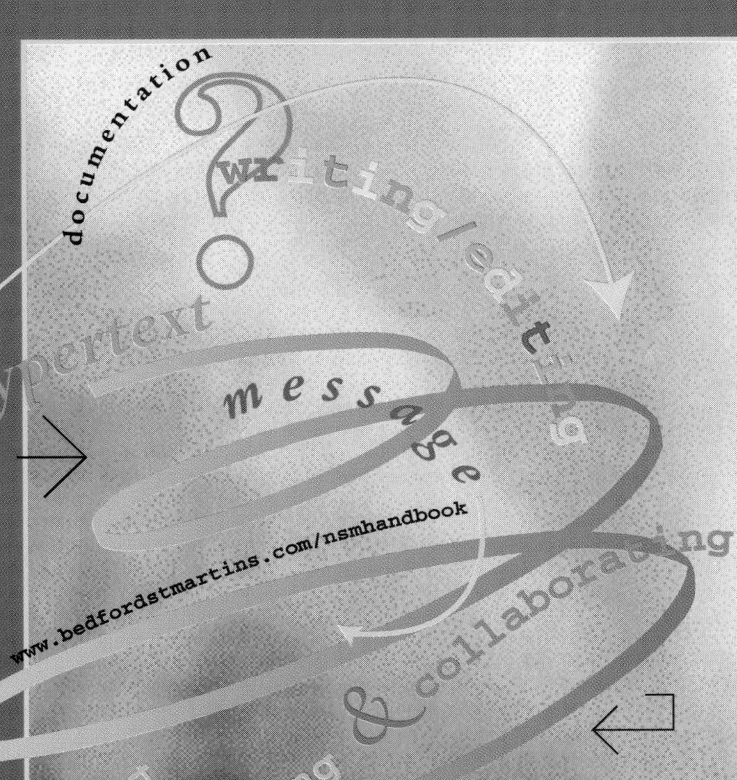

FAQ: Grammar Online

How do you deal with acronyms such as HTML or MOO that need to be made into verbs?

The digital revolution has spawned many acronyms that are used routinely by online writers. To make them into verb forms, just follow the grammar of English verbs, with a few variations.

- To make an acronym into a past-tense verb, add an apostrophe + *d:* FTP'd, HTML'd.
- To make an acronym into a present participle, just add *ing:* FTPing, CCing.
- To make an acronym into a past participle, add an apostrophe + *d:* CC'd, ID'd.

When you use acronyms in your online writing, keep your readers in mind: if they may not understand what an acronym stands for, or if you don't know them well enough to judge, it is better to write the term out.

What do the various parts of URLs mean? Is there an underlying "grammar" that helps you read them?

For many writers, Uniform Resource Locators (URLs) offer increasingly necessary ways to access information. Just as word order is important to the grammar of English sentences, so too is the order of the parts of a URL. You can read a URL for its meaning just as you can read a sentence, so knowing the "grammar" of URLs can help you use this locator, especially if you are trying to identify an error or typo in an address. The example below labels the parts of a URL: PROTOCOL, DOMAIN NAME, DIRECTORY PATH, and FILE NAME.

PROTOCOL — DOMAIN NAME — DIRECTORY PATH

http://www.bedfordstmartins.com/nsmhandbook/websites.html

FILE NAME

Of particular importance is the final designation of the domain name. In the United States, the following designations appear (note, however, that domain names differ in other countries):

com=commercial site

edu=education site

org=nonprofit organization site

gov=governmental site

The domain name may also identify a country of origin:

ca=Canada ar=Argentina ch=Switzerland

Most important of all, remember that a URL must be typed *exactly* as it appears, without any extra spaces, or you will not be able to access the site.

http://www.english.upenn.edu/~jlynch/Grammar/

Grammar and Style Notes *provides explanations of conventions of grammar, style, punctuation, and usage, broken into a file for each letter of the alphabet (click on "a" for information on adjectives and adverbs, for example).*

Constructing Grammatical Sentences

7

The fifteenth-century Holy Roman emperor Sigismund once answered a question about his Latin grammar by saying, "I am the Roman emperor and am above grammar." In one sense, all native speakers of a language are, like Sigismund, "above" grammar. All speakers, that is, learn the grammar of their language naturally as they learn to speak.

Then why bother to study it? In the first place, though all speakers know the basic grammatical "rules," these rules can generate a very broad range of sentences, some more artful and effective than others. Understanding grammatical structures can help you not simply write but write skillfully and successfully. In addition, because language is so closely related to thought, studying our language patterns, our grammar, can give us insight into our own ways of thinking. ■

7a Understanding the basic grammar of sentences

A **sentence** is a grammatically complete group of words that expresses a thought. To be grammatically complete, a group of words must contain two major structural components – a subject and a predicate. The **subject** identifies what the sentence is about, and the **predicate** says or asks something about the subject or tells the subject to do something.

SUBJECT	PREDICATE
I	have a dream.
We	shall overcome.
California	is a state of mind.
Puff, the magic dragon,	lived by the sea.

Some sentences contain only a one-word predicate with an implied, or "understood," subject (for example, *Stop!*). Most sentences, however, contain additional words that expand the basic subject and predicate. In the preceding example, for instance, the subject might have been simply *Puff;* the words *the magic dragon* say more about the subject. Similarly, the predicate of that sentence could grammatically be *lived;* the words *by the sea* expand the predicate by telling us where Puff lived.

A good way to examine your own sentences is by studying two or three examples of your own writing and classifying each sentence – grammatically, as simple, compound, complex, or compound-complex (7d1); functionally, as declarative, interrogative, imperative, or exclamatory (7d2); and (where applicable) rhetorically, as cumulative or periodic (22c3). Perhaps keep a tally of how many of each type of sentence you write, and then look for patterns.

1. Are your sentences varied, or do you rely heavily on one or two sentence patterns?
2. If you write mainly simple sentences, see if combining some to make compound or complex sentences makes your writing flow more smoothly.
3. If you have many compound sentences, see if revising some as complex sentences makes your writing easier to read.
4. If your sentences are all declarative, see if there is one you would like to emphasize, and try rephrasing it as a question or exclamation.
5. If you find several short sentences in a row, try combining them into one cumulative sentence.

EXERCISE 7.1

The following sentences are taken from "A Hanging," an essay by George Orwell. Identify the subject and predicate in each sentence, underlining the subject once and the predicate twice. Example:

One prisoner had been brought out of his cell.

1. We set out for the gallows.
2. He was an army doctor, with a gray toothbrush moustache and a gruff voice.
3. The rest of us, magistrates and the like, followed behind.
4. The dog answered the sound with a whine.
5. The hangman, a gray-haired convict in the white uniform of the prison, was waiting beside his machine.

7b Recognizing the parts of speech

If the basic sentence parts are subjects and predicates, the central elements of subjects and predicates are nouns and verbs. For example:

SUBJECT (NOUN) — PREDICATE (VERB)
A solitary figure waited on the platform.

Nouns and verbs are two of the eight **parts of speech,** one set of grammatical categories into which words may be classified. The other six parts of speech are pronouns, adjectives, adverbs, prepositions, conjunctions, and interjections. Many English words can function as more than one part of speech. Take the word *book,* for instance: when you *book a plane flight,* it is a verb; when you *take a good book to the beach,* it is a noun; and when you *have book knowledge,* it is an adjective.

The system of categorizing words by part of speech comes to English from Latin, but it is not as precise for English as it is for Latin. Even so, the parts of speech remain an important part of our grammatical vocabulary, and all dictionaries use them to label their entries. In this chapter, we will see how the various parts of speech are used in sentences.

1 Recognizing verbs

The word *verb* comes from the Latin *verbum,* which simply means "word." As their derivation suggests, **verbs** are among the most important words, for they move the meaning of sentences along by showing action (*glance, jump*), occurrence (*become, happen*), or a state of being (*be, live*). Verbs change form to show *time, person, number, voice,* and *mood.*

TIME	we *work,* we *worked*
PERSON	I *work,* she *works*
NUMBER	one person *works,* two people *work*
VOICE	she *asks,* she is *asked*
MOOD	we *see,* if we *saw*

Auxiliary verbs (also called **helping verbs**) combine with other verbs (often called **main verbs**) to create *verb phrases.* Auxiliaries include the forms of *be, do,* and *have,* which are also used as main verbs, and the words *can, could, may, might, must, shall, should, will,* and *would.*

See Chapter 9 for a complete discussion of verbs; for more on how verbs change form to show person and number, see 10a.

You *must get* some sleep tonight!

I *could have danced* all night.

She *would prefer* to take Italian rather than Spanish.

EXERCISE 7.2

Underline each verb or verb phrase in the following sentences. Example:

Terence should sing well in Sunday's performance.

1. My future does look bright.
2. The faucet had been leaking all day.
3. Within the next few weeks, we will receive the test results.
4. One person can collect sap, a second might run the evaporator, and a third should finish the syrup.
5. A job at an animal hospital would be great.

FOR MULTILINGUAL WRITERS

COUNT AND NONCOUNT NOUNS

Is the hill covered with grass or grasses? See 53a for a discussion of count and noncount nouns.

2 Recognizing nouns

The word *noun* comes from the Latin *nomen,* which means "name." That is what **nouns** do: they name things. Nouns can name persons (*aviator, child*), places (*lake, library*), things (*truck, suitcase*), or concepts (*happiness, balance*). **Proper nouns** name specific persons, places, things, or concepts: *Bill, Iowa, Supreme Court, Buddhism.* Proper nouns are capitalized. **Collective nouns** name groups: *team, flock, jury.*

For more on proper nouns, see 36b; for more on collective nouns, see 10d and 11b.

Most nouns can be changed from **singular** (one) to **plural** (more than one) by adding *-s* or *-es: horse, horses; kiss, kisses.* Some nouns, however, have irregular plural forms: *woman, women; alumnus, alumni; mouse, mice; deer, deer.* **Noncount nouns** cannot be made plural because they name something that cannot easily be counted: *dust, peace, prosperity.*

For more on plural forms, see 24e.

Nouns can also take a possessive form to show ownership. A writer usually forms the possessive by adding an apostrophe plus *-s* to a singular noun or just an apostrophe to a plural noun: *the horse's owner, the boys' department.*

For more on possessives, see 33a.

Nouns are often preceded by the **articles** *a, an,* or *the: a rocket, the launch.* Articles are also known as **noun markers** or **determiners.**

For a complete discussion of articles and determiners, see 53c and 53d.

EXERCISE 7.3

Identify the nouns, including possessive forms, and the articles in each of the following sentences. Underline the nouns once and the articles twice. Example:

The Puritans' hopes were dashed when Charles II regained his father's throne.

1. Nightlife begins in Georgetown even before the sun goes down.
2. Although plagiarism is dishonest and illegal, it does occur.
3. Thanksgiving is a grim season for turkeys.
4. Henderson's story is a tale of theft and violation.
5. In the front row sat two people, a man with slightly graying hair and a young woman in jeans.

3 Recognizing pronouns

Pronouns function as nouns in sentences and often take the place of specific nouns, serving as short forms so that we do not have to repeat a noun that has already been mentioned. A specific noun that a pronoun replaces or refers to is called the **antecedent** of the pronoun. In the following example, the antecedent of *she* is *Caitlin:*

For a complete discussion of pronouns and antecedents, see Chapters 11 and 13.

Caitlin refused the invitation even though *she* wanted to go.

Pronouns fall into several categories: personal, reflexive, intensive, indefinite, demonstrative, interrogative, relative, and reciprocal. **Personal pronouns** refer to specific persons or things. Each can take several different forms (for example, *I, me, my, mine*) depending on how it functions in a sentence.

For a discussion of the forms of personal pronouns, see Chapter 8.

I, you, he, she, it, we, they

After the scouts made camp, *they* ran along the beach.

Reflexive pronouns refer to the subject of the sentence or clause in which they appear. They end in *-self* or *-selves.*

myself, yourself, himself, herself, itself, oneself, ourselves, yourselves, themselves

The seals sunned *themselves* on the warm rocks.

Intensive pronouns have the same form as reflexive pronouns. They are used to emphasize their antecedents.

He decided to paint the apartment *himself.*

Indefinite pronouns do not refer to specific nouns, although they may refer to identifiable persons or things. They express the idea of a quantity (*all, some, any, none*) or an unspecified person or thing (*somebody, anything*). Indefinite pronouns are one of the largest categories of pronouns; the following is a partial list:

all, anybody, both, each, everything, few, most, none, one, some

Somebody screamed when the lights went out.

We gave them *everything* we had.

Demonstrative pronouns identify or point to specific nouns.

this, that, these, those

These are Peter's books.

Interrogative pronouns are used to ask questions.

who, which, what

Who can help set up the chairs for the meeting?

Relative pronouns introduce dependent clauses and "relate" the dependent clause to the rest of the sentence.

For more on dependent clauses, see 7c4.

who, which, that, what, whoever, whichever, whatever

Margaret owns the car *that* is parked by the corner.

The interrogative pronoun *who* and the relative pronouns *who* and *whoever* have different forms depending on how they are used in a sentence.

For a discussion of the forms of who *and* whoever, *see 8b.*

Reciprocal pronouns refer to the individual parts of a plural antecedent.

each other, one another

The business failed because the partners distrusted *each other.*

EXERCISE 7.4

Identify the pronouns and any antecedents in each of the following sentences, underlining the pronouns once and any antecedents twice. Example:

As identical twins, they really do understand each other.

1. She thanked everyone for helping.
2. The crowd that greeted the pope was the largest one I have ever seen.
3. Who knows better than Mark himself what he should do?
4. They have only themselves to blame.
5. People who are extremely fastidious often annoy those who are not.

4 Recognizing adjectives

Adjectives modify (limit the meaning of) nouns and pronouns, usually by describing, identifying, or quantifying those words.

The *red* Corvette ran off the road. [describes]

It was *defective.* [describes]

That Corvette needs to be repaired. [identifies]

We saw *several other* Corvettes race by. [quantifies]

In addition to their basic forms, most descriptive adjectives have other forms that are used to make comparisons: *small, smaller, smallest; foolish, more foolish, most foolish, less foolish, least foolish.*

This year's attendance was *smaller* than last year's.

This year's attendance was the *smallest* in ten years.

Many of the pronouns in 7b3 can function as adjectives when they are followed by a noun.

That is a dangerous intersection. [pronoun]

That intersection is dangerous. [adjective]

Other kinds of adjectives that identify or quantify are articles (*a, an, the*) and numbers (*three, sixty-fifth, five hundred*).

Proper adjectives are adjectives formed from or related to proper nouns (*Egyptian, Emersonian*). Proper adjectives are capitalized.

For more on proper adjectives, see 36b; for a complete discussion of adjectives, see Chapter 12.

5 Recognizing adverbs

Adverbs modify verbs, adjectives, other adverbs, or entire clauses. Many adverbs have an *-ly* ending, though some do not (*always, never, very, well*), and some words that end in *-ly* are not adverbs but adjectives (*friendly, lovely*). One of the most common adverbs is *not.*

David and Rebecca *recently* visited Maine. [modifies the verb *visited*]

They had an *unexpectedly* exciting trip. [modifies the adjective *exciting*]

They *very* soon discovered lobster. [modifies the adverb *soon*]

Frankly, they would have liked to stay another month. [modifies the independent clause that makes up the rest of the sentence]

Adverbs often answer the questions *when? where? why? how? to what extent?* In the first example on the preceding page, for instance, *recently* answers the question *when?* In the third sentence, *very* answers the question *to what extent?*

Many adverbs, like many adjectives, have different forms that are used in making comparisons: *forcefully, more forcefully, most forcefully, less forcefully, least forcefully.*

The senator spoke *more forcefully* than her opponent.

Of all the candidates, she speaks the *most forcefully.*

Conjunctive adverbs modify an entire clause and express the connection in meaning between that clause and the preceding clause (or sentence). Examples of conjunctive adverbs include *however, furthermore, therefore,* and *likewise.*

For more on conjunctive adverbs, see 7b7; for a complete discussion of adverbs, see Chapter 12.

EXERCISE 7.5

Identify the adjectives and adverbs in each of the following sentences, underlining the adjectives once and the adverbs twice. Remember that articles and some pronouns are used as adjectives. Example:

Inadvertently, the two agents misquoted their major client.

1. Because time had grown perilously short, I quickly prepared the final draft.
2. Hilariously, the sly villain revealed himself at the end of the first act.
3. The somewhat shy author spoke reluctantly to six exuberant admirers.
4. I unhappily returned the sleek new car to its owner.
5. The youngest dancer in the troupe performed a brilliant solo.

EXERCISE 7.6

Expand each of the following sentences by adding appropriate adjectives and adverbs. Delete *the* if need be. Example:

The veterinarians examined the patient.

Then the **three** veterinarians **thoroughly** examined the **nervous** patient.

1. A corporation can fire workers.
2. The heroine marries the prince.
3. In the painting, a road curves between hills.
4. Candles gleamed on the tabletop.
5. Feminists have staged demonstrations against the movie.

6 Recognizing prepositions

Prepositions are important structural words that express relationships – in space, time, or other senses – between nouns or pronouns and other words in a sentence.

We did not want to leave *during* the game.

The contestants waited nervously *for* the announcement.

Drive *across* the bridge, go *down* the avenue *past* three stoplights, and then turn left *before* the Gulf station.

Some common prepositions

about	at	down	near	since
above	before	during	of	through
across	behind	except	off	toward
after	below	for	on	under
against	beneath	from	onto	until
along	beside	in	out	up
among	between	inside	over	upon
around	beyond	into	past	with
as	by	like	regarding	without

Some prepositions, called compound prepositions, are made up of more than one word.

Some compound prepositions

according to	except for	instead of
as well as	in addition to	next to
because of	in front of	out of
by way of	in place of	with regard to
due to	in spite of	

If you are in doubt about which preposition to use, consult your dictionary. Frederich Wood's *English Prepositional Idioms* is a dictionary devoted to prepositions.

A **prepositional phrase** is made up of a preposition together with the noun or pronoun it connects to the rest of the sentence.

For more on prepositional phrases, see 7c3 and Chapter 55.

EXERCISE 7.7

Identify and underline the prepositions. Example:

In the dim interior of the hut crouched an old man.

1. A gust of wind blew through the window, upsetting the vase on the table.
2. He ran swiftly through the brush, across the beach, and into the sea.
3. A few minutes past noon, the police arrived at the scene.
4. During our trip down the river, a rivalry developed between us.
5. The book, by Anne Morrow Lindbergh, describes the flight the Lindberghs made to the Orient by way of the Great Circle route.

7 Recognizing conjunctions

Conjunctions connect words or groups of words to each other. There are four kinds of conjunctions: coordinating conjunctions, correlative conjunctions, subordinating conjunctions, and conjunctive adverbs.

Coordinating conjunctions

Coordinating conjunctions join equivalent structures – two or more nouns, pronouns, verbs, adjectives, adverbs, prepositions, conjunctions, phrases, or clauses.

For a discussion of how to use coordinating conjunctions effectively in writing, see 20a.

COORDINATING CONJUNCTIONS

and but or yet nor for so

A strong *but* warm breeze blew across the desert.

Please print *or* type the information on the application form.

Her arguments were easy to ridicule *yet* hard to refute.

He did not have much money, *nor* did he know how to get any.

Correlative conjunctions

Correlative conjunctions join equal elements, and they come in pairs.

CORRELATIVE CONJUNCTIONS

both . . . and	just as . . . so	not only . . . but also
either . . . or	neither . . . nor	whether . . . or

Both Bechtel *and* Kaiser submitted bids on the project.

Maisha *not only* sent a card *but also* visited me in the hospital.

Subordinating conjunctions

Subordinating conjunctions introduce adverb clauses and signal the relationship between the adverb clause and another clause, usually an independent clause. For instance, in the following sentence the subordinating conjunction *while* signals a time relationship, letting us know that the two events in the sentence happened simultaneously:

Sweat ran down my face *while* I frantically searched for my child.

SOME COMMON SUBORDINATING CONJUNCTIONS

after	if	though
although	in order that	unless
as	once	until
as if	since	when
because	so that	where
before	than	while
even though	that	

Unless sales improve dramatically, the company will soon be bankrupt.

My grandmother began traveling *after* she sold her house.

Conjunctive adverbs

Conjunctive adverbs connect independent clauses. As their name suggests, conjunctive adverbs can be considered both adverbs and conjunctions because they modify the second clause in addition to connecting it to the preceding clause. Like many other adverbs yet unlike other conjunctions, they can be moved to different positions in a clause. For example:

The cider tasted bitter; *however,* each of us drank a tall glass of it.

The cider tasted bitter; each of us, *however,* drank a tall glass of it.

The cider tasted bitter. Each of us drank a tall glass of it, *however.*

SOME CONJUNCTIVE ADVERBS

also	indeed	now
anyway	instead	otherwise
besides	likewise	similarly
certainly	meanwhile	still
finally	moreover	then
furthermore	namely	therefore
however	nevertheless	thus
incidentally	next	undoubtedly

Independent clauses connected by a conjunctive adverb must be separated by a semicolon or a period, not just a comma.

For more on independent clauses connected by conjunctive adverbs, see 15c.

Some of these problems could occur at any company; *however,* many could happen only here.

EXERCISE 7.8

Underline the coordinating, correlative, and subordinating conjunctions as well as the conjunctive adverbs in each of the following sentences. Example:

We used sleeping bags even though the cabin had sheets and blankets.

1. When we arrived at the pond, we saw many children playing there.
2. The shops along the waterfront were open, but business was slow.
3. The story was not only long but also dull.
4. Although I live in a big city, my neighborhood has enough trees and raccoons to make me feel as if I live in the suburbs.
5. Neither Henry nor Rachel could understand the story; therefore, they did not recommend it.

8 Recognizing interjections

Interjections express surprise or emotion: *oh, ouch, ah, hey.* Interjections often stand alone, as fragments. Even when they are included in a sentence, they are not related grammatically to the rest of the sentence. They are used mostly in speaking; in writing, they are used mostly in dialogue.

"Yes! All right!" The fans screamed, jumping to their feet.

The problem suggested, *alas,* no easy solution.

7c Recognizing the parts of a sentence

Knowing a word's part of speech helps us understand how to use that word, but we also have to look at the part it plays in a particular sentence. Every sentence has a grammatical pattern or structure, and certain parts of speech – nouns, pronouns, and adjectives – can function in more than one way depending on this structure.

SUBJECT
This description evokes the ecology of the Everglades.

DIRECT OBJECT
I read a description of the ecology of the Everglades.

Description is a noun in both of these sentences, yet in the first it serves as the subject of the verb *evokes,* while in the second it serves as the direct object of the verb *read.*

BASIC SENTENCE PATTERNS

1. **SUBJECT/VERB**

   S V
   Babies cry.

2. **SUBJECT/VERB/SUBJECT COMPLEMENT**

   S V SC
   Babies seem fragile.

3. **SUBJECT/VERB/DIRECT OBJECT**

   S V DO
   Babies drink milk.

4. **SUBJECT/VERB/INDIRECT OBJECT/DIRECT OBJECT**

   S V IO DO
   Babies give grandparents pleasure.

5. **SUBJECT/VERB/DIRECT OBJECT/OBJECT COMPLEMENT**

   S V DO OC
   Babies make parents proud.

This section examines the essential parts of a sentence – subjects, predicates, objects, complements, phrases, and clauses.

www •

http://deil.lang.uiuc.edu/web.pages/grammarsafari.html

The Grammar Safari *helps you get beyond the "safe confines of grammar books" to explore English on the Web. Want to hunt for adjective clauses in* Little Women? *The* Grammar Safari *will show you how.*

1 Recognizing subjects

As described in 7a, almost every sentence has a stated subject, which identifies whom or what the sentence is about. The **simple subject** consists of one or more nouns or pronouns; the **complete subject** consists of the simple subject with all its modifiers. Depending on the number and kinds of modifiers, subjects can be as plain as one word or far more complex. The following examples show the complete subjects in italics, with the simple subjects labeled *ss:*

ss
Baseball is a summer game.

ss
Sailing over the fence, the ball crashed through Mr. Wilson's window.

ss
Stadiums with real grass are hard to find these days.

ss
Those who sit in the bleachers have the most fun.

A **compound subject** contains two or more simple subjects joined with a coordinating conjunction (*and, but, or*) or a correlative conjunction (*both . . . and, either . . . or, neither . . . nor, not only . . . but also*).

Baseball and softball developed from cricket.

Both baseball and softball developed from cricket.

The simple subject usually comes before the predicate, or verb, but not always. Sometimes writers reverse this order to achieve a particular effect.

Up to the plate stepped *Casey.*

Great was the *anticipation* among Mudville fans.

In **imperative sentences,** which express requests or commands, the subject *you* is usually implied but not stated.

(*You*) Keep your eye on the ball.

In questions and certain other constructions, the subject usually appears between the auxiliary verb and the main verb.

Did *Casey* save the game?

Never have *I* known greater disappointment.

In sentences beginning with *there* or *here* followed by a form of the verb *be,* the subject always follows the verb. *There* and *here* are never the subject.

Here is the sad *ending* of the poem.

There was no *joy* in Mudville.

EXERCISE 7.9

Identify the complete subject and the simple subject in each sentence. Underline the complete subject once and the simple subject twice. Example:

The tall, powerful woman defiantly blocked the doorway.

1. The stories of Graham Greene probe the human psyche.
2. Has the new elevator been installed?
3. Here are some representative photographs.
4. The long, low, intricately carved table belonged to my aunt.
5. Some women worried about osteoporosis take calcium supplements.

2 Recognizing predicates

As we saw in 7a, in addition to a subject every sentence has a predicate, which asserts or asks something about the subject or tells the subject to do something. The "hinge," or key word, of most predicates is a verb. As we saw in 7b1, a verb can include auxiliary verbs (as in this sentence, where *can* is an auxiliary and *include* is the main verb). The **simple predicate** of a sentence is the main verb and any auxiliaries; the **complete predicate** includes the simple predicate and any modifiers of the verb and any objects or complements and their modifiers. In the following examples, the complete predicates are italicized, and the simple predicates are labeled *sp:*

SP

My roommate *seems wonderful.*

SP

Both of us *are planning to major in history.*

A **compound predicate** contains two or more verbs that have the same subject, usually joined by a coordinating or a correlative conjunction.

Charles *shut the book, put it back on the shelf, and sighed.*

The Amish *neither drive cars nor use electricity.*

On the basis of how they function in predicates, verbs can be divided into three categories: linking, transitive, and intransitive.

Linking verbs

A **linking verb** links, or joins, a subject with a **subject complement,** a word or word group that identifies or describes the subject. If it identifies the subject, the complement is a noun or pronoun (and is sometimes called a **predicate noun**). If it describes the subject, the complement is an adjective (and is sometimes called a **predicate adjective**). In the following examples, *a single mother* is a predicate noun, and *exhausted* is a predicate adjective:

S V SC
Christine is a single mother.

S V SC
She is exhausted.

The forms of *be,* when used as main verbs rather than as auxiliary verbs, are linking verbs (like *are* in this sentence). Other verbs, such as *appear, become, feel, grow, look, make, seem, smell,* and *sound,* can also function as linking verbs, depending on the sense of the sentence.

S V SC
The abandoned farmhouse had become dilapidated.

S V SC
It looked ready to fall down.

Transitive and intransitive verbs

If a verb is not a linking verb, it is either transitive or intransitive. A **transitive verb** expresses action that is directed toward a noun or pronoun, called the **direct object** of the verb.

S V DO
I will analyze three poems.

A direct object identifies what or who receives the action of the verb. In the preceding example, the subject and verb do not express a complete thought. The direct object completes the thought, saying *what* I will analyze.

A direct object may be followed by an **object complement,** a word or word group that describes or identifies it. Object complements may be adjectives, as in the next example, or nouns, as in the second example.

S V DO OC
I consider Marianne Moore's poetry exquisite.

S V DO OC
Her poems and personality made Moore a celebrity.

A transitive verb may also be followed by an **indirect object,** which tells to whom or what, or for whom or what, the verb's action is done. You might say the indirect object is the recipient of the direct object.

S V IO DO
Moore's poems about the Dodgers give me considerable pleasure.

An **intransitive verb** expresses action that is not directed toward an object. Therefore, an intransitive verb does not have a direct object.

S V
The Red Sox persevered.

S V
Their fans watched helplessly.

The action of the verb *persevered* has no object (it makes no sense to ask, *persevered what?* or *persevered whom?*), and the action of the verb *watched* is directed toward an object that is implied but not expressed.

Some verbs that express action can be only transitive or only intransitive, but most can be used both ways, with or without a direct object.

S V DO
A maid wearing a uniform opened the door. [transitive]

S V
The door opened silently. [intransitive]

EXERCISE 7.10

Underline the predicate in the following sentences. Then label each verb as linking, transitive, or intransitive. Finally, label all subject and object complements and all direct and indirect objects. Example:

TV DO OC
We considered city life unbearable.

1. California is dry in the summer.
2. The U.S. Constitution made us a nation.
3. A round of applause seemed appropriate.
4. Rock and roll will never die.
5. Advertisers promise consumers the world.

3 Recognizing and using phrases

A **phrase** is a group of words that lacks either a subject or a predicate or both. Phrases function in useful ways to add information to a sentence or shape it effectively. Look at the following sentence:

The new law will restrict smoking *in most public places.*

The basic subject of this sentence is a noun phrase, *the new law;* the basic predicate is a verb phrase, *will restrict smoking.* Additional information is provided by the prepositional phrase, *in most public places.* The prepositional phrase functions here as an adverb, telling *where* smoking will be restricted.

This section will discuss the various kinds of phrases: noun, verb, prepositional, verbal, absolute, and appositive.

Noun phrases

Made up of a noun and all its modifiers, a **noun phrase** can function in a sentence as a subject, object, or complement.

SUBJECT
Delicious, gooey peanut butter is surprisingly healthful.

OBJECT
Dieters prefer *green salad.*

COMPLEMENT
A tuna sandwich is *a popular lunch.*

Verb phrases

A main verb and its auxiliary verbs make up a **verb phrase,** which functions in a sentence in only one way: as a predicate.

Frank *had been depressed* for some time.

His problem *might have been caused* by tension between his parents.

Prepositional phrases

A **prepositional phrase** includes a preposition, a noun or pronoun (called the **object of the preposition**), and any modifiers of the object. Prepositional phrases usually function as adjectives or adverbs; occasionally they function as nouns.

ADJECTIVE	Our house *in Maine* was a cabin.
ADVERB	*From Cadillac Mountain,* you can see the northern lights.
NOUN	The best time to visit is *after lunch.*

Verbal phrases

Verbals are verb forms that do not function as verbs. Instead, they function as nouns, adjectives, or adverbs. There are three kinds of verbals: participles, gerunds, and infinitives.

The **participle** functions as an adjective. The **present participle** is the *-ing* form of a verb: *dreaming, being, seeing.* The **past participle** of most verbs ends in *-ed: dreamed, watched.* But some verbs have an irregular past participle: *been, seen, hidden, gone, set.*

For a list of irregular verbs and their past participles, see 9b.

A kiss awakened the *dreaming* princess.

The cryptographers deciphered the *hidden* meaning in the message.

The **gerund** has the same form as the present participle but functions as a noun.

SUBJECT	*Writing* takes practice.
OBJECT	The organization promotes *recycling.*

The **infinitive** is the *to* form of a verb: *to dream, to be, to see.* An infinitive can function as a noun, adjective, or adverb.

NOUN	She wanted *to write.*
ADJECTIVE	They had no more time *to waste.*
ADVERB	The corporation was ready *to expand.*

Verbal phrases are made up of a verbal and any modifiers, objects, or complements. Let us turn now to examine the forms and functions of the various kinds of verbal phrases.

PARTICIPIAL PHRASES

Participial phrases consist of a present participle or a past participle and any modifiers, objects, or complements. Participial phrases always function as adjectives.

Irritated by the delay, Louise complained.

A dog *howling at the moon* kept me awake.

GERUND PHRASES

Gerund phrases consist of a gerund and any modifiers, objects, or complements: *hoping for a victory, critical thinking.* Gerund phrases function as nouns.

SUBJECT

Opening their eyes to the problem was not easy.

DIRECT OBJECT

They suddenly heard *a loud wailing from the sandbox.*

INFINITIVE PHRASES

Infinitive phrases consist of an infinitive and any modifiers, objects, or complements: *to be happy, to go to a movie tonight.* They can function as nouns, adjectives, or adverbs.

NOUN/SC

My goal is *to be a biology teacher.*

ADJECTIVE

A party would be a good way *to end the semester.*

ADVERB

To perfect a draft, always proofread carefully.

Absolute phrases

An **absolute phrase** usually includes a noun or pronoun and a participle. It modifies an entire sentence rather than a particular word and is usually set off from the rest of the sentence with commas.

For more on commas with absolute phrases, see 30a.

I stood on the deck, *the wind whipping my hair.*

My fears laid to rest, I climbed into the plane for my first solo flight.

When the participle is *being,* it is often omitted.

The ambassador, *her head (being) high,* walked out of the room.

Appositive phrases

A noun phrase that renames the noun or pronoun that immediately precedes it is called an **appositive phrase.**

The report, *a hefty three-volume work,* included 150 recommendations.

We had a single desire, *to change the administration's policies.*

EXERCISE 7.11

Read the following sentences, and identify and label all of the prepositional, verbal, absolute, and appositive phrases. Notice that one kind of phrase may appear within another kind. Example:

ABSOLUTE — PREP
His voice breaking with emotion, Ed thanked us for the award.
PREP

1. Approaching the rope, I suddenly fell into the icy pond.
2. To listen to k. d. lang is sheer delight.
3. The figure outlined against the sky seemed unable to move.
4. Floating on my back, I ignored my practice requirements.
5. Jane stood still, her fingers clutching the fence.
6. Josúe, a sensitive child, was filled with a mixture of awe and excitement.
7. Shocked into silence, they kept their gaze fixed on the odd creature.
8. Basking in the sunlight, I was lost in reminiscence of birch trees.
9. Ana, the leader of the group, was reluctant to relinquish any authority.
10. His favorite form of recreation was taking a nap.

EXERCISE 7.12

Use prepositional, participial, infinitive, gerund, absolute, or appositive phrases to expand each of the following sentences. Example:

The apples dropped from the limb.

In response to my vigorous shake, the apples dropped from the limb.

1. Nancy jogged down Willow Street.
2. She looked healthy when he saw her the second time.
3. Tomas had lost almost all of his hair.
4. The Sunday afternoon dragged.
5. Zakiyyah looked at her mother.
6. The candidates shook hands with the voters.
7. We were uncertain what to do.
8. Ben often thought regretfully about the past.
9. The letter lay on the desk.
10. They lived in a trailer.

4 Recognizing and using clauses

A **clause** is a group of words containing a subject and a predicate. There are two kinds of clauses: independent and dependent. **Independent**

clauses (also known as **main clauses**) can stand alone as complete sentences.

The window is open.

The batter swung at the ball.

Pairs of independent clauses may be joined with a coordinating conjunction and a comma.

For a discussion and a list of coordinating conjunctions, see 7b7.

The window is open, *so* we'd better be quiet.

The batter swung at the ball, *and* the umpire called her out.

Like independent clauses, **dependent clauses** (also known as **subordinate clauses**) contain a subject and a predicate. They cannot stand alone as complete sentences, however, for they begin with a subordinating word – a subordinating conjunction or a relative pronoun – that connects them to an independent clause.

For discussions and lists of subordinating conjunctions and relative pronouns, see 7b7 and 7b3.

Because the window is open, the room feels cool.

In this combination, the subordinating conjunction *because* transforms the independent clause *the window is open* into a dependent clause. In doing so, it indicates a causal relationship between the two clauses.

Dependent clauses function as nouns, adjectives, or adverbs.

Noun clauses

Noun clauses can function as subjects, direct objects, subject complements, or objects of prepositions. Thus they are always contained within another clause. They usually begin with a relative pronoun (*that, which, what, who, whom, whose, whatever, whoever, whomever, whichever*) or with *when, where, whether, why,* or *how.*

S: That he had a college degree was important to her.

DO: She asked where he went to college.

SC: The real question was why she wanted to know.

OBJ OF PREP: She was looking for whatever information was available.

Notice that in each of these sentences the noun clause is an integral part of the independent clause that makes up the sentence; for example, in the second sentence the independent clause is not just *She asked* but *She asked where he went to college.*

Adjective clauses

Adjective clauses modify nouns and pronouns in another clause. Usually they immediately follow the words they modify. Most adjective clauses begin with the relative pronouns *who, whom, whose, that,* or *which.* Some begin with *when, where,* or *why.*

The surgery, *which took three hours,* was a complete success.

It was performed by the surgeon *who had developed the procedure.*

The hospital was the one *where I was born.*

Sometimes the relative pronoun introducing an adjective clause may be omitted, as in the following example:

That is one book *[that] I intend to read.*

Adverb clauses

Adverb clauses modify verbs, adjectives, or other adverbs. They begin with a subordinating conjunction. Like adverbs, they usually tell when, where, why, how, or to what extent.

For a discussion and a list of subordinating conjunctions, see 7b7.

We hiked *where there were few other hikers.*

My backpack felt heavier *than it ever had.*

I climbed as swiftly *as I could under the weight of my backpack.*

EXERCISE 7.13

Identify the independent and dependent clauses and any subordinating conjunctions and relative pronouns in each of the following sentences. Example:

DEPENDENT CLAUSE / INDEPENDENT CLAUSE
If I were going on a really long hike, I would carry a lightweight stove.

(*If* is a subordinating conjunction.)

1. The driver who won the race was driving a tan Pontiac.
2. The names they called my grandmother still haunt me.
3. When she was deemed old enough to understand, she was told the truth, and she finally knew why her father had left home.
4. The trip was longer than I had remembered.
5. I could see that he was very tired, but I had to ask him a few questions.

EXERCISE 7.14

Expand each of the following sentences by adding at least one dependent clause to it. Be prepared to explain how your addition improves the sentence. Example:

The books tumbled from the shelves.

As the earth continued to shake, the books tumbled from the shelves.

1. The last guests left.
2. The German government dismantled the Berlin Wall.
3. The new computer made a strange noise.
4. Rob always borrowed money from friends.
5. The streets were ringing with loud music.

7d Classifying sentences

Like words, sentences can be classified in several different ways: grammatically, functionally, or rhetorically. Grammatical classification groups sentences according to how many and what types of clauses they contain. Functional classification groups them according to whether they make a statement, ask a question, issue a command, or express an exclamation. Rhetorical classification groups them according to where in the sentence the main idea is located. These methods of classification can help you analyze and assess your sentences as you write and revise.

1 Classifying sentences grammatically

For more about using and punctuating these grammatical types of sentences, see Chapters 15, 20, 30, and 31.

Grammatically, sentences may be classified as *simple, compound, complex,* and *compound-complex.*

Simple sentences

A **simple sentence** consists of one independent clause and no dependent clause. The subject or the predicate, or both, may be compound.

The trailer is surrounded by a wooden deck.

Both my roommate and I had left our keys in the room.

At the country club, the head pro and his assistant give lessons, run the golf shop, and try to keep the members content.

Compound sentences

A **compound sentence** consists of two or more independent clauses and no dependent clause. The clauses may be joined by a comma and a coordinating conjunction, or by a semicolon.

Occasionally a car goes up the dirt trail, and dust flies everywhere.

Alberto is obsessed with soccer; he eats, breathes, and lives the game.

Complex sentences

A **complex sentence** consists of one independent clause and at least one dependent clause.

DEPENDENT CLAUSE
Many people believe that anyone can earn a living.

DEPENDENT CLAUSE
Those who do not like to get dirty should not go camping.

DEPENDENT CLAUSE
As I awaited my interview, I sat with other nervous candidates.

Compound-complex sentences

A **compound-complex sentence** consists of two or more independent clauses and at least one dependent clause.

IND CLAUSE — DEP CLAUSE — IND CLAUSE
I complimented Joe when he finished the job, and he seemed pleased.

IND CLAUSE — IND CLAUSE
Sister Lucy tried her best to help Martin, but he was an undisciplined boy
DEP CLAUSE
who drove many teachers to despair.

2 Classifying sentences functionally

In terms of function, sentences can be classified as **declarative** (making a statement), **interrogative** (asking a question), **imperative** (giving a command), or **exclamatory** (expressing strong feeling).

DECLARATIVE	Kira plays oboe for the Cleveland Orchestra.
INTERROGATIVE	How long has she been with them?
IMPERATIVE	Get me a ticket for her next performance.
EXCLAMATORY	What a talented musician she is!

www •

http://www.esc.edu/htmlpages/writer/workshop.htm

From Empire State College, this online writer's workshop offers good explanations and exercises. Click on Grammar Workout for advice on structuring sentences.

3 Classifying sentences rhetorically

Some sentences can be classified rhetorically as either cumulative or periodic sentences. The two patterns create very different rhythms and emphases. See 22c3 for an explanation of cumulative and periodic sentences.

EXERCISE 7.15

Classify each of the following sentences as simple, compound, complex, or compound-complex. In addition, note any sentences that could be classified as imperative, interrogative, or exclamatory.

1. The screen door creaked and banged when she ran into the house.
2. Should he admit his mistake, or should he keep quiet and hope to avoid discovery?
3. People go on safari to watch wild animals in their natural habitat.
4. Keeping in mind the terrain, the weather, and the length of the hike, decide what you need to take.
5. Dreams are necessary, but they can be frustrating unless you have the means to attain them.

THINKING CRITICALLY ABOUT SENTENCES

The following sentences come from the openings of well-known works. Identify the independent and dependent clauses in each sentence. Then choose one sentence, and write a sentence of your own imitating its structure clause for clause and phrase for phrase.

> She is an open and trusting child, unprepared for and unaccustomed to the ambushes of family life, and perhaps it is just as well that I can offer her little of that life.
>
> – JOAN DIDION, "On Going Home"

> Quogue was a year-round yet transient community, used to but indifferent toward the renters of summer cottages, so perhaps it was odd that we found it the most welcoming place on earth.

1. Most people who bother with the matter at all would admit that the English language is in a bad way, but it is generally assumed that we cannot by conscious action do anything about it. – GEORGE ORWELL, "Politics and the English Language"
2. We observe today not a victory of party but a celebration of freedom, symbolizing an end as well as a beginning, signifying renewal as well as change. – JOHN F. KENNEDY, Inaugural Address
3. Once in a long while, four times so far for me, my mother brings out the metal tube that holds her medical diploma. – MAXINE HONG KINGSTON, "Photographs of My Parents"

Understanding Pronoun Case

8

During the 1991 NCAA men's basketball tournament, two members of a winning team were being interviewed on CBS. Asked whether the players had "felt a win coming on," one of them responded: "Marcus and me — or Marcus and I, I should say — we definitely knew we could win. All we had to do was play our own game."

This player certainly would have been understood by the TV audience had he stuck with "Marcus and me," but he corrected himself because he realized that *I,* rather than *me,* should be used as a subject. Although most of us know intuitively most of the time when to use *I,* when to use *me,* and when to use *my,* almost everyone becomes confused at least occasionally by choices like those between *who* and *whom, we Texans* and *us Texans,* or *Marcus and me* and *Marcus and I.* ■

8a Using the three cases

The grammatical term **case** refers to the form a pronoun takes to indicate its function in a sentence. Pronouns functioning as subjects are in the subjective case; those functioning as objects are in the objective case; and those functioning as possessives are in the possessive case.

SUBJECTIVE PRONOUNS

I/we	you	he/she/it	they	who/ whoever

OBJECTIVE PRONOUNS

me/us	you	him/her/it	them	whom/ whomever

POSSESSIVE PRONOUNS

my/our	your	his/hers/its	their	whose
mine/ours	yours	his/hers/its	theirs	

1 The subjective case

A pronoun should be in the **subjective case** when it is a subject of a clause or a subject complement. (See 7c.)

SUBJECT OF A CLAUSE

They could either fight or face certain death with the lions.

Who wrote "Araby"?

GRAMMAR
Understanding Pronoun Case

→ Are all pronouns after forms of the verb *be* in the subjective case? (8a1)
→ To check for correct use of *who* and *whom* (and *whoever* and *whomever*), try answering the question or rewriting the clause using *he* or *him*. If *he* is correct, use *who* (or *whoever*); if *him*, use *whom* or *whomever.* (8b)
→ In compound structures, make sure pronouns are in the same case they would be in if used alone. (*Jake and she were living in Spain*). (8c)
→ When a pronoun follows *than* or *as,* complete the sentence mentally. If the pronoun is the subject of an unstated verb, it should be in the subjective case (*I like her better than he* [*likes her*]). If it is the object of an unstated verb, it should be in the objective case (*I like her better than* [*I like*] *him*). (8d)
→ Circle all the pronouns to see if you rely too heavily on any one pronoun or case, especially *I.* If you find that you do, try rewriting some sentences to change *I* to *me, she* to *her,* and so on.

www

http://linguistlist.org/~ask-ling/index.html

Not sure whether to use who *or* whom? *Go to the* Ask a Linguist *site, where a panel of linguists will answer questions about language.*

Roberto told the story to Carla, *who* told all her friends.

Our group appealed to *whoever* was willing to listen.

SUBJECT COMPLEMENT

Americans often use the objective case for subject complements, especially in conversation: *Who's there? It's* ***me.*** Nevertheless, you should use the subjective case in formal writing.

If I were *she,* I would worry about other things.

If you find the subjective case for a subject complement stilted or awkward, try rewriting the sentence using the pronoun as the subject.

She was the
▶ **~~The~~ first person to see Monty after the awards. ~~was she~~.**

2 The objective case

A pronoun should be in the **objective case** when it functions as a direct or indirect object (of a verb or verbal), a subject of an infinitive, or an object of a preposition.

For more about objects, see 7c2 and 7c3.

OBJECT OF A VERB OR VERBAL

The professor surprised *us* with a quiz. [direct object of *surprised*]

The grateful owner gave *him* a reward. [indirect object of *gave*]

Presidents usually rely on advisors *whom* they have known for years. [direct object of *have known*]

The Parisians were wonderful about helping *me.* [direct object of gerund]

SUBJECT OF AN INFINITIVE

The objective case is also used in sentences like the following, where the pronoun is preceded by a verb and followed by an infinitive. Though the pronoun in such constructions is called the subject of the infinitive, it is in the objective case because it is the object of the sentence's verb.

The students convinced *him* to vote for the school bond.

OBJECT OF A PREPOSITION

Several of my friends went with *me.*

3 The possessive case

A pronoun should be in the **possessive case** when it shows possession or ownership. Notice that there are two forms of possessive pronouns: adjective forms, which are used before nouns or gerunds (*my, your, his, her, its, our, their, whose*), and noun forms, which take the place of a noun (*mine, yours, his, hers, its, ours, theirs, whose*).

ADJECTIVE FORMS

Tarentino's movies put viewers on the edge of *their* seats.

Whose life is it, anyway?

The sound of *his* hammering echoed through the corridor.

NOUN FORMS

The responsibility is *hers.*

Whose is this blue backpack?

A pronoun that appears before a gerund should be in the possessive case (*my/our, your, his/her/its, their*). What can be tricky is distinguishing gerunds from present participles, for both are *-ing* forms of verbs. Notice the difference in meaning in the following examples:

I remember *his* singing.

I remember *him* singing.

In the first example, the memory is of *singing,* which is a gerund, modified by the possessive pronoun *his.* In the second, the memory is of *him,* which is a direct object of *remember* and thus is in the objective case; *singing* is a present participle modifying *him.* In sentences like these, use the possessive case if you want to emphasize the person; use the objective case if you want to emphasize the action.

8b Using *who, whoever, whom,* and *whomever*

A common problem with pronoun case is deciding whether to use *who* or *whom.* Even when traditional grammar requires *whom,* many Americans use *who* instead, especially in speech. Nevertheless, in formal written English, which includes most college writing, the case of the pronoun should reflect its grammatical function. *Who* and *whoever* are the subjective case forms and should be used when the pronoun is a subject or subject complement. *Whom* and *whomever* are the objective case forms and should be used when the pronoun is a direct or indirect object or the object of a preposition.

Most writers find that two particular situations can lead to confusion with *who* and *whom:* when they begin a question and when they introduce a dependent clause. In a dependent clause, you may also have to choose between *whoever* and *whomever.*

For a discussion of dependent clauses, see 7c4.

1 Beginning a question with *who* or *whom*

You can determine whether to use *who* or *whom* at the beginning of a question by answering the question using a personal pronoun. If the answer is in the subjective case, use *who;* if it is in the objective case, use *whom.*

Whom
► ~~**Who**~~ **did you visit?**

I visited *them. Them* is objective; thus *whom* is correct.

Who
► ~~**Whom**~~ **do you think wrote the story?**

I think *she* wrote the story. *She* is subjective; thus *who* is correct.

2 Beginning a dependent clause with *who, whoever, whom,* or *whomever*

GRAMMAR
Using *Who, Whoever, Whom,* and *Whomever*

The case of a pronoun in a dependent clause is determined by its function in the clause, no matter how that clause functions in the sentence. If the pronoun acts as a subject or subject complement in the clause, use *who* or *whoever.* If the pronoun acts as an object, use *whom* or *whomever.*

▶ **The new president was not ~~who~~ *whom* she had expected.**

Whom is the object of the verb *had expected* in the clause *whom she had expected.* Though the clause as a whole is the complement of the verb *was,* the pronoun should be in the objective case.

▶ **The center is open to ~~whomever~~ *whoever* wants to use it.**

Whoever is the subject of the clause *whoever wants to use it.* Though the clause as a whole is the object of the preposition *to,* the pronoun should be in the subjective case.

If you are not sure which case to use, try separating the dependent clause from the rest of the sentence and looking at it in isolation. Rewrite the clause as a new sentence with a personal pronoun instead of *who*(*ever*) or *whom*(*ever*). If the pronoun is in the subjective case, use *who* or *whoever;* if it is in the objective case, use *whom* or *whomever.*

▶ **The minister grimaced at (*whoever/whomever*) made any noise.**

Isolate the clause *whoever/whomever made any noise.* Substituting a personal pronoun gives you *they made any noise. They* is subjective case; therefore, *The minister grimaced at whoever made any noise.*

▶ **The minister smiled at (*whoever/whomever*) she greeted.**

Isolate and transpose the clause to get *she greeted whoever/whomever.* Substituting a personal pronoun gives you *she greeted them. Them* is in the objective case; therefore, *The minister smiled at whomever she greeted.*

Ignore such expressions as *he thinks* or *she says* when you isolate the clause.

▶ **The minister grimaced at (*whoever/whomever*) she thought made any noise.**

The clause is *whoever/whomever made any noise.* Substituting a personal pronoun gives you *they made any noise. They* is subjective case; therefore, *The minister grimaced at whoever she thought made any noise.*

EXERCISE 8.1

Insert *who, whoever, whom,* or *whomever* appropriately in the blank in each of the following sentences. Example:

She is someone *who* will go far.

1. _______ shall I say is calling?
2. _______ the voters choose faces an almost impossible challenge.
3. The manager promised to reward _______ sold the most cars.
4. Professor Quiñones asked _______ we wanted to collaborate with.
5. _______ will the new tax law benefit most?

8c Using case in compound structures

Most problems with the case of personal pronouns occur when the pronoun is part of a compound subject, complement, or object. Each part of a compound structure should be in the same case as it would if used alone. Pronouns in compound subjects and compound subject complements should be in the subjective case; pronouns in compound objects or compound subjects of infinitives should be in the objective case.

SUBJECTS AND SUBJECT COMPLEMENTS

▶ **When Zelda and ~~him~~** *he* **were first married, they lived in New York.**

▶ **The next two speakers will be Philip and ~~her~~** *she***.**

OBJECTS AND SUBJECTS OF INFINITIVES

▶ **The boss invited ~~she~~** *her* **and her family to dinner.**

▶ **They offered Gail and ~~she~~** *her* **a summer internship.**

▶ **This morning saw yet another conflict between my sister and ~~I~~** *me***.**

▶ **We asked Joan and ~~she~~** *her* **to attend the meeting.**

To decide whether to use the subjective or the objective case in a compound structure, make each part of the compound into a separate sentence.

► **Come to the park with Bob and ~~I.~~** *me*

Separating the compound structure gives you *come to the park with Bob* and *come to the park with me;* thus, *Come to the park with Bob and* *me.*

Pronoun case in a compound appositive is determined by the word the appositive renames. If the word functions as a subject or subject complement, the pronoun should be in the subjective case; if it functions as an object, the pronoun should be in the objective case.

► **All three panelists — Arlene, Tony, and ~~me~~** *I* **— were stumped by the question.**

Panelists is the subject of the sentence, so the pronoun in the appositive *Arlene, Tony, and I* should be in the subjective case.

► **The poker game produced two big winners, Aunt Rose and ~~I~~** *me***.**

Winners is the direct object of the verb *produced,* so the pronoun in the appositive *Aunt Rose and me* should be in the objective case.

8d Using case in elliptical constructions

Elliptical constructions, in which some words are left out but understood, are often used in comparisons with *than* or *as.* When sentences with such constructions end in a pronoun, the pronoun should be in the case it would be in if the construction were complete.

His brother has always been more athletic than *he* [is].

In some constructions like this, the case depends on the meaning intended. Use the subjective case if the pronoun is actually the subject of an omitted verb; use the objective case if it is an object of an omitted verb.

Willie likes Lily more than *she* [likes Lily].

Willie likes Lily more than [he likes] *her.*

8e Using *we* and *us* before a noun

If you are unsure about whether to use *we* or *us* before a noun, recasting the sentence without the noun will give you the answer. Use whichever pronoun would be correct if the noun were omitted.

► ~~Us~~ *We* **fans never give up hope.**

Fans is the subject, so the pronoun should be subjective.

► **The Orioles depend on ~~we~~** *us* **fans.**

Fans is the object of a preposition, so the pronoun should be objective.

EXERCISE 8.2

Choose the appropriate pronoun from the pair in parentheses in each of the following sentences. Example:

The possibility of (*their/them*) succeeding never occurred to me.

1. The relationship between (*they/them*) and their brother was often strained.
2. When I was in high school, I had one teacher (*who/whom*) I truly admired.
3. At the time, I had three friends who were more popular than (*I/me*).
4. The only candidates left in the race were (*he/him*) and Clinton.
5. Maria became more and more interested in (*his/him*) assisting her with planning her presentation.
6. When Jessica and (*she/her*) first met, they despised each other.
7. The two violinists, Sergei and (*he/him*), played as though they had a single musical mind.
8. Soap operas appeal to (*whoever/whomever*) is interested in intrigue, suspense, joy, pain, grief, romance, fidelity, sex, and violence.
9. Tomorrow (*we/us*) raw recruits will have our first on-the-job test.
10. The only experts (*who/whom*) they can recommend are the two magicians who trained them.

EXERCISE 8.3

Edit any of the following sentences with errors in pronoun case. Example:

Of the group, only ~~her~~ *she* and I finished the race.

1. The readers, her and me, agreed that the story was very suspenseful.
2. Just between you and I, this course is a disaster!
3. The people who Jay worked with were very cold and unsociable.
4. Who would have thought that twenty years later he would be king?
5. Roderigo becomes involved in the plot without him knowing it.
6. Only him, a few cabinet members, and several military leaders were aware of the steady advance Japan was making toward Pearl Harbor.

7. All of the job candidates were far more experienced than I.
8. As out-of-towners, my buddy and me did not know too many people.
9. I never got to play that role in front of an audience, but I am one of the few performers who really did break a leg.
10. Connor always lent money to whomever asked him for it.

THINKING CRITICALLY ABOUT PRONOUN CASE

Reading with an Eye for Pronoun Case

The poet e. e. cummings often broke the standard rules of grammar and word order to create particular effects in his poetry. Read the following poem, and note the function of each pronoun. Then rearrange the words of the poem so that they follow as closely as possible the normal order they would take in an ordinary sentence. How does pronoun case give you a clue to this arrangement?

> Me up at does
>
> out of the floor
> quietly Stare
>
> a poisoned mouse
>
> still who alive
>
> is asking What
> have i done that
>
> You wouldn't have — E. E. CUMMINGS

Thinking about Your Own Use of Pronoun Case

Research shows that one of the most overused words in any language is the word for *I*. Whenever you write anything that includes your own opinions, you probably rely to some degree on first-person pronouns, singular and plural. Read over some of your own paragraphs, paying attention to your use of pronouns. Do you find any patterns? If you find that you rely heavily on any one case — that half your sentences begin with *I*, for example — decide whether your writing seems at all monotonous as a result. If so, try revising some sentences to change *I* to *me* (or vice versa). Do the changes bring greater variety to your writing? If you keep a writing log, you might enter your work in it, noting what you have learned about your use of pronoun case.

9 Using Verbs

Used skillfully, verbs can be the heartbeat of prose, moving it along, enlivening it, carrying its action. Restaurant menus often spotlight verbs in action. One famous place in Boston, for instance, offers to bake, broil, pan-fry, deep-fry, poach, sauté, fricassee, blacken, or scallop any of the fish entrees on its menu. To someone ordering — or cooking — at this restaurant, important distinctions lie behind the verbs.

Verbs are extremely flexible, changing form to indicate tense (*walk, walked*), voice (*gives, is given*), and mood (*he is satisfied, if he were satisfied*). In addition, they can change form to show grammatical agreement with their subjects (*I work, she works*), a topic discussed in Chapter 10. Chapter 54 provides further details about English verbs for multilingual writers. ■

VERB FORMS

Except for be, all English verbs have five possible forms.

BASE FORM	PAST TENSE	PAST PARTICIPLE	PRESENT PARTICIPLE	-S FORM
talk	talked	talked	talking	talks
adore	adored	adored	adoring	adores
jog	jogged	jogged	jogging	jogs

The **base form** is the one listed in the dictionary. For all verbs except *be,* it is the form used to indicate an action or condition that occurs in the present when the subject is a plural noun; the pronoun *I, you, we,* or *they;* or a plural pronoun such as *these* or *many.*

During the ritual, the women *go* into trances.

The **past tense** is used to indicate an action or condition that occurred entirely in the past. For most verbs, it is formed by adding *-ed* or *-d* to the base form. Some verbs, however, have irregular past-tense forms. *Be* has two past-tense forms, *was* and *were.* (See 9b.)

The Globe *was* the stage for many of Shakespeare's works.

In 1613, it *caught* fire and *burned* to the ground.

The **past participle** is used to form perfect tenses, the passive voice (pp. 187 – 188), and adjectives. It usually has the same form as the past tense, though some verbs have irregular past participles. (See 9d – f and 9b.)

EDITING THE VERBS IN YOUR OWN WRITING

- → **Circle all forms of *be, do,* and *have* that you used as main verbs. Try in each case to substitute a stronger, more specific verb. (9a)**
- → **If you have trouble with verb endings, review the rules for using them on pp. 174 and 176.**
- → **Double-check forms of *lie* and *lay, sit* and *set, rise* and *raise.* See that the words you use are appropriate for your meaning. (9c)**
- → **If you have problems with verb tenses, use the guidelines on p. 184.**
- → **If you are writing about a literary work, you should refer to the action in the work in the present tense. (9d)**
- → **Check all uses of the passive voice for appropriateness. (9g)**
- → **Check all verbs used to introduce quotations, paraphrases, and summaries. If you rely on *say, write,* and other very general verbs, try substituting more vivid, specific verbs (*claim, insist, wonder,* for instance). (23a)**

GRAMMAR
Using Verbs

www •

http://www.urich.edu/~writing/concise.htm

A good, downloadable reference sheet gives Richard Lanham's system for identifying and editing out weak verbs.

She *had accomplished* the impossible. [past perfect]

No one *was injured* in the explosion. [passive voice]

Standardized tests usually require *sharpened* pencils. [adjective]

The **present participle** is constructed by adding *-ing* to the base form. Used with auxiliary verbs to indicate a continuing action or condition, it can also function as an adjective or noun (a gerund).

For more about gerunds, see 7c3.

Many students *are competing* in the race. [continuing action]

He tried to comfort the *crying* child. [adjective]

Climbing the mountain took all afternoon. [noun (gerund)]

Except for *be* and *have,* the **-*s* form** consists of the base form plus *-s* or *-es.* This form indicates an action or condition in the present for third-person singular subjects. All singular nouns; *he, she,* and *it;* and many other pronouns (such as *this* and *someone*) are third-person singular.

	SINGULAR	PLURAL
FIRST PERSON	I *wish*	we *wish*
SECOND PERSON	you *wish*	you *wish*
THIRD PERSON	he/she/it *wishes* Joe *wishes* someone *wishes*	they *wish* children *wish* many *wish*

The third-person singular form of *have* is *has.*

EDITING FOR -S AND -ES ENDINGS

If you tend to leave off or misuse the *-s* and *-es* verb endings in academic writing, you should check for them systematically.

1. **Underline every verb, and then circle all verbs in the present tense.**
2. **Find the subject of every verb you circled.**
3. **If the subject is a singular noun; *he, she,* or *it;* or a singular indefinite pronoun, be sure the verb ends in *-s* or *-es.* If the subject is not third-person singular, the verb should not have an *-s* or *-es* ending.**
4. **Be careful with auxiliary verbs such as *can* or *may.* (54d) These auxiliaries are used with the base form, never with the *-s* or *-es* form.**

FORMS OF *BE*

Be has three forms in the present tense (*am, is, are*) and two in the past tense (*was, were*).

Present tense

	SINGULAR	PLURAL
FIRST PERSON	I *am*	we *are*
SECOND PERSON	you *are*	you *are*
THIRD PERSON	he/she/it *is* Jane *is* somebody *is*	they *are* children *are* many *are*

Past tense

	SINGULAR	PLURAL
FIRST PERSON	I *was*	we *were*
SECOND PERSON	you *were*	you *were*
THIRD PERSON	he/she/it *was* Jane *was* somebody *was*	they *were* children *were* many *were*

ABSENCE OF *BE;* HABITUAL *BE*

My sister at work. She be there every day 'til five.

These sentences illustrate two common usages of *be.* The first shows the absence of *be;* the same sentence in standard academic English would read *My sister's at work.* The second shows the use of "habitual *be,*" indicating that something is always or almost always the case. The same sentence in standard academic English would read *She's there every day until five.*

These usages of *be* appear in the discourse of many African American speakers and some southern white speakers. You may have occasion to quote dialogue featuring these patterns in your own writing; doing so can be a good way to evoke particular regions or communities. Most academic writing, however, calls for standard academic English.

For more on using different varieties of English, see Chapter 28.

9a Using auxiliary verbs

Sometimes called helping verbs, **auxiliary verbs** are used with a base form, present participle, or past participle to create verb phrases. The base form or participle in a verb phrase is called the **main verb.** The most common auxiliaries are forms of *have, be,* and *do,* which are used to indicate completed or continuing action, the passive voice, emphasis, questions, and negative statements.

We *have considered* all viewpoints. [completed action]

The college *is building* a new dormitory. [continuing action]

We *were warned* to stay away. [passive voice]

I *do respect* your viewpoint. [emphasis]

Do you *know* the answer? [question]

He *does* not *like* wearing a tie. [negative statement]

Modal auxiliaries – *can, could, might, may, must, ought to, shall, will, should, would* – indicate future action, possibility, necessity, obligation, and so on.

They *will explain* the procedure. [future action]

You *can see* three states from the top of the mountain. [possibility]

I *must try* harder to go to bed early. [necessity]

She *should visit* her parents more often. [obligation]

FOR MULTILINGUAL WRITERS

USING MODAL AUXILIARIES

Why do we not say "Alice can to read Latin"? For discussion of *can* and other modal auxiliaries, see 54d.

9b Using regular and irregular verbs

A verb is **regular** when its past tense and past participle are formed by adding *-ed* or *-d* to the base form.

BASE FORM	PAST TENSE	PAST PARTICIPLE
love	loved	loved
honor	honored	honored
obey	obeyed	obeyed

EDITING FOR -ED OR -D ENDINGS

Speakers who skip over the *-ed* or *-d* endings in conversation may forget to include them in standard academic writing. If you tend to drop these endings, make a point of systematically checking for them when proofreading. Underline all the verbs, and then underline a second time any that are past tense or past participles. Check each of these for an *-ed* or *-d* ending. Unless the verb is irregular (see list following), it should end in *-ed* or *-d.*

Irregular verbs

A verb is **irregular** when it does not follow the *-ed* or *-d* pattern. If you are unsure about whether a verb is regular or irregular, or what the correct form is, consult the following list or a dictionary. Dictionaries list any irregular forms under the entry for the base form.

SOME COMMON IRREGULAR VERBS

BASE FORM	PAST TENSE	PAST PARTICIPLE
arise	arose	arisen
be	was/were	been
bear	bore	borne, born
beat	beat	beaten
become	became	become
begin	began	begun
bite	bit	bitten, bit
blow	blew	blown
break	broke	broken
bring	brought	brought
broadcast	broadcast	broadcast
build	built	built
burn	burned, burnt	burned, burnt
burst	burst	burst

BASE FORM	PAST TENSE	PAST PARTICIPLE
buy	bought	bought
catch	caught	caught
choose	chose	chosen
come	came	come
cost	cost	cost
cut	cut	cut
dig	dug	dug
dive	dived, dove	dived
do	did	done
draw	drew	drawn
dream	dreamed, dreamt	dreamed, dreamt
drink	drank	drunk
drive	drove	driven
eat	ate	eaten
fall	fell	fallen
feel	felt	felt
fight	fought	fought
find	found	found
fly	flew	flown
forget	forgot	forgotten, forgot
freeze	froze	frozen
get	got	gotten, got
give	gave	given
go	went	gone
grow	grew	grown
hang (suspend)[1]	hung	hung
have	had	had
hear	heard	heard
hide	hid	hidden
hit	hit	hit
keep	kept	kept
know	knew	known
lay	laid	laid

[1] *Hang* meaning "execute by hanging" is regular: *hang, hanged, hanged.*

BASE FORM	PAST TENSE	PAST PARTICIPLE
lead	led	led
leave	left	left
lend	lent	lent
let	let	let
lie (recline)[2]	lay	lain
lose	lost	lost
make	made	made
mean	meant	meant
meet	met	met
pay	paid	paid
prove	proved	proved, proven
put	put	put
read	read	read
ride	rode	ridden
ring	rang	rung
rise	rose	risen
run	ran	run
say	said	said
see	saw	seen
send	sent	sent
set	set	set
shake	shook	shaken
shoot	shot	shot
show	showed	showed, shown
shrink	shrank	shrunk
sing	sang	sung
sink	sank	sunk
sit	sat	sat
sleep	slept	slept
speak	spoke	spoken
spend	spent	spent
spread	spread	spread

[2]*Lie* meaning "tell a falsehood" is regular: *lie, lied, lied.*

BASE FORM	PAST TENSE	PAST PARTICIPLE
spring	sprang, sprung	sprung
stand	stood	stood
steal	stole	stolen
strike	struck	struck, stricken
swim	swam	swum
swing	swung	swung
take	took	taken
teach	taught	taught
tear	tore	torn
tell	told	told
think	thought	thought
throw	threw	thrown
wake	woke, waked	waked, woken
wear	wore	worn
win	won	won
wind	wound	wound
write	wrote	written

EXERCISE 9.1

Complete each of the following sentences by filling in each blank with the past tense or past participle of the verb listed in parentheses. Example:

They had already *eaten* (eat) the entree; later they *ate* (eat) the dessert.

1. Clearly this short story would not have _______ (be) so effective if it had been _______ (write) in the third person.
2. After she had _______ (make) her decision, she _______ (find) that the constant anxiety was no longer a factor in her daily life.
3. The process of hazing _______ (begin) soon after fraternities were formed.
4. Hearns _______ (lose) control of the fight, and Nolan _______ (take) advantage of this loss.
5. When Maria Callas _______ (make) her debut at the Metropolitan Opera, some people _______ (know) that music history was being made.
6. Katherine Dunn, a novelist who _______ (choose) thorny subjects, has now _______ (become) a cult figure.
7. Marisol _______ (shake) her head; she had _______ (bring) the evidence to disprove John's claim.

8. Roberto had _______ (throw) his hat into the ring and had assembled the best advisors he had _______ (be) able to find.
9. When Charles admitted that he had _______ (break) into the apartment, he said that he had _______ (lose) his keys.
10. I discovered that I had _______ (fall) into a rut; for several months I had neither _______ (break) my routines nor _______ (do) anything new.

9c Using *lie* and *lay*, *sit* and *set*, *rise* and *raise*

Three pairs of verbs – *lie* and *lay, sit* and *set,* and *rise* and *raise* – cause problems for many writers because both verbs in each pair have similar-sounding forms and somewhat related meanings. In each pair, one of the verbs is **transitive,** meaning that it takes a direct object; the other is **intransitive,** meaning that it does not take an object. The best way to avoid confusing the two is to memorize their forms and meanings – or to use synonyms. All these verbs except *raise* are irregular.

BASE FORM	PAST TENSE	PAST PARTICIPLE	PRESENT PARTICIPLE	-S FORM
lie	lay	lain	lying	lies
lay	laid	laid	laying	lays
sit	sat	sat	sitting	sits
set	set	set	setting	sets
rise	rose	risen	rising	rises
raise	raised	raised	raising	raises

Lie is intransitive and means "recline" or "be situated." *Lay* is transitive and means "put" or "place." This pair is especially confusing because *lay* is also the past-tense form of *lie.*

INTRANSITIVE He *lay* on the floor unable to move.

TRANSITIVE I *laid* the package on the counter.

Sit is intransitive and means "be seated." *Set* usually is transitive and means "put" or "place."

INTRANSITIVE She *sat* in the rocking chair, daydreaming.

TRANSITIVE She *set* the vase on the table.

Rise is intransitive and means "get up" or "go up." *Raise* is transitive and means "lift" or "cause to go up."

INTRANSITIVE He *rose* up in bed and glared at me.

TRANSITIVE He *raised* himself to a sitting position.

EXERCISE 9.2

Choose the appropriate verb form in each of the following sentences.

1. Sometimes she just (*lies/lays*) and stares at the ceiling.
2. He used whatever was (*lying/laying*) around the house.
3. I (*sat/set*) back, closed my eyes, and began to meditate.
4. (*Sitting/Setting*) in the sun too long can lead to skin cancer.
5. The Federal Reserve Bank is planning to (*rise/raise*) interest rates.

VERB TENSES

Tenses show when the action or condition expressed by a verb occurs. The three *simple tenses* are present tense, past tense, and future tense.

PRESENT TENSE	I *ask*
PAST TENSE	I *asked*
FUTURE TENSE	I *will ask*

More complex aspects of time are expressed through *progressive, perfect,* and *perfect progressive forms* of the simple tenses. Although such terminology sounds complicated, you regularly use all these forms.

PRESENT PERFECT	she *has asked*
PAST PERFECT	she *had asked*
FUTURE PERFECT	she *will have asked*
PRESENT PROGRESSIVE	she *is asking*
PAST PROGRESSIVE	she *was asking*
FUTURE PROGRESSIVE	she *will be asking*
PRESENT PERFECT PROGRESSIVE	she *has been asking*
PAST PERFECT PROGRESSIVE	she *had been asking*
FUTURE PERFECT PROGRESSIVE	she *will have been asking*

The perfect form of each tense expresses the idea of a *completed* action or condition in the present, past, or future; and the progressive form expresses the idea of a *continuing* action or condition. Finally, the perfect progressive form expresses the idea of an action or condition that *continues up to some point* in the present, past, or future.

9d Using the present-tense forms

The **simple present** indicates actions or conditions occurring at the time of speaking as well as those occurring habitually. In addition, with appropriate time expressions, the simple present can be used to indicate a scheduled future event.

They *are* very angry about the decision.

I *eat* breakfast every day at 8:00 A.M.

Love *conquers* all.

Classes *begin* next week.

General truths or scientific facts should be in the simple present, even when the predicate of the sentence is in the past tense.

▶ **Pasteur demonstrated that his boiling process ~~made~~ *makes* milk safe.**

Use the simple present, not the past tense, when writing about action in literary works.

▶ **Ishmael slowly ~~came~~ *comes* to realize all that ~~was~~ *is* at stake in the search for the white whale.**

In general, use the simple present when you are quoting, summarizing, or paraphrasing someone else's writing.

▶ **Keith Walters ~~wrote~~ *writes* that the "reputed consequences and promised blessings of literacy are legion."**

But in an essay using APA (American Psychological Association) style, the reporting of your experiments or another researcher's work should be in the past tense (*wrote, noted*) or the present perfect (*has reported*).

For more examples of APA style, see the essay at the end of Chapter 45.

▶ **Comer (1995) ~~notes~~ *noted* that protesters who deprive themselves of food (for example, Gandhi and Dick Gregory) are seen not as dysfunctional but rather as "caring, sacrificing, even heroic" (p. 5).**

The **present progressive** indicates actions or conditions that are ongoing or continuous in the present. It is typically used to describe an action that is happening at the moment of speaking, in contrast to the simple present, which more often indicates habitual actions.

PRESENT PROGRESSIVE	You *are driving* too fast.
SIMPLE PRESENT	I always *drive* carefully.

With an appropriate expression of time, the present progressive can also be used to indicate a scheduled event in the future.

We *are having* friends over for dinner tomorrow night.

The **present perfect** indicates actions or conditions begun in the past and either completed at some unspecified time in the past or continuing into the present.

Uncontrolled logging *has destroyed* many tropical forests.

The **present perfect progressive** indicates actions or conditions begun in the past and continuing into the present.

The two sides *have been trying* to settle the case out of court.

9e Using the past-tense forms

The **simple past** indicates actions or conditions that occurred at a specific time and do not extend into the present.

Germany *invaded* Poland on September 1, 1939.

The **past progressive** indicates continuing actions or conditions in the past, often with specified limits.

Lenin *was living* in exile in Zurich when the czar was overthrown.

The **past perfect** indicates actions or conditions completed by a specific time in the past or before some other past action occurred.

By the fourth century, Christianity *had become* the state religion.

The **past perfect progressive** indicates continuing actions or conditions in the past that began before a specific time or before some other past action began.

Carter *had been planning* a naval career until his father died.

9f Using the future-tense forms

The **simple future** indicates actions or conditions that have not yet begun.

The exhibition *will come* to Washington in September.

The **future progressive** indicates continuing actions or conditions in the future.

The loans *will be coming* due in the next two years.

The **future perfect** indicates actions or conditions that will be completed by or before some specified time in the future.

In ten years, the original investment *will have doubled.*

The **future perfect progressive** indicates continuing actions or conditions that will be completed by some specified time in the future.

In May, I *will have been living* in Tucson for five years.

EDITING VERB TENSES

Errors in verb tenses take several forms. If you have trouble with verb tenses, make a point of checking for these common errors as you proofread.

→ Errors of verb form: writing *seen* for *saw,* for example, which is an instance of confusing the past participle and past-tense forms (9b)
→ Omission of auxiliary verbs; for example, using the simple past (*Uncle Charlie arrived*) when meaning requires the present perfect (*Uncle Charlie has arrived*) (9d and e)
→ Other errors that result from using a regional or ethnic variety of English (*she nervous*) in situations calling for standard academic English (*she is nervous*). (See p. 175 and Chapter 28.)

EXERCISE 9.3

Complete each of the following sentences by filling in the blank with an appropriate form of the verb listed in parentheses. Since more than one form will sometimes be possible, be prepared to explain the reasons for your choices.

1. In spite of the poor turnout for today's referendum, local officials _______ (expect) the bond issue to pass.
2. Ever since the first nuclear power plants were built, opponents _______ (predict) disaster.
3. Thousands of Irish peasants _______ (emigrate) to America after the potato famine of the 1840s.
4. The newspaper _______ (arrive) late every day this week.
5. The committee _______ (meet) again next week.
6. President Kennedy was shot while he _______ (ride) in a limousine.
7. By eleven o'clock this morning, stock prices _______ (fall) fifteen points.
8. By the time a child born today enters first grade, he or she _______ (watch) thousands of television commercials.
9. In "The Road Not Taken," the poet _______ (come) to a fork in the road.
10. The supply of a product _______ (rise) when the demand is great.

9g Using verb tenses in sequence

Because tense is crucial to our understanding of when actions occur and because time relationships can be very complex, careful and accurate use of tenses is important to clear writing. Even the simplest narrative describes actions that take place at different times; using particular tenses for particular actions allows readers to follow such time changes readily.

The relationship between the tense of the verb in the independent clause of a sentence and the tense of a verb in a dependent clause or a verbal is called the **sequence of tenses.** Even though in general you can use almost any sequence of tenses, in a particular sentence the tense of the verb in a dependent clause or a verbal is limited by the meaning and by conventions about particular sequences.

1 Verb sequence with infinitives

The infinitive of a verb is *to* plus the base form (*to go, to be*). Use the **present infinitive** to indicate actions occurring at the same time as or later than the action of the predicate verb.

▶ **I *wanted to swim* in the ocean last summer.**

The wanting and the (imagined) swimming occurred at the same time in the past.

▶ **I *expect to swim* in the ocean next summer.**

The expecting is present; the swimming is in the future.

Use the **perfect infinitive** (*to have* plus the past participle) to indicate actions occurring before the action of the predicate verb.

He *was reported to have left* his fortune to his cat. [The leaving of the fortune took place before the reporting.]

2 Verb sequence with participles

Use the **present participle** (base form plus *-ing*) to indicate actions occurring at the same time as that of the predicate verb.

Seeking to relieve unemployment, Roosevelt *established* several public-works programs.

Use the **past participle** or the **present perfect participle** (*having* plus the past participle) to indicate action occurring before that of the predicate verb.

Flown to the front, the troops *joined* their hard-pressed comrades.

Having crushed all opposition at home, he *launched* a war of conquest.

3 Verb sequence and habitual actions

In conversation, people often use *will* or *would* to describe habitual actions. In writing, however, stick to the present and past tenses for this purpose.

▶ **When I have a deadline, I ~~will~~ work all night.**

▶ **While we sat on the porch, the children ~~would play.~~** *played.*

EXERCISE 9.4

Edit each of the following sentences to create the appropriate sequence of tenses.

He needs to ~~send~~ *have sent* in his application before today.

1. When he was twenty-one, he wanted to have become a millionaire by the age of thirty.
2. Leaving England in December, the settlers arrived in Virginia in May.
3. They hoped to plant their garden by now.
4. Cutting off contact with his family, he did not know whom to ask for help.
5. When he was in the shower, he would not hear the doorbell.

VOICE

Voice is the feature of transitive verbs that tells whether the subject is acting (*he questions us*) or being acted upon (*he is questioned*). When the subject is acting, the verb is in the **active voice;** when the subject is being acted upon, the verb is in the **passive voice.** The passive voice is formed, as in this sentence, by using the appropriate form of the auxiliary verb *be* followed by the past participle of the main verb: he *is being questioned,* he *was questioned,* he *will be questioned,* he *has been questioned.*

www •

http://www.io.com/~eighner/qa050152.html

This essay by Lars Eighner suggests a hierarchy for distinguishing weak from strong verbs.

Most contemporary writers use the active voice as much as possible because it makes prose more *active,* more lively. When passive-voice verbs pile up in a passage, that passage will generally be hard to understand and remember. In addition, writers sometimes use the passive voice to try to avoid taking responsibility for what they have written. A university president who announces that "it is recommended that fees rise substantially" skirts the pressing question: recommended by whom?

In spite of such questionable uses, however, the passive voice can work to good advantage in some situations. Reporters often use the passive voice to protect the confidentiality of their sources, as in the familiar phrase *it is reported that.* The passive voice is also appropriate when the performer of an action is unknown or less important than the recipient, as in the following passage:

> DALLAS, Nov. 22 – President John Fitzgerald Kennedy was shot and killed by an assassin today.
>
> He died of a wound in the brain caused by a rifle bullet that was fired at him as he was riding through downtown Dallas in a motorcade.
>
> Vice President Lyndon Baines Johnson, who was riding in the third car behind Mr. Kennedy's, was sworn in as the 36th President of the United States 99 minutes after Mr. Kennedy's death.
>
> – TOM WICKER, *New York Times*

Wicker uses the passive voice with good reason: to focus on Kennedy, not on who killed him, and on Johnson, not on who swore him in.

Much technical and scientific writing uses the passive voice effectively to highlight what is being studied rather than who is doing the studying. Look at the following example, from a description of geological movement:

> The Earth's plates are created where they separate and are recycled where they collide, in a continuous process of creation and destruction.
>
> – FRANK PRESS AND RAYMOND SIEVER, *Understanding Earth*

If you use the passive voice a great deal, however, practice shifting some of your sentences to the active voice. To do so, convert the subject of the verb into a direct or indirect object, and make the performer of the action into the subject.

For more about active and passive voice, see 14c and 23b.

The alarm clock *me*
► **~~I was~~ awakened ^ promptly at seven. ~~by the alarm clock.~~**

EXERCISE 9.5

Convert each sentence from active to passive voice or from passive to active, and note the differences in emphasis these changes make. Example:

Machiavelli advises the prince to gain the friendship of the people.

The prince **is advised by** Machiavelli to gain the friendship of the people.

1. Huge pine trees were uprooted by the storm.
2. Marianne avoided such things as elevators, subways, and closets.
3. For months, the baby kangaroo is protected, fed, and taught how to survive by its mother.
4. The lawns and rooftops were covered with the first snow of winter.
5. Flannery O'Connor employs the images of both a boxcar and a swinging bridge to show the inconsistencies between Mrs. Turpin's classification of people and God's classification of people.

EXERCISE 9.6

Look at several essays you have written recently or pieces of writing by others that you particularly like, and find examples of both the active voice and the passive voice. Convert each of the examples to the other voice, and note the difference in emphasis and rhythm the changes make.

MOOD

The **mood** of a verb indicates the attitude of the writer toward what he or she is saying or writing. Different moods are used to express a fact, opinion, or inquiry (**indicative mood**); a command or request (**impera-**

tive mood); or a wish, suggestion, requirement, or condition contrary to fact (**subjunctive mood**).

INDICATIVE I *did* the right thing.

IMPERATIVE *Do* the right thing.

SUBJUNCTIVE If I *had done* the right thing, I would not be in trouble now.

9h Using the subjunctive

The **present subjunctive** uses the base form.

It is important that children *be* psychologically ready for a new sibling.

The **past subjunctive** is the same as the past tense except for the verb *be,* which uses *were* for all subjects.

He spent money as if he *had* infinite credit.

If the store *were* better located, it would attract more customers.

Because the subjunctive can create a rather formal tone, many people today tend to substitute the indicative in informal conversation.

If I *was* a better typist, I would type my own papers.

Nevertheless, formal writing still requires the use of the subjunctive in the following kinds of dependent clauses:

Clauses expressing a wish

He wished that his mother *were* still living nearby.

If *clauses expressing a condition that does not exist*

If the sale of tobacco *were* banned, tobacco companies would suffer a great loss.

One common error is to use *would* in both clauses. Use the subjunctive in the *if* clause and *would* in the main clause.

► **If I ~~would have~~ *had* played harder, I would have won.**

As if *and* as though *clauses*

He started down the trail as if he *were walking* on thin ice.

FOR MULTILINGUAL WRITERS

USING THE SUBJUNCTIVE

"If you practiced writing every day, it would eventually seem much easier to you." For discussion of this and other uses of the subjunctive, see 56f.

- **That *clauses expressing a demand, request, requirement, or suggestion***

The job demands that the employee *be* in good physical condition.

EXERCISE 9.7

Revise any of the following sentences that do not use the appropriate subjunctive verb forms required in formal writing. Example:

> I saw how carefully he moved, as if he ~~was~~ *were* caring for an infant.

1. Her stepsisters treated Cinderella as though she was a servant.
2. Hamlet wishes he was not responsible for avenging his murdered father.
3. Freud recommended that an analyst use dreams as a means of studying the human personality.
4. If more money was available, we would be able to offer more scholarships.
5. It is necessary that the manager knows how to do any job in the store.

THINKING CRITICALLY ABOUT VERBS

Reading with an Eye for Verbs

Some years ago a newspaper in San Francisco ran the headline "Giants Crush Cardinals, 3–1," provoking the following friendly advice from John Updike about the art of baseball-headline verbs:

> The correct verb, San Francisco, is *whip*. Notice the vigor, force, and scorn obtained. . . . [These examples] may prove helpful: 3–1 — *whip,* 3–2 — *shade,* 2–1 — *edge.* 4–1 gets the coveted verb *vanquish.* Rule: Any three-run margin, *provided the winning total does not exceed ten,* may be described as a vanquishing.

Double-digit scores, Updike continues, merit such verbs as *annihilate, obliterate,* and *humiliate.* (Thus, "A's Annihilate O's, 13–2.") And if the home team is on the short end of the score, *shade* should become *squeak by.* Finally, Updike advises, use of *bow* (A's bow to O's) can allow the home team, while losing, "to be given the active position in the sentence and an appearance of graciousness as well."

Take the time to study a newspaper with an eye for its verbs. Copy down several examples of strong verbs as well as a few examples of weak or overused verbs. For the weak ones, try to come up with better choices.

Thinking about Your Own Use of Verbs

Writing that relies too heavily on the verbs *be, do,* and *have* almost always bores readers. Look at something you've written recently to see whether you rely too heavily on these verbs, and revise accordingly.

Maintaining Subject-Verb Agreement

10

In everyday terms, the word *agreement* refers to an accord of some sort: you reach an agreement with your boss about salary; friends agree to go to a movie; the members of a family agree to share household chores; the United States and Korea negotiate an agreement about nuclear arms. This meaning covers grammatical agreement as well. In academic varieties of English, verbs must agree with their subjects in number (singular or plural) and in person (first, second, or third). In practice, only a very few subject-verb constructions cause confusion. This chapter will look at those constructions in some detail. ■

10a Making verbs agree with third-person singular subjects

To make a verb in the present tense agree with a third-person singular subject, add *-s* or *-es* to the base form.

A vegetarian diet *lowers* the risk of heart disease.

To make a verb in the present tense agree with any other subject, use the base form of the verb.

I *miss* my family.

They *live* in another state.

Have and *be* do not follow the *-s* or *-es* pattern with third-person singular subjects. *Have* changes to *has; be* has irregular forms in both the present and past tenses and in the first person as well as the third person. (See Chapter 9.)

War *is* hell.

The soldier *was* brave beyond the call of duty.

In some varieties of African American English and some regional white English, third-person singular verb forms do not end with *-s* or *-es.*

She *go* to work seven days a week.

He *don't* take it to heart.

→ Check your drafts verb by verb, and identify the subject that goes with each verb.

▶ **The players on our side ~~is~~ *are* sure to win.**

Because the simple subject here is *players,* the verb needs to be *are.* When you take away the words between the subject and the verb, it is easier to identify agreement problems. (10b)

→ Check compound subjects. Those joined by *and* usually take a plural verb form. With those subjects joined by *or* or *nor,* however, the verb agrees with the part of the subject closest to the verb. *Neither the parents nor Claire plans to vote.* (10c)

→ Check collective-noun subjects. These nouns take a singular verb form when they refer to a group as a single unit but a plural form when they refer to the multiple members of a group. *The crowd screams its support. The team are wearing new uniforms.* (10d)

→ Check indefinite-pronoun subjects. Most take a singular verb form. *Both, few, many, others,* and *several* take a plural form; and *all, any, enough, more, most, none,* and *some* can be either singular or plural, depending on the noun they refer to. *Each of the singers rehearses for three hours daily. Most of the land was forested. Most of the people were farmers.* (10e)

In standard academic English, these verb forms are *she goes* and *he doesn't.* You will often see verb forms such as those in the preceding sentences in African American literature, especially in dialogue, and you may quote passages using these varieties of English in your own writing. In most academic writing, however, use the *-s* or *-es.*

10b Making subjects and verbs agree when separated by other words

Sometimes the simple subject is separated from the verb by other words. Make sure the verb agrees with the subject and not with another noun that falls in between.

A vase of flowers makes a room attractive.

▶ **Many books on the best-seller list ~~has~~ [have] little literary value.**

The simple subject is *books,* not *list.*

Be careful when you use phrases beginning with *as well as, along with, in addition to, together with,* or similar prepositions. They do not make a singular subject plural.

The president, along with many senators, *opposes* the bill.

▶ **A passenger, as well as the driver, ~~were~~ [was] injured in the accident.**

Though this sentence has a grammatically singular subject, it suggests the idea of a plural subject. The sentence makes better sense with a compound subject: *The driver and a passenger were injured in the accident.*

EXERCISE 10.1

Underline the appropriate verb form in each of the following sentences. Example:

The benefits of family planning (*is/are*) not apparent to many peasants.

1. Starving children and world peace (*is/are*) two of my concerns.
2. Dershowitz, together with his aide, (*presents/present*) a cogent argument.
3. Walls of glass (*characterizes/characterize*) much modern architecture.
4. The system of sororities and fraternities (*supplies/supply*) much of the social life on some college campuses.
5. The buck (*stops/stop*) here.
6. The soldiers, along with their commanding officer, (*was/were*) cited for bravery beyond the call of duty.
7. In many species, the male as well as the female (*cares/care*) for the offspring.
8. He (*holds/hold*) a controlling interest in the company.
9. The author of those stories (*writes/write*) beautifully.
10. Current research on AIDS, in spite of the best efforts of hundreds of scientists, (*leaves/leave*) serious questions unanswered.

www •

http://myst.hunter.cuny.edu/~rwcenter/writing/on-line/sva.html

A downloadable exercise from the Hunter College Writing Center *offers three ways to practice subject-verb agreement.*

10c Making verbs agree with compound subjects

Two or more subjects joined by *and* generally require a plural verb form.

Tony and his friend *commute* from Louisville.

▶ **A backpack, a canteen, and a rifle ~~was~~ *were* issued to each recruit.**

When subjects joined by *and* are considered a single unit or refer to the same person or thing, they take a singular verb form.

John Kennedy's closest friend and political ally *was* his brother.

▶ **Drinking and driving ~~remain~~ *remains* a major cause of highway fatalities.**

In this sentence, *drinking and driving* is considered a single activity, and a singular verb is used.

If the word *each* or *every* precedes subjects joined by *and,* the verb form is singular.

Each boy and girl *chooses* one gift to take home.

With subjects joined by *or* or *nor,* the verb agrees with the part closest to the verb.

Neither my roommate nor my neighbors *like* my loud music.

▶ **Either the witnesses or the defendant ~~are~~ *is* lying.**

If you find this sentence awkward, put the plural noun closest to the verb: *Either the defendant or the witnesses are lying.*

▶ **Either you or I ~~are~~ *am* wrong.**

10d Making verbs agree with subjects that are collective nouns or fractions

Collective nouns — such as *family, team, audience, group, jury, crowd, band, class,* and *committee* — refer to a group. Collective nouns can take either singular or plural verb forms, depending on whether they refer to the group as a single unit or to the multiple members of the group. The meaning of a sentence as a whole is your guide to whether a collective noun refers to a unit or to the multiple parts of a unit.

After deliberating, the jury *reports* its verdict.

The jury acts as a single unit.

The jury still *disagree* on a number of counts.

The members of the jury act as multiple individuals.

▶ **The family of ducklings ~~scatters~~ *scatter* when the cat approaches.**

Family here refers to the many ducks; they cannot scatter as one.

Treat fractions that refer to singular nouns as singular and those that refer to plural nouns as plural.

SINGULAR Two-thirds of the park *has* burned.

PLURAL Two-thirds of the students *were* commuters.

Treat phrases starting with *the number of* as singular and with *a number of* as plural.

SINGULAR The number of applicants for the internship *was* unbelievable.

PLURAL A number of applicants *were* put on the waiting list.

10e Making verbs agree with indefinite-pronoun subjects

Indefinite pronouns are those that do not refer to specific persons or things. Most take singular verb forms.

SOME COMMON INDEFINITE PRONOUNS

another	each	much	one
any	either	neither	other
anybody	everybody	nobody	somebody
anyone	everyone	no one	someone
anything	everything	nothing	something

Of the two jobs, neither *holds* much appeal.

▶ **Each of the plays ~~depict~~ *depicts* a hero undone by a tragic flaw.**

Both, few, many, others, and *several* are plural.

Though many *apply,* few *are* chosen.

▶ **Several articles in today's newspaper ~~contains~~ *contain* references to the deficit.**

All, any, enough, more, most, none, and *some* can be singular or plural, depending on the noun they refer to.

All of the cake *was* eaten.

All of the candidates *promise* to improve the schools.

10f Making verbs agree with the antecedents of *who, which,* and *that*

When the relative pronouns *who, which,* and *that* are used as a subject, the verb agrees with the antecedent of the pronoun.

Fear is an ingredient that *goes* into creating stereotypes.

Guilt, jealousy, and fear are ingredients that *go* into creating stereotypes.

Problems often occur with the words *one of the.* In general, *one of the* takes a plural verb, while *only one of the* takes a singular verb.

▶ **Carla is one of the employees who always ~~works~~ *work* overtime.**

Some employees always work overtime. Carla is among them. Thus *who* refers to *employees,* and the verb is plural.

▶ **Sam is the only one of the employees who always ~~work~~ *works* overtime.**

Only one employee always works overtime, and that employee is Sam. Thus *one,* and not *employees,* is the antecedent of *who,* and the verb form is singular.

10g Making linking verbs agree with their subjects, not their complements

A linking verb should agree with its subject, which usually precedes the verb, not with the subject complement, which follows it.

For an explanation of subject complements, see 7c2.

▶ **The signings of three key treaties ~~is~~ *are* the topic of my talk.**

The subject is *signings,* not *topic.*

▶ **Nero Wolfe's passion ~~were~~ *was* orchids.**

The subject is *passion,* not *orchids.*

10h Making verbs agree with subjects that are plural in form but singular in meaning

Some words that end in *-s* seem to be plural but are singular in meaning and thus take singular verb forms.

▶ **Measles still ~~strike~~ *strikes* many Americans.**

Some nouns of this kind (such as *statistics* and *politics*) may be either singular or plural, depending on context.

SINGULAR Statistics *is* a course I really dread.

PLURAL The statistics in that study *are* highly questionable.

10i Making verbs agree with subjects that follow them

In English, verbs usually follow subjects. When this order is reversed, it is easy to become confused. Make the verb agree with the subject, not with a noun that happens to precede it.

▶ **Beside the barn ~~stands~~ *stand* silos filled with grain.**

The subject is *silos;* it is plural, so the verb must be *stand.*

In sentences beginning with *there is* or *there are* (or *there was, there have been,* and so on), *there* serves only as an introductory word; the subject follows the verb.

There *are* five basic positions in classical ballet.

The subject, *positions,* is plural, so the verb must also be plural.

10j Making verbs agree with titles and words used as words

When the subject is the title of a book, film, or other work of art, the verb form is singular even if the title is plural in form.

One Writer's Beginnings describes Eudora Welty's childhood.

Similarly, a word referred to as a word requires a singular verb form even if the word itself is plural.

Steroids is a little word that packs a big punch in the world of sports.

www • http://webster.commnet.edu/hp/pages/darling/grammar_original.htm

Go to the Grammar and Writing Page *at Capital Community-Technical College, and click on* *Quiz on Subject-Verb Agreement.*

EXERCISE 10.2

Revise any of the following sentences as necessary to establish subject-verb agreement. (Some of the sentences do not require any change.) Example:

Into the shadows ~~dart~~ *darts* the frightened raccoon.

1. Every check and money order cost fifty cents.
2. Talking and getting up from my seat was my crime.
3. If rhythm and blues is your kind of music, try Mary Lou's.
4. His merry disposition and his success in business make him popular.
5. *The vapors* were a Victorian term for hypochondria.
6. Neither the lighting nor the frame display the painting well.
7. In the foreground is two women playing musical instruments.
8. Most of the voters support a reduction in nuclear weapons.
9. Each of the entrants rehearse for a minimum of three hours daily.
10. Neither her manner nor her tantrums intimidates the staff.
11. The audience always respond to Pavarotti.
12. My grandmother is the only one of my relatives who still goes to church.
13. *Our Tapes* were one of Fitzgerald's earlier titles for *Tender Is the Night.*
14. Sweden was one of the few European countries that was neutral in 1943.
15. Politics have been defined as the art of the possible.

THINKING CRITICALLY ABOUT SUBJECT-VERB AGREEMENT

Reading with an Eye for Subject-Verb Agreement

The following passage, from a 1990 essay questioning suggestions that our society is returning to more traditional values, especially marriage, includes several instances of complicated subject-verb agreement. Read the passage, paying close attention to the subjects and verbs and noting the rules governing subject-verb agreement in each case.

> For me, none of [these assumptions about marriage] add up. Between the public statistic and the private reality lies a sea of contradiction in which these pronouncements drown. Marriage seems to me more conflict-ridden than ever, and the divorce rate — with or without new babies in the house — remains constant. The fabric of men-and-women-as-they-once-were is so thin in places no amount of patching can weave that cloth together again. The longing for connection may be strong, but even stronger is the growing perception that only people who are real to themselves can connect. Two shall be as one is over, no matter how lonely we get.
>
> – Vivian Gornick, "Who Says We Haven't Made a Revolution?"

Thinking about Your Own Use of Subject-Verb Agreement

Visiting relatives is/are treacherous. Either of these verbs makes a grammatically acceptable sentence, agreeing with a subject, yet they result in two very different statements. Write a brief explanation of the two possible meanings. Then write a paragraph or two about visiting relatives. Using the information in this chapter, examine each subject and its verb. Have you maintained subject-verb agreement throughout? Revise to correct any errors you find, and then look for any patterns in your writing. If you find any, make a note to yourself (in a writing log, if you keep one) of things to look for routinely as you revise your writing.

11 Maintaining Pronoun-Antecedent Agreement

Pronouns "are tricky rather than difficult," says H. W. Fowler in *A Dictionary of Modern English Usage.* The "trickiness" Fowler notes comes primarily from the fact that pronouns usually stand in for another word, a noun or some other pronoun, called the *antecedent.* Making sure that the pronoun and its antecedent match up, or agree, is a task every writer faces.

Like a verb with its subject, a pronoun must agree with its antecedent in person and number. In addition, a third-person singular pronoun must agree with its antecedent in *gender* — masculine, feminine, or neuter. Fortunately, only a few kinds of antecedents cause problems with agreement. ■

11a Making pronouns agree with compound antecedents

A compound antecedent whose parts are joined by *and* requires a plural pronoun.

My parents and I tried to resolve *our* disagreement.

When a compound antecedent is preceded by *each* or *every,* however, it takes a singular pronoun.

Every plant and animal has *its* own ecological niche.

With a compound antecedent whose parts are joined by *or* or *nor,* the pronoun agrees with the nearest antecedent. If the parts of the antecedent are of different genders or persons, however, this kind of sentence can be awkward.

AWKWARD Neither Annie nor Barry got *his* work done.

REVISED Annie didn't get *her* work done, and neither did Barry.

With compound antecedents containing both singular and plural parts, the sentence may sound awkward unless a plural part comes last.

▶ **Neither the ~~radio stations~~ *newspaper* nor the ~~newspaper~~ *radio stations* would reveal ~~its~~ *their* sources.**

- → Check any subjects joined by *and, or,* or *nor* to be sure they are treated as singular or plural as appropriate. (11a) Recast any sentence in which agreement creates awkwardness.
- → Check any use of *anyone, each, everybody, many,* and other indefinite pronouns (see list in 10e) to be sure they are treated as singular or plural as appropriate. (11c)
- → If you find *he, his,* or *him* used to refer to persons of either sex, revise the pronouns, or recast the sentences altogether. (11d)

11b Making pronouns agree with collective-noun antecedents

When a collective-noun antecedent (*herd, team, audience*) refers to a single unit, it requires a singular pronoun.

> The audience fixed *its* attention on center stage.

When such an antecedent refers to the multiple parts of the unit, however, it requires a plural pronoun.

> The director chose this cast because *they* had experience in the roles.

Remember that collective nouns referring to single units require not only singular pronouns but also singular verb forms. Collective nouns referring to separate individuals in a unit, on the other hand, require plural pronouns and plural verb forms.

> Each generation *has its* own slang. [*generation* as single unit]
>
> That generation *have* sold *their* souls for money. [*generation* as individuals]

www •

http://www.columbia.edu/acis/bartleby/fowler

The King's English: *Check out the 1908 version of H. W. Fowler's classic work. Scroll the table of contents and click on* *number in the syntax chapter to see what Fowler has to say about pronoun-antecedent agreement.*

11c Making pronouns agree with indefinite-pronoun antecedents

A pronoun whose antecedent is an indefinite pronoun should agree with it in number. Indefinite pronouns may be always singular (as with *one*) or plural (as with *many*), or their number may depend on their context.

For more on indefinite pronouns, see 10e.

One of the ballerinas lost *her* balance.

Many in the audience jumped to *their* feet.

Some of the furniture was showing *its* age. [singular meaning for *some*]

Some of the farmers abandoned *their* land. [plural meaning for *some*]

11d Checking for sexist pronouns

For a list of indefinite pronouns, see 10e; for more on ways to avoid sexist language, see 29b.

Indefinite pronouns often refer to antecedents that may be either male or female. Writers used to use masculine pronouns, known as the generic *he,* in such cases. In recent decades, however, many people have pointed out that such wording ignores or even excludes females – and thus should be avoided.

www

http://vega.lib.vt.edu/ejournals/WILLA/fall94/h2-isele.html

Women Who Dared to Disturb the Lexicon: *an interview with two women who were among the first to question the generic use of* he.

***WAYS OF AVOIDING THE GENERIC USE OF* HE, HIS, *OR* HIM**

Look at the following sentence:

Every citizen should know *his* rights under the law.

Now consider three ways to express the same idea without *his:*

1. **Revise to make the antecedent plural.**

   All citizens should know their *rights under the law.*

2. **Revise the sentence altogether.**

   Everyone should have some knowledge of basic legal rights.

3. **Use both masculine and feminine pronouns.**

   Every citizen should know his or her *rights under the law.*

The last option, using both masculine and feminine pronouns, can be awkward, especially when repeated several times in a passage.

When an antecedent is an indefinite pronoun, such as *anybody* or *each,* some people avoid the generic *he* by using a plural pronoun. For example:

Everybody had *their* own theory about Nancy's resignation.

You will probably hear, and perhaps use, such sentences in conversation, but be careful about using them in writing. Although this usage – *everybody* with the plural pronoun *their* – is fast gaining acceptance, many readers still consider it excessively informal or even incorrect. *Everybody* is grammatically singular and hence calls for a singular pronoun.

EXERCISE 11.1

Revise the following sentences as needed to create pronoun-antecedent agreement and to eliminate the generic *he* and any awkward pronoun references. Some can be revised in more than one way, and some do not require any changes. Example:

Every graduate submitted his diploma card.

Every graduate submitted **his** or **her** diploma card.

All graduates submitted **their** diploma cards.

1. With tuition on the rise, a student has to save money wherever they can.
2. Not everyone gets along with his roommate, but the two can usually manage to tolerate each other temporarily.
3. Congress usually resists presidential attempts to encroach on what they consider their authority.
4. Either Tom or Teresa will always share their opinion.
5. If his own knowledge is all the reader has to go by, how can he identify one source as more reliable than another?
6. Every house and apartment has their advantages and their drawbacks.
7. Neither the scouts nor their leader knew their way out of the forest.
8. Our team no longer wears red and white.
9. A candidate attempts to generate favorable publicity about themselves.
10. I often turn on the fan and the light and neglect to turn it off.

THINKING CRITICALLY ABOUT PRONOUN AGREEMENT

Following is a paragraph from *Democracy in America,* Alexis de Tocqueville's classic critique of American institutions and culture, which was first published in 1835. Read the paragraph with an eye for pronouns. Does the use of the masculine pronoun to refer to both men and women seem odd to you? Revise the paragraph to eliminate this generic use of masculine pronouns.

> After the birth of a human being, his early years are obscurely spent in the toils or pleasures of childhood. As he grows up, the world receives him, when his manhood begins, and he enters into contact with his fellows. He is then studied for the first time, and it is imagined that the germ of the vices and the virtues of his maturer years is then formed. This, if I am not mistaken, is a great error. We must begin higher up; we must watch the infant in his mother's arms; we must see the first images which the external world casts upon the dark mirror of his mind, the first occurrences which he witnesses; we must hear the first words which awaken the sleeping powers of thought, and stand by his earliest efforts, — if we would understand the prejudices, the habits, and the passions which will rule his life. The entire man is, so to speak, to be seen in the cradle of the child.
>
> – ALEXIS DE TOCQUEVILLE, *Democracy in America*

12 Using Adjectives and Adverbs

As words that describe other words, adjectives and adverbs add liveliness and color to the flat gray surface of writing, helping writers *show* rather than just tell. See how much Dorothy West relies on them:

> *With a* long blackened fire-place *stick Mama* carefully *tilted the lid of the* three-legged *skillet to see if her cornbread was* done. . . . Gently *she let the lid drop.* . . .
>
> – DOROTHY WEST
> *The Living Is Easy*

Adjectives such as *blackened* and *three-legged* and adverbs such as *carefully* and *gently* create vivid images and a definite impression of West's own attitude about her subject. But adjectives and adverbs can also betray a writer who uses them inappropriately. Like any other part of speech, they usually follow certain rules and conventions. ■

12a Distinguishing adjectives from adverbs

Although adjectives and adverbs both modify other words, each modifies different parts of speech. **Adjectives** modify nouns and pronouns, answering the questions *which? how many?* or *what kind?* **Adverbs** modify verbs, adjectives, other adverbs, or entire clauses; they answer the questions *how? when? where?* or *to what extent?* Many adverbs are formed by adding *-ly* to adjectives (*slight, slightly*), but many are not (*outdoors, very*). And some words that end in *-ly* are adjectives (*lovely, homely*). Since adjectives and adverbs both act as modifiers, often have similar or even the same forms, and in some cases can occupy the same positions in sentences, sometimes the only way of identifying a word as one or the other is to identify its function in the sentence.

12b Using adjectives after linking verbs

When adjectives come after linking verbs, they usually serve as a subject complement, to describe the subject: *I am patient.* Note that in specific sentences, some verbs may or may not be linking verbs – *look, appear, sound, feel, smell, taste, grow,* and *prove,* for instance. When a word following one of these verbs modifies the subject, use an adjective; when it modifies the verb, use an adverb.

1. Scrutinize each adjective and adverb to see whether it is the best word possible. Considering one or two synonyms for each one might help you decide.
2. Is each adjective and adverb really necessary? See if a more specific noun would eliminate the need for an adjective (*mansion* rather than *enormous house,* for instance); do the same with verbs and adverbs.
3. Are there places where adding an adjective or adverb might make your writing more vivid or specific?
4. Do all adjectives modify nouns or pronouns and all adverbs modify verbs, adjectives, or other adverbs? (12a) Check especially for proper use of *good* and *well, bad* and *badly, real* and *really.* (12c)
5. Are all comparisons complete? (12d4)
6. If English is not your first language, check that adjectives are in the right order. (53e)

ADJECTIVE Dennis Rodman looked *angry.*

ADVERB He looked *angrily* at the referee.

Linking verbs suggest a state of being, not an action. In the preceding examples, *looked angry* suggests the state of being angry; *looked angrily* suggests an angry action.

12c Using adverbs to modify verbs, adjectives, and adverbs

In everyday conversation, you will often hear (and perhaps use) adjectives in place of adverbs. When you write in standard academic English, however, use adverbs to modify verbs, adjectives, and other adverbs.

▶ **You can feel the song's meter if you listen ~~careful.~~** *carefully.*

▶ **The audience was ~~real~~** *really* **disappointed by the show.**

GRAMMAR

Using Adverbs to Modify Verbs, Adjectives, and Adverbs

www •

http://english-www.hss.cmu.edu/langs/politics-english-language.txt

George Orwell's "Politics and the English Language." You can download this classic essay for Orwell's advice on adjectives, and also as a text well worth examining. Read closely to see if Orwell follows his own advice.

FOR MULTILINGUAL WRITERS

DETERMINING ADJECTIVE SEQUENCE

Should you write *these beautiful old-fashioned kitchen tiles* or *these old-fashioned beautiful kitchen tiles?* See 53e for guidelines on adjective sequence in English sentences.

Good and *well*, *bad* and *badly*

The modifiers *good, well, bad,* and *badly* cause problems for many writers because the distinctions between *good* and *well* and between *bad* and *badly* are often not observed in conversation. Problems also arise because *well* can function as either an adjective or an adverb. *Good* and *bad* are adjectives, and both can be used after a linking verb. Do not use them to modify a verb, an adjective, or an adverb; use *well* or *badly* instead.

The weather looks *good* today.

I feel *bad* for the Chicago fans.

▶ **He plays the trumpet ~~good~~ *well* and the trombone not ~~bad.~~ *badly.***

Badly is an adverb and can be used to modify a verb, an adjective, or another adverb.

In her first recital, the soprano sang *badly.*

Do not use it after a linking verb; use *bad* instead.

▶ **The clams tasted ~~badly.~~ *bad.***

As an adjective, *well* means "in good health"; as an adverb, it means "in a good manner" or "thoroughly."

ADJECTIVE	After a week of rest, Julio felt *well* again.
ADVERB	She plays *well* enough to make the team.

Right smart, way cool

Most regions have certain characteristic adjectives and adverbs. Some of the most colorful are intensifiers, adverbs meaning *very* or *absolutely.* In parts of the South, for example, and particularly in Appalachia, you are likely to hear the following:

He paid a *right* smart price for that car.

She was *plumb* tuckered out.

In each case, the adverb (*right, plumb*) acts to intensify the meaning of the adjective (*smart, tuckered out*). Consider two other examples, the first overheard in New York City, the second in Oakland, California:

It seems like *way* long ago that we were on vacation.

They looked *way* cool in their new sneakers.

As with all language, use of regional adjectives and adverbs is governed by appropriateness. In writing about a family member who lives in Minnesota, for example, you might well quote her, thus bringing some midwestern expressions into your writing. For most academic writing, however, you should use standard academic English.

For guidelines on using different varieties of language, see Chapter 28.

EXERCISE 12.1

Revise each of the following sentences to maintain correct adverb and adjective use. Then identify each adjective or adverb that you have revised, and point out the word each modifies.

The attorney delivered a ~~superb~~ *superbly* conceived summation.

1. Honest lawyers are not complete obsessed with status or money.
2. First he acts negative to her, and then in the next episode he proposes marriage!
3. Hypochondriacs call a doctor whenever they feel badly.
4. New Year's Day was real cold, and it was raining heavy.
5. The executive spoke forceful about the new union regulations.
6. Regrettably, the youngster was hurt bad in the accident.
7. The skater performed good despite the intense competition.
8. The instructor felt well about her presentation.
9. On the new stereo, many of the CDs, records, and tapes sounded differently.
10. They brought up their children very strict.

12d Using comparatives and superlatives

In addition to their simple, or positive, form, many adjectives and adverbs have two other forms, the **comparative** and **superlative,** that are used for making comparisons.

POSITIVE	COMPARATIVE	SUPERLATIVE
large	larger	largest
early	earlier	earliest
careful	more careful	most careful
happily	more happily	most happily

www

http://www.contrib.andrew.cmu.edu/user/bayer/humor/shakeinsult.html

Let thyself go: here you will find many inventive adjectives in a list of insults that sound Shakespearean.

Canada is *larger* than the United States.

My son needs to be *more careful* with his money.

They are the *most happily* married couple I know.

As these examples suggest, the comparative and superlative of most short (one-syllable and some two-syllable) adjectives are usually formed by adding *-er* and *-est*. *More* and *most* are sometimes used with short adjectives, however, to create a more formal tone. The only way to form the comparative and superlative of longer adjectives – three syllables or more – and of most adverbs is with *more* and *most*. If you are not sure whether a word has *-er* and *-est* forms, consult the dictionary entry for the simple form, where any *-er* and *-est* forms are usually listed.

1 Irregular forms

Some adjectives and adverbs have irregular comparative and superlative forms. Here is a list of them:

POSITIVE	COMPARATIVE	SUPERLATIVE
good, well	better	best
bad, badly, ill	worse	worst
little (quantity)	less	least
many, some, much	more	most

2 Comparatives vs. superlatives

The comparative is used to compare two things; the superlative, to compare three or more.

Rome is a much *older* city than New York.

Damascus is one of the *oldest* cities in the world.

In conversation, you will often hear the superlative form used even when only two things are being compared. *Of the two paintings, the one by Klee is the most interesting.* In college writing, however, use the comparative: *Of the two paintings, the one by Klee is the more interesting.*

3 Double comparatives and superlatives

Double comparatives and superlatives unnecessarily use both the *-er* or *-est* ending and *more* or *most*. Occasionally they can act to build a special emphasis, as in the title of Spike Lee's movie *Mo' Better Blues*. In college writing, however, make sure not to use *more* or *most* before adjectives or adverbs ending in *-er* or *-est.*

▶ **Paris is the ~~most~~ loveliest city in the world.**

▶ **Rome lasted ~~more~~ longer than Carthage.**

4 Incomplete comparisons

In speaking, we sometimes use incomplete comparisons – ones that specify only one of the things being compared – because the context makes the rest of the comparison clear. If after comparing your stereo with a friend's you say *Yours is better,* the context makes it clear that you mean *Yours is better than mine.* In writing, that context may not exist. So take time when editing to check for incomplete comparisons – and to complete them if they are unclear.

▶ **The patients taking the drug appeared healthier.** ^ *than those receiving a placebo.*

▶ **I consider Mozart the greatest.** ^ *of all composers.*

5 Absolute concepts

Some adjectives and adverbs – such as *perfect, final,* and *unique* – are absolute concepts, so it is illogical to form comparatives or superlatives of these words.

▶ **Max felt compelled to have ~~more~~ perfect control over his thoughts.**

▶ **Anne has ^ *a* ~~the most~~ unique sense of humor.**

12e Using nouns as modifiers

Sometimes a noun can function as an adjective by modifying another noun, as in *chicken soup* or *money supply.* If noun modifiers pile up, however, they can obscure meaning and should thus be revised.

AWKWARD The cold war–era Rosenberg espionage trial and execution continues to arouse controversy.

REVISED The Rosenbergs' trial and execution for espionage during the cold war continues to arouse controversy.

www •

http://www.cogsci.princeton.edu/~wn/

WordNet *is an online reference database of English nouns, verbs, adjectives, and adverbs that allows you to see words in many forms and to search for synonyms and antonyms (and much more).*

EXERCISE 12.2

Revise each of the following sentences to use modifiers correctly, clearly, and effectively. Many of the sentences can be revised in more than one way. Example:

He is sponsoring a housing project finance plan approval bill.

He is sponsoring **a bill to approve a financial plan for the housing project.**

1. Lady Macbeth is presented as the most ambitious of the two.
2. The article argued that walking is more healthier than jogging.
3. St. Francis made Assisi one of the famousest towns in Italy.
4. Most of the elderly are women because women tend to live longer.
5. Minneapolis is the largest of the Twin Cities.
6. Our college has the most unique work-study program.
7. My graduation day will be the most happiest day of my life.
8. The student cafeteria is operated by a college food service system chain.
9. Japanese cars captured much of the American market because American consumers found they were more reliable.
10. I think *Oedipus Rex* is a successfuler play than *Rent.*

THINKING CRITICALLY ABOUT ADJECTIVES AND ADVERBS

Reading with an Eye for Adjectives and Adverbs

> Gwendolyn Brooks "describes the 'graceful life' as one where people glide over floors in softly glowing rooms, smile correctly over trays of silver, cinnamon, and cream, and retire in quiet elegance."
>
> – MARY HELEN WASHINGTON, "Taming All That Anger Down"

Identify the adjectives and adverbs in the preceding passage, and comment on what they add to the writing. What would be lost if they were removed? What can you conclude about using adjectives and adverbs in your own writing?

Thinking about Your Own Use of Adjectives and Adverbs

Think of something you can observe or examine closely, and take a few minutes to study it. In a paragraph or two, describe your subject for someone who has never seen it. Using the guidelines at the beginning of the chapter, check your use of adjectives and adverbs, and revise your paragraphs. How would you characterize your use of adjectives and adverbs — do you overuse them? Put these thoughts in your writing log if you keep one.

PART 3

SENTENCES: MAKING CONVENTIONAL CHOICES

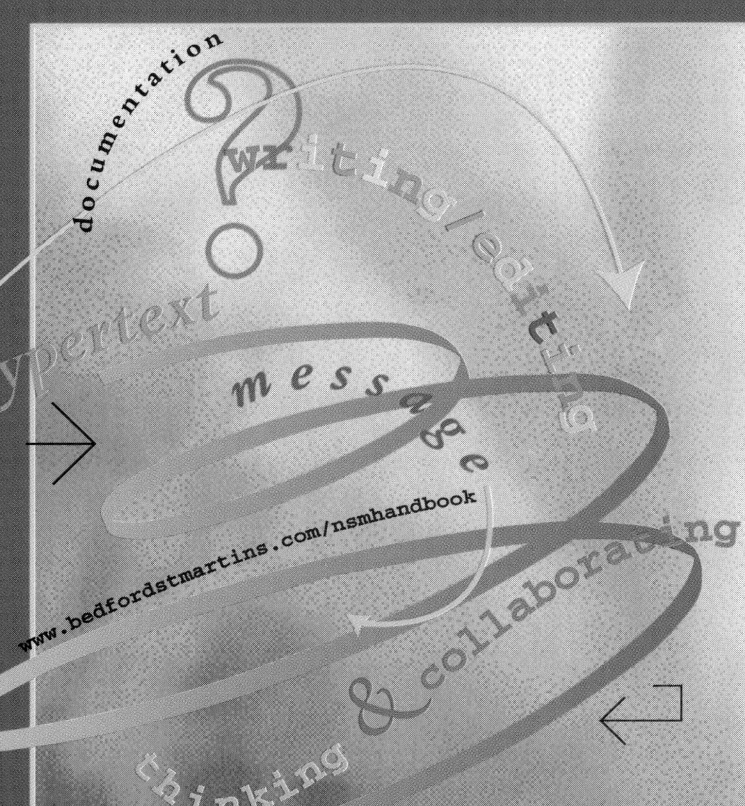

FAQ ········

FAQ: Sentence Conventions Online

How important are sentence conventions in email and other online writing?

The answer to this question depends on the kind of online writing you are doing (EMAIL? WEB PAGE? MOO? HYPERTEXT essay?) and on your rhetorical situation — the context of your writing, your purpose, your audience and their expectations, the genre you are using, and the level of formality appropriate to your message.

- **Email.** If in doubt, stick to the conventions of standard academic English, including clear, complete sentences, even if your diction is more informal. Much email is appropriately informal: it's often conversational, almost like talk: "Long time, no see — gimme some news, will you?" But if you're emailing your boss in response to a request, you will want to be more formal and to observe conventions: "I am responding to your request for an update on sales in the northern region."
- **Postings.** If you're posting to a LISTSERV or NEWSGROUP whose members are largely unknown to you, look for any available FAQs before you begin: the information there may provide ground rules for postings, including expectations about writing conventions. It's also a good idea to look at other postings for a few days to get a sense of style and audience before posting anything yourself. If you are too casual or don't pay attention to conventions, you may send a message that you don't intend — that you are satisfied with sloppy work, for instance.

  Remember that postings, like email, can easily be printed out and circulated OFFLINE. In print, carelessness about conventions may send unintentional signals to an even wider audience.
- **MOOs and MUDs.** In the fast-paced real-time communication of a MOO or MUD, paying careful attention to all conventions is very difficult. As a result, sentence fragments, comma splices, dangling modifiers, and so on are more likely to be ignored.

http://www.english.upenn.edu/~jlynch/Grammar/

Grammar and Style Notes *provides explanations of conventions of grammar, style, punctuation, and usage, broken into a file for each letter of the alphabet (click on "s" for information on sentence fragments, for example).*

13 Maintaining Clear Pronoun Reference

Take the Interstate until you come to Exit 3 and then Route 313. Go past it, and take the next exit, which will be Broadway.

These directions, intended to lead an out-of-towner to her friend's house, provide a good example of why it's important for most pronouns to refer clearly to another word, called the antecedent. The word *it* in this example could mean either Exit 3 or Route 313 — or are they perhaps the same thing? If the visitor doesn't already know, or if the exit *and* Route 313 aren't both clearly marked, she could have difficulty finding her way.

Avoiding such problems in your own writing is a fairly simple matter — of identifying each pronoun, finding the word(s) it substitutes for, or supplying such a word and making sure the pronoun cannot mistakenly refer to any other word as well. ■

13a Matching pronouns clearly to one antecedent

If more than one possible antecedent for a personal pronoun appears in a passage, the pronoun should refer clearly and unambiguously to only *one* of them. Look at the following examples:

▶ **The meeting between Bowman and Sonny makes ~~him~~** *Bowman* **compare his own unhappy life with one that is more emotionally secure.**

Who is the antecedent of *him* and *his:* Bowman or Sonny? The revision makes the reference clear by replacing a pronoun (*him*) with a noun (*Bowman*).

▶ **Kerry told Ellen ~~she should~~** *to* **be ready soon.**

Who should be ready soon: Kerry or Ellen? The revision makes the reference clear. It could also be revised for a different meaning: *Kerry told Ellen, "I should be ready soon."*

13b Keeping pronouns and antecedents close together

If a pronoun is too far from its antecedent, readers will have trouble making the connection between the two.

1. Find all the pronouns in your draft, and then identify the specific noun that is the antecedent of each one.
2. If you cannot find a noun antecedent, replace the pronoun with a noun, or supply an antecedent to which the pronoun clearly refers. (13a)
3. Look to see if any pronoun could be misunderstood to refer to a noun other than its antecedent. If so, replace the pronoun with the appropriate noun, or revise the sentence so that the pronoun can refer to only one possible antecedent. (13a)
4. Look at any pronoun that seems far from its antecedent. If a reader might have trouble relating the pronoun to its antecedent, replace the pronoun with the appropriate noun. (13b)
5. Check any use of *it, this, that,* and *which* to be sure each pronoun refers to a specific antecedent. (13c)
6. Be sure that any use of *you* refers to your specific reader or readers. (13e)

▶ **The right-to-life coalition believes that a *zygote,* an egg at the moment of fertilization, is as deserving of protection as is the born human being and thus that abortion is as much murder as is the killing of a child. The coalition's focus is on what ~~it~~ *the zygote* will become as much as on what it is now.**

13c Checking for vague use of *it, this, that,* and *which*

www •

http://webster.commnet.edu/hp/pages/darling/grammar/consistency.htm

This short page offers good examples of "things we have to remember about pronoun reference" along with links to quizzes and other grammar resources.

Writers are often tempted to use *it, this, that,* or *which* as a quick and easy way of referring to something mentioned earlier. But such shortcuts can often cause confusion. Make sure that these pronouns refer clearly to a specific antecedent.

▶ **When they realized the bill would be defeated, they tried to postpone the vote. However, ~~it~~ *the attempt* failed.**

▶ **Nancy just found out that she won the lottery, ~~which~~** *an event that* **explains her sudden resignation from her job.**

If *that* or *which* opens a clause that refers to a specific noun, put *that* or *which* directly after the noun, if possible.

▶ **We worked all night on the float ~~for the Rose Parade~~ that our club was going to sponsor** *for the Rose Parade*.

Does *that* refer to the float or the parade? The editing makes the meaning clear.

13d Checking for appropriate use of *who, which,* and *that*

Be careful to use the relative pronouns *who, which,* and *that* appropriately. *Who* refers primarily to people or to animals with names. *Which* refers to animals or to things, and *that* refers to animals, things, and occasionally anonymous or collective groups of people.

For more on that and which, see the Glossary of Usage.

Stephen Jay Gould, *who* has won many awards for his writing about science, teaches at Harvard.

The whale, *which* has only one baby a year, is subject to extinction because it reproduces so slowly.

Laboratories *that* harm animals have become controversial.

13e Checking for indefinite use of *you* and *they*

In conversation, we frequently use *you* and *they* in an indefinite sense, as in such expressions as *you never know* and *on television, they said.* In college writing, however, use *you* only to mean "you, the reader," and *they* only to refer to a clear antecedent.

▶ **Commercials try to make ~~you~~** *people* **buy without thinking.**

▶ *Most restaurants in* **~~In~~ France~~,~~ ~~they~~ allow dogs. ~~in most restaurants.~~**

13f Checking for implied antecedents

Though an adjective or possessive may clearly imply a noun antecedent, it does not serve as a clear antecedent.

▶ **In ~~Welty's~~ *her* story, ~~she~~ *Welty* characterizes Bowman as a man unaware of his own isolation.**

FOR MULTILINGUAL WRITERS

USING PRONOUN SUBJECTS

In some languages — Spanish and Russian, for instance — personal-pronoun subjects are largely unnecessary because the verb ending shows person and number. In other languages, such as Arabic, personal pronouns are added to the verbs as suffixes or prefixes. Native speakers of these languages sometimes "overcorrect" in English by doubling the subject, as in *Jaime he lives next door.* Such a double subject is inappropriate in English. Therefore, if you are using a pronoun as a subject, make sure that you have not used a proper noun subject as well: *He lives next door.*

EXERCISE 13.1

Revise each of the following items to clarify pronoun reference. Most of the items can be revised in more than one way. If a pronoun refers ambiguously to more than one possible antecedent, revise the sentence in at least two different ways, reflecting each possible meaning. Example:

After Jane left, Miranda found her keys.
Miranda found Jane's keys after Jane left.
Miranda found her own keys after Jane left.

1. Anna smiled at her mother as she opened the birthday package.
2. Lear divides his kingdom between the two older daughters, Goneril and Regan, whose extravagant professions of love are more flattering than the simple affection of the youngest daughter, Cordelia. The consequences of this error in judgment soon become apparent, as they prove neither grateful nor kind to him.
3. New England helped shape many aspects of American culture, including education, religion, and government. As New Englanders moved west, they carried its institutions with them.
4. When drug therapy is combined with psychotherapy, the patients relate better to their therapists, are less vulnerable to what disturbs them, and are more responsive to them.
5. Not long after the company set up the subsidiary, it went bankrupt.
6. In Texas, you often hear about the influence of big oil corporations.
7. A friend of mine recently had a conversation with a veteran that changed his view of the Persian Gulf War.
8. She dropped off a friend which had gone to the party with her.
9. Company policy prohibited smoking, which many employees resented.
10. In Tom Jobim's lyrics, he often describes the beaches of Rio.

EXERCISE 13.2 Revising to Clarify Pronoun Reference

Revise to establish a clear antecedent for every pronoun that needs one.

In Paul Fussell's essay "My War," he writes about his experience in combat during World War II, which he says still haunts his life. Fussell confesses that he joined the infantry ROTC in 1939 as a way of getting out of gym class, where he would have been forced to expose his "fat and flabby" body to the ridicule of his classmates. However, it proved to be a serious miscalculation. After the United States entered the war in 1941, other male college students were able to join officer training programs in specialized fields that kept them out of combat. If you were already in an ROTC unit associated with the infantry, though, you were trapped in it. That was how Fussell came to be shipped to France as a rifle-platoon leader in 1944. Almost immediately they sent him to the front, where he soon developed pneumonia because of insufficient winter clothing. He spent a month in hospitals; because he did not want to worry his parents, however, he told them it was just the flu. When he returned to the front, he was wounded by a shell that killed his sergeant, which had been with him since basic training.

THINKING CRITICALLY ABOUT PRONOUN REFERENCE

Reading with an Eye for Pronoun Reference

The following poem depends on its title to supply the antecedent for the pronouns that follow and that knit the poem together. Read the poem out loud, and then provide its two-word title. How did you know what the title should be? Try writing a poem (perhaps three or four verses) like this one, using pronouns and other words to give "clues" to your title.

His art is eccentricity, his aim
How not to hit the mark he seems to aim at,

His passion how to avoid the obvious,
His technique how to vary the avoidance.

The others throw to be comprehended. He
Throws to be a moment misunderstood.

Yet not too much. Not too errant, arrant, wild,
But every seeming aberration willed.

Not to, yet still, still to communicate
Making the batter understand too late.

– Robert Francis

Thinking about Your Own Use of Pronoun Reference

Turn to something you've written, and analyze your use of pronouns. Do any pronouns not refer clearly and directly to the correct antecedent? Could any antecedents be ambiguous? Using the guidelines on p. 214, revise as necessary. Note any patterns in your use of pronouns — in a writing log, if you keep one.

14 Recognizing Shifts

A shift in writing is an abrupt change of some sort that results in inconsistency. Sometimes writers shift deliberately, as Dave Barry does in saying he "would have to say that the greatest single achievement of the American medical establishment is nasal spray." Barry's shift in tone from the serious (the American medical establishment) to the banal (nasal spray) makes us laugh, as Barry wishes us to. Although writers sometimes deliberately make such shifts for good reasons, unintentional shifts can be jolting and confusing to readers. In addition to shifts in tense, among the most common kinds of unintentional shifts are those in verbs, in pronouns and nouns, and between direct and indirect discourses. ■

14a Checking for unnecessary shifts in tense

If the verbs in a passage refer to actions occurring at different times, they may require different tenses. Be careful, however, not to change tenses for no reason.

► **A few countries produce almost all of the world's illegal drugs, but addiction ~~affected~~** *affects* **many countries.**

14b Checking for unnecessary shifts in mood

Be careful not to shift from one mood to another without good reason. The mood of a verb can be indicative (he *closes* the door), imperative (*close* the door), or subjunctive (if the door *were closed*). (See Chapter 9.) Notice how the original version of the following sentence shifts unnecessarily from the imperative to the indicative:

► **Keep your eye on the ball, and ~~you should~~ bend your knees.**

The writer's purpose is to give orders, and the editing makes both verbs imperative.

- → If you shift from one verb tense to another, check to be sure there is a reason for doing so. (14a)
- → Do you see any shifts in mood — perhaps from an indicative statement to an imperative — and if so, are they necessary? (14b)
- → Check for shifts from active (*She asks questions*) to passive voice (*Questions are asked*). Are they intentional — and if so, for what reason? (14c)
- → Do you see any shifts in person or number — from *we* to *you*, for example — and if so, what are the reasons for the shifts? (14d)
- → Check your writing for consistency in tone. If your tone is serious, is it consistently so? (14f)

14c Checking for unnecessary shifts in voice

Do not shift without reason between the active voice (she *sold* it) and the passive voice (it *was sold*). Sometimes a shift in voice is justified, but often it may only confuse readers.

For more about voice, see Chapter 9 and 23b.

▶ **Two youths approached ~~me~~, and ~~I was~~ asked** *me* **for my wallet.**

The original sentence shifts from the active (*youths approached*) to the passive (*I was asked*), so it is unclear who asked for the wallet. Making both verbs active clears up the confusion.

14d Checking for unnecessary shifts in person and number

Unnecessary shifts between first-person point of view (*I, we*), second-person (*you*), and third-person (*he, she, it, one,* or *they*), or between singular and plural subjects can be very confusing to readers.

▶ *You* **~~One~~ can do well on this job if you budget your time.**

It was not clear whether the writer was making a general statement or giving advice to someone. Eliminating the shift eliminates this confusion.

▶ **Nurses receive much less pay than doctors, even though ~~a nurse has~~ *nurses have* the primary responsibility for daily patient care.**

The writer had no reason to shift from third-person plural (*nurses*) to third-person singular (*a nurse*).

Many shifts in number are actually problems with pronoun-antecedent agreement.

For a complete discussion of pronoun-antecedent agreement, see Chapter 11.

INCONSISTENT I have difficulty seeing another *person's* position, especially if *their* opinion contradicts mine.

REVISED I have difficulty seeing other *people's* positions, especially if *their* opinions contradict mine.

REVISED I have difficulty seeing another *person's* position, especially if *his* or *her* opinion contradicts mine.

14e Checking for unnecessary shifts between direct and indirect discourse

www

http://webster.commnet.edu/hp/pages/darling/grammar/consistency.htm

This short pages offers good examples of shifts in verb tense and also includes links to grammar exercises and other guidance.

When you quote someone's exact words, you are using **direct discourse:** *She said, "I'm an editor."* When you report what someone says without repeating the exact words, you are using **indirect discourse:** *She said she is an editor.* Shifting between direct and indirect discourse in the same sentence can cause problems, especially with questions.

▶ **Bob asked what *he* could ~~he~~ do to help~~?~~.**

The editing eliminates an awkward shift by rephrasing what Bob said. The sentence could also be edited to quote him: *Bob asked, "What can I do to help?"*

EXERCISE 14.1

Revise the following sentences to eliminate unnecessary shifts in tense, mood, voice, or point of view and between direct and indirect discourse. Most of the items can be revised in more than one way. Example:

When a person goes to college, you face many new situations.

When a person goes to college, he or she faces many new situations.

When people go to college, they face many new situations.

1. The fitness mania of the 1970s gave way to the greed of the 1980s, which in turn gives way to the occupational insecurity of the 1990s.
2. The coroner asked that we be quiet and that we should be attentive.

3. The physician moves the knee around to observe the connections of the cartilage and ligaments, and a fluid is injected into the joint.
4. According to the article, the ozone layer is rapidly dwindling, and "we are endangering the lives of future generations."
5. Suddenly we heard an explosion of wings off to our right, and you could see a hundred or more ducks lifting off from the water.
6. The first thing that is seen as we start down the slope is a green banner.
7. Although she enjoys rock music, jazz is preferred by her.
8. A cloud of snow powder rose as skis and poles fly in every direction.
9. The instructor told us, "Please read the next two stories before the next class" and that she might give us a quiz on them.
10. Workers with computer skills were in great demand, and a programmer could almost name their salary.
11. It is better that Grandfather die painlessly and with dignity than that he continues to live in terrible pain.
12. I liked the sense of individualism, the crowd yelling for you, and the feeling that I was in command.
13. Oscar Wilde wrote that books cannot be divided into moral and immoral categories and "books are either well written or badly written."
14. Place a test strip on the subject area; then you should expose the strip to light and develop it for two minutes.
15. The day is hot and stifling, a day when no one willingly ventured out onto the burning asphalt.

14f Checking for confusing shifts in tone and diction

Tone, the way a writer's attitude toward a topic or audience is expressed in writing, is related to **diction,** or word choice, and to the writer's overall level of formality or informality. Watch out for shifts in your tone or diction that could confuse readers and leave them wondering what your real attitude is.

See 4g4.

INCONSISTENT TONE

The question of child care forces a society to make profound decisions about its economic values. Can most families with children actually live adequately on only one salary? If some conservatives had their way, June Cleaver would still be stuck in the kitchen baking cookies for Wally and the Beaver and waiting for Ward to bring home the bacon, except that with only one income, the Cleavers would be lucky to afford hot dogs.

In the preceding version, the first two sentences set a serious, formal tone, discussing child care in fairly general, abstract terms. But in the third sentence, the writer shifts suddenly to sarcasm, to references to television characters, and to informal language like *stuck* and *bring home the bacon.* Readers cannot tell whether the writer is presenting a serious analysis or preparing for a humorous satire. See how the passage was revised to make the tone consistent.

REVISED

The question of child care forces a society to make profound decisions about its economic values. Can most families with young children actually live adequately on only one salary? Some conservatives believe that women with young children should not work outside the home, but many are forced to do so for financial reasons.

THINKING CRITICALLY ABOUT SHIFTS

Reading with an Eye for Shifts

The following paragraph includes several *necessary* shifts in person and number. Read the paragraph carefully, marking all such shifts. Notice how careful the author must be as he shifts back and forth among pronouns.

> It has been one of the great errors of our time to think that by thinking about thinking, and then talking about it, we could possibly straighten out and tidy up our minds. There is no delusion more damaging than to get the idea in your head that you understand the functioning of your own brain. Once you acquire such a notion, you run the danger of moving in to take charge, guiding your thoughts, shepherding your mind from place to place. *controlling* it, making lists of regulations. The human mind is not meant to be governed, certainly not by any book of rules yet written; it is supposed to run itself, and we are obliged to follow it along, trying to keep up with it as best we can. It is all very well to be aware of your awareness, even proud of it, but never try to operate it. You are not up to the job.
>
> – LEWIS THOMAS, "The Attic of the Brain"

Thinking about Any Shifts in Your Own Writing

Find an article about a well-known person you admire. Then write a paragraph or two about him or her, making a point of using both direct and indirect discourse. Using the information in 14e, check your writing for any inappropriate shifts between direct and indirect discourse, and revise as necessary.

Identifying Comma Splices and Fused Sentences

15

A **comma splice** occurs when two independent clauses are joined with only a comma. We often see comma splices in advertising, where they can give slogans a catchy rhythm.

Life's short, play hard.

– NIKE ADVERTISEMENT

In literary writing, another common construction is a **fused, or run-on, sentence,** which occurs when two independent clauses are joined with no punctuation or connecting word between them. The Nike advertisement as a fused sentence would be "Life's short play hard."

Despite the powerful effects comma splices or fused sentences can create in certain contexts, however, you should seldom use these constructions in academic writing. In fact, doing so will almost always be identified as an error. ■

15a Separating the clauses into two sentences

The simplest way to revise comma splices or fused sentences is to separate them into two sentences.

COMMA SPLICE **My mother spends long hours every spring tilling the soil and moving manure~~,~~. ~~t~~This part of gardening is nauseating.**

FUSED SENTENCE **My mother spends long hours every spring tilling the soil and moving manure. ~~t~~This part of gardening is nauseating.**

If the two clauses are very short, making them two sentences may sound abrupt and terse, and some other method of revision would probably be preferable.

15b Linking the clauses with a comma and a coordinating conjunction

If the ideas in the two clauses are fairly closely related and equally important, another alternative for revision is to use a comma and a coordinating conjunction: *and, but, or, nor, for, so,* or *yet.* The conjunction helps indicate what

Look for independent clauses — groups of words that can stand alone as a sentence — coming one after another. If you find no punctuation between two independent clauses, you have identified a fused sentence. If you find two such clauses joined only by a comma, you have identified a comma splice. Here are five methods of editing comma splices and fused sentences. To choose among these methods, you need to look at the sentences before and after the ones you are revising. Doing so will help you determine how a particular method will affect the rhythm of the passage.

1. Separate the clauses into two sentences. (15a)

   ▶ ***Education* is an elusive word, ~~it~~ *It* often means different things to different people.**

2. Link the clauses with a comma and a coordinating conjunction (*and, but, or, nor, for, so,* or *yet*). (15b)

   ▶ ***Education* is an elusive word, *for* it often means different things to different people.**

3. Link the clauses with a semicolon. (15c)

   ▶ ***Education* is an elusive word; it often means different things to different people.**

   If the clauses are linked only with a comma and a conjunctive adverb — a word like *however, then, therefore* — add a semicolon.

   ▶ ***Education* is an elusive word; indeed, it often means different things to different people.**

4. Recast the two clauses as one independent clause. (15d)

   ▶ *An elusive word, education* **~~*Education* is an elusive word, it~~ often means different things to different people.**

5. Recast one independent clause as a dependent clause. (15e)

   ▶ ***Education* is an elusive word *because* it often means different things to different people.**

kind of link exists between the two clauses. For instance, *but* and *yet* signal opposition or contrast (*I am strong, but she is stronger*); *for* and *so* signal cause-effect relationships (*The cabin was bitterly cold, so we built a fire*).

FUSED SENTENCE **I should pay my tuition, I need a new car.** (*but* inserted after "tuition,")

15c Linking the clauses with a semicolon

If the ideas in two spliced or fused clauses are closely related and you want to give them equal emphasis, you may want to link them with a semicolon.

COMMA SPLICE **This photograph is not at all realistic; it even uses dreamlike images to convey its message.**

Be careful when you link clauses with a conjunctive adverb or a transitional phrase. You must use such words and phrases with a semicolon, with a period, or with a comma combined with a coordinating conjunction. (See 7b7.)

SOME CONJUNCTIVE ADVERBS AND TRANSITIONAL PHRASES

also	indeed	now
anyway	instead	otherwise
besides	likewise	similarly
certainly	meanwhile	still
finally	moreover	then
furthermore	namely	therefore
however	nevertheless	thus
incidentally	next	undoubtedly
in fact	in contrast	in addition

Conjunctive adverbs and transitional phrases can appear in various positions in a clause. These words and expressions are usually set off from the rest of the clause by commas. (See 30a and 30e.)

FUSED SENTENCE **Many Third World countries have very high birthrates, therefore, most of their citizens are young.** (*and,* inserted after "birthrates,")

FOR MULTILINGUAL WRITERS

JUDGING SENTENCE LENGTH

If you speak a language that uses and values very long sentences, you may string together sentences in English in a way that results in comma-splice errors. (Arabic, Farsi, and Chinese are three such languages.) Note that in standard academic English, a sentence should contain only one independent clause, *unless* the clauses are joined by a comma and a coordinating conjunction, or by a semicolon.

15d Recasting the two clauses as one clause

Sometimes you can reduce two spliced or fused clauses to a single clause that is more direct and concise.

COMMA SPLICE — **Many people complain that ~~a large part~~** *most* **of their mail is advertisements,** *and* **~~most of the rest is~~ bills.**

15e Recasting one of the clauses as a dependent clause

When one of the spliced or fused clauses is more important than the other, try converting the less important one to a dependent clause.

For a discussion of dependent clauses, see 7c4.

FUSED SENTENCE — *Although* **Zora Neale Hurston is regarded as one of America's major novelists,** **she died in obscurity.**

The first clause stands in contrast to the second one: in contrast to Hurston's importance today (she is held in high esteem) are the circumstances of her death (obscurity). In the revision, the writer chose to emphasize the second clause and to make the first one into a dependent clause by adding the subordinating conjunction *although.*

COMMA SPLICE — **The arts and crafts movement** *, which reacted against mass production,* **called for handmade objects. ~~, it reacted against mass production.~~**

Both clauses discuss related aspects of the arts and crafts movement. In the revision, the writer chose to emphasize the first clause, the one describing what the movement advocated, and to make the second clause, the one describing what it reacted against, into a dependent clause.

EXERCISE 15.1

Revise to correct the comma splice or fused sentence using *two* of the methods in this chapter. Use each of the methods at least once. Example:

I had misgivings about the marriage, I did not attend the ceremony.
I had misgivings about the marriage, so I did not attend the ceremony.
Because I had misgivings about the marriage, I did not attend the ceremony.

1. I was sitting on a log bridge, the sun sank low in the sky.
2. Reporters today have no choice they must use computers.

www •

http://leo.stcloud.msus.edu/acad write/editing.html

Tips on how to proofread for comma splices and other common errors.

3. I completed the test, I was uncertain about the last essay question.
4. My mother taught me to read my grandmother taught me to *love* to read.
5. *David Copperfield* was written as a serial it is ideal for television.
6. Lincoln called for troops to fight the Confederacy, four more southern states seceded as a result.
7. The California condor is almost extinct scientists are trying to save it.
8. E. B. White died in 1985 his work continues to inspire readers.
9. Václav Havel was once imprisoned as a dissident, still, he eventually became president of Czechoslovakia.
10. The music lifted her spirits she stopped sighing and began to sing.

EXERCISE 15.2

Revise the following paragraph, eliminating all comma splices by using a period or a semicolon. Then revise the paragraph again, this time using any of the other methods in this chapter. Comment on the two revisions. What differences in rhythm do you detect? Which version do you prefer, and why?

My sister Mary decided to paint her house last summer, thus, she had to buy some paint. She wanted inexpensive paint, at the same time, it had to go on easily and cover well, that combination was unrealistic to start with. She had never done exterior painting before, in fact she did not even own a ladder. She was a complete beginner, on the other hand, she was a hard worker and was willing to learn. She got her husband, Dan, to take a week off from work, likewise she let her two teenage sons take three days off from school to help. Mary went out and bought the "dark green" paint for $6.99 a gallon, it must have been mostly water, in fact, you could almost see through it. Mary and Dan and the boys put one coat of this paint on the house, as a result, their white house turned a streaky light green. Dan and the boys rebelled, declaring they would not work anymore with such cheap paint. Mary was forced to buy all new paint, even so, the house did not really get painted until September.

EXERCISE 15.3

Revise the following paragraph, eliminating the comma splices and fused sentences by using any of the methods discussed in this chapter. Then revise the paragraph again, this time eliminating each comma splice and fused sentence by a *different* method. Decide which paragraph is more effective, and why. Finally, compare the revision you prefer with the revisions of several other students, and discuss the ways in which the versions differ in meaning.

Gardening can be very satisfying, it is also hard work people who just see the pretty flowers may not realize this. My mother spends long hours every spring tilling the soil, she moves many wheelbarrow-loads of disgusting cow manure and chicken droppings, in fact, the whole early part of gardening is nauseating. The whole garden area has to be rototilled every year, this process is not much like the ad showing people walking quietly behind the rototiller, on the contrary, my father has to fight that machine every inch of the way, sweating so much he looks like Hulk Hogan after a hard bout. Then the planting all must be done by hand, my back aches, my hands get raw, my skin gets sunburned. I get filthy whenever I go near that garden my mother always asks me to help, though. When harvest time comes the effort is *almost* worth it, however, there are always extra zucchinis I give away at school everybody else is trying to give away zucchinis, too. We also have tomatoes, lettuce, there is always more than we need and we feel bad wasting it wouldn't you like this nice bag of cucumbers?

THINKING CRITICALLY ABOUT COMMA SPLICES AND FUSED SENTENCES

Reading with an Eye for Special Effects

E. M. Forster is known as a careful and correct stylist, yet he often deviates from the "correct" to create special effects. Look, for example, at the way he uses a comma splice in the following passage:

> One of the evils of money is that it tempts us to look at it rather than at the things that it buys. They are dimmed because of the metal and the paper through which we receive them. That is the fundamental deceitfulness of riches, which kept worrying Christ. That is the treachery of the purse, the wallet and the bank-balance, even from the capitalist point of view. They were invented as a convenience to the flesh, they have become a chain for the spirit.
>
> – E. M. FORSTER, "The Last Parade"

Forster uses a comma splice in the last sentence to emphasize parallel ideas; any conjunction, even *and,* would change the causal relationship he wishes to show. Because the grammar is unexpected, it attracts just the attention that Forster wants for his statement.

Look through some stories or essays to find some comma splices and fused sentences. Copy down one or two and enough of the surrounding text to show context, and comment in writing on the effects they create.

Thinking about Any Comma Splices and Fused Sentences in Your Own Writing

Go through some essays you have written, checking for comma splices and fused sentences. Revise any you find, using one of the methods in this chapter. Comment on your chosen methods — in your writing log, if you are keeping one.

16

Recognizing Sentence Fragments

16a Revising phrase fragments

Phrases are groups of words that lack a subject, a verb, or both. (See 7c3.) When phrases are punctuated like a sentence, they become fragments. To revise these fragments, attach them to an independent clause, or make them a separate sentence.

▶ **NBC is broadcasting the debates~~.~~ *w*~~W~~ith discussions afterward.**

The second word group is a prepositional phrase, not a sentence. The editing combines the phrase with an independent clause.

▶ **One of our nation's most cherished ideals, ~~may be in danger.~~ *t*~~T~~he ideal of a good education for every child~~.~~***, may be in danger.*

The ideal of a good education for every child is an appositive phrase renaming the noun *ideals.* The editing attaches the fragment to the sentence containing the noun.

▶ **Vivian stayed out of school for three months after Linda was born.** *She did so to* **~~To~~ recuperate and to take care of her.**

To recuperate and to take care of her includes verbals, not verbs. The revision — adding a subject (*she*) and a verb (*did*) — turns the fragment into a separate sentence.

Our Lifetime Guarantee may come as a shock.

Or a strut. Or a muffler. Because once you pay to replace them, Toyota's Lifetime Guarantee covers parts and labor on any dealer-installed muffler, shock, or strut for as long as you own your Toyota! So if anything should ever go wrong, your Toyota dealer will fix it. Absolutely free.

This Toyota advertisement includes three fragments (underlined here) that grab our attention, the first two by creating a play on words and the third one by emphasizing that something is free. Sentence fragments are groups of words that are punctuated as sentences but lack some element grammatically necessary to a sentence, usually either a subject or a verb. Though you will often see fragments in literature and advertising and hear them in conversation, you will seldom want to use them in academic writing, where some readers might regard them as errors. ■

CONVENTIONS
Recognizing Sentence Fragments

A group of words must meet three criteria to form a complete sentence. If it does not meet all three, it is a fragment. Revise a fragment by combining it with a nearby sentence or by rewriting it as a complete sentence.

1. A sentence must have a subject. (7a)
2. A sentence must have a verb, not just a verbal. A verbal cannot function as a sentence's verb without an auxiliary verb. (7c3)

   VERB **The terrier *is barking*.**

   VERBAL **The terrier *barking*.**

3. Unless it is a question, a sentence must have at least one clause that does not begin with a subordinating word. Following are some common subordinating words:

although	if	when
as	since	where
because	that	whether
before	though	who
how	unless	why

▶ *In his* ~~**His**~~ **editorial making a plea for better facilities for severely handicapped children***, he pointed* ~~**. Pointed**~~ **out that these facilities are always located in poor areas.**

The first fragment lacked a verb (*making* is a verbal); the second lacked a subject.

Fragments beginning with transitions

Transitional expressions sometimes lead to fragments. If you introduce an example or explanation with one of the following transitions, be certain you write a sentence, not a fragment. Transitional words and phrases include:

again	but	like
also	finally	or
and	for example	specifically
as a result	for instance	such as
besides	instead	that is

www •

http://leo.stcloud.msus.edu/acad write/editing.html

This page offers strategies for editing and proofreading, including tips on dealing with fragments and other common errors.

▶ **Joan Didion has written on many subjects~~.~~, ~~Such~~ such as the Hoover Dam and migraine headaches.**

The second word group is a phrase, not a sentence. The editing combines it with an independent clause.

16b Revising compound-predicate fragments

A compound predicate consists of two or more verbs, along with their modifiers and objects, that have the same subject. Fragments occur when one part of a compound predicate is punctuated as a separate sentence although it lacks a subject. These fragments usually begin with *and, but,* or *or.* You can revise them by attaching them to the independent clause that contains the rest of the predicate.

▶ **They sold their house~~.~~ ~~A~~and moved into an apartment.**

EXERCISE 16.1

Revise each of the following items to eliminate any sentence fragments, either by combining fragments with independent clauses or by rewriting them as separate sentences. Example:

> Zoe looked close to tears. Standing with her head bowed.
>
> Standing with her head bowed, Zoe looked close to tears.
>
> Zoe looked close to tears. She was standing with her head bowed.

1. Small, long-veined, fuzzy green leaves. Add to the appeal of this newly developed variety of carrot.
2. Living with gusto. That is what many Americans yearn for.
3. The region has dry, sandy soil. Blown into strange formations by the ever-present wind.
4. The climbers had two choices. To go over a four-hundred-foot cliff or to turn back. They decided to make the attempt.
5. Connie picked up the cat and started playing with it. It scratched her neck. With its sharp little claws.
6. Clinton promoted one major reform. A plan to make health insurance coverage universal.
7. Trying to carry a portfolio, art box, illustration boards, and drawing pads. I must have looked ridiculous.
8. Organized crime has been able to attract graduates just as big business has. With good pay and the best equipment money can buy.

9. Joan Didion has investigated politics. And explored human emotions.
10. Wollstonecraft believed in universal public education. Also, in education that forms the heart and strengthens the body.

16c Revising dependent-clause fragments

For more about dependent clauses, see 7c4.

Dependent clauses contain both a subject and a verb, but they cannot stand alone as sentences because they depend on an independent clause to complete their meaning. Dependent clauses usually begin with words such as *after, because, before, if, since, though, unless, until, when, where, while, who, which,* and *that.* You can usually combine dependent-clause fragments with a nearby independent clause.

▶ **When I decided to work part-time, I gave up some earning potential.**

If you cannot smoothly attach a clause to a nearby independent clause, try deleting the opening subordinating word and turning the dependent clause into a sentence.

▶ **Injuries in automobile accidents occur in two ways. ~~When~~ An occupant either is hurt by something inside the car or is thrown from the car.**

EXERCISE 16.2

Identify all the sentence fragments in the following items, and explain why each is grammatically incomplete. Then revise each one in at least two ways. Example:

> Controlling my temper. That has been one of my goals this year.
>
> Controlling my temper has been one of my goals this year.
>
> One of my goals this year has been controlling my temper.

1. When Rick was in the fifth grade. His parents often left him with his sister.
2. The protagonist comes to a decision. To leave his family.
3. Fear, one of the basic emotions people have experienced throughout time.
4. We were thankful for a hot shower. After a week in the wilderness.
5. I plan to buy a computer. Which will help me organize my finances.
6. Forster stopped writing novels after *A Passage to India.* One of the greatest novels of the twentieth century.
7. Sylvia Plath achieved new status. Because of *Ariel,* her final poems.

8. I loved *Beloved.* And knew Toni Morrison deserved the Nobel Prize.
9. The president appointed five members. Who drew up a set of bylaws.
10. One might say that rebellion is normal. Because the younger generation often rejects the ways of its elders.

THINKING CRITICALLY ABOUT FRAGMENTS

Reading with an Eye for Fragments

Identify the fragments in the following passage. What effect does the writer achieve by using fragments rather than complete sentences?

> On Sundays, for religion, we went up on the hill. Skipping along the hexagon-shaped tile in Colonial Park. Darting up the steps to Edgecomb Avenue. Stopping in the candy store on St. Nicholas to load up. Leaning forward for leverage to finish the climb up to the church. I was always impressed by this particular house of the Lord.
>
> – KEITH GILYARD, *Voices of the Self*

Thinking about Any Fragments in Your Own Writing

Read through some essays you have written. Using the guidelines on p. 230, see whether you find any sentence fragments. If so, do you recognize any patterns? Do you write fragments when you're attempting to add emphasis? Are they all dependent clauses? phrases? Note any patterns you discover (in your writing log, if you keep one), and make a point of routinely checking your writing for fragments. Finally, revise any fragments to form complete sentences.

17 Placing Modifiers Appropriately

Modifiers enrich writing by making it more concrete or vivid, often adding important or even essential details. To be effective, however, modifiers should refer clearly to the words they modify and be positioned close to those words. Consider, for example, a sign seen recently in a hotel:

DO NOT USE
THE ELEVATORS
IN CASE OF FIRE.

Should we really avoid the elevators altogether, in case there is ever a fire? Repositioning the modifier *in case of fire* eliminates such confusion — and makes clear that we are to avoid the elevators only if there is a fire: IN CASE OF FIRE, DO NOT USE THE ELEVATORS. This chapter examines three types of problem modifiers — misplaced, disruptive, and dangling — and ways of revising them. ■

17a Revising misplaced modifiers

Misplaced modifiers are words, phrases, and clauses that cause ambiguity or confusion because they are not placed as close to the words they modify as they might be or because they could modify the words either before or after them. For example, in the sentence *Softly I could hear the tumbleweeds rustling in the wind,* the adverb *softly* seems to modify *could hear.* Yet the writer obviously meant it to modify *rustling* (because one cannot hear "softly"). Such confusion can be avoided by placing a modifier close to the word or words to which it actually refers.

> I could hear the tumbleweeds *softly* rustling in the wind.
>
> I could hear the tumbleweeds rustling *softly* in the wind.

Be especially careful with the placement of **limiting modifiers** like *almost, even, hardly, just, merely, nearly, only, scarcely,* and *simply.* In general, these modifiers should be placed right before the words they limit. Putting them anywhere else may produce not just ambiguity but a completely different meaning.

AMBIGUOUS	The court only hears civil cases on Tuesdays.
CLEAR	The court hears *only* civil cases on Tuesdays.
CLEAR	The court hears civil cases on Tuesdays *only.*

1. Identify all the modifiers in each sentence, and draw an arrow from each modifier to the word it modifies.
2. If a modifier is far from the word it modifies, try to move the two closer together. (17a)
3. Does any modifier seem to refer to a word other than the one it is intended to modify? If so, move the modifier so that it refers clearly to only the intended word. (17a and b)
4. If you cannot find the word to which a modifier refers, revise the sentence: supply such a word, or revise the modifier itself so that it clearly refers to a word already in the sentence. (17c)

CONVENTIONS

Revising Misplaced Modifiers

In the first sentence, placing *only* before the verb makes the meaning ambiguous. Does the writer mean that civil cases are the only cases heard on Tuesdays or that those are the only days when civil cases are heard? The other sentences each express one of these meanings clearly.

Phrases also should ordinarily be placed close to the words they modify. The most common type of phrase modifier, the prepositional phrase, usually appears right after the word it modifies.

on voodoo

▶ **She teaches a seminar ^ this term ~~on voodoo~~ at Skyline College.**

Surely the voodoo was not at the college.

Participial phrases usually appear right before or after the words they modify.

to my guests

▶ **I pointed out ^ the moose head ~~to my guests~~ mounted on the wall.**

The unedited sentence implies that the guests were mounted on the wall.

W *billowing from every window.*

▶ **~~Billowing from every window,~~ ~~w~~e saw clouds of smoke~~.~~ ^**

People cannot billow from windows.

Although you have more flexibility in the placement of dependent clauses than in the placement of modifying words and phrases, try whenever possible to place them close to what you wish them to modify. If you do not, unintended meanings can result.

www •

http://www.engr.trinity.edu/~Review/1995/gallman24.html

This poem of longing and memory by Geoff Alman includes the lovely line "yet even misplaced modifiers reveal a propensity for intention," which is the reason we point you to it.

▶ **The trees** *that line the walks are* **trimmed in the shapes of animals** ~~**that line the walks**~~ *and* **delight visitors.**

Do animals line the walks?

▶ *After he lost the 1962 race,* **Nixon said he would get out of politics.** ~~**after he lost the 1962 race.**~~

The unedited sentence implies that Nixon planned to lose the race.

EXERCISE 17.1

Revise each of the following sentences by moving any misplaced modifiers so that they clearly modify the words they are intended to. Example:

> *When they propose sensible plans, politicians* ~~Politicians~~ are supported by the people. ~~when they propose sensible plans.~~

1. The tenor captivated the entire audience singing with verve.
2. The city almost spent two million dollars on the new stadium.
3. On the day in question, the patient was not normally able to breathe.
4. The clothes were full of holes that I was giving away.
5. Elderly people and students live in the neighborhood surrounding the university, which is full of identical tract houses.
6. Doctors recommend a new test for cancer, which is painless.
7. I went through the process of taxiing and taking off in my mind.
8. I knew that the investment would pay off in a dramatic way before I decided to buy the stock.
9. The bank offered flood insurance to the homeowners underwritten by the federal government.
10. Revolving out of control, the maintenance worker shut down the turbine.

Squinting modifiers

If a modifier can refer to *either* the word(s) before it *or* the word(s) after it, it is called a **squinting modifier.** For example:

AMBIGUOUS Students who practice writing *often* will benefit.

Does the writer mean that students often benefit from practice or that they benefit from practicing often? Two revisions are possible, depending on meaning:

CLEAR Students who *often practice* writing will benefit.

CLEAR Students who practice writing *will often benefit.*

If a sentence could be read more than one way because of your placement of a modifier, put the modifier where it clearly relates to only a single term.

EXERCISE 17.2

Revise each of the following sentences in at least two ways. Move the squinting modifier so that it unambiguously modifies either the word(s) before it or the word(s) after it. Example:

The course we hoped would engross us completely bored us.

The course we hoped would completely engross us bored us.

The course we hoped would engross us bored us completely.

1. He remembered vividly enjoying the sound of Mrs. McIntosh's singing.
2. The mayor promised after her reelection she would not raise taxes.
3. The collector who owned the painting originally planned to leave it to a museum.
4. Doctors can now restore limbs that have been severed partially to a functioning condition.
5. The speaker said when he finished he would answer questions.

17b Revising disruptive modifiers

Disruptive modifiers interrupt the parts of a sentence or a grammatical structure, making it hard for readers to follow the progress of the thought. Be careful that modifiers do not disrupt the flow of a sentence. Most disruptive modifiers are adverbial clauses or phrases. In general, do not place such modifiers between the parts of a verb phrase, between a subject and verb, or between a verb and an object.

were discarded

▶ **The books, because the librarians had decided they were no longer useful, ~~were discarded.~~**

It was awkward to separate the subject *books* from the verb *were discarded.*

If they are cooked too long, vegetables will

▶ **~~Vegetables will, if they are cooked too long,~~ lose most of their nutritional value.**

Separating the parts of the verb phrase, *will* and *lose,* disrupts the flow of the sentence.

a secondhand car

▶ **He bought with his first paycheck. ~~a secondhand car.~~**

Separating the verb *bought* from the subject *a secondhand car* makes it hard to follow the thought.

Modifiers splitting an infinitive

In general, do not split an infinitive by placing a modifier between the *to* and the verb. Doing so makes it hard for readers to recognize that the two go together.

surrender

▶ **Hitler expected the British to fairly quickly. ~~surrender.~~**

In some cases, however, a modifier sounds awkward in any other position. To avoid a split infinitive in such cases, it may be best to reword the sentence to eliminate the infinitive altogether.

SPLIT I hope *to* almost *equal* my last year's income.

REWRITTEN I hope that I will earn almost as much as I did last year.

EXERCISE 17.3

Revise each of the following sentences by moving the disruptive modifier so that the sentence reads smoothly. Example:

During the 1980s, aggressive
~~Aggressive~~ investors discovered ~~during the 1980s~~ the real estate market.

1. Eastern North America was, when Europeans arrived, covered in forest.
2. The exhibit, because of extensive publicity, attracted large audiences.
3. The architect wanted to eventually design public buildings.
4. Bookstores sold, in the first week after publication, fifty thousand copies.
5. The stock exchange became, because of the sudden trading, a chaotic circus.

17c Revising dangling modifiers

Dangling modifiers are words that modify nothing in particular in the rest of a sentence. They often seem to modify something that is suggested or implied but not actually present in the sentence. Such modifiers are called dangling because they hang loosely from the rest of the sentence, attached to no specific element. They frequently appear at the beginnings or ends of sentences.

DANGLING Driving nonstop, Shalishan Lodge is two hours from Portland.

Who is driving? This sentence suggests inadvertently that Shalishan Lodge is the driver.

To revise dangling modifiers, you can add a subject that the modifier clearly refers to, or you can change the dangling modifier itself into a phrase or a nonelliptical clause that clearly modifies an existing part of the sentence. You could revise the above sentence two ways:

REVISED Driving nonstop from Portland, you can reach Shalishan Lodge in two hours.

REVISED If you drive nonstop, Shalishan Lodge is two hours from Portland.

family sold the
▶ **Bankrupt, the ^ land ~~was sold~~ to a neighboring farmer.**

Land cannot be bankrupt.

When he was
▶ **^ ~~As~~ a young boy, his aunt told stories of her years as a country doctor.**

His aunt was never a young boy.

M
▶ **~~Thumbing through the magazine,~~ ~~m~~y eyes automatically noticed the perfume ads ^.**
as I was thumbing through the magazine

Eyes cannot thumb through a magazine.

Even when cornered, a rabbit never uses its teeth for defense.
▶ **^ ~~A rabbit's teeth are never used for defense even when cornered~~.**

The teeth are not cornered.

he was
▶ **Although ^ a reserved and private man, everyone enjoyed his company.**

The elliptical clause cannot refer to *everyone* or to *his company.*

EXERCISE 17.4

Revise each of the following sentences to correct the dangling phrases. Example:

> *a viewer gets*
> Watching television news, ^ an impression ~~is given~~ of constant disaster.

1. High ratings are pursued by emphasizing fires and murders.
2. Interviewing grieving relatives, no consideration is shown for their privacy.
3. To provide comic relief, heat waves and blizzards are attributed to the weather forecaster.
4. Chosen for their looks, newscasters' journalistic credentials are often weak.
5. As a visual medium, complex issues are hard to present in a televised format.

EXERCISE 17.5

Revise each of the following sentences to correct the dangling elliptical clauses. Example:

> *I was impressed by*
> While cycling through southern France, ^ the Roman ruins. ^ ~~impressed me.~~

1. However unhappy, my part-time job helps pay my rent.
2. While attending a performance at Ford's Theater, Lincoln's assassination shocked the nation.
3. A waiter's job can become very stressful when faced with a busy restaurant full of hungry people.
4. Dreams are somewhat like a jigsaw puzzle; if put together in the correct order, organization and coherence become obvious.
5. No matter how costly, my family travels for two weeks every summer.

THINKING CRITICALLY ABOUT MODIFIERS

Reading with an Eye for Modifiers

E. B. White was a master of precise wording, choosing — and positioning — his words with great care. Read the following sentences by White, paying attention to the limiting modifier italicized in each one. Identify which word or words each one modifies. Then try moving the modifier to some other spot in the sentence, and consider how the meaning of the sentence changes as a result.

1. When we got back for a swim before lunch, the lake was exactly where we had left it, the same number of inches from the dock, and there was *only* the mere suggestion of a breeze. — "Once More to the Lake"

2. It was, among other things, the sort of railroad you would occasionally ride *just* for the hell of it, a higher existence into which you would escape unconsciously and without hesitation.
   – "Progress and Change"

Thinking about Your Own Use of Modifiers

Look at two pages of a draft, examining them for clear and effective modifiers. Can you identify any misplaced, disruptive, or dangling modifiers? Using the guidelines in this chapter, revise as need be. Then look for patterns – in the kinds of modifiers you use and in any problems you have placing them. Make a note of what you find.

18 Maintaining Consistent and Complete Grammatical Structures

About twenty years ago, a writing instructor who had studied thousands of student essays came to a simple but profound conclusion about many of the sentences in the essays. Though at first glance the sentences seemed incoherent or nonsensical, they actually fell into certain patterns. They could be better characterized, the instructor decided, either as (1) unsuccessful attempts to combine sentence structures that did not fit together grammatically or sensibly or as (2) sentences missing some element necessary to complete meaning.

In fact, many writers who produce garbled sentences do so in an attempt to use complex and sophisticated structures. What look like "errors," then, may be stepping-stones on a writer's way to greater stylistic maturity. This chapter will help you be sure your own sentences are consistent and complete. ■

18a Making grammatical patterns consistent

One inconsistency that poses problems for writers and readers is a **mixed structure,** which results from beginning a sentence with one grammatical pattern and then switching to another one. For example:

MIXED The fact that I get up at 5:00 A.M., a wake-up time that explains why I'm always tired in the evening.

The sentence starts out with a subject (*The fact*) followed by a dependent clause (*that I get up at 5:00 A.M.*). The sentence needs a predicate to complete the independent clause, but instead it moves to another phrase followed by a dependent clause (*a wake-up time that explains why I'm always tired in the evening*). Thus the independent clause is never completed, and what results is a fragment, or incomplete sentence.

REVISED The fact that I get up at 5:00 A.M. explains why I'm always tired in the evening

Deleting *a wake-up time that* changes the rest of the sentence into a predicate.

REVISED I get up at 5:00 A.M., a wake-up time that explains why I'm always tired in the evening.

Deleting *The fact that* turns the beginning of the sentence into an independent clause.

→ If you find an especially confusing sentence, check to see whether it has a subject (*The athletes swam and ran*) and a predicate (*The athletes swam and ran*). If not, revise as necessary. (18a) If you find both a subject and a predicate and you are still confused, see whether the subject and verb make sense together. If not, revise so that they do. (18b)

→ Revise any *is when, is where,* and *reason . . . is because* constructions. (18b)

▶ **Rio is ^*the city* where I learned Portuguese.**

→ Check all comparisons for completeness. (18e)

▶ **We like Marian better than ^*we like* Margaret.**

▶ **Because hope was the only thing left when Pandora finally closed up the mythical box, ~~explains why~~ we never lose hope no matter how bad life gets.**

The adverb clause beginning with *Because* is followed by a predicate (beginning with *explains*) which lacks a subject. Deleting *explains why* changes the original predicate into an independent clause to which the adverb clause can be attached.

18b Making subjects and predicates consistent

Another kind of mixed structure, called **faulty predication,** occurs when a subject and predicate do not fit together grammatically or simply do not make sense together. Many cases of faulty predication result from using forms of *be* when another verb would be stronger.

▶ **A characteristic that I admire is ^*generosity.* ~~a person who is generous.~~**

A person is not a characteristic.

▶ **The rules of the corporation ^*require that* ~~expect~~ employees ~~to~~ be on time.**

Rules cannot expect anything.

Is when, is where, *and* reason . . . is because

These constructions are inappropriate in academic writing because they use an adverb clause, rather than a noun or an adjective, as a subject complement.

an unfair characterization of
▶ **A stereotype is ~~when someone characterizes~~ a group. ~~unfairly.~~**

a place
▶ **A confluence is where two rivers join to form one.**

▶ **~~The reason~~ I like to play soccer ~~is~~ because it provides aerobic exercise.**

EXERCISE 18.1

Revise each of the following sentences in two ways to make its structures consistent in grammar and meaning. Example:

The fact that our room was cold we put a heater between our beds.

Because our room was cold, we put a heater between our beds.

The fact that our room was cold led us to put a heater between our beds.

1. My interest in a political career would satisfy my desire for public service.
2. The reason air-pollution standards should not be relaxed is because many people would suffer.
3. By not prosecuting white-collar crime as vigorously as violent crime encourages white-collar criminals to think they can ignore the law.
4. Hawthorne's short stories are experiences drawn from his own life.
5. One controversial element of the curriculum has been colleges with a required course in Western culture.

18c Using elliptical structures carefully

Sometimes writers omit certain words in compound structures. When the omission is common to all parts of the compound, this type of structure, known as an **elliptical structure,** is appropriate. In the following sentence, the omitted word is in brackets:

> That bell belonged to the figure of Miss Duling as though it grew directly out of her right arm, as wings grew out of an angel or a tail [grew] out of the devil.
> – EUDORA WELTY, *One Writer's Beginnings*

If the omitted word does not match other parts of the compound, however, the omission is inappropriate.

▶ **His skills are weak, and his performance ^ only average.** [inserted: *is*]

The omitted verb *is* does not match the verb in the other part of the compound (*skills are . . . performance is*), and so the writer must include it.

18d Checking for missing words

The best way to catch inadvertent omissions is to proofread carefully, reading each sentence slowly – and aloud.

▶ **The professor's heavy German accent made ^ difficult for the class ^ understand her lectures.** [inserted: *it*; *to*]

www •

http://www.vuse.vanderbilt.edu/~jgray/funny.html

This page offers a treasure trove of inconsistent and incomplete statements from the real world (one favorite: the ad offering "dress shirts for men with 16 necks"). Click on missing words.

18e Making comparisons complete, consistent, and clear

Check comparisons. When you compare two or more things, the comparison must be complete, logically consistent, and clear.

▶ **I was embarrassed because my parents were so different.** [period struck out; inserted: *from my friends' parents.*]

Different from what? Adding *from my friends' parents* tells readers what the comparison is being made to.

▶ **Woodberry's biography is better than ^ Fields.** [inserted: *the one by*]

This sentence illogically compares a book with a person. The editing makes the comparison logical.

UNCLEAR Ted felt more affection for his brother than his sister.

Did Ted feel more affection for his brother than his sister did – or more affection for his brother than he felt for his sister?

CLEAR Ted felt more affection for his brother than *he did for* his sister.

CLEAR Ted felt more affection for his brother than his sister *did.*

EXERCISE 18.2

Revise each of the following sentences to eliminate any inappropriate elliptical constructions; to make comparisons complete, logically consistent, and clear; and to supply any other omitted words that are necessary for meaning. Example:

> Most of the candidates are bright, and one ^*is* brilliant.

1. My new stepmother makes my father happier.
2. Argentina and Peru were colonized by Spain, and Brazil by Portugal.
3. She argued that children are even more important for men than women.
4. Was the dictatorship in Iraq any worse than many other countries?
5. The personalities of marijuana smokers are different from nonsmokers.

EXERCISE 18.3

Revise this paragraph to make every sentence grammatically and logically consistent and complete.

The reason I believe the United States should have a military draft is because draft would make us better citizens. By requiring the same sacrifice from every young person would make everyone feel part a common effort. In addition, a draft is fairer. When an army is made up of volunteers come mostly from the poor and minority groups. During the Persian Gulf War, news reports showed blacks were overrepresented among the troops, largely because their economic options were more limited than young whites and the military thus more attractive as a career. I also feel that women should be subject to the draft. A quality that the military needs is soldiers who are dedicated, and women soldiers have shown that they are more dedicated to their jobs than men. The requirements of a modern army also need skills that more women possess. Equality is when both sexes have equal responsibilities as well as equal opportunity.

THINKING CRITICALLY ABOUT CONSISTENCY AND COMPLETENESS

Thinking about Any Mixed or Incomplete Structures in Your Writing

Read over three or four paragraphs from a draft or completed essay you have written recently, checking for mixed sentences and incomplete or missing structures. Revise the paragraphs to correct any problems you find. If you find any, do you recognize any patterns? If so, make a note of them for future reference (in your writing log, if you keep one).

PART 4

SENTENCES: MAKING STYLISTIC CHOICES

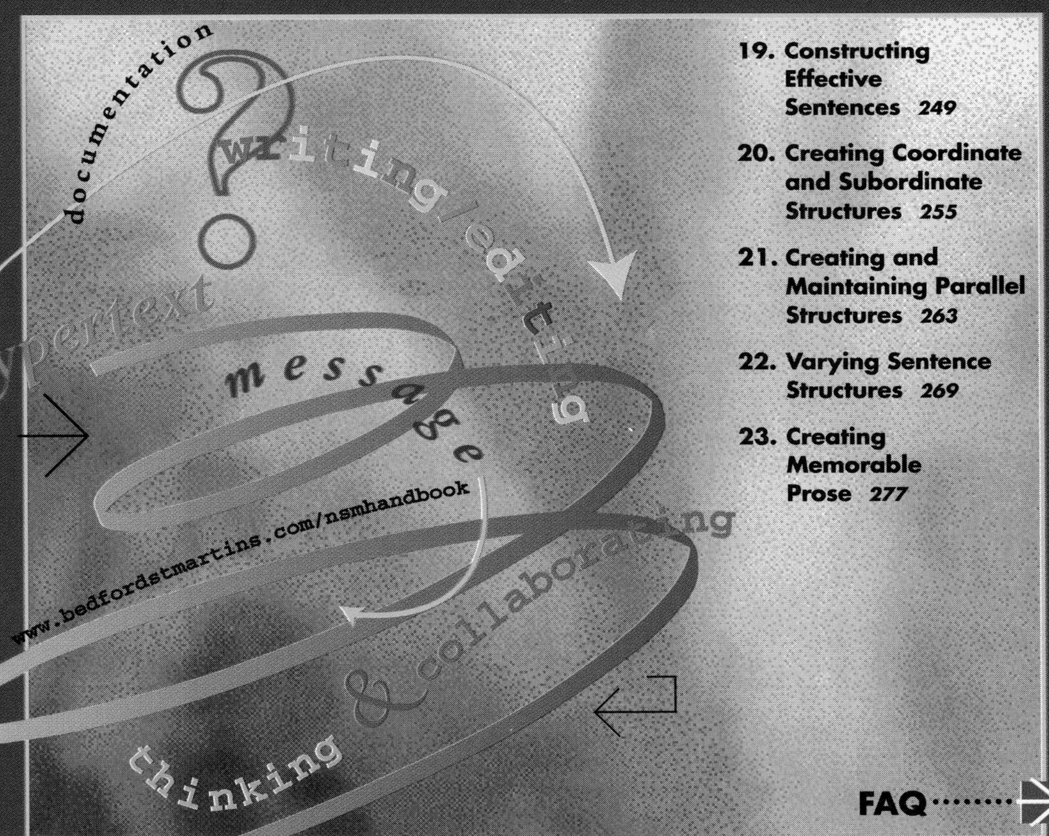

FAQ

FAQ: Sentence Style Online

Does all online writing need to be very concise?

Readers of online writing can't flip pages back and forth. Instead, they have to scroll down and back up, or print out and then read. Moreover, much online communication is meant to be instantaneous, composed of short exchanges and quick replies to queries. The speed of communication, small screens, even scarce BANDWIDTH — all encourage concise, directly stated messages. Unless your writing is meant to be DOWNLOADED and printed out, try to use screen space efficiently.

- **Homepages.** HOMEPAGES must use space to maximum effect, giving necessary information via images and words, and also including links to other pages and documents. Though these linked documents may be quite lengthy, the homepage leading you to them needs to be concise.
- **MOOs and MUDs.** Brevity is even more important in MOOs and MUDs, where many people interact simultaneously. MOOs and MUDs tend to invite very short exchanges, often just a sentence or two.

How much stylistic polishing does online writing call for?

As always, the answer depends on your rhetorical situation. If the outcome of a particular piece of online writing is very important to you (an award or promotion, say, or a contract, or a Web page you are responsible for designing), then the more polished your prose the better. Make sure it's correct, accurate, and persuasive.

Many EMAIL or NEWSGROUP postings, however, seek to convey particular pieces of information in the quickest and easiest way possible. Such messages need only be polished enough to be clear. And in MOOs and MUDs, writing contributions are so short and done so rapidly that polished prose is not expected.

http://www.columbia.edu/acis/bartleby/strunk

The Online Elements of Style *provides Strunk and White's classic advice on usage and style.*

http://www.emo.com/wwb/wwb_sty.html

Writer's Workbench Style Program *offers information on stylistic issues such as average sentence length, sentence type, voice of verbs, and kinds of sentence openers. It includes links to other programs on diction, spelling, punctuation, and so on.*

Constructing Effective Sentences

19

Put most simply, effective sentences have two main characteristics: they emphasize ideas clearly, and they do so as concisely as possible. We can see the importance of emphasis and conciseness in many sets of instructions. Look, for instance, at those found on one common prescription drug:

Take one tablet daily. Some nonprescription drugs may aggravate your condition, so read all labels carefully. If any include a warning, check with your doctor. Refill prescription only until 12/12/01.

Squeezing important information onto a three-inch label probably won't be a task you'll confront regularly, but more often than not, you will want to write as emphatically and concisely as you can — especially in academic writing. This chapter will help you to do so. ■

19a Emphasizing main ideas

When we speak, we achieve **emphasis** by raising our voices, putting extra stress on an important word, or drawing out a phrase. And much of the writing we see around us — in advertisements, on Web sites, in magazines — gains emphasis in similar fashion, with color or graphics or bold type, for instance. Much academic writing can't rely on such graphic devices for emphasis. Luckily, however, writers have other ways to let readers know which parts of sentences are most important.

1 Using closing and opening positions for emphasis

When you read a sentence, what are you likely to remember? Other things being equal, you remember the ending. This is the part of the sentence that should move the writing forward by providing new information, as it does in the following example:

> To protect her skin, she took along *plenty of sunblock lotion.*

A less emphatic but still important position in a sentence is the opening, which hooks up the new sentence with what has come before.

> When Rosita went to the beach, she was anxious not to get a sunburn. *To protect her skin,* she took along plenty of sunblock lotion.

FOR EMPHASIS

→ Identify the words you want to receive special emphasis. If those words are buried in the middle of a sentence, edit the sentence to change their position. Remember that the end and the beginning are generally the most emphatic. (19a1)

→ Note any sentences that include a series of three or more words, phrases, or clauses. Could the items in the series be arranged in climactic order, with the most important item last? (19a2)

FOR CONCISENESS

→ Look for redundant words. If you are unsure about a word, read the sentence without it; if the meaning is not affected, leave the word out.

→ Look for empty words – words like *aspect* or *factor, definitely* or *very.* Unless your meaning is unclear without them, leave them out. (19b2)

→ Do you use any wordy phrases? If so, see if you can replace them with a single word – instead of *because of the fact that,* try *because;* rather than *for the purpose of,* try *for.* (19b3)

→ Look for grammatical structures that might be simplified: adjective clauses that could be reduced to appositive phrases, expletive constructions that could be eliminated, passive-voice verbs that could be changed to the active voice, consecutive sentences with the same subject or predicate that could be combined into one sentence. (19b4)

The second sentence would lose emphasis if the key words, *plenty of sunblock lotion,* were buried in the middle, as in the following version:

> To protect her skin, she took along *plenty of sunblock lotion,* and she also planned to stay under an umbrella most of the time.

If you place relatively unimportant information in the memorable closing position of a sentence, you may undercut what you want to emphasize or give more emphasis to the closing words than you intend.

> ***Last month, she*** ... ***$500,000.***
>
> ▶ **~~She~~ gave ~~$500,000 to~~ the school capital campaign ~~last month.~~**
>
> Moving *$500,000* to the end of the sentence emphasizes the amount.

2 Using climactic order

Presenting ideas in **climactic order** means arranging them in order of increasing importance, power, or drama so that your writing builds to a climax.

> Dissidents risk social rejection, forced relocation, long imprisonment, and almost certain death.

> After they've finished with the pantry, the medicine cabinet, and the attic, [neat people] will throw out the red geranium (too many leaves), sell the dog (too many fleas), and send the children off to boarding school (too many scuffmarks on the hardwood floors).
>
> – SUSANNE BRITT, "Neat People vs. Sloppy People"

Each of these statements saves its most dramatic item for last, making its point forcefully. The original version of the next sentence fails to achieve strong emphasis because its verbs are not sequenced in order of increasing power; the editing provides climactic order.

offend our ears, *and*

▶ **Soap operas ^ assault our eyes, ^ damage our brains~~,~~^ ~~and offend our ears.~~**

EXERCISE 19.1

Revise each of the following sentences to highlight what you take to be the main or most important ideas. Example:

hybrids of coldblooded capabilities,

> Theories about dinosaurs run the gamut — simple lizards, ^ fully adapted warm-blooded creatures~~,~~^ ~~hybrids of coldblooded capabilities.~~

1. All medical papers, whether initial investigation, presentation of final statistics, or reports on work in progress, must undergo rigorous scrutiny.
2. Also notable is the image of chrysanthemums throughout the story.
3. Nancy Kerrigan went on to receive the silver medal in figure skating at the 1994 Winter Olympics, despite the preceding media circus.
4. The presence of the Indian in these movies always conjures up destructive stereotypes of bloodthirsty war parties, horse thieves, and drunkenness.
5. Victorian women were warned that if they smoked, they would become sterile, grow a moustache, die young, or contract tuberculosis.

19b Being concise

Usually you'll want to be **concise** – to make your point in the fewest possible words. Look at the following sentence:

> Her constant and continual use of vulgar expressions with obscene meanings indicated to her pre-elementary supervisory group that she was rather deficient in terms of her ability to interact in an efficient manner with peers in her potential interaction group.

Why write that sentence when you could instead write the following one?

> Her constant use of four-letter words told the day-care workers she might have trouble getting along with other four-year-olds.

1 Eliminating redundant words

Sometimes writers add words for emphasis, saying that something is large *in size* or red *in color* or that two ingredients should be combined *together*. The italicized words are **redundant,** or unnecessary for meaning, as are the deleted words in these examples:

▶ **~~Compulsory~~ *A*ttendance at assemblies is required.**

▶ **The auction featured ~~contemporary~~ "antiques" made recently.**

2 Eliminating empty words

Empty words are so general and so overused that they contribute no real meaning to a sentence.

EMPTY WORDS

angle, area, aspect, case, character, element, factor, field, kind, nature, scope, situation, thing, type

Many modifiers are so common that they have become empty words.

MEANINGLESS MODIFIERS

absolutely, awesome, awfully, central, definitely, fine, great, literally, major, quite, really, very

www •

http://www.columbia.edu/acis/bartleby/strunk

This classic 1918 style manual by Will Strunk, Jr., is now online; click on Omit needless words for his advice on being concise ("Vigorous writing is concise. . . .")

Because empty words tend to make writing dull as well as wordy, use them sparingly. When you cannot simply delete them, try to think of a more specific way to say what you mean.

▶ **~~The~~ *H*ousing ~~situation~~ can *strongly influence* ~~have a really significant impact on the social aspect of~~ a student's *social* life.**

3 Replacing wordy phrases

Wordy phrases are those that can be reduced to a word or two with no loss in meaning.

WORDY	CONCISE
at all times	always
at the present time	now/today
at that point in time	then
due to the fact that	because
in order to	to
in spite of the fact that	although
in the event that	if
for the purpose of	for

4 Simplifying sentence structure

Using the simplest grammatical structures possible will strengthen your sentences considerably.

▶ **Kennedy, ~~who was~~ only the second Roman Catholic ~~to be~~ nominated for the presidency by a major party, had to handle the religion issue** *delicately.* **~~in a delicate manner.~~** ^

Reducing a clause to an appositive, deleting unnecessary words, and replacing four words with one tighten the sentence and make it easier to read.

▶ **When ~~she was~~ questioned about her previous job, she seemed nervous/** *and* **~~She also~~ tried to change the subject.** ^

Reducing an adverb clause to an elliptical form and combining two sentences produces one concise sentence.

Other ways to simplify grammatical structures include using strong verbs and nouns, avoiding expletive constructions, and using the active rather than the passive voice. These methods are discussed in Chapter 23.

www •

http://www.english .upenn.edu:80/~jlynch /grammar.html

These notes on grammar and style are alphabetically arranged for easy access; click on wasted words and economy for notes on wordy phrases.

EXERCISE 19.2

Make each of the following sentences clear and concise by eliminating unnecessary words and phrases. Example:

> *summarize.*
> Let me ~~fill you in on the main points of the overall picture~~ here.

1. At the present time, many different forms of hazing occur, such as various forms of physical abuse and also mental abuse.
2. Many people have a tendency toward the expansion of their sentences by the superfluous addition of extra words that are not really needed for the meaning of the sentences.
3. One of the major problems that is faced at this point in time is that there is world hunger.
4. After I stopped the practice of exercising regularly, I became ten pounds heavier in weight in a relatively short amount of time.
5. There are numerous theories that have been proposed by scientists as to why dinosaurs reached the point of becoming extinct.

THINKING CRITICALLY ABOUT SENTENCES

Reading with an Eye for Sentence Style

Here are two sentences from "A Sweet Devouring," Eudora Welty's essay about the pleasures of reading. Each sentence makes a powerful statement. Read each one, and decide how Welty achieves such strong emphasis. Then read something by a favorite writer, looking for strong, emphatic sentences. Bring in one or two sentences to compare to those chosen by your classmates.

1. The pleasures of reading itself — who doesn't remember? — were like those of a Christmas cake, a sweet devouring.
2. And then I went again to the home shelves and my lucky hand reached and found Mark Twain — twenty-four volumes, not a series, and good all the way through.

Thinking about Your Own Sentences

Find two or three paragraphs you have written recently, and study them with an eye for empty words. Using 19b2 for guidance, eliminate meaningless words such as *aspect, factor, quite,* or *very.* Compare notes with one or two classmates to see what empty words, if any, you all tend to use. Finally, make a note of those you use (in your writing log, if you keep one) so that you can avoid them in the future.

Creating Coordinate and Subordinate Structures

20

20a Using coordination to relate equal ideas

When used well, **coordination** relates separate but equal elements, making clear the emphasis given to different ideas. The precise relationship is stated in the element that links the ideas, usually a coordinating conjunction (*and, but, for, nor, or, so, yet*) or a semicolon. The following sentences all use coordination, but note that the precise relationship between clauses differs in each sentence, as expressed in the connecting element (a coordinating conjunction or a semicolon):

> They acquired horses, *and* their ancient nomadic spirit was suddenly free of the ground.
>
> There is perfect freedom in the mountains, *but* it belongs to the eagle and the elk, the badger and the bear.
>
> No longer were they slaves to the simple necessity of survival; they were a lordly and dangerous society of fighters and thieves, hunters and priests of the sun.
>
> – N. Scott Momaday, *The Way to Rainy Mountain*

Coordination can help make more explicit the relationship between two ideas, as the following revision shows:

▶ **My son watches *The Simpsons* religiously~~.~~; ~~F~~forced to choose, he would probably choose Homer Simpson over his sister.**

If you think about how you build sentences, you may notice a difference between your spoken and your written language. In speech, people tend to use *and* and *so* as all-purpose connectors.

I'm going home now, and I'll see you later.

The meaning of this sentence may be perfectly clear in speech, which provides clues with voice, facial expressions, and gestures. But in writing, it could, for instance, have either of two rather different meanings.

Because I'm going home now, I'll see you later.

I'm going home now because I'll see you later.

These examples show two different ways of combining ideas in a sentence: coordinating conjunctions like *and* give the ideas equal emphasis, and subordinating conjunctions like *because* emphasize one idea more than another. As a writer, you must often decide whether to use coordinate structures, subordinate ones, both, or neither, depending on the emphasis and effect you want to achieve. ■

STYLE
Creating Coordinate and Subordinate Structures

How do your ideas flow from one sentence to another? Do they connect smoothly and clearly? Are the more important ideas given more emphasis than less important ones? These guidelines will help you edit with such questions in mind.

→ How often do you link ideas with *and*? If you use *and* a great deal in this way, consider whether the linked ideas are equally important. If they are not, edit to subordinate the less important ones. (20b)

→ Look for strings of short sentences that might be combined to join related ideas. (20a)

▶ **The report was short, ~~It~~ *but it* was persuasive; ~~It~~ *it* changed my mind.**

→ Are the most important ideas in independent clauses? If not, edit so that they are. (20b)

▶ **~~The~~ *Even though the* report was short, ~~even though~~ it changed my mind.**

www •

http://aix1.uottawa.ca/academic/arts/writcent/hypergrammar/conjunct.html co-ordinating conjunction

From the University of Ottawa's wonderful HyperGrammar *comes this clear and thorough advice on using coordinating and subordinating conjunctions.*

When you use coordination to connect ideas in a sentence, however, make sure that the connecting element clearly and accurately expresses the relationship between the ideas.

▶ **Watching television is a common way to spend leisure time, ~~and~~ *but* it makes viewers apathetic.**

The relationship between the two ideas in the original sentence is unclear: what does being a common form of leisure have to do with being apathetic? Changing *and* to *but* better relates the two ideas.

Using coordination for special effect

Coordination can be used to create special effects, as in a passage by Carl Sandburg describing the reaction of the American people to Abraham Lincoln's assassination.

> Men tried to talk about it and the words failed and they came back to silence.
>
> To say nothing was best.
>
> Lincoln was dead.
>
> Was there anything more to say?
>
> Yes, they would go through the motions of grief and they would take part in a national funeral and a ceremony of humiliation and abasement and tears.
>
> But words were no help.
>
> Lincoln was dead. – CARL SANDBURG, *Abraham Lincoln: The War Years*

Together with the other short simple sentences, the coordinate clauses, phrases, and words in the first and fifth sentences create a powerful effect. Everything in the passage is grammatically equal, flattened out by the pain and shock of the death. In this way, the sentence structure and grammar mirror the dazed state of the populace. The short sentences and clauses are almost like sobs that illustrate the thought of the first sentence, that "the words failed."

> Are you familiar with Motel 8? It's a chain of cheesy cheap motels across the South – twenty dollars a night gets you peeling beaverboard walls *and* thin pink blankets. There's no phone in the room, *but* a TV set that's always tuned to the Nashville Channel, *and* an air conditioner that's always got a screw or three loose *and* vibrates like a 747 on takeoff. You see piles of emptied cigarette butts in the parking lot, *and* always cigarette burns on the table, *and* more cigarette burns on the carpet, *and* a poorly repaired hole in the wall where some good old boy put his fist through it in anger at his pregnant sixteen-year-old wife who didn't wanna go out to the Ponderosa.

Here the use of *and* and *but* helps the writer catalog many colorful, if somewhat unsavory, details. By stringing together images in this way, the writer presents them in a kind of heap, which contributes to the overall impression of the Motel 8.

EXERCISE 20.1

Using the principles of coordination to signal equal importance or to create special emphasis, combine and revise the following twelve short sentences into several longer and more effective ones. Add or delete words as necessary.

> The bull-riding arena was fairly crowded.
>
> The crowd made no impression on me.

I had made a decision.
It was now time to prove myself.
I was scared.
I walked to the entry window.
I laid my money on the counter.
The clerk held up a Stetson hat filled with slips of paper.
I reached in.
I picked one.
The slip held the number of the bull I was to ride.
I headed toward the stock corral.

20b Using subordination to distinguish main ideas

Subordination allows you to distinguish major points from minor points or bring in supporting details. If, for instance, you put your main idea in an independent clause, you might then put any less significant ideas in dependent clauses, phrases, or even single words. Look at the following sentence, which shows the subordinated point in italics:

> Mrs. Viola Cullinan was a plump woman *who lived in a three-bedroom house somewhere behind the post office.* – MAYA ANGELOU, "My Name Is Margaret"

The dependent clause adds important information about Mrs. Cullinan, but it is grammatically subordinate to the independent clause, which carries the main idea: *Mrs. Viola Cullinan was a plump woman.*

Notice that the choice of what to subordinate rests with the writer and depends on the intended meaning. Angelou might have given the same basic information differently: *Mrs. Viola Cullinan, a plump woman, lived in a three-bedroom house somewhere behind the post office.* Subordinating the information about Mrs. Cullinan's size to that about her house would have resulted in a slightly different meaning, of course. As a writer, you must think carefully about where you want your emphasis to be and subordinate accordingly.

Besides adding information, subordination also helps establish logical relationships among ideas. These relationships are often specified by subordinating conjunctions – words such as *after, because,* or *so.* Look, for example, at another sentence by Maya Angelou, shown with the subordinate clause italicized and the subordinating conjunction underlined.

For more about subordinating conjunctions, see 7b7.

> She usually rested her smile until late afternoon *when her women friends dropped in and Miss Glory, the cook, served them cold drinks on the closed-in porch.*
> – MAYA ANGELOU, "My Name Is Margaret"

Subordination can be used to combine short sentences in ways that signal logical relationships. For example:

▶ *When the* **~~The~~ children opened the cage~~.~~, ~~T~~*t*he parrot flew out of the window~~.~~, *which* I had forgotten to close. ~~it.~~**

Finally, subordination can provide a useful alternative to coordination. Using too many coordinate structures can be monotonous and can make it hard for readers to recognize the most important ideas. Subordinating lesser ideas can help highlight the main ideas.

▶ **Many people come home tired in the evening, and so they turn on the TV to relax.** *Though they* **~~They~~ may intend to watch just the news, ~~but then~~ a game show comes on next,** *which* **~~and~~ they decide to watch ~~it~~ for just a short while~~,~~.** *Eventually,* **~~and~~ they get too comfortable to get up, and they end up spending the whole evening in front of the TV.**

By subordinating some of the less important ideas in the passage, the editing makes clear to the reader that some of the ideas are more important than others.

Like coordination, however, subordination can be used excessively. When too many subordinating structures, usually dependent clauses, are strung together, readers have trouble keeping track of the main idea expressed in the independent clause. Look, for example, at the following:

TOO MUCH SUBORDINATION

Philip II sent the Spanish Armada to conquer England, which was ruled by Elizabeth, who had executed Mary because she was plotting to overthrow Elizabeth, who was a Protestant, whereas Mary and Philip were Roman Catholics.

The long string of subordinate clauses makes the relationships among the ideas hard to follow — and also makes the main idea (in the independent clause at the beginning) hard for readers to remember. See how changing one of the dependent clauses to the independent clause in a new sentence and reducing two others to appositive phrases makes the meaning clearer.

REVISED

Philip II sent the Spanish Armada to conquer England, which was ruled by Elizabeth, a Protestant. She had executed Mary, a Roman Catholic like Philip, because Mary was plotting to overthrow her.

Depending on what grammatical structures you use to subordinate, you can call attention to a less important element of a sentence in various ways, as the following series demonstrates:

The parks report was persuasively written. It contained five typed pages. [no subordination]

The parks report, *which contained five typed pages,* was persuasively written. [clause]

The parks report, *containing five typed pages,* was persuasively written. [participial phrase]

The *five-page* parks report was persuasively written. [adjective]

The parks report, *five typed pages,* was persuasively written. [appositive]

EXERCISE 20.2

Combine each of the following sets of sentences into one sentence that uses subordination to signal the relationships among ideas. Example:

I was looking over my books.

I noticed that *Burr* was missing.

This book is a favorite of my roommate's.

While I was looking over my books, I noticed that *Burr,* one of my roommate's favorite books, was missing.

1. I walked into the shelter.
   Men, women, and children were slumped against the wall.
   Shopping carts containing families' belongings lay on their sides.
2. Barbra Streisand announced her first concert tour in years.
   Ticket sales were advertised.
   Fans lined up as many as forty-eight hours in advance.
3. We had dug a seventy-foot ditch.
   My boss would pour gravel into the ditch.
   I would level the gravel with a shovel.
4. *Working* was written by Studs Terkel.
   It is an important book.
   It examines the situation of the American worker.
5. The scenery there is beautiful.
   The mountains have caps of snow.

The lakes are deep and full of fish.
The pastures are green.
It is an ideal spot to spend spring break.

Using subordination for special effect

Carefully used subordination can create powerful effects. Some particularly fine examples come from Martin Luther King Jr. In the following passage, he piles up dependent clauses beginning with *when* to gain emphasis for his main statement, given in the independent clause:

> Perhaps it is easy for those who have never felt the stinging darts of segregation to say, "Wait." But *when* you have seen vicious mobs lynch your mothers and fathers at will and drown your sisters and brothers at whim; *when* you have seen hate-filled policemen curse, kick, and even kill your black brothers and sisters; . . . *when* you have to concoct an answer for a five-year-old son who is asking: "Daddy, why do white people treat colored people so mean?"; *when* you take a cross-country drive and find it necessary to sleep night after night in the uncomfortable corners of your automobile because no motel will accept you; . . . *when* your first name becomes "nigger," your middle name becomes "boy" (however old you are) and your last name becomes "John," and your wife and mother are never given the respected title "Mrs."; . . . *when* you are forever fighting a degenerating sense of "nobodiness" – then you will understand why we find it difficult to wait.
>
> – MARTIN LUTHER KING JR., "Letter from Birmingham Jail"

Look now at a student example that uses subordination.

> *Though* dogs are messy and hard to train, *though* they chew up my shoes and give me the blues, *though* they howl like wolves but jump at their own shadows, *though* they eat me out of house and home – still, I love them all.

A dependent clause can also be used to create an ironic effect, if it somehow undercuts the independent clause. Probably no American writer was better at using this technique than Mark Twain. In a tongue-in-cheek commencement address, Twain once opened a paragraph with this sentence.

> Always obey your parents, *when they are present.*
>
> – MARK TWAIN, "Advice to Youth"

Now look at a student writer's use of the same technique.

> Never eat fattening foods – *unless you are hungry.*

EXERCISE 20.3

Revise the following paragraph, using coordination and subordination where appropriate to clarify the relationships between ideas.

I stayed with my friend Louise. She owns a huge, mangy wolf. It is actually a seven-eighths wolf cross. The poor creature is allergic to everything. It looks like a shabby, moth-eaten exhibit of a stuffed wolf in a third-rate museum. Louise and Bill feed it rice and raw potatoes. It slavers all over everything. It never goes out of the house. It sleeps on the beds. They are covered with animal hair. It makes no sounds. It just looks at you with those sunken, wild eyes. It is not dangerous or ferocious. It is just completely miserable. This animal should never have been born. It's trying to tell you that with every twitch.

THINKING CRITICALLY ABOUT COORDINATION AND SUBORDINATION

Reading with an Eye for Coordination and Subordination

Read over the first draft of "The Smart One," in 3f, paying special attention to the coordination and subordination. Do you notice any patterns — is there some of each? more of one than the other? Analyze one paragraph, identifying the coordination and subordination. Are they used appropriately? If not, revise the paragraph following the guidelines in this chapter.

Thinking about Your Own Use of Coordination and Subordination

Analyze two paragraphs from one of your drafts. Do the independent clauses contain the main ideas? How many dependent clauses do you find? Should the ideas in the dependent clauses be subordinate to the ones in the independent clauses? Following the advice in this chapter, revise the paragraphs to use coordination and subordination effectively. What conclusions can you draw about your use of coordination and subordination? Note them down (in your writing log, if you keep one).

21 Creating and Maintaining Parallel Structures

Parallel grammatical structures are used in many of our most familiar phrases: *sink or swim, rise and shine, shape up or ship out.* But parallelism, expressing parallel elements in the same grammatical form, goes far beyond such clichés — and characterizes some of our most elegant writing. See how E. B. White uses parallel structures to describe the enchantment of watching a circus rider:

> *The enchantment grew not out of anything that happened or was performed but out of something that seemed to go round and around and around with the girl, attending her, a steady gleam in the shape of a circle — a ring of ambition, of happiness, of youth.*

Just as the young woman goes "round and around and around," balanced on her horse, so the sentence circles rhythmically too, balanced by a series of parallel phrases and clauses. This chapter will help you use parallelism to create pleasing rhythmic effects in your own writing. ■

21a Using parallel structures in series, lists, outlines, and headings

All items in a series should be in parallel form – all nouns, all prepositional phrases, all adverb clauses, and so on. Such parallelism makes a series both graceful and easy to follow.

> In the eighteenth century, armed forces could fight *in open fields* and *on the high seas.* Today, they can clash *on the ground anywhere, on the sea, under the sea,* and *in the air.*
>
> – Donald Snow and Eugene Brown, *The Contours of Power*

Notice how the parallel series of italicized prepositional phrases, as well as the parallel structure of the two sentences themselves, highlights the contrast between warfare in the eighteenth century and warfare today.

- ▶ **The quarter horse skipped, pranced, and ~~was sashaying~~** *sashayed* **onto the track.**
- ▶ **The children ran down the hill, skipped over the lawn, and** *jumped* **into the swimming pool.**
- ▶ **The duties of the job include baby-sitting, house-cleaning, and ~~preparation of~~** *preparing* **meals.**

STYLE

Creating and Maintaining Parallel Structures

→ Look for any series of three or more items, and make all of the items parallel in structure. If you want to emphasize one particular item, try putting it at the end of the series. (21a)

→ Check for places where two ideas are compared, contrasted, or otherwise paired in the same sentence. Often these ideas will appear on either side of *and, but, or, nor, for, so,* or *yet,* or after each part of *both . . . and, either . . . or, neither . . . nor, not only . . . but also, whether . . . or,* or *just as . . . so.* Edit to make the two ideas parallel in structure. (21b)

→ Check all parallel structures to be sure you have included all necessary words – articles, prepositions, the *to* of the infinitive, and so on. (21c)

→ Be sure items in lists are parallel in form. (21a)

→ Be sure all headings are parallel in form. (21a)

Items in a list should be parallel.

▶ **Kitchen rules: (1) Coffee to be made only by library staff. (2) Coffee service to be closed at 4:00 P.M. (3) Doughnuts to be kept in cabinet. (4) ~~No faculty members should handle coffee materials.~~** *Coffee materials not to be handled by faculty.* ^

For a discussion of formal outlines, see 3e.

Items on a formal outline and headings in a paper should be parallel. Each level should be parallel in form. You might center one level, underline another, and so on. Whatever form you decide on, be sure that all the items or headings in each level have the same form. They should also be parallel in wording – all nouns, all gerunds, all infinitive phrases, and so on.

21b Using parallel structures with pairs

www

http://www.columbia.edu/acis/bartleby/strunk

Go here for Will Strunk's advice on parallelism; click on Express co-ordinate ideas in similar form.

One effective use of parallel structures occurs in the pairing of two ideas. The more nearly parallel the two structures are, the stronger the connection between the ideas will be. Parallel structures are especially appropriate when two ideas are being compared or contrasted.

History became popular, and historians became alarmed. – WILL DURANT

We die. That may be the meaning of life. But we *do* language. That may be the measure of our lives. – TONI MORRISON

Writers are often more interesting on the page than in the flesh.

When two clauses in a sentence express compared or contrasted ideas in exactly or almost exactly parallel structures, they produce a **balanced sentence,** one with two parts that "mirror" each other. Balanced sentences create an especially forceful impression.

Mankind must put an end to war, or war will put an end to mankind. – JOHN F. KENNEDY

There is much in your book that is original and valuable — but what is original is not valuable, and what is valuable is not original. – SAMUEL JOHNSON

With coordinating conjunctions

In general, use the same grammatical structure on both sides of any of the coordinating conjunctions — *and, but, or, nor, for, so, yet.*

We performed *whenever folks would listen* and *wherever they would pay.*

who is
▶ **Consult a friend ^ in your class or who is good at math.**

With correlative conjunctions

Use the same structure after both parts of a correlative conjunction — *either . . . or, both . . . and, neither . . . nor, not . . . but, not only . . . but also, just as . . . so, whether . . . or.*

The organization provided both *scholarships for young artists* and *grants for established ones.*

to live
▶ **I wanted not only to go away to school but also ^ in New England.**

Balancing *to go* with *to live* links the two ideas and makes the sentence easier to read.

EXERCISE 21.1

Complete the following sentences, using parallel words or phrases in each case. Example:

The wise politician *promises the possible, effects the unavoidable,* and *accepts the inevitable.*

1. Before we depart, we must _______, _______, and _______.
2. My favorite pastimes include _______, _______, and _______.
3. We must either _______ or _______.
4. I want not only _______ but also _______.
5. Graduates find that the job market _______, _______, and _______.

EXERCISE 21.2

Revise the following sentences as necessary to eliminate any errors in parallel structure. Example:

I enjoy skiing, playing the piano, and ~~I cane~~ *caning* chairs.

1. I remember entering the stark canyon in North Dakota, searching the rubble by day, sleeping in a tent by night, and at last discovered dinosaur bones.
2. I will always remember how the girls dressed in green plaid skirts and the boys wearing green plaid ties.
3. It was a question of either reducing their staff, or they had to somehow find new customers for their baked potatoes.
4. To need a new pair of shoes and not being able to afford them is sad.
5. I'll never forget the good times we had — skiing, the swims, and especially that you taught me the basics of how to wind-surf.

21c Including all necessary words

In addition to making parallel elements grammatically similar, be careful to include any words — prepositions, articles, verb forms, and so on — that are necessary for clarity or grammar.

▶ **We'll move to a town near the ocean or ^*to* Mexico.**

To a town *near* Mexico or *to* Mexico? The editing makes the meaning clear.

▶ **I had never before ^*seen* and would never again see such a sight.**

In the unedited version, *had . . . see* is not grammatical.

▶ **I prefer the beaches in Brazil to ^*those in* the United States.**

The revision clearly compares beaches with beaches.

21d Using parallel structures for emphasis and effect

Parallel structures can help a writer emphasize the most important ideas in a sentence. Look at the following sentence:

> I would like to promise her that she will grow up with a sense of her cousins and of rivers and of her great-grandmother's teacups, would like to pledge her a picnic on a river with fried chicken and her hair uncombed, would like to give her *home* for her birthday, but we live differently now and I can promise her nothing like that. – JOAN DIDION, "On Going Home"

The first two parallel phrases, *would like to promise her . . . , would like to pledge her . . . ,* provide a series of specific, concrete details and images that leads up to the general statement in the last phrase, that Didion would like to give her daughter a sense of home. Although Didion could have stated this general point first and then gone on to illustrate it with concrete details, she achieves greater emphasis by making it the last in a series of parallel structures arranged in climactic order.

For more on ways to emphasize particular parts of a sentence, see 19a.

Besides emphasizing main ideas, parallel structures can create a number of different stylistic effects.

> At work, he may have time to gulp down a cup of coffee if the dining halls are running smoothly, if all the workers show up, and if the boss is not asking questions.

This sentence creates an impression of somewhat desperate activity as it piles up the three parallel *if* clauses.

EXERCISE 21.3

Revise the following paragraph to maintain parallelism and to supply all words necessary for clarity and grammar in parallel structures.

Growing up in a large city provides a very different experience from a suburban childhood. Suburban children undoubtedly enjoy many advantages over those who live in a city, including lawns to play ball on, trees for climbing, and often the schools are better. However, in recent years many people raised in the suburbs but who moved to large cities as young adults are deciding to bring up their own children in an urban setting. Their reasons for doing so include what they consider the cultural advantages of the city, the feeling that they will be able to spend more time with their children if they do not have to commute so far to work, and also they want to expose the children to a greater diversity of social and economic groups than most suburbs offer. Just as their own parents left the city for the space and calm of suburbia, so crowds and excitement are why today's parents are returning to it. Wherever they bring up their children, though, parents have never nor will they ever find utopia.

THINKING CRITICALLY ABOUT PARALLELISM

Reading with an Eye for Parallelism

Read the following paragraph about a bareback rider practicing her circus act, and identify all the parallel structures. Consider what effect they create on you as a reader, and try to decide why the author chose to put his ideas in such overtly parallel form. Try imitating the next-to-last sentence, the one beginning *In a week or two.*

> The richness of the scene was in its plainness, its natural condition – of horse, of ring, of girl, even to the girl's bare feet that gripped the bare back of her proud and ridiculous mount. The enchantment grew not out of anything that happened or was performed but out of something that seemed to go round and around and around with the girl, attending her, a steady gleam in the shape of a circle – a ring of ambition, of happiness, of youth. (And the positive pleasures of equilibrium under difficulties.) In a week or two, all would be changed, all (or almost all) lost: the girl would wear makeup, the horse would wear gold, the ring would be painted, the bark would be clean for the feet of the horse, the girl's feet would be clean for the slippers that she'd wear. All, all would be lost.
>
> – E. B. WHITE, "The Ring of Time"

Thinking about Your Own Use of Parallelism

Read carefully several paragraphs from a draft you have recently written, noting any series of words, phrases, or clauses. Using the guidelines at the beginning of this chapter, determine whether the series are parallel, and if not, revise them for parallelism. Then reread the paragraphs, looking for places where parallel structures would add emphasis or clarity, and revise accordingly. Can you draw any conclusions about your use of parallelism? Make a note of them (in your writing log, if you keep one).

Varying Sentence Structures

22

Row upon row of trees identical in size and shape may appeal at some level to a sense of orderliness, but those identical rows soon become boring. If variety is the spice of life, it is also the spice of sentence structure, where sameness can result in dull, listless prose.

We saw this principle in action in one particular college classroom. Although a peer-response group had worked on an essay for almost an hour, they felt stumped: it still seemed boring. Finally, one student exclaimed, "I've got it! Look at these sentences. They all look about the same length!"

And they were: every sentence in the essay was between twenty-two and twenty-five words long. Once the group realized this, they went to work again, carving some sentences into short ones and combining others to create new rhythms. With the resulting sentence variety, the essay took on new life. ■

22a Varying sentence length

Varying sentence length not only makes prose more readable and interesting but also creates a pleasing rhythmic effect, what some writers call "flow." Deciding how and when to vary sentence length is not always easy, however. How short is too short? How long is too long? Is there a "just right" length for a particular sentence or idea?

These questions are difficult to answer because the answers depend on, among other things, the writer's purpose, intended audience, and topic. A children's story, for instance, may call for mostly short sentences whereas an article on nuclear disarmament in the *Atlantic* may call for considerably longer ones. Many technical writers, particularly those who write manuals that will be translated into numerous languages, must follow stringent rules for sentence length and structure. Technical writers working for Hewlett-Packard, for example, are required to keep all sentences to fifteen words at most and to adhere strictly to subject-verb-object order.

Although series of short and of long sentences can both be effective in individual situations, frequent alternation in sentence length characterizes much memorable writing. After one or more long sentences that express complex ideas or images, the pith of a short sentence can be refreshing and arresting. For example:

Count the words in each sentence, and underline the longest and shortest sentences in each paragraph. If the difference between the longest and shortest sentences is fairly small – say, five words or fewer – consider revising the paragraph to create greater variety in length. Do not, however, change sentences arbitrarily. Think about the ideas you want to emphasize, and try to arrange your sentence lengths in a way that emphasizes them. Start by asking the following questions:

- **→ Do two or more short sentences in a row express closely related ideas? If so, could you make the relationship between these ideas clearer or more precise by combining them into a single longer sentence?**
- **→ Is there a long sentence that contains two or three important ideas? Would these ideas be more emphatic if each was expressed in a short sentence of its own?**

> The fire of, I think, five machine-guns was pouring upon us, and there was a series of heavy crashes caused by the Fascists flinging bombs over their own parapet in the most idiotic manner. It was intensely dark.
>
> – GEORGE ORWELL, *Homage to Catalonia*

Similarly, a long sentence that follows several short ones can serve as a climax or summation that relaxes the tension or fulfills the expectation created by the series, giving readers a sense of completion. For example:

> But it is under siege, too. Santa Fe, so recently hardly more than a remote and rather secretive village, is chic these days. The smart, the modish, the merely rich move in. The haven is embattled. The old hands watch thoughtfully as Santa Fe, *dear* Santa Fe, slowly but inexorably changes its character – as the condominiums spring up over the foothills, as the Soak Hot-Tub Club offers its twelve hot-tub suites with individual stereo and mood lighting, as downtown land reaches $100,000 an acre – as the triviality of things, the cuteness, the sham and the opportunism, spreads like a tinsel stain across the town.
>
> – JAN MORRIS, "Capital of the Holy Faith"

www •

http://www.esc.edu/htmlpages/writer/workshop.htm

An online writing workshop from Empire State College. Click on grammar workout and then ways to structure sentences.

EXERCISE 22.1

The following paragraph can be improved by varying sentence length. Read it aloud to get a sense of how it sounds. Then revise it, creating some short, emphatic sentences and combining other sentences to create more effective long sentences. Add words or change punctuation as you need to.

Before beginning to play bridge, it is necessary to have the proper materials, the correct number of people, and a knowledge of the rank of suits and cards. The necessary materials include a full deck of playing cards (minus the jokers) and a score pad, along with a pen or pencil. Bridge is played by four people grouped into two partnerships, which are usually decided by drawing cards from a shuffled deck. The two players who draw the highest cards and the two who draw the lowest are partners, and the partners sit across from each other. The person who draws the highest card during partnership is the first dealer. Starting with the person on his or her left and going clockwise, the dealer deals each person one card at a time, face down. The deal continues until all four players have thirteen cards apiece. After the deal, the players sort their cards by suit, usually alternating black and red suits. The players then arrange the cards in ranking order from the highest, the ace, to the lowest, the deuce. The five highest cards, the ace, king, queen, jack, and ten, are referred to as honors. There is one suit that has great power and outranks every other one, the trump suit, which is designated at the start of the game.

22b Varying sentence openings

In making prose readable and interesting, beginning sentences in different ways is just as important as writing sentences of different lengths. For instance, when each sentence begins with the subject of an independent clause, a passage may become monotonous or even hard to read.

▶ **The way football and basketball are played is as interesting as the**
Because football *e*
players. ~~Football~~ is a game of precision/, Each play is diagrammed to
however,
accomplish a certain goal. Basketball, is a game of endurance.
In fact, a
~~A~~ basketball game looks like a track meet; the team that drops of
exhaustion first loses. Basketball players are often compared to artists/;
their
~~The players'~~ moves and slam dunks are their masterpieces.

The editing adds variety by using subordinating words (*Because* in the second line) and a prepositional phrase (*In fact* in the fourth line), and by linking sentences. Varying sentence openings prevents the passage from seeming to jerk or lurch along.

You can add variety to your sentence openings by using transitions, various kinds of phrases, and introductory dependent clauses.

1 Using transitional expressions

See how transitions bring variety and clarity to this passage.

> In order to be alert Friday morning in New York, I planned to take the shuttle from Washington Thursday night. *On Thursday morning* it began to snow in Washington and to snow even harder in New York. *By mid-afternoon* I decided not to risk the shuttle and caught a train to New York. *Seven hours later* the train completed its three-hour trip. I arrived at Penn Station to find a city shut down by the worst blizzard since 1947.
>
> – LINDA ELLERBEE, "And So It Goes"

Here the transitional words establish chronology and help carry us smoothly through the paragraph.

Many other transitional expressions can be used to vary sentence openings. For a detailed list, see 6d4.

2 Using phrases

Prepositional, verbal, and absolute phrases can also provide variety in sentence openings.

PREPOSITIONAL PHRASES

At each desk, a computer printout gives the necessary data.

From a few scraps of wood in the Middle Ages to a precisely carved, electrified instrument in the 1990s, the guitar has gone through uncounted changes.

VERBAL PHRASES

Frustrated by the delays, the drivers started honking their horns.

To qualify for flight training, one must be in good physical condition.

ABSOLUTE PHRASES

Our hopes for snow shattered, we started home.

Baton raised in a salute, the maestro readied the orchestra.

In general, use a comma after these phrases when they open a sentence.

For more about commas after introductory phrases, see 30a.

3 Using dependent clauses

Dependent clauses are another way to open a sentence.

While the boss sat on his tractor, I was down in a ditch, pounding in stakes and leveling out the bottom.

For more about commas after adverb clauses, see 30a.

What they want is a place to call home.

Because the hills were dry, the fire spread rapidly.

In general, use a comma after an adverb clause that opens a sentence.

EDITING TO VARY SENTENCE OPENINGS

Underline the subject of each sentence. If most of your sentences begin with the subject, revise some of them so they open in other ways. Consider the following suggestions:

- **Look for sentences that are related to the preceding sentence in a specific chronological, spatial, or logical way that could be signaled by a transitional expression. (6d4 and 22b1)**
- **Try rewording some sentences to begin with a phrase. (7c3 and 22b2)**
- **If two consecutive sentences are closely related, see if it would be logical to combine them into one sentence, making one of the original sentences a dependent clause. (7c4 and 22b3)**

22c Varying sentence types

In addition to using different lengths and openings, you can help vary your sentence structures by using different *types* of sentences. Sentences can be classified in three different ways: grammatically, functionally, and rhetorically.

For more on grammatical and functional classification of sentences, see 7d1 and 7d2.

1 Grammatical types

Grammatically, sentences fall into four categories – **simple, compound, complex,** and **compound-complex** – based on the number of independent and dependent clauses they contain. Varying your sentences among these grammatical types can help you create readable, effective prose.

2 Functional types

Functional types of sentences can be **declarative** (making a statement), **interrogative** (asking a question), **imperative** (giving a command), and

exclamatory (expressing strong feeling). Most sentences are declarative, but occasionally a command, a question, or an exclamation of some kind is appropriate for your purpose. Note how each is used in the following examples:

COMMAND

Coal-burning plants undoubtedly harm the environment in various ways; among others, they contribute to acid rain. *But consider the alternatives.*

QUESTION

We kept pressing on. *And why? Why would sixteen middle-aged people try to backpack thirty-seven miles?* At this point, I was not at all sure.

EXCLAMATION

Divorcés! They were everywhere! Sometimes he felt like a new member of an enormous club, the Divorcés of America, that he had never before even heard of.

3 Rhetorical types

Periodic and cumulative sentences spotlight sentence endings and beginnings and can be especially helpful in achieving sentence variety. Although not all sentences can be classified as cumulative or periodic, these types can create strong effects.

Periodic sentences

Periodic sentences postpone the main idea (usually in an independent clause) until the very end of the sentence. Effectively written periodic sentences are especially useful for creating tension or building toward a climactic or surprise ending. Note in each of the following examples how the writer holds back the main idea, thus using the end of the sentence to shock or inspire:

> Early one morning, under the arc of a lamp, carefully, silently, in smock and leather gloves, *old Doctor Manza grafted a cat's head onto a chicken's trunk.*
>
> – DYLAN THOMAS

> Even though large tracts of Europe and many old and famous states have fallen or may fall into the grasp of the Gestapo and all the odious apparatus of Nazi rule, *we shall not flag or fail.*
> – WINSTON CHURCHILL

Look at the following sentence and its revision to see how periodic order can provide emphasis:

COMPLEX SENTENCE

> The nations of the world have no alternative but coexistence because another world war would be unwinnable and because total destruction would certainly occur.

REVISED AS A PERIODIC SENTENCE

> Because another world war would be unwinnable and because total destruction would certainly occur, the nations of the world have no alternative but coexistence.

Nothing is wrong with the first sentence, which conveys the information clearly. But to put greater emphasis on the idea in the independent clause of the sentence – *no alternative but coexistence* – the writer chose to revise using the periodic pattern.

Cumulative sentences

Cumulative sentences, which begin with an independent clause and then add details in phrases and other clauses, are far more common than periodic sentences. They are useful when you want to provide both immediate understanding of the main idea and a great deal of supporting detail. The writers of the following sentences use the cumulative pattern not only to add important detail but also to end with a strong image:

> From boyhood to manhood, *I have remembered him in a single image* – seated, asleep on the sofa, his head thrown back in a hideous corpselike grin, the evening newspaper spread out before him.
> – RICHARD RODRIGUEZ, "My Parents"

> *Powther threw small secret appraising glances at the coffee cup,* lipstick all around the edges, brown stains on the side where the coffee had dripped and spilled over, the saucer splotched with a whole series of dark brown rings.
> – ANN PETRY, *The Narrows*

→ Mark each sentence as simple, compound, complex, or compound-complex. If any one or two patterns predominate, combine, divide, and otherwise revise sentences to vary the grammatical types. (22c1)

→ Consider whether the ideas in any declarative sentences might be effective as commands, questions, or exclamations. (22c2)

→ Look for ideas with much detail or with colorful images. Would they be best expressed as cumulative sentences? Also look for ideas that could use greater emphasis — would they get such emphasis in periodic sentences? (22c3)

EXERCISE 22.2

Revise the following sentences twice, first as periodic and then as cumulative sentences.

1. Straggling hesitantly into the square, the survivors of the bombing carried their children, comforted the bereaved, and supported the injured.
2. I became the best salesperson in our store once I mastered the problems that I had encountered at the beginning and once I became thoroughly familiar with the stock.

EXERCISE 22.3

The following is an introductory paragraph from an essay. Analyze the paragraph carefully, noting for each sentence its length, its kind of opening, and its grammatical and rhetorical type. Then revise the paragraph to add variety in sentence length, sentence openings, and sentence types.

When we arrived at the accident scene, I could tell that the injuries were not minor. I walked up to the car nearest me to check the injuries of the people inside. I looked through the driver's window and saw the woman's body entangled in the steering wheel. I told dispatch, via two-way radio, to send medics "code red, lights and siren." I then went to see how the passenger in the car was. The passenger appeared to be in shock and had a broken leg. The officer walked over and checked the other vehicle. The driver of the other vehicle had received no injuries at all.

THINKING CRITICALLY ABOUT SENTENCE VARIETY

Read something by an author you admire. Analyze two paragraphs for sentence length, opening, and type. Compare the sentence variety in these paragraphs with that in one of your paragraphs. What similarities or differences do you recognize, and what conclusions can you draw about sentence variety?

Creating Memorable Prose

23

How many times have you read something so striking that you wanted immediately to share it with a friend? And how many times have you remembered the exact words of something you have read or heard? All of us recognize, and can even quote, certain passages from literature or history or music — the opening of Jane Austen's *Pride and Prejudice,* perhaps, or passages from Martin Luther King's "I Have a Dream," or lyrics to a well-known song. As students of writing, we can profit by examining some of the elements that help make such pieces memorable: strong verbs, active voice, and special effects such as repetition, antithesis, and inversion. This chapter will help you to use these elements in your own work, to make your writing not only worth reading but worth remembering. ■

23a Choosing strong verbs

The greatest writers in any language are those with a genius for choosing the precise words that will arrest and hold a reader's attention. In your own writing, you can help gain this attention by using precise nouns and adjectives instead of vague, empty ones. (See 19b2.) Perhaps even more important, however, you can use strong, precise verbs instead of weak, catchall verbs and instead of nouns.

1 Using precise verbs

Verbs serve as the real workhorses of our language. Take a look, for instance, at the strong, precise verbs in the following passage:

> A fire engine, out for a trial spin, *roared* past Emerson's house, hot with readiness for public duty. Over the barn roofs the martens *dipped* and *chittered.* A swarthy daughter of an asparagus grower, in culottes, shirt, and bandanna, *pedalled* past on her bicycle. – E. B. White, "Walden"

Instead of the italicized verbs, White could have used more general verbs such as *drove, flew, called,* and *rode.* But the more precise verbs are stronger because they give readers vivid sensory impressions of the actions they express. In White's verbs, readers can hear the roar of the fire engine, see the martens swooping downward and hear them chirping shrilly, and feel the young woman pushing on the pedals of her bicycle.

Some of the most common verbs in English – especially *be, do,* and *have* – carry little or no sense of specific action, but many writers tend to overuse them in situations where more precise verbs would be clearer and more effective. Look at how the following sentences are strengthened when precise verbs are used:

▶ **Constant viewing of rock videos ~~is harmful to~~ *stunts and distorts* children's development.**

▶ **In front of the hotel, an artist would ~~do~~ *etch* your portrait on glass.**

▶ **We ~~had~~ *sweated through* basic training at Fort Ord.**

Expletives

www • http://www.urich.edu/~writing/concise.htm
This downloadable reference sheet will help you identify and edit weak verbs.

One potentially weak verb construction to watch out for is the **expletive,** which begins with *there* or *it* followed by a form of *be* (*there are, it is,* and so on). Expletives can offer effective ways of introducing an idea with extra emphasis, as June Jordan does in the following sentence:

> *It is* for us, the living, to ensure that We the People shall become the powerful.
>
> – June Jordan, "Inside America"

Here the *it is* slows down the opening of the sentence and sets up a rather formal rhythm that adds emphasis to the main idea. Often, however, writers do not use expletive openings to add emphasis. Instead, they merely overuse them, creating sentences that needlessly bury action in nouns, verbals, or dependent clauses. Notice how the following sentences are strengthened by deleting the expletives:

▶ **~~There are~~ *M* ~~m~~any people ~~who~~ fear success because they believe they do not deserve it.**

▶ **~~It is necessary for~~ *P* ~~p~~residential candidates *must* ~~to~~ perform well on television.**

2 Changing nouns to verbs

Much modern writing tends to express action by using nouns that are formed from verbs, a process called **nominalization.** Although nominalization can help make prose clearer and more concise – for example, using *abolition* instead of *the process of abolishing* – it can also produce the opposite effect, making a sentence unnecessarily wordy and hard to read. Nominalization reduces the *active* quality of a sentence, burying the action in an abstract noun and forcing the writer to use weak, generalized verbs and too many prepositional phrases. Too often, writers use nominalizations not to make a complex process easier to talk about but to make an idea *sound* more complex and abstract than it really is. Bureaucratic writing especially tends to use nominalization in this way.

You can decide when to use a nominalized form and when to use the verb from which it derives by asking one question: which is most readily understandable? Look at the following sentence:

> The firm is now engaged in an assessment of its procedures for the development of new products.

This sentence scarcely impresses itself on our memories, and it sounds pretentious and stuffy as well. In contrast, note the more easily understood and forceful version.

> The firm is now assessing its procedures for developing new products.

23b Choosing between active and passive voice

In addition to choosing strong, precise verbs, you can help make your prose memorable by alternating those verbs appropriately between active and passive voice. Look at the following paragraph:

> A young man might go into military flight training believing that he was entering some sort of technical school in which he was simply going to acquire a certain set of skills. Instead, he found himself all at once enclosed in a fraternity. And in this fraternity, even though it was military, men were not rated by their outward rank as ensigns, lieutenants, commanders, or whatever. No, herein the world was divided into those who had it and those who did not. This quality, this *it,* was never named, however, nor was it talked about in any way.
>
> – Tom Wolfe, *The Right Stuff*

www •

http://www.english.upenn.edu:80/~jlynch/grammar.html

Alphabetically arranged notes on grammar and style; click on passive voice.

In this paragraph, Wolfe introduces the indefinable quality that he has made the title of his book. Notice that in the first sentence, the focus is on someone *doing* things: going into flight training, entering a school, acquiring skills. All of the verbs are in the active voice.

In the second sentence, the verb is still active. But notice that because the subject and object are the same person, because the subject of the verb *found* also receives the action of the verb, the sentence has the *feel* of being in the passive voice, as if *was enclosed* were the verb. And in the independent clauses of the last three sentences, the focus clearly shifts to things *being done* (or not done): men not being rated, the world being divided, and a quality never being named or talked about. The persons doing these things are unimportant or unknown; in fact, like the quality itself, they are never named, and the verbs are in the passive voice. Notice, however, that Wolfe uses the active voice when he focuses on the persons "who had it and those who did not."

Try to use the active voice whenever possible. Because the passive diverts attention from the performer of an action and because it is usually wordier than the active voice, its excessive use makes for dull and difficult reading. But as Wolfe's paragraph indicates, the passive can be used very effectively in certain situations: when the performer is unknown, unwilling to be identified, or less important than the recipient of the action. In the last sentence, for example, Wolfe could have written *No one ever named this quality, this* it, *however, nor did anyone talk about it in any way.* By using the passive voice, however, he focuses attention on the quality itself rather than on the persons who do not name or talk about it; in fact, by not mentioning them, he heightens the sense of a mysterious quality that cannot be defined.

For more about voice, see Chapter 9 and 14c.

EDITING VERBS AND NOUNS

1. **Underline all verbs, and look to see whether you rely too much on *be, do,* and *have.* If so, try to substitute more specific verbs. (23a1)**
2. **Note nouns whose meaning could be expressed by a verb. Try revising using the verb instead of the noun. (23a2)**
3. **Identify all expletives, and delete any that are not used to create special emphasis. (23a1)**
4. **Look for passive verbs, and decide whether they obscure the performer of the action or dull the sentence. If so, recast the sentence in the active voice. (23b)**

EXERCISE 23.1

Look at the following sentences, in which some of the verbs are active and some passive. Then rewrite each sentence in the other voice, and decide which version you prefer and why. Example:

> *I* ... *you*
> ~~You are~~ hereby relieve~~d~~ of your duties. ~~by me.~~

1. In Gower's research, it was found that pythons often dwell in trees and live near rivers.
2. They started shooting pool, and before Cathy knew it, she owed the kid ten dollars.
3. When I was eight, my father's crazy dreams uprooted our family from Florida to California.
4. For me, living in a dorm was more easily adjusted to than living in an apartment.
5. The image of American Indians has been totally distorted by Hollywood in most of its films about the West.

EXERCISE 23.2

Revise the following paragraph to eliminate weak verbs, unnecessary nominalizations and expletives, and inappropriate use of the passive voice.

There has long been resistance to the proposition that the effectiveness of educational methods and teachers must be measured in terms of the results secured. Those responsible for the evaluation of teachers have put emphasis on procedures in teaching and have seldom made an examination of the products, that is, the efficiency of the teacher as indicated by what can be done by his or her pupils following instruction. However, we are beginning to see an increasing number of bold proposals founded on the assumption that the American public has expectations of improved results from schooling. As public support of education increases, there will be greater insistence on making judgments about a teacher in the light of his or her ability to enhance the learning of pupils.

23c Creating special effects

Contemporary movies often succeed or fail on the basis of their special effects. Similarly, special effects like repetition, antithesis, and inversion can animate your prose and help make it memorable.

1 Using repetition

Carefully used, repetition of sounds, words, phrases, or other grammatical constructions serves as a powerful stylistic device. Orators in particular have long known its power. Here is a famous use of repetition, from one of Sir Winston Churchill's addresses to the British people during World War II:

> We shall not flag or fail, we shall go on to the end. We shall fight in France, we shall fight on the seas and oceans, we shall fight with growing confidence

> and growing strength in the air, we shall defend our island, whatever the cost may be; we shall fight on the beaches, . . . we shall fight in the fields and in the streets, . . . we shall never surrender.
> – WINSTON CHURCHILL

In this passage, the constantly hammering *we shall* accompanied by the repetition of *f* sounds (*flag, fail, fight, France, confidence, defend, fields*) has the effect of strengthening British resolve.

Though we may not be prime ministers, we can use repetition to equally good effect. Here are some examples:

> So my dream date turned into a nightmare. Where was the quiet, considerate, caring guy I thought I had met? In his place appeared this jerk. He strutted, he postured, he preened – and then he bragged, he bellowed, he practically brayed – just like the donkey he so much reminded me of.

> We need science, more and better science, not for its technology, not for leisure, not even for health or longevity, but for the hope of wisdom which our kind of culture must acquire for its survival.
> – LEWIS THOMAS, "Medical Lessons from History"

Be careful, however, to use repetition only for a deliberate purpose.

FOR MULTILINGUAL WRITERS

AVOIDING DOUBLE NEGATIVES

Many languages other than English, such as French and Russian, commonly use more than one negative word to make negative statements. In French, for example, there is no single word meaning "never"; instead, this concept is expressed by putting *ne* before the verb and *jamais* after the verb. If you are a native speaker of one of these languages, be especially careful in English to use only one negative word to express a negative meaning.

Multiple Negatives

One common way in which people use repetition for emphasis is to use more than one negative term in a negative statement. In "I can't hardly see you," for example, both *can't* and *hardly* carry negative meanings. Emphatic double negatives – and triple, quadruple, and more – are especially common in the South and among speakers of African American vernacular English, who may say, for example, "Don't none of my people come from up North."

Multiple negatives have a long history in English and can be found in the works of Chaucer and Shakespeare. In the eighteenth century, however, in an effort to make English more "logical," double negatives came to be labeled as incorrect. In college writing, you may well have reason to quote passages that include them (whether from Shakespeare, Toni Morrison, or your grandmother), but it would be safer to avoid other uses of double negatives.

EXERCISE 23.3

Go through the examples in 23c1, identifying the uses of repetition. Using one example as a model, write a passage of your own that uses repetition effectively.

2 Using antithesis

Another special effect that can contribute to memorable writing is **antithesis,** the use of parallel structures to highlight contrast or opposition. Like other uses of parallelism, antithesis provides a pleasing rhythm that calls readers' attention to the contrast, often in a startling or amusing way. For example:

For a complete discussion of parallelism, see Chapter 21.

> Love is an ideal thing, marriage a real thing.
>
> The congregation didn't think much of the new preacher, and what the new preacher thought of the congregation she didn't wish to say.
>
> It is a sin to believe evil of others — but it is not a mistake.
>
> – H. L. Mencken

EXERCISE 23.4

Using one of the preceding examples, create a sentence of your own that uses antithesis. Then consider whether the antithesis makes the sentence more memorable or effective. You might begin by thinking of opposites you could build on: hope/despair, good/evil, fire/ice. Or you might begin with a topic you want to write about: success, greed, generosity, and so on.

3 Using inverted word order

Inversion of the usual word order, such as putting the verb before the subject or the object before the subject and verb, can make writing memorable by creating surprise or emphasizing a particular word or phrase.

▶ ~~**Two dead birds plummeted**~~ *O* ~~**o**~~**ut of the tree***, plummeted two dead birds.*

> The inverted word order makes for a more dramatic sentence by putting the emphasis at the end, on *two dead birds.*

As with any unusual sentence pattern, inverted word order should be used sparingly, but it can indeed create special effects.

> Into this grey lake plopped the thought, I know this man, don't I?
>
> – Doris Lessing
>
> In a hole in the ground there lived a hobbit. – J. R. R. Tolkien
>
> Into her head flowed the whole of the poem she had found in that book.
>
> – Eudora Welty

EXERCISE 23.5

Look at something you have written, and find a sentence that might be more effective with inverted word order. Experiment with the word order, reading the results aloud and comparing differences in effect.

EXERCISE 23.6

Prose can be memorable for reasons quite different from those presented in this chapter. The Bulwer-Lytton Competition, known less formally as the Wretched Writing contest, challenges writers to produce an opening sentence to a novel, one that will celebrate the possibilities of "deliberate wretchedness" without hurting anyone's feelings. Here are two finalists.

1. It was the eve of the yearly whale-slaughtering festival, thought Mamook as her horny fingers relentlessly pushed the whalebone needle through the sole of the mukluk; and suddenly, unaccountably, uncontrollably, she began to blubber.
2. When the last of the afterglow faded and the air was still, John liked to sit in the porch swing, in the dark, and test his night vision by spitting through the banisters.

Write an opening sentence for a story. Try to make it a "wonderfully bad" sentence. And why not enter it in the contest? Just see the Web site listed in the margin for directions on how to submit your entry.

www •

http://www.bulwer-lytton.com/

Homepage of the Bulwer-Lytton Fiction Contest, including 1996 and 1997 winners and sample 1998 entries.

THINKING CRITICALLY ABOUT PROSE STYLE

Reading with an Eye for Prose Style

Chapters 19 – 23 have presented many elements that mark effective prose. One amusing way to practice these elements is to imitate them. Choose a writer you admire — Virginia Woolf, Chaucer, Leslie Silko, Stephen King, Salt 'n' Pepa, whoever. Reread this writer's work, getting a feel for the rhythms, the structures, the special effects. Make a list of the elements that contribute to the distinctive style. Then choose a well-known story, and retell it in that style. Following is the opening of "The Three Little Pigs" as one student imagined Edgar Allan Poe might have done it.

> It began as a mere infatuation. I admired them from afar, with a longing which only a wolf may know. Soon, these feelings turned to torment. Were I even to set eyes upon their porcine forms, the bowels of my soul raged, as if goaded by some festering poison. As the chilling winds of November howled, my gullet yearned for them. I soon feasted only upon an earnest and consuming desire for the moment of their decease.

Thinking about Your Own Prose Style

Read over something you have written, looking for memorable sentences. If few sentences catch your eye, choose some that show promise — ones with strong verbs or a pleasing rhythm, perhaps. Using this chapter for guidance, try revising one or two sentences to make them more effective and memorable. Finally, note some ways in which your writing is effective and some strategies for making it more effective. If you keep a writing log, make your notes there.

PART 5

SELECTING EFFECTIVE WORDS

documentation
writing/editing
hypertext
message
www.bedfordstmartins.com/nsmhandbook
collaborating
thinking & collaborating

FAQ ·······→

FAQ: Effective Words Online

How and when should digital jargon be used?

Like all jargon, the terms emerging in the digital age can be irritating and incomprehensible – or extremely helpful. If the jargon is concrete and specific, it can help clarify concepts, providing a useful shorthand for an otherwise lengthy explanation. Saying "Sorry, but for the time being I'm limited to asynchronous communication, primarily email" sends a pretty straightforward message, one that is faster to read than "Sorry, but for the time being I'm limited to the kinds of electronic communication in which there's a delay between the sending and receiving of messages, and primarily to email."

Frequently used terms (such as ASYNCHRONOUS COMMUNICATION and EMAIL) are the ones online writers should know. Other terms, like the jargon in this sentence – "Savvy wavelet compression is the fiber signpost of the virtual chillout room" – may be appropriate for techies talking to one another, but they are not very useful to those trying to communicate with a nontechnical or general audience. Before you use technical jargon, remember your readers: if they will not understand the terms, or if you don't know them well enough to judge, then take the time to say what you need to say in everyday language.

How do you spell the plurals of acronyms such as MOO or URL?

The digital revolution has also spawned many technical acronyms that are used routinely by online writers. To make them plural, just add a lowercase *-s* (without an apostrophe): MOOs, URLs. As with other jargon, though, if your readers may not understand what an acronym stands for, it is better to write the term out.

When is it appropriate to use digital acronyms like IMHO and F2F?

Along with the new jargon have come quite a few new acronyms that serve as a kind of shorthand for everyday expressions. Such acronyms may be appropriate for some informal online communication, but you should avoid them in most academic or other formal writing. Here are some of them:

BTW	by the way
FAQ	frequently asked questions
FWIW	for what it's worth
F2F	face-to-face
IMHO	in my humble opinion

http://c.gp.cs.cmu.edu:5103/prog/webster?

Webster's Dictionary Online *uses a* HYPERTEXT *interface that allows you to search for definitions of any word in the dictionary — and can help you if you're not sure how to spell the word you want.*

gopher://odie.niaid.nih.gov:70/77/.thesaurus/index

Roget's Thesaurus *can help you find synonyms.*

http://www.ccil.org/jargon/jargon.html

The New Hacker's Dictionary *includes definitions of online jargon and discussions of such topics as "how jargon works," "hacker writing style," and so on.*

http://www.hotwired.com/hardwired/wiredstyle/

Hotwired*'s URL allows you to order the print version of* Wired Style *and to amplify and update the printed book's advice on how to use the new language of the digital age.*

24 Attending to Spelling

When humorist Dave Barry quips that English spelling is "unusual" "because our language is a rich verbal tapestry woven together from the tongues of the Greeks, the Latins, the Angles, the Klaxtons, the Celtics, the 76ers, and many other ancient peoples, all of whom had severe drinking problems," he is exaggerating, of course — but not much. Indeed, the complex history of the English language makes spelling particularly challenging.

In addition, contemporary advertising makes use of many intentional misspellings — from a *Kountry Kitchen* restaurant to a *drive-thru* bank to a *lite* beer. But playful spelling will get you no points in most academic writing. So take a tip and learn some fairly straightforward spelling guidelines. And keep in mind: research shows that writers who use spell checkers make less than half as many spelling errors as those who do not. ■

24a The most commonly misspelled words

The three thousand first-year essays used in the research for this book revealed a fairly small number of persistently misspelled words. Look over the list of the fifty most common misspellings on p. 288 and compare it to words you have trouble spelling correctly.

EXERCISE 24.1

Choose the correct spelling from the words in parentheses in each of the following sentences. After checking your answers, make a list of the words you misspelled, and keep it near your typewriter or computer.

1. (*Their/There/They're*) going to put (*their/there/they're*) new stereo system over (*their/there/they're*) in the corner.
2. My little brother wants (*to/too*) go swimming (*to/too*).
3. The (*begining/beginning*) of school is (*a lot/alot*) earlier this year than last.
4. The temperature isn't (*noticable/noticeable*) (*until/untill*) the humidity rises.
5. The accident (*occured/occurred*) (*before/befour*) I could step aside.
6. We couldn't (*beleive/believe*) our team could (*loose/lose*) the playoffs.
7. In making your major life decisions, (*your/you're*) (*definately/definitely*) on (*your/you're*) own.

THE FIFTY MOST COMMONLY MISSPELLED WORDS

1. their/there/they're
2. too/to
3. a lot
4. noticeable
5. receive/-d/-s
6. lose
7. you're/your
8. an/and
9. develop/-s
10. definitely
11. than/then
12. believe/-d/-s
13. occurred
14. affect/-s
15. cannot
16. separate
17. success
18. through
19. until
20. where
21. successful/-ly
22. truly
23. argument/-s
24. experience/-s
25. environment
26. exercise/-s/-ing
27. necessary
28. sense
29. therefore
30. accept/-ed
31. heroes
32. professor
33. whether
34. without
35. business/-es
36. dependent
37. every day
38. may be
39. occasion/-s
40. occurrences
41. woman
42. all right
43. apparent/-ly
44. categories
45. final/-ly
46. immediate/-ly
47. roommate/-s
48. against
49. before
50. beginning

8. Nothing (*affects/effects*) (*success/sucess*) more (*than/then*) self-confidence or (*its/it's*) absence.
9. We (*received/recieved*) our notice (*threw/through*) the mail.
10. The group hopes to (*develop/develope*) a (*truely/truly*) (*succesful/successful*) fast-food franchise.
11. We (*can not/cannot*) easily (*separate/seperate*) fact and opinion.
12. Please tell me (*wear/where*) (*an/and*) when we should meet.
13. Our (*argumants/arguments*) (*against/aginst*) continuing to pollute the (*enviroment/environment*) fell on deaf ears.
14. Local (*busineses/businesses*) are (*dependant/dependent*) on the tourist trade.
15. (*Heroes/Heros*) are (*necesary/necessary*) to every culture's mythology.
16. Our first (*experiance/experience*) with aerobic (*exercise/exercize*) left us tired.
17. The (*professor/profesor*) agreed to (*accept/except*) our essays late.
18. She qualified for three (*catagories/categories*) in the (*final/finel*) gymnastics competition.
19. The two (*roomates/roommates*) would be lost (*without/witout*) each other.
20. We intend to celebrate the (*ocasion/occasion*) (*weather/whether*) or not the (*weather/whether*) cooperates.

21. The plane to Chicago (*may be/maybe*) late; (*therefore/therfore*), we don't need to leave for the airport (*imediately/immediately*).
22. A (*woman's/women's*) place is now wherever she wants it to be.
23. Police departments report (*occurences/occurrences*) of more and more burglaries (*every day/everyday*).
24. (*Its/It's*) not (*all right/alright*) to forgo common (*since/sense*).
25. (*Aparently/Apparently*), the shipment of books never arrived.

24b Recognizing homonyms

Of the words most often misspelled by college students, the largest number are **homonyms** – words that sound alike but have different spellings and meanings. English has many homonyms, but a relatively small number of them – eight pairs or trios – cause student writers frequent trouble. If you tend to confuse any of these words, now is a good time to study them, looking for some twist of memory to help you remember the differences.

THE MOST TROUBLESOME HOMONYMS

their (possessive form of *they*)
there (in that place)
they're (contraction of *they are*)

to (in the direction of)
too (in addition; excessive)
two (number between one and three)

weather (climatic conditions)
whether (if)

accept (to take or receive)
except (to leave out)

who's (contraction of *who is* or *who has*)
whose (possessive form of *who*)

its (possessive form of *it*)
it's (contraction of *it is* or *it has*)

your (possessive form of *you*)
you're (contraction of *you are*)

affect (an emotion; to have an influence)
effect (a result; to cause to happen)

OTHER HOMONYMS AND FREQUENTLY CONFUSED WORDS

advice (suggestion)
advise (to suggest [to])

allude (to refer)
elude (to avoid or escape)

(*continued on page 290*)

(continued from page 289)

allusion (reference)
illusion (false idea or appearance)

altar (sacred platform or table)
alter (to change)

are (form of *be*)
our (belonging to us)

bare (uncovered)
bear (animal; to carry or endure)

board (piece of lumber)
bored (uninterested)

brake (device for stopping)
break (interruption; to fragment)

buy (to purchase)
by (near; beside; through)

capital (principal city)
capitol (legislators' building)

cite (to refer to)
sight (seeing; something seen)
site (location)

coarse (rough or crude)
course (plan of study; path)

complement (something that completes; to make complete)
compliment (praise; to praise)

conscience (feeling of right and wrong)
conscious (mentally aware)

council (leadership group)
counsel (advice; to advise)

dairy (source of milk)
diary (journal)

desert (dry area; to abandon)
dessert (sweet course of a meal)

device (something planned or invented)
devise (to plan or invent)

die (to expire)
dye (color; to color)

elicit (to draw forth)
illicit (illegal)

eminent (distinguished)
immanent (inherent)
imminent (expected in the immediate future)

fair (just or right; light in complexion; an exposition)
fare (price of transportation; to go through an experience)

forth (forward; out into view)
fourth (between third and fifth)

gorilla (ape)
guerrilla (irregular soldier)

hear (to perceive with the ears)
here (in this place)

heard (past tense of *hear*)
herd (group of animals)

hoarse (sounding rough or harsh)
horse (animal)

know (to understand)
no (opposite of yes)

lead (a metal; to go before)
led (past tense of *lead*)

loose (not tight; not confined)
lose (to misplace; to fail to win)

meat (flesh used as food)
meet (to encounter)

(continued on page 291)

(continued from page 290)

passed (went by; received a passing grade)
past (beyond; events that have already occurred)
patience (quality of being patient)
patients (persons under medical care)
peace (absence of war)
piece (part)
personal (private or individual)
personnel (employees)
plain (simple; flat land)
plane (airplane; tool; flat surface)
presence (condition of being)
presents (gifts; gives)
principal (most important; head of a school)
principle (fundamental truth)
rain (precipitation)
rein (strap to control a horse)
reign (period of rule; to rule)
right (correct; opposite of left)
rite (ceremony)
write (to produce words on a surface)
road (street or highway)
rode (past tense of *ride*)
scene (setting; view)
seen (past participle of *see*)
sense (feeling; intelligence)
since (from the time that; because)
stationary (unmoving)
stationery (writing paper)
than (as compared to)
then (at that time; therefore)
threw (past tense of *throw*)
thorough (complete)
through (in one side of and out the other; by means of)
waist (part of the body)
waste (to squander)
weak (feeble)
week (seven days)
wear (to put onto the body)
were (past tense of *be*)
where (in what place)
which (what; that)
witch (woman with supernatural power)

EXERCISE 24.2

Choose the appropriate word in parentheses to fill each blank.

If _______ (*your/you're*) looking for summer fun, _______ (*accept/except*) the friendly _______ (*advice/advise*) of thousands of happy adventurers: spend three _______ (*weaks/weeks*) kayaking _______ (*threw/thorough/through*) the inside passage _______ (*to/too/two*) Alaska. For ten years, Outings, Inc., has _______ (*lead/led*) groups of novice kayakers _______ (*passed/past*) some of the most breathtaking scenery in North America. _______ (*Their/There/They're*) goal is simple: to give participants the time of _______ (*their/there/they're*) lives. As one of last year's adventurers said, "_______ (*Its/It's*) a trip I will remember vividly, one that _______ (*affected/effected*) me powerfully."

One special group of homonyms often misspelled by college writers is words written sometimes as one word and other times as two words. The correct spelling depends on the meaning. Note the differences illustrated here:

Of course, they did not wear *everyday* clothes *every day* of the year.

Ideally, children *always* love their parents – in *all ways*.

By the time we were *all ready* for the game to begin, the coach's patience was *already* exhausted.

We *may be* on time for the meeting, or *maybe* we won't be!

Nobody was surprised when the police officers announced that they had found *no body* at the scene of the crime.

24c Linking spelling and pronunciation

Even for words that are not homonyms, pronunciation often leads spellers astray. Pronunciation can vary considerably from one region to another, and the informality of spoken English allows us to slur or blur letters or syllables. The best way to link spelling and pronunciation is to learn to pronounce words mentally as they look, every letter and syllable included (so that, for example, you hear the *b* at the end of *crumb*) and to enunciate them slowly and clearly when you are trying to spell them.

Learning to "see" words with unpronounced letters or syllables will help you spell them correctly. Here are some frequently misspelled words of this kind with their unpronounced letters or syllables italicized:

can*d*idate	forei*g*n	prob*ab*ly
condem*n*	gover*n*ment	quan*t*ity
diff*e*rent	int*e*rest	rest*a*urant
drastic*al*ly	lib*r*ary	sep*a*rate (adjective)
enviro*n*ment	marr*i*age	su*r*prise
Feb*r*uary	mus*c*le	We*d*n*e*sday

In English words, *a, i,* and *e* often sound alike in syllables that are not stressed. Hearing the word *definite,* for instance, gives us few clues as to whether the vowels in the second and third syllables should be *i*'s or *a*'s. In this case, remembering how the related word *finite* looks or sounds helps us know that the *i*'s are correct. If you are puzzled about how to spell a word with unstressed vowels, try to think of a related word that will give you a clue to the correct spelling. Then check your dictionary.

FOR MULTILINGUAL WRITERS

RECOGNIZING AMERICAN SPELLINGS

Spelling varies slightly among English-speaking countries. If you have learned British English, you will want to be aware of some spelling differences in British and American English. For example:

AMERICAN	BRITISH
center	centre
check	cheque
color	colour
criticize	criticise
judgment	judgement

24d Taking advantage of spelling rules

Fortunately, English spelling does follow some general rules that can be of enormous help to writers. This section focuses on those rules closely related to commonly misspelled words.

1 Remembering "*i* before *e*"

Most of you probably memorized the "*i* before *e*" rule long ago. Here is a slightly expanded version.

i before *e* except after *c*
or when pronounced "ay"
as in *neighbor* or *weigh*
or in *weird* exceptions like *either* and *species*

I* BEFORE *E ach*ie*ve, br*ie*f, f*ie*ld, fr*ie*nd

EXCEPT AFTER *C* c*ei*ling, conc*ei*vable, dec*ei*t, rec*ei*ve

OR WHEN PRONOUNCED "AY" *ei*ghth, n*ei*ghbor, r*ei*gn, w*ei*gh

OR IN WEIRD EXCEPTIONS ancient, caffeine, conscience, either, foreign, height, leisure, neither, science, seize, species, weird

EXERCISE 24.3

Insert either *ei* or *ie* in the blank in each of the following words.

1. sl____gh
2. consc____nce
3. anc____nt
4. l____sure
5. p____rce
6. caff____ne
7. ch____f
8. rec____ve
9. ach____ve
10. h____ress

2 Adding prefixes

Prefixes are verbal elements placed at the *beginnings* of words to add to or qualify their meaning. Prefixes do not change the spelling of the words they are added to, even when the last letter of the prefix and the first letter of the word it is added to are the same.

dis- + service = disservice over- + rate = overrate

Some prefixes require the use of hyphens. For a discussion of such usage, see 39c.

3 Adding suffixes

Suffixes are elements placed at the *ends* of words to form related words. This section will provide guidance to spelling words with suffixes.

Words ending in unpronounced e

For words ending in an unpronounced *e* (*receive, lose, definite*), you must decide whether or not to drop the *e* when adding a suffix. In general, if the suffix starts with a vowel, *drop* the *e*.

explore + -ation = exploration
imagine + -able = imaginable
exercise + -ing = exercising
continue + -ous = continuous

If the suffix starts with a consonant, *keep* the *e*.

force + -ful = forceful
excite + -ment = excitement
state + -ly = stately
same + -ness = sameness

EXCEPTIONS

dye + -ing = dyeing
notice + -able = noticeable
argue + -ment = argument
judge + -ment = judgment
marriage + -able = marriageable
courage + -ous = courageous
true + -ly = truly
nine + -th = ninth

EXERCISE 24.4

Combine each of the following words and suffixes, dropping the unpronounced *e* when necessary.

1. future + -ism
2. whole + -ly
3. argue + -ment
4. lone + -ly
5. malice + -ious
6. dye + -ing
7. hope + -ful
8. continue + -ous
9. exercise + -ing
10. outrage + -ous

-ally *and* -ly

Use *-ally* if the base word ends in *ic*, *-ly* if it does not.

drastic + -ally = drastically
apparent + -ly = apparently
tragic + -ally = tragically
quick + -ly = quickly

EXCEPTION

public + -ly = publicly

-cede, -ceed, *and* -sede

The suffixes *-cede, -ceed,* and *-sede* are easy to use correctly because almost all words ending in the sound pronounced "seed" use the spelling *-cede.* Use *-sede* with only one word: *supersede.* Use *-ceed* with only three words: *exceed, proceed, succeed.* Use *-cede* with all other words ending in the "seed" sound.

accede	intercede	recede
concede	precede	secede

Words ending in y

When you add a suffix to words ending in *y,* you must sometimes change the *y* to *i.* In general, if it is preceded by a consonant, change the *y.*

bounty + -ful = bountiful
try + -ed = tried
silly + -er = sillier
breezy + -ness = breeziness
busy + -ly = busily

Keep the *y* if it is preceded by a vowel, if it is part of a proper name, or if the suffix begins with *i.*

joy + -ous = joyous
play + -ful = playful
dry + -ing = drying
Kennedy + -esque = Kennedyesque

EXCEPTIONS

day + -ly = daily
shy + -er = shyer
dry + -ly = dryly
gay + -ly = gaily
wry + -ness = wryness

EXERCISE 24.5

Combine each of the following words and suffixes, changing the final *y* to *i* when necessary.

1. lonely + -er
2. carry + -ing
3. defy + -ance
4. study + -ous
5. supply + -ed
6. duty + -ful
7. likely + -hood
8. obey + -ed
9. rainy + -est
10. coy + -ly

Words ending in a consonant

When a suffix beginning with a vowel is added to a word that ends in a consonant, the consonant is sometimes doubled. In general, if the word ends in consonant + vowel + consonant and the word contains only one syllable or ends in an accented syllable, double the final consonant.

stop + -ing = stopping
slap + -ed = slapped
hot + -est = hottest
run + -er = runner
begin + -ing = beginning
occur + -ence = occurrence
refer + -ing = referring

Do not double the consonant if it is preceded by more than one vowel or by another consonant, if the suffix begins with a consonant, if the word is not accented on the last syllable, or if the accent shifts from the last to the first syllable when the suffix is added.

sleep + -ing = sleeping
ship + -ment = shipment
benefit + -ing = benefiting
infer + -ence = inference
start + -ed = started
fit + -ness = fitness
fasten + -er = fastener
prefer + -ence = preference

EXERCISE 24.6

Combine each of the following words and suffixes, doubling the final consonant when necessary.

1. occur + -ed
2. fast + -est
3. skip + -er
4. refer + -ence
5. commit + -ment
6. regret + -able
7. submit + -ed
8. frantic + -ally
9. benefit + -ed
10. weep + -ing

24e Making words plural

Making singular nouns plural calls for the use of several different spelling guidelines. For most words, simply add *-s*. For words ending in *s*, *ch*, *sh*, *x*, or *z*, add *-es*.

pencil, pencils
Jones, Joneses
bus, buses
book, books
fox, foxes
church, churches
computer, computers
flash, flashes
buzz, buzzes

Words ending in o

Add *-es* if the *o* is preceded by a consonant. Add *-s* if the *o* is preceded by a vowel.

potato, potatoes	hero, heroes	veto, vetoes
rodeo, rodeos	patio, patios	zoo, zoos

EXCEPTIONS

memo, memos	piano, pianos	solo, solos

Words ending in f or fe

For some words ending in *f* or *fe,* change *f* to *v* and add *-s* or *-es.*

calf, calves	life, lives	leaf, leaves
half, halves	wife, wives	hoof, hooves
self, selves	shelf, shelves	knife, knives

Words ending in y

For words ending in *y,* change *y* to *i* and add *-es* if the *y* is preceded by a consonant. Keep the *y* and add *-s* if the *y* is preceded by a vowel or if the word is a proper name.

theory, theories	huckleberry, huckleberries
guy, guys	attorney, attorneys
Henry, Henrys	

Irregular plurals

Memorize irregular plurals you do not already know.

man, men	bacterium, bacteria	deer, deer
woman, women	locus, loci	sheep, sheep
child, children	alga, algae	moose, moose
foot, feet	basis, bases	series, series
tooth, teeth	datum, data	species, species

Compound words

For compound nouns that are written as one word, make the last part of the compound plural. For compound nouns that are written as separate words or hyphenated, make the most important part of the compound plural.

briefcase, briefcases

mailbox, mailboxes

brother-in-law, brothers-in-law

lieutenant governor, lieutenant governors

sergeant major, sergeants major

leap year, leap years

bus stop, bus stops

EXERCISE 24.7

Form the plural of each of the following words.

1. tomato
2. hoof
3. volunteer
4. baby
5. dish
6. spoof
7. beach
8. yourself
9. golf club
10. rose
11. stepchild
12. turkey
13. heir apparent
14. radio
15. phenomenon

24f Using a spell checker

www •

http://www.m-w.com/netdict.htm

Merriam-Webster's Dictionary on the Net *offers users wild card searches. Thus, if you recall how to spell only the beginning of* carabiner *(an oblong, hinged metal ring used in climbing), you can enter* carab* *and choose* carabiner *from the list of words that begin with* cara.

Some good news, perhaps, is that writers now have a special tool to help with spelling: the spell checker, a computer program that helps find incorrect spellings. We say *perhaps* this is good news, however, because a comparison of spelling errors in first-year essays produced these interesting results.

handwritten or typed	1.74 errors per essay
written on a computer *without* spell checker	3.81 errors per essay
written on a computer *with* spell checker	1.60 errors per essay

These findings make an important point about writing on a computer: seeing your words onscreen or in nice, neat typescript may make it difficult to "see" your spelling errors. Indeed, keyboarding often introduces new spelling errors, and the "clean" copy can, in a way, conceal these errors. If you use a computer without a spell checker, you probably need to proofread more carefully than ever before.

These results also tell us that spell checkers alone won't correct all spelling errors. Students using spell checkers misspelled almost as many words as did students who handwrote or typed their essays. To benefit from this tool, therefore, you must understand how to use a spell checker accurately and efficiently, and you must learn to adapt the spell checker to your own needs.

USING A SPELL CHECKER

1. Use your spell checker. Keep a dictionary near your computer, and look up *any* word the spell checker highlights that you aren't absolutely sure of.
2. Remember that spell-checker dictionaries are limited; they don't recognize most proper names, foreign words, or specialized language. If your program has a "learn" option, enter into your spell-checker dictionary any words you use regularly and have trouble spelling. Add also your own spelling "demons."
3. Remember that spell checkers do not recognize homonym errors (misspelling *there* as *their,* for example). (24b) If you know that you mix up certain words, check for them after running your spell checker. You may be able to use the search function to identify words you need to check – every *there, their,* and *they're,* for instance.
4. Remember that spell checkers are not sensitive to capitalization. If you write "president clinton," the spell checker won't question it.
5. Proofread carefully, even after you have used the spell checker.

24g Building on visualization and memory cues

Before the advent of printing – and photocopying machines – people learned to train their memories extensively. You can activate your memory first by **visualizing** correct spellings or making mental pictures of how a word looks. You can also learn to use memory cues, or **mnemonic devices** (named for the Greek goddess of memory, Mnemosyne), in mastering words that tend to trip you up. Here are one student's memory cues:

WORD; MISSPELLING	CUE
a lot; alot	I wouldn't write *alittle,* would I?
government; goverment	Government should serve those it *governs.*
separate; seperate	*Separate* rates two *a*'s.
definitely; definately	There are a *finite* number of ways to spell *definitely.*

EXERCISE 24.8 Revising for Spelling

Correct each misspelling in the following passage. Whenever possible, classify the misspelling according to one of the guidelines in this chapter. Then draw up three or four spelling tips you could give this particular student.

For me, the ideel ocupation is an arangement in which I would play with a band for six months and tour the other six months of the year. I wouldn't want to teach music because I would probly have to teach in a school where many students are forced by there parrents to take music. When children are forced to do something, its likly that they won't enjoy it. If I were able to both tour an teach, however, I would be happy.

I'm realy glad that I've gotten involved in music; it looks as if I'm destined to be a profesional musician. Surly I don't know what else I could do; I dout I'd be a good administrater or bussiness executive or lawyer. And the idea of being a doctor or denist and probing around people's bodys or looking at teeth that have huge, roting cavities isn't appealing to me. The more I think about it, the happyer I am with my music. I definately plan to pursue that career.

THINKING CRITICALLY ABOUT YOUR OWN SPELLING

If you are keeping a writing log, devote a section of it to a personal spelling inventory. Choose a sample of your recent writing, and identify every misspelling. If you have any drafts saved in a computer, use a spell checker. Then enter the word, your misspelling, and the guideline or pattern that relates to it (such as "homonym" or "final *e* + suffix"). For persistent misspellings, create a memory cue (see 24g), and enter it in the log along with the correct spelling.

Using Dictionaries

25

In the opening scene of Rex Stout's novel *Gambit,* master sleuth Nero Wolfe tears the pages out of a "subversive and intolerably offensive" book — the third edition of *Webster's New International Dictionary.* Wolfe claims that the dictionary threatens the very "integrity of the English language" and is, therefore, burning it page by page.

Dictionaries have, in fact, often been the cause of violent controversy, usually related to a tension between two basic and competing aims: to fix a standard of language by establishing clear "rights" and "wrongs" or, on the other hand, to record a full inventory of the language as it is actually used, without prescribing "right" and "wrong." What enraged Wolfe was one particular dictionary's focus on the second aim. Today, these dual aims persist in our dictionaries and may in fact influence your choice of which dictionary to use. ■

25a Exploring the dictionary

A good dictionary packs a surprising amount of information, including much more than correct spelling, into a relatively small space. Look at this entry in *Webster's New World Dictionary,* Third College Edition.

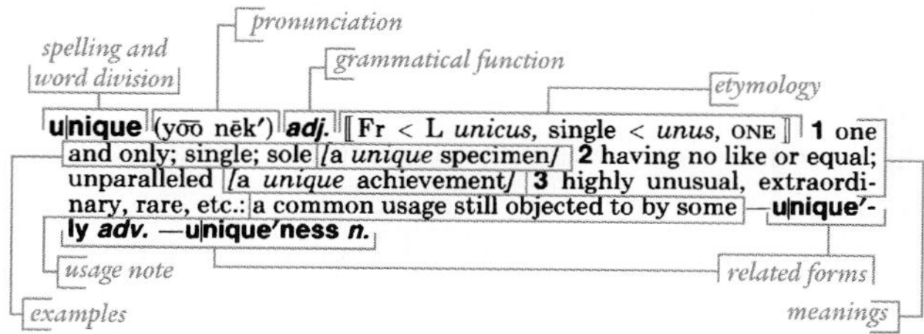

In fact, a dictionary entry may contain a dozen or more kinds of information about a word, the most common of which are listed here. The first six normally appear in all entries, the others only when relevant.

1. *Spelling,* including alternative spellings if they exist
2. *Word division,* with bars, dots, or spaces separating syllables and showing where a word may be divided at the end of a line
3. *Pronunciation,* including alternative pronunciations

4. *Grammatical functions and irregular forms* (if any), including plurals of nouns, principal parts of verbs, and comparative and superlative forms of adjectives and adverbs
5. *Etymology,* the languages and words that the word comes from
6. *Meanings,* in order of either development or frequency of use
7. *Examples* of the word in the context of a phrase or sentence
8. *Usage labels and notes* (See explanation in following section.)
9. *Field labels,* indicating that a word has a special meaning in a particular field of knowledge or activity
10. *Synonyms* and *antonyms*
11. *Related words* and their grammatical functions
12. *Idioms,* phrases in which the word appears and their meanings

Usage labeling and notes

For some words, many dictionaries include a kind of usage labeling, intended to let readers know that some or all meanings of the word are not considered appropriate in certain contexts. You can generally find such labels identified and described at the beginning of the dictionary. Here are some of the labels the *Webster's New World* uses:

1. *Archaic:* rarely used today except in specialized contexts
2. *Obsolete:* no longer used
3. *Colloquial:* characteristic of conversation and informal writing
4. *Slang:* extremely informal
5. *Dialect:* used mostly in a particular geographical or linguistic area, often one that is specified, such as Scotland or New England

In addition to labels, dictionaries sometimes include notes discussing usage in greater detail. In the *Webster's New World* entry for *unique,* notice that the third meaning includes a note that it is "common" but "still objected to by some."

EXERCISE 25.1

Look up the spelling, syllable division, and pronunciation of the following words in your dictionary. Note any variants in spelling and/or pronunciation.

1. process (noun)
2. heinous
3. exigency
4. schedule
5. whippet
6. crayfish
7. macabre
8. hurrah
9. greasy
10. theater

EXERCISE 25.2

Look up the etymology of the following words in your dictionary.

1. rhetoric
2. student
3. curry (noun)
4. whine
5. apple
6. sex
7. okra
8. tortilla
9. cinema
10. video

EXERCISE 25.3

Use your dictionary to find synonyms (and antonyms) of the following words.

1. coerce
2. prevaricate
3. parameter
4. odious
5. awesome
6. obfuscate

25b Distinguishing among dictionaries

Although you may use a portable paperback dictionary most often, you should be familiar with other kinds of dictionaries as well.

www •

http://www.bucknell.edu/~rbeard/diction.html

In addition to a searchable version of the Merriam-Webster's Collegiate Dictionary, *this site includes links to 400 dictionaries in over 130 languages.*

1 Abridged dictionaries

Abridged, or "abbreviated," **dictionaries** are the type most often used by college writers. Though they are not as complete as unabridged dictionaries, they are more affordable and more portable. Among the most helpful abridged dictionaries are *Webster's New World Dictionary, Random House Webster's College Dictionary,* and *The American Heritage Dictionary.*

Webster's New World Dictionary of American English, Third College Edition (New York: Prentice Hall, 1994), includes more than 170,000 entries; meanings are listed chronologically – in the order in which they entered the language. Geographical and biographical names appear with the regular entries, and more than 800 drawings are provided.

Random House Webster's College Dictionary, Second Edition (New York: Random House, 1997) has more than 180,000 entries, including words new to the language, from *acquaintance rape* to "Megan's law" to *zouk.* This work is notable for its attempt to eliminate sexist language from definitions, its usage notes intended to warn users when terms may be offensive or disparaging, and its appendix on "Avoiding Insensitive and Offensive Language."

The American Heritage College Dictionary, Third Edition (Boston: Houghton Mifflin, 1993), has more than 200,000 listings, augmented by

5,000 scientific and technical terms and over 3,000 illustrations. *The American Heritage* lists meanings in the order of most to least common. Notes on usage are extensive. Introductory essays provide a context for the usage notes in the form of a debate on the issue. Biographical and geographical sections, also liberally illustrated, follow the dictionary of general vocabulary, as does a section on abbreviations. The dictionary is also available on diskette or CD-ROM.

2 Unabridged dictionaries

Unabridged, or "unabbreviated," **dictionaries** are the royalty of their species – the most complete, richly detailed, and thoroughly presented dictionaries of English. Whereas good abridged dictionaries may include 175,000 items, unabridged dictionaries far more than double that figure. Because they are large and often multivolume – and hence expensive – you may not own one, but you will want and need to consult one on occasion. You can always find an unabridged dictionary in the library. Among the leading unabridged dictionaries are the *Oxford English Dictionary* and *Webster's Third New International Dictionary of the English Language.*

The Oxford English Dictionary, Second Edition, 20 volumes (New York: Oxford University Press, 1992). The grandparent of unabridged dictionaries in English, the *OED* began in Britain in the nineteenth century as an attempt to give a full history of each English word, recording its entry into the language and illustrating the development of its various meanings with dated quotations in chronological order. Volunteers all over the English-speaking world contributed quotations, and the first edition was published piecemeal over a period of more than forty years. The second edition traces more than half a million words and is unparalleled in its historical account of changes in word meanings and spellings. It is available on CD-ROM.

Webster's Third New International Dictionary of the English Language (Springfield, Mass.: Merriam-Webster, 1993). Containing more entries than any other dictionary except the *OED* – nearly half a million in all, with a special addenda section covering 14,000 new words and meanings – this one-volume work stirred considerable controversy at its publication because of its tendency, as mentioned in the introduction to this chapter, to *describe* rather than to *prescribe* usage. In all, the editors collected 6,165,000 examples of recorded usage, on which they drew for their usage notes. *Webster's Third* lists meanings in order of their entry into the language and quotes from over 14,000 different authors to provide illustrations of words in context.

EXERCISE 25.4

Look up the following words in at least one abridged and one unabridged dictionary, and compare the entries. Record any differences or disagreements you find, and bring this record to class for discussion.

1. dogmatism
2. alienate
3. discriminate
4. hopefully
5. humanism
6. culture

EXERCISE 25.5

Look up one of the following words in the *OED,* and write a paragraph describing any changes in meaning it has undergone since its entry into English.

1. cheerful
2. machine
3. vulgar
4. humor (noun)
5. honest
6. romance

25c Consulting specialized dictionaries

Abridged and unabridged dictionaries will provide you with an enormous amount of information. Sometimes, however, you will need to turn to additional sources for more specialized information. Such sources are available in dictionaries of usage, synonyms, and slang.

Dictionaries of usage

In cases where usage is disputed or where you feel unsure of your own usage, you may wish to consult a specialized dictionary of usage. The most widely used such work, although it is much more about British than American usage, is *The New Fowler's Modern English Usage,* Third Edition. First published in 1926 and edited by H. W. Fowler, the 1996 third edition has been edited by R. W. Burchfield.

Dictionaries of synonyms

All writers are sometimes stuck for just the right word, and at such times, a dictionary of synonyms or a thesaurus is a friend indeed. In these works, each entry is followed by words whose meanings are similar to that of the entry. A useful source is *Webster's Dictionary of Synonyms.*

A **thesaurus** (the word comes from a word meaning "treasure" or "storehouse") provides antonyms as well as synonyms. Two thesauri are particularly helpful: *Webster's Collegiate Thesaurus* and *The New Roget's Thesaurus of the English Language in Dictionary Form.*

www •

http://vancouver-webpages.com/synonyms.html

Type in a word and this online dictionary will find its synonym.

Remember, however, to use dictionaries of synonyms and thesauri carefully, because rarely in English are two words so close in meaning that they can be used interchangeably in radically different contexts. As Mark Twain put it, the difference between the right word and the almost right word is the difference between lightning and the lightning bug.

Dictionaries of etymology, regional English, slang, and neologisms

On some occasions, you may want or need to find out all you can about the origins of a word, to find out about a term used in only one area of the country, or to see whether a term is considered slang or jargon. The following specialized dictionaries can help you:

The Oxford Dictionary of English Etymology. Ed. C. T. Onions. New York: Oxford University Press, 1966.

Dictionary of American Regional English. Ed. Frederic G. Cassidy. Cambridge, Mass.: Belknap, Harvard University Press, 1985.

New Dictionary of American Slang. Ed. Robert L. Chapman. New York: Harper and Row, 1986. Revised edition of *Dictionary of American Slang,* compiled and edited by Harold Wentworth and Stuart Berg Flexner.

Trash Cash, Fizzbos, and Flatliners: A Dictionary of Today's Words. Eds. Sid Lerner and Gary F. Belkin. Boston: Houghton, 1993.

Dictionary of Computer Words, Revised Edition. Ed. American Heritage Dictionary. New York: Houghton Mifflin, 1995.

FOR MULTILINGUAL WRITERS

USING A LEARNER'S DICTIONARY

In addition to using a good college dictionary, you may want to invest in one of the following dictionaries intended especially for learners of English. The *Longman Dictionary of American English* presents the English spoken in the United States; the *Oxford Advanced Learner's Dictionary of Current English* covers British English.

These dictionaries provide information about count and noncount nouns, idioms and phrasal verbs, verbs that take a gerund and those that take an infinitive, and other topics important to learners of English. You should in general avoid using a bilingual dictionary, for you'll find more accurate and idiomatic information in an English dictionary than in, for example, a Spanish-English dictionary.

EXERCISE 25.6

Look up the following words in several specialized dictionaries, and find out as much as you can about their meanings, origins, and uses.

1. wazoo
2. tip
3. scam
4. jazz
5. whammy
6. advertorial

THINKING CRITICALLY ABOUT WORDS

In his autobiography, Malcolm X says that he taught himself to write by reading and copying the dictionary. Certainly you can teach yourself to be a better writer by paying careful attention to the way other writers use words that are unfamiliar to you. Choose a writer whose work you admire, and read that author's work for at least thirty minutes, noting six or seven words that you would not ordinarily have thought to use. Do a little dictionary investigative work on these words, and bring your results to class for discussion.

Enriching Vocabulary

26

In the Bible, how does God create the world? By naming it, creating a vocabulary for what was created. The word ***vocabulary*** comes, in fact, from a Latin term for "name" (*vocabulum*), which in turn comes from the Latin verb for "call." The connection between vocabulary and calling into being is what led a famous philosopher to declare that "the limits of my language are the limits of my world."

You can apply this insight to your own life by remembering a time when you learned the name of something new. Before that time, this thing did not exist for you; yet curiously enough, once you knew its name, you began to see it all around you. Such is the power of vocabulary in enriching not only our personal language but our lives as well. ■

26a Considering your vocabulary

At its largest, your English vocabulary includes all those words whose meanings you either recognize or can deduce from context. This, your **processing vocabulary,** allows you to interpret the meanings of many passages whose words you might not actively use yourself. Your **producing vocabulary** is more limited, made up of words you actually use in writing or speaking.

Part of what it means to mature intellectually is to broaden your mental horizons by learning how to name more things more accurately, to increase what the hero Beowulf called a "word hoard." Doing so involves consciously strengthening the bridges between your processing vocabulary and your producing vocabulary by beginning to use in your own speech and writing more of the words you recognize and can interpret in context. To accomplish this goal, you must become an investigative reporter of your own language and the language of others.

Charting the history of English

English has always been a hybrid language, what Daniel Defoe called "your Roman-Saxon-Danish-Norman English." Where did this hybrid come from, and how did it evolve? English, like one-third of all languages in the world, descends from Indo-European, a language spoken by groups of people whose original home was in some part of north-central Europe. Scholars began to argue for Indo-European as a "common source" and tried to identify its features when they noted striking resemblances among words in a number of languages.

English	Latin	Spanish	French	Greek	German	Dutch	Swedish
three	*tres*	*tres*	*trois*	*treis*	*drei*	*drie*	*tre*

A version of Indo-European was brought to Britain by the Germanic invasions following 449. This early language, called Anglo-Saxon or Old English, was influenced by Latin and Greek when Christianity was reintroduced into England beginning in 597, was later shaped by the Viking invasions beginning in the late 700s, and was transformed by French after the Norman Conquest (1066).

Although English continued to evolve in the centuries after the conquest, Latin and French were then the languages of the learned – of the church and court. In the late 1300s, it was Geoffrey Chaucer, writing *The Canterbury Tales* in the language of the people, who helped establish what is now called Middle English as the political, legal, and literary language of Britain. And after the advent of printing in the mid-1400s, that language became more accessible and more standardized. By about 1600, it had essentially become the Modern English we use today.

The following three versions of a biblical passage will give you an idea of how much English had evolved up to this time:

ANGLO-SAXON GOSPELS, AROUND A.D. 1000

And eft hē ongan hī æt þǣre sǣ lǣran. And him wæs mycel męnegu tō gegaderod, swā þæt hē on scip ēode, and on bǣre sǣ wæs; and eall sēo męnegu ymbe þē sǣ wæs on lande.

WYCLIFFE BIBLE, ABOUT 1380

And eft Jhesus bigan to teche at the see; and myche puple was gaderid to hym, so that he wente in to a boot, and sat in the see, and al the puple was aboute the see on the loond.

KING JAMES VERSION, 1611

And he began again to teach by the seaside: and there was gathered unto him a great multitude, so that he entered into a ship, and sat in the sea: and the whole multitude was by the sea on the land.

Note that in the Old English text, only a few words – *and, he, him, waes, on, lande* – look at all familiar. By the time of Chaucer and Wycliffe,

www •

http://www.m-w.com/mw/look.htm

"A Brief Look at the History of English." This short essay at Merriam-Webster's Web site provides a good summary of the evolution of English. Note the spelling variations displayed in the examples used to show changes in the language.

www •

http://peg.pegasus.oz.au/~toconnor/

A Web site that explores the history and origins of words and phrases; this site also includes a link to an online forum.

however, many words are recognizable. And by the time of Shakespeare, the language is easily readable.

In the last four hundred years, English has continued borrowing from many languages and, as a result, now has one of the world's largest vocabularies. Modern English, then, is a plant growing luxuriously in the soil of multiple language sources.

26b Recognizing word roots

As its name suggests, a **root** is a word from which other words grow, usually through the addition of prefixes or suffixes. From the Latin root *-dic-* or *-dict-* ("speak"), for instance, grows a whole range of words in English: *contradict, dictate, dictator, diction, edict, predict, dictaphone,* and others. Here are some other Latin (L) and Greek (G) roots. Recognizing them will help you recognize networks of words.

ROOT	MEANING	EXAMPLES
-audi- (L)	to hear	audience, audio
-bene- (L)	good, well	benevolent, benefit
-bio- (G)	life	biography, biosphere
-duc(t)- (L)	to lead or to make	ductile, reproduce
-gen- (G)	race, kind	genealogy, gene
-geo- (G)	earth	geography, geometry
-graph- (G)	to write	graphic, photography
-jur-, -jus- (L)	law	justice, jurisdiction
-log(o)- (G)	word, thought	biology, logical
-luc- (L)	light	lucid, translucent
-manu- (L)	hand	manufacture, manual
-mit-, -mis- (L)	to send	permit, transmission
-path- (G)	feel, suffer	empathy, pathetic
-phil- (G)	love	philosopher, bibliophile
-photo- (G)	light	photography, telephoto
-port- (L)	to carry	transport, portable
-psych- (G)	soul	psychology, psychopath
-scrib-, -script- (L)	to write	inscribe, manuscript
-sent-, -sens- (L)	to feel	sensation, resent
-tele- (G)	far away	telegraph, telepathy

ROOT	MEANING	EXAMPLES
-tend- (L)	to stretch	extend, tendency
-terr- (L)	earth	inter, territorial
-vac- (L)	empty	vacuole, evacuation
-vid-, -vis- (L)	to see	video, envision, visit

EXERCISE 26.1

Using the preceding list of roots, try to figure out the meaning of each of the following words. Write a potential definition for each one, and compare it to your dictionary's definition.

1. terrestrial
2. scriptorium
3. geothermal
4. lucent
5. beneficent
6. audiology
7. vacuous
8. pathogenic
9. juridical
10. graphology

26c Recognizing prefixes and suffixes

Originally individual words, prefixes and suffixes are groups of letters added to words or to word roots to create new words.

1 Prefixes

The word **prefix** appropriately demonstrates its own meaning: it is made up of a prefix (*pre-*) and a root (*-fix-*) and means literally "fasten before." Fastened to the beginnings of words or roots, prefixes modify and extend meanings. Recognizing common prefixes can often help you decipher the meaning of otherwise unfamiliar words.

Prefixes of negation or opposition

PREFIX	MEANING	EXAMPLES
a-, an-	without, not	ahistorical, anemia
anti-	against	antibody, antiphonal
contra-	against	contravene, contradict
de-	from, take away from	demerit, declaw
dis-	apart, away	disappear, discharge
il-, im-, in-, ir-	not	illegal, immature, indistinct, irreverent

PREFIX	MEANING	EXAMPLES
mal-	wrong	malevolent, malpractice
mis-	wrong, bad	misapply, misanthrope
non-	not	nonentity, nonsense
un-	not	unbreakable, unable

Prefixes of quantity

PREFIX	MEANING	EXAMPLES
bi-	two	bipolar, bilateral
milli-	thousand	millimeter, milligram
mono-	one, single	monotone, monologue
omni-	all	omniscient, omnipotent
semi-	half	semicolon, semiconductor
tri-	three	tripod, trimester
uni-	one	unitary, univocal

Prefixes of time and space

PREFIX	MEANING	EXAMPLES
ante-	before	antedate, antebellum
circum-	around	circumlocution, circumnavigate
co-, col-, com-, con-, cor-	with	coequal, collaborate, commiserate, contact, correspond
e-, ex-	out of	emit, extort, expunge
hyper-	over, more than	hypersonic, hypersensitive
hypo-	under, less than	hypodermic, hypoglycemia
inter-	between	intervene, international
mega-	enlarge, large	megalomania, megaphone
micro-	tiny	micrometer, microscopic
neo-	recent	neologism, neophyte
post-	after	postwar, postscript
pre-	before	previous, prepublication
pro-	before, onward	project, propel
re-	again, back	review, re-create

PREFIX	MEANING	EXAMPLES
sub-	under, beneath	subhuman, submarine
super-	over, above	supercargo, superimpose
syn-	at the same time	synonym, synchronize
trans-	across, over	transport, transition

EXERCISE 26.2

Using the preceding list of prefixes and the list of roots in 26b, try to figure out the meaning of each of the following words. Write a potential definition for each one, and compare it to your dictionary's definition.

1. remit
2. subterranean
3. translucent
4. monograph
5. distend
6. superscript
7. deport
8. neologism
9. inaudible
10. apathetic

2 Suffixes

Attached to the ends of words and word roots, **suffixes** modify and extend meanings, many times by altering the grammatical function or part of speech of the original word. Suffixes can, for example, turn the verb *create* into a noun, an adjective, or an adverb.

VERB	create
NOUNS	creat*or*/creat*ion*/creativ*ity*/creat*ure*
ADJECTIVE	creat*ive*
ADVERB	creative*ly*

Noun suffixes

SUFFIX	MEANING	EXAMPLES
-acy	state or quality	democracy, privacy
-al	act of	rebuttal, refusal
-ance, -ence	state or quality of	maintenance, eminence
-dom	place or state of being	freedom, thralldom
-er, -or	one who	trainer, investor
-ism	doctrine or belief characteristic of	liberalism, Taoism
-ist	one who	organist, physicist

SUFFIX	MEANING	EXAMPLES
-ity	quality of	veracity, opacity
-ment	condition of	payment, argument
-ness	state of being	watchfulness, cleanliness
-ship	position held	professorship, fellowship
-sion, -tion	state of being or action	digression, transition

Verb suffixes

SUFFIX	MEANING	EXAMPLES
-ate	cause to be	concentrate, regulate
-en	cause to be or become	enliven, blacken
-ify, -fy	make or cause to be	unify, terrify, amplify
-ize	cause to become	magnetize, civilize

Adjective suffixes

SUFFIX	MEANING	EXAMPLES
-able, -ible	capable of being	assumable, edible
-al	pertaining to	regional, political
-esque	reminiscent of	picturesque, statuesque
-ful	having a notable quality	colorful, sorrowful
-ic	pertaining to	poetic, mythic
-ious, -ous	of or characterized by	famous, nutritious
-ish	having the quality of	prudish, clownish
-ive	having the nature of	festive, creative, massive
-less	without	endless, senseless

EXERCISE 26.3

Using the preceding list of suffixes, figure out the meaning of each of the following words. (Use your dictionary if necessary.) Then choose two of the words, and use each one in a sentence.

1. contemplative
2. fanciful
3. impairment
4. liquefy
5. barrenness
6. defiance
7. merciless
8. redden
9. standardize
10. satirist

26d Building your vocabulary

Making good use of prefixes and suffixes will increase your vocabulary, but other methods will be even more helpful. These methods include analyzing contexts, reading actively, and learning the vocabulary of your field.

1 Analyzing word contexts

If you have ever run into a person you knew but could not place – until you remembered the place where you normally see the person (at the grocery store, say) – you know firsthand the importance of context in helping you identify people and things. The same principle holds true for words. So if a word is at first unfamiliar to you, look carefully at its context, paying attention to all the clues that the context can give; often you will be able to deduce the meaning.

For instance, if the word *accouterments* is unfamiliar in the sentence *We stopped at a camping-supply store to pick up last-minute accouterments,* the context – *a camping-supply store* and *last-minute* – suggests strongly that *equipment* or some similar word fits the bill. And that is what *accouterments* means.

EXERCISE 26.4

Identify the contextual clues that help you understand any unfamiliar words in the following sentences. Then write paraphrases of three of the sentences.

1. Before Prohibition, the criminal fringe in the United States had been a self-effacing, scattered class with little popular support.
2. The ambiguity of the evidence prevented the jury from determining which parts of it were extraneous. The jury asked for clarification.
3. The community's reaction to the preternatural creature in Shelley's *Frankenstein* shows that people are often more monstrous than a monster is.
4. My fifth-grade teacher was the epitome of what I wanted to be, and I began to imitate him scrupulously.
5. Aristarchus showed that the sun is larger than the earth and proposed a heliocentric model of the solar system. In the second century A.D., however, Ptolemy challenged this theory with his geocentric model, which came to dominate astronomy for the next fourteen hundred years.

As processors of information, we can read words alone, or we can read meanings. Reading meanings means filling in gaps, making connections, leaping ahead, asking questions, taking mental notes. Out of such activity, greater knowledge is born. Here are tips for building vocabulary:

→ Make a habit of paraphrasing or summarizing unfamiliar words or phrases. Then check the dictionary to see how accurate you were.
→ Practice naming the opposites of words. If you see abbreviation, for instance, try supplying its opposite – enlargement, elaboration, and so on.
→ Challenge authors by trying to come up with better words than the ones they used.
→ Read aloud to yourself from time to time, noting any words whose pronunciation you are unsure of. Check them in a dictionary.
→ Become a collector of words, choosing those you like best and making them part of your producing vocabulary. Begin by choosing a writer you admire and reading for as long as it takes to identify several words you like but have not yet used in speech or writing. Now analyze what you like about these words – their pronunciation, meaning, or usage.

2 Learning the vocabulary of your field

All occupations, professions, and disciplines rely on characteristic jargon: the vocabulary of medical fields, for example, includes technical terms such as *hematoma* and *carcinoid,* which the layperson might refer to simply as a "bruise" and a "tumor." In physics, the term *charm* indicates the quantum property assigned to the "charmed" quark. And in law, words quite often take on technical meanings associated with earlier legal decisions and precedents. In copyright law, for instance, the word *original* carries meanings and connotations that are much more highly specific and technical than those associated with the word in everyday use. You may want to keep a log of the language of your chosen field, noting both meanings and examples of each term's use.

For more about learning the vocabulary of a discipline, see 48b.

THINKING CRITICALLY ABOUT VOCABULARY

Reading with Attention to Vocabulary

Read each of the following passages, paying particular attention to the italicized words. See if you can determine the meaning of any words you don't know by using the clues suggested in this chapter — context, prefixes, roots, and suffixes. Check your understanding by looking up each word in a dictionary.

1. Now, I doubt that the imagination can be suppressed. If you truly *eradicated* it in a child, he would grow up to be an eggplant. Like all our evil *propensities,* the imagination will win out. – URSULA LEGUIN, "Why Are Americans Afraid of Dragons?"
2. Everything that comes alive seems to be in trade for something that dies, cell for cell. There might be some comfort in the recognition of *synchrony,* in the information that we all go down together, in the best of company. – LEWIS THOMAS, "Death in the Open"

Thinking about Your Own Vocabulary

Read over a piece of your writing. Underline any words you think could be improved on, and then come up with several possible substitutes. If you keep a writing log, list them there as a start to your own personal word hoard.

27 Considering Diction

One restaurant's "down-home beef stew" may look and taste much like another restaurant's "boeuf bourguignonne," but in each case the choice of language aims to say something not only about the food but also about the restaurant serving it. The difference is a matter of **diction** – literally, how you say or express something.

Effective diction involves many issues discussed elsewhere in this book, such as being concise, strengthening your vocabulary, and using varieties of English or other languages. Other aspects of good diction include choosing language appropriate to your purpose, topic, and audience; choosing words with the right denotations and connotations; balancing general and abstract words with specific and concrete ones; and using figurative language. ■

27a Choosing appropriate language

Musing on the many possible ways to describe a face, Ford Madox Ford notes,

> That a face resembles a Dutch clock has been said too often; to say that it resembles a ham is inexact and conveys nothing; to say that it has the mournfulness of an old smashed-in meat tin, cast away on a waste building lot, would be smart – but too much of that sort of thing would become a nuisance.
>
> – Ford Madox Ford

Ford here implies a major point about diction: effective word choice can be made only on the basis of what is appropriate to the writer's purpose, to the topic, and to the audience. What is appropriate may vary from one region to another, from one occupation to another, and from one social or ethnic group to another. In addition, the level of formality will vary depending on what is appropriate for a particular topic and audience. In an email or letter to a friend or close associate, informal language is often appropriate. For most academic and professional writing, however, more formal language is appropriate because you are addressing people you do not know well. Compare the following responses to a request for information about a job candidate:

→ Check to see that your language reflects the appropriate level of formality for your audience, purpose, and topic. If you use slang or colloquial language (such as *yeah*), is it appropriate? Is your language sufficiently courteous? (27a)
→ Check to be sure your audience will understand any jargon or other technical language. If not, either define the jargon, or replace it with words that will be understood. (27a)
→ Consider the connotations of words carefully to be sure they convey your intended meaning. If you say someone is *pushy,* be sure you mean to be critical; otherwise, use a word like *assertive.* (27b)
→ Be sure to use both general and concrete words. If you are writing about the general category of beds, for example, do you give enough concrete detail (*an antique four-poster bed*)? (27c)
→ Look for clichés, and replace them with fresher language. (27d)

EMAIL TO SOMEONE YOU KNOW WELL

Iris is great – hire her if you can!

LETTER OF RECOMMENDATION TO SOMEONE YOU DO NOT KNOW

I am pleased to recommend Iris Young. She will bring good ideas and extraordinary energy to your organization.

In deciding on the right words to use in a particular piece of writing, a writer needs to be aware of both the possibilities and the pitfalls of different kinds of language. Some specific kinds to keep in mind are slang and colloquial language; technical language; and pompous language, euphemisms, and doublespeak.

1 Slang and colloquial language

Slang, or extremely informal language, is often confined to a relatively small group and usually becomes obsolete rather quickly. Some slang gains wide use (*yuppie, bummer, Big Board*); it is often colorful or amusing (why pay with a dollar bill when you can hand over a *dead president* or a *frogskin*?). **Colloquial language,** such as *a lot, in a bind,* or *snooze,* is less informal, more widely used, and longer-lasting than slang.

Slang and colloquial language can expose a writer to the risk of not being understood or of not being taken seriously. If you are writing for a general audience about arms-control negotiations, for example, and you use the term *nukes* to refer to nuclear missiles, some readers may not know what you mean, and others may be distracted or irritated by what they see as a frivolous reference to a deadly serious subject.

EXERCISE 27.1

Choose something or someone to describe — a favorite cousin, a stranger on the bus, an automobile, a musical instrument, whatever strikes your fancy. Describe your subject using colloquial language and slang. Then rewrite the description, this time using neither of these. Read the two passages aloud, and note what different effects each creates.

2 Technical language

Some kinds of technical language originate in particular fields that have created special vocabularies or given common words special meaning. Businesspeople talk about *greenmail* and *upside movement,* biologists about *nucleotides* and *immunodestruction,* and baseball fans about *fielder's choices* and *suicide bunts.* You need to judge any use of technical language very carefully, making sure that your audience will understand your terms and replacing or defining those that they will not. Technical language can be divided into two overlapping categories: neologisms and jargon.

Neologisms

New words that have not yet found their way into dictionaries, **neologisms** can be very helpful to writers, especially in the sciences and applied disciplines. Terms like *thermosiphon hypertext,* for example, could not be easily replaced except by a much longer and more complex explanation. Some neologisms, however, do not meet a real need. Words like *deaccess* and *prioritization* could easily be replaced by existing words or phrases that general readers would understand.

www •

http://linguistlist.org/~ask-ling/index.html

Ask a Linguist. *A nationwide panel of linguists will answer questions about language. This site includes an archived list by subject of questions and answers.*

Jargon

Jargon is the special vocabulary of a trade or profession, enabling members to speak and write concisely to one another. It should be reserved as much as possible for a specific technical audience. Here is an example of jargon used inappropriately in writing addressed to general readers, and then revised to eliminate some of the jargon terms and define others:

JARGON

The VDT's in composition were down last week, so we had to lay out on dummies and crop and size the art with a wheel.

REVISED FOR A GENERAL AUDIENCE

The video display terminals were not working last week in the composing room, where models of the newspaper pages are made up for printing, so we had to arrange the contents of each page on a large cardboard sheet and use a wheel, a kind of circular slide rule, to figure out the size and shape of the pictures and other illustrations.

3 Pompous language, euphemisms, and doublespeak

Pompous language is unnecessarily formal for the purpose, audience, or topic. Hence it often gives writing an insincere or unintentionally humorous tone, making the writer's idea seem less significant or believable.

POMPOUS

Pursuant to the August 9 memorandum regarding petroleum supply exigencies, it is incumbent upon us to endeavor to make maximal utilization of telephonic communication in lieu of personal visitation.

REVISED

As of August 9, shortages of petroleum require us to use the telephone rather than make personal visits whenever possible.

FOR MULTILINGUAL WRITERS

AVOIDING FANCY DICTION

In writing standard academic English, which is fairly formal, you may be inclined to use the biggest and newest words in English that you know. Though your intention is good – to put new words to good use – you will be well advised to resist the temptation to use flowery or high-flown diction in your college writing. Academic writing calls first of all for clear, concise prose.

Euphemisms are terms designed to make an unpleasant idea more attractive or acceptable. *Your position is being eliminated* seeks to soften the blow of being fired or laid off; the British call this being *declared redundant,* whereas Canadians refer to being *made surplus.* Other euphemisms include *pass on* for *die* and *sanitation engineer* for *garbage collector.*

Use euphemisms with great care. Although they can appeal to readers by showing that the writer is considering their feelings, they can also sound pompous or suggest a wishy-washy, timid, or evasive attitude.

The name given by George Orwell to the language of Big Brother in his novel *1984,* **doublespeak** is the use of language to hide or distort the truth. During the massive layoffs and cutbacks in the corporate and business worlds in recent years, companies continued to speak of firings and layoffs as *work reengineering, employee repositioning, proactive downsizing,* and *special reprogramming.* The public – and particularly those who lost their jobs – recognized this use of doublespeak.

EXERCISE 27.2

Revise each of these sentences to use formal language consistently.

> *Although* *be excited* *as soon as*
> I can ~~get all enthused~~ about writing, ~~but~~ I sit down to write, ~~and~~ my mind
> *immediately* *blank.*
> goes ~~right to sleep~~.

1. Desdemona is a wimp; she just lies down and dies, accepting her death as inevitable.
2. All candidates strive for the same results: you try to make the other guy look gross and to persuade voters that you're okay for the job.
3. Often, instead of firing an incompetent teacher, school officials will transfer the person to another school to avoid hassles.
4. The more she flipped out about his actions, the more he rebelled and continued doing what he pleased.
5. My family lived in Trinidad for the first ten years of my life, and we went through a lot, but when we came to America, we thought we had it made.

27b Understanding denotation and connotation

Think of a stone tossed into a pool, and imagine the ripples spreading out from it, circle by circle. Or think of a note struck clear and clean, and the multiple vibrations that echo from it. In such images you can capture the distinction between **denotation,** the general meaning of a word, and **connotation,** the ripples, vibrations, and associations that accompany the word. As a writer, you want to choose words that are both denotatively and connotatively appropriate.

Words with similar denotations may have connotations that vary widely. The words *maxim, epigram, proverb, saw, saying,* and *motto,* for instance, all carry roughly the same denotation. Because of their different connotations, however, *proverb* would be the appropriate word to use in reference to a saying from the Bible; *saw* in reference to the kind of wisdom handed down anonymously; *epigram* in reference to a witty statement by someone like Dave Barry. *Pushy* and *assertive* also have much the same denotative meaning, but their connotations suggest different attitudes on the part of the writer, one negative, the other neutral or positive.

Because words with the wrong connotations for your intended meaning may not be as obvious as those with wrong denotations, take special

WWW •

http://www.thesaurus.com/

Roget's Thesaurus of English Words and Phrases on the Web. *A wonderful tool, this site does hypertextual searches of the famed thesaurus, allowing careful writers to better determine the connotations of words.*

care to avoid them. Look at the differences in connotation among the following three statements:

> Students Against Racism (SAR) erected a temporary barrier on the campus oval, saying it symbolizes "the many barriers to those discriminated against by university policies."
>
> Left-wing agitators threw up an eyesore right on the oval to try to stampede the university into giving in to their every demand.
>
> Supporters of human rights for all students challenged the university's investment in racism by erecting a protest barrier on campus.

As this example demonstrates, positive and negative connotations can shift meaning significantly. The first statement is the most neutral, merely stating facts (and quoting the assertion about university policy to represent it as someone's words rather than as "facts"); the second, by using words with negative connotations (*agitators, eyesore, stampede*), is strongly critical; the third, by using words with positive connotations (*supporters of human rights*) and presenting assertions as facts (*the university's investment in racism*), gives a favorable slant to the story. You should always pay attention to the connotations of the words you read or hear – including your own words. Try to use connotation to help make your meanings clear.

Many words carry fairly general connotations, evoking similar associational responses in most listeners or readers. But connotations can be personal or distinctive to a particular audience. If you have ever become ill right after eating a particular food, the mere mention of, say, peanut butter cookies carries powerful negative connotations for you.

The power of connotation to a particular audience was well illustrated by a meeting between presidential candidates Michael Dukakis and Jesse Jackson at the 1988 Democratic National Convention. Jackson was offended that Dukakis, who had clinched the party's nomination, had asserted his leadership by describing himself as "the quarterback on this team," a phrase that reminded African Americans of the stereotype that they were not intelligent enough to play quarterback on football teams. For his part, Dukakis was upset by Jackson's having told the new voters he had brought into the party that they were being used to "carry bales of cotton" up to "the big house," because the connotations of this language suggested that Dukakis was like a white plantation owner profiting from the labor of African American slaves. Whenever you write for a particular audience, try to be aware of the connotations your language will hold for that group of people.

"Wrong word" errors take so many different forms that it is very difficult to name any foolproof methods of checking for them. If you often find yourself using the wrong words, however, it will be well worth your time to go through each draft looking for them.

1. Check every word you are not absolutely sure of in a dictionary to see that you are using it properly.
2. Look for homonyms, words that sound like other words (such as *to, too,* and *two*). Using the information in 24b, make sure you are using the correct form.
3. Keep a list of any words you use incorrectly, including example sentences showing the way you have misused them. Make a point of proofreading carefully for them.

EXERCISE 27.3

Choose the word in parentheses whose denotative meaning makes most sense in the context of the sentence. Use a dictionary if necessary.

1. She listened (*apprehensively/attentively*) to the lecture and took notes.
2. Going swimming on a hot day can be a (*rapturous/ravenous*) experience.
3. Mark improved his windsurfing (*dramatically/drastically*) with lessons.
4. Franklin advised his readers to be (*feudal/frugal*) and industrious.

EXERCISE 27.4

Study the italicized words in each of the following passages, and decide what each word's connotations contribute to your understanding of the passage. Think of a synonym for each word, and see if you can decide what difference the new word would make to the effect of the passage.

1. The Burmans were already *racing* past me across the mud. It was obvious that the elephant would never *rise* again, but he was not dead. He was breathing very rhythmically with long *rattling gasps,* his great *mound* of a side painfully rising and falling. – GEORGE ORWELL, "Shooting an Elephant"
2. If boxing is a sport, it is the most *tragic* of all sports because, more than any human activity, it *consumes* the very excellence it *displays:* Its very *drama* is this consumption. – JOYCE CAROL OATES, "On Boxing"

FOR MULTILINGUAL WRITERS

LEARNING IDIOMS

Why do you wear a diamond *on* your finger but *in* your ear (or nose)? See 55a.

3. We caught two bass, *hauling* them in *briskly* as though they were mackerel, pulling them over the side of the boat in a *businesslike* manner without any landing net, and stunning them with a *blow* on the back of the head.
   – E. B. White, "Once More to the Lake"

4. Then one evening Miss Glory told me to serve the ladies on the porch. After I set the tray down and turned toward the kitchen, one of the women asked, "What's your name, *girl*?" – Maya Angelou, *I Know Why the Caged Bird Sings*

5. The Kiowas are a summer people; they *abide* the cold and keep to themselves; but when the season *turns* and the land becomes warm and *vital,* they cannot *hold still.* – N. Scott Momaday, "The Way to Rainy Mountain"

27c Balancing general and specific diction

Good writers move their prose along and help readers follow the meaning by balancing **general words,** those that refer to groups or classes of things, with **specific words,** those that refer to individual things. One kind of general words, **abstractions,** are words or phrases that refer to qualities or ideas, things we cannot perceive through our five senses. Specific words are often **concrete words;** they name things we can see, hear, touch, taste, or smell. Rarely can we draw a clear-cut line between general or abstract words on the one hand and specific or concrete ones on the other. Instead, most words fall somewhere between these two extremes.

GENERAL	LESS GENERAL	SPECIFIC	MORE SPECIFIC
book	dictionary	unabridged dictionary	my 1998 edition of *Webster's Dictionary*

ABSTRACT	LESS ABSTRACT	CONCRETE	MORE CONCRETE
culture	visual art	painting	Van Gogh's *Starry Night*

Because passages that contain mostly general terms or abstractions demand that readers supply most of the specific examples or concrete details with their imaginations, such writing is often hard to read. But writing that is full of specifics can also be tedious and hard to follow if the main point is not made clearly or is lost amid a flood of details. Strong writing must usually provide readers both with a general idea or overall picture and with specific examples or concrete details to fill in that picture.

In the following passage, for instance, the author might have simply made a general statement — *their breakfast was always liberal and good* — or simply described the breakfast. Instead, he does both.

> There would be a brisk fire crackling in the hearth, the old smoke-gold of morning and the smell of fog, the crisp cheerful voices of the people and their ruddy competent morning look, and the cheerful smells of breakfast, which was always liberal and good, the best meal that they had: kidneys and ham and eggs and sausages and toast and marmalade and tea.
>
> – THOMAS WOLFE, *Of Time and the River*

Here a student writer balances general statements with illustrative specific details:

GENERAL My neighbor is a nuisance.

SPECIFIC My next-door neighbor is a nuisance, poking and prying into my life, constantly watching me as I enter and leave my house, complaining about the noise when I am having a good time, and telling my parents whenever she sees me kissing my date.

EXERCISE 27.5

Rewrite each of the following sentences to be more specific and concrete.

1. The entryway of the building was dirty.
2. The sounds at dawn are memorable.
3. Sunday dinner was good.
4. The attendant came toward my car.
5. The child played on the beach.

27d Using figurative language

One good way to communicate with an audience is by using figurative language, or figures of speech. Such language paints pictures in our minds, allows us to "see" a point and hence understand more readily and clearly. Economists trying to explain the magnitude of the federal deficit use figurative language when they tell us how many hundred-thousand-dollar bills would have to circle the globe how many times to equal it. Scientists describing the way genetic data are transmitted use figurative language when they liken the data to a messenger that carries bits of information from one generation of cells to another and when they liken certain genetic variants to typographical errors. Far from being mere decoration, figurative language plays a crucial role in helping us follow a writer's meaning.

Particularly helpful in building understanding are figures of speech that compare one thing to another – similes, metaphors, and analogies. Other types of figurative language include allusion and signifying.

Similes

Similes (pronounced sim′əlēz) make explicit the comparison between two things by using *like, as, as if,* or *as though.*

> The comb felt as if it was raking my skin off. – MALCOLM X, "My First Conk"

> The Digital Revolution is sweeping through our lives like a Bengali typhoon.
> – LOUIS ROSSETTO

Metaphors

Metaphors (pronounced met′əfərz) are implicit comparisons, omitting the *like, as, as if,* or *as though* of similes.

> Black women are called, in the folklore that so aptly identifies one's status in society, "the mule of the world," because we have been handed the burdens that everyone else – everyone else – refused to carry.
> – ALICE WALKER, *In Search of Our Mothers' Gardens*

> Unix is the Swiss Army Knife of the Net. – THOMAS MANDEL

Analogies

For more on analogies, see 5h2.

Analogies compare similar features of two dissimilar things and are often extended to several sentences or paragraphs in length. The following sentence, for example, uses an analogy to help us understand the rapid growth of the computer industry:

> If the aircraft industry had evolved as spectacularly as the computer industry over the past twenty-five years, a Boeing 767 would cost five hundred dollars today, and it would circle the globe in twenty minutes on five gallons of fuel.

The analogy in the next passage helps us "see" an abstract point.

> One Hundred and Twenty-fifth Street was to Harlem what the Mississippi was to the South, a long traveling river always going somewhere, carrying something. – MAYA ANGELOU, *The Heart of a Woman*

Before you use an analogy, though, make sure that the two things you are comparing have enough points of similarity to justify the comparison and make it convincing to readers.

Clichés and mixed metaphors

Just as effective use of figurative language can create the impression the writer wants to create, so *ineffective* figures of speech can create the *wrong* impression by boring, irritating, or unintentionally amusing readers. Among the most common kinds of ineffective figurative language are clichés and mixed metaphors.

Cliché (pronounced klē shā′) comes from the French word for "stereotype," a metal plate cast from a page of type and used, before the invention of photographic printing processes, to produce multiple copies of a book or page without having to reset the type. So a **cliché** in language is an expression stamped out in duplicate to avoid the trouble of "resetting" the thought. Many clichés, like *busy as a bee* or *youth is the springtime of life,* are similes or metaphors.

By definition, we use clichés all the time, especially in speech, and the rhythm and alliteration of some continue to please, even if they are "unoriginal." Like anything else, however, clichés should be used in moderation: if your audience recognizes that you are using stereotyped, paint-by-numbers language to excess, they are likely to conclude that what you are saying is not very new or interesting – or true. The person who tells you that you look *pretty as a picture* uses a clichéd simile that may well sound false or insincere. Compare it with a more original compliment a grandmother once paid to her grandchildren: *You all look as pretty as brand-new red shoes.*

How can you check for clichés? Although one person's trite phrase may be completely new to another, one rule of thumb will serve you well: if you can predict exactly what the upcoming word(s) in a phrase will be, it stands a very good chance of being a cliché.

Mixed metaphors are comparisons that are not consistent. Instead of creating a clear and dominant impression, they confuse the reader by pulling against one another, often in unintentionally funny ways. Here is a mixed metaphor revised for consistency:

► **The lectures were like brilliant comets streaking through the night sky,** *dazzling* ~~**showering**~~ **listeners with** *flashes* ~~**a torrential rain**~~ **of insights.**

The images of streaking light and heavy precipitation were inconsistent; in the revised sentence, all of the images relate to light.

www •

http://www.nexus.edu.au/teachstud/dexed/docs/cliche.html

The account of an English teacher named Ms. English with an ax to grind who told her students to avoid clichés like the plague, this piece by Graeden Horsell says that sometimes clichés are needed, and that one should never say "never."

Allusions

Allusions, indirect references to cultural works, people, or events, can bring an entire world of associations to the minds of readers who recognize them. When a sports commentator said, *If Georgia Tech has an Achilles heel, it is their inexperience, their youth,* he alluded to the Greek myth in which the hero Achilles was fatally wounded in his one vulnerable spot, his heel.

You can draw allusions from history, from literature, from the Bible, from common wisdom, or from current events. Many current movies and popular songs are full of allusions. Remember, however, that allusions work only if your audience recognizes them.

Signifying

One distinctive use of figurative language found extensively in African American English is **signifying,** in which a speaker cleverly and often humorously needles or insults the listener. In the following passage, two African American men (Grave Digger and Coffin Ed) signify on their white supervisor (Anderson), who ordered them to discover the originators of a riot:

> "I take it you've discovered who started the riot," Anderson said.
>
> "We knew who he was all along," Grave Digger said.
>
> "It's just nothing we can do to him," Coffin Ed echoed.
>
> "Why not, for God's sake?"
>
> "He's dead," Coffin Ed said.
>
> "Who?"
>
> "Lincoln," Grave Digger said.
>
> "He hadn't ought to have freed us if he didn't want to make provisions to feed us," Coffin Ed said. "Anyone could have told him that."
>
> – CHESTER HIMES, *Hot Day, Hot Night*

Coffin Ed and Grave Digger demonstrate the major characteristics of effective signifying: indirection, ironic humor, fluid rhythm – and a surprising twist at the end. Rather than insulting Anderson directly by pointing out that he's asked a dumb question, they criticize the question indirectly by ultimately blaming a white man (and not just *any* white man, but one they're all supposed to revere). This twist leaves the supervisor speechless, teaching him something *and* giving Grave Digger and Coffin Ed the last word.

You will find examples of signifying in the work of many African American writers. You may also hear signifying in NBA basketball, for it is an important element of trash talking; what Grave Digger and Coffin Ed do to Anderson, Charles Barkley regularly does to his opponents on the court.

EXERCISE 27.6

Identify the similes and metaphors in the following passages, and decide how each contributes to your understanding of the passage it appears in.

1. John's mother, Mom Willie, who wore her Southern background like a magnolia corsage, eternally fresh, was robust and in her sixties.

   – MAYA ANGELOU, "The Heart of a Woman"

2. I was watching everyone else and didn't see the waitress standing quietly by. Her voice was deep and soft like water moving in a cavern.

   – WILLIAM LEAST HEAT-MOON, "In the Land of 'Coke-Cola'"

3. My horse, when he is in his stall or lounging about the pasture, has the same relationship to pain that I have when cuddling up with a good murder mystery — comfort and convenience have top priority.

   – VICKI HEARNE, "Horses in Partnership with Time"

EXERCISE 27.7

Return to the description you wrote in Exercise 27.1. Note any words that carry strong connotations, and identify the concrete and abstract language as well as any use of figurative language. Revise the description for better use of diction.

THINKING CRITICALLY ABOUT DICTION

Read the following brief poem. What dominant feeling or impression does the poem produce in you? Identify the diction, those specific words and phrases that help create that impression.

What happens to a dream deferred?

Does it dry up
Like a raisin in the sun?
Or fester like a sore —
And then run?
Does it stink like rotten meat?
Or crust and sugar over —
Like a syrupy sweet?

Maybe it just sags
Like a heavy load.

Or does it explode?

– LANGSTON HUGHES, "Harlem (A Dream Deferred)"

28 Considering Language Variety

A group of college students gathers outside a deli. "I'm having a hero," says one. "I'm ordering a submarine," says another. "You mean a hoagie?" asks a third. You might know this sandwich as a grinder, a poor boy, a cubano — or some other name. The differences suggest an important fact of our linguistic life: although all speakers of English share the same language, within this broad category are many differences. Indeed, many varieties of spoken and written English exist, distinguished by pronunciation, vocabulary and rhetorical and grammatical choices.

In addition to the many varieties of English, many other languages are spoken in the United States. Linguist Dell Hymes suggests that perhaps this multilingualism is what the Founders meant by choosing the Latin motto "E pluribus unum" (out of many, one): "E pluribus unum — bilingualism is . . . only as far away as the nearest nickel." ■

28a Recognizing different varieties of English

Everyone reading this text uses one or more varieties of English, whether they are those characteristic of particular *geographic regions,* of particular *occupations or professions,* or of particular *social, cultural, or ethnic groups.* In a given day, for example, one of the authors of this textbook might use a midwestern regional variety of English when talking with a group of students at Ohio State; an occupational variety characterized by highly specialized vocabulary when preparing a scholarly journal article; and an eastern Tennessee regional variety, which is strongly influenced by African American vernacular English, when talking on the phone with her grandmother. In each instance, the chosen language is appropriate. The question becomes, then, *when* to use a particular variety of English or shift from one variety to another — when to insert eastern Tennessee or African American vernacular patterns into a formal essay, for example, or when to use language from work in a conversation with friends.

Sometimes, in fact, our choices are limited or highly circumscribed by various kinds of pressures. An extreme but by no means isolated example is the tendency of many in our society to discriminate against those who fail to use an expected variety of English. Not only is there discrimination against those who don't speak "standard" English; there is also the rejection in other communities of those who sound affected, too proper, or "la-di-da." Used appropriately and wisely, however, *all* varieties of English can serve many purposes.

28b Using standard varieties of English

One variety of English, often referred to as the "standard," is that taught prescriptively in schools, used in the national media, and written and spoken widely by those thought to wield the most social and economic power. It is, in addition, the variety of English represented in this textbook (and in all textbooks). As the language used in most public institutions and in business and government, standard English is one variety you will no doubt want to be completely familiar with – all the while recognizing, however, that it is only one of many effective and powerful varieties of our language. As the linguist Steven Pinker says, "It makes sense to have a standard in the same way it makes sense for everyone to drive on the right-hand side of the road. But it's different from saying that the right side is the only true and justified side to drive on." In fact, the right-hand side of the road is not "right" in countries where the standard is to drive on the left. Similarly, what is agreed on as standard in U.S. English will not always be standard elsewhere.

But even standard English is hardly a monolith; the standard varies according to purpose and audience, from the very formal English used in academic writing and in prepared speeches to the informal English characteristic of casual conversation. Thus the notion that there is one absolutely correct and standard way to say or write something is in important ways a myth. Nevertheless, within this variation, a recognizable set of practices and conventions exists. These practices and conventions go by the shorthand name of standard English.

28c Using ethnic varieties of English

Whether you are a Native American or trace your ancestry to Germany, Italy, Ireland, Africa, China, Mexico, or elsewhere, you have an ethnic heritage that lives on in the English language. See how a Hawaiian writer uses an ethnic variety of English to paint a picture of young teens hearing a frightening, goose-bump-raising (or what he calls a "chicken skin") story about sharks from their grandmother.

FOR MULTILINGUAL WRITERS

GLOBAL ENGLISH

Like other world languages, English is used in many countries around the world, resulting in many global varieties. For example, if you have studied English outside the United States, you may well have learned a British variety. British English differs somewhat from U.S. English in certain vocabulary (*bonnet* for "hood" of a car), syntax (*to hospital* rather than "to the hospital"), spelling (*centre* rather than "center"), and of course pronunciation. If you have learned a British variety of English, you will want to recognize the ways in which it differs from the U.S. "standard."

> "– So, rather dan being rid of da shark, da people were stuck with many little ones, for dere mistake."
>
> Then Grandma Wong wen' pause, for dramatic effect, I guess, and she wen' add, "Dis is one of dose times. Dis is da time of da mano." She wen' look at my kid brother 'Analu and said, "Da time of da sharks."
>
> Those words ended another of Grandma's chicken skin stories. The stories she told us had been passed on to her by her grandmother, who had heard them from *her* grandmother. Always skipping a generation.
>
> – RODNEY MORALES, "When the Shark Bites"

Notice that the narrator of the story, the brother of 'Analu, uses both standard and ethnic varieties of English – presenting information necessary to the story line mostly in more formal standard English and using a more informal, local ethnic variety to represent spoken language.

This passage comes from fiction, but writers sometimes shift among varieties of English in nonfiction writing as well. Geneva Smitherman is particularly effective at using African American vernacular English to get the reader's attention, to create emphasis, and to make her point, all at the same time.

> Before about 1959 (when the first study was done to change black speech patterns), Black English had been primarily the interest of university academics, particularly the historical linguists and cultural anthropologists. In recent years, though, the issue has become a very hot controversy, and there have been articles on Black Dialect in the national press as well as in the educational research literature. We have had pronouncements on black speech from the NAACP and the Black Panthers, from highly publicized scholars of the Arthur Jensen – William Shockley bent, from executives of national corporations such as Greyhound, and from housewives and community folk. I mean, really, it seem like everybody and they momma done had something to say on the subject!
>
> – GENEVA SMITHERMAN, *Talkin and Testifyin*

Smitherman shifts into the African American vernacular English she is discussing in the last sentence of her paragraph, letting readers hear what she has been talking about. "Listen up," this shift says to the reader: "I'm making an important point here." And it dramatically illustrates that point by summarizing the content of the preceding academic language.

In each of these examples, the writers have full command of standard academic English, and yet at times they choose to shift to other varieties. In each case, one important reason for the shift is to demonstrate that the writer is a member of the community whose language he or she is representing and thus to build credibility with others in the community.

www •

http://ourworld.compuserve.com/homepages/JWCRAWFORD/home.htm

Language Policy Web Site & Emporium. *Maintained by James Crawford, a reporter and writer who specializes in the politics of languages, this site offers links to articles and Web sites on many language policy issues, including the English Only movement, bilingual education, Ebonics, endangered languages, and language rights.*

www •

http://www.cal.org/ebonics/

The Center for Applied Linguistics sponsors this page about African American vernacular English; it includes many useful links.

Take care, however, in using the language of communities other than your own. Used inappropriately, such language can have an opposite effect: that of destroying credibility and alienating your audience.

28d Using occupational varieties of English

From the fast-food business to taxi driving, from architecture to zoology, every job has its own special variety of English. Examples abound, from specialized words (*hermeneutics* in literary studies) to invented words (*quark* in physics). Here is an example from the computer world about a problem plaguing the World Wide Web:

> Right now, even if you're using a fully stocked Pentium and have a T1 line running into your bedroom, the Web can seem overloaded and painfully slow. Conventional wisdom says the solution lies in new network technologies like AIM and fiber optics. But researchers are investigating how to change the way computers communicate to minimize pauses, stutters, and false starts. After all, using the Internet isn't just a matter of shouting, "Hey, *www.hotwired.com,* shoot me that GIF!"
>
> – Steve G. Steinberg, *Wired*

The columnist writing here uses technical abbreviations (*T1*) and acronyms (*AIM, GIF*), as well as ordinary words that have special meanings, such as "pauses" and "stutters." He also uses a quotation to capture the sound and rhythm of speech and to help make his point: the Internet is governed by specific rules that can speed up – or slow down – communication.

Even within an occupation, there is room for variety. The language that sportscasters use, for instance, varies depending on whether the announcer is giving "play-by-play" commentary or "color" commentary. The following snippet, from a conversation between Pat Summerall (play-by-play) and John Madden (color) as they announce an Eagles-Giants football game, illustrates such variation:

> Summerall: Second and nine. Cunningham to throw it. Giles ducks to about a foot short of first. It looks like Cooks and Taylor on the stop.
>
> Madden: Jimmie Giles says, "I've been in a lot of big games" (he's a thirteen-year veteran), and the bad news for the Eagles was that they lost Keith Jackson, of course, but the good news is that they have Jimmie Giles. I'll tell you, Randall Cunningham feels very, very comfortable with Jimmie Giles.
>
> Summerall: And it's a first down by Giles from Cunningham.

Madden: Cunningham said to us yesterday – we were talking to him about Jimmie Giles, and he said he thinks he's twenty-seven. He wanted to know what that secret is where you just stay that one age all the time. You could bottle that and sell it.

Notice that the play-by-play commentary strings together units of words that exhibit combinations not found in ordinary language but that here are visually and linguistically meaningful to those watching the game. In addition, the play-by-play announcer provides specific technical information (*a first down*) and uses technical vocabulary (*second and nine, on the stop*). The color commentator, on the other hand, speaks in nearly complete sentences, provides interesting but tangentially related information, and does not use technical vocabulary. These differences reflect the different purposes of each announcer: one tries to sketch in exactly what is happening on the field; the other to color that sketch by commenting on it and on the players involved.

28e Using regional varieties of English

> "Ever'body says words different," said Ivy. "Arkansas folks says 'em different from Oklahomy folks says 'em different. And we seen a lady from Massachusetts, an' she said 'em differentest of all. Couldn' hardly make out what she was sayin'."
>
> – John Steinbeck, *The Grapes of Wrath*

Thus does Ivy point to the existence and significance of regional varieties of English. Like Ivy – and every other speaker of English – your language has been affected by region. In writing, such regional language provides an effective means of evoking a character or place.

Garrison Keillor, for instance, has become famous for his Lake Wobegon stories, which are peppered with the English spoken in parts of Minnesota. When Keillor says "Gimme a Wendy's," he refers not to a kind of hamburger but to Saint Wendell's beer, "brewed by the Dimmers family at the Old Dimmers Brewery in nearby Saint Wendell's for five generations."

In writing of her native Vermont, a student writer included the following piece of dialogue:

> "There'll be some fine music on the green tonight, don't ya know?"
> "Well, I sure do want to go."
> "So don't I!"

In both these instances, the regional English creates a homespun effect and captures some of the language used in a particular place.

Used to capture attention, to amuse, and to evoke the sounds of a particular place, the language in the following passage from a cookbook is characteristic of rural Alabama and other areas of Appalachia:

> Then there's Big Reba Culpepper, big because there's Little Reba also; Big Reba lives in Burnt Corn, Alabama. She is famous countrywide for Reba's Rainbow Icebox Cake. Not too far from Burnt Corn is a place called Flea Hop, Alabama. Big Reba said she has a relative buried "in a small family-type cemetery right out on the edge of town. He was some kind of Civil War hero and when he died he was a very rich man." His grave was richly and clearly marked with a big bronze obelisk "that went way up high," Reba said, "and all his wives (six of them), children, and grandchildren were buried within spittin' distance of his monument. The old cemetery was all growed up with pine trees and needed a whole lot of attention to make it look halfway decent," Reba said. . . . "So I took it on myself to get up a cemetery cleaning party, with rakes, shovels and hoes, fried chicken, Hoppin' John, biscuits, ice tea and, of course, my famous Rainbow Icebox Cake, enough to kill us all. We loaded down the car and took off like Moody's goose for Flea Hop, Alabama."
>
> – Ernest Matthew Mickler

In this example, the use of particular terms (*Hoppin' John,* for instance), expressions (*within spittin' distance, like Moody's goose*), and grammatical structures (*all growed up*) depicts regional pronunciations and rhythms, thus helping to capture the flavor of Big Reba's language as well as of Burnt Corn, Alabama. Notice that the regional language here is all *quoted* – that is, it is all spoken language.

EXERCISE 28.1

Try revising one of this chapter's examples of ethnic, occupational, or regional English. First, try to identify the purpose and audience for the original passage. Then rewrite the passage in order to remove all evidence of any variety of English other than standard academic. Compare your revised version to the original and to those produced by some of your classmates. What differences do you notice in tone (is it more formal? more distant? something else?) and in overall impression? Which version seems most appropriate for the intended audience and purpose? Which do you prefer – and why?

28f Bringing in other languages

Sometimes it may be appropriate for someone writing in English to use another language. You might do so for the same reasons you would use different varieties of English: to represent the actual words of a speaker, to make a point, to connect with your audience, to get the readers' attention.

See how Gerald Haslam uses Spanish to capture his great-grandmother's words as well as to make a point about his relationship to her.

> *"Expectoran su sangre!"* exclaimed Great-grandma when I showed her the small horned toad I had removed from my breast pocket. I turned toward my mother, who translated: "They spit blood."
>
> *"De los ojos,"* Grandma added. "From their eyes," mother explained, herself uncomfortable in the presence of the small beast.
>
> I grinned, "Awwwwwww."
>
> But my Great-grandmother did not smile. *"Son muy tóxicos,"* she nodded with finality. Mother moved back an involuntary step, her hands suddenly busy at her breast. "Put that thing down," she ordered.
>
> "His name's John," I said.
>
> – GERALD HASLAM, *California Childhood*

On some occasions, a writer may use a particularly apt foreign phrase that doesn't seem easily translatable or one that seems appropriate untranslated. See how the novelist Michele Herman uses Yiddish to evoke another grandmother's world.

> "Skip *shabes*?" Rivke chuckled. "I don't think this is possible. Once a week comes *shabes*. About this a person doesn't have a choice."
>
> "What I *mean*" – Myra's impatience was plain – "is skip the preparation. It's too much for you, it tires you out."
>
> *"Ach,"* Rivke said. "Too much for me it isn't." This wasn't true. For some time she had felt that it really was too much for her. It was only for *shabes* that she cooked; the rest of the week she ate cold cereal, fruit, pot cheese, crackers.
>
> – MICHELE HERMAN, *Missing*

In this passage, Rivke's syntax – the inversion of word order (*Once a week comes shabes,* for example, and *Too much for me it isn't*) – reflects Yiddish rhythms. In addition, the use of the Yiddish *shabes* carries a strong association with a religious institution, one that would be lost if it were translated to "sabbath." It is not "sabbath" to Rivke; it is *shabes.*

EXERCISE 28.2

We all shift regularly among varieties of English, often automatically and especially in speech, in response to changing situations and audiences. Try listening to yourself talk – at work, with parents or others in authority, with close friends, and so on. Take notes on your own use of language, noting any words and patterns that are from languages other than English or that are characteristic of a region or a job or a cultural group. Which of these might you use in writing as well as in speaking? Why would you use them, and for what effect?

28g Using varieties of language in academic writing

The key to shifting among varieties of English and among languages is appropriateness: when will such a shift reach your audience and help you make a particular point? Certain common college writing assignments – for example, writing about a person or place; writing based on sources; and oral presentation – might provide the opportunity to bring varieties of English or other languages into your academic writing.

See how an anthropologist weaves together regional and standard academic English in writing about one Carolina community.

> For Roadville, schooling is something most folks have not gotten enough of, but everybody believes will do something toward helping an individual "get on." In the words of one oldtime resident, "Folks that ain't got no schooling don't get to be nobody nowadays."
>
> – SHIRLEY BRICE HEATH, *Ways with Words*

See how Heath takes care to let a resident of Roadville speak her mind – and in her own words. She does so to be faithful to the person she is quoting as well as to capture some of the flavor of the spoken language.

In the following passage, a linguist uses Spanish in her discussion of literacy in a Mexican community in Chicago:

> *Gracia* (grace, wit) is used to refer to wittiness in talk; people who *tiene gracia* (have grace, are witty) are seen as clever and funny. Not everyone illustrates this quality, but those who do are obvious from the moment they speak. As one middle-aged male said,
>
> > *. . . cuando ellos empiezan a hablar, desde el momento que los oyes hablar, tienen gracia. Entonces, la gente que tiene gracia, se va juntando gente a oírlos. Y hay gente más desabrida, diría yo. No tiene, no le quedan sus chistes. Aunque cuente uno una charrita . . . ya no te vas a reír igual.*
>
> (. . . when they start to speak, from the moment that you hear them speak, they are witty. So then, the people who are witty begin to have a listening crowd gather about them. And then there are people who are more boring, I would say. They don't have, their jokes just don't make it. Even though they may tell a joke . . . you're not going to laugh in the same manner.)
>
> – MARCIA FARR, "Essayist Literacy and Other Verbal Performances"

Here Farr provides a translation of the Spanish, for she expects that many of her readers will not know Spanish. She evokes the language of the community she describes, however, by presenting the Spanish first.

Remember that using different languages and varieties of English can be a good way to reach out to an audience, as in the pope's use of various languages, but it can also exclude and alienate listeners or readers. Such a danger is particularly great when you shift to language that your audience may not understand or that is not your own. In such cases, you might be seen as attempting to keep others out, or to speak for others rather than letting them speak for themselves.

Translating

The question of whether or not to translate words or passages from another language into English depends on your purpose and audience. In general, you should not assume that all your readers will understand the other language. So in most cases, including a translation (as Marcia Farr does) is appropriate. Occasionally, however, the words from the other language will be clear from the context (as is *shabes* in Michele Herman's passage). A writer might at times leave something untranslated to make a point – to let readers know what it's like not to understand, for example.

To translate, as a general rule, underline or italicize foreign words, and put the translation in roman type, enclosed in parentheses or quotation marks.

THINKING CRITICALLY ABOUT LANGUAGE VARIETY

The following description of a supper features English characteristic of the Florida backwoods in the 1930s. Using this passage as an example, write a description of a memorable meal or other event from your daily life. Try to include some informal dialogue. Then look at the language you used – do you use more than one variety of English, and if so, which ones? What effect does your use of language have on your description?

> Jody heard nothing; saw nothing but his plate. He had never been so hungry in his life, and after a lean winter and a slow spring . . . his mother had cooked a supper good enough for the preacher. There were poke-greens with bits of white bacon buried in them; sandbuggers made of potato and onion and the cooter he had found crawling yesterday; sour orange biscuits and at his mother's elbow the sweet potato pone. He was torn between his desire for more biscuits and another sandbugger and the knowledge, born of painful experience, that if he ate them, he would suddenly have no room for pone. The choice was plain.
>
> – MARJORIE KINNAN RAWLINGS, *The Yearling*

29 Considering Others: Building Common Ground

East is East, and West is West, and never the twain shall meet. . . .

You say to-ma-to, and I say to-mah-to. . . .

These contrasting lines suggest a challenge every writer must face: many differences separate us. In the United States today, we are part of a richly diverse population representing just about every social, religious, linguistic, and cultural tradition imaginable — and yet all connected by a common citizenship. How can such different people ever build commonalities? Fortunately, careful language use can help us out. The words we use can and do build common ground, even if you say "to-ma-to" and I say "to-mah-to."

This chapter will get you started thinking about how your own language can work to respect differences and to build common ground with others. ■

29a Remembering the golden rule

As a child, you may have learned to "do to others what you would have them do to you." To that golden rule, we could add "say to others what you would have them say to you." Language has power. It can praise, delight, inspire. It can also hurt, offend, even destroy. Language that offends readers breaks the golden rule of language use, preventing them from identifying with you and thus damaging your credibility as a writer.

In many instances, avoiding such language is simple enough. We can safely assume, for instance, that no readers respond well to being referred to disparagingly — for example, as *slobs* or *nerds.* But other cases are more subtle and perhaps surprising. One student found, for example, that members of a group he had been referring to as *senior citizens* were irritated by that label, preferring more straightforward terms such as *elderly* or even *old.* Similarly, a recent survey of people with physical disabilities reported that most of them resented euphemisms like *physically challenged* because they saw them as trivializing their difficulties.

Because usage changes constantly and preferences vary, few absolute guidelines exist for using language that shows respect for differences and builds common ground. Two general rules, however, can help writers: consider carefully the sensitivities and preferences of others, and watch for words that carry stereotypes and betray unintended assumptions.

→ What unstated assumptions might come between you and your readers? Look, for instance, for language implying approval or disapproval and for the ways you use *we, you,* and *they.* (29a and b)

→ Does any language used to describe others carry offensive stereotypes or connotations? (29b)

→ Have you checked for use of masculine pronouns to refer to members of both sexes and for any other uses of potentially sexist language? (29b1)

→ Are your references to race, religion, gender, sexual orientation, and so on relevant or necessary to your discussion? If not, consider leaving them out. (29b2 and b3)

→ Are the terms you use to refer to groups accurate and acceptable? Because group labels and preferences are always changing, take care to use the most widely accepted terms. (29b2)

29b Watching for stereotypes and other assumptions

Children like to play; U.S. citizens value freedom; people who do not finish high school fare less well in the job market than those who graduate. These broad statements contain **stereotypes,** standardized or fixed ideas about a group. To some extent, we all think in terms of stereotypes, and sometimes they can be helpful in making a generalization. Stereotyping any individual on the basis of generalizations about a group can be dangerous, however, for it can lead to inaccurate and even hurtful conclusions.

Stereotyping becomes especially evident in language, in the words we choose to refer to or describe others. Stereotyped language can, and often does, break the links between writers and readers – or between speakers and listeners. An instructor who notes a male student's absence from her class on the morning after a big fraternity party and remarks, "Ah, he must be a fraternity man," is stereotyping the student on the basis of assumptions about "fraternity men." But such stereotyping may be far off the mark with this particular student – and with many other fraternity members. By indulging in it, this instructor may well be alienating some of her students and undermining her effectiveness as a teacher.

Very often based on half-truths, misunderstandings, and hand-me-down prejudices, stereotypes can lead to intolerance, bias, and bigotry.

Even apparently positive or neutral ones can hurt, for they inevitably ignore the uniqueness of an individual.

Other kinds of unstated assumptions that enter into our thinking and writing destroy common ground by ignoring differences between others and ourselves. For example, a student whose paper for a religion seminar uses *we* to refer to Christians and *they* to refer to members of other religions had better be sure that all the class members and the instructor are Christian, or some of them may feel left out of this discussion. In a letter to the editor of a newspaper about a current political issue, language implying that liberals are good and conservatives bad is likely to alienate some readers and prevent them from even considering the writer's argument about the specific issue.

Sometimes assumptions are so deeply ingrained that they have the effect of completely ignoring or "erasing" large groups of people, as students at the University of Kansas realized when they discovered that history books routinely reported only one survivor of General George Custer's Battle of Little Bighorn: Comanche, a horse (now stuffed and on display at their university). Several thousand Sioux survived that battle, yet the history books simply ignored them.

On the other hand, stereotypes and other assumptions often lead writers to mention a group affiliation unnecessarily when it has no relation to the point under consideration, as in *a woman bus driver* or *a Jewish doctor*. Decisions about whether to make a generalization about a group or to describe an individual as a member of a group are often difficult for writers. The following sections invite you to think about how your language can build – rather than destroy – common ground.

1 Considering assumptions about gender

An elementary teacher in Toronto got increasingly tired of seeing hands go up every time the children sang the line in Canada's national anthem, "true patriot love in all thy sons command." "When do we get to the part about the daughters?" the children inevitably asked. As a result of such questions, the House of Commons voted on a bill to change the line – to "true patriot love in all our hearts command."

These children's questions point to the ways in which powerful and often invisible gender-related elements of language affect our thinking and our behavior. We now know, for instance, that many young women at one time were discouraged from pursuing careers in medicine or engineering at least partially because speakers of our language, following stereotyped assumptions about gender roles in society, always referred to hypothetical doctors or engineers as "he" (and then labeled any woman who worked as a doctor a *woman doctor,* as if to say, “She’s an exception; doctors are normally male”). Equally problematic is the traditional use of *man* and *mankind* to refer to people of both sexes and the use of *he, him, his,* and *himself* to refer to people of unknown sex, as in *everyone must bring his own pencils.* Because such usage ignores half the human race – or at least seems to assume that the other half is more important – it hardly helps a writer build common ground. Similarly, labels like *male nurse* or *male secretary* may offend by reflecting stereotyped assumptions about proper roles for males.

Revising sexist language

www •

http://www.stetson.edu/~history/nongenderlang.html

This essay explores the origins of the practice of assigning masculine pronouns in gender-neutral or gender-inclusive situations and offers alternatives to the practice.

Sexist language, those words and phrases that stereotype or ignore members of either sex or that unnecessarily call attention to gender, can usually be revised fairly easily. For example, there are several alternatives to the use of masculine pronouns to refer to persons of unknown sex. One option is to recast the sentence using plural forms.

▶ ~~**A lawyer**~~ ^*Lawyers* **must pass the bar exam before** ~~**he**~~ ^*they* **can begin to practice.**

Another option is to substitute *he or she, him or her,* and so on.

▶ **A lawyer must pass the bar exam before he** ^*or she* **can begin to practice.**

Yet another way to revise the sentence is to eliminate the pronouns.

▶ **A lawyer must pass the bar exam before** ~~**he can begin**~~ ^*beginning* **to practice.**

INSTEAD OF	TRY USING
anchorman, anchorwoman	anchor
chairman, chairwoman	chair, chairperson
congressman	member of Congress, representative
mailman	mail carrier
male nurse	nurse
man, mankind	humans, human beings, humanity, the human race, humankind
manpower	workers, personnel
mothering	parenting
policeman, policewoman	police officer
steward, stewardess	flight attendant
woman engineer	engineer

For more discussion of nonsexist pronouns, see 11d.

1. Have you used *man* or *men* or words containing one of them to refer to people who may be female? If so, consider substituting another word – instead of *fireman,* for instance, try *firefighter.*
2. If you have mentioned someone's gender, is your doing so necessary? If you identify someone as a female architect, for example, do you (or would you) refer to someone else as a male architect? And if you then note that the female is an attractive blond mother of two, do you mention that the male is a muscular, square-jawed father of three? Unless gender and related matters – looks, clothes, parenthood – are relevant to your point, don't mention them.
3. Do you use any occupational stereotypes? Watch for the use of female pronouns for nurses, male ones for engineers, for example.
4. Have you used *he, him, his,* or *himself* to refer to people who may be female? Try revising with the help of the guidelines in 29b1.
5. Have you overused *he or she, him or her,* and so on? Frequent use of these pronoun pairs can bore or even irritate readers.

EXERCISE 29.1

The following excerpt is taken from the 1968 edition of Dr. Benjamin Spock's *Baby and Child Care.* Read it carefully, noting any language we might today consider sexist. Then try bringing it up-to-date by revising the passage, substituting nonsexist language as necessary.

399. Feeling his oats. One year old is an exciting age. Your baby is changing in lots of ways – in his eating, in how he gets around, in what he wants to do and in how he feels about himself and other people. When he was little and helpless, you could put him where you wanted him, give him the playthings you thought suitable, feed him the foods you knew were best. Most of the time he was willing to let you be the boss, and took it all in good spirit. It's more complicated now that he is around a year old. He seems to realize that he's not meant to be a baby doll the rest of his life, that he's a human being with ideas and a will of his own.

When you suggest something that doesn't appeal to him, he feels he **must** assert himself. His nature tells him to. He just says No in words or actions, even about things that he likes to do. The psychologists call it "negativism"; mothers call it "that terrible No stage." But stop and think what would happen to him if he never felt like saying No. He'd become a robot, a mechanical man. You wouldn't be able to resist the temptation to boss him all the time, and he'd stop learning and developing. When he was old enough to go out into the world, to school and later to work, everybody else would take advantage of him, too. He'd never be good for anything.

2 Considering assumptions about race and ethnicity

Generalizations about racial and ethnic groups can result in especially harmful stereotyping. Such assumptions can be seen in statements that suggest, for instance, that all African Americans are musically talented, that Asian Americans all excel in math and science, or that all Germans are efficiency experts. Negative stereotypes, of course, are even more damaging. In building common ground, writers must watch for any language that ignores not only differences among individual members of a race or ethnic group but among subgroups – for instance, the many nations to which Native Americans belong or the diverse places from which Americans of Spanish-speaking ancestry have emigrated.

Using preferred terms

For writers, avoiding stereotypes and other assumptions based on race or ethnicity is only a first step. Beyond that lies the task of attempting to refer to any group in terms that its members actually desire. Doing so is sometimes not an easy task, for preferences change and even vary widely.

The word *colored,* for example, was once widely used in the United States to refer to Americans of African ancestry (in fact, it still appears in the name of the NAACP, the National Association for the Advancement of Colored People). By the 1950s, the preferred term had become *Negro;* in the 1960s, however, *black* came to be preferred by most, though certainly not all, members of that community. Then, in the late 1980s, some leaders of the American black community urged that *black* be replaced by *African American.*

Similarly, the word *Oriental* is now often considered offensive when used to refer to people of East Asian descent. Many of those once referred to as *American Indians* now prefer to be called *Native Americans.* In Alaska and Canada, many of the native peoples once referred to as *Eskimos* now prefer *Inuit* (which is the official designated term in Canada). And among Americans of Spanish-speaking descent, the terms are many: *Chicano/Chicana, Hispanic, Latin American, Latino/Latina, Mexican American,* and *Puerto Rican,* to name but a few.

Clearly, then, ethnic terminology changes often enough to challenge the most careful writer. The best advice may be to consider your words carefully, to *listen* for the way members of groups refer to themselves (or *ask* their preferences), and to check any term you are unsure of in a current dictionary. The *Random House Webster's College Dictionary* includes particularly helpful usage notes about racial and ethnic designations.

3 Considering other kinds of difference

Gender, race, and ethnicity are among the most frequent challenges to a writer seeking to find common ground with readers, but you will face many others as well. The following section discusses some of them.

Age

Mention age if it is relevant, but be aware that age-related terms can carry derogatory connotations (*matronly, teenybopper, well-preserved,* and so on). Although describing Mr. Fry as *elderly but still active* may sound polite to you, chances are Mr. Fry would prefer being called *an active seventy-eight-year-old* – or just *a seventy-eight-year-old,* which eliminates the unstated assumption of surprise that he is active "at his age."

Class

Because you may not usually think about class as consciously as you do about age or race, for example, you should take special care to examine your words for stereotypes or assumptions about class. Such was the case in a *New York Times* column entitled "Young, Privileged, and Unemployed," written by a young woman who had lost her high-paying professional job. Unable to find other "meaningful work," the author wrote, she and others like her had been forced to accept "absurd" jobs like cleaning houses and baby-sitting.

The column provoked a number of angry letters to the *Times,* like this one: "So the young and privileged are learning what we of the working classes have always understood too well: there is no entitlement in life. We have always taken the jobs you label 'absurd.' Our mothers are the women who clean your mothers' houses. . . ." Thus did the writer destroy common ground with her readers by assuming that cleaning houses is an "absurd" way to make a living and that education or social standing entitles people to more "meaningful" occupations.

As a writer, then, do not assume that all your readers share your background or values – that your classmates' families all own their homes, for instance. And avoid using any words – *redneck, trailer trash,* and the like – that are bound to alienate.

Geographical areas

Though stereotypes related to geographical areas are not always insulting or even unpleasant, they are very often clichéd and exaggerated. New

Englanders are not all thrifty and tight-lipped; Florida offers more than retirement and tourism; Texans do not all wear cowboy boots and Stetson hats; midwesterners are not all hard-working; many Californians neither care about nor participate in the latest trends. Check your writing carefully to be sure it doesn't make such simplistic assumptions.

Check also that you use geographical terms like the following accurately.

America, American. Although many people use these words to refer to the United States alone, be aware that such usage will not necessarily be acceptable to people from Canada, Mexico, and Central or South America.

British, English. British should be used to refer to the island of Great Britain, which includes England, Scotland, and Wales, or to the United Kingdom of Great Britain and Northern Ireland. In general, do not use *English* for these broader senses.

Arab. This term refers only to people of Arabic-speaking descent. Note that Iran is not an Arab nation; its people speak Farsi, not Arabic. Note also that *Arab* is not synonymous with *Muslim* or *Moslem* (a believer in Islam). Most (but not all) Arabs are Muslim, but many Muslims (those in Pakistan, for example) are not Arab.

Physical ability or health

www •

http://www.ldonline.org/ld_indepth/technology/poor_richard_article.html

This essay by Richard Wanderman explains how using computers can help those with learning disabilities improve their writing in ways not possible with pen and paper.

The question to ask yourself when writing about a person with a serious illness or physical disability is whether to mention the disability at all if it is not relevant to your discussion. If you do, consider whether the words you use carry negative connotations. You might choose, for example, to say someone *uses* a wheelchair rather than to say he or she *is confined to* one. Similarly, you might note a subtle but meaningful difference between calling someone a *person with AIDS,* rather than an *AIDS victim.* Mentioning the person first, the disability second – for example referring to a *child with diabetes* rather than a *diabetic child* or a *diabetic* – is always a good idea. On the other hand, the survey of people with disabilities that was mentioned earlier shows that you also must be careful not to minimize the importance of a disability.

Religion

Religious stereotypes are very often inaccurate and unfair. Roman Catholics hold a wide spectrum of views on abortion, for example, Muslim women do not all wear veils, and many Baptists are not fundamentalists. In fact, not everyone believes in or practices a religion at all, so be careful of such assumptions. As in other cases, do not use religious labels without considering their relevance to your point, and make every effort to get them right – for example, *Reformed* churches but *Reform* synagogues.

Sexual orientation

Partly because sexual orientation is a topic that was "erased" from most public discourse until recent decades, the stereotypes and assumptions that surround it are particularly deep-seated and, often, unconscious. Writers who wish to build common ground, therefore, should not assume that readers all share any one sexual orientation – that everyone is attracted to the opposite sex, for example.

As with any label, reference to sexual orientation should be governed by context. Someone writing about Representative Barney Frank's economic views would probably have little if any reason to refer to his sexual orientation. On the other hand, a writer concerned with diversity in U.S. government might find it important to note that Frank is a member of Congress who has made his homosexuality public.

THINKING CRITICALLY ABOUT HOW LANGUAGE CAN BUILD COMMON GROUND

Reading with an Eye for Common Ground

The following poem is partially about finding common ground. Identify those places where the poet asserts his own individuality and those where he forges common ground with readers. How does the speaker address, perhaps indirectly, issues of racism? How does he deal with issues of difference without insulting readers? Does this poem relate to your experience with others? If so, how?

Theme for English B

The instructor said,

Go home and write
a page tonight.
And let that page come out of you –
Then, it will be true.

I wonder if it's that simple?

I am twenty-two, colored, born in Winston-Salem.
I went to school there, then Durham, then here
to this college on the hill above Harlem.

I am the only colored student in my class.
The steps from the hill lead down to Harlem,
through a park, then I cross St. Nicolas,
Eighth Avenue, Seventh, and I come to the Y,
the Harlem Branch Y, where I take the elevator
up to my room, sit down, and write this page:

It's not easy to know what is true for you or me
at twenty-two, my age. But I guess I'm what
I feel and see and hear. Harlem, I hear you:
hear you, hear me — we two — you, me talk on this page.
(I hear New York, too.) Me — who?
Well, I like to eat, sleep, drink, and be in love.
I like to work, read, learn, and understand life.
I like a pipe for a Christmas present,
or records — Bessie, bop, or Bach.

I guess being colored doesn't make me not like
the same things other folks like who are other races.
So will my page be colored that I write?
Being me, it will not be white.
But it will be
a part of you, instructor.
You are white —
yet a part of me, as I am a part of you.
That's American.

Sometimes perhaps you don't want to be a part of me.
Nor do I often want to be a part of you.
But we are, that's true!
As I learn from you,
I guess you learn from me —
although you're older — and white —
and somewhat more free.

This is my page for English B.

– Langston Hughes

Thinking about How Your Language Builds Common Ground

Like you, generations of college students have found themselves in classes filled with people both like them and different from them. Take time now to examine where you've come from — your age, ethnicity, hometown, religion, and so on. Then do the same for one or more of your classmates. Write a paragraph about the differences *and* the common ground you see. Finally, study your paragraph for any assumptions your language reveals.

PART 6

UNDERSTANDING PUNCTUATION CONVENTIONS

FAQ

FAQ: Punctuation Online

What do the punctuation marks in electronic addresses indicate?

/ The **forward slash** separates parts of URLS.

• The **dot** separates parts of email addresses and URLS.

@ The **"at" sign** is part of every email address, indicating that you are "at" an electronic address.

<> **Angle brackets** can be used in printed texts to frame email addresses and URLS, making it possible to use them within sentences and with other punctuation.

_ The **underscore** is used in many URLS (and around titles in online text in place of italics).

~ The **tilde** appears in many URLS as an indicator of the user or owner of the DIRECTORY PATH.

These marks are crucial for finding what you want, so treat them with care — they are not optional!

What are the strange combinations of punctuation marks that you often see in online writing?

Some online writers combine punctuation marks and other keyboard characters to create (when viewed sideways) "facial expressions" that signal tone or attitude: a smile **:-)** signals a friendly hello or nod, whereas a frown **:-(** or a wink **;-)** or a laugh **:-D** signal other emotions. These little online punctuation marks, called EMOTICONS (or *smileys*), are used primarily for fun, or to tease and puzzle readers. You should use them as you would other marks: only if they are appropriate to your topic and purpose, and only if they will be understood and accepted by your audience. As a general rule, leave emoticons out of most academic writing.

http://www.english.upenn.edu/~jlynch/Grammar/

Grammar and Style Notes *provides explanations of conventions of grammar, style, punctuation, and usage, broken into a file for each letter of the alphabet (click on* c *for information on commas, for example).*

http://sti.larc.nasa.gov/html/Chapt3/

The chapter on punctuation in Mary McCaskil's Grammar, Punctuation, and Capitalization: A Handbook for Technical Writers and Editors *is available online.*

http://www.emo.com/wwb/wwb_sty.html.

This site offers a helpful program on punctuation.

30 Using Commas

It's hard to go through a day without encountering commas. Even the directions for making hot cereal depend on the careful placement of a comma: *Add Cream of Wheat slowly, stirring constantly.* Here the comma tells the cook to *add the cereal slowly.* If the comma came before the word *slowly,* however, the cook might add the cereal all at once and *stir slowly* — perhaps ending up with lumpy cereal.

In fact, the comma is the most frequently used punctuation mark in English — and so commas count in your writing. However, reducing comma use to hard and fast rules is difficult because the comma can play a number of different roles in a sentence. More important, many decisions about commas relate to matters of purpose, rhythm, and style rather than to grammar alone. This chapter provides guidelines and examples to help you use commas effectively. ■

30a Using commas after introductory elements

A comma usually follows an introductory word, expression, phrase, or clause. These introductory elements include adverbs (see 7b5); conjunctive adverbs (see 7b7); transitional expressions (see 6d4); participles, infinitives, and prepositional, participial, infinitive, and absolute phrases (see 7c3); and adverb clauses (see 7c4).

- **Slowly, Drue became conscious of her predicament.**
- **Nevertheless, the hours of a typist are flexible.**
- **In fact, only Lindsay was prepared.**
- **Frustrated, he wondered whether he should change jobs.**
- **In Fitzgerald's novel, the color green takes on great symbolic qualities.**
- **Sporting a pair of specially made running shoes, Jamie prepared for the race.**
- **To win the contest, Connor needed luck.**
- **Pens poised in anticipation, the students waited for the test to be distributed.**

Research has shown that five of the most common errors in college writing involve commas. Check your writing for these five errors:

1. Check every sentence that doesn't begin with the subject to see whether it opens with an introductory element (a word, phrase, or clause that tells when, where, how, or why the main action of the sentence occurs). An introductory element needs to be followed by a comma, separating the introduction from the main part of the sentence. (30a)
2. Look at every sentence that contains one of the conjunctions *and, but, or, nor, for, so,* or *yet.* If the group of words before and after the conjunction each functions as a complete sentence, you have a compound sentence. Make sure to use a comma before the conjunction. (30b)
3. Look at all adjective clauses beginning with *which, who, whom, whose, when,* or *where,* and at phrases and appositives (7c3 and 7c4). Consider each element, and decide whether it is essential to the meaning of the sentence. If the rest of the sentence would be unclear without it, you should *not* set off the element with commas. (30c)
4. Identify all adjective clauses beginning with *that,* and make sure they are *not* set off with commas. (30c and j)
5. Check every *and* and *or* to see if it comes before the last item in a series of three or more words, phrases, or clauses. Be sure that each item in a series (except the last) is followed by a comma. (30d)

► **Since my mind was not getting enough stimulation, I decided to read some good literature.**

After certain introductory elements — adverbs, infinitives, prepositional and infinitive phrases, and adverb clauses — some writers omit the comma if the element is short and does not seem to require a pause after it. However, you will seldom be wrong if you use a comma.

At the racetrack Henry lost nearly his entire paycheck.

If the introductory element is followed by inverted word order, with the verb preceding the subject, do not use a comma.

► **From directly behind my seat came huge clouds of cigar smoke.**

EXERCISE 30.1

In the following sentences, add any commas that are needed after the introductory element.

1. In one of his most famous poems Frost asks why people need walls.
2. Unfortunately the door to the kennel had been left open.
3. Unable to make such a decision alone Katie asked John for help.
4. If you follow the instructions you will be able to install your radio.
5. Therefore answering the seemingly simple question is very difficult.
6. With the fifth century came the fall of the Roman Empire.
7. Their bags packed they waited for the taxi to the airport.
8. To become an Olympic competitor an athlete must train for years.
9. After the hurricane moved on the citizens of the town assessed the damage.
10. Startled by the explosion the workers dropped to the ground.

30b Using commas in compound sentences

A comma usually precedes a coordinating conjunction (*and, but, or, for, nor, so,* or *yet*) that joins two independent clauses in a compound sentence.

▶ **The title may sound important, but *administrative clerk* is only a euphemism for *photocopier*.**

▶ **The show started at last, and the crowd grew quiet.**

You may want to use a semicolon rather than a comma when the clauses are long and complex or contain other punctuation.

> When these early migrations took place, the ice was still confined to the lands in the far north; but eight hundred thousand years ago, when man was already established in the temperate latitudes, the ice moved southward until it covered large parts of Europe and Asia. – ROBERT JASTROW, *Until the Sun Dies*

With very short clauses, writers sometimes omit the comma before *and* or *or*. You will never be wrong to include it, however.

> She saw her chance and she took it.

Always use the comma if there is any chance the sentence will be misread without it.

▶ **The game ended in victory, and pandemonium erupted.**

Be careful not to use *only* a comma between independent clauses. Doing so is usually considered a serious grammatical error, called a comma splice. Either use a coordinating conjunction after the comma, or use a semicolon.

For more about comma splices, see Chapter 15.

COMMA SPLICE Do not say luck is responsible for your new job, give yourself the credit you deserve.

REVISED Do not say luck is responsible for your new job, *but* give yourself the credit you deserve.

REVISED Do not say luck is responsible for your new job; give yourself the credit you deserve.

EXERCISE 30.2

Use a comma and a coordinating conjunction (*and, but, or, for, nor, so,* or *yet*) to combine each of the following pairs of sentences into one sentence. Delete or rearrange words if necessary. Example:

I had finished studying for the test, so I went to bed.

1. Max Weber was not in favor of a classless society. He thought it would lead to the expansion of the power of the state over the individual.
2. Joan Didion's nonfiction is renowned. Her novels are also worthwhile.
3. I studied ten of Verdi's operas. I have only begun to appreciate the wealth of his creativity.
4. The playwright disliked arguing with directors. She avoided rehearsals.
5. Tropical fish do not bark. They are not cuddly pets.

30c Using commas to set off nonrestrictive elements

Nonrestrictive elements – clauses, phrases, and words that do *not* limit, or "restrict," the meaning of the words they modify – are set off from the rest of the sentence with commas. **Restrictive elements** *do* limit meaning and are *not* set off with commas.

RESTRICTIVE Drivers *who have been convicted of drunken driving* should lose their licenses.

NONRESTRICTIVE The two drivers involved in the accident, *who have been convicted of drunken driving,* should lose their licenses.

In the first sentence, the clause *who have been convicted of drunken driving* is essential to the meaning because it limits the word it modifies, *Drivers,* to only those drivers who have been convicted of drunken driving. Therefore, it is not set off by commas. In the second sentence, the same clause is not essential to the meaning because it does not limit what it modifies, *The two drivers involved in the accident,* but merely provides additional information about these drivers. Therefore, it *is* set off with commas.

Notice how using or not using commas to set off such an element can change the meaning of a sentence.

The bus drivers rejecting the management offer remained on strike.

The bus drivers, rejecting the management offer, remained on strike.

In the first sentence, not using commas to set off the phrase *rejecting the management offer* makes the phrase restrictive, limiting the meaning of *The bus drivers.* This sentence says that only some of the total group of bus drivers, the ones who rejected the offer, remained on strike, implying that other drivers went back to work. In the second sentence, the commas around the phrase make it nonrestrictive, implying that *The bus drivers* refers to all of the drivers and that all of them remained on strike.

To decide whether an element is restrictive or nonrestrictive, mentally delete the element, and then decide whether the deletion changes the meaning of the rest of the sentence or makes it unclear. If it does, the element is probably restrictive and should not be set off with commas. If it does not, the element is probably nonrestrictive and requires commas.

www •

http://www.fas.harvard.edu/~wricntr/comma.html

This handy page on "the mysterious comma" offers four tips for comma use, including some very clear and useful advice about using commas with nonrestrictive elements.

1 Adjective and adverb clauses

Adjective clauses begin with *who, whom, whose, which, that, when, where,* or *why.* Adverb clauses begin with *when, where,* or another subordinating conjunction, such as *because, although,* or *before.* Adverb clauses are usually essential to the meaning of the sentence; in general, do not set them off with commas unless they precede the independent clause or begin with *although, even though, while,* or another conjunction expressing the idea of contrast.

For more about adjective clauses, see 7c4.

For more about subordinating conjunctions, see 7b7; for more about adverb clauses, see 7c4.

NONRESTRICTIVE CLAUSES

▶ **The city renovated Straus Park, which soon became a popular gathering place.**

The adjective clause beginning with *which* is not essential to the meaning of *Straus Park* and therefore is set off with a comma.

▶ **The park soon became a popular gathering place, although some nearby residents complained about the noise.**

The adverb clause *although some nearby residents complained about the noise* expresses the idea of contrast; therefore, it is set off with a comma.

RESTRICTIVE CLAUSES

▶ **I grew up in a house *where the only regular guests were my relations.***

– **RICHARD RODRIGUEZ, "Aria: Memoir of a Bilingual Childhood"**

▶ **The claim *that men like seriously to battle one another to some sort of finish* is a myth.** – **JOHN MCMURTRY, "Kill 'Em! Crush 'Em! Eat 'Em Raw!"**

An adjective clause that begins with *that* is always restrictive and is not set off with commas. An adjective clause beginning with *which* may be either restrictive or nonrestrictive; however, some writers prefer to use *which* only for nonrestrictive clauses.

2 Participles and phrases

Participles and participial phrases may be either restrictive or nonrestrictive. Prepositional phrases are usually restrictive but sometimes are not essential to the meaning of a sentence and are therefore set off with commas.

NONRESTRICTIVE PHRASES

▶ **Stephanie, amazed, stared at the strange vehicle.**

The participle *amazed* does not limit the meaning of *Stephanie.*

For more about participles and participial and prepositional phrases, see 7c3.

▶ **The "synfuels" program, launched at the height of the energy crisis, languished with the drop in fuel prices.**

The participial phrase beginning with *launched* does not limit the meaning of *The "synfuels" program* or change the central meaning of the sentence.

▶ **The bodyguards, in dark suits and matching ties, looked quite intimidating.**

The prepositional phrase *in dark suits and matching ties* does not limit the meaning of *The bodyguards.*

RESTRICTIVE PHRASES

▶ **A penny *saved* is a penny *earned.***

Without *saved* and *earned,* the sentence has a very different meaning.

▶ **Wood *cut from living trees* does not burn as well as dead wood.**

The participial phrase *cut from living trees* is essential to the meaning.

▶ **The bodyguards were the men *in dark suits and matching ties.***

The prepositional phrase *in dark suits and matching ties* is essential to the meaning.

3 Appositives

An appositive is a noun or noun substitute that renames a nearby noun or noun substitute. When an appositive is not essential to identify what it renames, it is set off with commas.

NONRESTRICTIVE APPOSITIVES

▶ **Ms. Baker, my high school chemistry teacher, inspired my love of science.**

Ms. Baker's name identifies her; the appositive simply provides extra information.

▶ **Beethoven's opera, *Fidelio,* includes the famous "Prisoners' Chorus."**

Beethoven wrote only one opera, so its name is not essential.

▶ **The editorial cartoonist *Thomas Nast* helped bring about the downfall of the Tweed ring in New York City.**

The appositive *Thomas Nast* identifies the specific cartoonist.

▶ **Mozart's opera *The Marriage of Figaro* was considered revolutionary.**

The appositive is restrictive because Mozart wrote more than one opera.

EXERCISE 30.3

Use commas to set off nonrestrictive clauses, phrases, and appositives in any of the following sentences that contain such elements.

1. Anyone who is fourteen years old faces strong peer pressure every day.
2. Embalming is a technique that preserves a cadaver.
3. I would feel right at home in the city dump which bears a striking resemblance to my bedroom.
4. The musical *West Side Story* was based on Shakespeare's play *Romeo and Juliet.*
5. A house overlooking the ocean costs $1,500,000.
6. The Zunis an ancient tribe live in New Mexico.
7. The president elected for a six-year term acts as head of state.
8. Karl Marx an important nineteenth-century political philosopher believed that his role as a social thinker was to change the world.
9. Birds' hearts have four chambers whereas reptiles' have three.
10. Britain and France agreed to aid each other if one of them was attacked.

30d Using commas to separate items in a series

A comma is used between items in a series of three or more words, phrases, or clauses.

> I bumped into professors, horizontal bars, agricultural students, and swinging iron rings.
> – JAMES THURBER, "University Days"

> He has plundered our seas, ravaged our coasts, burnt our towns, and destroyed the lives of our people.
> – THOMAS JEFFERSON, Declaration of Independence

You may see a series with no comma after the next-to-last item, particularly in newspaper writing. Occasionally, however, omitting the comma can cause confusion, and you will never be wrong if you include it.

▶ **Diners had a choice of broccoli, green beans, peas, and carrots.**

Without the comma after *peas,* you wouldn't know if there were three choices (the third being a *mixture* of peas and carrots) or four.

When the items in a series contain commas of their own or other punctuation, separate them with semicolons rather than commas.

For more about using semicolons to separate items in a series, see 31b.

Coordinate adjectives, those that relate equally to the noun they modify, should be separated by commas.

The *long, twisting, muddy* road led to a shack in the woods.

In a sentence like *The cracked bathroom mirror reflected his face,* however, *cracked* and *bathroom* are not coordinate because *bathroom mirror* is the equivalent of a single word, which is modified by *cracked.* Hence they are *not* separated by commas.

You can usually determine whether adjectives are coordinate by inserting *and* between them. If the sentence makes sense with the *and,* the adjectives are coordinate and should be separated by commas.

▶ **They are sincere *and* talented *and* inquisitive researchers.**

The sentence makes sense with the *and*'s, so the adjectives *sincere, talented,* and *inquisitive* should be separated by commas.

▶ **Byron carried an elegant *and* gold *and* pocket watch.**

The sentence does not make sense with the *and*'s, so the adjectives *elegant, gold,* and *pocket* should not be separated by commas.

EXERCISE 30.4

Revise any of the following sentences that require commas to set off words, phrases, or clauses in a series.

1. They found employment in truck driving farming and mining.
2. We bought zucchini peppers and tomatoes at the market.
3. James Joyce wrote novels short stories and poetry.
4. The daddy longlegs's orange body resembles a colored dot amidst eight long black legs.

5. A prestigious car a large house and membership in an exclusive club are taken as signs of success.
6. Superficial observation does not provide accurate insight into people's lives — how they feel what they believe in how they respond to others.
7. The ball sailed over the fence across the road and through the Wilsons' living room window.
8. I timidly offered to help a loud overbearing lavishly dressed customer.
9. Ellen is an accomplished freelance writer.
10. These Cosell clones insist on calling every play judging every move and telling everyone within earshot exactly what is wrong with the team.

30e Using commas to set off parenthetical and transitional expressions

Parenthetical expressions are added comments or information. Because they often interrupt or digress, they are usually set off with commas. Transitional expressions are also usually set off with commas. They include conjunctive adverbs such as *however* and *furthermore* and other words and phrases used to connect parts of sentences.

For full lists of transitional expressions, see 7b7 and 6d4.

Some studies, *incidentally,* have shown that chocolate, *of all things,* helps prevent tooth decay.

Roald Dahl's stories, *it turns out,* were often inspired by his own childhood.

Ceiling fans are, *moreover,* less expensive than air conditioners.

Ozone is a byproduct of dry cleaning, *for example.*

30f Using commas to set off contrasting elements, interjections, direct address, and tag questions

Contrasting elements

On official business it was she, *not my father,* one would usually hear on the phone or in stores.

– Richard Rodriguez, "Aria: A Memoir of a Bilingual Childhood"

Interjections

My God, who wouldn't want a wife? – JUDY BRADY, "I Want a Wife"

We had hiked for, *say,* seven miles before stopping to rest.

Direct address

My friends, I must say to you that we have not made a single gain in civil rights without determined legal and nonviolent pressure.
– MARTIN LUTHER KING JR., "Letter from Birmingham Jail"

Tag questions

The governor did not veto the unemployment bill, *did she?*

EXERCISE 30.5

Revise each of the following sentences, using commas to set off parenthetical and transitional expressions, contrasting elements, interjections, words used in direct address, and tag questions.

1. One must consider the society as a whole not just its parts.
2. The West in fact has become solidly Republican in presidential elections.
3. Her friends did not know about her illness did they?
4. The celebration will alas conclude all too soon.
5. Ladies and gentlemen I bid you farewell.

30g Using commas with dates, addresses, titles, and numbers

Commas are used according to established rules with dates, addresses and place-names, and numbers. Commas are also used to separate personal and professional titles from the names preceding them.

Dates

For dates, use a comma between the day of the week and the month, between the day of the month and the year, and between the year and the rest of the sentence, if any.

The war began on *Thursday, January 17, 1991,* with air strikes on Iraq.

Do not use commas with dates in inverted order or with dates consisting of only the month and the year.

> 18 October 1998
>
> Thousands of Germans swarmed over and through the wall in *November 1989* and effectively demolished it.

Addresses and place-names

In addresses and place-names, use a comma after each part, including the state if no ZIP code is given. A ZIP code, however, is not preceded by a comma.

> Forward my mail to the Department of English, The Ohio State University, Columbus, Ohio 43210.
>
> Portland, Oregon, is much larger than Portland, Maine.

Titles

Use commas to set off a title such as *M.D., Esq.,* and so on from the name preceding it and from the rest of the sentence. The titles *Jr.* and *Sr.,* however, are often *not* set off by commas.

> Jaime Mejia, *Ph.D.,* will speak about his anthropological research.
>
> Martin Luther King *Jr.* was one of this century's greatest orators.

Numbers

In numbers of five digits or more, use a comma between each group of three digits, starting from the right.

> The city's population rose to *17,126* in the 1990 census.

Do not use a comma within house or building numbers, ZIP codes, or page numbers.

> My parents live at *11311* Wimberly Drive, Richmond, Virginia *23233*.
>
> Turn to page *1566*.

The comma is optional within numbers of four digits but is never used in years with four digits. Use a comma with numbers of more than four digits.

The college has an enrollment of *1,789* [or *1789*] this semester.

The French Revolution began in *1789*.

EXERCISE 30.6

Revise each of the following sentences, using commas appropriately with page numbers, dates, addresses and place-names, titles, and numbers.

1. In my dictionary, the rules of punctuation begin on page 1560.
2. Ithaca New York has a population of about 30000.
3. The *Titanic* hit an iceberg on April 14 1912 and sank in about two hours, drowning 1503 people.
4. MLA headquarters are at 10 Astor Place New York New York 10003.
5. The nameplate read *Donald Good R.N.* and looked quite impressive.

30h Using commas with quotations

Commas set off a quotation from words used to introduce or identify the source of the quotation. A comma following a quotation goes *inside* the closing quotation mark.

"No one becomes depraved all at once," wrote Juvenal.

A German proverb warns, "Go to law for a sheep, and lose your cow."

"All I know about grammar," said Joan Didion, "is its infinite power."

When a quoted question or exclamation is followed by explanatory words, do not use a comma after the question mark or exclamation point.

► **"What's a thousand dollars?," asks Groucho Marx in *Cocoanuts*. "Mere chicken feed. A poultry matter."**

► **"Out, out, damned spot!," cries Lady Macbeth.**

Do not use a comma when a quotation is introduced by *that* or when the rest of the sentence includes more than the words used to introduce or identify the source of the quotation.

▶ **The writer of Ecclesiastes concludes that, "all is vanity."**

▶ **People who say, "Have a nice day" irritate me.**

Do not use a comma before an indirect quotation, one that does not use the speaker's exact words.

▶ **In a famous speech, Patrick Henry declared, that he wanted either liberty or death.**

▶ **Abigail Adams said that, all men would like to be tyrants.**

EXERCISE 30.7

Insert a comma in any of the following sentences that require one.

1. "The public be damned!" William Henry Vanderbilt was reported to have said. "I'm working for my stockholders."
2. Joseph Epstein admits "I prefer not to be thought vulgar in any wise."
3. Who remarked that "youth is wasted on the young"?
4. "Neat people are lazier and meaner than sloppy people" according to Suzanne Britt.
5. "Who shall decide when doctors disagree?" asked Alexander Pope.

30i Using commas to facilitate understanding

Sometimes a comma is necessary to make a sentence much easier to read or understand.

▶ **The members of the dance troupe strutted in, in matching tuxedos and top hats.**

▶ **Before, I had planned to major in biology.**

30j Checking for unnecessary commas

Excessive use of commas can spoil an otherwise fine sentence.

Around restrictive elements

Do not use commas to set off restrictive elements, which limit, or restrict, the meaning of the words they modify or refer to.

For more about restrictive elements, see 30c.

▶ **I don't let my children watch TV shows~~,~~ that are violent.**

▶ **A law~~,~~ requiring the use of seat belts~~,~~ was passed in 1987.**

▶ **My only defense~~,~~ against my allergies~~,~~ is to stay indoors.**

▶ **The actress~~,~~ Emma Thompson~~,~~ played herself on *Ellen*.**

Between subjects and verbs, verbs and objects or complements, and prepositions and objects

Do not use a comma between a subject and its verb, a verb and its object or complement, or a preposition and its object. This rule holds true even if the subject, object, or complement is a long phrase or clause.

▶ **Watching movies on my VCR late at night~~,~~ has become an important way for me to relax.**

▶ **Parents must decide~~,~~ how much TV their children may watch.**

▶ **The winner of~~,~~ the trophy for outstanding community service stepped forward.**

In compound constructions

Do not use a comma before or after a coordinating conjunction joining the two parts of a compound construction.

▶ **A buildup of the U.S. military, and deregulation of major industries were the Reagan administration's goals.**

▶ **Meridel Le Sueur worked as a stuntwoman, and trained as an actress and a writer.**

In a series

Do not use a comma before the first or after the last item in a series.

▶ **The auction included, furniture, paintings, and china.**

▶ **The swimmer took slow, powerful, strokes.**

EXERCISE 30.8

Revise each of the following sentences, deleting unnecessary commas.

1. The four types of nonverbal communication are, kinesic, haptic, proxemic, and dormant, communication.
2. Observers watch facial expressions and gestures, and interpret them.
3. We could see nothing, except jagged peaks, for miles around.
4. Our supper that evening, consisted of stale bologna sandwiches.
5. Clothes, that had to be ironed, were too much trouble.
6. As we sat around the campfire, we felt boredom, and disappointment.
7. Magazines, like *Modern Maturity,* are aimed at retired people.
8. The photographer, Edward Curtis, is known for his depiction of the West.
9. We all took panicked, hasty, looks at our notebooks.
10. Driving a car, and talking on the car phone at the same time demand care.

THINKING CRITICALLY ABOUT COMMAS

Reading with an Eye for Commas

The following poem uses commas to create rhythm and guide readers. Read the poem aloud, listening especially to the effect of the commas at the end of the first and fifth lines. Then read it again as if those commas were omitted, noting the difference. What is the effect of the poet's decision *not* to use a comma at the end of the third line?

Some say the world will end in fire,
Some say in ice.
From what I've tasted of desire
I hold with those who favor fire.
But if it had to perish twice,
I think I know enough of hate
To say that for destruction ice
Is also great
And would suffice.

– ROBERT FROST, "Fire and Ice"

Thinking about Your Own Use of Commas

The following passage has had all of the author's commas removed. Punctuate the passage with commas as seems appropriate to you, and then explain in writing why you put commas where you did. Finally, check over your use of commas, consulting this chapter for guidance and noting any problems or observations.

> And here was another strange thing about Myers. He not only did nothing for a living but he appeared to have no history. He came from Elkhart Indiana but beyond this fact nobody seemed to know anything about him – not even how he had met my aunt Margaret. Reconstructed from his conversation a picture of Elkhart emerged for us that showed it as a flat place consisting chiefly of ball parks poolrooms and hardware stores. Aunt Margaret came from Chicago which consisted of the Loop Marshall Field's assorted priests and monsignors and the black-and-white problem. How had these two worlds impinged? Where our family spoke freely of its relations real and imaginary Myers spoke of no one not even a parent. At the very beginning when my father's old touring car which had been shipped on still remained in our garage Myers had certain seedy cronies whom he took riding in it or who simply sat in it in our driveway as if anchored in a houseboat; but when the car went they went or were banished. Uncle Myers and Aunt Margaret had no friends no couples with whom they exchanged visits – only a middle-aged black-haired small emaciated woman with a German name and a yellowed skin whom we were taken to see one afternoon because she was dying of cancer. . . .
>
> – MARY MCCARTHY, *Memories of a Catholic Girlhood*

31 Using Semicolons

If you've ever pored over the fine print at the bottom of an ad for a big sale looking for the opening hours or the address of the store nearest you, then you've seen plenty of semicolons in action. Here's an example from a Bloomingdale's ad:

Stores & Hours —
Short Hills: SUN., 12 – 6; MON., 10 – 9:30;
TUES., 10 – 5; WED. through FRI., 10 – 9:30; SAT., 10 – 8.

The semicolons separate the information for one day's hours from the next. Semicolons, which have the effect of creating a pause stronger than that of a comma but not as strong as that of a period, are used primarily to link independent clauses and to separate items in a series.

This chapter will help you use semicolons effectively in your own writing. ■

31a Using semicolons to link independent clauses

You can join independent clauses in several ways: with a comma and a coordinating conjunction (see 30b), with a colon (see 35d), with a dash (see 35c), or with a semicolon. Semicolons provide writers with subtle ways of signaling closely related clauses. The second clause often restates an idea expressed in the first, and it sometimes expands on or presents a contrast to the first. As a writer, you must choose when and where to use semicolons to signal such relationships. Note, for instance, the following examples:

> Immigration acts were passed; newcomers had to prove, besides moral correctness and financial solvency, their ability to read. – Mary Gordon, "More Than Just a Shrine"

> The problem, of course, is that it is one thing to urge somebody else to take on those anxiety-producing challenges; it is quite another to get ourselves to do it.
> – James Lincoln Collier
> "Anxiety: Challenge by Any Other Name"

In the first sentence, Gordon uses a semicolon to lead to a clause that expands on the statement made in the first clause. She might have joined the two clauses with *and* or *so,* but the lack of a conjunction gives the sentence an abrupt, clipped rhythm that suits the topic: laws that

1. Note any semicolons. If you find few or none, look at each sentence together with the one that follows. Are there any pairs of sentences that express closely related ideas that would be stronger if combined into one sentence using a semicolon? (31a)
2. Make sure semicolons are used only between independent clauses or between items in a series. If you have used a semicolon between an independent clause and a dependent clause or a phrase, change it to a comma. If you have used a semicolon before the *first* item in a series, change it to a colon. (31b and d)
3. Do semicolons separate more than three independent clauses in a sentence, or do they separate clauses in more than two consecutive sentences? If so, would making some clauses into separate sentences make the writing smoother or less monotonous? (31c)

imposed strict requirements. In the second example, the semicolon links two contrasting clauses; the logical connection between them is far more subtle and immediate than if Collier had used *but* or used a period to separate the clauses into two sentences.

A semicolon can also be used to link independent clauses joined by conjunctive adverbs such as *therefore, however,* or *indeed* or transitional expressions such as *in fact, in addition,* or *for example.*

For more about conjunctive adverbs and transitional expressions, see 7b7 and 6d4.

> The circus comes as close to being the world in microcosm as anything I know; in a way, it puts all the rest of show business in the shade.
>
> – E. B. WHITE, "The Ring of Time"

If two independent clauses joined by a coordinating conjunction contain commas, you may use a semicolon instead of a comma before the conjunction to make the sentence easier to read.

> Every year, whether the Republican or the Democratic Party is in office, more and more power drains away from the individual to feed vast reservoirs in far-off places; and we have less and less say about the shape of events which shape our future.
>
> – WILLIAM F. BUCKLEY JR., "Why Don't We Complain?"

EXERCISE 31.1

Use one of the four examples in 31a as a model for a sentence of your own. Bring your sentence to class, and compare it to those written by your classmates.

EXERCISE 31.2

Combine each of the following pairs of sentences into one sentence by using a semicolon. Example:

> Take the bus to Henderson Street; meet me under the clock.

1. Establishing your position in an office is an important task. Your profile will mold your relationships with other staff members.
2. City life offers many advantages. In many ways, however, life in a small town is much more pleasant.
3. Florida's mild winter climate is ideal for bicycling. In addition, the terrain is very flat.
4. Physical education forms an important part of a university's program. Nevertheless, few students and professors clearly recognize its value.
5. The debate over political correctness affects more than the curriculum. It also affects students' social relationships.

31b Using semicolons to separate items in a series

For more about using commas with items in a series, see 30d.

Ordinarily, commas separate items in a series. But when the items themselves contain commas or other punctuation, using semicolons to separate the items will make the sentence clearer and easier to read. Such a series is best placed at the *end* of a sentence.

> Anthropology encompasses several fields: archaeology, the study of ancient civilizations through artifacts; linguistics, the study of the structure and development of language; and cultural anthropology, the study of the way of life of various peoples, especially small, nonindustrialized societies.

Note that a semicolon should never be used to *introduce* a series; use a colon instead.

31c Checking for overused semicolons

If semicolons are used too often, they distract readers by calling attention to themselves instead of to what the writer is saying. In addition, sentence upon sentence punctuated with semicolons will sound monotonous and jerky.

► **Like many people in public life, he spoke with confidence~~;~~, perhaps ~~he~~ even ~~spoke~~ with arrogance; yet I noted a certain anxiety~~; it~~ *that* touched and puzzled me~~;~~. *H*~~h~~e seemed too eager to demonstrate his control of a situation and his command of the necessary data.**

EXERCISE 31.3

Revise the following passage, substituting other punctuation for some of the semicolons. Add or delete words if necessary.

Remember when the neighborhood kids played football out in the vacant lot; they were there every Saturday, having a good time. Whatever happened to just playing for a good time? Now uniformed coaches yell at young players to win; they put more and more pressure on them; and parents join in the chant of win, win, win; in fact, if the child is not a winner, he or she must be — that's right — a loser. The young athlete is constantly told that winning is everything; what used to be fun is now just like a job; play to win, the adults say, or do not play at all.

31d Checking for misused semicolons

A comma, not a semicolon, should separate an independent clause from a dependent clause or a phrase.

► **The police found a set of fingerprints~~;~~, which they used to identify the thief.**

A colon, not a semicolon, should introduce a series.

► **The tour includes visits to the following art museums~~;~~: the Prado, in Madrid; the Louvre, in Paris; and the Rijksmuseum, in Amsterdam.**

31e Using semicolons with quotation marks

Ordinarily, a semicolon goes *outside* closing quotation marks.

Jackson's most famous story is "The Lottery"; it is a horrifying allegory about the power of tradition and the search for scapegoats.

THINKING CRITICALLY ABOUT SEMICOLONS

Reading with an Eye for Semicolons

The author of the following paragraph describes a solar eclipse in elaborate detail, using semicolons to separate each part of her description. Read the paragraph with attention to the use of semicolons. What different effect would the paragraph have if the author had used periods instead of semicolons? Imagine also that she had used commas and coordinating conjunctions. What is the effect of all the semicolons?

> You see the wide world swaddled in darkness; you see a vast breadth of hilly land, and an enormous, distant, blackened valley; you see towns' lights, a river's path, and blurred portions of your hat and scarf; you see your husband's face looking like an early black-and-white film; and you see a sprawl of black sky and blue sky together, with unfamiliar stars in it, some barely visible bands of cloud, and over there, a small white ring. The ring is as small as one goose in a flock of migrating geese — if you happen to notice a flock of migrating geese. It is one 360th part of the visible sky. The sun we see is less than half the diameter of a dime held at arms' length.
>
> – ANNIE DILLARD, "Solar Eclipse"

Thinking about Your Own Use of Semicolons

Think of something you might take five or ten minutes to observe — a football game, a brewing storm, an ant awkwardly carrying a crumb — and write a paragraph describing your observations point by point and using semicolons to separate each point, as Annie Dillard does in the preceding paragraph. When you have finished, look at the way you used semicolons. Are there places where a period or a comma and a coordinating conjunction would better serve your meaning? Revise appropriately. What can you conclude about effective ways of using semicolons? If you keep a writing log, record your thoughts there.

Using End Punctuation

32

Periods, question marks, and exclamation points often appear in advertising to create special effects or draw readers along from line to line. For example:

The experts say America Online is a well-designed, easy-to-use service.

So what are you waiting for?

Get your hands on America Online today!

End punctuation tells us how to read each sentence — as a matter-of-fact statement, an ironic query, or an emphatic order. Although you may have thought of periods, question marks, and exclamation points as punctuation marks you can use almost automatically, without paying much attention to them, in fact you often do have to make choices about whether to use one of these marks or which one to use. This chapter will help you to make such choices. ■

32a Using periods

Use a period to close sentences that make statements or give mild commands.

> Books are like mountaintops jutting out of the sea.
> – JEROME BRUNER, *Acts of Meaning*

> Never use a foreign phrase, a scientific word or a jargon word if you can think of an everyday English equivalent.
> – GEORGE ORWELL, "Politics and the English Language"

A period also closes indirect questions, which report rather than ask questions.

> I asked how old the child was.
>
> Many parents ask if autism is an inherited disorder.

In American English, periods are also used with most abbreviations.

Mr.	Jr.	Ph.D.
Ms.	B.C.E.	M.D.
Mrs.	A.D.	M.B.A.
A.M./a.m.	ibid.	R.N.
P.M./p.m.	Dr.	Sen.

→ If you find that all or almost all of your sentences end with periods, see if any of them might be phrased more effectively as questions or exclamations. (32a, b, and c)
→ Check to be sure you use question marks appropriately. (32b)
→ Do you use exclamation points? If so, consider carefully whether they are justified. Does the sentence call for extra emphasis? If in doubt, use a period instead. (32c)

Some abbreviations do not require periods. Among them are the postal abbreviations of state names, such as *FL* and *TN* (though the traditional abbreviations, such as *Fla.* and *Tenn.*, do call for periods), and most groups of initials (*GE, CIA, AIDS, UNICEF*). If you are not sure whether a particular abbreviation should include periods, check a dictionary.

For more about abbreviations, see Chapter 37.

EXERCISE 32.1

Revise each of the following sentences, inserting periods in the appropriate places. Example:

Ms.^ Maria Jordan received both a Ph.^D.^ in chemistry and an M.^Ed.^

1. Please attend the meeting on Tuesday at 10:00 AM in Room 401.
2. Cicero was murdered in 43 BC
3. "Have you lost something, Charles?" I inquired
4. She asked whether Operation PUSH had been founded by Jesse Jackson
5. A voluntary effort by the AMA could help contain hospital costs

32b Using question marks

A question mark closes sentences that ask direct questions.

If you own things, what's their effect on you? – E. M. FORSTER, "My Wood"

Who will be left to celebrate a victory made of blood and fire?
– THICH NHAT HANH, "Our Green Garden"

Question marks do not close *indirect* questions, which report rather than ask questions. Indirect questions close with a period.

▶ **She asked whether I opposed his nomination~~?~~.^**

Do not use a comma or a period after a question mark that ends a direct quotation.

► **"Am I my brother's keeper?," Cain asked.**

► **Cain asked, "Am I my brother's keeper?."**

A polite request phrased as a question can be followed by a period rather than a question mark.

Would you please close the door.

Questions in a series may have question marks even when they are not separate sentences.

I often confronted a difficult choice: should I go to practice? finish my homework? spend time with my friends?

A question mark in parentheses can be used to indicate that a writer is unsure of a date, a figure, or a word.

Quintilian died in A.D. 96 (?).

EXERCISE 32.2

Revise each of the following sentences, adding question marks and substituting them for other punctuation where appropriate. Not all of the sentences require question marks. Example:

She asked the travel agent, "What is the air fare to Greece/?"

1. Social scientists face difficult questions: should they use their knowledge to shape society, merely describe human behavior, try to do both.
2. Are people with so many possessions really happy.
3. "Can I play this" asked Manuel.
4. I looked at him and asked what his point was.
5. The judge asked, "What is your verdict."

32c Using exclamation points

Exclamation points close sentences that show surprise or strong emotion: emphatic statements, interjections, and emphatic commands.

www •

http://b11.edu.aca.mmu.ac.uk/Punct/Misc.html

This punctuation miscellany offers useful tips on exclamation points, including advice from F. Scott Fitzgerald to cut them all out; he said that using an exclamation point is "like laughing at your own jokes."

> In those few moments of geologic time will be the story of all that has happened since we became a nation. And what a story it will be!
>
> – James Rettie, "But a Watch in the Night"

> Ouch!

> Look out!

Use exclamation points very sparingly because they can distract your readers or suggest that you are exaggerating the importance of what you are saying. Do not, for instance, use them with mild interjections or to suggest sarcasm or criticism. In general, try to create emphasis through diction and sentence structure rather than with exclamation points.

For more on creating emphasis through diction and sentence structure, see Chapter 27 and 19a.

► **This university is so large, so varied, that attempting to tell someone everything about it would take three years!.**

Do not use a comma or a period after an exclamation point that ends a direct quotation.

► **"Happiness hates the timid!" according to Eugene O'Neill, who went on to add, "So does Science!"/**

EXERCISE 32.3

Revise each of the following sentences, adding or deleting exclamation points where appropriate and removing any other unnecessary punctuation you find. Example:

> Look out/! The tide is coming in fast/!

1. Jessica is such a bright ten-year-old that even her parents have trouble keeping up with her!
2. I screamed at Jamie, "You rat. You tricked me."
3. "This time we're starting early!," she shouted.
4. Stop, thief.
5. Oh, no. We've lost the house.

THINKING CRITICALLY ABOUT END PUNCTUATION

Reading with an Eye for End Punctuation

Consider the use of end punctuation in the following paragraph. Then experiment with the end punctuation. What would be the effect of deleting the exclamation point from the quotation by Cicero or of changing it to a question mark? What would be the effect of changing Cicero's question to a statement?

> To be admired and praised, especially by the young, is an autumnal pleasure enjoyed by the lucky ones (who are not always the most deserving). "What is more charming," Cicero observes in his famous essay *De Senectute,* "than an old age surrounded by the enthusiasm of youth! . . . Attentions which seem trivial and conventional are marks of honor — the morning call, being sought after, precedence, having people rise for you, being escorted to and from the forum. . . . What pleasures of the body can be compared to the prerogatives of influence?" But there are also pleasures of the body, or the mind, that are enjoyed by a greater number of older persons.
>
> – MALCOLM COWLEY, *The View from 80*

Thinking about Your Own Use of End Punctuation

Look through something you have written recently, noting its end punctuation. Using the guidelines at the beginning of this chapter, see if your use of end punctuation follows any patterns. Try revising the end punctuation in a paragraph or two to emphasize (or de-emphasize) some point. What conclusions can you draw about ways of using end punctuation to draw attention to (or away from) a sentence? If you keep a writing log, note your observations there.

33 Using Apostrophes

The little apostrophe can sometimes make a big difference in meaning. A friend of ours found that out when he agreed to look after a neighbor's apartment while she was out of town. "I'll leave instructions on the kitchen counter," the neighbor said as she gave him her key. Here are the instructions he found: "(1) Please water the plants in the living room — once will be fine. (2) The cat's food is on the counter. Once a day on the patio. Thanks. I'll see you Friday."

Because the note said *cat's,* he expected one cat — and when he saw one, he put it and the food outside on the patio. When the neighbor returned, she found one healthy cat — and a second, very weak one that had hidden under the bed. The difference between *cat's* and *cats'* in this instance almost cost his neighbor a cat. This chapter will help you use apostrophes carefully. ■

33a Using apostrophes to signal possessive case

The possessive case denotes ownership or possession of one thing by another. (See 8a3.) Apostrophes are used in the possessive case of nouns and some pronouns.

Singular nouns and indefinite pronouns

Add an apostrophe and *-s* to form the possessive of most singular nouns, including those that end in *-s,* and of indefinite pronouns.

▶ **Marilyn Monroe's early movies are considered classics.**

▶ **The reading list included ~~Brooks~~ *Brooks's* poem.**

▶ **Anyone's guess is as good as mine.**

Apostrophes are not used with the possessive forms of *personal* pronouns: *yours, his, hers, its, ours, theirs.*

Plural nouns

For plural nouns that do not end in *-s,* add an apostrophe and *-s.*

▶ **Robert Bly helped to popularize the ~~mens'~~ *men's* movement.**

For plural nouns ending in *-s,* add only the apostrophe.

▶ **The three ~~clown's~~ clowns' costumes were bright green and orange.**

Compound words

For compound words, make the last word in the group possessive.

The *secretary of state's* speech was televised.

Both her *daughters-in-law's* birthdays fall in July.

My *in-laws'* disapproval dampened our enthusiasm for the new house.

Two or more nouns

To signal individual possession by two or more owners, make each noun possessive.

There are great differences between *John Wayne's* and *Henry Fonda's* westerns. [Wayne and Fonda appeared in different westerns.]

To signal joint possession, make only the last noun possessive.

MacNeil and Lehrer's program focused on current issues. [MacNeil and Lehrer appeared on the same program.]

EDITING FOR POSSESSIVE APOSTROPHES

1. **Circle all the nouns that end in *-s.* Then check each one that shows ownership or possession to see that it has an apostrophe in the right place, either before or after the *-s.***
2. **Then underline all the indefinite pronouns, such as *someone* and *nobody.* (See 7b3 for a list.) Any that end in *-s* should have an apostrophe before the *-s.***

www •

http://b11.edu.aca.mmu.ac.uk/Punct/Misc.html

This punctuation page offers amusing but thought-provoking observations, including notes on "the problematic apostrophe." At least one British English professor has suggested abolishing it altogether.

EXERCISE 33.1

Write a brief paragraph, beginning "I've always been amused by my neighbor's ________." Then note every use of an apostrophe.

EXERCISE 33.2

Complete each of the following sentences by inserting *'s* or an apostrophe alone to form the possessive case of the italicized words.

1. Grammar is *everybody* favorite subject.
2. *Maria Callas* opera performances are now the stuff of legend.
3. I was having a good time at *P.J.*, but my friends wanted to go to *Sunny*.
4. *Carol and Jim* income dropped drastically after Jim lost his job.
5. Parents often question their *children* choice of friends.
6. Many smokers disregard the *surgeon general* warnings.
7. How the economy will recover is *anyone* guess.
8. The *governors* attitudes changed after the convention.
9. This dog has a *beagle* ears and a *St. Bernard* nose and feet.
10. *My friend and my brother* cars have the same kind of stereo system.

33b Using apostrophes to signal contractions and other omissions

Contractions are two-word combinations formed by leaving out certain letters, which are indicated by an apostrophe. For example:

it is/it's	I would/I'd	will not/won't
was not/wasn't	he would/he'd	let us/let's
I am/I'm	would not/wouldn't	who is, who has/who's
he is, he has/he's	do not/don't	cannot/can't
you will/you'll	does not/doesn't	

Contractions are common in conversation and informal writing. Some academic work, however, calls for greater formality.

Distinguishing its *and* it's

Do not confuse the possessive pronoun *its* with the contraction *it's*. *Its* is the possessive form of *it*. *It's* is a contraction for *it is*.

▶ **This disease is unusual; it's symptoms vary from person to person.**

▶ **It's a difficult disease to diagnose.**

1. Check each *its.* If it does not show possession, add an apostrophe before the *-s.*
2. Check each *it's.* Does it mean "it is"? If not, remove the apostrophe.

Signaling omissions

An apostrophe signals omissions in some common phrases:

ten of the clock	rock and roll	class of 1998
ten o'clock	rock 'n' roll	class of '98

In addition, writers can use an apostrophe to signal omitted letters in approximating the sound of speech or some specific dialect. Note the way Mark Twain uses the apostrophe to form contractions and signal omitted letters in the following passage, in which Huckleberry Finn tells Jim about King Henry VIII:

> S'pose people left money laying around where he was – what did he do? He collared it. S'pose he contracted to do a thing; and you paid him, and didn't set down there and see that he done it – what did he do? He always done the other thing. S'pose he opened his mouth – what then? If he didn't shut it up powerful quick, he'd lose a lie, every time. That's the kind of a bug Henry was; and if we'd 'a' had him along 'stead of our kings, he'd 'a' fooled that town a heap worse than ourn done.
>
> – MARK TWAIN, *The Adventures of Huckleberry Finn*

33c Using apostrophes to form certain plurals

An apostrophe and *-s* are used to form the plural of numbers, letters, symbols, and words referred to as such.

The gymnasts need marks of *8*'s and *9*'s to qualify for the finals.

Several Cessna *150*'s were lined up for takeoff.

Many *Ph.D.*'s cannot find jobs as college teachers.

The computer prints *e*'s whenever there is an error in the program.

I marked special passages with a series of three *'s.

The five *Shakespeare*'s in the essay were spelled five different ways.

Note that numbers, letters, and words referred to as words are usually italicized; but the plural ending is not, as in the examples here.

The plural of years is usually written without an apostrophe (*1990s*).

EXERCISE 33.3

The following sentences, from which all apostrophes have been deleted, appear in Langston Hughes's "Salvation." Insert apostrophes where appropriate.

"Sister Reed, what is this child's name?"

1. There was a big revival at my Auntie Reeds church.
2. I heard the songs and the minister saying: "Why dont you come?"
3. Finally Westley said to me in a whisper: "Im tired o sitting here. Lets get up and be saved."
4. So I decided that maybe to save further trouble, Id better lie. . . .
5. That night, . . . I cried, in bed alone, and couldnt stop.

THINKING CRITICALLY ABOUT APOSTROPHES

Reading with an Eye for Apostrophes

In the following rhyme, Zora Neale Hurston uses apostrophes to form contractions and signal omitted letters. They help create the rhythms and cadences of African American vernacular English. To get a sense of this effect, try reading the lines aloud with the missing letters filled in.

Ah got up 'bout half-past fo'
Forty fo' robbers wuz 'round mah do'
Ah got up and let 'em in
Hit 'em ovah de head wid uh rollin' pin.

– ZORA NEALE HURSTON, *Jonah's Gourd Vine*

Thinking about Your Own Use of Apostrophes

As a tool for presenting contractions and omitted letters, apostrophes play a larger role in informal writing than in formal writing. You may need to learn to write with few or no contractions, a task that requires some effort because we all use contractions in conversation. To get an idea of the difference between spoken and written language, try transcribing a "paragraph" or so of your own spoken words. Use apostrophes whenever you use a contraction or otherwise omit a letter. Look over your paragraph to see how many apostrophes you used, and then revise the piece to make it more formal, eliminating all or most apostrophes. What conclusions can you draw about ways you should and should not use apostrophes?

Using Quotation Marks

34

As a way of bringing other people's words into our own, quotation can be a powerful writing tool. For example:

Mrs. Macken urges parents to get books for their children, to read to them when they are "li'l," and when they start school to make certain they attend regularly. She holds herself up as an example of a "millhand's daughter who wanted to be a schoolteacher and did it through sheer hard work."

– Shirley Brice Heath
Ways with Words

The writer could have paraphrased, but by quoting, she lets her subject speak for herself – and lets us as readers hear that person's voice. Quotation marks are also used to mark certain titles, to set off definitions, to quote poetry, to signal dialogue, and to highlight words used ironically. ■

34a Using quotation marks to signal direct quotations

In American English, double quotation marks signal a direct quotation.

> Bush called for a "kinder, gentler" America.
>
> She smiled and said, "Son, this is one incident I will never forget."

Single quotation marks enclose a quotation within a quotation. Open and close the quoted passage with double quotation marks, and change any quotation marks that appear *within* the quotation to single quotation marks.

> In "The Uses of the Blues," Baldwin says, "The title 'The Uses of the Blues' does not refer to music; I don't know anything about music."

Do not use quotation marks for *indirect* quotations, which do not repeat someone's exact words.

▶ **Dad smiled and said that "he would never forget the incident."** (quotation marks deleted)

1 Quoting longer passages

If the passage you wish to quote exceeds four typed lines, set it off from the rest of the text by starting it on a new

→ Use quotation marks around direct quotations and titles of short works. (34a and b)

→ Do not use quotation marks around set-off quotations of more than four lines of prose or three lines of poetry, or around titles of long works. (34a and b)

→ Check other punctuation used with closing quotation marks. (34e)
- Periods and commas should be *inside* the quotation marks.
- Colons, semicolons, and footnote numbers should be *outside.*
- Question marks, exclamation points, and dashes should be *inside* if they are part of the quoted material, *outside* if they are not.

→ Never use quotation marks around indirect quotations. (34a)

▶ **Keith said that "he was sorry."**

→ Do not rely on quotation marks to add emphasis to words. (34d)

line and indenting each line ten spaces from the left margin. This format, known as **block quotation,** does not require quotation marks.

> In *Winged Words: American Indian Writers Speak,* Leslie Marmon Silko describes her early education:
>
> > I learned to love reading, and love books, and the printed page, and therefore was motivated to learn to write. The best thing [. . .] you can have in life is to have someone tell you a story [. . .] but in lieu of that [. . .] I learned at an early age to find comfort in a book, that a book would talk to me when no one else would. (145)

This block quotation, including the bracketed ellipses and the page number in parentheses at the end, follows the Modern Language Association's (MLA) style. The American Psychological Association (APA) and *The Chicago Manual of Style* have different guidelines for setting off block quotations.

FOR MULTILINGUAL WRITERS

QUOTING IN AMERICAN ENGLISH

American English and British English offer opposite conventions for double and single quotation marks. Writers of British English use single quotation marks first and, when necessary, double quotation marks for quotations within quotations. If you have studied British English, be careful to follow the U.S. conventions governing quotation marks: double quotation marks first and, when necessary, single quotation marks within double.

2 Quoting poetry

If the quotation is fewer than four lines, include it within your text, enclosed in double quotation marks. Separate the lines of the poem with slashes, each preceded and followed by a space.

> In one of his best-known poems, Robert Frost remarks, "Two roads diverged in a wood, and I — / I took the one less traveled by, / And that has made all the difference."

If the poetic quotation is longer, start it on a new line, indent each line ten spaces from the left margin, and do not use quotation marks.

> The duke in Robert Browning's "My Last Duchess" is clearly a jealous, vain person, whose arrogance is illustrated through his statement:
>
> She thanked men – good! but thanked
> Somehow – I know not how – as if she ranked
> My gift of a nine-hundred-years-old name
> With anybody's gift.

When you quote poetry, take care to follow the indentation, spacing, capitalization, punctuation, and other features of the original passage.

EXERCISE 34.1

Quoting someone else's words can contribute authority, texture, and even irony to your writing in that it adds other voices and images to your own. See how one writer uses a quotation in the following passage about Wyoming:

Most characteristic of the state's landscape is what a developer euphemistically describes as "indigenous growth right up to your front door" – a reference to waterless stands of salt sage, snakes, jackrabbits, deerflies, red dust, a brief respite of wildflowers, dry washes, and no trees.

– Gretel Ehrlich, *The Solace of Open Spaces*

Spend a few minutes reading an article on a topic you know something about. Then write a paragraph on that topic, quoting the article at least once. Choose something worded in a memorable way or someone whose voice will lend weight to your own words. Finally, check your use of quotation marks against the guidelines in this chapter.

WWW •

http://www.amazon.com/exec/obidos/recent-interviews-chrono

Amazon.com, the WWW-based bookseller, offers this site where you can read interviews of authors. It's a good place to go for quotes on writing by published writers.

3 Signaling dialogue

When you write dialogue or quote a conversation, enclose the words of each speaker in quotation marks, and mark each shift in speaker by beginning a new paragraph, no matter how brief the quoted remark may be.

> "But I can see you're bound to come," said the father. "Only we ain't going to catch us no fish, because there ain't no water left to catch 'em in."
>
> "The river!"
>
> "All but dry."
>
> – Eudora Welty, "Ladies in Spring"

Beginning a new paragraph with each change in speaker helps readers follow the dialogue. In the preceding example, we know when the father is speaking and when the child is speaking without the author's having to repeat *said the father, the child said,* and so on.

34b Using quotation marks to signal titles and definitions

Quotation marks are used to enclose the titles of short poems, short stories, articles, essays, songs, sections of books, and episodes of television and radio programs.

> "Dover Beach" moves from calmness to sadness. [poem]
>
> Alice Walker's "Everyday Use" is about more than just quilts. [short story]
>
> In "Photography," Susan Sontag considers the role of photography in our society. [essay]
>
> The *Atlantic* published an article entitled "Illiberal Education." [article]
>
> In the chapter called "Complexion," Rodriguez describes his sensitivity about his skin color. [section of book]

For a discussion of the use of italics for titles, see 38a.

Use italics rather than quotation marks for the titles of longer works, such as books and magazines. Do not use either in titling your own writing unless your title is or includes another title or a quotation.

Definitions are sometimes set off with quotation marks.

> The French phrase *idée fixe* means literally "fixed idea."

34c Using quotation marks to signal irony and coinages

One way of showing readers that you are using a word or a phrase ironically is to enclose it in quotation marks.

> The "banquet" consisted of dried-out chicken and canned vegetables. [The quotation marks suggest that the meal was anything but a banquet.]

Quotation marks are also used to enclose words or phrases made up by the writer, as is *forebirth* in the following example:

> Your whole first paragraph or first page may have to be guillotined in any case after your piece is finished: it is a kind of "forebirth."
>
> – JACQUES BARZUN, "A Writer's Discipline"

EXERCISE 34.2

Revise each of the following sentences, using quotation marks appropriately to signal titles, definitions, irony, or coinages.

1. Kowinski uses the term mallaise to mean physical and psychological disturbances caused by mall contact.
2. In Flannery O'Connor's short story Revelation, colors symbolize passion, violence, sadness, and even God.
3. The little that is known about gorillas certainly makes you want to know more, writes Alan Moorehead in his essay A Most Forgiving Ape.
4. The fun of surgery begins before the operation ever takes place.
5. Wolfe's article Radical Chic satirizes wealthy liberals.
6. Big Bill, a section of Dos Passos's *U.S.A.,* opens with a birth.
7. Amy Lowell challenges social conformity in her poem Patterns.
8. The Beatles song Love Me Do catapulted the band to international stardom.
9. My dictionary defines *isolation* as the quality or state of being alone.
10. In the episode Driven to Extremes, *48 Hours* takes a humorous look at driving in New York City.

34d Checking for misused quotation marks

Use quotation marks only when there is a reason for them. Do not use them just to emphasize particular words or phrases.

▶ **Michael said that his views may not be ~~"~~politically correct,~~"~~ but that he wasn't going to change them for anything.**

▶ **Much time was spent speculating about their ~~"~~relationship.~~"~~**

Do not use quotation marks with slang or colloquial language; they create the impression that you are apologizing for using such language. Instead, try to express the idea in formal language. If you have a good reason to use a slang or colloquial term, use it without quotation marks.

For a discussion of slang and colloquial language, see 27a.

▶ **After their twenty-mile hike, the campers were** *exhausted* **~~"wiped out"~~ and ready to** *go to bed.* **~~"hit the sack."~~**

34e Using quotation marks with other punctuation

Periods and commas go *inside* closing quotation marks.

"Don't compromise yourself," said Janis Joplin, "you are all you've got."

Colons and semicolons go *outside* closing quotation marks.

Everything is dark, and "a visionary light settles in her eyes"; this vision, this light, is her salvation.

I felt only one emotion after finishing "Eveline": pity.

Question marks, exclamation points, and dashes go *inside* closing quotation marks if they are part of the quotation, *outside* if they are not.

PART OF THE QUOTATION

Gently shake the injured person while asking, "Are you all right?"

"Jump!" one of the firefighters shouted.

"Watch out – watch out for – " Jessica began nervously.

NOT PART OF THE QUOTATION

What is the theme of "The Birth-Mark"?

How tired she must be of hearing "God Save the Queen"!

"Break a leg" – that phrase is supposed to bring good luck to a performer.

Footnote numbers go *outside* closing quotation marks.

Tragedy is defined by Aristotle as "an imitation of an action that is serious and of a certain magnitude."[1]

For more information on footnotes and for examples of quotation marks in bibliographical references, see Chapters 44 – 47.

EXERCISE 34.3

Revise the following paragraph to use quotation marks appropriately.

In his poem The Fly, William Blake uses the image of the poet as a fly to make a "profound statement" about the fragility of human life and thought. "Addressing" the fly, the poet regrets that "he has killed it as it was playing" and goes on to ask "whether he is not a fly, too": "For I dance, / And drink, & sing / Till some blind hand / Shall brush my wing." This image "echoes" Shakespeare's play *King Lear,* in which the character Gloucester says, "As flies to wanton boys are we to th' gods; / They kill us for their sport". Apparently, Blake is less "stressed out" by the thought of himself as a helpless "bug", since he concludes the poem, "Then am I / A happy fly, / If I live / Or if I die. But in his essay “Moral Vision in “The Fly”,” Sylvester Pritchard argues that “Blake’s closing image of death suggests a despair no less deep than that of Gloucester in his terrible blind sight[2]”.

THINKING CRITICALLY ABOUT QUOTATION MARKS

Reading with an Eye for Quotation Marks

Read the following passage about the painter Georgia O’Keeffe, paying particular attention to the use of quotation marks. What effect is created by the author’s use of quotation marks with *hardness, crustiness,* and *crusty*? How do the quotations by O’Keeffe help support the author’s description of her?

> “Hardness” has not been in our century a quality much admired in women, nor in the past twenty years has it even been in official favor for men. When hardness surfaces in the very old we tend to transform it into “crustiness” or eccentricity, some tonic pepperiness to be indulged at a distance. On the evidence of her work and what she has said about it, Georgia O’Keeffe is neither “crusty” nor eccentric. She is simply hard, a straight shooter, a woman clean of received wisdom and open to what she sees. This is a woman who could early on dismiss most of her contemporaries as “dreamy,” and would later single out one she liked as “a very poor painter.” (And then add, apparently by way of softening the judgment: “I guess he wasn’t a painter at all. He had no courage and I believe that to create one’s own world in any of the arts takes courage.”) This is a woman who in 1939 could advise her admirers that they were missing her point, that their appreciation of her famous flowers was merely sentimental. “When I paint a red hill,” she observed coolly in the catalogue for an exhibition that year, “you say it is too bad that I don’t always paint flowers. A flower touches almost everyone’s heart. A red hill doesn’t touch everyone’s heart.”
>
> – JOAN DIDION, “Georgia O’Keeffe”

Thinking about Your Own Use of Quotation Marks

Choose a topic that is of interest on your campus, and interview one of your friends about it for ten or fifteen minutes. On the basis of your notes from the interview, write two or three paragraphs about your friend’s views, using as many direct quotations as possible. Then look to see how closely you followed the conventions for quotation marks explained in this chapter. Note any usages that caused you problems – in your writing log, if you keep one.

35 Using Other Punctuation Marks

Parentheses, brackets, dashes, colons, slashes, and ellipses are all around us. Pick up the television listings, for instance, and you will find all these punctuation marks in abundance, helping viewers preview programs in a clear and efficient way.

❼⑧ **College Football** ***3:30*** 501019/592361 — Northwestern Wildcats at Ohio State Buckeyes. The Buckeyes are looking for their 20th straight win over Northwestern. (Live) [Time approximate.]

This chapter will guide you in deciding when you can use these marks of punctuation to signal relationships among sentence parts, to create particular rhythms, and to help readers follow your thoughts. ■

35a Using parentheses

Parentheses enclose material that is of minor or secondary importance in a sentence – material that supplements, clarifies, comments on, or illustrates what precedes or follows it. Parentheses also enclose numbers or letters that precede items in a list, and sometimes they enclose source citations or publication information.

Enclosing less important material

> Normal children do not confuse reality and fantasy – they confuse them much less often than we adults do (as a certain great fantasist pointed out in a story called "The Emperor's New Clothes").
>
> – Ursula LeGuin, "Why Are Americans Afraid of Dragons?"

> Boxing is a purely masculine world. (Though there are female boxers – the most famous is the black champion Lady Tyger Trimiar with her shaved head and tiger-striped attire – women's role in the sport is extremely marginal.)
>
> – Joyce Carol Oates, "On Boxing"

As the preceding examples demonstrate, a period may be placed either inside or outside a closing parenthesis, depending on whether the parenthetical text is part of a larger sentence. A comma, however, is always placed *outside* a closing parenthesis (and never before an opening one).

- → Be sure that any material set off with dashes or enclosed in parentheses requires special treatment. Then check to see that the dashes or parentheses don't make the sentence difficult to follow. (35a and c)
- → Decide whether you have chosen the right punctuation: parentheses tend to de-emphasize material they enclose; dashes add emphasis.
- → Check to see that you use square brackets to enclose parenthetical elements in material that is already within parentheses and to enclose words or comments inserted into a quotation. (35b)
- → Check to see that you have not used a colon between a verb and its object or complement, between a preposition and its object, or after such expressions as *such as, especially,* or *including.* (35d)
- → Check to be sure you've used slashes to mark line divisions in poetry quoted within text. (35e)
- → Make sure you've used ellipses (three equally spaced dots) to indicate omissions from quoted passages. If you are following MLA style, enclose ellipses in brackets to distinguish them from ellipsis points the author may have used. (35f)
- → If you are writing an online communication, check your use of slashes in addresses and of angle brackets to enclose email and World Wide Web addresses. (35b) Make sure you use emoticons sparingly. (35g)

> Gene Tunney's single defeat in an eleven-year career was to a flamboyant and dangerous fighter named Harry Greb ("The Human Windmill"), who seems to have been, judging from boxing literature, the dirtiest fighter in history.
>
> – Joyce Carol Oates, "On Boxing"

If the material in parentheses is a question or an exclamation, use a question mark or exclamation point inside the closing parenthesis.

> Our laughing (so deep was the pleasure!) became screaming.
>
> – Richard Rodriguez, "Aria: A Memoir of a Bilingual Childhood"

Use parentheses judiciously, for they break up the flow of a sentence or passage, forcing readers to hold the original train of thought in their minds while considering a secondary one.

www •

http://b11.edu.aca.mmu.ac.uk/Punct/Misc.html

This page from the United Kingdom offers examples, wry quotes, and intriguing historical facts about punctuation. (Did you know that until recently most British legal documents had no punctuation at all?)

Enclosing numbers or letters in a list

> Five distinct styles can be distinguished: (1) Old New England, (2) Deep South, (3) Middle American, (4) Wild West and (5) Far West or Californian.
>
> – Alison Lurie, *The Language of Clothes*

Enclosing textual citations or publication information

> Freud and his followers have had a most significant impact on the ways abnormal functioning is understood and treated (Joseph, 1991).
>
> – RONALD J. COMER, *Abnormal Psychology*

```
     1. John A. Garraty, Quarrels That Have Shaped the
Constitution (New York: Harper and Row, 1987), 7-14.
```

35b Using brackets

Square brackets are used to enclose parenthetical elements in material that is within parentheses and to enclose explanatory words or comments that are inserted into a quotation. If you are using a keyboard that does not include keys for square brackets, draw them in by hand.

Setting off material within parentheses

> Eventually the investigation had to examine the major agencies (including the previously sacrosanct National Security Agency [NSA]) that were conducting covert operations.

Inserting material within quotations

In the following sentence, the bracketed words replace the words *he* and *it* in the original quotation:

> As Curtis argues, "[Johnson] saw [the war] as a game or wrestling match in which he would make Ho Chi Minh cry 'uncle.' "

In the following sentence, the bracketed material explains what the *that* in the quotation means:

> In defending his station's inferior children's programs, a network executive states, "If we were to do that [supply quality programs in the afternoon, one of the demands of ACT], a lot of people might say: 'How dare they lock the kids up for another two and a half hours.' "
>
> – MARIE WINN, *The Plug-in Drug: Television, Children, and the Family*

In the quotation in the following sentence, the artist Gauguin's name is misspelled. The bracketed word *sic,* which means "so," tells readers that the person being quoted – not the writer – made the mistake.

> One admirer wrote, "She was the most striking woman I'd ever seen – a sort of wonderful combination of Mia Farrow and one of Gaugin's [*sic*] Polynesian nymphs."

Use angle brackets to enclose email and Internet addresses in other text.

> For further information, visit our Web site at <http://www.bedfordstmar tins.com>.

EXERCISE 35.1

Revise the following sentences, using parentheses and brackets correctly. Example:

> She was in fourth grade (or was it third?) when she became blind.

1. One incident of cruelty was brought to public attention by the Animal Liberation Front ALF.
2. During my research, I found that a flat-rate income tax a single-rate tax with no deductions has its problems.
3. The health care expert informed readers that "as we progress through middle age, we experience intimations of our own morality *sic*."
4. Many researchers used the Massachusetts Multiphasic Personality Inventory the MMPI for hypnotizability studies.
5. Some of the alternatives suggested include 1 tissue cultures, 2 mechanical models, 3 in vitro techniques, and 4 mathematical and electrical models.

35c Using dashes

Pairs of dashes allow a writer to interrupt a sentence to insert a comment or to highlight particular material. In contrast to parentheses, dashes give more rather than less emphasis to the material they enclose. On most typewriters and with some computer software, a dash is made with two hyphens (--) with *no* spaces before, between, or after. In some software, a solid dash can be typed as it is in this book (—). In some computer programs, two typed hyphens are automatically converted into a solid dash.

Inserting a comment

> The pleasures of reading itself – who doesn't remember? – were like those of Christmas cake, a sweet devouring. – EUDORA WELTY, "A Sweet Devouring"

Emphasizing explanatory material

Mr. Angell is addicted to dashes and parentheses — small pauses or digressions in a narrative like those moments when the umpire dusts off home plate or a pitcher rubs up a new ball — that serve to slow an already deliberate movement almost to a standstill.

– JOEL CONARROE, *New York Times Book Review*

A single dash sets off a comment or emphasizes material at the end of a sentence. It may also mark a sudden shift in tone, introduce a summary or explanation of what has come before, or indicate a hesitation in speech.

Emphasizing material at the end of a sentence

In the twentieth century it has become almost impossible to moralize about epidemics — except those which are transmitted sexually.

– SUSAN SONTAG, *AIDS and Its Metaphors*

Marking a sudden change in tone

New York is a catastrophe — but a magnificent catastrophe. – LE CORBUSIER

Introducing a summary or explanation

In walking, the average adult person employs a motor mechanism that weighs about eighty pounds — sixty pounds of muscle and twenty pounds of bone. – EDWARD WAY TEALE

Indicating hesitation in speech

As the officer approached his car, the driver stammered, "What — what have I done?"

In introducing a summary or explanation, the difference between a single dash and a colon is a subtle one. In general, however, a dash is less formal. In fact, you should use dashes very carefully in college writing because too many of them create a jerky, disconnected effect that makes it hard for readers to follow your thought.

EXERCISE 35.2

Punctuate the following sentences with dashes where appropriate. Example:

> He is quick, violent, and mean—they don't call him Dirty Harry for nothing—but appealing nonetheless.

1. Many people would have ignored the children's taunts but not Ace.
2. Even if smoking is harmful and there is no real proof of this assertion it is unjust to outlaw smoking while other harmful substances remain legal.
3. Saving old theaters how many have we already lost? is a cultural necessity.
4. Union Carbide's plant in Bhopal, India, sprang a leak a leak that killed more than 2,000 people and injured an additional 200,000.
5. Fair-skinned people and especially those with red hair should use a strong sunscreen.

35d Using colons

A colon is used to introduce something: an explanation, an example, an appositive, a series, a list, or a quotation. Colons also separate elements such as hours, minutes, and seconds; biblical chapter numbers and verses; and titles and subtitles.

Introducing an explanation, an example, or an appositive

> And we are all on our own when it comes to keeping those lines open to ourselves: your notebook will never help me, nor mine you.
>
> – Joan Didion, "On Keeping a Notebook"

> The men may also wear the getup known as Sun Belt Cool: a pale beige suit, open-collared shirt (often in a darker shade than the suit), cream-colored loafers and aviator sunglasses. – Alison Lurie, *The Language of Clothes*

Introducing a series, a list, or a quotation

> At the baby's one-month birthday party, Ah Po gave him the Four Valuable Things: ink, inkslab, paper, and brush. – Maxine Hong Kingston, *China Men*

> We began a series of workshops on nonviolence, and we repeatedly asked ourselves: "Are you able to accept blows without retaliation?"
>
> – Martin Luther King Jr., "Letter from Birmingham Jail"

Separating elements

SALUTATIONS IN FORMAL LETTERS

Dear Dr. Chapman:

HOURS, MINUTES, AND SECONDS

4:59 P.M.
2:15:06

RATIOS

a ratio of 5:1

BIBLICAL CHAPTERS AND VERSES

I Corinthians 3:3 – 5

TITLES AND SUBTITLES

The Joy of Insight: Passions of a Physicist

CITIES AND PUBLISHERS IN BIBLIOGRAPHIC ENTRIES

New York: St. Martin's, 1998

Checking for misused colons

Except when it is used to separate the standard elements discussed in the preceding section, a colon should be used only at the end of an independent clause. Do not put a colon between a verb and its object or complement, unless the object is a quotation. Do not put a colon between a preposition and its object or after such expressions as *such as, especially,* or *including.*

▶ **Some natural fibers are~~:~~ cotton, wool, silk, and linen.**

▶ **In poetry, additional power may come from devices such as~~:~~ simile, metaphor, and alliteration.**

EXERCISE 35.3

Insert a colon or colons in each of the following items that needs them. Some of the items do not require a colon. Example:

Images:^ *My Life in Film* includes revealing material written by Ingmar Bergman.

1. The sonnet's structure is effective in revealing the speaker's message love has changed his life and ended his depression.
2. Another example is taken from Psalm 139 16.
3. Nixon claimed that throughout the Watergate investigation he believed it was his duty to stay on as president "to make every possible effort to complete the term of office to which you elected me."
4. Shifting into German, Kennedy declared "Ich bin ein Berliner."

5. Education can alleviate problems such as poverty, poor health, and the energy shortage.
6. Gandhi urged four rules tell the truth even in business, adopt more sanitary habits, abolish caste and religious divisions, and learn English.
7. Solid vocal technique is founded on the correct use of head position, diaphragm control, muscle relaxation, and voice placement.
8. *Signs of Trouble and Erosion A Report on Education in America* was submitted to Congress and the president in January 1984.
9. Even more important was what money represented success, prestige, and power.
10. Two buses go to Denver: one at 9 38 A.M. and one at 2 55 P.M.

35e Using slashes

Slashes are used to mark line divisions in poetry quoted within text, to separate two alternative terms, and to separate the parts of fractions and Internet addresses. When used to separate lines of poetry, the slash should be preceded and followed by a space.

See 34a2.

Marking line divisions in poetry

In Sonnet 29, the persona states, "For thy sweet love rememb'red such wealth brings / That then I scorn to change my state with kings."

Separating alternatives

"I'm not the typical wife/girlfriend of a baseball player – those women you see on TV with their hair done up and their Rose Bowl Parade wave to the crowds."

– ROGER ANGELL, "In the Country"

Separating parts of fractions

The structure is 138½ feet high.

Separating parts of Internet addresses

http://www.bedfordstmartins.com/nsmhandbook

35f Using ellipses

Ellipses, or ellipsis points, are three equally spaced dots. Most often used to indicate that something has been omitted from a quoted passage, they can also be used to signal a pause or hesitation in speech in the same way that a dash can.

Indicating omissions

Just as you should carefully use quotation marks around any material that you quote directly from a source, so you should carefully use an ellipsis to indicate that you have left out part of a quotation that otherwise appears to be a complete sentence. The fifth edition of the Modern Language Association's (MLA) handbook (1999) recommends placing brackets around ellipses you have inserted to distinguish them from ellipsis points the author may have used. Note that brackets are not necessary if you are using a citation style other than MLA. Look at the following example:

ORIGINAL TEXT

> The quasi-official division of the population into three economic classes called high-, middle-, and low-income groups rather misses the point, because as a class indicator the amount of money is not as important as the source.
> – PAUL FUSSELL, "Notes on Class"

WITH ELLIPSES

> As Paul Fussell argues, "The quasi-official division of the population into three economic classes [. . .] rather misses the point [. . .] ."

In this example, the ellipses are used to indicate two different omissions – one in the middle of the sentence and one at the end. When you omit the last part of a quoted sentence, add a period after the ellipsis – for a total of four dots. Be sure a complete sentence comes before and after the four points. If you are using MLA style and your quotation ends with a source documentation (such as a page number, a name, or a title), follow these steps:

1. Leave a space before the first bracket and use three ellipsis points but no period after the closing bracket.
2. Add the closing quotation mark, closed up to the closing bracket.
3. Add the source documentation in parentheses.
4. Use a period to indicate the end of the sentence.

Hawthorne writes, "My friend, whom I shall call Oberon — it was a name of fancy and friendship between him and me [. . .]" (575).

If you are not using MLA style, omit the brackets.

Indicating a pause or a hesitation

Then the voice, husky and familiar, came to wash over us — "The winnah, and still heavyweight champeen of the world . . . Joe Louis."

– MAYA ANGELOU, *I Know Why the Caged Bird Sings*

35g Using emoticons

If you participate in any computer bulletin boards, discussion groups, or other electronic forms of communication, you will already have come in contact with **emoticons,** also known as *smileys.* These are combinations of keyboard characters that, when looked at sideways, "punctuate" a passage by indicating the mood of the sender. Following are some commonly used emoticons:

the smile:	:-)	the wink:	;-)
the frown:	:-(	the laugh:	:-D

These marks are sometimes also used to express something about the sender's appearance. How, for instance, might a writer indicate that she or he wears glasses, has a mustache, or wears a turban? As these questions suggest, many emoticons are used simply for fun, to tease and puzzle readers. Their growing use, however, suggests that some of these symbols may well become standard punctuation marks.

In the meantime, if you are using emoticons in your writing, follow the same rules you would use for other marks: Are they appropriate to your topic and purpose? Will they be readily understood and accepted by your audience? In general, you will probably not use them in most college writing.

WWW •

http://www.windweaver.com/emoticon.htm

This good list of emoticons is indexed by emotion: click on happy, trying to communicate, and so on. Compiled by Tracy Marks, it includes links to the sources where she learned about emoticons.

EXERCISE 35.4

Complete the following sentence by incorporating two parts of one of the sentences in the passage below, using ellipsis points to indicate what you omit: "In 'Shopping and Other Spiritual Adventures,' Phyllis Rose says of Americans' attitudes toward shopping, ______________________________."

We Americans are beyond a simple, possessive materialism. We're used to abundance and the possibility of possessing things. The things, and the possibility of possessing them, will still be there next week, next year. So today we can walk the aisles calmly. – PHYLLIS ROSE, "Shopping and Other Spiritual Adventures"

EXERCISE 35.5

The following sentences use the punctuation marks presented in this chapter very effectively. Read the sentences carefully; then choose one, and use it as a model for writing a sentence of your own, making sure to use the punctuation marks in the same way in your sentence.

1. The dad was — how can you put this gracefully? — a real blimp, a wide load, and the white polyester stretch-pants only emphasized the cargo.
   – GARRISON KEILLOR, "Happy to Be Here"
2. I took exercise daily (as I still do), did not smoke (and still don't), and though excessively fond of wine, seldom drank spirits, not much liking the taste of them. – JAN MORRIS, "To Everest"
3. Not only are the distinctions we draw between male nature and female nature largely arbitrary and often pure superstition: they are completely beside the point. – BRIGID BROPHY, "Women"
4. A few traditions, thank heaven, remain fixed in the summer state of things — the June collapse of the Giants, Gaylord Perry throwing (or not throwing) spitballs, Hank Aaron hitting homers, and the commissioner . . . well, commissioning. – ROGER ANGELL, *Five Seasons*

EXERCISE 35.6

The following paragraph uses many parentheses and dashes. Using the guidelines in this chapter, revise the paragraph to make it flow more smoothly, and emphasize appropriate elements by deleting some of the parentheses and dashes, replacing one with the other, or substituting other punctuation.

By the time we reached Geneva, we had been traveling more than seven weeks — it seemed like seven months! — and were getting rather tired of one another's company. (We had been only casual acquaintances before the trip.) Since there was not a great deal to see in the city — especially on Sunday — we decided to take the train to Chamonix (France) to see Mont Blanc — Europe's second-highest mountain (a decision that proved to be a disaster). After an argument about the map (the kind of argument we were having more and more often), we wandered around endlessly before finding the train station, only to discover that it was the wrong one. So we had to walk even farther — back to the other train station. Despite an exhausting pace, we just missed the train — or so we thought — until we learned that there was no train to Chamonix that day — because it was Sunday. I have never (for obvious reasons) gone back to Geneva.

THINKING CRITICALLY ABOUT PUNCTUATION

Reading with an Eye for Punctuation

In the following passage, Tom Wolfe uses dashes, parentheses, an ellipsis, and a colon to create rhythm and build momentum in a very long (178-word) sentence. The editorial comment inserted in brackets calls attention to the fact that the "right stuff" was, in the world Wolfe describes here, always male. Look carefully at how Wolfe and the editors use these punctuation marks, and then try writing a description of something that effectively uses as many of them as possible. Your description should be about the same length as Wolfe's passage, but it need not be all one sentence.

> Likewise, "hassling" — mock dogfighting — was strictly forbidden, and so naturally young fighter jocks could hardly wait to go up in, say, a pair of F-100s and start the duel by making a pass at each other at 800 miles an hour, the winner being the pilot who could slip in behind the other one and get locked in on his [never *her* or *his or her!*] tail ("wax his tail"), and it was not uncommon for some eager jock to try too tight an outside turn and have his engine flame out, whereupon, unable to restart it, he has to eject . . . and he shakes his fist at the victor as he floats down by parachute and his million-dollar aircraft goes *kaboom!* on the palmetto grass or the desert floor, and he starts thinking about how he can get together with the other guy back at the base in time for the two of them to get their stories straight before the investigation: "I don't know what happened, sir. I was pulling up after a target run, and it just flamed out on me."
>
> – TOM WOLFE, *The Right Stuff*

Thinking about Your Own Use of Punctuation

Look through a draft you have recently written or are working on, and check your use of parentheses, brackets, dashes, colons, slashes, and ellipses. Have you followed the conventions presented in this chapter? If not, revise accordingly. Then read through the draft again, looking especially at all the parentheses and dashes. Are there too many? Check the material in parentheses to see if it could use more emphasis and thus be set off instead with dashes. Then check any material in dashes to see if it could do with less emphasis and thus be punctuated with commas or parentheses. If you keep a writing log, enter some examples of this work in your log.

PART 7

UNDERSTANDING MECHANICAL CONVENTIONS

documentation

writing/editing

hypertext

message

www.bedfordstmartins.com/nsmhandbook

thinking & collaborating

FAQ

FAQ: Mechanics Online

How do you show italics online? Can you use underlining instead?

For programs that don't allow you to use italics, you can substitute other devices.

- To add emphasis to a word or phrase, use asterisks:

  The company homepage simply *must* be updated!

- To indicate a title, use the underline mark before and after the title:

  Thanks for the copy of _EasyWriter_, which arrived today.

Because underlining on the World Wide Web signals an active HYPERTEXT LINK, you should not underline text to signal italics in Web documents.

Are there special rules for using capital letters online?

In general, follow the same conventions online that you would in print, capitalizing the first word of each sentence and proper nouns and adjectives. Some writers treat EMAIL almost like talk, writing hurriedly and not using any capital letters. This practice can be hard on your readers, however, and can result in text that looks unprofessional if it is printed out. Since email *is* often printed out, you should ordinarily follow the print conventions of capitalization. Here are some other tips for using capital letters online:

- **Electronic addresses.** Follow the capitalization *exactly* in address lines: systems that are case sensitive may not recognize <Lunsford .8@Osu.edu> if the actual address is <lunsford.8@osu.edu>.
- **Shouting.** Capitalizing whole words or phrases for emphasis comes across to readers as SHOUTING. So instead of uppercase letters, use asterisks to add emphasis: "Sorry for the abrupt response, but I am *very* busy."
- **InterCaps.** Some contemporary companies use capitals in the middle of their own or their products' names, often turning two words into one. Leave the capitals in, following the style you see in company advertising or on the product itself — *HotJava, WordPerfect, EasyWriter.*

How do you know when to use hyphens with new compound words that are not yet in any dictionaries?

Many new compounds, especially those pertaining to technology, appear as one word, without hyphenation. Helpful advice comes from *Wired Style:* "When in doubt, close it up." Hence *videogame, desktop, workstation, download, toolbar.*

http://www.english.upenn.edu/~jlynch/Grammar/

Grammar and Style Notes *provides explanations of conventions of grammar, style, punctuation, and usage, broken into a file for each letter of the alphabet (click on* n *for information on numbers, for example).*

http://sti.larc.nasa.gov/html/Chapt4/

The chapter on capitalization in Mary McCaskill's Grammar, Punctuation, and Capitalization: A Handbook for Technical Writers and Editors *is available online.*

How do you break a URL if it won't all fit on one line of printed text?

First, remember to signal the beginning and end of the URL with angle brackets (<>). Then, in general, break it in one of the following places:

- *after* the beginning PROTOCOL: <http://
- *before* a punctuation mark: <http://www.bedfordstmartins .com/nsmhandbook>

If absolutely necessary, break the URL in the middle of a word:

> http://www.bedfordstmar
> tins.com/nsmhandbook

If you are documenting sources using MLA style, however, and you need to break a URL within an entry in your Works Cited list, break it only after a slash:

> http://www.bedfordstmartins.com/

Wherever you break a URL, be sure not to add a hyphen at the break and to delete a hyphen added by your word-processor. Otherwise, readers will not know whether or not the hyphen is part of the URL.

How do you deal with money, weights and measurements, and phone numbers on the Internet?

Because the INTERNET reaches readers around the globe, you may need to use non-U.S. units. When using monetary figures online, use the currency of the nation you are writing about or to. For weights and measures, remember that the system of inches and pounds is largely limited to the United States; use metric measurements (meters, grams) when they are appropriate for the nation you are discussing. Begin phone numbers with a plus sign (+) followed by the international access code; then add the area, province, or city code in parentheses; and then add the local number, with spaces between:

> +1 (212) 846 3119
> +81 (5) 9232 6722

36 Using Capitals

Capital letters are a key signal in everyday life. Look around any store to see their importance: you can shop for cola or for Coke; for running shoes or for Nikes; for a house brand of tissues or for Kleenex. In each case, the capital letter is critical to the meaning – and to the corporation that makes the product, which may spend thousands of dollars to defend its exclusive legal right to the name. A published writer who treats a trade name in a generic way, referring, perhaps, to a *frisbee,* may receive a stern letter, or even a subpoena, from the product's manufacturer. On the other hand, capitalizing too freely can also get a writer into trouble; online, for example, readers usually dislike HAVING TO READ TEXT LIKE THIS. With capitalization, then, as with other "mechanical" aspects of writing, it is usually best to follow established conventions. ■

36a Capitalizing the first word of a sentence or line of poetry

Capitalize the first word of a sentence.

> Posing relatives for photographs is a challenge.
>
> Could you move to the left a little?

If you are quoting a full sentence, capitalize its first word.

> Everyone was asking, "What will I do after I graduate?"

Capitalization of a sentence following a colon is optional.

> Gould cites the work of Darwin: The [*or* the] theory of natural selection incorporates the principle of evolutionary ties between all animals.

A sentence that is set off within another sentence by dashes or parentheses should not be capitalized. Note, however, that a sentence within parentheses that stands by itself *is* capitalized.

> Those assigned to transports were not humiliated like washouts – *somebody* had to fly those planes – nevertheless, they, too, had been *left behind* for lack of the right stuff. Or a man could go for a routine physical one fine day, feeling like a million dollars, and be grounded for *fallen arches.* It happened! – just like that! (And try raising them.)
>
> – Tom Wolfe, *The Right Stuff*

- → **Make sure to capitalize the first letter of each sentence. If you quote a poem, follow its original capitalization. (36a)**
- → **Check to make sure you have appropriately capitalized proper nouns and proper adjectives. (36b)**
- → **If you have used titles of people or of works, see that they are capitalized correctly. (36b and c)**
- → **Double-check the capitalization of geographical directions (*north* or *North?*), family relationships (*dad* or *Dad?*), and seasons of the year (*spring*, never *Spring*). (36e)**

The first word of each line in a poem is also traditionally capitalized.

> Loveliest of trees, the cherry now
> Is hung with bloom along the bough,
> And stands about the woodland ride
> Wearing white for Eastertide.
>
> – A. E. HOUSMAN, "Loveliest of Trees"

Some poets do not capitalize each line. When citing poetry, therefore, be careful to follow the original capitalization.

> Morning sun heats up the young beech tree
> leaves and almost lights them into fireflies
>
> I wish I could dig up the earth to plant apples
> pears or peaches on a lazy dandelion lawn
>
> I am tired from this digging up of human bodies
> no one loved enough to save from death
>
> – JUNE JORDAN, "Aftermath"

36b Capitalizing proper nouns and proper adjectives

Capitalize **proper nouns** (those naming specific persons, places, and things) and **proper adjectives** (those formed from proper nouns). In general, do not capitalize **common nouns** (those naming general classes of people, places, and things) unless they begin a sentence or are used as part of a proper noun. Do not capitalize articles (*a, an,* or *the*) or prepositions preceding or within proper nouns or proper adjectives.

www •

http://sti.larc.nasa.gov/newhtml/sp7084ch4.html

This chapter from Mary McCaskill's Handbook for Technical Writers and Editors, *located at NASA's Langley Research Center Web site, includes advice on capitalizing list items, chart and graph categories, and headlines.*

PROPER NOUNS	COMMON NOUNS
Alfred Hitchcock, Hitchcockian	the director, directorial
Brazil, Brazilian	the nation
Golden Gate Bridge	the bridge

SOME COMMONLY CAPITALIZED TERMS

NAMES OF INDIVIDUALS

Morgan Freeman	Louise Erdrich
Aristotelian logic	Petrarchan sonnet form

GEOGRAPHIC NAMES

Asia	Pacific Ocean
Nepal	Sugarloaf Mountain
St. Louis	Michigan Avenue
African art	Parisian fashions

STRUCTURES AND MONUMENTS

Flatiron Building	Gateway Arch
Fort McHenry Tunnel	Coit Tower

SHIPS, TRAINS, AIRCRAFT, AND SPACECRAFT

S.S. Titanic	Metroliner
Spirit of St. Louis	*Challenger*

INSTITUTIONS, ORGANIZATIONS, AND BUSINESSES

Library of Congress	National Organization for Women
St. Martin's Press	United Auto Workers
General Motors Corporation	Democratic Party

HISTORICAL EVENTS, ERAS, AND CALENDAR ITEMS

Shays's Rebellion	Saturday
Great Depression	July
Middle Ages	Memorial Day

(continued on page 409)

(continued from page 408)

RELIGIONS AND RELIGIOUS TERMS

Buddhism, Buddhists	Allah
Catholicism, Catholics	Jesus Christ
Islam, Muslims *or* Moslems	God
Judaism, Jews	the Bible
United Methodist Church, Methodists	the Koran
	Bhagavad Gita

ETHNIC GROUPS, NATIONALITIES, AND LANGUAGES

African American	Arab	Iraqi
Chicano/Chicana	English	Latin
Slavic	Chinese	

TRADE NAMES

Reebok	Cheerios	Levi's
Xerox	Huggies	Walkman

Titles of individuals

Capitalize titles used before a proper name. Used alone or following a proper name, most titles are not capitalized. The only exceptions are titles of some very high officials – for example, many writers capitalize the word *president* when it refers to the President of the United States.

Governor George Bush	George Bush, governor of Texas
Professor Lisa Ede	Lisa Ede, an English professor
Doctor Edward A. Davies	Edward A. Davies, our doctor

Academic institutions and courses

Capitalize the names of specific schools, departments, or courses but not the common nouns referring to institutions or subject areas.

University of California (*but* a California university)
History Department (*but* a history department)
Political Science 102 (*but* a political science course)

36c Capitalizing titles of works

Capitalize most words in titles of books, articles, stories, essays, plays, poems, documents, films, paintings, and musical compositions. Articles (*a, an, the*), prepositions, conjunctions, and the *to* in an infinitive are not capitalized unless they are the first or last words in a title or subtitle.

Walt Whitman: A Life
"June Recital"
"Shooting an Elephant"
Our Town
"Lovely to Look At"
Magna Carta
In the Line of Fire
The Magic Flute

36d Capitalizing *I* and *O*

Always capitalize the pronoun *I* and the interjection *O*. Be careful, however, to distinguish between the interjections *O* and *oh*. *O* is an older form that is usually used for direct address in very formal speech. It is always capitalized, whereas *oh* is not unless it begins a sentence or is part of a title.

In fact, I don't know the answer.

Grant us peace, O Lord.

36e Checking for unnecessary capitalization

Do not capitalize a compass direction, unless the word designates a specific geographical region.

The nation was at that time divided into three competing economic sections: the Northeast, the South, and the West.

▶ **John Muir headed ~~W~~*w*est, motivated by the need to explore.**

Do not capitalize a word indicating a family relationship, unless the word is used as part of the name or as a substitute for the name.

I could always tell when Mother was annoyed with Aunt Rose.

▶ **When she was a child, my ~~M~~*m*other shared a room with her ~~A~~*a*unt.**

FOR MULTILINGUAL WRITERS

LEARNING ENGLISH CAPITALIZATION

Capitalization systems vary considerably among languages, and some languages (Arabic, Chinese, and Hebrew, for example) do not use capital letters at all. English used to capitalize more nouns than it does now (see the Declaration of Independence for one good example). As a result, the system of capitalization commonly used in standard academic English may pose challenges for speakers of other languages.

Do not capitalize seasons of the year and parts of the academic year.

spring	fall semester
winter	winter term
autumn	spring quarter

EXERCISE 36.1

Capitalize words as needed in the following sentences. Example:

T S E T W L F F
t. s. eliot, who wrote *the waste land,* was an editor at faber and faber.

1. the town in the south where i was raised had a statue of a civil war soldier in the center of main street.
2. we had a choice of fast-food, chinese, or italian restaurants.
3. I caught a glimpse of president bill clinton and his family.
4. the council of trent was convened to draw up the catholic response to the protestant reformation.
5. We drove east over the hudson river on the tappan zee bridge.
6. i wondered if my new levi's were faded enough.
7. accepting an award for his score for the film *the high and the mighty,* dmitri tiomkin thanked beethoven, brahms, wagner, and strauss.
8. i will cite the novels of vladimir nabokov, in particular *pnin* and *lolita.*
9. the battle of lexington and concord was fought in april 1775.
10. my favorite song by cole porter is "you'd be so nice to come home to."

THINKING CRITICALLY ABOUT CAPITALIZATION

The following poem uses capitalization in an unconventional way. Read it over a few times, at least once aloud. What effect does the capitalization have on your understanding and recitation of the poem? Why do you think the poet chose to use capitals as she did?

A little Madness in the Spring
Is wholesome even for the King,
But God be with the Clown —
Who ponders this tremendous scene —
This whole Experiment of Green —
As if it were his own!

– EMILY DICKINSON

37 Using Abbreviations and Numbers

Any time you open up a telephone book, you see an abundance of abbreviations and numbers, as in the following movie theater listing from the telephone book in Berkeley, California :

Oaks Theater 1875 Solano Av Brk

Abbreviations and numbers allow writers to present detailed information in a small amount of space and allow readers to process information quickly and efficiently. In academic writing, you will want to follow certain conventions in using abbreviations and numbers, conventions that vary from field to field

This chapter provides guidelines and examples to help you use abbreviations and numbers appropriately, especially in English and other humanities courses. ■

ABBREVIATIONS

37a Abbreviating titles and academic degrees

When used before or after a name, some personal and professional titles and academic degrees are abbreviated, even in academic writing.

Ms. Steinem	Henry Louis Gates Jr.
Mr. Guenette	Paul Irvin, M.D.
Dr. C. William McCurdy	Jamie Barlow Kayes, Ph.D.

Other titles, including religious, military, academic, and government titles, should always be spelled out in academic writing. In other writing, they may be abbreviated when they appear before a full name but should be spelled out if they appear before only a surname.

Gen. Colin Powell	General Powell
Prof. Beverly Moss	Professor Moss
Sen. Barbara Mikulski	Senator Mikulski

Academic degrees may be abbreviated when used alone, but personal or professional titles used alone are never abbreviated.

She received her *Ph.D.* this year.

▶ **He was a rigorous ~~prof.,~~ *professor,* and we worked hard.**

→ Make sure you use abbreviations and numbers according to the conventions of a specific field. For example, *57%* might be acceptable in a math paper, but *57 percent* may be more appropriate in a sociology essay.
→ If you use an abbreviation readers might not understand, make sure you spell out the term the first time you use it and give the abbreviation in parentheses.
→ If you use an abbreviation more than once, make sure you use it consistently.

Use either a title or an academic degree, but not both, with a person's name.

INAPPROPRIATE	Dr. James Dillon, Ph.D.
REVISED	Dr. James Dillon
REVISED	James Dillon, Ph.D.

37b Using abbreviations with years and hours

The following abbreviations are acceptable when used with numerals. Notice that A.D. precedes the numeral; all other abbreviations follow the numeral.

399 B.C. ("before Christ")
A.D. 49 (*anno Domini,* Latin for "year of our Lord")
210 B.C.E. ("before the common era")
49 C.E. ("common era")
11:15 A.M. *or* a.m. (*ante meridiem,* Latin for "before noon")
9:00 P.M. *or* p.m. (*post meridiem,* Latin for "after noon")

37c Using acronyms and initial abbreviations

Abbreviations that can be pronounced as words are called **acronyms:** OPEC, for example, is the acronym for the Organization of Petroleum Exporting Countries. **Initial abbreviations** are those that are

www •

http://home3.inet.tele.dk/hgaarde/Acronyms.html

This Internet acronyms dictionary lists acronyms commonly used in email, Usenet, real-time discussions, and Web-based bulletin boards. It also includes many acronyms that are used mostly by insiders. Still, if you ever run into AWGTHTGTATA, you'll know where to look it up.

pronounced as separate initials: NRA for National Rifle Association, for instance. Many well-known acronyms and initial abbreviations come from business, government, and science: NASA, PBS, DNA, GE, UNICEF, AIDS, SAT.

As long as you can be sure your readers will understand them, you can use such abbreviations in much of your college writing. If you are using a term only once or twice, you should spell it out; but when you need to use a term repeatedly, abbreviating it will serve as a convenience for you and your readers alike. If the abbreviation may be unfamiliar to your readers, however, spell out the term at the first use, and give the abbreviation in parentheses. After that, you can use the abbreviation by itself.

> The Comprehensive Test Ban (CTB) Treaty was first proposed in the 1950s. For those nations signing it, the CTB would bring to a halt all nuclear-weapons testing.

www •

http://www.onelook.com/browse.shtml#all_acronym

Part of the OneLook Site *(<http://www.onelook.com/>), this collection of acronym dictionaries includes general interest, military, and Internet acronyms, and many other useful word search tools as well.*

37d Using other kinds of abbreviations

The following guidelines will help you use some other common abbreviations. Especially in science courses, however, you may also want to check with your instructor about special conventions for abbreviations in a particular field. In general, you should not use any type of abbreviation not discussed in this chapter in an academic writing assignment. For example:

▶ **The ~~bio~~ *biology* lab was deserted on ~~Fri.~~ *Friday* nights.**

Company names

Use such abbreviations as *Inc., Co.,* and *Corp.* and the ampersand (&) if they are part of a company's official name. You should not, however, use them in most other contexts.

▶ **Sears, Roebuck & Co. was the only big ~~corp.~~ *corporation* in town.**

Reference information

Though it is conventional to abbreviate such words as *chapter* (ch.), *page* (p.), or *pages* (pp.) in source citations, it is not conventional to do so in the body of a paper.

▶ **The preface to the 1851 ~~ed.~~ [edition] of *Twice-Told Tales* states that the stories are not autobiographical.**

Latin abbreviations

In general, avoid these abbreviations except when citing sources:

cf.	compare (*confer*)
e.g.	for example (*exempli gratia*)
et al.	and others (*et alia*)
etc.	and so forth (*et cetera*)
i.e.	that is (*id est*)
N.B.	note well (*nota bene*)

▶ **Many firms have policies to help working parents — ~~e.g.,~~ [for example,] flexible hours, parental leave, day care.**

Geographical terms and months

Place-names and months of the year are often abbreviated in source citations, but they should always be written out within sentences.

For examples of abbreviations in source citations, see Chapters 44 – 47

▶ **In ~~Aug.,~~ [August,] I moved from Lodi, ~~Calif.,~~ [California,] to ~~L.A.~~ [Los Angeles.]**

Common exceptions are *Washington, D.C.*, and *U.S.* The latter is acceptable as an adjective but not as a noun.

The *U.S. delegation* negotiated the treaty.

▶ **The exchange student enjoyed the ~~U.S.~~ [United States.]**

Symbols

Symbols such as ¢, #, %, +, and = should generally not be used in the body of a paper, though they are commonly used in graphs and tables. The dollar sign ($) is acceptable before specific figures, and the "at" sign (@) is used in Internet addresses.

▶ **Only 50~~%~~ [percent] of applicants are accepted.**

Units of measure

Except in scientific and technical writing, most units of measure should not be abbreviated in the body of a paper.

► **The ball sailed 425 ~~ft.~~ *feet* over the fence.**

EXERCISE 37.1

Revise each of the following sentences to eliminate any abbreviations that would be inappropriate in most academic writing. Example:

The population of the ~~U.S.~~ *United States* grew about 10~~%~~ *percent* in the 1980s.

1. The old NBC show is set in a fictional L.A. law firm.
2. An MX missile, which is 71 ft. long and 92 in. around, weighs 190,000 lbs.
3. The waiters prefer the A.M. shift because customers usually order just coffee, tea, doughnuts, etc.
4. Bill Bradley has been a U.S. sen. from NJ as well as a star of the NBA.
5. A large corp. like AT&T may help finance an employee's M.B.A.
6. Unfortunately, the five-¢ candy bar is a relic of the past.
7. Founded in 1966, NOW fights discrimination against women.
8. The local NPR station has a broadcast range of seventy-five mi.
9. After less than a yr. at U.Va., Poe left and joined the U.S. Army.
10. Dostoyevsky was influenced by many European writers — e.g., Dickens, Stendhal, and Balzac.

NUMBERS

37e Spelling out numbers

If a number can be written as one or two words, spell it out.

The victim's screams were heard by *thirty-eight* people, none of whom called the police.

Police arrested the assailant *six* days later.

When a sentence begins with a number, either spell out the number or rewrite the sentence.

INAPPROPRIATE 277,000 hours (or 119 years) of CIA labor cost taxpayers sixteen million dollars.

HARD TO READ Two hundred seventy-seven thousand hours (or 119 years) of CIA labor cost taxpayers sixteen million dollars.

REVISED Taxpayers spent sixteen million dollars for 277,000 hours (or 119 years) of CIA labor.

37f Using figures for numbers

Numbers that cannot be written in one or two words should be expressed in figures.

> Did you know that a baseball is wrapped in 174 yards of blue-gray wool yarn and is held together by 216 red stitches?

If one of several numbers of the same kind in the same sentence needs to be expressed in figures, all the numbers should be expressed that way.

▶ **A complete audio system can range in cost from ~~one hundred dollars~~** *$100* **to $2,599; however, a reliable system can be purchased for approximately ~~five hundred dollars.~~** *$500.*

37g Using figures according to convention

Conventions for expressing numbers vary from field to field, and you will want to make sure you understand the conventions of your own field — and follow them closely. For rules on using numbers in a particular discipline, the *MLA Handbook for Writers of Research Papers* or *The Chicago Manual of Style* is usually followed in the humanities; the *Publication Manual of the American Psychological Association,* in the social sciences; and the *CBE Style Manual: A Guide for Authors, Editors, and Publishers in the Biological Sciences,* in the natural sciences. The following examples show *MLA Handbook* style:

ADDRESSES

23 Main Street; 175 Fifth Avenue, New York, NY 10010

DATES

September 17, 1951; 4 B.C.; the 1860s; the sixties

DECIMALS, FRACTIONS, AND PERCENTAGES

65.34; 8½; 77 percent

DIVISIONS OF BOOKS AND PLAYS

volume 5, pages 81 – 85 (*not* 81 – 5)
Act III, Scene ii (*or* Act 3, Scene 2), lines 3 – 9

SPECIFIC AMOUNTS OF MONEY

$7,348; $1.46 trillion; $2.50; thirty-five cents

SCORES AND STATISTICS

an 8 – 3 Red Sox victory; a verbal score of 600
an average age of 22; a mean of 53; a ratio of 3 to 1

TIME OF DAY

6:00 A.M.; 5:45 P.M.; 12:01
five in the morning; four o'clock; four-thirty

EXERCISE 37.2

Revise the numbers in the following sentences as necessary for correctness and consistency. If a sentence is correct, circle its number. Example:

twenty-first
Does the ~~21st~~ century begin in 2000 or 2001?

1. 307 miles long and 82 miles wide, the island offered little of interest.
2. Time will provide perspective on the stock-market boom of the '90s.
3. You could travel around the city for only 65 cents.
4. The invasion of Kuwait began on August second, 1990.
5. The department received 1,633 calls and forty-three letters.
6. Cable TV is now available to seventy-two percent of the population.

7. Walker signed a three-year, $4.5-million contract.
8. In the 35-to-44 age group, the risk is estimated to be about 1 in 2,500.
9. The parents considered twenty-five cents enough for a five-year-old.
10. The amulet measured one and one-eighth by two and two-fifths inches.

THINKING CRITICALLY ABOUT ABBREVIATIONS AND NUMBERS

Reading with an Eye for Abbreviations and Numbers

The paragraph by Roger Angell at the end of Chapter 39 follows the style of the *New Yorker* magazine, which often spells out numbers in situations where this chapter recommends using figures. Read the paragraph carefully, and then consider whether it would have been easier to read if figures had been used for some of the numbers. If so, which ones? Then consider how the paragraph would have been different if Angell had used *semi-professional* instead of *semi-pro*. What effect does the abbreviated form create?

Thinking about Your Own Use of Abbreviations and Numbers

Look over an essay or two that you have written, noting all abbreviations and numbers. Check your usage for correctness, consistency, and appropriateness. If you discover anything you have done wrong, make a note of it (in your writing log, if you are keeping one) so that you will do it correctly the next time.

38 Using Italics

The slanted type known as *italics* is more than just a pretty typeface. Indeed, italics give words special meaning or emphasis. In the sentence "Many people read *People* on the subway every day," the italics (and the capital letter) tell us that *People* is a publication.

You may use a computer that produces italic type; if not, underline words that you would otherwise italicize. If neither italics nor underlining is available, as is sometimes the case in online communication, use asterisks before and after words you need to emphasize ("Her homepage *must* be updated") and the underscore symbol before and after other words you would normally italicize ("Have you read Bill Gates's _The Road Ahead_"?). ■

38a Using italics for titles

In general, italics are used to signal the titles of long or complete works; shorter works or sections of works are set off with quotation marks. (See 34b.) Use italics for the following kinds of works:

BOOKS	*Beloved*
CHOREOGRAPHIC WORKS	Agnes de Mille's *Rodeo*
FILMS AND VIDEOS	*Shine*
LONG MUSICAL WORKS	*Brandenburg Concertos*
LONG POEMS	*The Waste Land*
MAGAZINES AND JOURNALS	*Newsweek*, the *New England Journal of Medicine*
NEWSPAPERS	the Cleveland *Plain Dealer*, the *New York Times*
PAINTINGS AND SCULPTURE	Georgia O'Keeffe's *Black Iris*
PAMPHLETS	Thomas Paine's *Common Sense*
PLAYS	*Rent*
RADIO SERIES	*All Things Considered*
RECORDINGS	the Fugees' *The Score*
SOFTWARE AND WEB SITES	*Quicken*, *Purdue Online Writing Lab*
TELEVISION SERIES	*The Simpsons*

Note that sacred books, such as the Bible and the Koran, and public documents, such as the Constitution and the

- → Check that all titles of long or complete works are italicized. (38a)
- → If you refer to any words, letters, or numbers as words, make sure they are in italics. (38b)
- → Italicize any non-English words or phrases that are not in an English dictionary. (38c)
- → If you use italics to emphasize words, check to be sure you really need them. If so, use them sparingly. (38e)

Magna Carta, are *not* italicized. Notice also with magazines and newspapers that an initial *the* is neither italicized nor capitalized, even if part of the official name.

38b Using italics for words, letters, and numbers referred to as words

Italicize words, letters, or numbers referred to as words.

> What's vulgar? Some people might say that the contraction of the words *what* and *is* itself is vulgar. – JOSEPH EPSTEIN, "What Is Vulgar?"

> One characteristic of some New York speech is the absence of postvocalic *r*, with some New Yorkers, for example, pronouncing *four* as "fouh."

> The first four orbitals are represented by the letters *s, p, d,* and *f.*

> On the back of his jersey was the famous *24.*

38c Using italics for foreign words and phrases

Italicize words and phrases from other languages unless they are so frequently used by English speakers that they have come to be considered a part of English, such as the French word *bourgeois* and the Italian *pasta.* As a rule, if the word is in an English dictionary, it need not be italicized.

> At last one of the phantom sleighs gliding along the street would come to a stop, and with gawky haste Mr. Burness in his fox-furred *shapka* would make for our door. – VLADIMIR NABOKOV, *Speak, Memory*

Note that Latin genus and species names are always italicized.

> The caterpillars of *Hapalia,* when attacked by the wasp *Apanteles machaeralis,* drop suddenly from their leaves and suspend themselves in air by a silken thread. – STEPHEN JAY GOULD, "Nonmoral Nature"

38d Using italics for the names of vehicles

Italicize names of specific aircraft, spacecraft, ships, and trains. Do not italicize types and classes, such as Learjet, space shuttle, and Concorde.

AIRCRAFT AND SPACECRAFT	*Spirit of St. Louis, Discovery*
SHIPS	the *Santa Maria,* U.S.S. *Iowa*
TRAINS	the *Orient Express,* Amtrak's *Silver Star*

38e Using italics for special emphasis

Italics can help create emphasis in writing, but use them sparingly for this purpose. It is usually better to create emphasis with sentence structure and word choice.

> Great literature and a class of literate readers are nothing new in India. What is new is the emergence of a gifted generation of Indian writers *working in English.* – SALMAN RUSHDIE

www •

http://counterpoint.mit.edu/staff/writer/index.html

Counterpoint, *a journal from Wellesley and MIT, offers guidelines to writers who submit text via email. Go there for sound advice on when to use italics as well as unique advice on how to indicate when* italics *should be used.*

EXERCISE 38.1

In each of the following sentences, underline any words that should be italicized and circle any italicized words that should not be. Example:

Critics debated whether Thelma & Louise was a feminist film.

1. Hawthorne's story *My Kinsman, Major Molineux* bears a striking resemblance to Shakespeare's play A Midsummer Night's Dream.
2. Is Samuel Beckett's play Endgame a sequel to Shakespeare's King Lear?
3. Georgetown offers a *potpourri* of cultures and styles.
4. The word veterinary comes from the Latin *veterinarius.*
5. Niko Tinbergen's essay *The Bee-Hunters of Hulshorst* is a diary of experiments on *Philanthus triangulum Fabr,* the *bee-killer wasp.*
6. Flying the Glamorous Glennis, named for his wife, Chuck Yeager was the first pilot to fly faster than the speed of sound.

7. The Washington Post provides extensive coverage of Congress.
8. The Waste Land is a long and difficult but ultimately rewarding poem.
9. If you have seen only a reproduction of Picasso's Guernica, you can scarcely imagine the impact of the original painting.
10. The White Star liner Titanic sank in the North Atlantic in 1912.

THINKING CRITICALLY ABOUT ITALICS

Reading with an Eye for Italics

The following passage about a graduate English seminar uses italics in several different ways — for emphasis, for a foreign phrase, and for a title. Read the passage carefully, particularly noting the effects created by the italics. How would it differ without any italic emphasis? What other words or phrases might the author have italicized?

> To get into this seminar, you had to submit to a grilling wherein you renounced all former allegiance to the then-current literary religion, New Criticism, which considered that only the text existed, not the world. I passed the interview by lying — cunningly, and against my real convictions. I said that probably the world *did* exist — and walked triumphantly into the seminar room.
>
> There were four big tables arranged in a square, with everyone's feet sticking out into the open middle of the square. You could tell who was nervous, and how much, by watching the pairs of feet twist around each other. The Great Man presided awesomely from the high bar of the square. His head was a majestic granite-gray, like a centurion in command; he *looked* famous. His clean shoes twitched only slightly, and only when he was angry.
>
> It turned out he was angry at me a lot of the time. He was angry because he thought me a disrupter, a rioter, a provocateur, and a fool; also crazy. And this was twenty years ago, before these things were *de rigueur* in the universities. Everything was very quiet in those days: there were only the Cold War and Korea and Joe McCarthy and the Old Old Nixon, and the only revolutionaries around were in Henry James's *The Princess Casamassima.*
>
> – CYNTHIA OZICK, "We Are the Crazy Lady"

Thinking about Your Own Use of Italics

Write a paragraph or two describing the most eccentric person you know. Make a point of italicizing some words for special emphasis. Read your passage aloud to hear the effect of the italics. Consider italicizing any other words you wish to emphasize. Now explain each use of italics, stating in words the reason for them. If you find yourself unable to give a reason, ask yourself whether the word should in fact be italicized at all.

Then revise the passage to eliminate *all but one* use of italics. Try revising sentences and choosing more precise words to convey emphasis without italics. Compare the two versions, and decide which is more effective. Can you reach any conclusions about using italics for emphasis?

39 Using Hyphens

Hyphens show up every time you listen to hip-hop, wear a T-shirt, make a left-hand turn, eat Tex-Mex food, get one-on-one tutoring, or worry about a long-term relationship. Sometimes the dictionary will tell you whether to hyphenate a word. Other times, you will have to apply some general rules or think about your intended meaning.

As Hall of Fame pitcher Jim Palmer once said, "The difference between *re-sign* and *resign* is a hyphen." This statement, heard on a televised baseball game, shows how important a hyphen can be. This chapter will help you use hyphens appropriately and correctly. ■

39a Using hyphens to divide words at the end of a line

It is best not to divide words between lines, but when you must do so, break words between syllables. The word *metaphor,* for instance, is made up of three syllables (*met-a-phor*), and you could break it after either the *t* or the *a*. All dictionaries show syllable breaks, so the best advice for dividing words correctly is simply to look them up. In addition, you should follow certain other conventions.

- *Never divide one-syllable words,* even relatively long words.
- *Divide compound words only between the parts.* Words such as *anklebone* or *mother-in-law* should be broken between their parts (*ankle-bone*) or at their hyphens (*mother-in-law*).
- *Divide words with prefixes or suffixes after the prefix or before the suffix.* The word *disappearance,* then, might be broken as *dis-appearance* or *disappear-ance.* Prefixed or suffixed words that include a hyphen, such as *self-righteous* or *mayor-elect,* should be divided at the hyphen.
- *Never divide abbreviations, contractions, or figures.* Though such "words" as *NASA, didn't,* and *150,000* have audible syllables, do not divide them in writing.
- *Leave at least two letters on each line when dividing a word.* Words such as *acorn* (*a-corn*) or *scratchy* (*scratch-y*) may not be divided at all, and a word such as *Americana* (*A-mer-i-can-a*) can be broken only after the *r* or *i.*

→ Check that words broken at the end of a line are divided at an appropriate point. (39a)
→ Double-check compound words to be sure they are properly closed up, separated, or hyphenated. If in doubt, consult a dictionary. (39b)
→ Check all terms that have prefixes or suffixes to see whether you need hyphens. (39c)

EXERCISE 39.1

Divide each of the following words into syllables, first referring to your dictionary. Then indicate with a hyphen the places where you might break each word at the end of a line. Indicate any words that cannot be divided into syllables or broken at the end of a line.

1. passable
2. retract
3. stripped
4. military
5. antechamber
6. inner-directed
7. haven't
8. dimming
9. anonymous
10. attitude

39b Using hyphens with compound words

Compound words are made up of more than one word. Some compounds are written as one word (*rowboat*), some as separate words (*floppy disc*), and some with hyphens (*up-to-date*). In general, consult a dictionary if you have any doubt about how to spell a compound. There are, in addition, some conventions that can guide you in using hyphens with compound words.

www •

http://www.computertips.com/

This Computer Tips *site exists to help you find answers to computer-use problems. If turning the automatic hyphenating function of your word processor on and off is a problem, go to this site and use the word* hyphenating *as a search term to get help.*

Compound adjectives

Often you will use adjectives made up of word combinations that are not listed in a dictionary. The guiding principle then is to hyphenate most compound adjectives that precede a noun but not those that follow a noun.

a *well-liked* boss	My boss is *well liked.*
a *six-foot* plank	The plank is *six feet* long.

In general, the reason for hyphenating such compound adjectives is to facilitate reading.

► **The designers used potted palms as living-room dividers.**

Without the hyphen, *living* may seem to modify *room dividers.*

Commonly used compound adjectives do not usually need to be hyphenated for clarity – *income tax reform* or *first class mail* would seldom if ever be misunderstood. Never hyphenate a combination of an adverb ending in *-ly* and an adjective: *a radically different approach.*

Compound adjectives formed from compound proper nouns are hyphenated if the noun is hyphenated: *Austro-Hungarian history*, but *Latin American literature.*

Coined compounds

You may sometimes want to use hyphens to link words that would not normally be hyphenated but that you are using in an unexpected way, especially as an adjective. Such combinations are called **coined compounds.**

It was an established Daddy-said-so fact. . . .

Before it reached the top of the porch it went off, a piece of tin shot God-is-whipping-you straight for Eddy's eye. – MAXINE CLAIR, "Cherry Bomb"

Fractions and compound numbers

To write out fractions, use a hyphen to join the numerator and denominator. Also use hyphens to spell out whole numbers from twenty-one to ninety-nine, both when they stand alone and when they are part of larger numbers. (Usually such larger numbers should be written as numerals.)

one-seventh	thirty-seven
seven-sixteenths	three hundred fifty-four thousand

Suspended hyphens

A series of compound words that share the same base word can be shortened by the use of suspended hyphens.

Each student should do the work *him-* or *herself.*

39c Using hyphens with prefixes and suffixes

Most words with prefixes or suffixes are written without hyphens: *antiwar, gorillalike.* Only in the following cases do you need a hyphen:

WITH CAPITALIZED BASE WORDS

pro-Clinton, un-American, non-Catholic

WITH FIGURES

pre-1960, post-1945

WITH CERTAIN PREFIXES AND SUFFIXES

all-state, self-possessed, quasi-legislative, mayor-elect, fifty-odd

Hyphens are also used with *ex-* and *-some* when these mean "former" and "approximately," respectively: *ex-husband, twenty-some.*

WITH COMPOUND WORDS

pre-high school, pro-civil rights, post-cold war

FOR CLARITY OR EASE OF READING

re-cover, anti-inflation, troll-like

Re-cover means "cover again"; the hyphen distinguishes it from *recover,* meaning "get well." In *anti-inflation* and *troll-like,* the hyphens separate confusing clusters of vowels and consonants.

EXERCISE 39.2

Using the dictionary as a reference, insert hyphens as needed.

1. deescalate
2. pre World War II
3. pre and post-Wall Berlin
4. happily married couple
5. a what me worry look
6. self important
7. president elect
8. seven hundred thirty three
9. a hard working farmer
10. a politician who is fast talking

EXERCISE 39.3

Insert or delete hyphens as necessary, and correct any incorrect word divisions in the following sentences. Use your dictionary if necessary.

1. Stress can lead to hypertension and ulcers.

2. The drum-beating and hand-clapping signaled that the parade was near.
3. The carpenter asked for a two pound bag of three quarter inch nails.
4. Suicide among teen-agers has tripled in the past thirty five years.
5. We urged him to be open minded and to temper his insensitive views.
6. Both pro and antiState Department groups registered complaints.
7. One of Mikhail Baryshnikov's favorite dancers was none other than Fred A-staire.
8. In Bizet's *Carmen,* the ill-fated Carmen is betrayed by her fickle-ness.
9. The governor elect joked about the preelection polls.
10. The beautifully-written essay earned high praise.

THINKING CRITICALLY ABOUT HYPHENATION

The following paragraph uses many hyphens. Read it carefully, and note how the hyphens make the paragraph easier to read. Why do you think *semi-pro* is hyphenated? Why is *junior-college* hyphenated in the last sentence?

> All semi-pro leagues, it should be understood, are self-sustaining, and have no farm affiliation or other connection with the twenty-six major-league clubs, or with the seventeen leagues and hundred and fifty-two teams . . . that make up the National Association – the minors, that is. There is no central body of semi-pro teams, and semi-pro players are not included among the six hundred and fifty major-leaguers, the twenty-five-hundred-odd minor-leaguers, plus all the managers, coaches, presidents, commissioners, front-office people, and scouts, who, taken together, constitute the great tent called organized ball. (A much diminished tent, at that; back in 1949, the minors included fifty-nine leagues, about four hundred and forty-eight teams, and perhaps ten thousand players.) Also outside the tent, but perhaps within its shade, are five college leagues, ranging across the country from Cape Cod to Alaska, where the most promising freshman, sophomore, and junior-college ballplayers . . . compete against each other. . . .
>
> – Roger Angell, "In the Country"

PART 8

DOING RESEARCH AND USING SOURCES

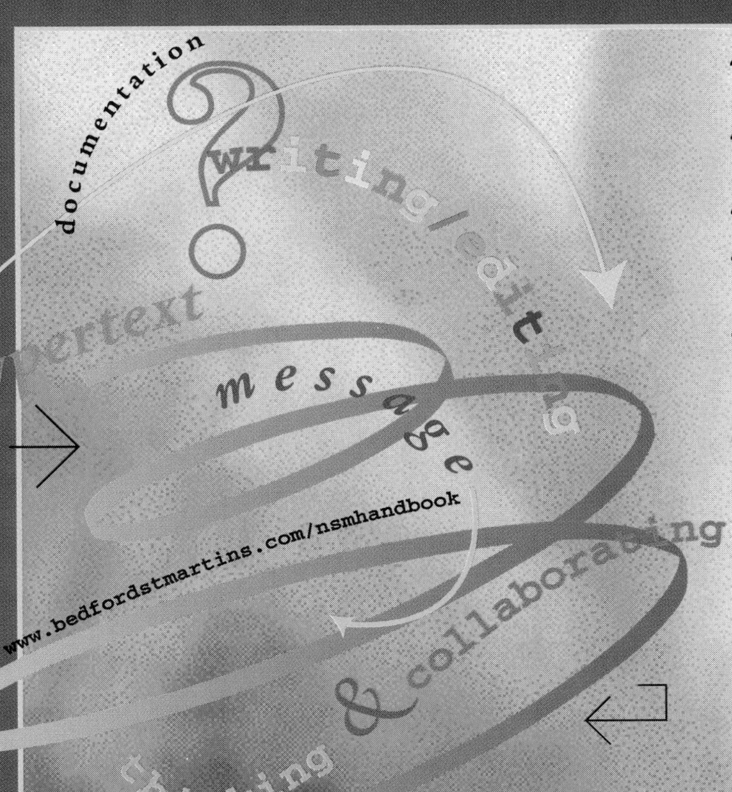

FAQ ....→

FAQ: Research Online

How do you gain access to the Internet?

In addition to a computer, you'll need two basic tools: a MODEM and a BROWSER, such as Netscape Navigator, Lynx, Mosaic, or Microsoft Explorer. Then you'll need an INTERNET service provider (ISP) — a school computing center, telephone or cable company, or other communal or government service — to connect your computer to the Internet and provide you with a USERNAME and password. Your campus computer lab is a good place to find people who can help you get started. For establishing your own Internet connection, check out the *Internet Starter Kit* by Adam Engst, a text that has versions for both Mac and Windows. It is available online at:

<http://www.mcp.com/hayden/iskm/iskw2/index.html>
for Windows

<http://www.mcp.com/hayden/iskm/iskm3/index.html>
for Mac

Where can you get more information and detailed help on navigating the Internet and the Web?

Check out Andrew Harnack and Eugene Kleppinger's *Online! A Reference Guide to Using Internet Sources.* An online version is also available:

<http://www.smpcollege.com/online-4styles~help>

Another helpful online source can be found at:

<http://www.yahoo.com/Computers_and_Internet/World_Wide_Web>

How do you do online research efficiently?

Narrow your topic, and then come up with a list of specific KEYWORDS as soon as possible. Rather than searching for instances of a broad term like *cancer,* for example — which would call up thousands of possibilities — begin with the most specific topic you can, such as "metastatic colon cancer in teenagers."

How do you begin searching the Web?

Start by choosing the most appropriate and efficient SEARCH ENGINES for your topic; you can find a catalog of all search engines listed by category at <www.search.com>.

- **Subject Directory Search Engines.** The following sources index WORLD WIDE WEB contents by subject and are especially helpful if you need to narrow a general topic to a specific subtopic.

Yahoo! offers links to various fields (art, education, sports, and so on):

<http://www.yahoo.com>

The *Internet Services List* offers links in alphabetical order, from agriculture to the Web:

<http://www.spectracom/islist>

WWW Virtual Library provides links to Library of Congress topics:

<http://www.w3.~org/pub/DataSources/bySubject/Overview.html>

The Library of Congress WorldWideWeb HomePage provides links to information on all Internet sources:

<http://lcweb.loc.gov>

- **Text Index Search Engines.** The following tools help you look for specific keywords and give links to documents containing those words. These engines are particularly helpful when you have already carefully limited your topic.

  AltaVista is huge, indexing millions of WEB PAGES and NEWSGROUP messages; it allows you to search for a single term or for terms in combinations:

  <http://altavista.digital.com>

  Other popular and user-friendly engines include:

  ***Excite* <http://www.excite.com>**

  ***HotBot* <http://www.hotbot.com>**

  ***Infoseek* <http://guide.infoseek.com>**

  ***Lycos* <http://www.lycos.com>**

  ***Net Search* <http://home.netscape.com/home/internet-search/html>**

  ***WebCrawler* <http://webcrawler.com>**

How do you evaluate online sources?

Because almost anything — regardless of quality — may be published on the Internet and the Web, online research calls for very careful evaluation of sources. The questions that follow will help you assess online sources.

- **Authorship.** Who is the author of this site? What are the author's credentials? Who or what does the author represent? Check for a HYPERLINK to information about the author and for information at the bottom of a Web page. Also try entering the author's name in a search engine to see what links it provides; if the author has a HOMEPAGE, you'll find it this way. On Usenet, you can try using DejaNews to search for other messages written by the author.

- **Sponsor.** Who sponsors the site? Read the Web address for clues. If a comparative review of new VCRs, for example, gives an address of <maritav@mitsubishi.com>, the review *may* favor Mitsubishi products. The final suffix in a DOMAIN NAME also tells something about the kind of group sponsoring the site.

  .com (commercial)

  .org (nonprofit organizations)

  .edu (educational institutions, usually universities)

  .gov (government agencies)

  .mil (military groups)

  .net (networks)

  Note also that geographical domains indicate country of origin: .ca (Canada), .IE (Republic of Ireland), and so on.
- **Links to Other Sources.** Does the site provide references and links to other sources? If possible, check out those sources.
- **Verifiability and Currency.** Can the information in the site be verified? How accurate and complete is the information? How current is it? Many sites include links to the sources of their information; check these out whenever possible. Remember, too, that the date when a source is posted is *not* necessarily the date when it was composed. Sites with no date are generally less reliable than those that are updated regularly.

Do you need permission to use online texts, graphics, or images in your own work?

The concept of "fair use" in copyright law allows you to use brief excerpts of copyrighted material (generally 300 words from a book, 150 words from an article, or 4 lines from a poem — or even more if your work is for a class and not intended to be "published"), as long as you provide a full citation. To cite personal communications such as EMAIL or for LISTSERV POSTINGS, however, you should ask permission of the writer before you include any of his or her material in your own text. To use someone else's graphics or images in your text, it is safest to request permission from the creator or owner. Here are two sample email permission requests:

MAIL TO: litman@mindspring.com
CC TO: lunsford.2@osu.edu
SUBJECT: Request for permission

Dear Professor Litman:

I am writing to request permission to quote from your essay, "Copyright, Owners' Rights, and Users' Privileges on the Internet: Implied Licenses, Caching, Linking, Fair Use, and Sign-on Licenses." I want to quote some of your work in a hypertext essay I am writing for students in my composition class in order to explain the complex debates over ownership on the Internet and to argue that students in my class should be participating in these debates. My essay, like all the others in my class, will be linked to our class Web page. I will give full credit to you and will cite the URL where I first found your work: <http://www.msen.com/~litman/dayton/htm>.

Please let me know if you are willing to grant me permission to quote from your essay. Thank you very much for considering my request.

Raul Sanchez <sanchez.32@osu.edu>

MAIL TO: fridanet@aol.com
CC TO: lunsford.2@osu.edu
SUBJECT: Request for permission

Dear Kimberley Masters:

I am a student at Ohio State University and am writing to request your permission to download and use your photograph of Frida Kahlo in a three-piece suit <fridanet/suit.htm#top>. This illustration would be used in a project I and two other students are working on for members of our composition class about the later work of Frida Kahlo. In the report on our project, which we will post on our class's Web page, we will cite <http://members.aol.com/fridanet/kahlo.htm> as the URL, unless you want us to use a different source.

Thank you very much for considering our request.

Jennifer Fox <fox.360@osu.edu>

In all cases, remember the difference between the fair use of a document for an assignment that you will submit to a teacher and classmates and one that you will post or publish on the Internet or in print. For your class, you might include the text of an entire song in an essay, but you cannot put such an essay — with the copyrighted song — on the Internet without infringing on the rights of the copyright owner.

http://www.onlineinc.com/onlinemag/MayOL/zorn5.html

For advice on doing online research, consult Great Web Searching: Tricks of the Trade, *by Peggy Zorn, Mary Emanoil, Luc Marshall, and Mary Panek.*

http://www.marlboro.edu/~nickc/research/evallist.html

Mary D. Been provides a list of Web Site Evaluation Guides.

http://www.cohums.ohio-state.edu/english/People/Locker.1/research.htm

Professor Kitty Locker's Doing Research on the Web, *which is linked to her homepage, provides useful step-by-step guidance to online research.*

http://www.apa.org/journals/webref.html

The APA Web Site *contains a link to student FAQs that can help you cite information from the Web using APA style.*

http://www.smpcollege.com/online-4styles~help/toc.html

The electronic version of Andrew Harnack and Eugene Kleppinger's Online! *provides guidelines for documenting online sources using four different styles — MLA, APA, Chicago, and CBE.*

http://www.cas.usf.edu/english/walker.mla.html

Janice Walker also provides Citations of Electronic Sources.

http://www.nlc-bnc.ca/ifla/I/training/citation/citing.htm

Eric Crump offers a list of Citation Guides for Electronic Documents.

What if page numbers aren't included in an online source you want to cite?

If the source has internal divisions such as parts, paragraphs, or screens, you can include the number or name of the division(s) you are citing, such as (Selfe, par. 8) or (Selfe, abstract). But be careful not to list divisions that come from your browsing software. Here are some additional examples, following MLA style (see Chapter 44):

> As Richard deCordova notes in a memorable phrase, the studios wanted to convince millions of moviegoers that "the real hero behave[d] just like the reel hero" (qtd. in Gallagher, part 2).
>
> Brian Gallagher cites a remark by Cary Grant that sums up the strain many stars must have felt: "Everybody wants to be Cary Grant. Even I want to be Cary Grant" (part 3).

Here is the works-cited entry for these citations:

> Gallagher, Brian. "Some Historical Paradoxes of Stardom in the American Film Industry, 1910-1960." Images: A Journal of Film and Popular Culture 3 (1997): 7 parts. 7 Aug. 1997 <http://www.qni.com/~ijournal/issue03/infocus/stars1.htm>.

How do you cite texts that may exist in different versions or that are subject to change?

If possible, include the *date of print publication,* if any; the *publication date on the Web* – sometimes a version number or revision date; and the *date you accessed the document.* This information lets readers know that any material you used was part of the document on the date you accessed it – and it allows them to look at other versions to see whether changes have occurred.

> Brewer, E. Cobham. The Dictionary of Phrase and Fable. London, 1894. 1996. Bibliomania. 9 Oct. 1997 <http://www.bibliomania.com/Reference/PhraseAndFable/>.

Becoming a Researcher

40

Research is formalized curiosity. It is poking and prying with a purpose.

– Zora Neale Hurston

Research provides the primary way of exploring a subject. As the editors of a famous encyclopedia put it, without research, "no authoritative words could have been written, no scientific discoveries or inventions made, no theories of any value propounded."

Work in many professions – engineering, news reporting, law, medicine, criminal justice – relies heavily on research. But the process of investigating sources, compiling data, and drawing conclusions pervades our personal lives as well as our work. We find something out, and then we act on it. This chapter and the three that follow will help you understand and carry out the process of academic research. ■

40a Understanding the research process

This chapter rests on the assumption that we are all researchers. From this basic assumption come five important premises.

1. *You already know how to do research.* You act as a researcher whenever you investigate something – whether a college, a course, a cosmetic, a computer, or a car – by reading up on it, discussing its features with your friends or with experts, or perhaps checking several stores to see what is in stock and how much it costs. Therefore, you already have essential research skills. You know how to combine experience, observation, and new information when you solve a problem, answer a question, make a decision, analyze a situation, or make an "educated guess."

2. *Good research makes you a genuine expert.* If you approach your research with serious intent, you may gradually become someone who knows more than anyone else on campus about new uses for metal hybrids or Jackie Robinson's place in sports history. And you will be able to add your knowledge to the educated conversation taking place all around you.

3. *Research is usually driven by a purpose.* Research is rarely an end in itself. Whether for common everyday needs or in an academic setting, researchers seek out facts and opinions for a reason – to make a discovery; to

answer a question, solve a problem, or prove something; to teach; or to advocate a position. Your main purpose in college research will most often be to fulfill a specific assignment: for example, to compare literary texts, to trace the causes of the Civil War, or to survey and summarize students' feelings about mandatory drug testing of athletes. Sometimes, however, you may be asked to determine your own purpose for research.

4. *Your purpose influences the research you do, which in turn refines your purpose.* When you begin any research, it is impossible to know exactly what you will find out. The evidence you gather, for example, may prove so startling that it calls for you to persuade – to advocate a solution to a problem – when you originally had meant only to explain the problem. In turn, as you refine your purpose, that purpose will help guide you in choosing additional sources and organizing material.

5. *Research rarely progresses in a neat line from start to finish.* You begin with a question that you may or may not be able to answer. Then your background research and investigation may lead you to start all over – or to refer to other sources. This additional research may focus your idea even more, leading you to more specific sources – or it may lead you to change directions yet again. Wherever the process takes you, however, your overriding goal remains the same: to develop a strong critical understanding of the information you are gathering.

www •

http://www.mbnet.mb.ca/~mstimson/

This site clusters resources under steps in the research process, among them Wondering, Seeking, and Choosing. Even though it was designed for elementary and high school students, many of the links will prove most useful for the college researcher as well.

One student's experience illustrates how ideas can change and develop during the research process. Assigned to write an essay on any topic, he began by puzzling over whether modern rock-guitar styles could be traced to the electric-guitar styles developed in the 1940s and 1950s by Chicago blues groups. Starting with background reading about modern rock guitarists such as Eric Clapton and Pete Townshend, he found repeated references to Muddy Waters, Howlin' Wolf, Buddy Guy, Albert King, and other Chicago blues artists. He listened to a number of records and found repeated riffs (musical phrases) and clear derivations. And he began to make notes for an essay.

Then, in several sources on the Chicago electric blues tradition, the student found references to country blues and southern race records as influences on the Chicago artists. He was not sure what these terms meant, but then he discovered that blues music harks back to nineteenth-century slave songs, that country blues was nearly always played on a single acoustic guitar, and that the history of country blues guitar styles traces back to the 1920s. Clearly the story was older and the traditions deeper than he had imagined.

The student then searched the Internet using keywords and found a number of Web sites with information about southern and country blues musicians of the 1920s and 1930s like Leadbelly and Mississippi John Hurt. He began to consider the differences between electric and acoustic instruments. Finally, he looked for recordings by some of the early country blues musicians. To his amazement, he heard on these early recordings some of the exact riffs and techniques he so admired in the work of contemporary guitarists.

Thus did this student arrive at a deeper idea to develop, a far better grasp of music history, and more research sources. He had also accumulated enough information to begin crafting a fine essay.

Research for writing

College research may range from a couple of hours spent gathering background about a topic for a brief essay to weeks or months of full-scale exploration for a term paper. Chapters 40 – 45 provide guidelines to help you with *any* research done for the purpose of writing. In addition, Chapters 40 – 43 show examples of work by Shannan Palma, a student whose complete essay appears in Chapter 44. An additional complete essay appears in Chapter 45.

40b Analyzing a research assignment

Before you begin research in response to a writing assignment, be sure you understand the requirements and limits of the assignment. For an introductory writing course, Shannan Palma received the following assignment:

> Choose a subject of interest to you, and use it as the basis for a research essay that makes and substantiates a claim.

Pay close attention to the exact wording of the assignment. If it asks you to choose your own topic, consider any requirements for purpose, audience, scope of research, and length as you do so. Then try to map out a rough schedule for your research, consulting the one on p. 439.

For more on choosing topics, see 40c.

In response to questions, Shannan Palma's instructor clarified some requirements of the assignment: the essay should use information from both print and online sources to support the claim; it should be roughly ten to fifteen pages in length; and it should be written for members of the writing class.

Identifying the purpose

Read through the assignment for **cue words,** such as *describe, survey, analyze, explain, classify, compare,* or *contrast,* that specify the pattern the essay is to follow. What do such words mean in this field? Keeping these meanings in mind as you begin researching will help you identify sources that are appropriate for your purpose.

For a discussion of ways to assess purpose, see 2d.

Identifying the audience

Find out whether your assignment specifies an audience other than the instructor. Then answer the following questions:

- Who will be interested in the information you gather, and why?
- What do you know about their backgrounds?
- What will they want to know? What will they already know?
- What response do you want to elicit from them?
- What assumptions might they hold about the topic?
- What kinds of evidence will you need to present to convince them?
- What will your instructor expect in a strong essay on this topic?

For additional questions to consider about your audience, see 2h.

Considering your rhetorical stance

Think about your own attitude toward your topic, your stance. Are you just curious about it? Do you like it? dislike it? find it bewildering? What influences have shaped your stance?

For additional questions to consider about your rhetorical stance, see 2g.

Gauging the scope of your research

Next consider the kind of research you will need to do. Does the assignment specify how many or what kind(s) of library sources you should use? Does it suggest any field research – interviewing, surveying, or observing? Will the Web be a good (or bad) place to look?

Noting the length of the essay

The amount of research and writing time you need for a five-page essay differs markedly from that for a fifteen-page essay. And you may need more time if materials are not available or if you discover that you must do more research. The best plan is to begin work as soon as possible.

Working toward the deadline

When is the project due? Are any preliminary materials – a working bibliography, a thesis, an outline, a first draft – due before this date?

Keeping a research log

You might set up a **research log** – either print or electronic – for keeping track of your work. In the log, jot down thoughts about your topic, lists of things to do, and ideas about possible sources, and keep track of library materials.

SCHEDULING A RESEARCH PROJECT

Assignment date: ________ Try to do by:

Analyze assignment; decide on primary purpose and audience; choose topic if necessary. ________

Arrange library time; decide on keywords, and develop search strategy. ________

Do background reading and online searches; narrow topic if necessary. ________

Decide on research question, tentative hypothesis. ________

Start working bibliography; track down sources in the library and online. ________

Develop working thesis and rough outline. ________

If necessary, conduct interviews, make observations, or distribute and collect questionnaires. ________

Read and evaluate sources; take notes. ________

Draft explicit thesis and outline. ________

Prepare first draft. ________

Obtain and evaluate critical responses. ________

Do more research if necessary. ________

Revise draft; prepare list of works cited. ________

Edit revised draft; use spell checker if available. ________

Prepare final draft. ________

Do final proofreading. ________

Final draft due: ________

www •

http://www.csbsju.edu/advising/helplist.html

From the academic advising office of the College of St. Benedict/St. John's University comes this site full of study skills advice and with 21 links to tips on time management, taking an essay exam, effective reading and note-taking, and other academic skills.

40c Choosing a topic

If your assignment does not specify a topic, you can best begin articulating one by keeping in mind any specifications about purpose, audience, scope, length, and deadline and by considering the following questions:

- What subjects do you know something about?
- What subjects might you like to become an expert on?
- What subjects evoke a strong reaction from you – intense attraction, puzzlement, or skepticism?

In addition, do some surfing on the Internet, or skim through your textbooks or class notes, current magazines or journals, or standard reference works, looking for some topic or question that intrigues you. You may find the techniques presented in 3a for exploring a topic useful for discovering one. Even if your instructor has assigned a broad topic, these questions and methods may help you decide what aspect of it to research.

Getting responses to your topic

When you have a topic, describe it in several sentences. Then try to get responses from your instructor and some classmates by asking the following questions:

- Would you be interested in reading about this topic?
- Does the topic seem manageable?
- Can you suggest any interesting angles or approaches?
- Can you suggest any good sources of information on this topic?

www •

http://www.ipl.org/teen/aplus/stepfirst.htm

From the Internet Public Library comes this site that offers a step by step approach to doing research. This page focuses on the beginning of research: preparing the assignment, discovering information, formulating a thesis, and gathering information. This site has many useful links.

40d Narrowing and focusing a topic

Any topic you choose to research must be manageable – must suit the scope, audience, length, and time limits of your assignment. Making a topic manageable often requires narrowing it, but narrowing is not always sufficient in itself. Rather than simply reducing a large subject to a smaller one, then, *focus* on a particular slant, looking for a governing question to guide your research. One good way to work toward such a question is by brainstorming to generate a series of questions you might ask about your topic. You can then evaluate them and choose one or two that seem most interesting and most manageable.

Shannan Palma knew that she wanted to study changes in the ideal of the hero in U.S. movies, and she originally wanted to discuss this topic in the context of social and economic changes in the United States in the second half of the twentieth century. In working on this angle, however, she realized that doing justice to the social and economic contexts would more than double the length of her essay. She decided, therefore, to narrow her focus and concentrate solely on movies and heroes.

Asking a research question and developing a hypothesis

The result of the focusing process is a **research question** that can be tentatively answered by a **hypothesis,** a statement of what you anticipate your research will show. Like a working thesis, a hypothesis must be not only manageable but interesting and specific. In addition, it must be arguable, a debatable proposition that can be proved or disproved by research evidence. For example, a statement like this one is not arguable since it merely states a widely known fact: "Senator Joseph McCarthy attracted great attention with his anti-Communist crusade during the 1950s." On the other hand, this statement is an arguable hypothesis since it can be proved or disproved: "Roy Cohn's political views and biased research while he was an assistant to Senator Joseph McCarthy were largely responsible for McCarthy's anti-Communist crusade."

For a discussion of a working thesis, see 3b.

In moving from a general topic of interest, such as Senator Joseph McCarthy's anti-Communist crusade of the 1950s, to a useful hypothesis, such as the one in the previous paragraph, you first focus on a single manageable issue, such as Roy Cohn's role in the crusade. After background reading, you then raise a question about that issue ("To what extent did Cohn's political views and research contribute to McCarthy's crusade?") and devise a possible answer, your hypothesis.

For more on judging whether a hypothesis is arguable, see 5b2.

Here is how Shannan Palma moved from general topic to hypothesis:

TOPIC Heroes in U.S. films

ISSUE Changes in heroes in U.S. films

RESEARCH QUESTION How have heroes changed since they found a home in Hollywood?

HYPOTHESIS As real-life heroes have been dethroned in popular U.S. culture over the last century, so have film heroes, and current films suggest that the hero may not have a future at all.

The hypothesis that tentatively answers the research question is precise enough to be supported or challenged by a manageable amount of research.

40e Investigating what you already know about your topic

Once you have narrowed and focused a topic, you need to marshal everything you already know about it. Here are some strategies for doing so:

- *Brainstorming.* Take five minutes to list, in words or phrases, everything you think of or wonder about your hypothesis. You may find it helpful to do this in a group, with other students. (See 3a1.)
- *Freewriting in favor of your hypothesis.* For five minutes, write about every reason for believing your hypothesis is true. (See 3a2.)
- *Freewriting in opposition to your hypothesis.* For five minutes, write down every argument you can think of, no matter how weak or improbable, that someone opposed to your hypothesis might make.
- *Freewriting about your audience.* Write for five minutes about your readers, including your instructor. What do you think they currently believe about your topic? What sorts of evidence will convince them to accept your hypothesis? What sorts of sources will they respect?
- *Tapping your memory for sources.* List everything you can remember about *where* you learned about your topic: computer bulletin boards, email, books, magazines, courses, conversations, television. Much of what you know may seem like common knowledge, but common knowledge comes from somewhere, and "somewhere" can serve as a starting point for investigation.

40f Moving from hypothesis to working thesis

As you gather information and begin reading sources, your research question is likely to be refined, and your hypothesis is likely to change significantly. Only after you have explored it, tested it, and sharpened it by reading and writing does the hypothesis become a **working thesis.**

In Shannan Palma's case, she found that her hypothesis that the hero has no future in U.S. films did not hold up after her full examination of contemporary films. Thus she shifted her attention to what forms future heroes might take and developed the following working thesis: "Although a case of mistaken identity dealt a near-fatal blow to the hero in U.S. films, a study of recent movies suggests that the hero lives on – in two startlingly different forms."

In doing your own research, you may find that your interest shifts, that a whole line of inquiry is unproductive, that a work you need in order to complete an argument is not available, or that your hypothesis is simply wrong. In each case, the process of research pushes you to learn more and more about your hypothesis, to make it more focused and more precise, to become an expert on your topic.

THINKING CRITICALLY ABOUT RESEARCH

If you have done research for an essay before, go back and evaluate the work you did as a researcher and as a writer in light of the principles developed in this chapter. What was the purpose of the research? Who was your audience? How was your topic focused? What kinds of sources did you use? What about your research and your essay pleased you most? What pleased you least? What would you do differently if you were to revise the essay now?

41 Conducting Research

A few minutes' thought may bring to mind some piece of everyday research you have done. One couple we know with a passion for ice cream, for instance, wanted to write an article for a local magazine on the best ice cream in their city. Their guiding research questions ("Who has the best ice cream in town, and what makes it the best?") led them first to the library, where they did background reading on the history of ice cream and the way it is made, and later to the World Wide Web, where they searched for discussion groups for ice-cream lovers. Finally, they went into the field, systematically tasting ice cream at many stores and interviewing local ice-cream makers. This chapter offers advice for doing all of these three basic kinds of research — in the library, on the Internet, and in the field. ■

41a Beginning to explore library and database resources

The library is one of a researcher's best friends, especially in an age of electronic communication. Your college library houses a great number of print materials: books, journals and periodicals, reference works of all kinds. In addition, computer terminals there will give you access to electronic catalogs and indexes – and access to many other libraries via the Internet. You can best begin a research project, then, by acquainting yourself with the resources in your own particular library. How are its holdings cataloged? What encyclopedias, indexes, and databases can you search in the library on CD-ROM? What online databases and other archives (such as the index to the *New York Times*) are available to you there?

If you have your own computer and an Internet connection, you can do some of your research from home. In addition, you can probably access the library from computers in computer labs on campus; if you don't have your own computer, find these labs and make a note of their hours.

When Shannan Palma, the student whose research project we followed in Chapter 40, began her research, she spent several hours in the campus library, learning how to use the circulation computer and how to gain access to the Internet from the library's terminals. She discovered that her library provides a free instructional program for students that is full of lessons, examples, and guides for those learning to use the Internet for research. In addition, she spoke with a reference librarian about collections in the library related to the history of film. Your college library probably has similar programs and services: check them out.

DIRECTORY OF LIBRARY RESOURCES

guides to reference books and databases (41b2, c, and e)
encyclopedias (41c)
biographical resources (41c)
almanacs, yearbooks, and atlases (41c)
book indexes (41c)
periodical indexes (41c)
library catalog (41d)
vertical file (41d)
special collections (41d)
audio and video collections (41d)
art collections (41d)
interlibrary loans (41d)
Internet and World Wide Web (41f and g)
computer databases (41e)

41b Developing a research strategy

Especially in an age of information, having a set of clear research strategies is invaluable to any researcher.

1 Thinking about the kinds of sources you need

Where should you begin your research? with an overview, looking first at an encyclopedia? with the library catalog and periodical indexes? with a

Web search? Before you plunge into your research project, ask yourself these questions:

- Will you need **primary sources** (historical documents, literary works, diaries, letters, eyewitness accounts, raw data from experiments), **secondary sources** (accounts produced by other investigators, such as lab reports, biographies, reviews), or both? Often what constitutes a primary or secondary source will depend on your purpose or field. A critic's evaluation of a painting, for example, serves as a secondary work if you are writing an essay on that painting but as a primary work if you are conducting a study of the critic's writing.
- What kinds of sources does the assignment require? If you must use primary or nonprint sources, find out where they are and whether they are readily available or whether you must make special arrangements to see or examine them. If you need to use sources from the World Wide Web or elsewhere on the Internet, make sure you have good access to those electronic media and that you know how to use them. (See 41f.) On the other hand, if your instructor or the nature of your topic requires that you rely primarily on print sources found in the library or on your own field research (observations, interviews, or surveys), you may not need – or even be able – to do much of your research online.
- How current do your sources need to be? If you must investigate the latest findings in your field, you will want to check the Web and periodicals. If you need broader, more detailed coverage and background information, you may need to look more to books.
- Do you need to consult sources contemporary with an event or a person's life? If your research deals with a specific time period, you may need to examine newspapers, magazines, and books written during that period.
- How many sources should you consult? You can expect to look at many more sources than you will actually end up using. Make sure you have enough sources to support your hypothesis or prove your thesis, and check to see whether your assignment specifies a minimum (or maximum) number of sources.

2 Listing preliminary keywords for a search

Looking through indexes or databases will go more efficiently if you have identified **keywords** to look for – synonyms for your topic, general terms that would include it, or appropriate subtopics. Information on ice cream, for instance, might appear under the headings of frozen desserts, dairy products, or sherbet. A good place to check for keywords is in the *Library of Congress Subject Headings*, which lists the headings under which books are cataloged in most libraries. As you search a particular print index or computer database, check its list of keywords, or **descriptors,** because many indexes and databases use terms peculiar to their systems. Also check the glossary and index of appropriate textbooks.

When Shannan Palma searched one computer database, she began with the keywords *film* and *hero.*

3 Thinking about logistics

For most research projects you will carry out, whether in college or on the job, you will be working against a deadline. Considering logistics can help you complete a project in the time allowed. If you have only two weeks to do research, for instance, you will need to be very selective. If you have several months, however, you can follow a broader course, perhaps conducting some field research. Also consider issues of access: can you get to the materials, people, works of art, or other items you need in the time allowed? How can you speed up access? For library work, find out whether you can print the results of the searches you conduct (some libraries charge a fee for printing or limit the number of pages you can print on any one day) and whether you can copy these results onto your own disc. Finally, consider any advance contacts you may need to make — to set up an interview, to secure materials through interlibrary loan, to use a friend's computer with a speedy ethernet connection, to see materials in a rare-book room.

For guidelines on conducting field research, see 41h.

Shannan Palma had the entire term to work on her research project. Consequently, she decided to include background reading about the history of U.S. film in her set of strategies. In addition, she knew she wanted to conduct a full search of the Web, see a number of movies (either on video or on the "big screen"), and conduct at least one interview with an expert in film studies.

4 Consulting others

Your most valuable source at the library is the highly trained staff, especially the reference librarians and those skilled in electronic searches. To get the most helpful advice, pose *specific* questions: not "Where can I find information about computers?" but "Where can I find information on the history of computers?" or "Where can I find the *Gale Directory of Databases*?" If you are having difficulty asking clear and precise questions, you probably need to do some general background research on your topic. Then work again on narrowing and focusing your topic, clarifying the issue, asking a more specific research question, formulating a sharper hypothesis. On a second trip to the library, you will be able to ask more specific questions and get more helpful answers.

Of course, many sources are available beyond the walls of the library. Don't forget that brainstorming with friends and classmates can help you explore your topic and focus your reading. In addition, email allows you to send queries about your topic to people in far-flung places. And online listservs, newsgroups, and MOOs and MUDs are still other places to gather pertinent information or consult with others. Consider all these sources as you develop your full research strategy.

For a discussion of these online resources, see 41g2, 3, and 4.

41c Considering reference works

www

http://www.n2h2.com/KOVACS/

This directory of e-conferences holds the best searchable data base of scholarly and professional discussions, covering both email lists and Usenet groups and offering a good forum for finding people interested and knowledgable in your research area. Diane Kovacs updates the site regularly.

Your library's reference collection includes two broad types of **reference materials:** those that are general in scope and those that deal with specific disciplines (music, zoology, political science, and so on). Guides to reference books can help you identify the ones that suit your purpose. Your research question can then help you choose the best sources to use. Among the types of sources most often consulted are encyclopedias, biographical dictionaries, summaries of current events, and book indexes. Many of these reference materials are available either online or on CD-ROM; your librarian can help you access them.

Gale Directory of Databases. 1993 – . Published yearly, this two-volume resource (one volume for online databases, the other for CD-ROM) is the most comprehensive index and guide to databases available.

Guide to Reference Books. 10th ed. 1986. Edited by Eugene P. Sheehy, this large book is usually just called Sheehy. It supplies annotated lists of general reference works and specialized bibliographies and is divided into five sections: General Reference; Humanities; Social and Behavioral Sciences; History and Area Studies; and Science, Technology, and Medicine. Each section is further subdivided into areas and then into special approaches. Full bibliographic information, including the Library of Congress call number, is provided for each entry.

Walford's Guide to Reference Material. 4th ed. 3 vols. 1980 – 86. *Walford's* three volumes deal with Science and Technology; Social and Historical Sciences, Philosophy, and Religion; and Generalities, Languages, the Arts, and Literature.

Encyclopedias

For general background on a subject, **encyclopedias** are a good place to begin, particularly because many include bibliographies. Though some encyclopedias do provide in-depth information, more often they serve as a place to start, not as a major source of information. Note that many general encyclopedias are available, often in elegant multimedia, on CD-ROM, or by online subscription.

GENERAL ENCYCLOPEDIAS

Compton's Interactive Encyclopedia <www.comptons.com>
Microsoft Encarta <www.encarta.com>
Encyclopædia Britannica <www.eb.com>
Grolier Multimedia Encyclopedia <www.grolier.com>

SPECIALIZED ENCYCLOPEDIAS

Compared with general encyclopedias, **specialized encyclopedias** usually provide more detailed articles by authorities in the field as well as extensive bibliographies for locating sources. Again, you should rely on these books more for background material than as major sources of information.

Cambridge Ancient History
Cambridge History of Africa
Cambridge Medieval History
Encyclopedia of Anthropology
Encyclopedia of Asian History
Encyclopedia of Banking and Finance
Encyclopedia of Bioethics
Encyclopedia of Biological Sciences
Encyclopedia of Business Information Sources
Encyclopedia of Chemistry
Encyclopedia of Computer Science and Technology
Encyclopedia of Crime and Justice
Encyclopedia of Education
Encyclopedia of Management
Encyclopedia of Philosophy
Encyclopedia of Physical Education, Fitness, and Sports
Encyclopedia of Physics
Encyclopedia of Religion
Encyclopedia of Social Work
Encyclopedia of World Architecture

Encyclopedia of World Art
Encyclopedia of World History
Harvard Guide to American History
International Encyclopedia of the Social Sciences
McGraw-Hill Dictionary of Earth Sciences
McGraw-Hill Dictionary of Modern Economics
McGraw-Hill Encyclopedia of Economics
McGraw-Hill Encyclopedia of Science and Technology
McGraw-Hill Encyclopedia of World Drama
New Cambridge Modern History
New Grove Dictionary of Music and Musicians
Oxford Classical Dictionary
Oxford Companion to American Literature
Oxford Companion to English Literature

Consult a reference librarian about other specialized encyclopedias that may relate to the discipline you are researching.

Biographical resources

The lives and historical settings of famous people are the topics of biographical dictionaries and indexes. Here are a few examples of biographical reference works; many others, particularly volumes specialized by geographic area or field, are available.

African American Biographies
American Men and Women of Science
Biography Index
Contemporary Authors
Current Biography
Dictionary of American Biography
Dictionary of National Biography
International Who's Who
Notable American Women
Webster's New Biographical Dictionary
Who's Who
Who's Who in America

Almanacs, yearbooks, and atlases

Almanacs, yearbooks, atlases, and other sources provide information on current events and statistical and geographic data.

ALMANACS, YEARBOOKS, NEWS DIGESTS

Facts on File: News Digest
Information Please Almanac
Statesman's Year-Book
Statistical Abstracts of the United States
World Almanac and Book of Facts

ATLASES

Atlas of World Cultures: A Geographical Guide to Ethnographic Literature
Hammond Medallion World Atlas
National Geographic Atlas of the World
The New International World Atlas
The New York Times Atlas of the World

Book and review indexes

Other useful sources include **book indexes,** which can be helpful for quickly locating complete information on a book when you know only one piece of it – the author's last name, perhaps, or the title. These sources can also be valuable for alerting you to other works by a particular author or on a particular subject. Note that such indexes are available online or on CD-ROM.

Books in Print
Cumulative Book Index
Paperbound Books in Print

Consider also using a **review index** to check the relevance of a source or to get a thumbnail sketch of its contents.

Book Review Digest
Book Review Index
Index to Book Reviews in the Humanities
Index to Book Reviews in the Social Sciences

Periodical indexes

Periodical indexes are guides to articles published in periodicals. Each index covers a specific group of periodicals, usually identified at the beginning of the index or volume. In addition to printed indexes, your library may have indexes available on CD-ROM or in microform. Microform indexes cover only the past three or four years, however, so if you are searching for earlier material, check the printed or CD-ROM indexes.

GENERAL INDEXES

General indexes of periodicals – usually located in the periodicals reading room – list articles from current general-interest magazines (such as *Time* and *Newsweek*), newspapers, or a combination of these. General indexes will usually provide current sources on your topic, though these sources may not treat the topic in sufficient depth for your purposes.

Access: The Supplementary Index. Indexes magazines not covered by the *Readers' Guide to Periodical Literature.*

Alternative Press Index. Indexes alternative and radical publications.

InfoTrac. Indexes roughly 2,000 publications related to business, government, and education.

NewsBank. Includes over one million articles from 500 U.S. newspapers.

Newspaper Abstracts Ondisc. Contains abstracts from eight major newspapers.

New York Times Index

NEXIS/LEXIS. NEXIS contains full texts and abstracts of newspapers, magazines, wire services, newsletters, company and industry analyst reports, and broadcast transcripts. LEXIS contains legal, legislative, and regulatory information.

Nineteenth Century Readers' Guide to Periodical Literature

Periodical Abstracts. Contains abstracts of articles from over 1,000 periodicals and journals in science, social science, humanities, and business. At the top of the next page is an example of an entry Shannan Palma found in an online version of *Periodical Abstracts,* using the keywords *film* and *hero:*

SAMPLE ENTRY FROM *PERIODICAL ABSTRACTS*

Author	Firstenberg, Jean Picker
Title	**From the Director: On Heroes and the Media**
Appears in	American Film 1987, v13n1, Oct p. 67

Click here to see which OhioLINK libraries have this journal

Abstract	The idea that today's images of **film** and television have had an enormous impact on the evolution of the modern **hero** is expressed in an opinion
Subject	Heroism & heroes Motion picture industry
Note	Availability: American Film Subscription Service, PO Box 966, Farmingdale NY 11737-9866 Article Length: Medium (10-30 col inches) Article Type: Commentary

Poole's Index to Periodical Literature. Indexes nineteenth-century British and American periodicals.

Readers' Guide to Periodical Literature. Indexes articles from over 170 magazines. Here is a *Readers' Guide* entry for the subject heading "Heroes and Heroines in Motion Pictures":

HEROES AND HEROINES IN MOTION PICTURES
Cowardly heroes. il *Premiere* v6 p101-2 Ag '93
title of article — From El Cid to Arnold: the superhero in crisis [C. Heston] G. Fuller. il por *Interview* v23 p98 S '93

author — *title of periodical* — *volume and page numbers* — *date of publication*

Silver Platter. Indexes periodicals in the social and health sciences.

Times Index (London).

SPECIALIZED INDEXES AND ABSTRACTS

Many disciplines have **specialized indexes** and **abstracts** to help researchers find detailed information. In general, such works list articles in scholarly journals for that discipline, but they may include other publications as well; check the beginning of the volume. To use these resources most efficiently, ask a reference librarian to help you identify those most likely to address your topic.

America: History and Life

Applied Science and Technology Index

Art Index
Arts and Humanities Citation Index
Biological Abstracts
Biological and Agricultural Index
Business Periodicals Index
Chemical Abstracts
Chicano Index
Cumulative Index to Nursing and Allied Health Literature
Current Index to Journals in Education
Dissertation Abstracts International
Education Index
Engineering Index
ERIC (Educational Resources Information Center)
Essay and General Literature Index
General Science Index
Hispanic American Periodicals Index (HAPI)
Historical Abstracts
Humanities Index
Index Medicus
Index to Legal Periodicals
Index to Periodicals by and about Blacks
MLA International Bibliography of Books and Articles on the Modern Languages and Literature
Music Index: A Subject-Author Guide to Music Periodical Literature
Philosopher's Index
Physics Abstracts
PsycLIT
Psychological Abstracts
Public Affairs Information Service (PAIS)
Science Citation Index
Social Sciences Citation Index
Social Sciences Index
Sociological Abstracts
United States Government Publications
Women's Studies Index

41d Using the library catalog

A **library catalog** lists all the library's materials. Some libraries still have their catalogs on cards or microfiche, but most have transferred (or are in the process of transferring) their holdings to a **circulation computer,** which allows you to use public terminals to search for material. If your library is in the process of computerizing its catalog, ask a reference librarian which catalog to check for recently published materials.

In whatever form, library catalogs follow a standard pattern of organization. Each holding is identified by three kinds of entries: one headed by the author's name, one by the title, and one or (usually) more by the subject. If you can't find a book under one of these headings, try the others; sometimes entries are lost or misfiled.

Using the circulation computer

Most circulation computers provide clear instructions on how and when to type in information. You can search for holdings by author, title, or subject. Here is an example of a circulation-computer entry. Note that many circulation computers, like the one this example comes from, indicate whether a book has been checked out and, if so, when it is due to be returned.

```
AUTHOR          Rushing, Janice Hocker.
TITLE           Projecting the shadow : the cyborg hero
                  in American film / Janice Hocker Rush-
                  ing, Thomas S. Frentz.
PUBLISH INFO    Chicago : University of Chicago Press,
                  1995.
DESCRIPTION     x, 261 p. : ill. ; 24 cm.
SERIES          New practices of inquiry.
NOTES           Includes bibliographical references
                  (p. 222-244) and index.
SUBJECTS        Cyborgs in motion pictures.
                Myth in motion pictures.
ADD AUTHORS     Frentz, Thomas S.
OCLC #          32737837.
ISBN            0226731669 (cloth : alk. paper)
    LOCATION      CALL NO.          YEAR   STATUS
1 > JOU Stacks   PN1995.9.C9 R57   1995   DUE 01-05-98
```

Identifying subjects for your search

Subjects in the library catalog are usually identified and arranged according to the system presented in the *Library of Congress Subject Headings* (LCSH). This three-volume reference work may be kept at the reference desk and is also available online. (An advantage of accessing an online catalog through the Web is that doing so always allows you to download the information in some way.) In it, you can check the exact wording of subject headings and define key terms of interest to you. You may find that the LCSH identifies headings that have not readily occurred to you. Under most headings, you'll find other subjects that are treated (identified by *UF,* "use for"), broader headings that include the subject (*BT,* "broader topic"), and narrower headings that might be relevant (*NT,* "narrower topic").

After entering the Library of Congress Web site, <http://www.loc.gov>, Shannan Palma clicked on this series of links: "library services," "cataloging," "search online catalogs," "other public access," and "advanced word search," which allowed her to search for the subject "film and hero in books." Here is one of the sources that search yielded:

BOOKS[AND(film[1,4,4,2]|hero[1,4,4,2])](1-1)

Records 1 through 1 of 6 returned.

```
Author:         Gerbner, George.
Title:          The film hero : a cross-cultural study
                  / George Gerbner.
Published:      [Lexington, Ky.] : Association for
                  Education in Journalism, 1969.
Description:    54 p. ; 23 cm.
Series:         Journalism monographs ; no. 13
LC Call No.:    PN4722 .J6 no. 13 PN1995.9.C36
Dewey No.:      070/.08 s 791.43/0909/27
ISSN:           4159662
Notes:          Cover title.
Subjects:       Characters and characteristics in
                  motion pictures.
Series Entry:   Journalism monographs (Austin, Tex.) ;
                  no. 13.
Control No.:    76352849 //r882
```

Searching only for subject entries is likely to be inefficient, however, because the headings are usually so broad. If the best Library of Congress heading you can identify does not match your particular needs or is so broad that your search yields many books but only a few that are useful, use other leads. Look to bibliographies, book indexes, reference books, periodical indexes, and notes in other publications for potentially useful authors and titles.

Using call numbers

Besides identifying a book's author, title, subject, and publication information, each catalog entry also lists a **call number** – the book's identification number. Most academic libraries now use the Library of Congress system, which begins call numbers with letters of the alphabet. Some libraries, however, still use the older Dewey decimal system, utilizing all numerals; the others combine systems. Once you have printed out the circulation-computer entry for the book or written down the call number, look for a library map or shelving plan to tell you where your book is housed. When you find it, take the time to browse through the books around it. Very often you will find the immediate area a more important treasure trove than any bibliography or index.

If the computer tells you that the book is checked out or if your book is not on the shelf, ask about it at the circulation desk. The book may not circulate, or it may be in an area closed to the public. If someone has checked it out, the library might recall it for you. Consider your deadline, and determine whether it is realistic to request a recall.

Using other library resources

In addition to books and periodicals, libraries hold other useful materials that might be appropriate for your research. For example:

- *vertical file:* pamphlets and brochures from government and private agencies, usually kept in file cabinets
- *special collections:* manuscripts, rare books, local literature, memorabilia
- *audio collections:* records, audiocassettes, and CDs of all kinds of music, readings, and speeches
- *video collections:* slides, filmstrips, and videocassettes
- *art collections:* drawings, paintings, engravings, and photographs

Many libraries will also borrow books from another library for you. Be aware, however, that interlibrary loans often take some time and may involve some cost to you.

41e Searching databases

As the preceding pages have demonstrated, many important resources are now available to you in databases, either online or on CD-ROMs. To search such databases, as Shannan Palma's research shows, you need to use authors' names, other titles, or keywords. Especially if you have to pay a fee for these searches, it is important to limit each search as much as you can.

Choosing keywords

If you are preparing a class report on military technology in Shakespeare's plays, you can begin, for instance, by checking the *Gale Directory of Databases* to find databases that might index works related to your topic. From there, you might identify and then search the *MLA International Bibliography* for the terms *Shakespeare* and *cannon* or *firearms,* thereby finding references to articles that mention Shakespeare in conjunction with one of these words. Doing efficient database searches requires that you choose your keywords carefully. Sometimes you may search by author or title – then the keywords are obvious. More often, however, you will probably be searching subject headings. Luckily, most databases include a thesaurus of keywords to help you as you start your search.

Shannan Palma's searches focused on two major keywords, *film* and *hero.* She sometimes narrowed a search further by adding a third term, *United States.*

Using database search logic

Reading the instructions for searching the particular database you are using is also a good idea, since to search efficiently you need to understand a database's **search logic.** For instance, using *and* usually indicates that two items (Shakespeare *and* guns) must be present for an article to be called up. *Or* instructs the computer to include every article in which either one word *or* the other shows up. And *not* indicates that when a particular word appears, the article should be excluded (firearms *not* swords). Another element of search logic is the use of parentheses or quotation marks to indicate key terms with more than one word; if you are searching for information on Lois Lane, for example, you would type in (*Lois Lane*) or "*Lois Lane.*" Other devices enable you to call up every instance in which a keyword (*Clinton,* for example) appears near another keyword (*veto,* for example).

When Shannan Palma accessed the *MLA International Bibliography* database, she entered the key term *film hero,* and the database quickly replied with sixteen initial entries, including the following one:

```
You searched for the WORD: film hero                    MLA
                                               Record 2 of 81

AUTHOR          Abele, Elizabeth.
TITLE           Rescuing the Hero: Shifting Expectations
                  for  Men in the '90s.

APPEARS IN      The Mid-Atlantic Almanac: The Journal of
                  the  Mid-Atlantic Popular/American Cul-
                  ture Association, 1996, 5, p. 107-22
                  MAA 1063-1763 Greencastle, PA.

PUB TYPE        journal article.
LANGUAGE        English.

SUBJECT         dramatic arts -- film -- treatment of
                  masculinity -- of hero.
ISSN            1063-1763.
SEQUENCE #      96-4-225.
UPD CODE        9601.
```

Continuing her search, Shannan Palma used the same key term to search two other CD-ROM databases: *PsycLIT* and *ERIC.* The *PsycLIT* search yielded five entries, and the *ERIC* search yielded six; a sample entry from each of these searches is shown on pages 460 and 461.

Record 1 of 1 in PsycLIT Journal Articles 1991-6/97

DOCUMENT TITLE
It's not such a Wonderful Life : The neurotic George Bailey.

AUTHOR(S)
Gordon,-Andrew

INSTITUTIONAL AFFILIATION OF FIRST AUTHOR
U Florida, Dept of English, Gainesville, US

JOURNAL NAME
American-Journal-of-Psychoanalysis; 1994 Sep Vol 54(3) 219-233;

ISSN 00029548

LANGUAGE
English

PUBLICATION YEAR
1994

ABSTRACT
Argues that the **film** It's a Wonderful Life exposes the dark side of the American dream and that the **hero,** George Bailey, is a supremely divided neurotic who embodies 2 incompatible longings of the American character: the desire to serve the family and the community selflessly and the desire for personal financial success. Horneyan theory is used to explain the nature of Bailey's neurosis as the character's move toward others (selflessness) conflicts with his move against others (personal success). Bailey's attempted suicide is both a response to his hopelessness about ever actualizing his idealized image and a way to punish himself for failure. The film's "forced" happy ending serves to reinforce Bailey's neurotic conflict by proving to the **hero** that he is both loved and needed and that he is not a failure. (PsycLIT Database Copyright 1995 American Psychological Assn, all rights reserved)

KEY PHRASE
Horneyan perspective on neurosis in character G. Bailey in **film** "It's a Wonderful Life"

DESCRIPTORS
PSYCHOANALYTIC-INTERPRETATION; MOTION-PICTURES-ENTERTAINMENT; NEUROSIS-; PSYCHOANALYTIC-THEORY

CLASSIFICATION CODE(S)
2610; 26

POPULATION
Human

UPDATE CODE
9502

PSYC ABS. VOL. AND ABS. NO.
82-04826

JOURNAL CODE
1051

Record 1 of 1 in ERIC 1992-6/97

ACCESSION NUMBER
EJ517706

CLEARINGHOUSE NUMBER
CS751232

PERSONAL AUTHOR
Prats,-Armando-J.

TITLE
Back from the Sunset: The Western, the Eastwood **Hero,** and "Unforgiven."

PUBLICATION YEAR
1995

JOURNAL CITATION
Journal-of-Film-and-Video;v47 n1-3 p106-23 Spr-Fall 1995;

INTERNATIONAL STANDARD SERIAL NUMBER
ISSN-0724-4671

DOCUMENT TYPE
Opinion Papers (120); Reports – Evaluative (142); Journal Articles (080)

LANGUAGE
English

MINOR DESCRIPTORS
Comparative-Analysis; Mythology-

MAJOR DESCRIPTORS
*Characterization-; *Film-Criticism; *Films-

MINOR IDENTIFIERS
Heroes-

MAJOR IDENTIFIERS
*Eastwood-Clint; *Westerns-Films

ABSTRACT ISSUE
CIJJUN96

ABSTRACT
Explores the prevalence of the gunfighter as mythic **hero.** Compares the depictions of Clint Eastwood's characters from the beginning of Eastwood's career ("A Fistful of Dollars" and "Pale Rider") to "Unforgiven," finding similarities and differences in each character. (PA)

CLEARINGHOUSE
CS

SOURCE FILE
EJ

DOCUMENT TYPE NUMBER
120; 142; 080

41f Navigating the Internet and World Wide Web

Most databases, along with a wealth of other sources for research, are available to you through the Internet and the World Wide Web. As explained in Chapter 2, the Internet is essentially a global patchwork quilt of linked computer networks. The World Wide Web is a part of the Internet that is hypertextual, allowing users to leap from place to place by moving a cursor arrow onto parts of the computer screen called *links* (usually designated by highlighting or underlining) and clicking a mouse.

1 Access to the Internet

Today most college students can get direct access to the Internet and the Web from the library or from a campus computer center or lab. In addition, some dormitory rooms are now wired for immediate ethernet connections for students who own computers. But in most dormitories – and almost certainly at home – Internet access requires a modem and a software package, which is usually available at the campus bookstore for a low fee. With a modem, you can either access your college computer system or subscribe to an Internet provider, such as America Online, CompuServe, or Prodigy. In addition to Internet and Web access, these companies often offer "bonus" features, such as encyclopedias and various kinds of software. But commercial services can be quite expensive, so you may want to ask at computer stores about other local sources, some of which are labeled *Freenet*.

Every site on the Internet has its own address, called a **Uniform Resource Locator (URL),** which must be typed *exactly* as it appears – using the exact capital or lowercase letters, spacing, and so on. Here, for example, is the URL for a helpful Web site that offers answers to a multitude of questions about computer terminology:

<http://whatis.com>

The first part of this address, (http:), is the **protocol,** or **hypertext transfer protocol,** which announces the kind of Internet link that is being made; the next part (whatis.com) is the **domain name,** which announces the owner of the site and identifies it, in this case, as a commercial site (com). Some addresses have a third part, a **directory path,** which leads you to a particular part of the larger site. Throughout this book, URLs in the margins of pages direct you to online sources of additional information about material discussed in that part of the text.

For a more detailed explanation of URLs, see p. 136.

2 Web browsers and search engines

Software programs called **browsers** allow you easy access to the Web and also let you move swiftly from one Web site to another. Today most computers in the United States are served by the browsers Netscape Navigator and Microsoft Explorer, which offer access to multimedia – graphics, video, audio, real-time discussion – as well as text on the Web. Browsers also give you access to powerful **search engines** that allow you to carry out keyword searches or that list what is available in a series of directories.

Some of the most widely used search engines are listed on p. 464. If your library has a Web page, you can check there to see which search engines the librarians have recommended. Or you can click on the link on the browser itself that takes you to search engines used by that browser. Here is an example of a Netscape screen on which Shannan Palma clicked on "Net Search":

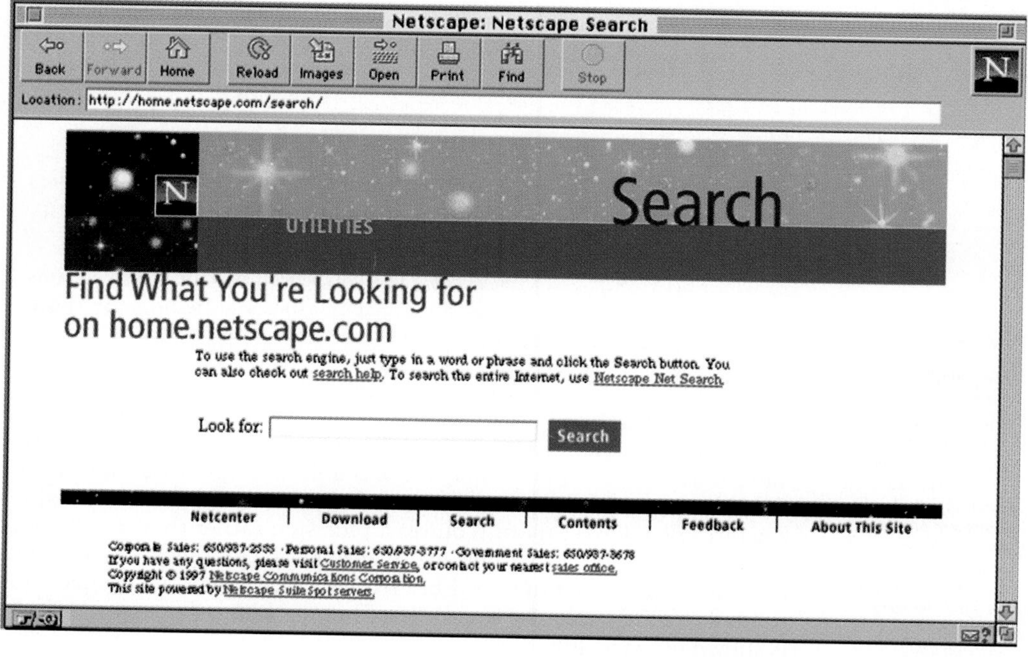

Yahoo! <*http://www.yahoo.com*> is a Web guide that allows you either to search directories of sites related to particular subjects (such as entertainment or education) or to enter keywords that Yahoo! forwards to nine search engines, which send back the results.

Alta Vista <*http://altavista.digital.com*> lets you search the entire Web, using either a single keyword or multiple keywords.

Excite <*http://www.excite.com*> allows you to do simple searches of over sixty thousand Web sites.

HotBot <*http://www.hotbot.com*> let you search for individual words or phrases, names, or URLs in forty-five million Web sites and to narrow the search to specific dates, media, and other criteria.

Infoseek <*http://guide.infoseek.com*> lets you choose a part of the Internet to search – such as the Web, directories of email addresses, or Usenet groups.

Lycos <*http://www.lycos.com*> allows you to search a huge catalog of Web sites and includes multimedia documents.

Magellan <*http://www.magellan.com*> allows you to search the entire Web or Web sites that have been evaluated for the quality of their content and organization.

Open Text <*http://www.opentext.com*> offers access to five million sites classified into forty categories, including the Web, gopher and ftp, and even multilingual sites using non-Roman characters.

WebCrawler <*http://webcrawler.com*> lets you search two million Web sites with an easy-to-use procedure that is especially helpful for those new to keyword searching.

For her research, Shannan Palma found Yahoo! best suited to entertainment-related subjects. By clicking on "Search Options" within Yahoo! as shown on page 465, she was able to limit her search to only those listings added during the past three years. When she entered her key term *film+hero* (Yahoo! requires a plus sign rather than *and* between keywords to indicate that both words need to be present), Yahoo! found twenty-one sites that matched her request, including one she definitely wanted to follow up. The first page of her printout of the search results is shown on page 466.

WWW •

http://www.lib.berkeley.edu/TeachingLib/Guides/Internet/FindInfo.html

From the University of California at Berkeley's library, this site is consistently updated and keeps track of new trends in search engine protocols and browser developments, incorporating them into self-directed tutorials.

WWW •

http://daphne.palomar.edu/TGSEARCH/

How to Search the Web: A Guide to Search Tools. *Knowing how to use different search engines, how to phrase and punctuate your search terms, will determine the quality of your WWW searches. This guide by Terry Gray offers expert advice on using ten powerful search engines, as well as links to other resources for search advice.*

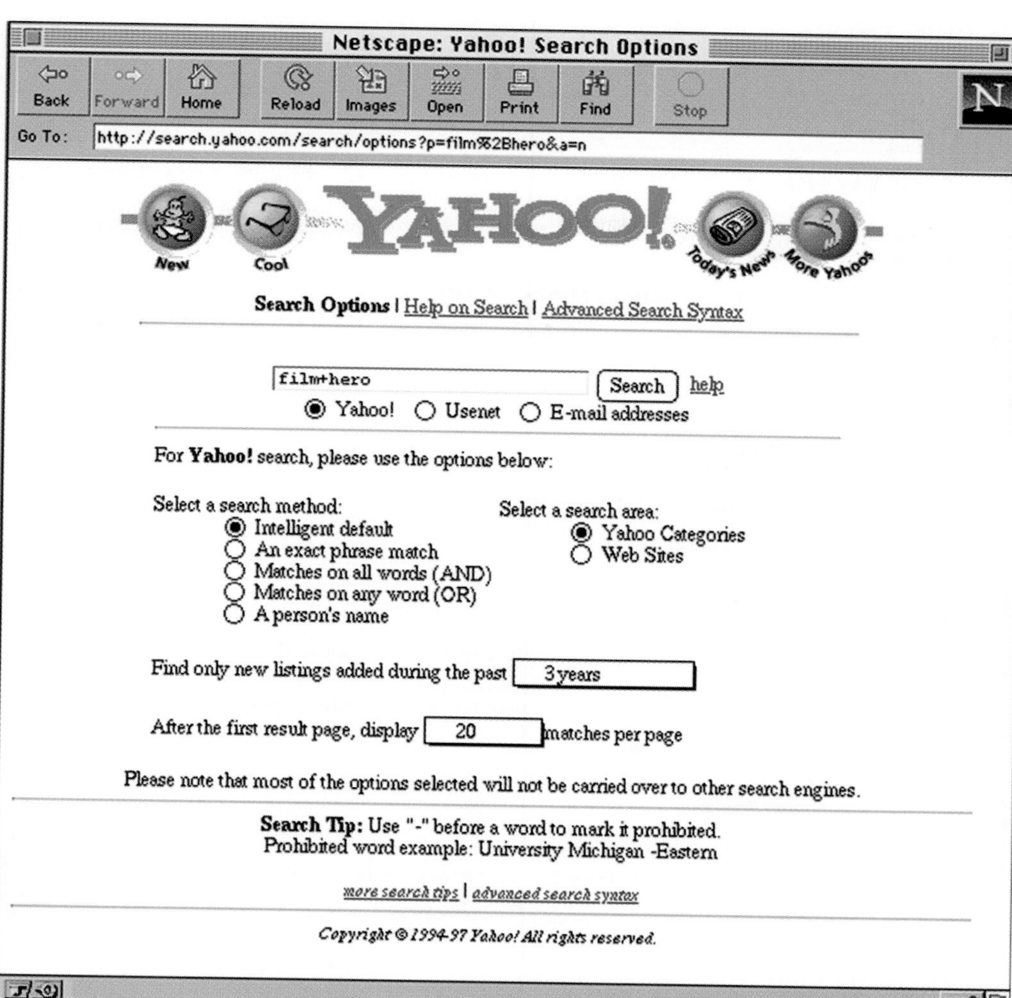
Netscape: Yahoo! Search Options
Back
Forward
Home
Reload
Images
Open
Print
Find
Stop
Go To: http://search.yahoo.com/search/options?p=film%2Bhero&a=n
New
Cool
YAHOO!
Today's News
More Yahoos
Search Options | Help on Search | Advanced Search Syntax
film+hero
Search
help
Yahoo!
Usenet
E-mail addresses
For Yahoo! search, please use the options below:
Select a search method:
Intelligent default
An exact phrase match
Matches on all words (AND)
Matches on any word (OR)
A person's name
Select a search area:
Yahoo Categories
Web Sites
Find only new listings added during the past 3 years
After the first result page, display 20 matches per page
Please note that most of the options selected will not be carried over to other search engines.
Search Tip: Use "-" before a word to mark it prohibited.
Prohibited word example: University Michigan -Eastern
more search tips | advanced search syntax
Copyright © 1994-97 Yahoo! All rights reserved.

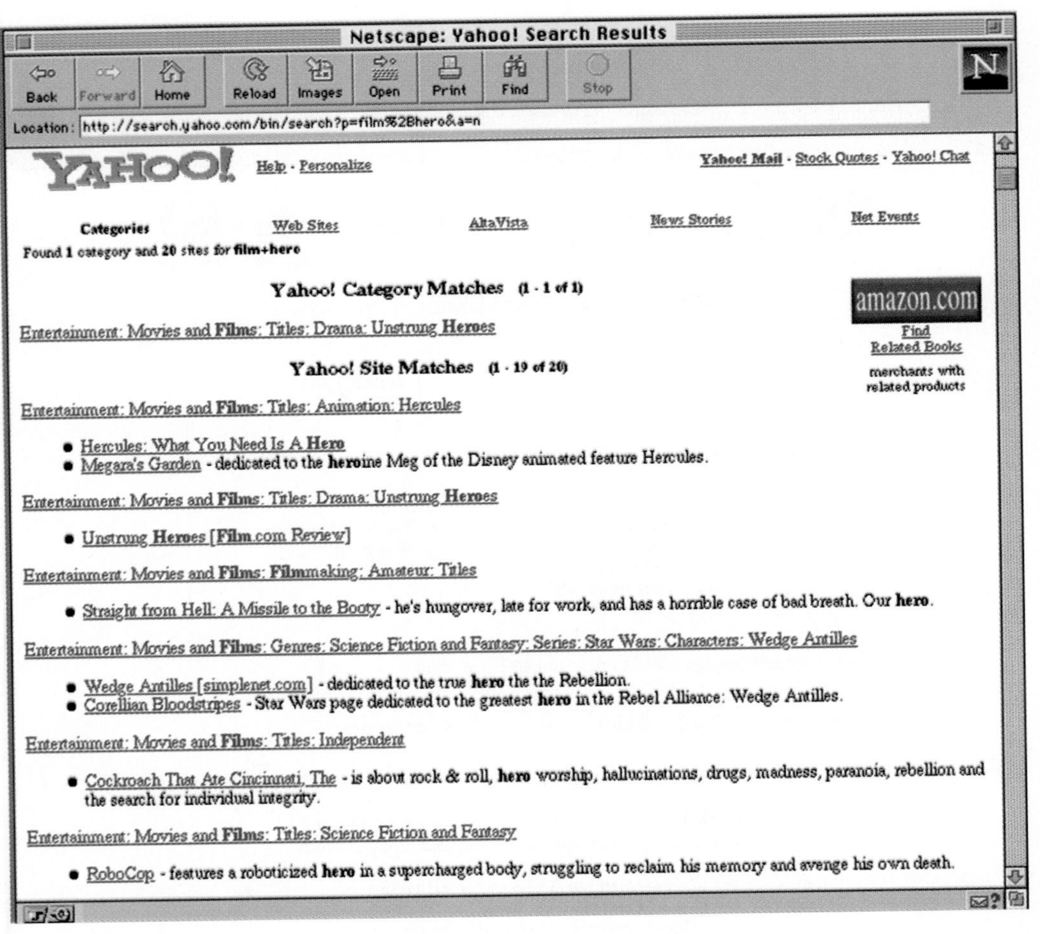

41g Using other parts of the Internet for research

The Internet provides access not only to the Web but to a number of other applications, including gopher, FTP, and telnet; email; listservs and Usenet newsgroups; and MOOs, MUDs, and IRCs. Some of these may be helpful to you in doing certain kinds of research.

1 Gopher, FTP, and telnet

Until recently, gopher, FTP, and telnet could be accessed only through special software for each one. Now, however, they are assimilated into most Web browsers.

Using **gopher,** a software browser, often involves following a path from one menu to another before you get to a specific document. At times, you may lose track of how you actually located the material of interest to you. To simplify matters, you can use a **bookmark** to identify an important gopher location you want to revisit. Over time, you may create a **bookmark list,** a sort of custom menu, that makes it easy for you to get to particular gopher sites. You can use the search engines Veronica or Jughead to conduct keyword searches on gopher.

File transfer protocol (FTP) is a method for calling up and copying (at no cost) a huge number of public files from host computers all over the Internet. The files, which may not be available via gopher or the Web, can be short documents (such as government statistics), whole books, or online magazines that include graphics, sound, and video. The search engine Archie allows you to search FTP sites for access to artwork, books, journals, photographs, sound tracks, and much more. In addition, Archie tells you how to locate the file so that you can copy or download it.

The **telnet** system allows you to make a telephone connection with another computer on the Internet. Through telnet, you can access on your computer the resources that are available on the other one. To be able to log on to telnet, you usually need an account on the other computer, but some sites, such as libraries, allow you to log on as a guest.

2 Email

Email (short for "electronic mail"), a sped-up postal system that allows you to communicate with people or groups all over the world via the Internet, can also be very helpful in conducting research. Some search engines contain "phone books" of email addresses, and some have a "who is" search function.

www •

http://www.ipl.org/

The Internet Public Library. *The American Library Association <www.ala.org> recommends this site, which organizes information according to subject categories and, more important, does a good job of choosing worthwhile sources (though you should still be independently critical) and of keeping links updated.*

3 Listservs and Usenet newsgroups

Listservs are groups that use email to carry on a discussion among people who have similar interests – and you can find a listserv on the Internet for almost every subject under the sun. You can check out potentially interesting listservs by using the subject directory on a search engine such as AltaVista. To join a listserv, you must subscribe by sending a message to a subscription address. After subscribing, you should read postings for a few days before becoming an active participant; this "lurking" will give you a sense of the discussion and of the rules, if any, that are governing it. Once you feel comfortable posting a message, you can use the listserv to get responses to questions or tips on other resources related to your topic of interest.

Usenet is a network with links to thousands of discussion **newsgroups** that, unlike listservs, are open to visitors without subscriptions. Although you can visit a newsgroup by using a Web browser or search engine, you must subscribe to receive postings from it automatically. Like listservs, newsgroups can be very helpful in conducting research. But you should be aware that the information on them is only as reliable as the people who are doing the posting. For this reason, you should look carefully at a group's **frequently asked questions,** or **FAQs,** which will tell you something about its topics of interest and procedures, and read postings for a while so that you can test their reliability and credibility. Be aware also that Usenet postings are kept on a school's site only for a limited time; make a copy of anything you find useful.

In her research, Shannan Palma decided to check out some newsgroup sites. To do so, she used the search engine WebCrawler, on whose homepage she could click on "Newsgroups" (and then hit "return"), which took her to a screen called "Newsgroup search." Here she typed "Hollywood movie hero" in the search line and clicked on "find Newsgroups," which took her to a list of newsgroups ranked in order of how well they fit her keywords. Clicking on the first newsgroup listed, "rec.arts.movies.current-films," then took her to a list of messages within that newsgroup that matched her keywords. After scanning these messages, she selected a posting titled "Re: In which movie DID the bad guy win??" The next page shows the original posting and a reply that focuses on the film *Chinatown* as an antihero movie. With this new information, Shannan Palma could look further for information regarding this film.

4 MUDs, MOOs, and IRCs

www •

http://139.182.93.1Ø7/jrgst7/MOOcentral.html

The MOO Central Help Page. *Written by Jeff Galin, this site offers links and leads on how to find and use educational MOOS and MUDS.*

Whereas communication via email is **asynchronous,** meaning that there is a time gap between the posting and the receiving of a message, communication via the Internet software systems for MUDs, MOOs, and IRCs is **synchronous,** with messages received as they are being typed. **MUDs** (multi-user domains or dungeons) are probably most familiar as online versions of role-playing games like Dungeons and

Newsgroups

Reference

home | my page | email | help

Newsgroup search powered by DEJA NEWS

Previous Article | Next Article | Current Results | View Thread | Post Message

Subject: Re: In which movie DID the bad guy win??
From: Raj <rkrminac@jetform.com>
Date: 1997/09/11
Message-ID: <341856EF.1824@jetform.com>
Newsgroups: rec.arts.movies.current-films
[More Headers]

> >
> > I just read a post where everyone was mentioning movies in which they
> > wanted the bad guy to win. But are there any movies in which the bad
> > guy really wins? I can only think of one, "The Silence Of The Lambs".
> > I did want to see Anthony Hopkins eat Jodi Foster with some soya
> > beans!! I also wanted King Kong to win but unfortunately they did kill
> > him in the end. Do you know some movies in which the bad guy DO win?
> >

I am suprised that no on has mentioned the classic CHINA TOWN. At the end of this brilliant film, one of the most despicable villians ever in the history of cinema not only gets away with murder but also manages to swindle an entire city and fathers a child with his OWN daughter. The **hero** of the film, played by Jack Nicholson, losses everything in the end, yet the villian triumphs and only suffers a minor bullet wound in the shoulder. One of the opening lines of the **movie** is "You have to be rich to get away with murder" and with conviction that would be almost impossible in today's **Hollywood** the director, Roman Polanski, follows through with this premise. I have to admit that this is one of my all time favourite endings, and in a strange way this is an ending that is far more satisfying than eny "happy" ending I have seen.

Previous | Next | Results | View Thread | Author Profile | Post Message | Post Reply | Send Email

Dragons, but they are now being used for distance education and other academic projects. **MOOs** (MUDs, object-oriented) let participants create complex virtual spaces for conferencing and all kinds of collaborations. **IRCs** (internet relay chats), also called *chat rooms,* allow people at far-flung sites to talk or hold a conference, but without the role-playing aspect of MOOs and MUDs.

Many college computer labs and classrooms now are equipped with the software necessary to conduct IRCs and thus offer the potential for holding an interview, for example, with several experts on a subject you are researching. MOOs and MUDs are less frequently supported on college campuses, though some educational MOOs can be reached through other Web sites.

41h Conducting field research

For many research projects, particularly those in the social sciences and business, you will need to collect field data. The "field" may be many things – a classroom, a church, an ice-cream parlor, a laboratory, or the corner grocery store. As a field researcher, you will need to discover *where* you can find relevant information, *how* to gather it, and *who* might be your best providers of information.

Extensive field research almost certainly lies beyond your grasp as an undergraduate since it requires prolonged observation (often over several years) and complex analysis. Nevertheless, you may be able to use several field-research techniques, including observation and interviewing, to very good advantage.

1 Observing

"What," you might ask, "could be easier than observing something?" You just choose a subject, look at it closely, and record what you see and hear. Yet experience shows that several people who have observed the same scene or phenomenon will most often offer contradictory "evidence." Trained observers tell us that getting down a faithful record of an observation requires intense concentration and mental agility.

Moreover, observation is never neutral. Just as the camera has an angle on its subject and the person behind the camera must choose what to include and what to leave out, so an observer always has an angle on what he or she is looking at. If, for instance, you decide to conduct a formal observation of your writing class, the field notes you take will reflect your status as an insider. Consequently, you will need to question or second-guess your observations to see what your participation in the class may have obscured or led you to take for granted.

In other instances, when you need to observe situations or phenomena in which you are not an insider, you will aim for optimal objectivity, keeping yourself out of the picture and altering as little as possible the phenomena you are looking at – all the while remembering that you will always alter them somewhat. Much professional writing – for example, a doctor's diagnostic notes, a reporter's news article, or a social worker's case study – depends on such careful observation. You can observe anything in this way, from the use of bicycle paths on campus to the kinds of products advertised during Saturday morning television shows to the growth of chicks in an agriculture lab.

Before you conduct any observation, decide exactly what you want to find out and anticipate what you are likely to see. Are you going to observe an action repeated by many people (such as pedestrians crossing a street), a sequence of actions (such as a medical procedure), or the interactions of a group (such as a church congregation)? Also decide exactly what you want to record and how to do so. In a grocery store, for instance, decide whether to observe shoppers or store employees and what you want to note about them – what they say, what they buy, how they are dressed, how they respond to one another, and so on.

CONDUCTING OBSERVATION

1. **Determine the purpose of the observation, and be sure it relates to your research question and hypothesis.**
2. **Make plans as far in advance as possible. Brainstorm about what you are looking for and what you expect to see. Have a sense of what you are looking for, but be flexible.**
3. **If necessary, make appointments and gain permissions to observe.**
4. **Develop an appropriate system for recording your data. For field notes taken during observation, consider using a "split" notebook or page: on one side, record your observations directly; on the other, record your own thoughts and interpretations.**
5. **Gather plenty of materials for note-taking: notebooks, pens, a camera, tape recorder, or videocassette recorder. Be aware that your way of recording data will inevitably affect your final report, if only in respect to what you include in your notes and what you leave out.**

(continued on page 472)

(continued from page 471)

6. **Review the steps you plan to take, going through the motions of observing and note-taking. Then conduct a trial run, taking field notes throughout. These activities will help you identify and solve potential problems before your formal observation.**
7. **After taking field notes, go back and question your observations, remaining open to various interpretations.**

2 Interviewing

Some information is best obtained by **interviewing.** If you can talk with an expert in person, on the telephone, or online, you might get information you could not have obtained through any other kind of research. In addition to getting "expert opinion," you might ask for firsthand accounts or suggestions of other places to look or other people to consult. You also may wish to conduct follow-up interviews with some people you've observed.

Finding people to interview

Check first to see whether your research has generated the names of people you might contact directly. Next brainstorm for names. In addition to authorities on your topic, consider people in your community – faculty members, lawyers, librarians, government officials, or corporate executives. Once you identify some promising possibilities, write, telephone, or email them to see whether interviews might be arranged.

Composing questions

To prepare useful questions, you need to know your topic well, and you need to know a fair amount about your interviewee. Try to learn as much as you can about his or her experience and opinions. You will probably want to ask several kinds of questions. **Factual questions** elicit specific answers, ones that do not invite expansion or opinion.

What flavors of ice cream does your company produce?

How many people contributed to this year's United Way campaign?

In contrast, **open-ended questions** lead the interviewee to think out loud, to go in directions that interest him or her, and to give additional details.

> How would you characterize the atmosphere of the campaign finance hearings?
>
> How do you feel now about your decision to go to Canada in 1968 rather than be drafted?

Avoid questions that encourage vague or rambling answers (*What do you think of youth today?*) or yes/no answers (*Should the campaign finance laws be changed?*). Instead, ask questions that must be answered with supporting details (*Why should the campaign finance laws be changed?*).

By looking through the course offerings bulletin, Shannan Palma learned of a professor on her campus who regularly taught film and film criticism courses. She then checked her university homepage to find the email address for this professor, Morris Beja, and wrote to him requesting an interview about her research on the development of the hero in Hollywood films. When he agreed to the interview, she prepared specific questions so she could be sure of using the hour-long interview efficiently.

PLANNING AN INTERVIEW

1. **Determine your exact purpose, and be sure it relates to your research question and hypothesis.**
2. **Set up the interview in advance. Specify how long it will take, and if you wish to tape-record the session, ask permission to do so.**
3. **Prepare a written list of questions you can use to structure the interview. Brainstorming or freewriting techniques can help you come up with questions. (3a)**
4. **If possible, try out your questions on one or two people to determine how best to sequence them, how clear and precise they are, and how long answers will take.**
5. **Prepare a final copy of your questions, leaving plenty of space for notes after each one.**
6. **Check out all equipment beforehand – pens, notebook, tape recorder, and so on. Record the subject, date, time, and place of the interview at the beginning of all tapes and on all handwritten notes.**

Conducting an interview

Be prompt, and dress appropriately. Even if you use a tape recorder, write down the answers to your questions and any other notes you wish to make. Do not feel bound to your prepared questions as long as the interview proceeds in a direction that seems fruitful. Be flexible. Note the time, and be careful not to take up more time than you said you would. End the interview with a thank-you – and follow up with a letter or formal email message thanking the person for taking the time to meet with you. Spend some time reviewing your notes, clarifying them and adding your comments.

3 Surveying opinion

Surveys, another common field-research strategy, can take the form of interviews, but more often they depend on **questionnaires.** A student investigating campus parking for motorcycles surveyed his dormitory's residents to learn how many owned motorcycles and how many had difficulty finding parking spaces. Though he sent questionnaires to everyone in the dorm, such extensive surveying is often unwieldy and even unnecessary. All you need is a representative sample of people and a questionnaire whose questions will elicit the information you need.

Questions should be clear and easy to understand and designed so that you will be able to analyze the answers easily. For example, questions that ask respondents to say yes or no or to rank something on a five-point scale of most to least desirable are easy to tabulate.

DESIGNING A QUESTIONNAIRE

1. Write out your purpose, and review your research question and hypothesis to determine the kinds of questions to ask.
2. Determine the audience for your questionnaire, and figure out how you will reach the potential respondents.
3. Using brainstorming, freewriting, or another strategy from 3a, draft some potential questions.
4. Check each question to see that it calls for a short, specific answer.
5. Test the questions on several people – including your instructor, if possible. Which questions are hard to answer? How much time do the answers require? Revise the questions as necessary.

(continued on page 475)

6. If the questionnaire is to be mailed, draft a cover letter explaining your purpose and asking the recipient to complete the questionnaire. Provide an addressed, stamped return envelope.
7. If the questionnaire is to be distributed electronically, make sure you introduce it and state your purpose clearly. In addition, thank the people or group in advance for their responses, and provide clear instructions on how they should return them to you (to your own email address or some other one?).
8. Be sure to state a deadline.
9. Consider adding a question that asks for comments.
10. Type the questionnaire, leaving adequate space for answers if it is being distributed in print form.
11. Proofread the questionnaire.

4 Analyzing and synthesizing data from field research

To make sense of the information you gather and determine its significance, first analyze it to identify what you want to look at: kinds of interactions? kinds of language? comparisons between men's and women's responses? The point is to find a focus, since you can't pay equal attention to everything. See if your instructor could recommend similar research you could check to see how it was analyzed.

Then synthesize by looking at the relationships among pieces of data. Look for recurring words or ideas that fall into patterns. Establish a system for coding your information, labeling each pattern you identify – a *V* for every use of violent language, for example, or a plus sign for every positive response. Ask one or two classmates to review your notes or data; they may notice other patterns or question your findings in helpful ways. Also consider showing your findings to some of your subjects, whose responses might help you revise your analysis and synthesis. Finally, sum up the meaning of what you have found. What is the significance of your finding?

THINKING CRITICALLY ABOUT RESEARCH

Return to the exercise you completed on p. 443. Add to it by examining the ways in which you conducted your research: What use did you make of primary and secondary sources? What library, online, and field work did you carry out? What aspect of the research process was most satisfying? What was most disappointing or irritating? How could you do research more efficiently?

42 Using Sources

All research builds on the astute, judicious, and sometimes inspired use of sources — that research work done by others. As Isaac Newton noted, those researchers who see the farthest do so "by standing up on the shoulders of giants." And while researchers cannot always count on a giant's shoulders to stand on, the quality of their insights is often directly related to how well they have understood and used the source materials — the shoulders — they have relied on.

As a reader, you will want to make the most of your sources, using the insights you gain from them in creating powerful prose of your own. This chapter offers advice on choosing and assessing sources, taking useful notes on them, acknowledging them appropriately, and interpreting them so that you can present data clearly to your readers. ■

42a Choosing sources

Experienced researchers know that all sources are not created equally useful, that some are more helpful or more provocative than others. One of your goals, therefore, is to learn to make good judgments about sources.

1 Building a working bibliography

One important result of choosing sources for research is the creation of a **working bibliography** — a list of books, articles, Web sites, and other sources that seem likely to address your research question. The emphasis here is on *working* — for this list will include materials that may end up not being useful. As you use reference books, bibliographic sources, periodical indexes, computer databases, search engines, or the circulation computer, make a bibliography entry for every source you think you might use.

Before you begin a working bibliography, check your assignment or ask your instructor to see whether you are to follow a particular style for documenting the sources you use. Chapters 44 – 47 provide guidelines on four major documentation styles — MLA, APA, CBE, and Chicago. If you familiarize yourself with the style now and follow it carefully, you will have, in the proper format, all the information necessary to prepare your final list of sources cited.

1. Decide on a format: index cards (one for each source), a notebook, or a computer file you can store on your disc. If you use cards or notebook pages, record information on one side only so that you can arrange the entries alphabetically when preparing the list of sources cited. Most word-processing programs will sort the entries for you.
2. For each book, record the following:
   - call number or other location information
   - author and/or editor
   - title and subtitle, if any
   - publisher's name and location
   - year of publication
   - other information — translator, volume, edition, and so on
   - inclusive page numbers for chapters or short works
3. For each article, list the following:
   - author and/or editor
   - article title and subtitle, if any
   - periodical name, volume number, and date
   - inclusive page numbers for the article
4. For entries from bibliographic or periodical indexes, list the name of the index in case you need to check the information again, and add the call number or other location information when you find the source in your library catalog.
5. For entries from electronic sources, get a printout, making sure that it includes all of the following items of information about the source that are applicable and available:
   - author
   - title
   - name and/or URL of discussion group
   - date published online or last updated
   - publication information for the print version of the source
   - URL and other protocol information
   - inclusive page, paragraph, screen, or other section numbers, or the total number of sections
   - date accessed
   - copyright information

(continued on page 478)

(continued from page 477)

6. **For nonprint sources such as films, recordings, or works of art, list the information required by the documentation system you are using (see Chapters 44 – 47), and note where you found the information.**
7. **When you examine print sources, check the accuracy of your information by consulting the title and copyright pages of a book and the table of contents and first page of a journal or magazine article. For a Web site, check the homepage.**

For a discussion of MLA style, see Chapter 44.

For her research essay, Shannan Palma, who was using the Modern Language Association style of documentation, decided to record her sources on index cards. Here is one of the cards she created for a book. Notice that it includes the library call number at the top.

BOOK

PN1995.9
R57
1995

Rushing, Janice Hocker, and Thomas S. Frentz. Projecting the Shadow: The Cyborg Hero in American Film. Chicago: U Chicago P, 1995.

Here is one of the cards Shannan Palma created for a periodical article. Notice that it includes the name of the database where she found the article.

ARTICLE

Prats, Armando J. "Back from the Sunset: The Western, the Eastwood Hero, and 'Unforgiven.'" Journal of Film and Video. Sp-Fall 1995: 106 – 23. ERIC Database.

2 Assessing the usefulness of a source

Since you want the information you glean from sources to be reliable and persuasive, you must evaluate each potential source carefully. Use these critical-thinking guidelines to assess the usefulness of a source:

- *Relevance.* Is the source closely related to your research question?
- *Author's and publisher's credentials and stance.* Is the author an expert on the topic? What is the author's stance on the issue(s) involved, and how does this influence the information in the source? Does the author support or challenge your own views? If you are evaluating a book published by a corporation, government agency, or interest group, what is the publisher's position on the topic? If you are evaluating an article, what kind of periodical published it? popular? academic? alternative?
- *Date of publication.* Recent sources are often more useful than older ones, particularly in the sciences. However, in some fields, the most authoritative works may be the older ones.
- *Level of specialization.* General sources can be helpful as you begin your research, but you may then need the authority or currentness of more specialized sources. On the other hand, extremely specialized works may be too hard to understand.
- *Audience.* Was the source written for the general public? specialists? advocates or opponents?

- *Cross-referencing.* Is the source cited in other works?
- *Length.* Is the source long enough to provide adequate detail?
- *Availability.* Do you have access to the source?

You can determine many of these characteristics just by quickly looking at the parts of a source that are listed here. If you then want to explore the source more thoroughly, these elements can also help you read critically.

- *Title and subtitle.* If you are investigating coeducation in the nineteenth century and find a book called *Women in Education,* the subtitle *The Challenge of the 1970s* will tell you that you almost certainly do not need to examine the book.
- *Copyright page.* In a book, this page will show you when the book was originally published, whether it is a revised edition, and who published it.
- *Abstract.* Abstracts are concise summaries of articles or books. They routinely precede articles in some journals and are included in certain periodical or bibliographic guides. Abstracts can help you decide whether to read the entire work; use them accordingly.
- *Table of contents.* Part and chapter titles can show you what a book contains. Try to determine whether the chapter topics are specific enough to be useful. In a periodical, the table of contents often includes brief descriptions of articles and can give you a general impression of the periodical itself.
- *Preface or foreword.* Very often these specify in detail the writer's purposes, range of interests, intended audience, topic restrictions, research limitations, and thesis.
- *Subheadings.* Subheadings in the text can give you an idea of how much detail is given on a topic and whether that detail would be helpful to you.
- *Conclusion or afterword.* Some books and articles end with a summary of the contents and a statement of significance that could help you decide how appropriate that source is for your project.
- *Note on the author.* Check the dust jacket of a book, the first and last few pages of a work, or an article itself for information about the author.
- *Index.* Check the index for words and topics key to your project; then see whether they seem to have much importance in the book. Are the listings for your key terms many or few?
- *Bibliography and/or footnotes.* Lists of references, usually at the end of a book or article, show how carefully a writer has investigated the subject. In addition, they may help you find other sources.

3 Evaluating electronic sources

Unlike most library-based research tools, much material on the Internet in general and the World Wide Web in particular is still the work of enthusiastic amateurs or commercial entrepreneurs. Advertisements, one-sided statements, and misleading or even false information are all jumbled together with good, reliable data. In this frontier electronic environment, you must rely on the same kind of critical thinking you use to assess the usefulness of any source. In addition, keep some key questions in mind.

- Who has posted this message or sponsors this site – an individual? an interest group? a company? a government agency? What can you determine about the credibility of the source? The following abbreviations within the URL can give important clues:

  .com – a commercial entity
  .edu – an educational institution
  .gov – a government agency
  .org – a nonprofit organization

  Country codes (.ca for Canada, for example) identify non-U.S. addresses.
- Who can be held accountable for the information in the source? How well and thoroughly does it credit its own sources?
- How effectively is the source designed? How user-friendly is it? If it is a Web site, are the links helpful? What effects do design, visuals, and sound have on the message?
- What is missing or omitted from the source? Do such exclusions affect how or whether you can use the information?
- What perspectives are represented? If only one perspective is represented, are other views acknowledged? Note that in Web sources, the links can tell you something about the site's perspective.

www

http://www.slu.edu/departments/english/research/

Designed by Craig Branham, this site offers tips for evaluating Web sources and reading a Web page, with discussion of different types of Web pages and a full tutorial on Web search strategies.

42b Reading sources with a critical eye

Because of time constraints and the wealth of material available on most topics, you probably will not have time to read completely through all of your potential material. Thus, reading with a critical eye can make your research process more efficient. The following considerations can guide your critical reading:

For additional information on critical reading, see 1b2.

Reading with your research question in mind

A good way to focus your attention is to read with your research question in mind. Use the index and the table of contents to zero in on the parts of a book that will help you answer your research question. Consider the following questions as you read:

- How does this material address your research question?
- In what ways does it provide support for your hypothesis?
- How might particular quotations help support your thesis?
- Does the source include counterarguments to your hypothesis that you will need to answer? If so, what answers can you provide?

Identifying the author's stance and tone

Every author holds opinions that affect his or her discussion of an issue, opinions that you as a reader must try to recognize and understand. Even the most seemingly factual report, such as an encyclopedia article, is necessarily filled with judgments, often unstated. Read with an eye for the author's overall rhetorical stance, or perspective on the topic, as well as for facts or explicit opinions. The rhetorical stance is closely related to the author's tone, the way his or her attitude toward the topic and audience is conveyed.

For a discussion of rhetorical stance, see 2g.

Alertness to perspective and tone will help you more fully understand a source and decide how (or whether) to use it. The following questions can help as well:

- Is the author an enthusiastic advocate of something, a strong opponent, a skeptical critic, an amused onlooker, a confident specialist in the field? Are there any clues to why the author takes this stance? What forces in society may have shaped or influenced it?
- How does this stance affect the author's presentation?
- If the author has a professional affiliation, how might the affiliation affect his or her stance?
- In what ways do you share – or not share – the author's stance?
- What is the author's tone? Is it cautious, angry, flippant, serious, impassioned? What words express this tone?

In the following paragraph, which appeared in a *Parade* magazine essay about nuclear war, the author's stance is obvious from the first sentence: he sees his topic, the possibility of nuclear war, as "an unprecedented human catastrophe." His dismissal of those who disagree with him as "fools and madmen" indicates the depth of his feelings, but his overall tone is restrained and objective because he assumes ("everyone knows") that the great majority of his readers share his view.

> Except for fools and madmen, everyone knows that nuclear war would be an unprecedented human catastrophe. A more or less typical strategic warhead has a yield of 2 megatons, the explosive equivalent of 2 million tons of TNT. But 2 million tons of TNT is about the same as all the bombs exploded in World War II – a single bomb with the explosive power of the entire Second World War but compressed into a few seconds of time and an area 30 or 40 miles across. . . .
>
> – CARL SAGAN, "The Nuclear Winter"

Assessing the author's argument and evidence

Just as every author has a point of view, every piece of writing has what may be called an argument, a position it takes. Even a report of scientific data implicitly "argues" that we should accept it as reliably gathered and reported. As you read, then, try to identify the author's argument, the reasons given in support of his or her position. Then try to decide *why* the author takes this position. Considering the following questions as you read can help you recognize – and assess – the points being argued in your sources:

- What is the author's main point?
- How much and what kind of evidence supports that point?
- How persuasive do you find the evidence?
- Can you offer counterarguments to or refutations of the evidence?
- Can you detect any questionable logic or fallacious thinking? (See 5g.)

Questioning your sources

Because all sources make an explicit or implicit argument, they often disagree with one another. Disagreements among sources arise sometimes from differences about facts, sometimes from differences about how to interpret facts. For instance, if an authoritative source says that the chances of a nuclear power plant melting down are 1 in 100,000, commentators could interpret that statistic very differently. A critic of nuclear power could argue that nuclear accidents are so terrible that this chance is too great to take, while a supporter of nuclear power could argue that such a small chance is essentially no chance at all.

The point is that all knowledge is interpreted subjectively. A writer may well tell nothing but the truth, but he or she can never tell the *whole* truth because people are not all-knowing. Thus you must examine all sources critically, using them not as unquestioned authorities but as contributions to your own informed opinion, your own truth.

Reading for connections

As you work with your sources, growing more familiar with them and with the ways in which they vary from – or agree with – one another, you should begin to see interesting patterns and connections emerging. This kind of critical thinking is crucial to your ability to use your sources in pursuit of your own goals, rather than just stacking them up as unconnected bits of information.

As Shannan Palma researched the development of the hero in Hollywood movies, she soon began to notice some patterns: the film star both as somehow bigger than life and as a flawed or "damaged human," as she came to call this kind of star. Shannan Palma was able to recognize these patterns because she was thinking critically, synthesizing, and comparing her sources. She then began to record her own ideas about these patterns, ideas that could further guide her research.

42c Taking notes

After you have decided that a source is useful, you will need to take careful notes on it. Note-taking methods vary greatly from one researcher to another. Whatever method you adopt, however, your goals will include (1) getting down enough information to help you recall the major points of the source; (2) getting down the information in the form in which you are most likely to want to incorporate it into your essay; and (3) getting down all the information you will need in order to cite the source accurately. Taking careful and complete notes will help you digest the source information as you read and will help you incorporate the material into your essay without inadvertently plagiarizing the source.

For a discussion of incorporating source materials into an essay, see 43d.

TAKING ACCURATE NOTES

1. **Using index cards, a notebook, or a computer file, list the author's name and a shortened title of the source. Your working bibliography entry for the source should contain full publication information (42a1), so you need not repeat it in your notes.**

(continued on page 485)

(continued from page 484)

2. Record exact page references. If the note refers to more than one page, indicate page breaks so that if you decide to use only part of the note, you will know which page to cite. For online sources without page numbers, record the paragraph, screen, or other section number(s) if indicated.
3. Label each note with a subject heading.
4. Identify the note as a quotation, a paraphrase, a summary, a combination of these forms, or some other form – such as your own critical comment – to avoid any confusion later. Mark quotations accurately with quotation marks, and paraphrase and summarize completely in your own words to be sure you do not inadvertently plagiarize the source. (42d)
5. Read over each completed note carefully to recheck the accuracy of quotations, statistics, and specific facts.

Most of your notes will probably take the form of direct quotation, paraphrase, or summary. Deciding what material to include and whether to quote, paraphrase, or summarize it is an outgrowth of reading with a critical eye. You may use some sources for background information and others as support for your thesis, and these different purposes may guide you to take one kind of note rather than another – summarizing background information, for example, but quoting statements that support your views. Likewise, as you read, you will want to evaluate the usefulness of each source and begin to decide what role it will play in your paper. You may then decide to eliminate some sources that do not prove useful.

DECIDING WHETHER TO QUOTE, PARAPHRASE, OR SUMMARIZE

QUOTE

→ wording that is so memorable or expresses a point so perfectly that you cannot change it without weakening the meaning you need
→ authors' opinions you wish to emphasize
→ respected authorities whose opinions support your ideas
→ authors whose opinions challenge or vary greatly from those of others in the field

(continued on page 486)

(continued from page 485)

PARAPHRASE

→ **passages you do not wish to quote but whose details you wish to note fully**

SUMMARIZE

→ **long passages whose main points you wish to record selectively**

1 Quoting

Quoting involves noting a source's *exact words.* Direct quotations can be effective for catching your readers' attention – for example, including a well-turned phrase in your introduction or giving an eyewitness's account in arresting detail. In a research essay, quotations from respected authorities can help establish your credibility as a researcher by showing that you've sought out experts in the field. In addition, allowing authors to speak for themselves, particularly if they hold opinions counter to yours or to those of other experts, helps demonstrate your fairness.

For more about establishing credibility, see 5f.

Finally, well-chosen quotations can broaden the appeal of your essay by drawing on emotion as well as logic, appealing to the reader's mind and heart. A student writing on the ethical issues of bullfighting, for example, might introduce an argument that bullfighting is not a sport by quoting Ernest Hemingway's striking comment that "the formal bull-fight is a tragedy, not a sport, and the bull is certain to be killed."

For more about using logical and emotional appeals in an argument, see 5g and 5h.

Here is an example of an original passage and Shannan Palma's note card recording a quotation from it. Notice how Palma uses ellipses to mark author's words she omitted. As she is using MLA style, she encloses the ellipses in square brackets to distinguish them from ellipsis points the author may have used. She also uses brackets to show an added word, changed capitalization, and which part of the quotation came from which page.

For more on using ellipses to indicate omissions and other changes in quotations, see 35b and 35f.

> It is not clear who makes and who is made in the relation between human and machine. It is not clear what is mind and what body in machines that resolve into coding practices. In so far as we know ourselves in both formal discourse (for example, biology) and in daily practice (for example, the homework economy in the integrated circuit), we find ourselves to be cyborgs, hybrids, mosaics, chimeras. Biological organisms have become biotic systems, communications devices like others. There is no fundamental, ontological

separation in our formal knowledge of machine and organism, of technical and organic. The replicant Rachel in the Ridley Scott film *Blade Runner* stands as the image of a cyborg culture's fear, love, and confusion.

– DONNA J. HARAWAY, *Simians, Cyborgs, & Women* (177 – 78)

Cyborg heroes

Haraway, Simians, pp. 177 – 178

[177]"In so far as we know ourselves [. . .], we find ourselves to be cyborgs, hybrids [. . .] [178][Thus, t]he replicant Rachel in the Ridley Scott film Blade Runner *stands as the image of a cyborg culture's fear, love, and confusion."*

Quotation

QUOTING ACCURATELY

→ Copy quotations *carefully*, with punctuation, capitalization, and spelling exactly as in the original.

→ Use square brackets if you introduce words of your own into a quotation or make changes in it, and use ellipses if you omit material. If you are following MLA style, enclose the ellipsis points in brackets. (35b and f) If you later incorporate the quotation into your essay, copy it faithfully, brackets, ellipses, and all.

→ It is especially important to enclose the quotation in quotation marks; don't rely on your memory to distinguish your own words from those of the source.

→ Record the author's name, shortened title, and page number(s) on which the quotation appeared. For online sources without page numbers, record the paragraph, screen, or other section number(s) if indicated.

→ Make sure you have a corresponding working bibliography entry with complete source information. (42a1)

→ Label the note with a subject heading.

2 Paraphrasing

A **paraphrase** accurately states all the relevant information from a passage *in your own words and phrasing,* without any additional comments or elaborations. A paraphrase is useful when the main points of a passage, their order, and at least some details are important but – unlike passages worth quoting – the particular wording is not. Unlike a summary, a paraphrase always restates *all* the main points of a passage in the same order, and often in about the same number of words.

Paraphrasing material helps you digest a passage, because chances are you can't restate the passage in your own words unless you grasp its full meaning. When you incorporate an accurate paraphrase into your essay, you show readers that you understand that source.

In order to paraphrase without plagiarizing inadvertently, *use your own words and sentence structures;* do not simply substitute synonyms, and do not imitate an author's style. If you wish to cite some of an author's words within a paraphrase, enclose them in quotation marks. A good way of assuring your originality is to paraphrase without looking at the source; then check to see that the paraphrase accurately presents the author's meaning and that you have used your own words and phrasing.

Writing acceptable paraphrases

Looking at the following examples of paraphrases that resemble the original too closely will help you understand how to write acceptable paraphrases. Be aware that even for acceptable paraphrases you must include a citation in your essay identifying the source of the information.

ORIGINAL

> It is not clear who makes and who is made in the relation between human and machine. It is not clear what is mind and what body in machines that resolve into coding practices. In so far as we know ourselves in both formal discourse (for example, biology) and in daily practice (for example, the homework economy in the integrated circuit), we find ourselves to be cyborgs, hybrids, mosaics, chimeras. Biological organisms have become biotic systems, communications devices like others. There is no fundamental, ontological separation in our formal knowledge of machine and organism, of technical and organic. The replicant Rachel in the Ridley Scott film *Blade Runner* stands as the image of a cyborg culture's fear, love, and confusion.
>
> – DONNA J. HARAWAY, *Simians, Cyborgs, & Women*

UNACCEPTABLE PARAPHRASE: USING THE AUTHOR'S WORDS

> As Haraway explains, in a high-tech culture like ours, *who makes and who is made, what is mind or body, becomes unclear.* When we look at ourselves in relation to the real or the mechanical world, we must admit we are cyborgs, and even *biological organisms* are now *communications systems.* Thus our beings can't be separated from machines. A fine example of this cyborg image is Rachel in Ridley Scott's *Blade Runner.*

Because the italicized phrases are either borrowed from the original without quotation marks or changed only superficially, this paraphrase plagiarizes.

UNACCEPTABLE PARAPHRASE: USING THE AUTHOR'S SENTENCE STRUCTURES

> As Haraway explains, it is unclear who is the maker and who is the made. It is unclear what in the processes of machines might be the mind and what the body. Thus in order to know ourselves at all, we must recognize ourselves to be cyborgs. Biology then becomes just another device for communicating. As beings, we can't separate the bodily from the mechanical anymore. Thus Rachel in Ridley Scott's *Blade Runner* becomes the perfect symbol of cyborg culture.

Although this paraphrase does not rely on the words of the original, it does follow the sentence structures too closely. Substituting synonyms for the major words in a paraphrase is not enough to avoid plagiarism. The paraphrase must represent your own interpretation of the material and thus must show your own thought patterns.

Now look at two paraphrases of the same passage that express the author's ideas accurately and acceptably, the first completely in the writer's own words and the second including a quotation from the original.

ACCEPTABLE PARAPHRASE: IN THE WRITER'S OWN WORDS

> As Haraway's entire chapter demonstrates, today the line between person and machine is forever blurred, especially in terms of the binary coding systems used by computers to "know." If knowing thyself is still important, we must know ourselves as a mixture of body, mind, and machine. Moviemaker Ridley Scott provides a good example of this mixture in the character of Rachel in *Blade Runner.*

ACCEPTABLE PARAPHRASE: QUOTING SOME OF THE AUTHOR'S WORDS

As Haraway's entire chapter demonstrates, today the line between person and machine is forever blurred, especially in terms of the binary coding systems used by computers to "know." If knowing thyself is still important, then, we must know ourselves as "cyborgs, hybrids, mosaics, chimeras." Moviemaker Ridley Scott provides a good example of this mixture in the character of Rachel in *Blade Runner.*

Here is an example of an original passage and Shannan Palma's note card recording a paraphrase of the passage:

> Cyborg imagery can help express two crucial arguments in this essay: first, the production of universal, totalizing theory is a major mistake that misses most of reality, probably always, but certainly now; and second, taking responsibility for the social relations of science and technology means refusing an anti-science metaphysics, a demonology of technology, and so means embracing the skilful task of reconstructing the boundaries of daily life, in partial connection with others, in communication with all of our parts. It is not just that science and technology are possible means of great human satisfaction, as well as a matrix of complex dominations. Cyborg imagery can suggest a way out of the maze of dualisms in which we have explained our bodies and our tools to ourselves.
>
> – DONNA J. HARAWAY, *Simians, Cyborgs, & Women* (181)

Cyborg heroes

Haraway, Simians, p. 181

Dreams of organic unity and coherence are futile, as are temptations to blame science and machinery for our problems. In place of these dreams and temptations, Haraway recommends the cyborg figure, which can give us a way to reconnect to parts of ourselves as well as others. In addition, it can give us a new dream of ourselves as multiple, surpassing either body or machine.

Paraphrase

On page 14 of the research essay at the end of Chapter 44, Shannan Palma uses part of this paraphrase: "In one of the essays in her anthology *Simians, Cyborgs, & Women,* historian of science Donna J. Haraway claims that our dreams of organic unity and coherence are futile. In their place, she recommends the cyborg figure, which can give us a new dream of ourselves as multiple, surpassing either body or machine."

PARAPHRASING ACCURATELY

- → **Include all main points and any important details from the original, in the same order in which they were presented.**
- → **State the meaning in your own words and sentence structures. If you want to include especially memorable language from the original, enclose it in quotation marks.**
- → **Leave out your own comments, elaborations, or reactions.**
- → **Record the author, shortened title, and the page number(s) on which the original material appeared. For online sources without page numbers, record the paragraph, screen, or other section number(s) if indicated.**
- → **Make sure you have a corresponding working-bibliography entry for the material. (42a1)**
- → **Label the note with a subject heading, and identify it as a paraphrase to avoid confusion with a summary.**
- → **Recheck to be sure that the words and sentence structures are your own and that they express the author's meaning accurately.**

3 Summarizing

A **summary** is a significantly shortened version of a passage, a section, or even a whole chapter or work that *captures main ideas in your own words.* Unlike a paraphrase, a summary uses just enough information to record the main points or the points you wish to emphasize. You needn't include all the author's points or any details, but be sure not to distort his or her meaning. The length of a summary depends on the length of the original and on how much information you will need to use. Your goal is to keep the summary as brief as possible, capturing only the gist of the original.

For a short passage, try reading it carefully and, without looking at the text, writing a one- or two-sentence summary. For a long passage or an entire chapter, skim the headings and topic sentences, and make notes of each; then write your summary in a paragraph or two. For a whole book, you may want to refer to the preface and introduction as well as chapter titles, headings, and topic sentences – and your summary may take a page or more.

Following is a note card recording a summary of the Haraway passage on page 488. Notice that it states the author's main points selectively – and without using her words.

Cyborg heroes

Haraway, Simians, pp. 177 – 78

Haraway says humans today are already part machine, and she cites the Ridley Scott movie Blade Runner *as an example.*

Summary

SUMMARIZING ACCURATELY

- → **Include just enough information to recount the main points you wish to cite. A summary is usually far shorter than the original.**
- → **Use your own words. If you include language from the original, enclose it in quotation marks.**
- → **Record the author, shortened title, and page number(s) on which the original material appeared. For online sources without page numbers, record the paragraph, screen, or other section number(s) if indicated.**
- → **Make sure you have a corresponding working-bibliography entry.**
- → **Label the note with a subject heading, and identify it as a summary to avoid confusion with a paraphrase.**
- → **Recheck to be sure you have captured the author's meaning and that your words are entirely your own.**

Combination notes

Often your reading will lead you to take a **combination note** – perhaps a paraphrase with some quotations, like the one on p. 490, or a summary of an entire chapter with a paraphrase of a key paragraph. If you combine forms, be sure to follow the guidelines for each kind of note, and label clearly which material is in which form.

Other kinds of notes

Many researchers take notes that do not fall into the preceding categories. Some take **key-term notes,** which may include names, dates, short statements – anything to jog their memories when they begin drafting. Others record **personal** or **critical notes** – thoughts, questions, disagreements, criticisms – striking ideas that come to mind as they read. Still others adopt systems peculiar to their research project. Shannan Palma kept a separate note for each of the movies that dealt with the themes she pursued in her essay. By labeling these notes with subject headings, she could easily determine how often each theme appeared. For research that is not library or Web based, you will probably need to take **field notes.**

For a discussion of field research, see 41h.

You may find reason to keep notes of various kinds in addition to those described here. Whatever form your notes take, always list the source's title, author, and page number(s) to document the material accurately. In addition, check that you have carefully distinguished your own thoughts and comments from the source's.

Photocopying and downloading source material

Nearly all libraries provide photocopying machines that you can use to copy pages or even whole articles or chapters. You can then annotate the photocopies with your thoughts and questions and highlight interesting quotations and key terms. However, try not to rely too heavily on photocopying – you still need to read the material carefully. And resist the temptation to treat photocopied material as notes, an action that could lead to inadvertent plagiarizing as well as to wasting time looking for information you only vaguely remember having read. If you read and take careful notes on your sources rather than relying primarily on photocopies, your drafting process will be more efficient. If you do photocopy material, note on the photocopy all the information you need to cite the material in your list of sources cited. (And check that the page numbers are clearly legible.)

If you are downloading source material from the Internet, check to see whether you are allowed to copy the source without asking for permission. Many sites include copyright guides. Most sites allow students to download one copy for personal use; do not email copies of material to discussion lists or other public forums without first getting permission. In addition, remember that Web sites change frequently, so what is there one day may not be there the next. It's especially important, then, to print out or take down all the information you will need to document those sources you download. For specific guidelines and help in requesting permission to use materials on the Internet, see p. 432.

42d Recognizing plagiarism and acknowledging sources

www •

http://www.ombuds.org/narrative1.html

This narrative from the Online Ombudsman <www.ombuds.org> describes a case involving a person whose Web site included summaries of a particular newspaper's articles. The debate provides a good example of how complex the issues of plagiarism and copyright can be in cyberspace.

"There is," the Bible says, "no new thing under the sun." In a way, this saying is true of research as well as of life: whatever research we do is influenced and affected by everything we have already read and experienced. Giving full acknowledgment to those sources presents a challenge, but trying to do so is important for several reasons. First, acknowledging your sources allows you to thank those whose work you have built on and thus avoid plagiarism. Second, it helps readers by placing your research in the context of other thinking and research; it shows how your research is part of a larger conversation and lets readers know where they can find more information. Finally, acknowledging your sources helps you critically examine your own research and thinking. How timely and reliable are your sources? Have you used them appropriately and accurately?

Acknowledging sources fully and generously, then, provides a means of establishing your *ethos* or your credibility as a researcher. Failure to credit sources breaks trust with both the research "conversation" and your readers; as a sign of dishonesty, it can easily destroy the credibility of the researcher and the research.

For more on credibility, see 5f.

1 Recognizing plagiarism

Plagiarism, the use of someone else's words or ideas as your own without crediting the other person, can result in serious consequences. At some colleges, students who plagiarize fail the course automatically; at others, they are expelled. Outside academic life, eminent political, business, and scientific leaders have been stripped of candidacies, positions, and awards following charges of plagiarism.

You are probably already aware of cases of deliberate plagiarism – handing in a paper that a friend wrote for a similar course or that was "purchased" online, copying passages directly from source materials. In addition, however, you should be aware of unintended plagiarism – a quotation accidentally used without quotation marks, a paraphrase that too closely resembles the original, background details used without acknowledgment in the mistaken belief that none was necessary. By understanding what material you must document, taking systematic, accurate notes, and giving full credit to sources in both parenthetical citations and your list of sources cited, you can avoid unintended plagiarism. Doing so for every idea you build on, however, is impossible. Where, then, do you draw the line?

2 Knowing which material requires acknowledgment

Some of the information you use does not need to be credited to another source because it is well known or because you gathered the data yourself. The following discussion should help you determine which materials you need to credit and which ones you can use without credit.

Materials not requiring acknowledgment

Common knowledge. If most readers would be likely to know something, you need not cite it. You do not need to credit a source for the statement that Bill Clinton was reelected president in 1996, for example. If, on the other hand, you give the exact number of popular votes he received in the 1996 election, you should cite the source for that figure.

Facts available in a wide variety of sources. If a number of encyclopedias, almanacs, or textbooks include a certain piece of information, you need not cite a specific source for it. For instance, you would not need to cite a source for the fact that the Japanese bombing of Pearl Harbor on December 7, 1941, destroyed most of the base except for the oil tanks and submarines. You would, however, need to credit a source that argued that the failure to destroy the submarines meant that Japan was destined to lose the subsequent war with the United States.

Your own feelings from field research. If you conduct observation, interviews, or surveys, simply announce your findings as your own.

FOR MULTILINGUAL WRITERS

PLAGIARISM AS A CULTURAL CONCEPT

Many cultures do not recognize Western notions of plagiarism, which rest on a belief that language can be owned by writers. Indeed, in many countries, and even within some communities in the United States, using the words of others without attribution is considered a sign of deep respect as well as an indication of knowledge. In academic writing in the United States, however, you should credit all materials but those that are common knowledge, that are available in a wide variety of sources, or that are your own findings from field research.

Materials requiring acknowledgment

For material that does not fall under the preceding categories, credit sources as fully as possible, using quotation marks where appropriate, citing the source in a customary fashion, and if necessary, including it in a list of sources.

For guidelines on documenting sources, see Chapters 44 – 47.

Direct quotations. Whenever you use another person's words directly, credit the source. If two quotations from the same source appear close together, you can use one citation after the second quotation. If you quote some of the author's words within a paraphrase or summary, you need to cite the quotation separately, after the closing quotation mark.

Facts that are not widely known or assertions that are arguable. If your readers would be unlikely to know a fact or if an author presents as fact an assertion that may or may not be true, cite the source. To claim, for instance, that Switzerland is amassing an offensive nuclear arsenal would demand the citation of a source because Switzerland has long been an officially neutral state. If you are not sure whether a fact will be familiar to your readers or a statement is debatable, citing the source is advisable.

Judgments, opinions, and claims of others. Whenever you summarize or paraphrase anyone else's opinion, give the source for that summary or paraphrase. Even though the wording should be completely your own, you need to acknowledge the source.

Statistics, charts, tables, and graphs from any source. Credit all statistical and graphic material not derived from your own field research, even if you yourself create the graph from data in another source.

Help provided by friends, instructors, or others. A conference with an instructor may give you the idea you need to clinch an argument. Give credit. Friends may help you conduct surveys, refine questionnaires, or think through problems. Credit them, too.

If your working bibliography contains complete entries that you double-checked as you examined each source and if your notes clearly identify direct quotations, paraphrases, and summaries that you double-checked for accuracy as you took the notes, the task of acknowledging the source of each piece of information you incorporate into your essay will be much easier.

→ Maintain an accurate and thorough working bibliography. (42a1)
→ Establish a consistent note-taking system, listing sources and page numbers and clearly identifying all quotations, paraphrases, summaries, statistics, and graphics. (42c)
→ Identify all quotations with quotation marks – both in your notes and (except for block quotations) in your essay.
→ Be sure that you summarize and paraphrase using your own words and sentence structures.
→ In your essay, give a citation for each quotation, paraphrase, summary, arguable assertion or opinion, statistic, and graph that is from a source. (44a, 45a, 46a, and 47a)
→ Prepare an accurate and complete list of sources cited according to the required documentation style. (44c, 45c, 46b, and 47b)

42e Interpreting sources

Your task as a reader is to identify and understand sources and sets of data as completely as possible. As a writer, your aim must be to present data and sources *to other readers* so that they can readily understand the point you are making. Doing so calls for you to notice patterns in your sources and to develop your own interpretation of them.

Synthesizing data and drawing inferences

Throughout the research process, you are **synthesizing** – grouping similar pieces of data together, looking for patterns or trends, and identifying the gist, or main points, of the data. Shannan Palma began by grouping the movie heroes she was studying into types: the traditional romantic hero; the fantasy hero; the loner or misfit hero, and so on. These group categories allowed her to note differences and similarities between them, an act characteristic of synthesizing and critical thinking.

Often, such synthesizing will lead you to make **inferences** – conclusions that are not explicitly stated in but that follow logically from the data given. For example, as Shannan Palma looked at the similarities among her groups of heroes, she began to notice a pattern: many of the stars who played the heroes seemed to be viewed by moviegoers as heroes themselves. What started as a hunch turned into an inference she later made, that the Hollywood star system led to a case of "mistaken identity" that blurred the lines between fictional characters and real-life heroes.

Recording your thoughts and ideas

Perhaps the most exciting part of the research process occurs when the materials you are reading spark something in your mind and new ideas take hold, ideas that can become part of your thesis or argument. *Don't let them get away.* Jot them down, perhaps in a special section of your writing log or research log, if you are keeping one. Some ideas may be thrown away later because they do not suit the final shape your essay takes, but others will likely *provide* the shape. Disagreements among sources can provide particularly fruitful areas to consider and may encourage you to discover new insights of your own. Consequently, you need to pay close attention to all your sources' arguments – those you agree with as well as those you do not agree with.

THINKING CRITICALLY ABOUT PARAPHRASES AND SUMMARIES

If you are working on a research essay, choose an important source, and prepare a paraphrase of two or three paragraphs, using your own words and sentence structures. Analyze your paraphrase using the guidelines on p. 492. Then summarize the same passage, and check to see how well you followed the guidelines on p. 492. Note any mistakes you made in paraphrasing or summarizing, and list ways you can avoid such mistakes in the future. Record these notes along with the revised paraphrase and summary in your writing log or research log, if you are keeping one.

Writing a Research Essay

43

A nineteenth-century author remarked that "in research the horizon recedes as we advance. . . . And research is always incomplete." But while you may continue to pursue a research question for a long time, there comes a time to draw the strands of research together and articulate your conclusions in writing.

You will probably do most of your final organizing and drafting when your research is largely complete and you have most of the facts, evidence, quotations, and other data you think you need. For most college research essays, the process of drafting a final version should begin *at least* two weeks before the deadline, to allow time for responses to the draft, further research, revision, and editing. This chapter will help guide you through this process. ■

43a Refining your plans

Throughout your research, you have generated notes that answer your research question and reflect on your hypothesis. Your growing understanding of the subject has no doubt led you to gather other information, which may have altered your original question. This somewhat circular process, a kind of research spiral, is at the heart of all research-based writing.

You should by now have a fair number of notes containing facts, opinions, paraphrases, summaries, quotations, and other material. You probably also have thoughts about the connections among these many pieces of information. And you should have some sense of whether your hypothesis has been established sufficiently to serve as the thesis of an essay. Reconsider now your purpose, audience, stance, and working thesis.

1 Reconsidering your purpose, audience, stance, and working thesis

Given what you now know about your research question, reconsider questions such as the following:

1. What is your central purpose? What other purposes, if any, do you have?
2. What is your stance toward your topic? Are you an advocate, a critic, an observer ? (See 2g.)

3. What audience(s) other than your instructor might you be addressing?
4. How much about your research question does your audience know already? How much background will you need to present?
5. What sorts of supporting information are your readers likely to find convincing – examples? precedents? quotations from authorities? statistics? direct observation? data drawn from interviews? (See 5g.)
6. What tone will most appeal to them? Should you present yourself as a colleague, an expert, a student?
7. How can you establish common ground with your readers and show consideration of points of view other than your own? (See 5f2 and Chapter 29.)
8. What is your working thesis trying to establish? How likely is your audience to accept it?

2 Developing an explicit thesis

One useful way of relating your purpose, audience, and thesis before you begin a full draft is by writing out an **explicit thesis statement.** Such a statement allows you to articulate all your major lines of argument and to see how well those arguments carry out your purpose and appeal to your audience. At the drafting stage, try to develop your working thesis into an explicit statement, which might take the following form:

> In this essay, I plan to (explain/argue/demonstrate/analyze, and so on) for an audience of ____
> that ____
> because/if____________________________, ____________________________,
> ____________________________.

Shannan Palma developed the following explicit thesis statement:

> In this essay, I plan to demonstrate for an audience of classmates from my first-year writing class that current trends in Hollywood films signal not the death of the hero but the evolution of the hero into two very different images.

3 Testing your thesis

Writing out an explicit thesis will often confirm your research and support your hypothesis. It may, however, reveal that your hypothesis is invalid, inadequately supported, or insufficiently focused. In such cases, you must then rethink your original research question, perhaps do further research, and work toward revising your hypothesis and thesis. To test your thesis, consider the following list of questions:

1. How can you state the topic of your thesis or your comment about the topic more precisely or more clearly (3b)?
2. In what ways will your thesis interest and appeal to your audience? What can you do to increase that interest (5h)?
3. How could the wording of your thesis be more specific? Could you use more concrete nouns (27c) or stronger verbs (23a)? Should you add qualifying adjectives or adverbs (Chapter 12)?
4. Is your thesis going to be manageable, given your limits of time and knowledge? If not, what can you do to make it more manageable?
5. What evidence from your research supports each aspect of your thesis? What additional evidence do you need?

43b Organizing information

In discussing her process of writing, writer Marie Winn talks about the challenge of transforming a tangle of ideas and information "into an orderly and logical sequence on a blank piece of paper." This is the task of organization, of grouping information effectively. Experienced writers differ considerably in the ways they go about this task, and you will want to experiment until you find an organizational method that works well for you. This section will discuss two organizing strategies — grouping material by subject headings and outlining.

1 Grouping notes by subject headings

During your research, you have been taking notes and listing ideas. To group these materials, examine them for connections, finding what might be combined with what, which notes will be more useful and which less useful, which ideas lend support to the thesis and which should be put aside. Brainstorm about your research question one last time, and add the resulting notes to your other materials, looking to see whether they fit with any of the materials you already have.

If you have been keeping notes on cards, you can arrange the cards in groups by subject headings, putting the ones with your main topics in the center and arranging any related cards around them. If you have been taking notes in a notebook, you can cut the pages apart and group the slips of paper in a similar manner. If your notes are in a computer file, you can sort them by subject headings or search for particular headings — or print them out, cut them up, and group them yourself.

Grouping your notes in this way will help you identify major ideas and see whether you have covered all the areas you need to cover. It will also help you decide whether you have too many ideas, whether you can omit some of your less useful sources, or whether you need to do more research in some area. Most important, it will allow you to see how the many small pieces of your research fit together.

Once you have established initial groups, skim through the notes looking for connections you can use to organize your draft. For example, Shannan Palma noticed that the notes on one of her main topics, contemporary movie heroes, seemed to be related to another set of notes, on movie characters who are only partially human. She thus decided to see whether this connection revealed a new category of hero.

2 Outlining

Outlines can be used in various ways. Some writers group their notes, write a draft, and then outline the draft to study its tentative structure. Others develop a working outline from their notes, listing the major points in a tentative order with support for each point. Such a working outline may see you through the rest of the process, or you may decide to revise it as you go along. Still other writers prefer to plot out their organization early on in a formal outline.

For further discussion of outlines, see 3e.

Shannan Palma drew up an informal outline of her ideas while she was still doing research on her topic, thinking that this simple structure would help keep her focused on the information she still needed to find. Here is that informal outline:

Development of the hero
- in legend, literature, film
- film heroes and "mistaken identity"
- the emerging Hollywood star
- the confusion between the star and the hero/character
- examples

Beyond heroes
- what possibilities??

Because she knew she was required to submit a formal outline with her essay, Shannan Palma kept adding to this informal outline as her research and writing progressed. She did not complete the formal outline (which appears on p. 541) until after her essay was completely drafted, however, when it served as a way to analyze and revise the draft.

43c Drafting your essay

When you are ready to draft your essay, set yourself a deadline, and structure your work with that deadline in mind. Gather your notes, outline, and sources and read through them, "getting into" your topic. Most writers find that some sustained work (perhaps two or three hours) pays off at this point. Begin drafting a part of the essay that you feel confident about. For example, if you are not sure how you want to introduce the essay but do know how you want to approach one point, begin with that, and return to the introduction later. The most important thing is to get started.

The drafting process itself varies considerably among researchers, and no one else can determine what will work best for you. The tips offered in 3f, however, can help. No matter what process you use to produce a draft, remember to include sources (including summaries, paraphrases, and quotations) as you go; doing so during drafting will save time later and help you produce your list of works cited.

Chances are that you will be doing most of your drafting with a word-processing program. If so, remember that most software programs now come with an outlining function as well as capabilities for formatting endnotes, footnotes, and lists of sources cited. You may want to begin by pasting or copying your informal (or formal) outline into a new document and using it to help guide your drafting: you can always jump back and forth from one part of the outline to the next. You can also open up more than one window, putting notes in one window, your draft in another, your bibliography in another, your outline in yet another. If you have been keeping your notes in a computer file, you can copy them directly into your document and then rework them so that they fit appropriately into your draft. And if you have kept your source information in a computer file as well, you can have that file handy as you add entries to your list of sources cited.

www •

http://www.researchpaper.com/forums/Writers_Corner/index.html

Discuss writing strategies and tips with other students and researchers who are working on their own research projects. Follow the URL back to <http://www.researchpaper.com/forums/> and you'll find links to research discussions organized by subject area.

1 Drafting a working title and introduction

The title and introduction play special roles, for they set the context for what is to come. Ideally, the title announces the subject of the essay in an intriguing or memorable way. The introduction should draw readers into the essay and provide any background they will need to understand the discussion. You can find general advice on titles in 4f1 and on introductions in 4f2 and 6f1. Also consider the following specifics when drafting an introduction to a research essay:

- It is often effective to *open with a question,* especially your research question. Next, you might explain what you will do to answer the question and then *end with your thesis* (in essence, the answer).
- Because you will be bringing together several distinct points from various sources, you will probably want to *forecast your main points,* to help readers get their bearings.
- You will want to *establish your own credibility* as a research writer by revealing your experience and demonstrating what you have done to become an expert on your topic.
- In general, you may *not* want to open with a quotation – though it can be a good attention-getter. In a research essay, you usually want to quote several sources to support your ideas, and opening with a quotation from one source may give the impression that you will be presenting that writer's ideas rather than using them in support of your own.

Shannan Palma wanted to use lyrics from a well-known song at the very beginning of her essay, both because she knew that the song and the singer (Jewel) would be known to her classmates and because the song poses a provocative question: "where's my hope now that my heroes have gone?" She begins by affirming the importance of this question and then builds interest in its answer by noting the central role heroes have played throughout U.S. history. After establishing that she has conducted extensive research on this question and its possible answers, she provides an overview of her goals for the essay, concluding with her thesis. Because she had to set the scene for her essay and provide necessary background information, she decided to use two paragraphs for her full introduction. (See her introduction on p. 544.)

2 Drafting your conclusion

A good conclusion to a research essay helps readers know what they have learned. Its job is not to persuade (the body of the essay should already have done that), but it can contribute to the overall effectiveness of your argument. General advice on writing conclusions can be found in 4f3 and 6f2, but the following specific strategies are especially appropriate for research essays:

- A specific-to-general pattern is frequently appropriate. Open with a reference to your thesis, and then expand to a more general conclusion that reminds readers of the significance of your discussion.
- If you have covered several main points, you may want to remind readers of them. Be careful, however, to provide more than a mere summary.

- Try to end with something that will have an impact — a provocative quotation or question, a vivid image, a call for action, or a warning. Remember, however, that readers generally don't like obvious preaching.
- Tailor your conclusion to the needs of your readers, in terms of both the information you include and the tone and style you adopt.

Shannan Palma's conclusion summarizes the main points of her essay and then ends with an assertion of her topic's importance to our culture. Her use of the pronoun *our* invokes a kinship with readers who are also wondering what kind of heroes the twenty-first century will bring.

43d Incorporating source materials

When you reach the point of drafting your essay, a new task awaits: weaving your source materials into your writing. The challenge is to use your sources yet remain the author — to quote, paraphrase, and summarize other voices while remaining the major voice in your essay.

You tentatively decided to quote, paraphrase, or summarize material when you took notes on your sources. As you choose which sources to use in your essay and how to use them, however, you may reevaluate those decisions. For example, you may decide to summarize in your essay what you paraphrased in your notes, to use only a quotation you included in the midst of a summary, or not to use a particular quotation at all. To avoid plagiarizing, document any source material you do include with a citation within your text and an entry in your list of sources.

For guidelines on critical reading and note taking, see 42b and c.

For guidelines on documenting sources, see Chapters 44 – 47.

1 Using direct quotations

Your essay must be your own work, and you should depend on other people's words as little as possible, limiting quotations to those *necessary* to your argument or *memorable* for your readers. Reasons to use direct quotations include the following:

- to incorporate a statement expressed so effectively by the author that it cannot be paraphrased without altering the meaning
- to allow the words of an authority on your topic to contribute to your own credibility as a writer
- to allow an author to defend his or her position in his or her own words
- to create a particular effect

Consider, then, how to work any quotations into your text.

Enclosing brief quotations within your text

Prose quotations of no more than four lines (MLA style) or fewer than forty words (APA style) should be worked into your text, enclosed by quotation marks. For example:

> In Miss Eckhart, Welty recognizes a character who shares with her "the love of her art and the love of giving it, the desire to give it until there is no more left" (10).

> In Russia, however, the men who took control had hardly any experience in military or administrative fields at all. As Edward Crankshaw explained, "They were a disciplined set of revolutionary conspirators who had spent most of their adult lives in exile in Russia or abroad" (44).

Notice that both examples alert readers to the quotations by using **signal phrases** that include the author's name. When you cite a quotation in this way, you need put only the page number in parentheses.

When you introduce a quotation without mentioning the author's name, place the name in parentheses before the page number. Be sure, however, that you always distinguish where someone else's words begin. For example:

> In *The Third Life of Grange Copeland,* Grange's inability to respond to his son is evident "even in private and in the dark and with his son, presumably asleep" when he "could not bear to touch his son with his hand" (Walker 121).

These are but two ways of introducing a quotation. Both MLA and APA styles specify what should appear in parenthetical citations in what circumstances and how they should be punctuated. See 44a and 45a for guidelines.

Setting off long quotations

Prose quotations longer than four lines (MLA style) or forty words (APA style) should be set off from the regular text. Begin such a quotation on a new line, and indent every line one inch or ten spaces (MLA) or five to seven spaces (APA) from the left margin. Because this indentation sets off the quotation clearly, no quotation marks are necessary. Type the quotation to the right margin, and double-space it as you do the regular text. Long quotations are usually introduced by a signal phrase or a sentence followed by a colon. The following example shows MLA style.

```
A good seating arrangement can prevent problems;
however, "withitness," as defined by Woolfolk, works
even better:
          Withitness is the ability to communicate to
          students that you are aware of what is
          happening in the classroom, that you "don't
          miss anything."  With-it teachers seem to have
          "eyes in the back of their heads."  They avoid
          becoming too absorbed with a few students,
          since this allows the rest of the class to
          wander. (359)
This technique works, however, only if students actually
believe that their teacher will know everything that
goes on.
```

Note that with long quotations, the parenthetical citation comes after the period at the end of the quotation and does not have a period after it.

Though long quotations are often necessary in research essays, use them cautiously. Too many of them may suggest that you did not rely on your own thinking. In addition, long quotations can make an essay seem choppy, and they can distract from your analysis of the material. If you think you may be overusing long quotations, substitute paraphrases or summaries for some of them.

Integrating quotations into your text

In college writing, quotations need to be smoothly and clearly linked to the surrounding sentences in your essay. In most cases, you need to use a signal phrase to provide such a link. For example:

WITHOUT A SIGNAL PHRASE

In *Death of a Salesman,* Willy Loman dreams the wrong dreams and idealizes the wrong ideals. "He has lived on his smile and on his hopes, survived from sale to sale, been sustained by the illusion that he has countless friends in his territory, that everything will be all right [. . .]" (Brown 97).

See how the following revision uses a signal phrase to make the link between quotation and text far easier to recognize. Note also how the shift in verb tenses from text to quotation is smoothed out in the revision.

WITH A SIGNAL PHRASE

In *Death of a Salesman,* Willy Loman dreams the wrong dreams and idealizes the wrong ideals. His misguided perceptions are well captured by Brown: "He has lived on his smile and on his hopes, survived from sale to sale, been sustained by the illusion that he has countless friends in his territory, that everything will be all right [. . .]" (97).

Introducing a quotation with the author's name and a **signal verb** is another way of integrating a quotation into your text. Remember, however, that the verb must be appropriate to the idea you are expressing.

As Richard deCordova notes in a memorable phrase, the studios wanted to convince millions of movie-goers that "the real hero behave[d] just like the reel hero" (qtd. in Gallagher, part 2).

In this sentence from Shannan Palma's essay, her use of the signal verb *notes* makes it clear that the quotation is by deCordova – and that she agrees with it. If she had wanted to indicate that the author's point is more open to disagreement – that other authorities might disagree with it, or that she herself does – she might have used a different verb, such as *claims* or *asserts.* If she had wanted to take a neutral stance, a verb like *says* or *remarks* would have been appropriate.

Verbs like *notes* or *claims* or *says* can be used by themselves following the author's name. But other verbs, like *interprets* or *opposes,* require more complex phrasing.

In her essay, Haraway strongly opposes those who condemn technology outright, arguing that we must not indulge in a "demonology of technology" (181).

In any case, the signal verb you choose allows you to characterize the author's viewpoint or perspective as well as your own, so you should choose with care.

SIGNAL VERBS

acknowledges	answers	claims	criticizes
advises	asserts	concludes	declares
agrees	believes	concurs	describes
allows	charges	confirms	disagrees

(continued on page 509)

(continued from page 508)

discusses	lists	remarks	says
disputes	objects	replies	states
emphasizes	observes	reports	suggests
expresses	offers	responds	thinks
interprets	opposes	reveals	writes

Indicating changes with square brackets and ellipses

Sometimes, for the sake of clarity or length, you will wish to alter a direct quotation in some way – to make a verb tense fit smoothly into your text, to replace a pronoun with a noun, to eliminate unnecessary detail, to change a capital letter to lowercase or vice versa. Enclose any changed or added words in square brackets, and indicate any deletions with ellipsis points. If you are following MLA style, enclose the ellipsis points in brackets to distinguish them from ellipses the author may have used. Because most quotations that you integrate into your essay come from longer passages, you need not use ellipses at the beginning or end of a quotation unless the last sentence as you cite it is incomplete.

> A farmer, Jane Lee, spoke to the Nuclear Regulatory Commission about the occurrences. "There is something wrong in the [Three Mile Island] area. It is happening within nature itself," she said, referring to human miscarriages, stillbirths, and birth defects in farm animals ("Legacy" 33).

> Economist John Kenneth Galbraith has pointed out that "large corporations cannot afford to compete with one another. Their survival is predicated upon [. . .] market segmentation. In a truly competitive market someone loses [. . .]. American big business has finally learned that everybody has to protect everybody else's investment" (Key 17).

Be careful that any changes you make in a quotation do not alter its meaning. Even if an error occurs in the original, do not correct it, but alert readers to it by inserting *sic* ("thus") in square brackets after it.

> As the reviewer for *Gumshoe* remarks, "This absorbing mystery offers an attractively sardonic heroin [*sic*] and a humdinger of a plot" (31).

In any event, use brackets and ellipses sparingly; too many of them make for difficult reading and might suggest that you have changed the meaning by removing some of the context.

For more on using brackets and ellipses to indicate omissions and other changes in quotations, see 35b and 35f.

2 Using paraphrases and summaries

When you want to use others' ideas but have no need to quote their exact words, paraphrase or summarize. Reasons for using paraphrases and summaries include the following:

- to present background information and other facts that your readers may not know
- to explain various positions on your topic

Integrating paraphrases and summaries

As with quotations, you need to introduce paraphrases and summaries clearly, usually with a signal phrase that includes the name of the author of the source. Using the author's name also helps lend authority to the material. Sometimes, in fact, you will want to highlight the source even more prominently. Notice how the writer of the following example focuses on one authority, first introducing her by name and title and then both quoting and summarizing her work:

> On the other hand, some observers of the battle of the sexes are trying to arrange cease-fires. Professor of linguistics Deborah Tannen says that she offers her book *That's Not What I Meant!* to "women and men everywhere who are trying their best to talk to each other" (19). Tannen goes on to illustrate how communication between women and men breaks down and then to suggest that a full awareness of "genderlects" can improve relationships (297).

In the following example, on the other hand, the writer focuses more on the information paraphrased, identifying the authors only parenthetically:

> Three areas of established differences in cognitive abilities are recognized by the majority of researchers: verbal ability, mathematical ability, and spatial ability (Block 517). As shown by current research, a specific cognitive sex difference exists in verbal ability; in general, females are superior to males in this area starting in early childhood (Weitz 99).

Remember that indicating the sources of paraphrases and summaries is important. Even unintentional failure to cite sources for materials that are not in quotation marks but that you could not have known or arrived at by yourself constitutes plagiarism. Make certain that you record the sources of general background information as well as sources of specific quotations, facts, viewpoints, and so forth. If any of your

For a discussion of how to avoid plagiarism, see 42d.

notes are incomplete or unclear, relocate and reread the appropriate sources to clarify the information. If you are unable to do so, you would be wise to leave out the material rather than risk plagiarism.

3 Checking for excessive use of source material

Exactly how much you should use sources in an essay depends on your purpose, your audience, and the section of the essay. In general, your essay should not be a patchwork of quotations, paraphrases, and summaries from other people. You need a rhetorical stance, a perspective that represents you as the author. If you are overquoting and overciting, your own voice will disappear. The following passage illustrates this problem:

> The United States is one of the countries with the most rapid population growth. In fact, rapid population increase has been a "prominent feature of American life since the founding of the republic" (Day 31). In the past, the cause of the high rate of population growth was the combination of large-scale immigration and a high birth rate. As Day notes, "Two facts stand out in the demographic history of the United States: first, the single position as a receiver of immigrants; second, our high rate of growth from natural increase" (31).
>
> Nevertheless, American population density is not as high as in most European countries. Day points out that the Netherlands, with a density of 906 persons per square mile, is more crowded than even the most densely populated American states (33).

Most readers will think that the source, Day, is much too prominent here. If this passage were a background discussion or a survey of the literature on a topic, with each source being different, such a large number of citations might be acceptable. But all these citations are from the same source, and readers are likely to conclude that the source is primary and the author of the essay only secondary.

43e Reviewing your draft

Because a research essay involves a complex mix of your thoughts and materials from outside sources, it calls for an especially careful review before you begin revising. As with most kinds of writing, however, taking a break after drafting the essay is important, so that when you reread it, you can bring a fresh eye to the task.

When you return to the draft, read it straight through, without stopping. Then read it again slowly, reconsidering five things: purpose, audience, stance, thesis, and support. You might find that outlining your draft (see 3e) helps you analyze it at this point.

- From your reading of the draft, what do you now see as its *purpose*? How does this compare to your original purpose? Does the draft do what your assignment requires?
- What *audience* does your essay address?
- What is your *stance* toward the topic?
- What is your *thesis*? Is it clearly stated?
- What *evidence* supports your thesis? Is the evidence sufficient?

Answer these questions as best you can, since they are the starting point for revision. Next, you need a closer reading of your essay and probably the comments of other readers. Consider asking friends or classmates to read and respond to your draft.

The advice from readers may be most helpful if you ask questions specific to your essay. If you are unsure about whether to include a particular point, how to use a certain quotation, or where to add more examples, ask readers specifically what they think you should do.

For more on getting critical responses to a draft, see 4c.

43f Revising and editing your draft

Using any responses you have gathered and your own analysis, turn now to your final revision. It is advisable to work in several steps.

- *Considering responses.* Have readers identified problems you need to solve? If so, have they made specific suggestions about ways to revise? Have they identified strengths that might suggest ways of revising? For example, if they showed great interest in one point but no interest in another, consider expanding the first and deleting the second.
- *Reconsidering your original purpose, audience, and stance.* Judging from your readers' comments, do you feel confident that you have achieved your purpose? If not, what is missing? How have you appealed to your readers? How have you established common ground with them? How have you satisfied any special concerns they may have? Has your rhetorical stance toward your topic changed in any way? If so, what effect has that change had on your essay?
- *Assessing your own research.* If you conducted experiments, surveys, interviews, observations, or other field research, do the results stand up to your own and readers' analyses? Are all the data accurate and your conclusions warranted? What part did you play in the research, and how could your role have influ-

enced your findings? If your research involved interviewing or surveying other people, how appropriate are their credentials or characteristics to the thesis you are arguing? Have you obtained their permission to quote them (by name if you want to do so)? If you quoted from email, Usenet, a MOO, or an IRC, did you get permission from the writer to use their words?

- *Gathering additional material.* If you need to strengthen any points, go back to your notes to see whether you have the necessary information. If you failed to consider opposing viewpoints adequately, for instance, you may need to find more material.
- *Deciding on changes you need to make.* Figure out everything you have to do to perfect your draft, and make a list. With your deadline firmly in mind, plan your revision.
- *Rewriting your draft.* Word-processing software has the great advantage of allowing you to move text around and to delete or change passages easily. Experienced writers usually prefer to revise first on hard copy, however, so that they can see the entire essay spread out before them. However you revise, be sure to keep copies of each successive draft. And begin with the major work: changing content, adding examples or evidence, addressing section- or paragraph-level concerns. Then turn to sentence-level work and to individual word choice. Also revise for clarity and to sharpen the dominant impression your essay creates.
- *Reconsidering your title, introduction, and conclusion.* In light of the reevaluation and revision of your draft, reread these important parts to see whether they still serve their purpose. Does the introduction accurately predict, and the conclusion accurately restate, what the body of the final essay discusses? If not, do you need to forecast your main points in the introduction or summarize them in the conclusion? Does your introduction capture readers' attention? Does your conclusion help them see the significance of your argument? Is your title specific enough to let your readers know about your research question and engaging enough to make them want to read your answer to it?
- *Checking your documentation.* Have you included a citation in your text for every quotation, paraphrase, and summary you incorporated, following consistently the required style? (See 42d and Chapters 44 and 45.)
- *Editing your draft.* Now is the time to attend carefully to grammar, usage, spelling, punctuation, and mechanics. If you are using a computer, take the time to use the spell checker – but be aware that it will miss many errors (such as homonyms like *to, two,* and *too*). If you have persistent problems with certain words or phrases, use the "Search" command to find them, and then double-check their spelling and usage. If you are using a style or grammar checker, be aware that such programs cannot make rhetorical choices and often miss problem passages or phrases – or identify perfectly acceptable ones as problems – because they aren't yet equal to the complexity of English. Use them with great caution.

43g Preparing a list of sources

Once you have a final draft with your source materials in place, you are ready to prepare your list of works cited (MLA style), your references (APA and CBE styles), or your bibliography (Chicago style). Follow the guidelines for your required style carefully, creating an entry for each source used in your essay. Double-check your draft against your list of sources cited to see that you have listed every source mentioned in the parenthetical citations and (unless you are listing all the sources you consulted) that you have not listed any sources not cited in your essay. See Chapters 44 – 47 for guidelines on preparing a list of sources.

Almost all word-processing software programs now provide templates for formatting endnotes, footnotes, or lists of sources. They will alphabetize for you and insert some of the necessary formatting, such as italics.

43h Preparing and proofreading your final copy

www •

http://www.ualr.edu/~owl/proofrd.htm

Item 1 makes this short list of proofreading tips worth consulting and printing out for later reference.

Your final rough draft may end up looking very rough indeed. So your next task is to create a final perfectly clean copy. This is the version of the paper you will submit to your instructor, the one that will represent all your work and effort.

To make sure that this final version puts your best foot forward, proofread extremely carefully. For proofreading, it is best to work with a hard copy, since reading onscreen often leads to inaccuracies and especially to missed typos. In addition, you may want to read backward, going word for word, or to use a ruler, lowering it as you read each line. Finally, proofread once again for content, for the flow of your argument, to make sure you haven't mistakenly deleted whole lines, sentences, paragraphs, or sections.

Preparing the final copy, especially if you are working with a computer, can allow for interesting possibilities in the layout and design of your essay. For a discussion of these issues, see Chapter 51.

After your manuscript preparation and proofreading are complete, take some time to celebrate your achievement: your research and hard work have paid off and produced a piece of writing you can, and should, take pride in.

THINKING CRITICALLY ABOUT RESEARCH ESSAYS

Reading with an Eye for Research

The research essays at the end of Chapters 44 and 45 were written by two students, the first of whom you've followed since Chapter 40. The first essay, which follows MLA style, was written for a composition class; the second, which follows APA style, was written for a psychology class. Read these essays carefully, and study the marginal annotations. Compare your research essay with these, noting differences in approach, style, format, and use of sources.

Thinking about Your Own Research Essay

Pause now to reflect on the research essay you have written. How did you go about organizing your information? What would you do to improve this process? What problems did you encounter in drafting? How did you solve these problems? How many quotations did you use, and how did you integrate them into your text? When and why did you use summaries and paraphrases? What did you learn from revising?

44

Documenting Sources: MLA Style

Adam was the only man who, when he said a good thing, knew that nobody had said it before him.

– MARK TWAIN

No writer since Adam, in other words, has had the luxury of not having to document his or her sources. In your writing, full and accurate documentation is important because it helps build your credibility as a writer and researcher by giving credit to those people whose works influenced your own ideas.

Although all documentation styles require the same basic information, you will want to use the style favored in a particular field or required by a particular instructor. Following specific rules of punctuation and format ensures consistency and helps protect you from plagiarizing because of omitted source information. This chapter discusses the Modern Language Association (MLA) style of documentation, widely used in literature and languages as well as other fields. ■

For further reference on MLA style, consult the MLA's Web site, <http://www.mla.org>, or one of the following. The second is intended primarily for advanced scholars but includes the MLA's latest guidelines for citing electronic sources.

Gibaldi, Joseph. *MLA Handbook for Writers of Research Papers.* 5th ed. New York: MLA, 1999.

Gibaldi, Joseph. *MLA Style Manual and Guide to Scholarly Publishing.* 2nd ed. New York: MLA, 1998.

44a MLA format for parenthetical citations

MLA style uses **parenthetical citations** in the text of an essay to document every quotation, paraphrase, summary, or other material requiring documentation. (See 42d.) Parenthetical citations refer to full bibliographic entries in a list of works cited at the end of the text.

In general, make your parenthetical citations short, including just enough information for your readers to locate the full citation in the works-cited list. Place a parenthetical citation as near the relevant material as possible without disrupting the flow of the sentence, usually before the punctuation mark at the end of the sentence or phrase containing the material. Place any punctuation mark *after* the closing parenthesis. If your citation refers to a quotation, place the citation *after* the closing

44a. Parenthetical citations

44b. Explanatory and bibliographic notes

44c. List of works cited

1. BOOKS

(Continued on page 518)

(Continued from page 517)

44d. A sample research essay, MLA style

quotation mark but *before* any other punctuation mark. For block quotations, place the citation two spaces after the final punctuation mark. Here are examples of the ways to cite various kinds of sources:

1. AUTHOR NAMED IN A SIGNAL PHRASE Ordinarily, use the author's name in a signal phrase to introduce the material, and simply cite the page number(s) in parentheses. Use the full name the first time you cite a source. For later citations, use just the last name.

> Herrera indicates that Kahlo believed in a "vitalistic form of pantheism" (328).

2. AUTHOR NAMED IN A CITATION When you do not name the author in the text, include the author's last name before the page number(s) in the parenthetical citation.

> In places, Beauvoir "sees Marxists as believing in subjectivity as much as existentialists do" (Whitmarsh 63).

3. TWO OR THREE AUTHORS Use all the last names in a signal phrase or parenthetical citation.

> Gortner, Hebrun, and Nicolson maintain that "opinion leaders" influence other people in an organization because they are respected, not because they hold high positions (175).

4. FOUR OR MORE AUTHORS Use the first author's name and *et al.* ("and others") in a signal phrase or parenthetical citation, or, preferably, name all the authors.

> Similarly, as Belenky, Clinchy, Goldberger, and Tarule assert, examining the lives of women expands our understanding of human development (7).

5. CORPORATE OR GROUP AUTHOR Give the corporation's name or a shortened form in a signal phrase or parenthetical citation.

> In fact, one of the leading foundations in the field of higher education supports the recent proposals for community-run public schools (Carnegie Corporation 45).

6. UNKNOWN AUTHOR Use the title of the work or a shortened version in a signal phrase or parenthetical citation.

> "Hype," by one analysis, is "an artificially engendered atmosphere of hysteria" ("Today's Marketplace" 51).

7. AUTHOR OF TWO OR MORE WORKS If your list of works cited includes another work by the same author, give the title of the work you are citing or a shortened version in a signal phrase or parenthetical citation.

> Gardner presents readers with their own silliness through his description of a "pointless, ridiculous monster, crouched in the shadows, stinking of dead men, murdered children, and martyred cows" (Grendel 2).

8. TWO OR MORE AUTHORS WITH THE SAME SURNAME If your list of works cited includes works by authors with the same surname, always include the author's first name in the signal phrases or parenthetical citations for those works.

> Children will learn to write if they are allowed to choose their own subjects, James Britton asserts, citing the Schools Council study of the 1960s (37-42).

9. MULTIVOLUME WORK In the parenthetical citation, note the volume number first and then page number(s), with a colon and one space between them.

> Modernist writers prized experimentation and gradually even sought to blur the line between poetry and prose, according to Forster (3: 150).

If you name only one volume of the work in your list of works cited, you need include only the page number in the parentheses.

10. LITERARY WORK Because literary works are often available in many different editions, first cite the page number(s) from the edition you used followed by a semicolon, and then give other identifying information that will lead readers to the passage in any edition. Indicate the act and/or scene in a play (*37; sc. 1*). For a novel, indicate the part or chapter (*175; ch. 4*).

> Resisting gossip, Wharton's character Lily says, "What is truth? Where a woman is concerned, it's the story that's easiest to believe" (215; bk. 2, ch. 4).

For a poem, instead of page numbers cite the part (if there is one) and line(s), separated by a period. If you are citing only line numbers, use the word *line(s)* in the first citation of the poem (*lines 33–34*).

On dying, Whitman speculates "All goes onward and outward, nothing collapses, / And to die is different from what any one supposed, and luckier" (6.129-30).

For a verse play, give only the act, scene, and line numbers, separated by periods.

As Macbeth begins, the witches greet Banquo as "Lesser than Macbeth, and greater" (1.3.65).

11. WORK IN AN ANTHOLOGY For an essay, short story, or other piece of prose reprinted in an anthology, use the name of the author of the work, not the editor of the anthology, but use the page number(s) from the anthology.

Narratives of captivity play a major role in early writing by women in the United States, as demonstrated by Silko (219).

12. BIBLE Identify quotations by giving the title of the Bible, the book, chapter, and verse. Spell out the names of books mentioned in your text. In a parenthetical citation, use an abbreviation for books with names of five or more letters (*New Oxford Annotated Bible,* Prov. 16.18.).

13. INDIRECT SOURCE Use the abbreviation *qtd. in* to indicate that you are quoting from someone else's report of a conversation, interview, letter, or the like.

As Arthur Miller says, "When somebody is destroyed everybody finally contributes to it, but in Willy's case, the end product would be virtually the same" (qtd. in Martin and Meyer 375).

14. TWO OR MORE SOURCES IN THE SAME CITATION Separate the information with semicolons.

Some economists recommend that employment be redefined to include unpaid domestic labor (Clark 148; Nevins 39).

15. ENTIRE WORK OR ONE-PAGE ARTICLE Include the reference in the text without any page numbers or parentheses.

Thomas Hardy's tragic vision is given full vent in his Jude the Obscure.

16. WORK WITHOUT PAGE NUMBERS If a work has no page numbers but has another kind of numbered sections, such as parts or paragraphs, include the name and number(s) of the section(s) you are citing. (For paragraphs, use the abbreviation *par.* or *pars.*) If such a citation includes the author's name, use a comma after the name.

```
A remark by Cary Grant sums up the strain many stars
must have felt: "Everybody wants to be Cary Grant. Even
I want to be Cary Grant" (qtd. in Gallagher, part 3).
```

17. NONPRINT SOURCE Give enough information in a signal phrase or parenthetical citation for readers to locate the source in the list of works cited. Usually use the name or title under which you list the source. Specify a source's page, section, paragraph, or screen numbers in parentheses, if numbered.

```
Describing children's language acquisition, Pinker
explains that "what's innate about language is just a way
of paying attention to parental speech" (Johnson, sec. 1).
```

44b MLA format for explanatory and bibliographic notes

For other examples of explanatory and bibliographic notes, see the "Notes" to Shannan Palma's essay *(p. 560).*

MLA style allows **explanatory notes** for information or commentary that would not readily fit into the text but is needed for clarification or further explanation. In addition, MLA style permits **bibliographic notes** for citing several sources for one point and for offering thanks to, information about, or evaluation of a source. Superscript numbers are used in the text to refer readers to the notes, which may appear as endnotes (typed under the heading "Notes" on a separate page after the text but before the list of works cited) or as footnotes at the bottom of the page (typed four lines below the last text line). For example:

SUPERSCRIPT NUMBER IN TEXT

```
Stewart emphasizes the existence of social contacts in
Hawthorne's life so that the audience will accept a
different Hawthorne, one more attuned to modern times
than the figure in Woodberry.[3]
```

NOTE

```
     [3] Woodberry does, however, show that Hawthorne was
often an unsociable individual. He emphasizes the
```

seclusion of Hawthorne's mother, who separated herself from her family after the death of her husband, often even taking meals alone (28). Woodberry seems to imply that Mrs. Hawthorne's isolation rubbed off onto her son.

44c MLA format for a list of works cited

A list of **Works Cited** is an alphabetical list of the sources cited in your essay. (If your instructor asks that you list everything you have read as background, call the list "Works Consulted.") Start your list on a separate page after the text of your essay and any notes (see 44b). Number each page, continuing the page numbers of the text. Center the heading an inch from the top of the page; do not underline or italicize it or enclose it in quotation marks. Double-space between the heading and the first entry, and double-space the entire list. Start each entry flush with the left margin, and indent any additional lines one-half inch, or five typewriter spaces.

List your sources alphabetically by author's (or editor's) last name. If the author of a source is unknown, alphabetize the source by the first word of the title, disregarding *A, An,* or *The.* If you cite two or more works by the same author(s), arrange the entries alphabetically by title. List the name(s) of the author(s) in the first entry, but in subsequent entries use three hyphens followed by a period instead.

Lorde, Audre. A Burst of Light. Ithaca: Firebrand, 1988.

---. Sister Outsider. Trumansburg: Crossing, 1984.

If you cite a work by one author who is also listed as the first coauthor of another work you cite, list the single-author work first, and repeat the author's name in the entry for the coauthored work. Also repeat the author's name if you cite a work in which that author is listed as the first of a different set of coauthors. Use three hyphens only when the work is by *exactly* the same author(s) as the previous entry.

On the following pages, you will find sample entries that follow the MLA specifications for various kinds of sources.

1 Books

The basic entry for a book includes three elements, each followed by a period.

- *Author.* List the last name first, followed by a comma and the first name.

- *Title.* Underline or (if your instructor permits) italicize the title and any subtitle, and capitalize all major words. (See 36c for more on capitalizing titles.)
- *Publication information.* Give the city of publication followed by a colon, a space, and a shortened version of the publisher's name – dropping *Press, Publishers, Inc.,* and so on (*HarperCollins* for *HarperCollins Publishers*), using only the first surname (*Harcourt* for *Harcourt Brace*), and abbreviating *University Press* (*Oxford UP* for *Oxford University Press*). The publisher's name is followed by a comma and the year of publication.

Here is an example of a basic entry for a book:

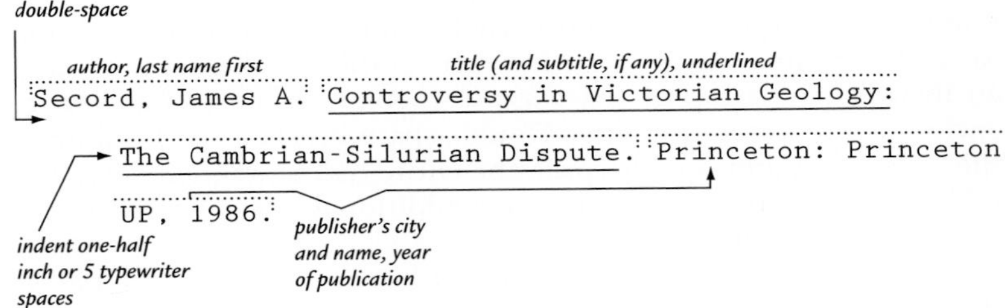

1. ONE AUTHOR

deCordova, Richard. Picture Personalities: The Emergence of the Star System in America. Urbana: U of Illinois P, 1990.

2. TWO OR THREE AUTHORS List the first author, last name first; then list the name(s) of the other author(s) in regular order, with a comma between authors and an *and* before the last one.

Appleby, Joyce, Lynn Hunt, and Margaret Jacob. Telling the Truth about History. New York: Norton, 1994.

3. FOUR OR MORE AUTHORS Give the first author listed on the title page, followed by a comma and *et al.* ("and others"), or list all the names, since the use of *et al.* diminishes the importance of the other contributors.

Belenky, Mary Field, Blythe Clinchy, Jill Goldberger, and Nancy Tarule. Women's Ways of Knowing. New York: Basic, 1986.

4. CORPORATE OR GROUP AUTHOR Give the name of the group listed on the title page as the author, even if the same group published the book.

American Chemical Society. Handbook for Authors of Papers in the American Chemical Society Publications. Washington: American Chemical Soc., 1978.

5. UNKNOWN AUTHOR Begin the entry with the title.

The New York Times Atlas of the World. New York: New York Times Books, 1980.

6. EDITOR OR EDITORS Treat an editor as an author, but add a comma and *ed.* (or *eds.* for more than one editor).

Wall, Cheryl A., ed. Changing Our Own Words: Essays on Criticism, Theory, and Writing by Black Women. New Brunswick: Rutgers UP, 1989.

7. AUTHOR AND EDITOR If you have cited the body of the text, begin with the author's name, and list the editor's name, introduced by *Ed.,* after the title.

James, Henry. Portrait of a Lady. Ed. Leon Edel. Boston: Houghton, 1963.

If you have cited the editor's contribution to the work, begin with the editor's name followed by a comma and *ed.,* and list the author's name, introduced by *By,* after the title.

Edel, Leon, ed. Portrait of a Lady. By Henry James. Boston: Houghton, 1963.

8. SELECTION IN AN ANTHOLOGY OR CHAPTER IN A BOOK WITH AN EDITOR List the author(s) of the selection or chapter; its title; the title of the book in which the selection or chapter appears; *Ed.* and the name(s) of the editor(s); the publication information; and the inclusive page numbers of the selection or chapter. For inclusive page numbers up to 99, note all digits in the second number. For numbers above 99, note only the last two digits and any others that change in the second number (115 – 18, 1378 – 79, 296 – 301).

Gordon, Mary. "The Parable of the Cave." The Writer on Her Work. Ed. Janet Sternburg. New York: Norton, 1980. 27-32.

If the selection was originally published in a periodical and you are asked to supply information for this original source, use the following format. *Rpt.* is the abbreviation for "Reprinted."

For guidelines on citing a periodical article, see 44c2.

Didion, Joan. "Why I Write." New York Times Book Review. 9 Dec. 1976: 22. Rpt. in The Writer on Her Work. Ed. Janet Sternburg. New York: Norton, 1980. 3-16.

9. TWO OR MORE ITEMS FROM AN ANTHOLOGY Include the anthology itself in your list of works cited.

Donalson, Melvin, ed. Cornerstones: An Anthology of African American Literature. New York: St. Martin's, 1996.

Then list each selection by its author and title, followed by a cross-reference to the anthology.

Baker, Houston A., Jr. "There Is No More Beautiful Way." Donalson 856-63.

Ellison, Ralph. "What America Would Be Like without Blacks." Donalson 737-41.

10. TRANSLATION Give the translator's name, preceded by *Trans.,* after the title.

Zamora, Martha. Frida Kahlo: The Brush of Anguish. Trans. Marilyn Sode Smith. San Francisco: Chronicle, 1990.

If you cite a translated selection in an anthology, add *Trans.* and the translator's name before the title of the anthology.

Horace. The Art of Poetry. Trans. Burton Raffel. The Critical Tradition: Classic Texts and Contemporary Trends. Ed. David H. Richter. New York: Bedford-St. Martin's, 1989. 66-77.

11. EDITION OTHER THAN THE FIRST Add the information, in abbreviated form, after the title.

Kelly, Alfred H., Winfred A. Harbison, and Herman Belz. The American Constitution: Its Origins and Development. 6th ed. New York: Norton, 1983.

12. ONE VOLUME OF A MULTIVOLUME WORK Give the volume number after the title, and list the number of volumes in the complete work after the date, using the abbreviations *Vol.* and *vols.*

Foner, Philip S., and Ronald L. Lewis, eds. The Black Worker. Vol. 3. Philadelphia: Lippincott, 1980. 8 vols.

13. TWO OR MORE VOLUMES OF A MULTIVOLUME WORK Give the number of volumes in the complete work after the title, using the abbreviation *vols.*

Foner, Philip S., and Ronald L. Lewis, eds. The Black Worker. 8 vols. Philadelphia: Lippincott, 1980.

14. PREFACE, FOREWORD, INTRODUCTION, OR AFTERWORD List the author of the item, the item title (not underlined, italicized, or in quotation marks), the title of the book, and its author's name, preceded by the word *By.* If the same person wrote both the book and the cited item, use just the last name after *By.* List the inclusive page numbers of the item at the end of the entry.

Schlesinger, Arthur M., Jr. Introduction. Pioneer Women: Voices from the Kansas Frontier. By Joanna L. Stratton. New York: Simon, 1981. 11-15.

15. ENTRY IN A REFERENCE WORK List the author of the entry, if there is one. If no author is identified, begin with the title. For a well-known work, just note any edition number and date after the name of the work. If the entries in the work are in alphabetical order, no volume or page numbers are needed.

Johnson, Peder J. "Concept Learning." Encyclopedia of Education. 1971.

"Hero." The New Merriam-Webster Dictionary. 1989.

16. BOOK THAT IS PART OF A SERIES Cite the series name as it appears on the title page, followed by any series number.

Moss, Beverly J., ed. Literacy across Communities. Written Language Series 2. Cresskill: Hampton, 1994.

17. **REPUBLICATION** To cite a modern edition of an older book, add the original publication date, followed by a period, after the title.

Scott, Walter. Kenilworth. 1821. New York: Dodd, 1956.

18. **GOVERNMENT DOCUMENT** Begin with the author, if identified. If no author is given, start with the name of the government followed by the agency and any subdivision. Use abbreviations if they can be readily understood. Then list the title, underlined or italicized. For congressional documents, cite the number, session, and house of Congress (using *S* for Senate and *H* or *HR* for House of Representatives), and the type (Report, Resolution, Document), in abbreviated form, and number of the material. If you cite the *Congressional Record,* give only the date and page number. Otherwise, end with the publication information; the publisher is often the Government Printing Office (GPO).

New Hampshire. Dept. of Transportation. Right of Way Salinity Reports, Hillsborough County, 1985. Concord: New Hampshire Dept. of Transportation, 1986.

United States. Cong. House. Report of the Joint Subcommittee on Reconstruction. 39th Cong., 1st sess. H. Rept. 30. 1865. New York: Arno, 1969.

U.S. Bureau of the Census. Historical Statistics of the United States, Colonial Times to 1870. Washington: GPO, 1975.

19. **PAMPHLET** Treat a pamphlet as you would a book.

Why Is Central America a Conflict Area? Opposing Viewpoints Pamphlets. St. Paul: Greenhaven, 1984.

20. **PUBLISHED PROCEEDINGS OF A CONFERENCE** Treat proceedings as a book, but add information about the conference if it is not part of the title.

Martin, John Steven, and Christine Mason Sutherland, eds. Proceedings of the Canadian Society for the History of Rhetoric. Calgary, Alberta: Canadian Soc. for the History of Rhetoric, 1986.

21. **BOOK PUBLISHED BEFORE 1900** Omit the publisher's name, and add a comma between the place of publication and the date.

Randolph, Peter. From Slave Cabin to the Pulpit. Boston, 1893.

22. **PUBLISHER'S IMPRINT** If a book was published by a publisher's imprint (indicated on the title page), hyphenate the imprint and the publisher's name.

Rose, Phyllis. Parallel Lives: Five Victorian Marriages. New York: Vintage-Random, 1984.

23. **TITLE WITHIN THE TITLE** Do not underline or italicize the title of a book within the title of a book you are citing. Enclose in quotation marks the title of a short work within a book title, and underline or italicize it as you do the rest of the title.

Gilbert, Stuart. James Joyce's Ulysses. New York: Vintage-Random, 1955.

24. **SACRED BOOK** Begin the entry with the title, underlined or italicized. For versions of the Bible in which the version is not part of the title, list the version after the title.

The Jerusalem Bible. Garden City, NY: Doubleday, 1966.

Holy Bible. King James Version. Nashville: Broadman, 1940.

2 Periodicals

The basic entry for a periodical includes three elements, each followed by a period.

- *Author.* List the author's last name first, followed by a comma and the first name.
- *Article title.* Enclose the title and any subtitle in quotation marks, and capitalize all major words. (See 36c for more on capitalizing titles.) The closing period goes inside the closing quotation mark.
- *Publication information.* Give the periodical title (excluding any initial *A, An,* or *The*), underlined or italicized and with all major words capitalized; the volume number and issue number if appropriate; and the date of publication. For journals, list the year in parentheses followed by a colon, a space, and the inclusive page numbers. For magazines and newspapers, list the month (abbreviated, except for May, June, and July) or the day and month before the year, and do not use parentheses. Do not use *p.* or *pp.* before the page numbers. For inclusive page numbers, note all digits for numbers 1 to 99, and note only the last two digits and any others that change for numbers above 99 (24 – 27, 134 – 45).

Here is an example of a basic entry for an article in a journal:

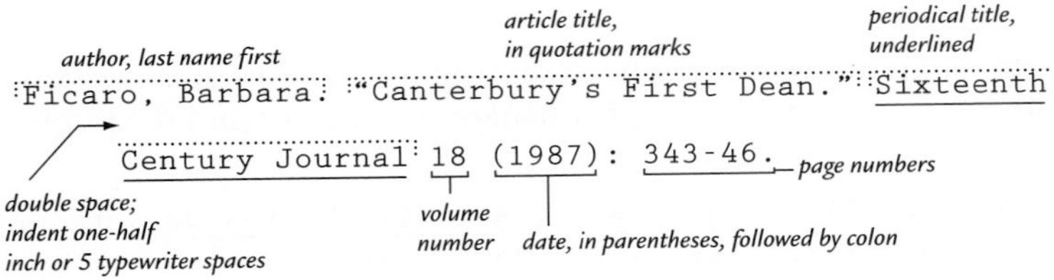

author, last name first · article title, in quotation marks · periodical title, underlined

```
Ficaro, Barbara. "Canterbury's First Dean." Sixteenth
     Century Journal 18 (1987): 343-46.
```

double space; indent one-half inch or 5 typewriter spaces · volume number · date, in parentheses, followed by colon · page numbers

25. ARTICLE IN A JOURNAL PAGINATED BY VOLUME Follow the journal title with the volume number in arabic numerals.

Norris, Margot. "Narration under a Blindfold: Reading Joyce's 'Clay.'" PMLA 102 (1987): 206-15.

26. ARTICLE IN A JOURNAL PAGINATED BY ISSUE Put a period and the issue number after the volume number.

Loffy, John. "The Politics at Modernism's Funeral." Canadian Journal of Political and Social Theory 6.3 (1987): 89-96.

27. ARTICLE IN A MONTHLY MAGAZINE Put the month (or months, hyphenated) before the year. Do not include volume or issue numbers.

Weiss, Philip. "The Book Thief: A True Tale of Bibliomania." Harper's Jan. 1994: 37-56.

28. ARTICLE IN A WEEKLY MAGAZINE Include the day, month, and year in that order, with no commas between them. Do not include volume or issue numbers.

Daly, Steve. "Face to Face." Entertainment Weekly 20 June 1997: 20-24.

29. ARTICLE IN A NEWSPAPER Give the name of the newspaper, underlined or italicized, as it appears on the front page but without any initial *A*, *An*, or *The*. Add the city in brackets after the name if it is not part of the name. Then give the date and the edition (if listed), followed by a colon, a space, the section number or letter (if listed), and the page number(s). If the article appears on discontinuous pages, give the first page followed by a plus sign.

Markoff, John. "Cyberspace's Most Wanted: Hacker Eludes F.B.I. Pursuit." New York Times 4 July 1994, late ed.: A1+.

30. EDITORIAL OR LETTER TO THE EDITOR Use the label *Editorial* or *Letter,* not underlined, italicized, or in quotation marks, after the title or after the author's name if there is no title.

Magee, Doug. "Soldier's Home." Editorial. Nation 26 Mar. 1988: 400-01.

Crews, Frederick. "Was Freud a Fraud?" Letter. New York Times Book Review 27 Mar. 1994: 27.

31. UNSIGNED ARTICLE Begin with the article title, alphabetizing the entry according to the first word after any initial *A, An,* or *The.*

"The Odds of March." Time 15 Apr. 1985: 20+.

32. REVIEW List the reviewer's name and the title of the review, if any, followed by *Rev. of* and the title and author or director of the work reviewed. Then add the publication information for the periodical in which the review appears.

Solinger, Rickie. "Unsafe for Women." Rev. of Next Time, She'll Be Dead: Battering and How to Stop It, by Ann Jones. New York Times Book Review 20 Mar. 1994: 16.

33. ARTICLE WITH A TITLE WITHIN THE TITLE Enclose in single quotation marks the title of a short work within an article title. Underline or italicize the title of a book within an article title.

Frey, Leonard H. "Irony and Point of View in 'That Evening Sun.'" Faulkner Studies 2 (1953): 33-40.

3 Electronic sources

Electronic sources such as CD-ROMs, World Wide Web sites, and email differ from print sources in the ease with which they can be – and the frequency with which they are – changed, updated, or even eliminated. In addition, as the *MLA Style Manual* notes, "few standards currently govern the presentation of electronic publications," so that it is often hard to identify information that can direct a reader to the source. In recommending the following guidelines for some of the most common kinds of electronic sources, the *Manual* adds, "If you cannot find some of this information, cite what is available."

Note that MLA style requires that if a URL within an entry in a Works Cited list will not all fit on one line, it should be broken only after a slash.

WWW •

http://www.mla .org/set_stl.htm

The MLA's Online Advice about Citing Online Sources, *with up-to-date advice and standards for citing WWW-based sources. Also of use is a link to frequently asked questions about the MLA format.*

34. PERIODICALLY REVISED DATABASE ON CD-ROM Include the author's name; publication information for the print version of the text (including its title and date of publication); the title of the database, underlined or italicized; the medium (*CD-ROM*); the name of the company producing it; and the electronic publication date (month and year, if possible).

Natchez, Gladys. "Frida Kahlo and Diego Rivera: The Transformation of Catastrophe to Creativity." Psychotherapy-Patient 4.1 (1987): 153-74. PsychLIT. CD-ROM. SilverPlatter. Nov. 1994.

35. SINGLE-ISSUE CD-ROM, DISKETTE, OR MAGNETIC TAPE Cite this kind of source like a book or, if you are citing only a part of it, as you would a part of a book; but before the place of publication include the medium and, if appropriate, the number of the electronic edition, release, or version. If you are citing only a part of the source, end with the page, paragraph, screen, or other section numbers of the part if they are indicated in the source – either the range of numbers (*pp. 78 – 83*) or, if each section is numbered separately, the total number of sections in the part (*8 screens*).

"Poem." The Oxford English Dictionary. 2nd ed. CD-ROM. Oxford: Oxford UP, 1989.

36. MULTIDISC CD-ROM In citing a CD-ROM publication of more than one disc, include either the total number of discs or, if you use material from only one, the number of that disc.

The 1998 Grolier Multimedia Encyclopedia. CD-ROM. 2 discs. Danbury: Grolier Interactive, 1997.

The 1998 Grolier Multimedia Encyclopedia. CD-ROM. Disc 2. Danbury: Grolier Interactive, 1997.

37. SCHOLARLY PROJECT OR REFERENCE DATABASE Include the title of the project or database, underlined or italicized; the name of the editor, if any, preceded by *Ed.*; the version number, if relevant and not part of the title; the date of electronic publication or of the latest update; the name of any sponsoring institution or organization; the date of access; and the URL, in angle brackets.

The Orlando Project: An Integrated History of Women's Writing in the British Isles. 1997. U of Alberta. 9 Oct. 1997 <http://www.ualberta.ca/ORLANDO/>

To cite a poem, essay, article, or other short work within a scholarly project, begin with the author's name and the title of the work, in quotation marks, and give the URL of the short work rather than that of the project if they differ.

Scott, Walter. "Remarks on Frankenstein, or the Modern Prometheus: A Novel." Romantic Circles. Ed. Neil Fraistat, Steven Jones, Donald Reiman, and Carl Stahmer. 1996. 15 Apr. 1998 <http://www.udel.edu/swilson/mws/bemrev.html>.

To cite an anonymous article from a reference database, begin with the article title, in quotation marks, and give the URL of the article rather than that of the database if they differ.

"Sasquatch." The Encyclopedia Mythica. Ed. Micha F. Lindemans. 1998. 31 Mar. 1998 <http://www.pantheon.org/mythica/areas/folklore/>.

38. GENERAL WEB SITE Include the name of the person who created the site, if relevant; the title of the site, underlined or italicized, or (if there is no title) a description such as *Home page,* not underlined or italicized or in quotation marks; the name of any institution or organization associated with the site; the date of access; and the URL, in angle brackets.

Classical Myth: The Ancient Sources. Dept. of Greek and Roman Studies, U of Victoria. 28 Mar. 1998. <http://www.wesleyan.edu/~cbays/homepage.html>.

Kim, Angela. Home page. 9 Oct. 1997 <http://www.cohums.ohio-state.edu/english/people/kim.1/>.

39. ONLINE BOOK Begin with the name of the author or, if only an editor, a compiler, or a translator is identified, the name of that person followed by a comma and *ed., comp.,* or *trans.* Then give the title, underlined or italicized, and the name of any editor, compiler, or translator not listed earlier, preceded by *Ed., Comp.,* or *Trans.* If the online version of the text has not been published before, give the date of electronic publication and the name of any sponsoring institution or organization. Then give any publication information (city, publisher, and/or year) for the original print version that is given in the source. End with the date of access and the URL, in angle brackets.

Riis, Jacob A. How the Other Half Lives: Studies among the Tenements of New York. Ed. David Phillips. New York: Scribner's, 1890. 26 Mar. 1998 <http://www.cis.yale.edu/amstud/inforev/riis/title.html>.

If you are citing a poem, essay, or other short work within a book, include its title, in quotation marks, after the author's name. Give the URL of the short work, not of the book, if they differ. If the book is part of a scholarly project, give the information about the project (title, editor, date, and sponsor) after the information about the print version. Give the URL of the book, not of the project, if they differ.

> Dickinson, Emily. "The Grass." Poems: Emily Dickinson. Boston, 1891. Humanities Text Initiative American Verse Collection. Ed. Nancy Kushigian. 1995. U of Michigan. 9 Oct. 1997 <http://www.planet.net/pkrisxle/emily/poemsOnline.html>.

40. ARTICLE IN AN ONLINE PERIODICAL To cite an article in an online scholarly journal, magazine, or newspaper, follow the guidelines given on pages 529 – 531 for citing articles in print periodicals, but adapt them as necessary to the online medium. Include the author's name; the title, in quotation marks; the name of the periodical, underlined or italicized; the volume, issue, or other identifying number, if any; the date of publication; the page numbers of the article or the total number of pages, paragraphs, parts, or other numbered sections, if any; the date of access; and the URL, in angle brackets.

For an example of how to cite an online periodical article with numbered sections, see p. 562.

> Browning, Tonya. "Embedded Visuals: Student Design in Web Spaces." Kairos: A Journal for Teachers of Writing 2.1 (1997). 9 Oct. 1997 <http://english.ttu.edu/kairos/current/toc.html>.

> Gawande, Atul. "Drowsy Docs." Slate. 9 Oct. 1997. 10 Oct. 1997 <http://www.slate.com/MedicalExaminer/97-10-09/MedicalExaminer.asp>.

41. POSTING TO A DISCUSSION GROUP In citing an online posting, begin with the author's name; the title of the document, in quotation marks; the date of posting; and the description *Online posting,* not underlined or italicized or in quotation marks. For a listserv posting, then give the name of the listserv; the number of the posting, if any; the date of access; and the URL of the listserv or the email address of its moderator or supervisor. Always cite an archival version of the posting if possible.

Chagall, Nancy. "Web Publishing and Censorship." 2 Feb. 1997. Online posting. ACW: The Alliance for Computers and Writing Discussion List. 10 Oct. 1997 <http://english.ttu.edu/acw-1/archive.htm>.

For a posting to a newsgroup, end with the date of access and the name of the newsgroup, in angle brackets, with the prefix *news.* Always cite an archival version of the posting if possible.

Gill, David. "Environmental Archaeology in the Aegean." 9 Jan. 1996. Online posting. 28 Mar. 1998 <http://www.umich.edu/~classics/archives/aegeanet/>.

42. WORK FROM AN ONLINE SUBSCRIPTION SERVICE To cite an article from an online subscription service to which you subscribe personally such as America Online, begin with the author's name, if known, and the title of the work, in quotation marks. Give the title of the online service, underlined, along with the date of access, the work *Keyword*, followed by the keyword used.

Weeks, W. William. "Beyond the Ark." Nature Conservancy Mar.-Apr. 1999. America Online. 2 Apr. 1999. Keyword: Ecology.

For a work from an online service to which a library subscribes, list the information about the work, followed by the name of the service, the library, the date of access, and the URL of the service, in angle brackets.

"Breaking the Dieting Habit: Drug Therapy for Eating Disorders." Psychology Today Mar. 1995: 12+. Electric Lib. Main Lib., Columbus, OH. 31 Mar. 1999 <http://www.elibrary.com/>.

43. EMAIL Include the writer's name; the subject line of the message, in quotation marks; a description of the message that mentions the recipient; and the date of the message.

Talbot, Casey J. "Do This." Email to the author. 10 May 1996.

Lunsford, Andrea A. "New Examples." Email to Kristin Bowen. 26 Jan. 1997.

44. SYNCHRONOUS COMMUNICATION In citing a posting in a forum such as a MOO, MUD, or IRC, include the name(s) of any specific speaker(s) you are citing; a description of the event; its date; the name of the forum; the date of access; and the URL, with the prefix *telnet.*

Seminar discussion on netiquette. 28 May 1996. LambdaMOO. 28 May 1996 <telnet://lambda.parc.xerox.edu.8888>.

Always cite an archival version of the posting if possible.

Patuto, Jeremy, Simon Fennel, and James Goss. The Mytilene Debate. 9 May 1996. MiamiMOO. 28 Mar. 1998 <http://moo.cas.muohio.edu/cgi-bin/moo?look+4085>.

45. OTHER ELECTRONIC SOURCES In citing other kinds of electronic sources, follow the guidelines given on pages 537 – 539, but adapt them as necessary to the electronic medium. Here are examples of citations for a work of art, a film, and an interview.

Aleni, Guilio. K'un-yu t'u-shu. ca. 1620. Vatican, Rome. 28 Mar. 1998 <http//:www.ncsa.uiuc.edu/SDG/Experimental/vatican.exhibit/exhibit/full-images/i_rome_to_china/china02.gif>.

The Godfather. Dir. Francis Ford Coppola. 28 Mar. 1998 <http://UK.imdbj.com/Title?Godfather,+The+[1972]>.

Dyson, Esther. Interview. Hotseat 23 May 1997 <http://www.hotwired.com/packet/hotseat/97/20/index4a.html>.

46. FTP (FILE TRANSFER PROTOCOL), TELNET, OR GOPHER SITE Substitute *ftp, telnet,* or *gopher* for *http* at the beginning of the URL.

Korn, Peter. "How Much Does Breast Cancer Really Cost?" Self Oct. 1994. 5 May 1997 <gopher://nysernet.org:70/00/BCTC/Sources/SELF/94/how-much>.

47. WORK IN AN INDETERMINATE MEDIUM If you are not sure whether material accessed through a local electronic network is stored on the central computer's hard drive or on a CD-ROM, use the label *Electronic.* Include any publication information that is available, the name of the network or of its sponsoring organization, and the date of access.

The Oxford English Dictionary. 2nd ed. Oxford: Oxford UP, 1989. Electronic. OhioLink, Ohio State U Lib. 15 Apr. 1998.

4 Other kinds of sources

48. UNPUBLISHED DISSERTATION Enclose the title in quotation marks. Add the identification *Diss.,* the name of the university or professional school, a comma, and the year the dissertation was accepted.

LeCourt, Donna. "The Self in Motion: The Status of the (Student) Subject in Composition Studies." Diss. Ohio State U, 1993.

49. PUBLISHED DISSERTATION Cite a published dissertation as a book, adding the identification *Diss.* and the name of the university. If the dissertation was published by University Microfilms International, add *Ann Arbor: UMI,* and the year, and list the UMI number at the end of the entry.

Botts, Roderic C. Influences in the Teaching of English, 1917-1935: An Illusion of Progress. Diss. Northeastern U, 1970. Ann Arbor: UMI, 1971. 71-1799.

50. ARTICLE FROM A MICROFORM Treat the article as a printed work, but add the name of the microform and information for locating it.

Sharpe, Lora. "A Quilter's Tribute." Boston Globe 25 Mar. 1989. Newsbank: Social Relations 12 (1989): fiche 6, grids B4-6.

51. INTERVIEW List the person interviewed and then the title of the interview, if any, in quotation marks (or underlined or italicized if the interview is a complete work). If the interview has no title, use the label *Interview* (not underlined, italicized, or in quotation marks), and identify the source. If you were the interviewer, use the label *Telephone interview, Personal interview,* or *Internet interview.* End with the date the interview took place.

Schorr, Daniel. Interview. Weekend Edition. Natl. Public Radio. WEVO, Concord. 26 Mar. 1988.

Beja, Morris. Personal interview. 2 Oct. 1997.

52. LETTER If the letter was published, cite it as a selection in a book, noting the date and any identifying number after the title.

Frost, Robert. "Letter to Editor of the Independent." 28 Mar. 1894. Selected Letters of Robert Frost. Ed. Lawrance Thompson. New York: Holt, 1964. 19.

If the letter was sent to you, follow this form:

Anzaldúa, Gloria. Letter to the author. 10 Sept. 1997.

53. FILM OR VIDEOCASSETTE In general, start with the title, underlined or italicized; then name the director, the company distributing the film or videocassette, and the date of its release. Other contributors, such as writers or actors, may follow the director. If you cite a particular person's work, start the entry with that person's name. For a videocassette, include the original film release date (if relevant) and the label *Videocassette.*

Face/Off. Dir. John Woo. Perf. John Travolta and Nicholas Cage. Paramount, 1997.

Weaver, Sigourney, perf. Aliens. Dir. James Cameron. 20th Century Fox, 1986.

The Star. Dir. Lawrence Pitkethly. Videocassette. CBS/Fox Video, 1995.

54. TELEVISION OR RADIO PROGRAM In general, begin with the title of the program, underlined or italicized. Then list the narrator, director, actors, or other contributors, as necessary; the network; the local station and city, if any; and the broadcast date. If you cite a particular person's work, begin the entry with that person's name. If you cite a particular episode, include any title, in quotation marks, before the program's title. If the program is part of a series, include the series title (not underlined, italicized, or in quotation marks) before the network.

Box Office Bombshell: Marilyn Monroe. Writ. Andy Thomas, Jeff Schefel, and Kevin Burns. Dir. Bill Harris. Nar. Peter Graves. A&E Biography. Arts and Entertainment Network. 23 Oct. 1997.

Travanti, Daniel J., perf. Hill Street Blues. NBC. WNBC. New York. 15 Jan. 1981.

55. SOUND RECORDING Begin with the name of the composer, performer, or conductor, depending on whose work you are citing. Next give the title of the recording, which is underlined or italicized, or the title of the composition, which is not. End with the manufacturer, a comma, and the year of issue. If you are not citing a compact disc, give the medium before the manufacturer. If you are citing a particular song, include its title, in quotation marks, before the title of the recording.

Grieg, Edvard. Concerto in A minor, op. 16. Cond. Eugene Ormandy. Philadelphia Orch. LP. RCA, 1989.

Kilcher, Jewel. "Amen." Pieces of You. A&R, 1994.

56. WORK OF ART List the artist; the work's title, underlined or italicized; the name of the museum or other location; and the city.

Kahlo, Frida. Self-Portrait with Cropped Hair. Museum of Modern Art, New York.

57. LECTURE OR SPEECH List the speaker, the title in quotation marks, the name of the sponsoring institution or group, the place, and the date. If the speech is untitled, use a label such as *Lecture* or *Keynote speech.*

Lu, Min-Zhan. "The Politics of Listening." Conference on College Composition and Communication. Palmer House, Chicago. 3 Apr. 1998.

58. PERFORMANCE List the title, other appropriate details (such as composer, writer, director), the place, and the date. If you cite a particular person's work, begin the entry with that person's name.

Frankie and Johnny in the Clair de Lune. By Terrence McNally. Dir. Paul Benedict. Westside Arts Theater, New York. 18 Jan. 1988.

59. MAP OR CHART Cite a map or chart as you would a book with an unknown author, adding the label *Map* or *Chart.*

Pennsylvania. Map. Chicago: Rand, 1985.

60. CARTOON List the cartoonist's name, the title of the cartoon (if it has one), the word *Cartoon,* and the usual publication information.

Trudeau, Garry. "Doonesbury." Cartoon. Philadelphia Inquirer. 9 Mar. 1988: 37.

44d A sample research essay, MLA style

Shannan Palma's final essay appears on the following pages. In preparing this essay, she followed the MLA guidelines described in this chapter. She was required to prepare a title page. Had she not needed a separate title page, she would have followed MLA instructions for a heading at the top of the first page of her essay (see Chapter 51 for an example). Note that, to annotate this essay, we have reproduced it in a narrower format than you will have on a standard (8½" × 11") sheet of paper.

For the first page of an essay that does not use a title page, see 51e.

Title centered one-third of way down page

Hollywood and the Hero:
Solving a Case of Mistaken Identity

Writer's name centered three or four lines below title

by Shannan Palma

Course number, professor's name, and date centered three or four lines below writer's name

English 167
Professor Lunsford
18 November 1998

Palma i

Outline

Thesis statement: Recent films strongly suggest that the hero of the twenty-first century will most likely appear not as a Hollywood star or a mythical manifestation but as a combination of mortal and machine--in short, a cyborg.

I. Originally relying on earlier heroes from the realms of myth and history, Hollywood studios gradually developed a system for transforming actors into star-heroes.
   A. Moviegoers began to identify a favorite hero-character with the particular actor who played him or her.
   B. The studios recognized the financial possibilities of the mass idolization of a commercialized hero and set out to manufacture this "product" efficiently.
      1. The persona that a studio developed to turn an actor into a star was the only public identity that actor was allowed to have.
      2. Early examples of the star-hero included Douglas Fairbanks and Mary Pickford.

II. As the studio system disintegrated in the 1950s and 1960s, and the stars lost the publicity shield it had provided, the problems of stardom became obvious to the public.

Student's last name and page number in upper right-hand corner; roman numerals used for outline page numbers

Heading centered

Thesis stated

First major point in support of thesis

Subpoint

Subpoint followed by two supporting details

Second major point in support of thesis

Subpoint followed by two supporting details

Subpoint

Subpoint

Third major point in support of thesis

Subpoint

Subpoint

Palma ii

A. Films from this period show that the movie industry was self-mockingly aware of its pitfalls.
   1. Sunset Boulevard showed what happened when a hero-image was no longer popular and the system abandoned the star it had made.
   2. A Star Is Born showed how the system created a perfect image and forced a human being to become it.

B. Widely publicized scandals like that surrounding the death of Marilyn Monroe further increased the public's knowledge of star-hero failings.

C. Although scandals seemed only to increase public adoration of stars by giving their images an air of tragic martyrdom, public perception of star-heroes as ideals began to fade.

III. More recent decades have seen the confusion of identity between film characters and stars take a new form, which has further contributed to the decline of the hero.

A. The last vestiges of the studio system's image-projection and -protection have vanished, leaving the public with few illusions about the lives of star-heroes.

B. Rather than admire stars for their heroic achievements and personal qualities, the public envies them for their lifestyle.

Palma iii

C. Profound cynicism toward the hero as ideal is reflected in current films, such as The Ref, which encourage audiences to identify heroes with the stars that portray them rather than vice versa.

Subpoint

D. The disappearance of the hero-ideal has led to a lack of lasting empathy with the hero among movie audiences.

Subpoint followed by two supporting details

1. After audiences see a movie, they no longer associate the character and the film, but rather the actor and the film.
2. To re-create that lasting empathy in a modern context, we need heroes who can overcome the problem of mistaken identity and who are believable and relevant to today's world.

IV. The 1997 film Face/Off can serve as one prototype for overcoming these obstacles.

Final major point in support of thesis

A. The film turns mistaken identity against itself, with the two lead actors switching roles in such a way that the audience has its preconceptions of the relationships between star and character challenged and develops a lasting empathy with the hero.

Subpoint

B. With its portrayal of a hero who resorts to advanced technology to take on the face of his enemy, the film also provides a prototype for the cyborg hero, a form that the twenty-first-century hero may take.

Subpoint

Writer's last name and page number in upper right-hand corner

Title centered; announces topic, engages reader interest

Opening quotation appeals to student readers and poses question that essay will try to answer

First paragraph of introduction provides background

Reference book cited, with page number in parentheses immediately following quotation

Second paragraph introduces major theme of "mistaken identity" and explains what writer will do in essay

1"

Palma 1

Hollywood and the Hero:

Solving a Case of Mistaken Identity

Where are my angels?
Where's my golden one?
And where's my hope
now that my heroes
have gone?

The song is "Amen" from Jewel Kilcher's best-selling album Pieces of You. The questions are ones worth asking. For the hero, what The New Merriam-Webster Dictionary defines as "a man admired for his achievements and qualities" (348), seems to have vanished from American culture. From Hercules to Robin Hood, from Joan of Arc to Scarlett O'Hara, male and female heroes alike have reflected the ideals and the most admired traits of their respective times: brute strength or sharply honed cunning, devotion to duty or desire for rebellion. Throughout history, and specifically U.S. history, the hero-ideal has endured--until now. The twentieth century, which started off with the promising evolution of the hero from figure of legend and literature to star of the silver screen, now seems to be ending with the near death of the hero as ideal.

The eclipse of the hero results from a case of what I will call "mistaken identity," which has caused film heroes' fates to become inextricably intertwined with the fates of the actors who portray them. In this research essay, I will explore whether today's films truly signal the end of the hero-ideal and preview a hero-less future, or whether they instead help the hero evolve to a different, perhaps more realistic, level. If the latter is true, the question then becomes one of what form the new hero will take onscreen. In this essay, I argue that recent films strongly suggest that the hero of the twenty-first century will most likely appear not as a Hollywood star or a mythical manifestation but as a combination of mortal and machine--in short, a cyborg.[1]

Explicit thesis stated

Superscript refers readers to bibliographic note

Before either of these questions can be addressed, however, a brief history of Hollywood's relationship with the hero is necessary. Our heroes once came primarily from the fantasy of myth and the remove of history and literature. King Arthur, the Three Musketeers, Jo March of Little Women, Annie Oakley--all have spent time on the hero's pedestal. With the development of motion pictures in the early twentieth century, many of these heroes made the transition from legend to life, or at least to life on the screen. Soon moviegoers were able not only to read about and imagine their heroes in action but also to see them in the most glamorous incarnations Hollywood could create. Fans began to identify a favorite hero-character with the particular actor who played him or her, and this burgeoning case of mistaken iden-

Transition to first main point: Hollywood studios transformed the hero

First subpoint: fans confused characters with actors ("mistaken identity")

Palma 3

tity did not go unnoticed for long. Film historian Morris Beja notes that although the studios, then the most powerful force in Hollywood, had originally hoped to give actors as little influence as possible over the studios' operations, it quickly became obvious that "movie stars sold tickets." Recognizing the enormous financial possibilities inherent in the mass idolization of a commercialized hero, "the industry" set out to manufacture this "product" as efficiently as possible. As a 1995 video on the star system in Hollywood explains:

> In the old days of the studio system there was a structure for developing stars. Players were owned body and soul, signed to long-term contracts. With the powerful publicity machine run by the studio they could reach an audience of millions. But that alone did not guarantee success. The problem for the studio was to find the one persona out of many possible character roles that would boost a character to stardom. (The Star)

Studios found that manufacturing movie stars was not easy. It required an actor with just the right combination of style, charisma, and talent, and it required just the right roles and public persona to make that actor a star. When it succeeded, however, the mistaken identity was complete. The star became an icon--an ideal--a

Quotation from interview

Quotation marks used to signal irony

Second subpoint: heroes became "products"

Block quotation introduced by phrase with signal verb

Videocassette title cited in parentheses; for set-off quotation, parenthetical citation follows final punctuation

Palma 4

hero. Many fictional hero "types" (such as the romantic hero and the western hero) carried over from the prefilm era; but new kinds of heroes also emerged, identified even more closely by the public with the stars who originated them. Early examples of the star-hero included silent film stars Douglas Fairbanks and Mary Pickford. "The swashbuckler was born with [. . .] Fairbanks," according to Beja, who also sees Pickford as the prototype of the brave or "plucky" movie heroine. As Richard deCordova notes in a memorable phrase, the studios wanted to convince millions of moviegoers that "the real hero behave[d] just like the reel hero" (qtd. in Gallagher, part 2). Therefore, the persona that a studio developed to turn a working actor into a star was the only public identity that actor would be allowed to have. Film historians like Beja and deCordova, who explores this topic in his book Picture Personalities: The Emergence of the Star System in America, say that the public's conceptual link between the hero and the star is the reason studios tried so hard to encourage the idea that stars like Fairbanks and Pickford had no private personalities separate from those of their onscreen characters. (See Figure 1.)

As silent films gave way to "talkies" and Hollywood cinema emerged as a cultural force in and of itself, new names replaced those of Fairbanks and Pickford on theater marquees. The star system,

Examples of star-hero

Sentence combining quotation and paraphrase from interview, with bracketed ellipsis indicating words omitted from quotation

Square brackets enclose material altered so tense of quotation fits into writer's sentence

Indirect online source without page numbers cited using qtd. in *and part number*

No page numbers needed for citation of interview or entire book

Parenthetical reference directs readers to figure

Transition to second main point: public exposure of star-hero failings in the 1950s and 1960s

Caption relates figure to text

Figure 1. Hollywood studios tried to stage-manage the image of stars like Mary Pickford to create public illusions of heroic, almost mythological beings.

however, only grew more deeply entrenched. As long as the star-hero stayed separate from the public, buffered by studios in order to keep the image intact, his or her fictional self remained safe. But the strain of living up to a legend instead of living a life took a toll on the private, "real" selves. Brian Gallagher cites a remark by Cary Grant that sums up the strain many stars must have felt: "Everybody wants to be Cary Grant. Even I want to be Cary Grant" (part 3). As the studio system disintegrated in the 1950s and the 1960s and the stars lost the publicity shield it had provided, this toll became glaringly obvious to their adoring public.

Part number cited for online source without page numbers

Films from this period show that the movie industry was self-mockingly aware of its pitfalls. Sunset Boulevard, released in 1950, showed what happened when a hero-image was no longer profitable and the system abandoned the star it had made. Gloria Swanson played the fictional silent film star Norma Desmond, once young and adored, now aging and forgotten, who tries in vain to recapture her lost glory and ends her quest in tragedy. A Star Is Born, remade in 1954 with Judy Garland in the lead role, chronicled the rise of a young woman from nobody to star, showing the reality of how the system created a perfect image and forced a human being to become it (Corey and Ochoa 353, 347). Yet even though these films showed the artificiality and destructiveness of the star system, at the same time they helped to perpetuate it. After all, the fictional star was played by a real-life one--and thus fiction and truth became even further intertwined.

Subpoint: movie industry's self-awareness, with two examples

Citation with two page references covers two preceding sentences; comma separates pages

Ironic consequence of star system exposés pointed out

Approximately a decade later, in 1962, Marilyn Monroe died of what was officially ruled an accidental overdose of sleeping pills. And in the words of a television biography, "almost instantly,

Subpoint: scandals surrounding stars, with an example

the lurid circumstances of [her] death made national headlines around the world [. . .]. Marilyn Monroe was dead. Marilyn the Myth was born" (Box Office Bombshell). The supposedly idyllic life stars lived was being steadily exposed as false through both fictional tragedies and actual scandals, yet paradoxically the public did not turn against the stars but only focused their fascination in a slightly different way. Singer and songwriter Elton John immortalized the unique cult of fame that overshadowed Monroe's death in his 1973 song "Candle in the Wind," when he wrote of his own youthful feelings toward her: "Your candle burned out long before, your legend never did."[2] Rather than serving to separate the hero from the star, in fact, scandals only bound the two more closely together, lending a tragic, martyred cast to the star's image. The public's adoration of their stars did not diminish. Their perception of their heroes as ideals, however, began to fade.

Superscript refers readers to explanatory note

Ironic consequence of scandals pointed out

Transition to next main point

Fast forward from the fifties and sixties to the present: forty, almost fifty, years later. A brief excerpt from the celebrity gossip-fest Hollywood Confidential shows that the last vestiges of the studio system's image-projection and -protection have vanished:

Imperative sentence with film jargon used to introduce third main point: a new form of mistaken identity and the continued decline of the hero

Subpoint: disappearance of stars' image-protection

> Well into the throes of drug addiction by the time she was thirteen,

> Drew Barrymore attempted suicide by cutting her wrists with a kitchen knife.
>
> Rosemary Clooney was addicted to prescription drugs and, after two embattled marriages to José Ferrer, was admitted to a psych ward.
>
> Francis Ford Coppola takes lithium.
>
> Patty (Call Me Anna) Duke is a manic-depressive. (Amende 247)

Quotation from popular magazine cites author in parentheses rather than in signal phrase

No longer do stars try to hide their personal lives from the public, and every scandal, every lie is exposed in the short run. Thus today's public hold very few illusions about the lives of their star-heroes. Although stars are still "living heroes," the relationship between the two terms has changed: rather than admiring stars for their heroic achievements and personal qualities, the public simply envies them for their lifestyle--their immense power, wealth, and fame. A profound cynicism exists toward the hero as ideal, and this cynicism is reflected in the portrayal of the fictional hero in current American films. It is a portrayal that perpetuates the problem of mistaken identity I identified earlier, but in reverse, with heroes being identified with the stars that portray them, rather than vice versa.

Subpoint: stars are now envied rather than admired

Subpoint: current films reflect cynicism about hero-ideal and perpetuate a new form of mistaken identity

The 1994 film The Ref offers a striking example of this reversal and of the cynicism it

Extended example illustrates cynicism and reversal of mistaken identity

Neutral signal verb introduces description of film

Ellipses indicate omissions in quotation

Bracketed comment indicates underlining added by writer for emphasis

Author's name cited alone for one-page, one-paragraph source

Concept of antihero introduced

both grows out of and feeds into. As a review on the ABC News Web site Mr. Showbiz notes:

> Judy Davis and Kevin Spacey are a married couple who for the life of them can't stop bickering. Denis Leary is the burglar who's taken them hostage on Christmas Eve. Writers Marie Weiss and Richard LaGravanese have built a [. . .] platform [. . .] from which Leary can freely launch himself into the mad stand-up monologues of outrage and spleen that are his trademark [emphasis mine]. (Feeney)

A closer look at this film tells us more. It is Christmas Eve, a traditional time of sharing and harmony among loved ones, yet the married couple in the film and the relatives who descend upon them for the holidays are all so bitter, sarcastic, and self-absorbed that even a hardened criminal is appalled by them. As the values associated with Christmas are turned on their ear and exposed as empty vanity in today's society, the criminal becomes a cynical sort of antihero: unlike his hostages, he at least remembers what a family is supposed to act like. The film's message was emphasized by the casting of comedian Leary in the title role, casting that capitalized on his reputation as a one-man mouthpiece for the Middle-American cynicism or anti-ideals of the nineties.

Palma 10

The fictional commentary of Leary's character was made more believable to the audience because the majority of them were familiar with its similarities to the actual commentary made famous by Leary himself. Rather than the hero creating the star, the star now forms the hero.

The disappearance of the hero-ideal as a separate entity from, or as a model for, the star has led to a second and perhaps more complex problem: with most modern films, there is a peculiar absence of lasting empathy of the audience with the hero. Apart from the rare phenomenon such as Luke Skywalker in Star Wars (1977), not only do "modern" movie heroes not exist apart from actors in audiences' minds, but they do not stay there for long. Think of Sigourney Weaver as Ripley, savior of humanity from Aliens (1986), or Harrison Ford as president of the United States in Air Force One (1997). In fact, this wording reveals just how most moviegoers do think of those heroes--the roles are indistinguishable from the stars--and after audiences see a movie, they no longer associate the character and the film, but rather the actor and the film. The difference between the short shelf life of modern "heroes" and the staying power of their old-style predecessors is evident if we look at film remakes of novels like Little Women and The Three Musketeers, in which the characters do supersede the actors in importance. But such

Transition to next subpoint: absence of lasting audience empathy with most modern film heroes

Two examples cited

New films contrasted to remakes of novels

Palma 11

films only cater to audience nostalgia for the time when those heroes gave cause for belief and hope, when the culture on which they were based held some ideals. These classic heroes may endure in memory, but they will never again have the mythic power that they did once upon a time. To re-create that lasting empathy in a modern context, we need films that can overcome mistaken identity and that contain heroes who are believable and relevant to today's world. Fortunately, in 1997 such a film, and such a hero, came to the screen.

Transition to last main point: remakes cater to nostalgia for old heroes, but we need new ones

Think of the current film hero as, to borrow a term from The Princess Bride (1987), "mostly dead." Not having died, the hero needs not rebirth but revival or regeneration. To begin regenerating the hero, then, it is necessary to overcome (1) the audience's preconceptions about the stars' relationships to the characters they play, and (2) the failure of recent hero-characters to invoke a lasting empathy in the public. The 1997 film Face/Off can serve as one prototype for overcoming both of these obstacles and thus for resolving once and for all the problem of mistaken identity.

Parenthetical numbers used to define regeneration of the hero as a two-part challenge

Introduction of prototype for solution to problem: Face/Off

First, the plot and characterization of this film provide an opportunity to prove that it is possible for a character to exist and be identified apart from the star who plays him or her. During the course of the story, the two main characters, hero Sean Archer and villain Castor Troy, undergo

Subpoint: Face/Off turns mistaken identity against itself

Figure 2. Nicholas Cage and John Travolta switched roles partway through Face/Off, a technique that helped audiences see their characters as figures independent of the actors portraying them.

surgery that exchanges their faces. The two stars of the film start off playing particular characters, John Travolta as Archer and Nicholas Cage as Troy; but approximately twenty minutes into the film they switch roles. (See Figure 2.) In an interview for a magazine article, Travolta described his take on imitating his costar:

> [Cage's walk is] a saunter almost. It's very specific to Nick's natural gait. And I said if you don't mind, maybe we could use that Nick Cage cadence for the bad guy's voice, too, and I could just

Bracketed words clarify beginning of quotation to fit writer's introduction

> adapt that. You know, the way Nick slows down and <u>enunciates</u> and <u>pronunciates</u>. He's almost poetic in his talking. (qtd. in Daly 24)

Parenthetical citation indicates indirect source

Director John Woo and others involved in the making of <u>Face/Off</u> seem to have used audience preconceptions about actor-idiosyncrasies being identical to character-idiosyncrasies, purposely emphasized in the beginning of the film, to make the switch-off of actors and roles that much more shocking and "real" to the audience. They turned mistaken identity against itself. Moviegoers who had seen Cage and Travolta act before, who associated their faces with their body language, found that when the body language remained the same, even with a new face, it was convincing. This disassociation of actor from character negates the second obstacle to regeneration of the hero as well. Without mistaken identity to cloud the issue, Archer was able to create a lasting empathy with the audience. Even after the audience left the darkness of the theater, his character could not be viewed on anything but its own terms.

Transition to second subpoint: creating a believable contemporary hero is difficult

With the complex problem of mistaken identity overcome, what remains is to create a believable hero who is relevant to today's world. In this context, the major challenge is that the model for the old hero, in Western culture at least, is based on the view that a human being is essentially a

Palma 14

unified organic whole and can be labeled in some way: as epic hero, romantic hero, tragic hero, swashbuckling hero, western hero, detective hero, and so on. In the contemporary world, we can no longer believe in such a one-dimensional being. In one of the essays in her anthology Simians, Cyborgs, & Women, historian of science Donna J. Haraway claims that our dreams of organic unity and coherence are futile. In their place, she recommends the cyborg figure, which can give us a new dream of ourselves as multiple, surpassing either body or machine (181). In fact, Haraway argues that with our thinking computers, our routine organ transplants and high-technology prostheses, human beings in the late twentieth century already live in a world of cyborgs--"hybrid[s] of machine and organism, [creatures] of social reality as well as [creatures] of fiction" (149). Much of Haraway's analysis can be applied to the emerging film hero.

Paraphrase of source; signal verbs indicate disputable statements

Concept of cyborg introduced and explained

Summary of source that incorporates a quotation; square brackets enclose material added by writer

The reel hero can no longer exist as a contained organic whole in today's fractured, technology-driven society. The human aspect of the hero has been damaged by mistaken identity to the extent that moviegoers will no longer put an extraordinary amount of faith in it. They no longer want the lie of static perfection given by classic heroes such as Hercules or Robin Hood and betrayed by film stars of Monroe's, and later

Cyborg concept applied to film heroes

Earlier points summarized

Return to example of Face/Off

Introductory phrase calls attention to striking quotation and cites source title related to writer's point

Barrymore's, generations, but neither will a hero as openly damaged as such stars suffice in and of itself. Within their realistic heroes, people still want to hold firm to a core of something untainted by human frailties. At just this moment, the cyborg hero has emerged in film.

Again, Face/Off offers a useful demonstration. The character of Archer, a tortured FBI agent who spends years tracking the criminal (Troy) who gunned down his little boy, is not a hero, in the classic sense of the word, nor is he an antihero, in the modern sense of the word. Instead, he is a prototype for the emerging twenty-first-century hero, a figure whose humanity is not perfect but rather is damaged beyond repair (like the American culture's belief in the hero-ideal). To defeat "evil," Archer must use technology to "become" his enemy--literally wear his face and take his place in the world. As Janice Rushing and Thomas Frentz put it in their book Projecting the Shadow: The Cyborg Hero in American Film, "to survive, a man must be technological, and to thrive, he must be technologically adept" (147). The new heroes cannot be sustained without the props of the modern world. Technology supplements their human frailties with cyborg prosthetics that give them an inhuman capacity for human salvation. The cyborg image metaphorically compensates for the modern dissonance between the technological and the organic; it uses technology to weld together the fractured nature of contemporary human beings, creating one inhuman whole that is capable of obtaining a limited perfection precisely because of its inhuman state. Archer achieves this state and triumphs--maybe not an angel, not a "golden one," but certainly a cause for hope.

Allusions to opening song quotation

The emergence of cyborg figures in films is not limited to Face/Off. Over the past two decades, the different facets of the cyborg character have been explored in films as diverse as Blade Runner (1982) and Star Trek: First Contact (1996). These portrayals reflect a deep ambivalence, since many in our culture see the cyborg as a symbol not of hope but of dehumanization, the dead end of the modern world. In Blade Runner, the human hero's job is to hunt down and "cancel" android "replicants" that are "more human than human"; and in First Contact, humans battle to resist "assimilation into the [cy]Borg collective." In both cases, though, the films offer positive images of cyborgs as well, suggesting that their future could go either way--or continue to go both ways. Jewel asked the question: "And where's my hope now that my heroes have gone?" Perhaps the 1991 film Terminator 2: Judgment Day provides the answer, one that speaks to the eventual triumph of the cyborg as hero. Turning to human heroes Sarah and John Connor, the cyborg Terminator says simply, "Come with me if you want to live."

Conclusion cites additional examples of cyborgs in films and raises issue of cultural ambivalence toward them

Restatement of opening quotation/question

Closing example suggests answer

Heading centered

Indent five spaces to superscript number

Bibliographic note acknowledges help

Explanatory note offers additional comments on cult of fame surrounding celebrities

1"

Palma 17

Notes

[1] I want to thank those who have contributed to my thinking on this topic, including my professors and classmates, Professor Morris Beja, and two consultants from the Ohio State University Writing Center, Melissa Goldthwaite and Nels Highberg.

[2] The rewritten version of "Candle in the Wind" that John sang at the funeral of Diana, Princess of Wales, in 1997 is now the best-selling recorded single of all time. Although Diana was not in movies, she was constantly in public view--in newspapers and magazines and on television; she too was caught up in the cult of fame that Monroe experienced. As Diana the person died, Diana the myth was born.

1"

Palma 18

Works Cited

Amende, Coral. Hollywood Confidential: An Inside Look at the Public Careers and Private Lives of Hollywood's Rich and Famous. New York: Penguin, 1997.

Beja, Morris. Personal interview. 2 Oct. 1997.

Blade Runner. Dir. Ridley Scott. Warner Bros./Ladd, 1982.

Box Office Bombshell: Marilyn Monroe. Writ. Andy Thomas, Jeff Schefel, and Kevin Burns. Dir. Bill Harris. Nar. Peter Graves. A&E Biography. Arts and Entertainment Network. 23 Oct. 1997.

Corey, Melinda, and George Ochoa. The Dictionary of Film Quotations: 6,000 Provocative Movie Quotes from 1,000 Movies. New York: Crown, 1995.

Daly, Steve. "Face to Face." Entertainment Weekly 20 June 1997: 20-24.

deCordova, Richard. Picture Personalities: The Emergence of the Star System in America. Urbana: U of Illinois P, 1990.

Face/Off. Dir. John Woo. Perf. John Travolta and Nicholas Cage. Paramount, 1997.

Feeney, F. X. Rev. of The Ref, dir. Ted Demme. Mr. Showbiz: A World of Entertainment from ABCNEWS.com. 18 Aug. 1997 <http://www.mrshowbiz.com/reviews/moviereviews/movies/32363.html>.

Heading centered

First line of entry flush with left margin; subsequent lines indented one-half inch or 5 spaces

Interview

Film

Television program

Book

Article in a weekly magazine

Review in a Web site

Palma 19

Article in an online journal

Essay in a collection

Book with an editor

Entry in a well-known reference work

Sound recordings

Photograph obtained from agency

Ford, Harrison, perf. Air Force One. Dir. Wolfgang Petersen. Columbia, 1997.

Gallagher, Brian. "Some Historical Reflections on the Paradoxes of Stardom in the American Film Industry, 1910-1960." Images: A Journal of Film and Popular Culture 3 (1997): 7 parts. 7 Aug. 1997 <http://www.qni.com/~ijournal/issue03/infocus/stars1.htm>.

Haraway, Donna J. "A Cyborg Manifesto: Science, Technology, and Socialist Feminism in the Late Twentieth Century." Simians, Cyborgs, & Women. New York: Routledge, 1991. 149-81.

Henry, Lewis C., ed. Five Thousand Quotations for All Occasions. Garden City: Doubleday, 1945.

"Hero." The New Merriam-Webster Dictionary. 1989.

John, Elton. "Candle in the Wind." Goodbye Yellow Brick Road. Audiocassette. MCA, 1973.

Kilcher, Jewel. "Amen." Pieces of You. A&R, 1994.

Little Women. Dir. Gillian Armstrong. Columbia Tri-Star, 1994.

Photograph of Mary Pickford. Undated. Photofest, New York.

Photograph of Nicholas Cage and John Travolta in Face/Off. Photofest, New York.

The Princess Bride. Dir. Rob Reiner. 20th Century-Fox, 1987.

The Ref. Dir. Ted Demme. Perf. Denis Leary, Judy Davis, and Kevin Spacey. Touchstone, 1994.

Palma 20

Rushing, Janice Hocker, and Thomas S. Frentz. Projecting the Shadow: The Cyborg Hero in American Film. Chicago: U of Chicago P, 1995.

The Star. Dir. Lawrence Pitkethly. Videocassette. CBS/FOX Video, 1995.

A Star Is Born. Dir. George Cukor. Perf. Judy Garland. Warner Bros., 1954.

Star Trek: First Contact. Dir. Jonathan Frakes. Paramount, 1996.

Star Wars. Dir. George Lucas. 20th Century Fox, 1977.

Sunset Boulevard. Dir. Billy Wilder. Perf. Gloria Swanson. Paramount, 1950.

Terminator 2: Judgment Day. Dir. James Cameron. Tri-Star, 1991.

The Three Musketeers. Dir. Stephen Herek. Disney, 1993.

Weaver, Sigourney, perf. Aliens. Dir. James Cameron. 20th Century Fox, 1986.

Book with two authors

Videocassette

Performer in a film

45

Documenting Sources: APA Style

It's all "a matter of style," as the old adage suggests, in academic disciplines as in fashion and design. Indeed, the conventions of style vary among disciplines, according to what a discipline values and how it credits work. As a prospective member of one or more academic disciplines, you will have occasion to follow various disciplinary styles, particularly when you need to use their guidelines for citing and documenting sources in your own writing. One of the most important documentation styles is that of the American Psychological Association (APA), which is widely used in psychology and other social sciences. ■

For further reference on APA style, consult the following volume:

> American Psychological Association. *Publication Manual of the American Psychological Association.* 4th ed. Washington, D.C.: APA, 1994.

45a APA format for parenthetical citations

APA style requires **parenthetical citations** in the text to document quotations, paraphrases, summaries, and other material from a source (42d). These in-text citations correspond to full bibliographic entries in a list of references at the end of the text.

1. AUTHOR NAMED IN A SIGNAL PHRASE Generally, use the author's name in a signal phrase to introduce the cited material, and place the date, in parentheses, immediately after the author's name. For a quotation, the page number, preceded by *p.,* appears in parentheses after the quotation. For electronic texts or other works without page numbers, paragraph numbers may be used instead.

```
Key (1983) has argued that the placement of
women in print advertisements is
subliminally important.
```

(Continued on page 566)

(Continued from page 565)

As Briggs (1970) observed, parents play an important role in building their children's self-esteem because "children value themselves to the degree that they have been valued" (p. 14).

For a long, set-off quotation, position the page reference in parentheses two spaces after the final punctuation.

2. AUTHOR NAMED IN A PARENTHETICAL CITATION When you do not name the author in your text, give the name and the date, separated by a comma, in parentheses at the end of the cited material.

One study has found that only 68% of letters received by editors were actually published (Renfro, 1979).

3. TWO AUTHORS Use both names in all citations. Join the names with *and* in a signal phrase, but use an ampersand (&) instead in a parenthetical reference.

Murphy and Orkow (1985) reached somewhat different conclusions by designing a study that was less dependent on subjective judgment than were previous studies.

A recent study that was less dependent on subjective judgment resulted in conclusions somewhat different from those of previous studies (Murphy & Orkow, 1985).

4. THREE TO FIVE AUTHORS List all the authors' names for the first reference.

Belenky, Clinchy, Goldberger, and Tarule (1986) suggest that many women rely on observing and listening to others as ways of learning about themselves.

In any subsequent references, use just the first author's name plus *et al.* ("and others").

From this experience, observe Belenky et al. (1986), women learn to listen to themselves think, a step toward self-expression.

5. SIX OR MORE AUTHORS Use only the first author's name and *et al.* ("and others") in every citation, including the first.

As Mueller et al. (1980) demonstrated, television holds the potential for distorting and manipulating consumers as free-willed decision makers.

6. CORPORATE OR GROUP AUTHOR If the name of the organization or corporation is long, spell it out the first time you use it, followed by an abbreviation in brackets. In later citations, use the abbreviation only.

FIRST CITATION (Centers for Disease Control [CDC], 1990)

LATER CITATIONS (CDC, 1990)

7. UNKNOWN AUTHOR Use the title or its first few words in a signal phrase or a parenthetical citation.

The school profiles for the county substantiate this trend (Guide to secondary schools, 1983).

8. TWO OR MORE AUTHORS WITH THE SAME SURNAME If your list of references includes works by different authors with the same surname, include the authors' initials in each citation.

G. Jones (1994) conducted the groundbreaking study of retroviruses.

9. TWO OR MORE SOURCES IN THE SAME PARENTHETICAL CITATION If you cite more than one source at once, list works in alphabetical order by author's surname, separated by semicolons; list works by the same author in chronological order, separated by commas.

```
(Chodorow, 1978; Gilligan, 1982)
(Gilligan, 1977, 1982)
```

10. SPECIFIC PARTS OF A SOURCE Use abbreviations (*chap., p.,* and so on) in a parenthetical citation to name the part of a work you are citing.

```
Montgomery (1998, chap. 9) argues that his research
yielded the opposite results.
```

11. PERSONAL COMMUNICATION Cite any personal letters, email, telephone conversations, or interviews with the person's initial(s) and last name, the identification *personal communication,* and the date.

```
J. L. Morin (personal communication, October 14, 1990)
supported the claims made in her recent article with new
evidence.
```

45b APA format for content notes

APA style allows content notes for information you wish to include to expand or supplement your text. Indicate such notes in the text by superscript numerals in consecutive order throughout the text. Type the notes themselves on a separate page after the last page of the text, under the heading "Footnotes," centered at the top of the page. Double-space all entries. Indent the first line of each note five to seven spaces, but begin subsequent lines at the left margin.

SUPERSCRIPT IN TEXT

```
The age of the children involved in the study was an
important factor in the selection of items for the
questionnaire.[1]
```

FOOTNOTE

```
     [1]Marjorie Youngston Forman and William Cole of the
Child Study Team provided great assistance in
identifying appropriate items.
```

45c APA format for a list of references

The alphabetical list of the sources cited in your essay is called **References.** (If your instructor asks that you list everything you have read as background, call the list "Bibliography.") Here are some guidelines for preparing such a list:

- Start your list on a separate page after the text of your document but before any appendices or notes. Number each page, continuing the numbering of the text.
- Type the heading "References," not underlined or italicized or in quotation marks, centered one inch from the top of the page.
- Double-space, and begin your first entry. Double-space the entire list.
- List sources alphabetically by authors' (or editors') last names. If a source has no known author or editor, alphabetize it by the first major word of the title, disregarding *A, An,* or *The.* If the list includes two or more works by the same author, see the examples on pages 572 and 573.

1 Books and periodicals

For source materials from books and periodicals, the APA style specifies the treatment and placement of four basic elements – author, publication date, title, and publication information. Each element is followed by a period.

- *Author.* List *all* authors last name first, and use only initials for first and middle names. Separate the names of multiple authors with commas, and use an ampersand before the last author's name.
- *Publication date.* Enclose the date in parentheses. Use only the year for books and journals; use the year, a comma, and the month or month and day for magazines. Do not abbreviate the month.
- *Title.* Underline or italicize titles and subtitles of books and periodicals. Do not enclose titles of articles in quotation marks. For books and articles, capitalize only the first word of the title and subtitle and any proper nouns or proper adjectives. Capitalize all major words in a periodical title. (See 36c for more information on capitalization.)
- *Publication information.* For a book, list the city of publication (and the country or postal abbreviation for the state if the city is unfamiliar), a colon, and the publisher's name, dropping any *Inc., Co.,* or *Publishers.* For a periodical, follow the periodical title with a comma, the volume number (underlined), the issue number (if appropriate) in parentheses, a comma, and the inclusive page numbers of the article. For newspaper articles and for articles and chapters in books, include the abbreviations *p.* ("page") or *pp.* ("pages").

Consult the following sample entries for information on where in an entry you should place other information. These entries are in a "hanging indent" format, where the first line flushes left and the subsequent lines indent one-half inch or five spaces. This is the customary APA format for final copy, including student papers. Unless your instructor suggests otherwise, it is the format we recommend. Note, however, that for manuscripts being submitted to journals, APA requires the reverse (first lines indented, subsequent lines flushed left), assuming that it will be converted by a typesetting system to a hanging indent.

1. BOOK BY ONE AUTHOR

Lightman, A. (1993). Einstein's dreams. New York: Warner.

2. BOOK BY TWO OR MORE AUTHORS

Newcombe, F., & Ratcliffe, G. (1978). Defining females--The nature of women in society. New York: Wiley.

3. BOOK BY A CORPORATE OR GROUP AUTHOR

Institute of Financial Education. (1983). Income property lending. Homewood, IL: Dow Jones-Irwin.

Use the word *Author* as the publisher when the organization is both the author and the publisher.

American Chemical Society. (1978). Handbook for authors of papers in American Chemical Society publications. Washington, DC: Author.

4. BOOK BY AN UNKNOWN AUTHOR

National Geographic atlas of the world. (1988). Washington, DC: National Geographic Society.

5. BOOK PREPARED BY AN EDITOR

Solomon, A. P. (Ed.). (1980). The prospective city. Cambridge, MA: MIT Press.

6. SELECTION IN A BOOK WITH AN EDITOR

West, C. (1992). The postmodern crisis of the Black intellectuals. In L. Grossberg, C. Nelson, & P. Treichler (Eds.), Cultural studies (pp. 689-705). New York: Routledge.

7. TRANSLATION

Durkheim, E. (1957). Suicide (J. A. Spaulding & G. Simpson, Trans.). Glencoe, IL: Free Press of Glencoe.

8. EDITION OTHER THAN THE FIRST

Kohn, M. L. (1977). Class and conformity: A study in values (2nd ed.). Chicago: University of Chicago Press.

9. ONE VOLUME OF A MULTIVOLUME WORK

Baltes, P., & Brim, O. G. (Eds.). (1980). Life-span development and behavior (Vol. 3). New York: Basic Books.

10. ARTICLE IN A REFERENCE WORK

Ochs, E. (1989). Language acquisition. In International encyclopedia of communications (Vol. 2, pp. 390-393). New York: Oxford University Press.

If no author is listed, begin with the title.

11. REPUBLICATION

Piaget, J. (1952). The language and thought of the child. London: Routledge & Kegan Paul. (Original work published 1932)

12. GOVERNMENT DOCUMENT

U.S. Bureau of the Census. (1975). Historical statistics of the United States, colonial times to 1870. Washington, DC: U.S. Government Printing Office.

13. TWO OR MORE BOOKS BY THE SAME AUTHOR(S) List two or more books by the same author in chronological order. Repeat the author's name in each entry.

Macrorie, K. (1968). Writing to be read. New York: Hayden.

Macrorie, K. (1970). Uptaught. New York: Hayden.

14. ARTICLE IN A JOURNAL PAGINATED BY VOLUME

Shuy, R. (1981). A holistic view of language. Research in the Teaching of English, 15, 101-111.

15. ARTICLE IN A JOURNAL PAGINATED BY ISSUE

Maienza, J. G. (1986). The superintendency: Characteristics of access for men and women. Educational Administration Quarterly, 22(4), 59-79.

16. ARTICLE IN A MAGAZINE

Gralla, P. (1994, April). How to enter cyberspace. PC Computing, 60-62.

17. ARTICLE IN A NEWSPAPER

Browne, M. W. (1988, April 26). Lasers for the battlefield raise concern for eyesight. The New York Times, pp. C1, C8.

18. UNSIGNED ARTICLE

What sort of person reads creative computing? (1985, August). Creative Computing, 8, 10.

19. EDITORIAL OR LETTER TO THE EDITOR

Russell, J. S. (1994, March 27). The language instinct [Letter to the editor]. The New York Times Book Review, 27.

20. REVIEW

Larmore, C. E. (1989). [Review of the book Patterns of moral complexity]. Ethics, 99, 423-426.

21. PUBLISHED INTERVIEW

McCarthy, E. (1968, December 24). [Interview with Boston Globe Washington staff]. Boston Globe, p. B27.

22. TWO OR MORE WORKS BY THE SAME AUTHOR IN THE SAME YEAR List two or more works by the same author published in the same year alphabetically, and place lowercase letters (*a, b,* etc.) after the dates.

Murray, F. B. (1983a). Equilibration as cognitive conflict. Developmental Review, 3, 54-61.

Murray, F. B. (1983b). Learning and development through social interaction. In L. Liben (Ed.), Piaget and the foundations of knowledge (pp. 176-201). Hillsdale, NJ: Erlbaum.

2 Internet sources

With the exception of guidelines for citing some kinds of electronic sources, such as an online journal article available via email or FTP, the APA's *Publication Manual* does not have guidelines for citing World Wide Web sites and other Internet sources. The following formats – adapted from APA style to include Internet sources – are from *Online! A Reference Guide to Using Internet Sources,* by Andrew Harnack and Eugene Kleppinger.

The basic entry for most sources you access via the Internet should include the following elements in the order given. Each element except the address is followed by a period.

- *Author.* List all authors last name first, and use only initials for first and middle names. Separate the names of multiple authors with commas, and use an ampersand before the last author's name.
- *Date of publication.* Enclose the date in parentheses. Give the year of Internet publication or of the most recent update, if available, followed by a comma and the month and day, if these are available. Do not abbreviate the month.
- *Title.* List the title of the document or the subject line of the message or posting. Do not underline or italicize the title or enclose it in quotation marks. Capitalize only the first word of the title and subtitle and any proper nouns or proper adjectives.
- *Address.* Give the URL, in angle brackets, or other retrieval information.
- *Date of access.* Enclose the date in parentheses. Include the year, a comma, and the month and day; do not abbreviate the month.

www •

http://www.smpcollege.com/online-4styles~help

The site for Harnack and Kleppinger's Online! *provides more details and examples of their adaptation of APA style to Internet sources.*

www •

http://www.apa.org/journals/webref.html

This page gives the APA's own current advice about citing Internet and Web sources.

23. WORLD WIDE WEB SITE After the document title, include the title of the complete work of which it is a part, if any, underlined.

```
Mullins, B. (1995). Introduction to Robert Hass.
     Readings in Contemporary Poetry at Dia Center for
     the Arts. <http://www.diacenter.org/prg/poetry/95
     -96/interhass.html> (1997, April 24).

Shade, L. R. (1993). Gender issues in computer
     networking. <http://www.mit.edu:8001/people
     /sorokin/women/lrs.html> (1996, May 28).
```

24. LINKAGE DATA To cite a file or document accessed through a link with a source document, provide information on both the cited document and the source. After the title of the document, include the abbreviation *Lkd.* and the title of the source document, underlined. Then give additional linkage details, if applicable, indicated by *at,* and the source's URL.

```
Williams, T. T. The politics of place. Lkd. Insight &
     Outlook: A Program of Ideas, at "Transcripts."
     <http://www.west.net/~insight/> (1997, May 1).
```

25. FTP (FILE TRANSFER PROTOCOL) SITE After the title of the document, use the abbreviation *ftp* followed by the address of the FTP site, with no closing punctuation, and the full path to follow to find the document, with no closing punctuation.

```
Altar, T. W. (1993). Vitamin B12 and vegans. ftp
     wiretap.spies.com Library/Article/Food/b12.txt
     (1996, May 28).
```

26. TELNET SITE After the title of the document, include the title of the full work, if applicable, underlined and followed by a period. Then include the word *telnet,* followed by the complete telnet address, with no closing punctuation, and directions to access the document.

```
Aquatic Conservation Network. (n.d.). About the Aquatic
     Conservation Network. National Capital Freenet.
     telnet freenet.carleton.ca login as guest, go acn,
     press 1 (1996, May 28).
```

27. GOPHER SITE Include any print publication information, underlined where appropriate. Then give the URL, or list the word *gopher,* the site name, and the path followed to access information, with slashes to indicate menu selections.

Korn, P. How much does breast cancer really cost? Self. October 1994. <gopher://nysernet.org:70/00/BCIC/Sources/SELF/94/how-much> (1997, May 5).

28. LISTSERV MESSAGE Include the author's email address, in angle brackets. The subject line from the posting is followed by the address of the listserv, in angle brackets.

Lackey, N. <eeinly@ath.ericsson.se> (1995, January 30). From Clare to here. <nanci@world.std.com> (1997, May 1).

To cite a file that can be retrieved from a list's server or Web address, after the publication date, include the address of the listserv, in angle brackets, and the address or URL for the list's archive, indicated by *via,* in angle brackets.

Lackey, N. <eeinly@ath.ericsson.se> (1995, January 30). From Clare to here. <nanci@world.std.com> via <http://www.rahul.net/frankf/Nancy/archives/95130.html> (1997, May 1).

29. NEWSGROUP MESSAGE Include the author's email address (if known), in angle brackets. The subject line from the posting is followed by the name of the newsgroup, in angle brackets.

Sand, P. <psand@unh.edu> (1996, April 20). Java disabled by default in Linux Netscape. <keokuk.unh.edu> (1996, May 10).

30. EMAIL MESSAGE The APA's *Publication Manual* discourages including email in a list of references and suggests citing email only in text. It is good practice, however, to document email messages in the list of references, especially when their content is scholarly. In citing email correspondence, include the author's email address, in angle brackets, after the author's name. After the subject line from the posting, include the kind of communication (*Personal email, Office communication*) in square brackets.

Talbot, C. J. <ctalbot@pop.interport.net> (1996, January 26). Do this [Personal email]. (1996, May 10).

31. SYNCHRONOUS COMMUNICATION To cite postings in MOOs, MUDs, and IRCs, provide the speaker's name, if known, or the name of the site; the date of the event, in parentheses; its title, if appropriate; and the kind of communication (*Group discussion, Personal interview*), if necessary, in square brackets. Include the URL or command-line directions and the date of access, in parentheses.

LambdaMOO. (1996, May 28). Seminar discussion on netiquette. <telnet://lambda.parc.xerox.edu:8888> (1996, May 28).

3 Other sources

32. CD-ROM ABSTRACT

Natchez, G. (1987). Frida Kahlo and Diego Rivera: The transformation of catastrophe to creativity [CD-ROM]. Psychotherapy-Patient, 8, 153-174. Abstract from: SilverPlatter File: PsycLIT Item: 76-11344

33. MATERIAL FROM AN INFORMATION SERVICE OR DATABASE

Belenky, M. F. (1984). The role of deafness in the moral development of hearing impaired children. In A. Areson & J. De Caro (Eds.), Teaching, learning and development. Rochester, NY: National Institute for the Deaf. (ERIC Document Reproduction Service NO. ED 248 646)

34. TECHNICAL OR RESEARCH REPORTS AND WORKING PAPERS

Wilson, K. S. (1986). Palenque: An interactive multimedia optical disc prototype for children (Working Paper No. 2). New York: Center for Children and Technology, Bank Street College of Education.

35. PAPER PRESENTED AT A MEETING OR SYMPOSIUM, UNPUBLISHED Cite the month of the meeting, if it is available.

Engelbart, D. C. (1970, April). *Intellectual implications of multi-access computing.* Paper presented at the meeting of the Interdisciplinary Conference on Multi-Access Computer Networks, Washington, DC.

36. DISSERTATION, UNPUBLISHED

Leverenz, C. A. (1994). *Collaboration and difference in the composition classroom.* Unpublished doctoral dissertation, Ohio State University, Columbus.

37. POSTER SESSION

Ulman, H. L., & Walborn, E. (1993, March). *Hypertext in the composition classroom.* Poster session presented at the Annual Conference on College Composition and Communication, San Diego, CA.

38. FILM OR VIDEOTAPE

Hitchcock, A. (Producer & Director). (1954). *Rear window* [Film]. Los Angeles: MGM.

39. TELEVISION PROGRAM, SINGLE EPISODE

Kuttner, P. K., Moran, C., & Scholl, E. (1994, July 19). Passin' it on (W. Chamberlain, Executive Director). In D. Zaccardi (Executive Producer), *P.O.V.* New York: Public Broadcasting Service.

40. RECORDING Begin with the writer's name, followed by the date of copyright. Give the recording date if it is different from the copyright.

Colvin, S. (1991). I don't know why. [Recorded by A. Krauss and Union Station]. On *Every time you say goodbye* [Cassette]. Cambridge, MA: Rounder Records. (1992)

45d A sample research essay, APA style

An essay by Leah Clendening appears on the following pages. She followed the APA guidelines described in 45a – c.

Shortened title and page number appear on every page

Heading centered and double-spaced

A Content Analysis of Letters
to the Editor

Leah Clendening
Professor Garrett
Psychology 201
May 20, 1997

Abstract

This study analyzed the content of 624 letters to the editor in two newspapers--one published in a city of over 500,000, the other in a city of about 15,000--in order to explore the relationship between community size and subject matter of letters. A researcher read all of the letters printed in the newspapers on the weekdays of three nonconsecutive months in late 1987 and early 1988 and then classified them according to whether they dealt with local or national issues and recorded the findings on a category sheet. Results indicate a significant difference: letters in the smaller community concentrated almost entirely on local issues, whereas those in the larger community concentrated more frequently on national than on local issues.

No paragraph indent

Key words embedded in abstract to help readers identify the article

Title centered

Paragraphs indented five spaces

Previous work surveyed

Double spacing used throughout

Minimum of one-inch margin on all sides

First-level heading centered

Research question stated

Hypothesis stated

A Content Analysis of Letters to the Editor

Research has indicated that the average person who writes letters to an American newspaper tends to be a conservative, well-adjusted white male who is middle-aged or older and a longtime resident of his community (Singletary & Cowling, 1979). One study concluded that 71.4% of the letters printed were written by people who wished to inform or persuade by writing their letters. Most of the remainder, 27%, wished only to use the letter as a means of self-expression; the other 1.6% wished to arouse readers to action (Lemert & Larkin, 1979).

Problem

But what are the major concerns of these letter writers? Are they more concerned about events in their local communities or about national issues? Does the size of the community have some influence on the subjects of letters its members write? These questions led to the following hypothesis: people living in a small community (with a population of about 15,000) tend to be concerned more with local than with national issues. People living in a large community (with a population over 500,000) show more concern for national than for local issues.

Method

Newspapers

The two newspapers that served as data sources, the Mount Vernon News and the Cleveland Plain Dealer, were chosen mainly for convenience and availability. Cleveland has a population of 573,822 and a weekly distribution of the Plain Dealer of 482,564. Mount Vernon has a population of 14,380 and a weekly distribution of the Mount Vernon News of 10,936 (1985 IMS/Ayer Directory, 1985). Each newspaper's letters were read for the weekdays of October 1987, December 1987, and February 1988. Sunday issues were not taken into account.

A category sheet of possible subjects for the letters to the editor was adapted from the coding sheet of Donohew's study on Medicare (Budd, Thorp, & Donohew, 1967, p. 41). One column recorded national issues and a second, local issues. The sheet was constructed with a space for the newspaper's abbreviation, the date, and the letter number(s). The Mount Vernon News was given the abbreviation MVN and the Cleveland Plain Dealer, the abbreviation CPD.

Procedure

After the category sheet was finished and approved, observation began. The letters were read and marked for content in a library setting. Each

Second-level heading underlined and flush left

Subjects of study identified; passive voice used to focus on the research rather than the researcher

Right margin not justified

Short title used to identify source with no author

Materials described

Page noted for specific source

Steps in carrying out research explained

letter was then classified on the category sheet that had been titled with the proper abbreviations, date, and letter number. As observation progressed, constraints of time demanded a change from filling out a separate sheet for each letter to recording each day's letters on the same category sheet. The space left for recording the letter number was used to record the total number of letters for each particular day. After all observation was finished, the counts for each of the newspapers were totaled for each month and overall.

Results

Results from first newspaper analyzed statistically

During the three months, 60 letters were read from the Mount Vernon News. Fifty-three pertained to local issues, and seven pertained to national issues. A Chi-square test with an adjustment for continuity was used on these data to find whether there was a statistically significant difference between concern with local issues and concern with national issues. Results showed an overwhelming difference between issues, even at the .01 probability level. A graph (Figure 1) was also constructed to show the number of national and local issues for each month for the MVN.

Results from second newspaper analyzed statistically

Of a total of 564 letters read from the Cleveland Plain Dealer, 248 pertained to local

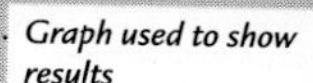

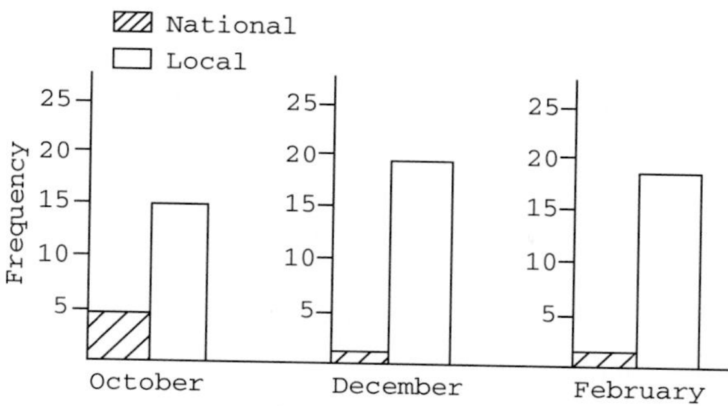

Figure 1. Frequency of national and local issues for the MVN

issues and 316 to national issues. A Chi-square test with an adjustment for continuity was also used on these data and, once again, showed a statistically significant difference. A graph (Figure 2) was constructed to show the frequency of national and local issues for each month for the CPD.

One interesting side note is that 21.6% of the letters from the Plain Dealer expressed grievances or appreciation, compared with 36% of the letters from the Mount Vernon News. These findings differ considerably from those of Lister, who found that only 5% of letters to the editor were of this particular type (Lister, 1985).

Findings counter to previous research noted

Graph used to show results

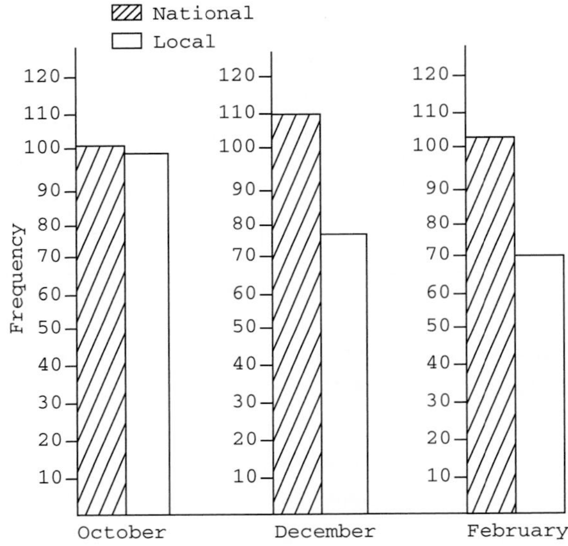

Figure 2. Frequency of national and local issues for the CPD

Discussion

The findings of this study generally supported the hypothesis, especially in the smaller community, where letters concentrated overwhelmingly on local issues. Perhaps residents of such a community do not see themselves as strongly affected by national politics and events. For the larger community, the findings were not as clear; one possibility is that many of the letters were

Results interpreted

not from the larger community itself but from smaller communities surrounding it.

If more time had been permitted, an entire year's letters could have been categorized, perhaps yielding more representative information. In addition, use of a second reader could have reduced bias on the part of a single reader in the categorization of letters. It was found as the study progressed that a few categories could have been added, such as religion and local and state elections; the lack of these categories, however, did not severely affect the study. Another bias that would be difficult to account for is editorial bias: one study has found that only 68% of letters received by editors were published (Renfro, 1979). The only way to eliminate this bias would be to read all the letters received instead of only those that are printed.

Biases and possible improvements in the study listed

Conclusion

This study raises some interesting questions that further study would probably help to answer. Does gender or age influence whether people are interested in local or national issues? What is the causal relationship between residence in small towns and apparent greater interest in local affairs? Future studies may answer such questions, building on the information here.

Larger questions noted in conclusion

Heading centered on new page

Entries listed alphabetically by author, last names first; initials used for first and middle names

Title beginning with a number alphabetized as if the number were spelled out

First line of each entry flushes left with margin

Subsequent lines indent five spaces

References

Budd, R. W., Thorp, K., & Donohew, L. (1967). Content analysis of communications. New York: Macmillan.

Lemert, J. B., & Larkin, J. P. (1979). Some reasons why mobilizing information fails to be in letters to the editor. Journalism Quarterly, 56, 504-512.

Lister, L. (1985). An analysis of letters to the editor. Social Work, 30, 77-78.

The 1985 IMS/Ayer Directory of Publications (117th ed.). (1985). Fort Washington, PA: IMS Press.

Renfro, P. C. (1979). Bias in selection of letters to the editor. Journalism Quarterly, 56, 822-826.

Singletary, M. W., & Cowling, M. (1979). Letters to the editor of the non-daily press. Journalism Quarterly, 56, 165-168.

Documenting Sources: CBE Style

46

In the sciences, it's often very important to track reported findings to their source. If the study that produced the findings is flawed — or if it cannot be replicated to yield the same results — then the findings are suspect at best. Careful documentation of sources is very important in the sciences, then, and the **CBE style** is widely used to do just that. This chapter illustrates CBE style and guides you in the use of such documentation in your own writing. ■

For further reference on CBE style, consult the following volume:

Council of Biology Editors. *Scientific Style and Format: The CBE Manual for Authors, Editors, and Publishers,* 6th edition. New York: Cambridge UP, 1994.

46a CBE format for in-text citations

In CBE style, citations within an essay follow one of two formats.

- The **citation-sequence format** calls for a superscript number (^{1}) or a number in parentheses after any mention of a source.
- The **name-year format** calls for the last name of the author and the year of publication in parentheses after any mention of a source. If the last name appears in a signal phrase, the name-year format allows for giving only the year of publication in parentheses.

Dr. Edward Huth, chairperson of the CBE Style Manual Committee, recommends either the name-year or the superscript system rather than the number-in-parentheses system – and suggests that student writers check a current journal in the field or ask an instructor about the preferred style in a particular course or discipline.

1. IN-TEXT CITATION USING CITATION-SEQUENCE SUPERSCRIPT FORMAT

```
In his lengthy text, Gilman[1] provides the most complete
discussion of this phenomenon.
```

For the citation-sequence system, you would also use a superscript ([1]) for each subsequent citation of this work by Gilman.

2. IN-TEXT CITATION USING NAME-YEAR FORMAT

```
In his lengthy text, Gilman provides the most complete
discussion of this phenomenon (Gilman 1994).

Maxwell's two earlier studies of juvenile obesity (1988,
1991) examined only children with diabetes.

The classic examples of such investigations (Morrow
1968; Bridger and others 1971; Franklin and Wayson 1972)
still shape the assumptions of current studies.
```

46b CBE format for a list of references

The citations in the text of an essay correspond to items on a list called **References.** If you use the citation-sequence superscript format, number and list the references in the sequence in which the references are *first* cited in the text. If you use the name-year format, list the references, unnumbered, in alphabetical order.

The following examples show both the citation-sequence format and the name-year format for various types of sources. You will see that the citation-sequence format calls for listing the date after the publisher's name in references for books and after the periodical name in references for articles. The name-year format calls for listing the date immediately after the author's name in any kind of reference.

DIRECTORY TO CBE STYLE FOR A LIST OF REFERENCES

1. BOOKS

(Continued from page 588)

1 Books

For a book, the basic entry includes the following items: the author, with the last name first, no comma, and initials without periods for the first and middle names; the title, with only the first word and proper nouns and adjectives capitalized and without underlining, italics, or quotation marks; the place and year of publication; the publisher; and the number of pages in the book.

1. ONE AUTHOR

[1]Freidson E. Profession of medicine. New York: Dodd-Mead; 1972. 802 p.

Freidson E. 1972. Profession of medicine. New York: Dodd-Mead. 802 p.

2. TWO OR MORE AUTHORS

[2]Stalberg E, Trontelj JV. Single fiber electromyography: studies in healthy and diseased muscle. New York: Raven; 1994. 291 p.

Stalberg E, Trontelj JV. 1994. Single fiber electromyography: studies in healthy and diseased muscle. New York: Raven. 291 p.

3. ORGANIZATION AS AUTHOR Any organization abbreviation is placed at the beginning of the name-year entry and is used in the corresponding in-text citation.

[3]World Health Organization. World health statistics annual: 1993. Geneva: World Health Organization; 1994.

[WHO] World Health Organization. 1994. World health statistics annual: 1993. Geneva: WHO.

4. BOOK PREPARED BY EDITOR(S)

[4]Berge ZL, Collins MP, editors. Computer mediated communication and the online classroom. Cresskill, NJ: Hampton Pr; 1995. 230 p.

Berge ZL, Collins MP, editors. 1995. Computer mediated communication and the online classroom. Cresskill, NJ: Hampton Pr. 230 p.

5. SECTION OF A BOOK WITH AN EDITOR

[5]Adler M. Stroke. In: Dulbecco R, editor. Encyclopedia of human biology. San Diego: Academic; 1991. p 299-308.

Adler M. 1991. Stroke. In: Dulbecco R, editor. Encyclopedia of human biology. San Diego: Academic. p 299-308.

6. CHAPTER OF A BOOK

[6]Castro J. The American way of health: how medicine is changing and what it means to you. Boston: Little, Brown; 1994. Chapter 9, Why doctors, hospitals, and drugs cost so much; p 131-53.

Castro J. 1994. The American way of health: how medicine is changing and what it means to you. Boston: Little, Brown. Chapter 9, Why doctors, hospitals, and drugs cost so much; p 131-53.

7. PUBLISHED PROCEEDINGS OF A CONFERENCE

[7][Anonymous]. International Conference on the Bus '86; 1986 Sep 9-10; London. [London]: Institution of Mechanical Engineers; 1986. 115 p.

The place of publication was not stated but inferred and placed in brackets.

[Anonymous]. 1986. International Conference on the Bus '86; 1986 Sep 9-10; London. [London]: Institution of Mechanical Engineers. 115 p.

2 Periodicals

For a journal article, the basic entry includes the author, with the last name first, no comma, and initials without periods for the first and middle names; the article title, with only the first word and proper nouns and adjectives capitalized; the journal title, abbreviated; the date of the issue; the volume number; the issue number, if any; and the inclusive page numbers. For newspaper and magazine articles, the entry includes the section designation and column number, if any. For rules on abbreviating journal titles, consult *The CBE Manual,* or ask an instructor or librarian to refer you to other examples. Following are examples using both superscript and name-year systems:

8. ARTICLE IN A JOURNAL PAGINATED BY VOLUME

[8]Finkel MJ. Drugs of limited commercial value. New Engl J Med 1980;302:643-4.

Finkel MJ. 1980. Drugs of limited commercial value. New Engl J Med 302:643-4.

9. ARTICLE IN A JOURNAL PAGINATED BY ISSUE

[9]Fagan R. Characteristics of college student volunteering. J Vol Admin 1992;11(1):5-18.

Fagan R. 1992. Characteristics of college student volunteering. J Vol Admin 11(1):5-18.

10. ARTICLE IN A WEEKLY JOURNAL

[10]Kerr RA. How many more after Northridge? Science 1994 Jan 28;263(5146):460-1.

Kerr RA. 1994 Jan 28. How many more after Northridge? Science 263(5146):460-1.

11. ARTICLE IN A MAGAZINE

[11]Jackson R. Arachnomania. Natural History 1995 Mar:28-31.

Jackson R. 1995 Mar. Arachnomania. Natural History:28-31.

12. ARTICLE IN A NEWSPAPER

[12]Christopher T. Grafting: playing Dr. Frankenstein in the garden. New York Times 1995 Feb 19;Sect Y:21(col 1).

Christopher T. 1995 Feb 19. Grafting: playing Dr. Frankenstein in the garden. New York Times; Sect Y:21(col 1).

3 Electronic sources

13. ELECTRONIC JOURNAL ARTICLES

[13]Harrison CL, Schmidt PQ, Jones JD. Aspirin compared with acetaminophen for relief of headache. Online J Therap [serial online] 1992 Jan 2;Doc nr 1:[4320 words; 10 paragraphs]. 5 figures; 10 tables. (Accessed 1992 Dec 26).

The abbreviation *nr* stands for "number."

Harrison CL, Schmidt PQ, Jones JD. 1992 Jan 2. Aspirin compared with acetaminophen for relief of headache. Online J Therap [serial online];Doc nr 1: [4320 words; 10 paragraphs]. 5 figures; 10 tables. (Accessed 1992 Dec 26).

14. ELECTRONIC BOOKS (MONOGRAPHS)

[14]Martindale online [monograph online]. London: Pharmaceutical Society of Great Britain; 1989 [updated 1989 Dec]. Available from: Dialog. Dialog. Accessed 1990 Jan 10.

[PSGB] Pharmaceutical Society of Great Britain. 1989. Martindale online [monograph online]. London: PSGB; [updated 1989 Dec]. Available from: Dialog. Accessed 1990 Jan 10.

4 Internet sources

With the exception of guidelines for citing electronic journal articles and books, some of which are available on the World Wide Web and by FTP and gopher, *The CBE Manual* does not have guidelines for citing Internet sources. The following formats, adapted from CBE style, are from *Online! A Reference Guide to Using Internet Sources,* by Andrew Harnack and Eugene Kleppinger. These examples use the citation-sequence system; to adapt them to the name-year system, simply delete the superscripts and alphabetize the entries.

The basic entry for most sources you access through the Internet should include the following elements:

- *Author.* Give the author's name, if available, last name first, followed by the initial(s) and a period.
- *Date of publication.* Give the year of Internet publication or most recent update, if available, followed by a period. If no date is available, use *n.d.*
- *Title.* List the title of the document or subject line of the message, followed by a period.
- *Address.* Include the URL, in angle brackets, or other retrieval information.
- *Date of access.* The date should be preceded by *Accessed* and followed by a period.

15. WORLD WIDE WEB SITE Include the title of the complete work, if applicable, after the document title.

[15]Brail S. n.d. Newsflash! Spider woman: an online community & resource for women web designers. <http://www.amazoncity.com/spiderwoman/web.html> Accessed 1997 May 22.

16. EMAIL MESSAGE Include the author's email address, in angle brackets, after the author's name, and the type of communication (*Personal email, Office communication*), in square brackets, after the subject line.

[16]Mitchell D. <mitcheld@ucs.orst.edu> 1997 May 28. PhD decisions [Personal email]. Accessed 1997 May 28.

www •

http://www.smpcollege.com/online-4styles~help

The site for Harnack and Kleppinger's Online! *provides more details and examples of their adaptation of CBE style to electronic sources.*

www •

http://www.apsu.edu/~lesterj/CYBER6.HTM

The CBE does not have information about citing electronic sources on its own site; however, this advice by James D. Lester is brief and cogent, and makes a good quick reference.

17. HYPERNEWS POSTING Include the author's email address, in angle brackets, after the author's name, and the type of message (if appropriate), in square brackets, after the subject line or title.

[17]Cyrus. <yku@moe.ac.sg> 1996 October 21. Students as creative users of multimedia [reply to Multimedia--students as users or creators? by Mark Christie]. <http://www.smedia.com.sg/HyperNews/get.cgi/TeachTalk/30/1.html> Accessed 1997 May 28.

18. LISTSERV MESSAGE Include the author's email address, in angle brackets, after the author's name, and the address of the listserv, in angle brackets, after the subject line.

[18]Fisher-Wirth A. <afwirth@sunset.backbone.olemiss.edu> 1997 May 27. Deserts. <asle@unr.edu> Accessed 1997 May 28.

19. NEWSGROUP MESSAGE Include the author's email address, in angle brackets, after (or instead of) the author's name, and the name of the newsgroup, in angle brackets, after the subject line.

[19]<kunk@astro.phys.unm.edu> 1997 May 30. What did the vandals learn? <soc.history.ancient> Accessed 1997 June 2.

20. SYNCHRONOUS COMMUNICATION Cite the name(s) of the speaker(s), if known, or the name of the site; the date of the event; its title, if appropriate; the kind of communication (*Group discussion, Personal interview*), if not indicated elsewhere in the entry, in square brackets; and the address, using either a URL or command-line directions.

[20]MediaMoo. 1997 May 13. Netoric's Tuesday cafe on Megabyte University: a look back; a look ahead. <telnet://purple-crayon.media.mit.edu:8888> Accessed 1997 June 5.

[21]Bauman M. 1997 Apr 15. Collaborative software environments: what's on your wish list? [Group discussion]. telnet purple-crayon.media.mit.edu/port=8888 Accessed 1997 June 5.

21. TELNET SITE After the document title, include the title of the full work, if applicable, followed by a period. Then include the word *telnet* and the complete telnet address, with no closing punctuation, and directions for accessing the document, with no closing punctuation.

> [22]Virginia's Public Education Network. n.d. Legislation tracking report. Virginia Department of Education legislative tracking analysis. telnet pen 1.pen .k12.va.us login as guest, press 3, press 4, press 2 Accessed 1997 May 29.

22. FTP (FILE TRANSFER PROTOCOL) SITE If the date of publication is unknown, use *n.d.* After the document title, include the abbreviation *ftp* followed by the address of the FTP site, with no closing punctuation. Then give either the URL or the command, address, and path elements used to find the document, with no closing punctuation.

> [23]Wang Z. 1992 June. EIP: the extended Internet protocol: a long-term solution to Internet address exhaustion. <ftp://munnari.OZ.AU/big-internet /eip.txt> Accessed 1997 June 5.

23. GOPHER SITE After the document title, include any print publication information. Then give either the URL or the word *gopher,* the site name, and the path followed to access the document, with slashes to indicate menu selections.

> [24]Martinots S. 1995. Spectors of Sartre: Nancy's romance with ontological freedom. gopher Journals and Newsletters/OSU Libraries' Electronic Serials /Postmodern Culture/pmcv6n1/review 4 Accessed 1997 May 29.

46c A sample research essay, CBE style

An introductory biology class was asked to analyze an unknown cob of corn to find out the most likely genetic cross that produced it and to write a report on the findings. Excerpts from Lesley Shaffer's research report follow. Her report follows a standard format recommended in the natural sciences, and the citations and references follow the CBE guidelines described in 46a and b.

The Determination of the Most Probable Genetic Cross Which Produced an Unknown Cob of Corn (*Zea mays*)

Abstract summarizes research and conclusions

Abstract

The analysis of an unknown cob of corn was conducted to determine the most probable genetic cross that produced it. Phenotypes for aleurone color and starch content were recognized for each of the total 460 kernels. Alleles for aleurone color were found to be dominant for purple (R) and recessive for yellow (r). Alleles for endosperm starch content were found to be dominant for starchy endosperms (Su) and recessive for sweet endosperms (su). The phenotypic ratio of the unknown cob of corn was 1.04:1.00:1.03:1.16 for R_Su_, R_susu, rrSu_, and rrsusu kernels respectively. The most probable genetic cross was RrSusu rrsusu or Rrsusu rrSusu.

Introduction briefly reviews other relevant research and explains purpose of experiment

Introduction

The foundation of modern genetics can be attributed, in large part, to the work of Gregor Mendel. He conducted hybridization experiments on the garden pea, determining dominant and recessive alleles in peas. Using mathematics and probabilities, he also found that the genotypic ratios of the offspring from hybrid crosses could be predicted. This was based on the possible alleles that could be donated in the gametes of each parent organism (Gardner 1960).

Source and date cited in parentheses

Mendel's work can also be applied to the genetics of corn. However, there is greater complexity in hybrid crosses than Mendel's experiments reveal. In 1911, G. N. Collins and J. H. Kempton found the first clearly recognized linkage in corn, discovering that the gene for the waxy endosperm is linked to the gene for aleurone color (Gardner 1960). This discovery led to the concept of crossing-over, in which segments of homologous chromosomes break and exchange genes creating genetic recombinations. Therefore, the genotypic ratios for the offspring of hybrid crosses do not always coincide with Mendelian ratios.

The purpose of my experiment was to analyze the phenotypes expressed in the kernels of an unknown cob of corn and determine the most probable genetic cross that produced it.

Methods and Materials

Methods and materials section briefly describes experiment

A cob of corn of unknown parentage was analyzed. Analysis consisted of counting individual kernels and categorizing them according to phenotypes of aleurone color and starch content. A total of 460 kernels were counted and placed in categories of either purple aleurone / starchy endosperm, purple aleurone / sweet endosperm, yellow aleurone / starchy endosperm, or yellow aleurone / sweet endosperm.

Dominant and recessive alleles for aleurone color were determined by the analysis of a separate cob of corn. Each kernel was counted according to color. Phenotypic ratios were calculated from which the monohybrid cross was deduced. Dominant and recessive alleles for starch content were determined with the analysis of another cob of corn in which the kernels were counted for each phenotype. Phenotypic ratios were calculated, and the monohybrid cross was deduced.

A phenotypic ratio for the unknown was then calculated, and the hypothesis for the most probable genetic cross of the parent corn was deduced.

Results section explains what experiment produced

Results

The monohybrid corn cob analyzed for dominant and recessive alleles for aleurone color had 106 yellow kernels and 282 purple kernels out of a total 388 kernels. The phenotypic ratio was 1:2.7. The calculated Chi-square value was 1.113 for the hypothesis of a heterozygous cross.

The monohybrid corn analyzed to determine dominant and recessive alleles for starch content had 110 sweet kernels and 317 starchy kernels out

5

of a total 427 kernels. The phenotypic ratio was 1:2.9. The calculated Chi-square value was 0.132 for the hypothesis of a heterozygous cross.

The unknown cob of corn analyzed had kernels that exhibited phenotypes of purple or yellow aleurones, and starchy or sweet endosperms. Of the total 460 kernels, 24.6% were purple starchy, 23.7% purple sweet, 24.3% yellow starchy, and 27.4% yellow sweet (Table 1). The phenotypic ratio was 1.04:1.00:1.03:1.16.

Discussion and Conclusions

Discussion and Conclusions examine two possible dihybrid crosses and conclude that both hypotheses are acceptable

The development of the endosperm starts with the initial triploid nucleus, which begins rapid divisions within two to four hours after fertilization (Knowles 1990). Sixteen to thirty days after pollination, genes are activated that specify the increase of enzymes involved in the synthesis of stored products, such as starch. From thirty-one to fifty days after pollination, there is continued synthesis of the major storage products. The endosperm changes as structures specialized for the storage of starch enlarge (Walden 1978).

[Eight more paragraphs of discussion and conclusions follow.]

References

Book

Gardner EJ. 1960. Principles of genetics. New York: Wiley. 386 p.

Hayward HE. 1938. Structure of economic plants. New York: Macmillan. 674 p.

Journal article

Knowles RV, Sprienc F, Phillips RL. 1990. Endoreduplication of nuclear DNA in the developing maize endosperm. Dev Genet 11:125-32.

Walden DB. 1978. Maize breeding and genetics. New York: Wiley, 794 p.

Documenting Sources: Chicago Style

47

The practice of documenting sources is at least as old as ancient libraries, where some kind of systematic listing was desirable. With the explosion of information in print-based societies, more formal kinds of documentation systems became necessary. One of the oldest and most widely respected of such systems is the one referred to simply as **Chicago style,** which has long been used in history as well as other areas of the arts and humanities. This chapter illustrates Chicago style and guides you in the use of such documentation in your own writing. ■

The fourteenth edition of the style guide of the University of Chicago Press, published in 1993 and called *The Chicago Manual of Style,* provides a complete guide to Chicago style. For further reference, you can also consult *The Chicago Manual* or the following much shorter volume intended for student writers:

> Turabian, Kate L. *A Manual for Writers of Term Papers, Theses, and Dissertations.* 6th ed. Rev. John Grossman and Alice Bennett. Chicago: U of Chicago P, 1996.

47a Chicago format for in-text citations and notes

Chicago style uses superscript numbers ([1]) to mark citations in the text. Citations are numbered sequentially throughout the text and correspond to notes that contain either publication information about the sources cited or explanatory or supplemental material that the writer chooses not to include in the main text. The sources are often also listed in a bibliography at the end of the text.

In the text, the superscript number for each note is placed near the cited material – at the end of the relevant quotation, sentence, clause, or phrase. The number is typed after any punctuation mark except the dash, and no space is left between the superscript and the preceding letter or punctuation mark.

47a. In-text citations and notes

47b. Bibliographic entries

(Continued on page 603)

(Continued from page 602)

3. INTERNET SOURCES

The notes themselves can be **footnotes** (each typed at the bottom of the page on which the citation for it appears in the text) or **endnotes** (all typed on a separate page at the end of the text under the heading "Notes"). Be sure to check your instructor's preference. The first line of each note is indented like a paragraph and begins with a number followed by a period and one space before the first word of the entry. All remaining lines of the entry are typed flush with the left margin. Type footnotes single-spaced with a double space between each note. Type all endnotes double-spaced. See p. 617 for an example of endnotes.

IN THE TEXT

```
As Luftig notes, true friendship between the sexes may
simply not be possible.[1]
```

IN THE NOTE

```
     1. Victor Luftig, Seeing Together: Friendship
between the Sexes in English Writing (Palo Alto, Calif.:
Stanford University Press, 1993), 1.
```

The first note for any source gives full information about the source, whereas subsequent notes are shortened. Here are some guidelines for the format of notes in Chicago style:

1 Books

A note for a book typically includes four elements, separated by commas: the author's name, in normal order; the title and subtitle, underlined or italicized; the publication information, including the city of publication, a shortened form of the publisher's name, and the date, all enclosed in parentheses; and the page number(s) to which the note refers, followed by a period.

1. ONE AUTHOR

1. Hayden Herrera, Frida: A Biography of Frida Kahlo (New York: Harper and Row, 1983), 356.

2. MORE THAN ONE AUTHOR

2. John T. McNeill and Helena M. Gamer, Medieval Handbooks of Penance (New York: Octagon Books, 1965), 139.

3. UNKNOWN AUTHOR

3. The New York Times Atlas of the World (New York: New York Times Books, 1980), 67.

4. EDITOR

4. C. Vann Woodward, ed., Mary Chesnut's Civil War (New Haven, Conn.: Yale University Press, 1981), 214.

5. SELECTION IN AN ANTHOLOGY, OR CHAPTER IN A BOOK, WITH AN EDITOR

5. Mary Gordon, "The Parable of the Cave," in The Writer on Her Work, ed. Janet Sternburg (New York: W. W. Norton, 1980), 30.

6. EDITION OTHER THAN THE FIRST

6. Alfred H. Kelly, Winfred A. Harbison, and Herman Belz, The American Constitution: Its Origins and Development. 6th ed. (New York: W. W. Norton, 1983), 187.

7. MULTIVOLUME WORK

7. Philip S. Foner and Ronald L. Lewis, eds., The Black Worker (Philadelphia: W. P. Lippincott, 1980), 3:134.

2 Periodicals

A note for a periodical typically includes the following elements, separated by commas: the author's name, in normal order; the article title, in quotation marks; and the periodical title, underlined or italicized. The format for the rest of the publication information, including the volume and issue numbers (if any), the date of publication, and the page number(s) to which the note refers, varies according to the type of periodical.

8. ARTICLE IN A JOURNAL PAGINATED BY VOLUME

8. Margot Norris, "Narration under a Blindfold: Reading Joyce's 'Clay,'" PMLA 102 (1987): 206.

9. ARTICLE IN A JOURNAL PAGINATED BY ISSUE

9. John Lofty, "The Politics at Modernism's Funeral," Canadian Journal of Political and Social Theory 6, no. 3 (1987): 89.

10. ARTICLE IN A MAGAZINE

10. Sarah Ferguson, "The Comfort of Being Sad: Kurt Cobain and the Politics of Suicide," Utne Reader, July-August 1994, 60.

11. ARTICLE IN A NEWSPAPER

11. Dennis Kelly, "A Financial Report Card for Colleges," USA Today, 5 July 1994, sec. D, p. 1.

3 Internet sources

The Chicago Manual does not include guidelines for citing Internet sources. The following formats, adapted from Chicago style, are from *Online! A Reference Guide to Using Internet Sources,* by Andrew Harnack and Eugene Kleppinger.

The basic entry for most sources you access through the Internet should include the following elements:

- *Author.* Give the author's name, if available, in normal order, followed by a comma.
- *Title.* Give the title of the document or subject line of the message, enclosed in quotation marks and followed by a comma.

www •

http://www.smpcollege.com/online-4styles~help
The site for Harnack and Kleppinger's *Online!* provides more details and examples of their adaptation of Chicago style to Internet sources.

- *Date of publication.* List the date of Internet publication or the most recent update, if available, followed by a comma. (If no date is available, use *n.d.*)
- *Address.* Include the URL, in angle brackets, or other retrieval information.
- *Date of access.* Enclose the date in parentheses, followed by a comma or by a period if it is the last item in the entry.
- *Text division.* List the page number or other internal division of the source, if applicable, followed by a period.

www •

http://www.press.uchicago.edu/Misc/Chicago/cmosfaq.html

The Chicago Manual of Style, *FAQ (and not-so-FAQ). Go here for the most current advice about* Chicago *style, and to submit your own questions about style.*

12. WORLD WIDE WEB SITE After the document title, include the title of the complete work, if applicable, italicized or underlined.

12. Stephanie Brail, "Newsflash!" Spider Woman: An Online Community & Resource for Women Web Designers, n.d., <http://www.amazoncity.com/spiderwoman/web.html> (22 May 1997).

13. EMAIL MESSAGE Include the author's email address, in angle brackets, after the author's name, and the type of communication (*Personal email, Distribution list*) after the subject line.

13. Danielle Mitchell, <mitcheld@ucs.orst.edu> "PhD Decisions," 28 May 1997, Personal email (28 May 1997).

14. HYPERNEWS POSTING Include the author's email address, in angle brackets, after the author's name, and the type of message (if appropriate), followed by a comma, after the publication date.

14. Cyrus, "Students as Creative Users of Multimedia," <yku@moe.ac.sg> 21 October 1996, reply to "Multimedia--Students as Users or Creators?" by Mark Christie, <http://www.smedia.com.sg/HyperNews/get.cgi/TeachTalk/30/1.html> (28 May 1997).

15. LISTSERV MESSAGE Include the author's email address, in angle brackets, after the author's name, and the address of the listserv, in angle brackets, after the publication date.

15. Ann Welpton Fisher-Wirth, <afwirth@sunset.backbone.olemiss.edu> "Deserts," 27 May 1997 <asle@unr.edu> (28 May 1997).

16. NEWSGROUP MESSAGE Include the author's email address, in angle brackets, after (or instead of) the author's name, and the name of the newsgroup, in angle brackets, after the publication date.

16. <kunk@astro.phys.unm.edu> "What Did the Vandals Learn?" 30 May 1997, <soc.history.ancient> (2 June 1997).

17. SYNCHRONOUS COMMUNICATION Cite the name of the speaker(s), if known, or the name of the site, followed by a comma; the title of the event, if appropriate, enclosed in quotation marks and followed by a comma; the date of the event, followed by a comma; the type of communication (*Group discussion, Personal interview*), if not indicated elsewhere in the entry, followed by a comma; the address, using either a URL or command-line directions; and the date of access, in parentheses, followed by a period.

17. MediaMoo, "Netoric's Tuesday Cafe on Megabyte University: A Look Back; a Look Ahead," 13 May 1997, <telnet://purple-crayon.media.mit.edu:8888> (5 June 1997).

18. Marcy Bauman, "Collaborative Software Environments: What's on Your Wish List?" Group discussion, 15 April 1997, <telnet purple-crayon.media .mit.edu/port=8888> (5 June 1997).

18. TELNET SITE After the document title, include the full title of the work, if applicable, italicized or underlined and followed by a comma. After the publication date, include the word *telnet* and the complete telnet address, with no closing punctuation, and directions for accessing the document, with no closing punctuation.

19. Virginia's Public Education Network, "Legislation Tracking Report," <u>Virginia Department of Education Legislative Tracking Analysis</u>, n.d., telnet pen1.pen.k12.va.us login as guest, press 3, press 4, press 2 (29 May 1997).

19. FTP (FILE TRANSFER PROTOCOL) SITE After the publication date, include the abbreviation *ftp* followed by the address of the FTP site, with no closing punctuation, and either the URL or the command, address, and path elements used to find the document, with no closing punctuation.

20. Zheng Wang, "EIP: The Extended Internet Protocol: A Long-Term Solution to Internet Address Exhaustion," June 1992, <ftp://munnari.OZ.AU /big-internet/eip.txt> (5 June 1997).

20. GOPHER SITE After the document title, include any print publication information, italicized or underlined where appropriate. Then give either the URL or the word *gopher,* the site name, and the path followed to access the document, with slashes to indicate menu selections.

21. Steve Martinots, "Spectors of Sartre: Nancy's Romance with Ontological Freedom," September 1995, gopher Journals and Newsletters/OSU Libraries' Electronic Serials/Postmodern Culture/pmcv6n1/review 4 (29 May 1997).

21. LINKAGE DATA After the document title, give the abbreviation *lkd.;* the title of the document to which the file is linked, italicized or underlined; and additional linkage information, if applicable, preceded by *at* and followed by a comma. After the publication date, give the URL for the source document.

22. Meredith Goldstein-LeVande, "Elizabeth Cady Stanton," lkd. Introduction, at "To learn about Elizabeth Cady Stanton, click here," n.d., <http://www .history.rochester.edu/class/suffrage/home.htm> (2 June 1997).

4 Subsequent notes for previously cited sources

After giving a full citation the first time you refer to a work, for any additional reference to that work you need list only the author's name followed by a comma, a shortened version of the title, a comma, and the page number. If the reference is to the same source cited in the previous note, you can use the Latin abbreviation *Ibid.* instead of the name and title.

23. Herrera, Frida, 32.

24. Ibid., 33.

25. Foner and Lewis, Black Worker, 138-39.

26. Ferguson, "Comfort of Being Sad," 63.

27. Martinots, "Spectors of Sartre."

47b Chicago format for bibliographic entries

An alphabetical list of sources in Chicago style is usually titled **Bibliography.** If "Sources Consulted," "Works Cited," or "Selected Bibliography" better describes your list, however, any of these titles is acceptable. Begin the list on a separate page following the main text and any endnotes. Continue the consecutive numbering of pages. Type the title (without underlining or quotation marks), and center it two inches below the top of the page. Double-space, and begin each entry at the left margin. Indent the second and subsequent lines of each entry five spaces. Double-space the entire list.

List sources alphabetically by authors' last names (or by the first major word in the title if the author is unknown). See p. 618 for an example of a bibliography in Chicago style.

The bibliographic entry for a source includes the same information as the first note for that source, except for the specific page reference. However, the author's name is given last name first; the main elements of the entry are separated by periods rather than commas; and the publication information for books and periodical articles is not enclosed in parentheses. The following examples demonstrate how to arrange the elements of bibliographic entries according to Chicago style:

1 Books

1. ONE AUTHOR

Herrera, Hayden. <u>Frida: A Biography of Frida Kahlo</u>. New York: Harper and Row, 1983.

2. MORE THAN ONE AUTHOR

McNeill, John T., and Helena M. Gamer. <u>Medieval Handbooks of Penance</u>. New York: Octagon Books, 1965.

3. UNKNOWN AUTHOR

<u>The New York Times Atlas of the World</u>. New York: New York Times Books, 1980.

4. EDITOR

Woodward, C. Vann, ed. <u>Mary Chesnut's Civil War</u>. New Haven, Conn.: Yale University Press, 1981.

5. SELECTION IN AN ANTHOLOGY, OR CHAPTER IN A BOOK, WITH AN EDITOR

Gordon, Mary. "The Parable of the Cave." In The Writer on Her Work, edited by Janet Sternburg, 30-45. New York: W. W. Norton, 1980.

6. EDITION OTHER THAN THE FIRST

Kelly, Alfred H., Winfred A. Harbison, and Herman Belz. The American Constitution: Its Origins and Development, 6th ed. New York: W. W. Norton, 1983.

7. MULTIVOLUME WORK

Foner, Philip S., and Ronald L. Lewis, eds. The Black Worker. Vol. 3. Philadelphia: W. P. Lippincott, 1980.

2 Periodicals

8. ARTICLE IN A JOURNAL PAGINATED BY VOLUME

Norris, Margot. "Narration under a Blindfold: Reading Joyce's 'Clay.'" PMLA 102 (1987): 206-15.

9. ARTICLE IN A JOURNAL PAGINATED BY ISSUE

Lofty, John. "The Politics at Modernism's Funeral." Canadian Journal of Political and Social Theory 6, no. 3 (1987): 89-96.

10. ARTICLE IN A MAGAZINE

Ferguson, Sarah. "The Comfort of Being Sad: Kurt Cobain and the Politics of Suicide." Utne Reader, July-August 1994, 60-62.

11. ARTICLE IN A NEWSPAPER

Kelly, Dennis. "A Financial Report Card for Colleges." USA Today, 5 July 1994, sec. D, p. 1.

3 Internet sources

12. **WORLD WIDE WEB SITE**

Brail, Stephanie. "Newsflash!" Spider Woman: An Online Community & Resource for Women Web Designers. n.d. <http://www.amazoncity.com/spiderwoman/web.html> (22 May 1997).

13. **EMAIL MESSAGE**

Mitchell, Danielle. <mitcheld@ucs.orst.edu> "PhD Decisions." 28 May 1997. Personal email (28 May 1997).

14. **HYPERNEWS POSTING**

Cyrus. "Students as Creative Users of Multimedia." <yku@moe.ac.sg> 21 October 1996. Reply to "Multimedia--Students as Users or Creators?" by Mark Christie. <http://www.smedia.com.sg/HyperNews/get.cgi/TeachTalk/30/1.html> (28 May 1997).

15. **LISTSERV MESSAGE**

Fisher-Wirth, Ann Welpton. <afwirth@sunset.backbone.olemiss.edu> "Deserts." 27 May 1997. <asle@unr.edu> (28 May 1997).

16. **NEWSGROUP MESSAGE**

<kunk@astro.phys.unm.edu> "What Did the Vandals Learn?" 30 May 1997. <soc.history.ancient> (2 June 1997).

17. **SYNCHRONOUS COMMUNICATION**

MediaMoo. "Netoric's Tuesday Cafe on Megabyte University: A Look Back; a Look Ahead." 13 May 1997. <telnet://purple-crayon.media.mit.edu:8888> (5 June 1997).

Bauman, Marcy. "Collaborative Software Environments: What's on Your Wish List?" Group discussion. 15 April 1997. <telnet purple-crayon.media.mit.edu/port=8888> (5 June 1997).

18. TELNET SITE

Virginia's Public Education Network. "Legislation Tracking Report." Virginia Department of Education Legislative Tracking Analysis. n.d. telnet penl.pen.k12.va.us login as guest, press 3, press 4, press 2 (29 May 1997).

19. FTP (FILE TRANSFER PROTOCOL) SITE

Wang, Zheng. "EIP: The Extended Internet Protocol: A Long-Term Solution to Internet Address Exhaustion." June 1992. <ftp://munnari.OZ.AU/big-internet/eip.txt> (5 June 1997).

20. GOPHER SITE

Martinots, Steve. "Spectors of Sartre: Nancy's Romance with Ontological Freedom." September 1995. gopher Journals and Newsletters/OSU Libraries' Electronic Serials/Postmodern Culture/pmcv6n1/review 4 (29 May 1997).

21. LINKAGE DATA

Goldstein-LeVande, Meredith. "Elizabeth Cady Stanton." Lkd. Introduction, at "To learn about Elizabeth Cady Stanton, click here." n.d. <http://www.history.rochester.edu/class/suffrage/home.htm> (2 June 1997).

47c A sample research essay, Chicago style

An introductory history course on U.S. civilization to 1877 called on students to write an essay "of no more than six pages focusing on a controversial issue related to the First Amendment." Kelly Darr chose to review the 1803 *Marbury v. Madison* decision and to relate that decision to the growth of the Supreme Court's powers. Following are the first four paragraphs of her essay, excerpted, and her endnotes and bibliography, which follow the guidelines in 47a and b.

Marbury v. Madison and the Origins of Judicial Review

The Supreme Court of the United States is a very prestigious and powerful branch of American government today. It has not always held this position, however. When the government system was developed in the late-eighteenth century, the powers of the judicial branch were fairly undefined. In 1803, Chief Justice John Marshall, with his decision in Marbury v. Madison, began to define the duties of the Court by claiming for the Supreme Court the power of judicial review. Judicial review has been upheld ever since, and many people take the practice for granted. There is controversy around Marshall's decision, however, with some claiming that judicial review was not the intent of the Framers. Two questions must be asked: Did Marshall overstep his bounds when he declared judicial review for the Court? If so, why has his decision been upheld for almost two hundred years? An examination of the actual case, Marbury v. Madison, and of Marshall's reasons for his decision is the first step to answering these questions.

Opening paragraph concludes with thesis in the form of two questions

This case was surrounded by personal and political opposition. It was brought to Court by William Marbury, whose commission as justice of the

1

peace by John Adams was withheld by Thomas Jefferson when he became president. Jefferson's act was prompted by Adams's attempt to fill the national judiciary with Federalist judges on the eve before Jefferson took office. Due to a mistake by John Marshall himself (at the time the secretary of state under Adams), however, the commissions were not delivered. Jefferson, who did not appreciate the last-minute attempt to fill the offices with Federalists, refused to deliver the commissions after he took office. Marbury and a few other men sued James Madison, secretary of state under Jefferson. Marshall, now the chief justice, was eager to try the case and attack Jefferson, his political enemy.[1]

Source cited using superscript numeral

By the time the case went to trial in 1803, two of the five years of the term for justice of the peace had expired. It was no longer a case over undelivered commissions; it was a case testing the power of the courts against the executive. . . . If Marshall issued a writ of mandamus requiring Madison to hand over the commissions, Jefferson could have him impeached.[2] If Marshall ruled in favor of Jefferson, he would make the judicial branch look even more powerless than it already did. Marshall was in a no-win situation, and he was aware of this predicament when he set out to make his decision.[3]

He finally made his decision on February 24, 1803, and it was based on two concerns: the ethics of withholding Marbury's commission, and the right of the Supreme Court to issue a writ of mandamus to the president.[4] Marshall broke the issue into three questions. The first question addressed whether Marbury had a right to the commission. Marshall said that he did have the right to it because it had been signed by the president at the time and sealed with the seal of the United States. Second, Marshall asked, if Marbury had a right to the commission, did the laws of the land protect his right to the appointment? Marshall reasoned that withholding his commission would be in violation of his personal rights, so the laws must protect those rights. Third, Marshall asked if the laws protected Marbury in the form of a writ of mandamus from the Supreme Court. Marshall reasoned that the Court could not issue a writ of mandamus even though the Judiciary Act of 1789 said that it could. According to this law, the Supreme Court could issue writs of mandamus to people under the authority of the United States, which Marbury clearly was; however, if the Court could not issue a writ of mandamus, then this law was unconstitutional. He went on to say that the Supreme Court only had appellate jurisdiction (except in a few specific cases) and this case had been brought before the Court for original jurisdiction.

Therefore he declared that the law stating that the Supreme Court could issue writs of mandamus was unconstitutional. In other words, Congress did not have the legal power to give the Court that right. He went on to say that the Constitution is the supreme law of the land, and since it was the judicial branch's duty to say what the law is, the Court had the power to declare acts unconstitutional. Thus Marshall denied mandamus for Marbury and ruled in favor of Madison. At the same time, however, he took a big step toward strengthening the judicial branch by establishing judicial review for the Supreme Court.[5]

[In the next paragraph, Darr sums up the strengths and weaknesses of Marshall's decision. She then discusses the effects of *Marbury v. Madison* and its status today.]

Notes

1. John A. Garraty, Quarrels That Have Shaped the Constitution (New York: Harper and Row, 1987), 7-14.

2. Ibid., Quarrels, 19.

3. William C. Louthan, The United States Supreme Court: Lawmaking in the Third Branch of Government (Englewood Cliffs, N.J.: Prentice-Hall, 1991), 51.

4. Thomas J. Higgins, Judicial Review Unmasked (West Hanover, Mass.: Christopher Publishing House, 1981), 40-41.

5. Marbury v. Madison, 1 Cranch, 137 (1803).

6. Louthan, Supreme Court, 51.

7. Ibid., 51.

8. Ibid., 50-51.

9. Higgins, Judicial Review, 40-41.

10. Ibid., 32.

11. Ibid., 34.

First line of each note indented 5 spaces

Book

Author's last name and shortened title used for source already cited

Ibid. *used to cite same source as in previous note*

5

First line of each source flush left, subsequent lines indented five spaces

Bibliography

Garraty, John A. Quarrels That Have Shaped the Constitution. New York: Harper and Row, 1987.

Higgins, Thomas J. Judicial Review Unmasked. West Hanover, Mass.: Christopher Publishing House, 1981.

Louthan, William C. The United States Supreme Court: Lawmaking in the Third Branch of Government. Englewood Cliffs, N.J.: Prentice-Hall, 1991.

Marbury v. Madison, 1 Cranch, 137 (1803).

6

PART 9

ACADEMIC WRITING

documentation
writing/editing
hypertext
message
www.bedfordstmartins.com/nsmhandbook
thinking & collaborating

FAQ

FAQ: Academic Writing Online

What online resource can you turn to for information about a particular discipline or field?

The World Wide Web offers an embarrassment of riches when it comes to learning about fields of study. Here are a few sites that can help you start to investigate the following disciplines:

ART WWW Virtual Library — Art
<http://www.fisk.edu/vl/Literature/Overview.html>
An excellent collection of links to art sites; includes links to other virtual libraries.

BIOLOGY and BIOSCIENCES WWW Virtual Library — Biosciences
<http://golgi.harvard.edu/biopages.html>
Categorizes information by provider and subject. A good place to begin research, this site includes many links to journals, FTP sites, and subdisciplines.

BUSINESS A Business Researcher's Interests
<http://www.brint.com/interest.html>
Provides links to articles, papers, magazines, tools, and many other resources for "contemporary business, management, and information technology issues."

CHEMISTRY ChemCenter
<http://www.chemcenter.org/>
From the American Chemical Society; includes links to education, industry, publications, and searchable databases.

COMMUNICATION ACA Homepage
<http://www.americancom.org/>
Sponsored by the American Communication Association; includes links to the different subfields that make up communications.

ENGINEERING WWW Virtual Library — Engineering
<http://arioch.gsfc.nasa.gov/wwwvl/engineering.html>
Lists links to many relevant sources across engineering fields, including all the engineering VLs, from acoustic engineering to welding engineering.

HISTORY The History Net
<http://www.theHistoryNet.com/>
A project of the National Historical Society; provides a historical magazine as well as a search service.

MATHEMATICS AMS Mathematics on the Web
<http://www.ams.org/mathweb/>
Offers literature guides and links both on- and offline, references, topical guides, and links to individuals. See also the Math Archives Undergrads Page at <http://archives.math.utk.edu/undergraduates.html>.

MUSIC Sibelius Academy Music Resources
<http://www.siba.fi/Kulttuuripalvelut/music.html>
Provides links to every aspect of music appreciation, production, and education.

PHYSICS Physics News
<http://www.het.brown.edu/news/index.html>
Lists the latest work being done in physics, including NASA's Hot Topics and the newsletter The Scientist; *science news from wire services; and links to journals and magazines.*

POLITICAL SCIENCE Political Science Virtual Library
<http://spirit.lib.uconn.edu/PoliSci/polisci.htm>
Includes links to departments, libraries, journals, government agencies, newsgroups, listservs, and related fields.

PSYCHOLOGY American Psychological Association
<http://www.apa.org>
The APA homepage, with access to its PsychNet document site and information for students in psychology.

SOCIOLOGY WWW Virtual Library – Sociology
<http://www.ixpres.com/lunatic/soc.html>
Provides links to sites covering research centers, discussion groups, ejournals, organizations, and university departments.

What particular resources would help with writing about literature?

To learn about the major terms used in writing about literature, see the site *In Other Words: A Lexicon of the Humanities* at <http://www.sil.org/humanities>.

To begin research related to writing about literature, a useful site is *Resources in English Language and Literature* at <http://www.lib.cmich.edu/bibliographers/billmiles/english.htm>.

48 Understanding Disciplinary Discourse

A recent survey confirmed that good writing plays an important role in almost every profession, and in some it is crucial to success. As one MBA wrote, "Those who advance quickly in my company are those who write and speak well." But writing works in different ways in different disciplines, and you may begin to get a sense of such differences as you prepare essays or other written assignments for various courses. Certainly by the time you choose a major, you should be ready to familiarize yourself with the expectations, vocabularies, styles, methods of proof, and conventional formats used in your field. This chapter will help you to begin this process of familiarization. ■

48a Analyzing academic assignments and expectations

Academic assignments vary widely from course to course and even from professor to professor. Thus the directions this section offers can only be general, but the best advice is really very simple: make sure you are in control of the assignment rather than letting the assignment be in control of you. To take control, you need to understand the assignment fully and to understand what professors in the particular discipline expect in response.

When you receive an assignment in *any* discipline, your first job is to make sure you understand what that assignment is asking you to do. Some assignments may be as vague as "Write a five-page essay on one aspect of the Civil War." Others, like this psychology assignment, will be fairly specific: "Collect, summarize, and interpret data drawn from a sample of letters to the editor published in two newspapers, one in a small rural community, and one in an urban community, over a period of three months. Organize your research report according to APA requirements." (See 45d for one student's essay in response to this assignment.) Whatever the assignment, you must take charge of analyzing it. Answering the following questions can help you do so:

1. *What is the purpose of the assignment?* Does it serve an informal purpose – as a basis for class discussion or as a way to brainstorm about a topic? Or is the purpose more formal, a way to demonstrate your mastery of certain material and your competence as a writer?
2. *What is the assignment asking you to do?* Are you to summarize, explain, evaluate, interpret, illustrate, define? If the assignment asks you to do more than one of these things, does it specify the order in which you are to do them? (Note that the preceding psychology assignment does specify the activities to be carried out and the general topic to be covered in the report.)
3. *Do you need to ask for clarification of any terms?* Students responding to the psychology assignment might well ask the instructor, for instance, to discuss the meaning of *collect* or *interpret* and perhaps to give examples. Or they might want further clarification of the term *urban community* or the size of a suitable *sample.*
4. *What do you need to know or find out to do the assignment?* Students doing the psychology assignment need to develop a procedure – a way to analyze or categorize the letters to the editor. Furthermore, they need to know how to do simple statistical analyses of the data.
5. *Do you understand the expectations regarding background reading and preparation, method of organization and development, format, and length?* The psychology assignment mentions no reading, but in this field an adequate statement of a problem usually requires setting that problem in the context of other research. A student might well ask how extensive this part of the report is to be.
6. *Can you find an example of an effective response to a similar assignment?* If you can, you can analyze its parts and use it as a model for developing your approach to the current assignment.
7. *Does your understanding of the assignment fit with that of other students?* Talking over an assignment with classmates is one good way to test your understanding.

EXERCISE 48.1

Here is an assignment from a communications course. Read it carefully, and then use the seven questions in 48a to analyze the assignment.

Assignment: Distribute a questionnaire to twenty people (ten male, ten female) asking these four questions: (1) What do you expect to say and do when you meet a stranger? (2) What don't you expect to say and do when you meet a stranger? (3) What do you expect to say and do when you meet a very close friend? (4) What don't you expect to say and do when you meet a very close friend? When you have collected your twenty questionnaires, read them over and answer the following questions.

1. What, if any, descriptions were common to all respondents' answers?
2. How do male and female responses compare?
3. What similarities and differences were found between the responses to the stranger and to the very close friend situations?
4. What factors (environment, time, status, gender, and so on) do you think have an impact on these responses?
5. Discuss your findings, using concepts and theories explained in your text.

48b Understanding disciplinary vocabularies

The rhetorician Kenneth Burke describes how people become active participants in the "conversation of humankind" in the following way. Imagine, he says, that you enter a crowded room in which everyone is talking and gesturing animatedly. You know no one there and cannot catch much of what is being said. Slowly you move from group to group listening, and finally you take a chance and interject a brief statement into the conversation. Others listen to you and respond. Thus, slowly but surely, do you come to *participate* in, rather than to observe, the conversation.

Entering into an academic discipline or a profession is much like entering into such a conversation. At first you feel like an outsider, and you do not catch much of what you hear or read. Trying to enter the new "conversation" takes time and careful attention. Eventually, however, the vocabulary becomes familiar, and participating in the conversation seems easy and natural.

Of course, this chapter cannot introduce you to the vocabulary of every field. The point is that *you* must make the effort to enter into the conversation, and that again means taking charge of the situation. To get started, one of the first things you need to do is to study the vocabulary.

Determine how much of what you are hearing and reading depends on specialized or technical vocabulary. Try highlighting key terms in your

www •

http://myst.hunter.cuny.edu/~rwcenter/writing/on-line/invention.html

From the Hunter College writing center, this essay on invention techniques offers questions and ways of thinking about issues that can be applied across disciplines and discourse communities. Included, you'll note, is Burke's Pentad, five questions for examining people's actions.

reading or your notes to help you distinguish the specialized vocabulary. If you find little specialized vocabulary, try to master the new terms quickly by reading your textbook carefully, by asking questions of the instructor and other students, and by looking up a few key words or phrases.

If you find a great deal of specialized vocabulary, however, you may want to familiarize yourself with it somewhat methodically. Any of the following procedures may prove helpful:

- Keep a log of unfamiliar or confusing words *in context.* To locate definitions, check the terms in your textbook's glossary or index.
- Review your class notes each day after class. Underline important terms, review their definitions, and identify anything that is unclear. Use your textbook or ask questions to clarify anything confusing before the class moves on to a new topic.
- Check to see if your textbook has a glossary of terms or sets off definitions in italics or boldface type. Study pertinent sections to master the terms.
- Try to start using or working with key concepts. Even if they are not yet entirely clear to you, working with them will help you come to understand them. For example, in a statistics class, try to work out (in words) how to do an analysis of *covariance,* step by step, even if you are not sure of the precise definition of the term. Or try to plot the narrative progression in a story even if you are still not entirely sure of the definition of *narrative progression.*
- Find the standard dictionaries or handbooks of terms for your field. Students beginning the study of literature, for instance, can turn to several guides such as *A Dictionary of Literary, Dramatic, and Cinematic Terms,* or *A Handbook to Literature.* Those entering the discipline of sociology may refer to the *Dictionary of the Social Sciences,* while students beginning statistical analysis may turn to *Statistics without Tears.* Ask your instructor or a librarian for help finding the standard references in your field.
- If you belong to online listservs or discussion groups – or even if you are browsing sites on the Internet and World Wide Web related to a particular field – take special note of the ways technical language or disciplinary vocabulary is used there.

Whatever your techniques for learning a specialized vocabulary, begin to use the new terms whenever you can – in class, in discussions with instructors and other students, and in your assignments. This ability to *use* what you learn in speaking and writing is crucial to your full understanding of and participation in the discipline.

48c Identifying the style of a discipline

Becoming familiar with technical vocabulary is one important way to initiate yourself into a discipline or field of study. Another method is to identify stylistic features of the writing in that field. You will begin to assimilate these features automatically if you immerse yourself in reading and thinking about the field. To get started, study some representative pieces of writing in the field with the following questions in mind:

- How would you describe the overall *tone* of the writing? Is it very formal, somewhat formal, informal?
- To what extent do writers in the field strive for a somewhat distanced, objective stance?
- In general, how long are the sentences? How long are the paragraphs?
- Are verbs generally active or passive — and why?
- Do the writers use first person (*I*) or prefer terms such as *one* or *the investigator*? What is the effect of this stylistic choice?
- Does the writing use visual elements such as graphs, tables, charts, computer-based graphics, or maps? How are these integrated into the text?
- What bibliographical styles (such as MLA, APA, CBE, or Chicago) are used? (See Chapters 44 – 47.)

www •

http://info.lib.uh.edu/wj/webjour.html

Journals are a good way to get a sense of how a field presents and defines its own discourse. Some libraries carry more journals than others, however; therefore, if you're at a smaller school, this site will be especially helpful in finding a journal in a given field.

Of course, writings within a single discipline may have different purposes and different styles. Although a research report is likely to follow a conventional form, a published speech greeting specialists at a convention may well be less formal and more personal no matter what the field. Furthermore, answering questions such as the preceding ones will not guarantee that you can produce a piece of writing similar to the one you are analyzing. Nevertheless, looking carefully at writing in the field brings you one step closer to writing effectively in that discipline.

48d Understanding the use of evidence

"Good reasons" form the core of any writing that argues a point, for they provide the *evidence* for the argument. Chapter 5 explains how to formulate good reasons. However, what is acceptable and persuasive evidence in one discipline may be more or less so in another. Observable, quantifiable data may constitute the very best evidence in, say, experimental psychology, but the same kind of data may be less appropriate — or even impossible to come by — in a historical study. As you grow familiar with any area of study, you will develop a sense of just what it takes to prove a point in that field. You can speed up this process, however, by doing some investigating and questioning of your own. As you read your textbook and other assigned materials, make a point of noticing the use of evidence. The following questions are designed to help you do so:

- How do writers in the field use precedent and authority? What or who counts as an authority in this field? How are the credentials of an authority established?
- What use is made of quantitative data (things that can be counted and measured)? What kinds of data are used? How are such data gathered and presented?
- What use is made of qualitative data (things that can be systematically observed)?
- How are statistics used and presented? Are tables, charts, or graphs common? How much weight do they carry?
- How is logical reasoning used? How are definition, cause and effect, analogies, and examples used in this discipline?
- How does the field use primary and secondary sources? What are the primary materials – the firsthand sources of information – in this field? What are the secondary materials – the sources of information derived from others? How is each type of source likely to be presented?
- What other kinds of textual evidence are cited? Web sites? electronic journals or databases? personal experiences or personal correspondence?
- How are quotations used and integrated into the text?

In addition to carrying out your own investigation, ask your instructor how you can best go about making a case in this field.

WWW •

http://www-english.tamu.edu/wcenter/journal.html

From Texas A&M's Writing Center, this help sheet of questions to ask in analyzing a journal or article will provide a way for you to discern the conventions and styles of a discipline.

EXERCISE 48.2

Do some reading in books and journals associated with your prospective major or a discipline of particular interest to you, using the preceding questions to study the use of evidence in that discipline. If you are keeping a writing log, make an entry in it summarizing what you have learned.

48e Using conventional disciplinary patterns and formats

You can gather all the evidence in the world and still fail to produce effective writing in your discipline if you do not know the field's generally accepted formats for organizing and presenting evidence. Again, these formats vary widely from discipline to discipline and sometimes from instructor to instructor, but patterns do emerge. The typical laboratory report, for instance, follows a fairly standard organizational framework whether it is in botany, chemistry, or parasitology. A case study in sociology or education or anthropology likewise follows a typical organizational plan.

Your job in any discipline is to discover its conventional formats and organizing principles so that you can practice using them. This task is easy enough to begin. Ask your instructor to recommend some excellent examples of the kind of writing you will do in the course. Then analyze these examples in terms of format and organization. You might also look at major scholarly journals in your field, checking to see what types of formats seem most common and how each is organized. Study these examples, keeping in mind these questions about organization and format:

- What types of essays, reports, or documents are common in this field? What is the purpose of each type? Are these types produced mainly in print, or mainly online?
- What can a reader expect to find in each type? What does each type assume about its readers?
- How is a particular type of text organized? What are its main parts? Are they labeled with conventional headings? What logic underlies this sequence of parts?
- How does a particular type of essay, report, or document show the connections among ideas? What assumptions of the discipline does it take for granted? What points does it emphasize?

THINKING CRITICALLY ABOUT THE DISCOURSE OF A DISCIPLINE

Reading with an Eye for Disciplinary Discourse

Here is an introductory passage of a college textbook. Read it carefully to see what you can infer about the discourse of chemistry — about its characteristic vocabulary, style, use of evidence, and so on.

> At one time it was easy to define chemistry. The traditional definition goes something like this: Chemistry is the study of the nature, properties, and composition of matter, and how these undergo changes. That served as a perfectly adequate definition as late as the 1930s, when natural science (the systematic knowledge of nature) seemed quite clearly divisible into the physical and biological sciences, with the former being comprised of physics, chemistry, geology, and astronomy and the latter consisting of botany and zoology. This classification is still used, but the emergence of important

fields of study such as oceanography, paleobotany, meteorology, and biochemistry, for example, have made it increasingly clear that the dividing lines between the sciences are no longer at all sharp. Chemistry, for instance, now overlaps so much with geology (thus we have *geochemistry*), astronomy (*astrochemistry*), and physics (*physical chemistry*) that it is probably impossible to devise a really good modern definition of chemistry, except, perhaps, to fall back on the operational definition: chemistry is what chemists do. (And what chemists do is what this book is all about!) . . .

To make a very long story short, copper and bronze gave way to iron and steel, the latter being an iron-carbon alloy. Metals were very important in early civilization and the practice of metallurgy provided a wealth of chemical information. Egyptians, for example, learned how to obtain many different metals from their ores, and according to some experts the word *chemistry* is derived from an ancient word *khemeia,* which may refer to the Egyptians' name for their own country, *Kham*. However, some experts believe *chemistry* came from the Greek word *chyma,* which means "to melt or cast a metal." . . .

– JOHN B. RUSSELL, *General Chemistry*

Thinking Critically about Your Writing in a Discipline

Choose a piece of writing you have produced for a particular discipline — a hypertext history essay, a laboratory report, a review of the literature in some particular field, or any other written assignment. Examine your writing closely for its use of that discipline's vocabulary, style, methods of proof, and conventional formats. How comfortable are you writing a piece of this kind? In what ways are you using the conventions of the discipline easily and well? What conventions give you difficulty, and why? You might interview an instructor in this field about the conventions and requirements for writing in the discipline. Make notes about what you learn about being a better writer in the field.

49 Writing about Literature

Are you intrigued by virtual reality and the idea that it might enable you to broaden your experience in heretofore hard-to-imagine ways? This chapter is about an early forerunner of virtual reality: the world's literature. Literature presents us with a range of "virtual" realities that go far beyond our own time-and-place-bound experience. Especially during a time of frenetic movement and change such as ours, literature can help us think carefully and critically about the human condition, about what it means to be human, or even to be "virtually" human. Thus does the study of literature offer a wealth of insight into human motives, character, and potential — and help us explore our own humanity. ■

49a Becoming a strong reader of literature

As a reader of literature, you are not a neutral observer, not an empty cup into which the "meaning" of a literary work is poured. If such were the case, literary works would have exactly the same meanings for all of us, and reading would be a fairly boring affair. If you have ever gone to a movie with a friend and each come away with a completely different understanding or response, you already have ample evidence that a story never has just one meaning.

Nevertheless, you may have been willing to accept the first meaning to occur to you, or to take a piece of literature at face value, failing to question or puzzle over it. The following guidelines aim to help you exercise your interpretive powers, to build your strength as a reader of literature:

FOR READING LITERATURE

1. *Read the work first for an overall impression.* Read it straight through, and jot down your first impressions. How did the work make you feel? What about it is most remarkable or memorable? Are you confused about anything in it?
2. *Reread the work, annotating* in the margins to "talk back," asking questions, pointing out anything that seems out of place or ineffective.

3. *What is the genre* – gothic fiction? tragic drama? hypertext fiction? lyric poetry? creative nonfiction? What is noteworthy about the form of the work?
4. *What is the point of view, and who is (are) the narrator(s)?* How reliable and convincing does the narrator seem? What in the work makes the narrator seem reliable or unreliable? How does the narrator's point of view affect your response to the work?
5. *What do you see as the major themes* of the work, the points the author seems to want to make? What evidence in the text supports these themes? Consider plot, setting, character, point of view, imagery, and sound.
6. *What may have led the author to address these themes?* Consider the time and place represented in the work as well as when and where the writer lived. Also consider social, political, or even personal forces that may have affected the writer.
7. *Who are the readers the writer seems to address?* Do they include you? Do you sympathize with a particular character – and if so, why?
8. *Review your notes,* highlighting the ideas that most interest you. Then freewrite for fifteen minutes or so about your overall response to this work and about the key point you would like to make about it.

One student's annotations of a poem

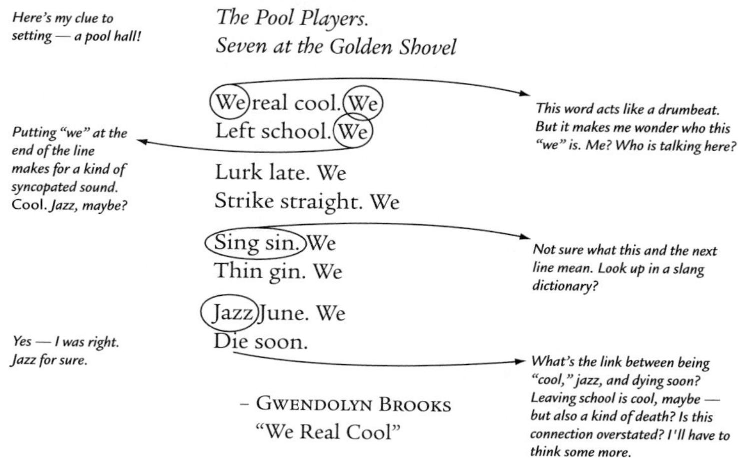

This student went on to freewrite about the way the poem draws her into the "we," in spite of the fact that she feels little connection to the pool players at first.

49b Understanding the language of literary interpretation

www •

http://www.lib.lsu.edu/hum/lit.html

Collected by Steven Harris, the material in this site offers excellent links for literary and literature resources. Truncate the URL to <http://www.lib.lsu.edu/hum/> for wider humanities resources.

In writing about literature, you may need to use a number of special terms. The following list includes terms that are frequently used in the close reading of literary works to analyze their structure and style:

A GLOSSARY OF LITERARY TERMS

To analyze the sounds in a literary work, you might use the following terms:

alliteration the repetition of sound to create special emphasis or rhythm, as in this sentence from Eudora Welty: *Monsieur Boule inserted a delicate dagger in Mademoiselle's left side and departed with a posed immediacy.*

meter the rhythm of verse, as determined by the kind and number of feet (groups of syllables) in a line. Iambic pentameter indicates five feet of two syllables, with the stress falling on the second of the two, as in *An aged man is but a paltry thing.*

onomotopoeia the use of words whose sounds call up or "echo" their meaning: *hiss* or *sizzle,* for example.

rhyme scheme the pattern of end rhymes in a poem, usually designated by the letters *a, b, c.* The Emily Dickinson poem at the end of Chapter 36 has a rhyme scheme of *aabccd.* A Shakespearean sonnet typically follows a rhyme scheme of *abab cdcd efef gg.*

rhythm in poetry, the beat or pattern of stresses; in prose, the effect created by repetition, parallelism, and variation of sentence length and structure. Robert Frost's "Fire and Ice" (at the end of Chapter 30) uses a basic iambic rhythm, with every other syllable stressed: ˘/˘/˘.

stanza a division of a poem: a four-line stanza is called a *quatrain;* a two-line stanza, a *couplet.* Robert Francis's poem at the end of Chapter 13 contains five two-line stanzas.

(Continued on page 633)

Literary language is sometimes distinguished from the nonliterary by its intensely purposeful use of imagery, vivid descriptions that evoke a picture or appeal to other senses. Often imagery is used to defamiliarize or "make strange" the ordinary so that readers can look at it in new ways. In discussing imagery, you might use the following terms:

allusion an indirect (unacknowledged) reference in a work to another work, such as a biblical passage, or to a historical event, a contemporary issue, a mythological character, and so on.

analogy a comparison of two things that are alike in some respect, often to explain one of the things or to represent it more vividly by relating it to the second. At the end of Chapter 10, Vivian Gornick compares traditional relationships between men and women to a thin fabric that *no amount of patching can weave . . . together again.*

figurative language the use of metaphor, simile, signifying, and other figures of speech that enrich description and create meaning. (5h2 and 27d)

symbolism the use of one thing to represent other things or ideas, as the flag symbolizes patriotism or as ice symbolizes hate in Frost's "Fire and Ice." (in Chapter 30)

The codes and structures of narrative are very important to literary interpretation. You might want to examine the complexities that arise from representations of the author, the characters and their relationships, or the structures of time and space in a work. Some helpful terms for doing so include the following:

characters the people in a story, who may act, react, and change accordingly during the course of a story. In Amy Dierst's essay on *The Third Life of Grange Copeland,* she examines the characters in the novel as one way of interpreting its meaning. (49d)

dialogism a term associated with the critic Mikhail Bakhtin, describing the rich social, cultural, and historical context surrounding any word or phrase, which is inevitably *in dialogue with* and responding to that context. The word *democracy,* for instance, carries a whole history of meanings and usages that any writer using the word must contend with.

dialogue the conversation among characters, which can show how they interact and suggest why they act as they do. The passage from

(Continued on page 634)

(Continued from page 633)

Eudora Welty in 34a3 is some dialogue from a story. A *monologue* is a long speech by one character, spoken to him- or herself or aloud to another character.

heteroglossia a term referring to the many voices present in a work of literature. In Charles Dickens's *Hard Times,* for example, the "voice" of mass education speaks alongside the voices of fictional characters.

implied author the "author" that is inferred from or implied by the text, as distinct from the real person/author. In *The Adventures of Huckleberry Finn,* for example, the real author is Samuel Clemens (or Mark Twain); the implied author is the "author" we imagine as Clemens presents himself in the text.

intertextuality the system of references in one text to other texts through quotations, allusions, parodies, or thematic references. Gary Larson's *The Far Side* Frankenstein cartoons, for example, refer intertextually to the original novel *Frankenstein* as well as to many movie versions and to other works focusing on the dangers or limits of science.

irony the use of language to suggest the opposite, or nearly the opposite, of what the words usually mean, as in saying that being caught in a freezing downpour is "delightful."

narrator the person telling a story, who may be a character or an omniscient voice with a viewpoint outside the story itself. In *The Adventures of Huckleberry Finn,* for example, the narrator is Huck Finn himself. In poetry, the narrator is known as the speaker. Both narrator and speaker may be referred to as the *persona.* See also *point of view.*

parody an imitation intended for humorous or satiric effect, as in a takeoff on the magazine *Martha Stewart Living* entitled *Is Martha Stewart Living?* At the end of Chapter 23 is an example of a student parody of Edgar Allan Poe's style.

plot the events selected by a writer to reveal the conflicts among or within the characters, often arranged in chronological order but sometimes including flashbacks to past events or even using episodic or spiraling progressions. Traditionally, the plot begins with exposition, which presents background information; rises to a

(Continued on page 635)

(Continued from page 634)
climax, the point of greatest tension; and ends with a resolution and denouement, which contain the outcome. In her essay on *The Third Life of Grange Copeland,* Amy Dierst describes events of the plot. (49d)

point of view the perspective from which a work is presented — in fiction, by a narrator outside the story or a character speaking in first or third person; in poetry, by the poet or a role assumed by the poet. In "Theme for English B" (at the end of Chapter 29), the point of view is that of the student.

protagonist the hero, heroine, or main character, often opposed by an *antagonist,* as Othello is opposed by Iago in Shakespeare's play *Othello.*

setting the scene of a literary work, including the time, physical location, and social situation. "Theme for English B" (in Chapter 29) is set in Harlem during the 1950s.

style a writer's choice of words and sentence structures. Two devices characteristic of John F. Kennedy's style are repetition and inverted word order.

theme a major and often recurring subject or topic. Amy Dierst discusses the theme of conflict between men and women in her essay about *The Third Life of Grange Copeland.* (49d) The predominant theme often reveals the larger meaning of the work, including any thoughts or insights about life or people in general.

tone a writer's attitude, conveyed through specific word choices and structures. In her essay arguing that students should consider designing their own majors, Jennifer Georgia's tone is earnest and serious. (5j3)

49c Considering your assignment, purpose, and audience

In most writing about literature, you will be responding to an assignment given by an instructor.

- Study the assignment carefully, with special attention to any key terms (for example, *analyze* or *discuss*). Note any requirements about use of sources and length.

www •

http://www.english.upenn.edu/~jlynch/Lit/

Literary Research Tools on the Net *is a searchable collection of excellent sources maintained by Jack Lynch. Make sure also to visit Lynch's* Resources for Writers and Writing Teachers *at <http://www.english.upenn.edu/~jlynch/writing.html>.*

- The assignment may well imply a specific purpose. *Analyze,* for example, implies that your purpose will be to look at one or more parts of the literary work and to argue or explain their relationship to a point or theme of the work.
- As in all academic work, you will also want to consider the audience for your essay – your instructor, most likely, and perhaps others as well.

49d Developing a critical stance and a thesis

www •

http://humanitas.ucsb.edu/

The Voice of the Shuttle. *By Alan Liu, this is one of the richest humanities sites. The literature resources <http://humanitas.ucsb.edu/shuttle/english.html> include cross links to world literature and minority literatures and offer searches by subject and period. In addition, this site has an extensive literary theory page that is very useful for undergraduates.*

Just as all your reading is based to some extent on your personal history and knowledge and reasons for reading, so your writing about literature is based to some extent on your own **critical stance,** what you've read and where you're coming from as a writer. What perspective do you bring? How do you approach the text you're writing about? Your critical stance will help lead you to your **thesis,** the major point or claim you wish to make about a literary work. In general, student writers tend to adopt one of three primary stances: a ***text-based stance*** that builds an argument by focusing on specific features of the literary text in question; a ***context-based stance*** that builds an argument by focusing on the context in which a literary text exists; a ***reader-based stance*** that focuses on the personal response of a particular reader to the text and the interpretation that grows out of that response; or some combination of these approaches.

The writer of the following essay, Amy Dierst, took a text-based stance in responding to an assignment for an introductory literature class that asked her to "analyze some aspect of one of the works read this term." This is a fairly open-ended assignment, and so she checked with her instructor to make sure that her chosen focus, "the role of men," would qualify as an aspect of a work to be analyzed. Note that because the assignment called for an analysis of a work read by the entire class, she did not need to review the plot. As a student in a literature class, she could assume that analyzing characters and themes was an appropriate form of interpretation.

This kind of literary interpretation, based largely on specific evidence from the literary text itself, is the approach most students take in writing about literature. Amy Dierst makes a claim – her thesis – about the role of men in *The Third Life of Grange Copeland* that she then substantiates by citing passages from the primary source, the novel itself, as well as from secondary sources (other interpretations of the novel).

The Role of Men in
The Third Life of Grange Copeland

Many observers of American society charge that it has created a distorted definition of manhood and produced men who, in their need to assert control of their lives, release their frustration at the expense of women. In her novel The Third Life of Grange Copeland, Alice Walker addresses this theme from the point of view of black men and women, for whom racism heightens the distortion and its consequences. She suggests that by stifling black men's sense of freedom and control, a racist society creates frustrations that are released in family violence and inherited by their children. Because his wife and children are the only aspect of the black man's life that he can control, they become the scapegoat upon which his frustrations are released. As Walker's title suggests, she sees redemption, or spiritual rebirth into a new life, as the best defense against society's injustice. Though Walker's male characters have been labeled by some as either heartlessly cruel or pathetically weak (Steinem 89), many of them, like Grange Copeland, do change during the course of a work. Individual transformation stimulates the potential for change in the social system as a whole.

In this novel, Walker shows how the social and economic system of the 1920s offered a futile existence to southern black families. Grange Copeland, like most southern black men of his era, lived and worked on a farm owned and operated by a white man. This system, called sharecropping, did not allow for future planning or savings, for everything earned was returned to the white man's pocket for rent. Thus sharecropping, like slavery before it, contributed to the black man's feelings of powerlessness. In his desperation and helplessness, Grange turns to exert power in the one place he is dominant, his home. He releases his frustration by abusing his family in a weekly cycle of cruelty:

> By Thursday, Grange's gloominess reached its peak and he grimaced respectfully, with veiled eyes, at the jokes told by the man who drove the truck [the white farm owner, Mr. Shipley]. On Thursday night, he stalked the house from room to room, pulled himself up and swung from the rafters. Late Saturday night Grange would come home lurching drunk, threatening to kill his wife and Brownfield [his son], stumbling and shooting his shotgun. (Walker 12)

At other times, Grange displays his frustration through neglect, a more psychologically disturbing device that later affects Brownfield's emotional stability. Grange's inability to rise above his own discontent with his life and express feeling toward his son becomes his most abusive act. Eventually, he abandons his family completely for a new life in the North. Even when he says good-bye, "even in private and in the dark and with his son, presumably asleep, Grange could not bear to touch his son with his hand" (Walker 121).

Brownfield picks up where Grange left off, giving his father's violent threats physical form by beating his own wife and children regularly. Although he, too, blames the whites for driving him to brutality, Walker suggests that his actions are not excusable on these grounds. By the time he reaches adulthood, sharecropping is not a black man's only option and cannot be used as a scapegoat. Nevertheless, he chooses to relinquish his freedom and work for Mr. Shipley.

By becoming the overseer on Mr. Shipley's plantation, Brownfield positions himself for the same failure that ruined his father. As Trudier Harris notes, over time Brownfield's loss of control of his life turns his feelings of depression and lost pride into anger, and his own destructive nature turns him toward violence and evil (240). Unable or unwilling to take responsibility for himself, Brownfield blames his own inadequacies on his wife, Mem, who bears the brunt of his anger:

> Brownfield beat his once lovely wife now, regularly, because it made him feel briefly good. Every Saturday night he beat her, trying to pin the blame for his failure on her by imprinting it on her face, and she [. . .] repaid him by becoming a haggard [. . .] witch. (Walker 55)

Brownfield demonstrates his power by stripping Mem, a former schoolteacher, of anything that would threaten his manhood. Reasoning that her knowledge is a power that he cannot have and therefore she does not deserve, he wants her to speak in her old dialect so that she will not appear to be more intelligent than he does. He also wants her to be ugly because her ugliness makes it easier for him to justify beating her. He wants her to reach a state of ultimate degradation where any strength of her character will be quickly extinguished by a blow to the face or a kick in the side. In fact, "he rather enjoyed her desolation because in it she had no hopes. She was totally weak, totally without view, without a sky" (Walker 59). In a final attempt to release his frustration, as Paul Theroux suggests, Brownfield kills Mem, literally and symbolically obliterating the remainder of her identity--her face (2).

But in the face of this brutality and degradation, Walker raises the possibility of a different fate for black men and women. While in the North, Grange undergoes a spiritual rebirth and, as Karen Gaston notes, comes to understand that white injustice is not alone responsible for the cruelty of black men toward their families (278). He also realizes that to weaken and destroy a wife and family is not a sign of manhood:

> You gits just as weak as water, no feeling of doing nothing yourself, you begins to destroy everybody around you, and you blame it on crackers [whites]. Nobody's as powerful as we make out to be, we got our own souls, don't we? (Walker 207)

Grange redeems his spirit in his "third life" with his granddaughter, Ruth. His objective now is not to destroy what he loves but to cherish it. When a judge orders Ruth to go back to live with Brownfield after his release from prison, Grange kills him before this horror becomes a reality. Although Grange is shot to death as he tries to escape the police, he dies a redeemed man and passes his inner strength of hope on to his granddaughter.

The impact of the racist system of the South unquestionably pervades the lives of Walker's black characters. Nevertheless, she does not portray as justifiable the destructive need of black men to exert their strength at the expense of the weak. It is necessary to be aware of societal injustices and their effects but not to use them as excuses for individual cruelty. Through her characters, Walker gives us faith that cruelty turns back on itself. Some meet tragic endings, but the redemption of Grange shows Walker's faith in change. She envisions the children of tomorrow inheriting not hatred and selfishness but compassion and honesty. Her affirmative voice demonstrates the potential for social change through individual transformation.

Works Cited

Gaston, Karen C. "Women in the Lives of Grange Copeland." College Language Association Journal 24 (1981): 276-86.

Harris, Trudier. "Violence in The Third Life of Grange Copeland." College Language Association Journal 19 (1975): 238-47.

Steinem, Gloria. "Do You Know This Woman? She Knows You--A Profile on Alice Walker." Ms. June 1982: 89-94.

Theroux, Paul. Rev. of The Third Life of Grange Copeland, by Alice Walker. Bookworld 4 Sept. 1970: 2.

Walker, Alice. The Third Life of Grange Copeland. New York: Harcourt, 1970.

EDITING YOUR WRITING ABOUT LITERATURE

- → What is your thesis? How could it be stated more clearly?
- → What support do you offer for your thesis? Check to be sure you include concrete instances drawn from the text you are writing about.
- → How do you organize your essay? Do you move chronologically through the work of literature? Do you consider major elements such as images or themes or characters one by one? If you cannot discern a clear relationship among your points, you may have to rearrange them, revise your materials, or substitute better evidence in support of your thesis.
- → Check all quotations to make sure each supports your thesis and that you have properly used signal phrases, indentations (necessary for longer quotations), and citations in parentheses.
- → If you quote, paraphrase, or summarize secondary sources, do you cite and document thoroughly and accurately following MLA guidelines? (Chapters 41 – 44)
- → Be sure to use present-tense verbs when discussing works of literature: *Alice Walker's Grange Copeland displays his frustration through neglect.* Use past tense only to describe historical events: *Thus sharecropping, like slavery before it, contributed to the black man's feeling of powerlessness.*

THINKING CRITICALLY ABOUT LITERATURE

Reading Literature with a Critical Eye

Using this chapter, read a literary work that has been assigned to your class. Compare your notes and annotations to those done by two or three classmates. Compare your understandings of the work as well as your tentative interpretations. What do all of your readings have in common? How do they differ?

Thinking about Your Own Writing about Literature

Carefully analyze writing you have done about a literary work, using the preceding guidelines. What could you add to strengthen your argument? Make a list of tips you would give yourself for writing a better essay about literature.

PART 10

CONSIDERING MEDIA

FAQ

FAQ: Considering Media Online

How can I use images and graphics from the Web?

Graphic browsers (Microsoft Explorer, Netscape Communicator, HotJava) let you roam the Web in search of images or graphics to use, and many of them are in the "public domain," meaning that you can use them without requesting permission or paying a fee. Several sources of graphics are listed in the left margin of this page.

Choose images and graphics to download selectively: many will take a long time to download. In addition, it's easy to indulge in overkill, especially with clip art, which many people find irritating or clichéd. Choose only those images or graphics that are thoroughly relevant to your topic, and integrate them into your text so that they support but do not dominate the point you are trying to make.

If an image or graphic you want to use is marked with a copyright symbol (©), and if you are going to disseminate your text in print or on the Web, you will need to ask permission and acknowledge its use in any list of references. (See p. 433 for sample letters of permission.)

What art or drawing programs exist for developing effective graphics?

Almost all contemporary software programs now allow you to create simple visuals such as charts or graphs. Other packages such as Microsoft Excel, ClarisWorks, or FrontPage offer increasingly sophisticated image composers. In addition, drawings you make by hand can be quickly scanned into your computer and inserted into any document, including hypertext.

http://www.fciencias.unam.mx/ejemplo/index_bkgr.html

Background patterns for Web sites.

http://www.yahoo.com/Computers_and_Internet/Graphics

Links to buttons, clip art, and other graphics.

http://www.ncsa.uiuc.edu/General/Internet/WWW/HTML Primer.html

A beginner's guide to learning HTML.

50 Making Oral Presentations

When the Gallup Poll reports on what U.S. citizens say they fear most, the findings are always the same: public speaking is apparently even scarier than an attack from outer space. Perhaps it is not surprising, then, that students who use this handbook have consistently asked for information on giving oral presentations.

Successful speakers point to three elements crucial to their effectiveness:

- *a thorough knowledge of the subject at hand*
- *careful attention to the interactive nature of speaking and thus to the needs of the audience*
- *practice, practice, and more practice*

This chapter provides some detailed guidance on how to bring these elements to your own presentations. ■

50a Considering the assignment, purpose, and audience

You will be wise to begin preparing for an oral presentation as soon as you get the assignment. Consider the assignment carefully, noting how much time you have to prepare, how long the presentation is to be, and whether any visual aids, handouts, or other materials are required to accompany the presentation. Consider whether you are to make the presentation alone or as part of a group so that you can plan and practice accordingly. (See 1f.) Finally, make sure that you understand the criteria for evaluation – how will the presentation be graded or assessed?

To understand your assignment fully, you must think about the rhetorical situation. In particular, consider the goal or purpose your presentation is supposed to accomplish. Are you to lead a discussion? teach a lesson? give a report? engage the class in an activity? And who will be the audience? Since your instructor will almost certainly be an important member of the audience, you will want to think about what he or she expects you to do – and do well. As the other class members will also probably be part of the audience, ask yourself what they know about your topic, what opinions they probably hold about it, and what they need to know and understand to follow your presentation and perhaps accept your point of view. For more on thinking about audience, see Chapter 2.

→ How does your presentation accomplish the specifications of the assignment? (50a)
→ How does your presentation appeal to your audience's experiences and interests? Does it achieve your purpose? (50a)
→ How does the introduction get the audience's attention? Does it provide any necessary background information? (50b)
→ What organizational structure informs your presentation? (50b)
→ Check for signpost language that can guide listeners. Are there explicit transitions? Do you repeat key words or ideas? (50b)
→ Have you used mostly straightforward sentences? Consider revising any long or complicated sentences to make your talk easier to follow. Check your words as well for too much abstraction. Substitute concrete words for abstract ones as often as you can. (50b)
→ Have you marked your text for pauses and emphasis? (50b)
→ Have you prepared visuals? If so, how do they contribute to your presentation? Are they large enough to be seen? If you have not prepared visuals, can you identify any information that would be enhanced by them? (50c)

50b Writing to be heard

Writing to be heard rather than read has several special requirements, among them a memorable introduction and conclusion, explicit structure and signpost language, straightforward syntax and concrete diction, and a well-prepared text.

Composing a memorable introduction and conclusion

Remember that listeners, like readers, tend to remember beginnings and endings most readily. Work extra hard, therefore, to make these elements memorable. Consider, for example, using a startling statement, opinion, or question; a vivid anecdote; a powerful quotation; a vivid visual image; see 6f for examples. Shifting language, especially into a variety of language that your audience will identify with, is another effective way to catch their attention; Chapter 28 provides examples. Whenever you can link your subject to the experiences and interests of your audience, do so.

CONSIDERING MEDIA
Writing to be Heard

Using structure and signpost language

Use a clear organizational structure, and give an overview of your main points toward the beginning of your presentation. (You may wish to recall these points again toward the end of the talk.) Throughout, it will be helpful to pause between major points and to use **signpost language** to mark your movement from one topic to the next. Signpost language, which acts as an explicit transition in your talk, should be clear and concrete: *The second crisis point in the breakup of the Soviet Union occurred hard on the heels of the first* instead of *The breakup of the Soviet Union came to another crisis point....* In addition to such explicit transitions as *next, on the contrary,* or *finally,* you can offer signposts to your listeners by carefully repeating key words and ideas as well as by sticking to concrete topic sentences to introduce each new idea.

For a list of transitions, see 6d4.

Considering syntax and diction

Avoid long, complicated sentences, and use straightforward syntax (subject-verb-object) as much as possible. Remember also that listeners can hold on to concrete verbs and nouns more easily than they can grasp abstractions. You will probably need to deal with abstract ideas, but try to illustrate them with concrete examples.

For a discussion of abstract and concrete language, see 27c.

Preparing your text

You will almost certainly want to rely on some written material. Depending on the assignment, the audience, and your personal preferences, you may even decide to prepare a full text of your presentation. If so, double- or triple-space it, and use fairly large print so that it will be easy to read. Try to end each page with the end of a sentence, so you won't have to pause while you turn a page. In addition, you may decide to mark spots where you want to pause and to highlight words you want to emphasize.

On the other hand, you may prefer to work from a detailed topic or sentence outline, from points listed on an overhead, or from note cards. If so, use the same basic techniques so that you can easily follow the material. Whatever kind of text you decide to prepare (and each kind can be highly successful), you will want to pay special attention to the task of *writing to be heard.*

Look carefully at the following paragraphs. The first is from an essay about the importance of thinking critically before choosing a course of

www

http://www.uark.edu/depts/comminfo/www/rhetoric.html

Maintained by the American Communication Association, this site links to speeches, literature, rhetoric, and guides to public speaking.

study; the full essay appears in 5j. The second paragraph presents the same information, this time written to be heard. See how the second text uses signpost language, repetition, vivid concrete examples, and simple syntax to make it easy to follow orally. Note also how the writer has marked her text for emphasis and pauses that will help her listeners follow the oral text.

A PARAGRAPH FROM A WRITTEN ESSAY

The decision about a major or other course of study is crucial because it determines both what we study and how we come to think about the world. The philosopher Kenneth Burke explains that we are inevitably affected not only by our experiences but also by the terminologies through which our perceptions of those experiences are filtered. Burke calls these filters "terministic screens" and says that they affect our perception, highlighting some aspects of an experience while obscuring others. Thus the terminologies (or languages) we use influence how we see the world and how we think about what we see.

THE PARAGRAPH REVISED FOR AN ORAL PRESENTATION

Why is our decision about a major so crucial? I can give two important reasons. First, our major determines what we study. *Pause* ^ Second, it determines how we come to think about the world. The philosopher Kenneth Burke explains these influences this way: our experience, he says, influences what we think about ideas and the world. But those experiences are always filtered through language, through words and terminologies. Burke calls these terminologies "terministic screens," a complicated-sounding term for a pretty simple idea. Take, for example, the latest hike in student fees on our campus. The Board of Trustees and the administration use one kind of term to describe the hike: "modest and reasonable," they call it. Students I know use entirely different terms: "exorbitant and unjust," they call it. Why the difference? Because their terministic screens are entirely different. *Pause* ^ Burke says we all have such screens made up of language, and these screens act to screen out some things for us and to screen in, or highlight, others. Burke's major point is this: the terms and screens we use have a big influence on how we see the world and how we think about what we see.

50c Using visuals

Visuals may be an integral part of an oral presentation, and they should be prepared with great care. Do not think of them as add-ons but as one of your major means of conveying information. Whatever visuals you decide to use (charts, graphs, photographs, summary statements, or lists), they must be large enough to be easily seen by your audience. Many speakers use PowerPoint or overhead projections throughout a presentation to help keep themselves on track and to guide their audience. If you don't have access to this technology, you might prepare a poster or flip chart, or you could simply use a chalkboard.

For a discussion of multimedia presentations, including PowerPoint and overhead projections and poster presentations, see Chapter 52.

Most important, make sure that your visuals engage and help your listeners, rather than distract them from your message. One good way to test the effectiveness of the visuals you plan to use is by trying them out on classmates, friends, or roommates. If these colleagues do not clearly grasp the meaning of the visuals, revise them and try again.

You may also want to prepare handouts for your audience: pertinent bibliographies, for example, or text too extensive to be presented otherwise. Unless the handouts include material you want your audience to use while you speak, distribute them at the end of the presentation.

50d Practicing the presentation

CONSIDERING MEDIA
Making Oral Presentations

www •

gopher://gopher.vt.edu:10010/02/39/24

Aristotle's Rhetoric. *This text version of Aristotle's famous advice on how to present an argument explains why "some speakers succeed."*

In oral presentations as with many other things in life, practice makes perfect. Prepare a draft of your presentation, including all visuals, far enough in advance to allow for several run-throughs. Some speakers audio- or videotape their rehearsals and then base their revisions on the tape-recorded performance. Others practice in front of a mirror or in front of friends. Do whatever works for you – just as long as you practice!

Make sure you can be heard clearly. If you are soft-spoken, concentrate on projecting your voice. If your voice tends to rise when you are in the spotlight, you may want to practice lowering your pitch. If you speak rapidly, practice slowing down and enunciating words clearly. If you practice with friends or classmates, ask them how well they can hear you and what advice they have for making your voice clearer and easier to listen to.

One student who taped her rehearsal found, to her great surprise, that she had used the word *like* 32 times in her 8-minute presentation, even though the word never appeared in her notes. In this case, it took a lot of practice to break the *like* habit.

Once you are comfortable giving the presentation, make sure you will stay within the allotted time. One good rule of thumb is to allow roughly two and a half minutes per double-spaced 8½″ × 11″ page of text (or one and a half minutes per 5″ × 7″ card). The only way to be sure about your time, however, is to time yourself as you practice. Knowing that your presentation is neither too short nor too long will help you relax and gain self-confidence; and when the members of your audience sense your self-confidence, they will become increasingly receptive to your message.

50e Making the presentation

Experienced speakers say they always expect to feel some anxiety before an oral presentation – and they develop strategies for dealing with it. In addition, they note that some nervousness can act to a speaker's advantage: adrenaline, after all, can provide a little extra jolt and help you perform well.

The best strategy seems to be to know your material well. Having confidence in your own knowledge will go a long way toward making you a confident presenter. In addition to doing your homework, however, you may be able to use the following strategies to good advantage: (1) Visualize your presentation with the aim of feeling comfortable during it; go over the scene of your presentation in your mind, and think it through completely. (2) Get some rest before the presentation, and avoid consuming an excessive amount of caffeine. (3) Consider doing some deep-breathing exercises right before the presentation. Concentrate on relaxing.

Move around the room if you are comfortable doing so. If you are more comfortable in one spot, at a table or a lectern, then stand with both feet flat on the floor. If you are standing at a lectern, rest your hands on it. Many speakers find that this stance keeps them from fidgeting.

Pause before you begin your presentation, concentrating on your opening lines. During your presentation, interact with your audience as much as possible. You can do so by facing the audience at all times and making eye contact as often as possible. You may want to choose two or three people to look at and "talk to," particularly if you are addressing a large group. Allow time for the audience to respond and ask questions. Try to keep your answers short so that others may participate in the conversation. At the conclusion of your presentation, remember to thank your audience.

THINKING CRITICALLY ABOUT ORAL PRESENTATIONS

Study the text of an oral presentation you've prepared or given. Using the preceding guidelines, see how your text appeals to your audience. Look in particular at how well you catch and hold their attention. What do you conclude about the differences between spoken and written text?

Alternatively, look over a piece of your writing. Using this chapter, revise your writing to be heard.

51 Designing Documents

The electronic revolution has dramatically affected the delivery of information. Known in the ancient Greek world as *actio,* delivery was an art every educated person needed to master, for how a speaker delivered a speech — tone and volume of voice, use of gestures, and so on — was of great importance to how it would be received. Today, computers have given us new ease in presenting our written texts, allowing us to use headings, lists, graphics, and other visuals. Because these visual elements can be fundamental to readability and to helping us get and keep a reader's attention, they bring a whole new dimension to writing — what some refer to as *visual rhetoric.*This chapter will help you to use visual rhetoric effectively in creating various documents, including online documents that can be printed out. (The next chapter discusses how to design hypertext and multimedia presentations.) ■

51a Creating a visual structure

Those who study visual rhetoric tell us that effective writers use visual elements to guide readers, presenting them with documents that are easy on the eye — and easy to understand. In thinking about the overall visual structure of a document, you may well begin by considering how you use white space and color, what kind of paper you use, and how you type or print out the final document.

Using white space to frame information

The white space around text acts as a frame and leads the reader through the text. For most documents, you will want to frame your page with margins of white space of between one inch and one and one-half inches — depending on the purpose of the document, its content, and its audience. Since the eye takes in only so many chunks of data in one movement, very long lines can be hard to read. Wider margins help, particularly if the information is difficult or dense. In your college papers, such margins give your instructor room to make comments. Within the page, you can also use white space in other ways — around graphics or lists, for example.

Whatever the case, your goal is to make each page look inviting to your readers. Each page, therefore, should be a unit, leading the reader smoothly to the next. You would not want to put a heading at the very bottom of a page, for the reader would have to turn the page to get to the text that the heading is announcing. Nor would you want to end a page with a hyphenated word, leaving readers to guess at the second part as they turn the page.

Using color

Many software programs and printers now offer the possibility of using color in print documents. As with all decisions, ones about color depend to a large extent not only on the kind of equipment you are using but also on the purpose(s) of your document and its intended audience. As you design your print documents, keep in mind the following tips about the effective use of color:

- Use color to draw attention to elements you want to emphasize: headings and subheadings, bullets, text boxes, parts of charts or graphs.
- For most documents, keep the number of colors to a minimum (one or two, in addition to white and black); too many colors can create a busy or confused look. In addition, avoid putting colors that clash next to one another.
- Be consistent in your use of color; use the same color for all subheads, for example.

Selecting appropriate paper and print

The quality of the paper and the readability of the print affect the overall look and feel of your document. Although you may well want to use inexpensive paper for your earlier drafts, when your college writing is ready for final presentation use 8½″ × 11″ good-quality white bond paper. On some occasions, you may wish to use a parchment or cream-colored bond – for a résumé perhaps. For brochures and posters, colored paper may be most appropriate. If you are working on a computer, seek out the best-quality printer available to you for your final product. This may mean using a laser printer in one of the campus computing centers or libraries.

51b Using consistency to lead readers through a document

Especially in longer documents, you can help readers a great deal by maintaining consistency of design, including the placement of page numbers, style of the typeface, spacing of lines, and width of margins.

Paginating your document

Except for a separate title page, which is usually left unnumbered, number every page of your document. Your instructor may ask that you follow a particular format (APA or MLA, for example); if not, number each page consecutively with arabic numerals, beginning with the first page of text. Place your last name and the page number in the upper-right-hand corner of the page, about one-half inch from the top and flush with the right margin. Do not put the number in parentheses or follow it with a period. Most personal computers will paginate a document for you.

For examples of pagination formats in MLA and APA styles, see 44d and 45d.

Selecting type

Most personal computers allow writers to choose among a great variety of type sizes and typefaces, or **fonts.** For most college writing, the easy-to-read ten- or eleven-point type size is best, as is a **serif** font (this is serif type; this is sans serif type). Although a smaller or more unusual style — such as *italics* or *cursive* — might seem attractive at first glance, readers may find such styles distracting and/or hard to read. Most important, be consistent in the size and style of typeface you choose. Unless you are striving for some special effect, shifting sizes and fonts can give an appearance of disorderliness.

Considering spacing and margins

Final drafts for most of your college writing should be double-spaced, with the first line of paragraphs indented one-half inch or five spaces. Certain kinds of writing for certain disciplines may call for different spacing. Letters and memorandums, for example, are usually single-spaced, with no paragraph indentation. Lab reports in some disciplines are also single-spaced, and some long reports may be printed with one-and-a-half-line spacing to save paper. Other kinds of documents, such as flyers and newsletters, may call for multiple columns of print. If in doubt, consult your instructor.

Computers allow you to decide whether or not you want both side margins **justified,** or squared off — as they are on this page. Except in posters and other writing where you are trying to achieve a distinctive visual effect, you should always justify the left margin, though you may decide to indent lists and blocks of text that are set off. However, most writers — and many instructors — prefer the right margin to be "ragged," or unjustified.

www

http://www.slip.net/~graphion/style.html

Part of Graphion's Online Type Museum, this site provides good advice about indenting, using capitals, and spacing, both within and between lines. Hyperlinked definitions and examples round out the presentation.

51c Using headings

For brief essays and reports, you may need no headings at all. For longer documents, however, these devices serve as friendly signposts for readers, calling attention to the organization of the text and thus aiding comprehension. Some genres of reports have set headings, which readers expect (and writers therefore must provide); see 46c for an example. If you use headings, you need to decide on type size and font, wording, and placement.

CONSIDERING MEDIA
Using Headings

WWW •

http://www.slip.net/~graphion/gloss.html

This glossary of typographic terms offers a good starting point for anyone interested in design and layout for both print and online venues.

Choosing type size and style

If you look through this book, which is a long and complex document, you will note the use of various levels of headings. This chapter, for example, uses four levels of headings, distinguished by different type sizes and fonts as well as by color:

1 First-level heading

2 Second-level heading

Third-level heading

FOURTH-LEVEL HEADING

For your college writing, you might distinguish levels of headings using type — all capitals for the first-level headings, capital and lowercase underlined for the second level, plain capitals and lowercase for the third level, and so on. With a computer, you have even more options. For example:

ON A TYPEWRITER:	**ON A COMPUTER:**
`FIRST-LEVEL HEADING`	FIRST-LEVEL HEADING
<u>`Second-Level Heading`</u>	**Second-Level Heading**
`Third-Level Heading`	<u>Third-Level Heading</u>
	Third-Level Heading

Phrasing headings

Heading styles often follow discipline-specific conventions, but as a general rule look for the most succinct way to word your headings. Most often, this means stating the topic in a *single word*, usually a noun (*Toxicity*); in a *phrase*, usually a noun phrase (*Levels of Toxicity*) or a gerund phrase (*Measuring Toxicity*); in a *question* that will be answered in the text (*How can toxicity be measured?*); or – especially in writing about a process – in an *imperative* that tells readers what steps to take (*Measure the toxicity*). Whichever structure you choose, make sure you use it consistently for all headings of the same level: all questions, for example, or all gerund phrases and *not* a mixture of the two.

For more on maintaining parallel structure in headings, see 21a.

Positioning headings

Typically, major headings are placed at the left margin. The first level of subhead may then be indented five spaces from the left, and the second level may be centered. Other positions are possible; just remember to place each level of head consistently throughout your paper.

51d Using visuals

www

http://www.plumbdesign.com/thesaurus/

Visual Thesaurus. *This is a strange and captivating site that gives a visual representation of synonyms. You have to see it and spend some time with it to appreciate the beauty of it — and you'll need a high-end computer with Java capability to do so.*

Using visuals in a written composition can both draw readers into your argument and help persuade them to accept your claim. In some cases, visuals may even be the primary text you present; in other cases, they will be of equal or supplemental importance to your text. In every case, they can help make a point vividly and emphatically by presenting information more succinctly and more clearly than words alone could.

Visuals fall into two categories: **tables,** which present information in columns and rows of numbers or words, and **figures,** which include all other visuals – pie, bar, and line charts; line and bar graphs; photographs; maps; and drawings. Many software packages offer help creating visuals.

In deciding when and where to use visuals, the best rule of thumb is simply to use ones that will make your points most emphatically and will most help your readers understand your document. Researchers who have studied the use of visuals offer some tips about when a particular kind of visual is most appropriate.

- *Use tables* to draw readers' attention to particular numerical information.
- *Use graphs or charts* to draw readers' attention to relationships among data. *Pie charts* compare a part to the whole. *Bar charts and line graphs* compare one element to another, compare elements over time, demonstrate correlations, and/or illustrate frequency.
- *Use drawings or diagrams* to draw readers' attention to dimensions and to specific details.
- *Use maps* to draw readers' attention to location and to spatial relationships.
- *Use cartoons* to illustrate or emphasize a point dramatically or to amuse.
- *Use photographs* to draw readers' attention to a graphic scene (such as devastation following an earthquake) or to depict people or objects.

For examples of the use of photographs in an essay, see 44d.

In choosing visuals, you will inevitably be making important rhetorical choices. Tables, for example, express certain kinds of information more precisely than do figures, but if they are long and complex, readers will have difficulty processing the information. Figures, though less precise, can more easily be taken in at a glance. You should make your choices, then, based on your purpose and on the needs of your audience. In any case, remember that your visuals need to be numbered (*Table 1*) and given titles (*Word Choice by Race*) and perhaps captions or subtitles that provide a link to the text (Seesaw *and* Teeter-totter, *Chicago 1986*). Following are examples of several kinds of visuals and some guidelines for using them.

WWW

http://nilesonline.com/stats/

Stats Every Writer Should Know. *This site describes concepts writers should know as they seek to understand and interpret statistical data. After visiting it, go to Princeton's Survey Research Center at <http://www.princeton.edu/~abelson/> to apply what you've learned (and to learn more about surveys).*

TABLE

Table 1
Word Choice by Race:
Seesaw and *Teeter-totter,* Chicago 1986

	Black	*White*	*Total*
Seesaw	47 (78%)	4 (15%)	51
Teeter-totter	13 (22%)	23 (85%)	36
Total	60	27	87

Source: Michael I. Miller, "How to Study Black Speech in Chicago." *Language Variation in North American English.* Ed. A. Wayne Glowka and Donald M. Lance. New York: MLA, 1993. 166.

PIE CHART

Figure 1
Racial and Ethnic Origin in the United States, 1990

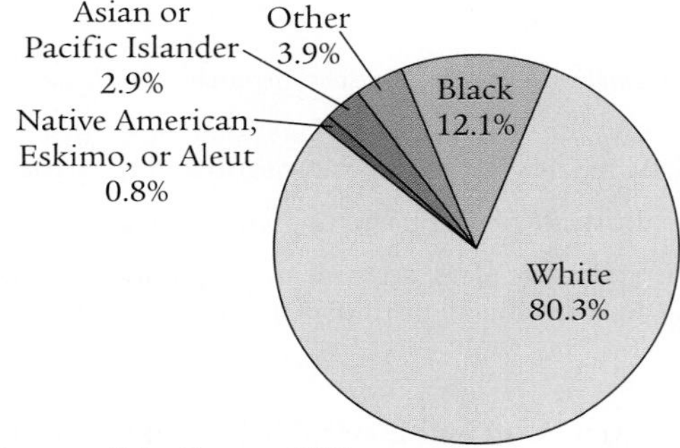

Source: U.S. Bureau of the Census, 1991.

BAR GRAPH

Figure 2
Church Growth by Denomination, 1700 – 1780

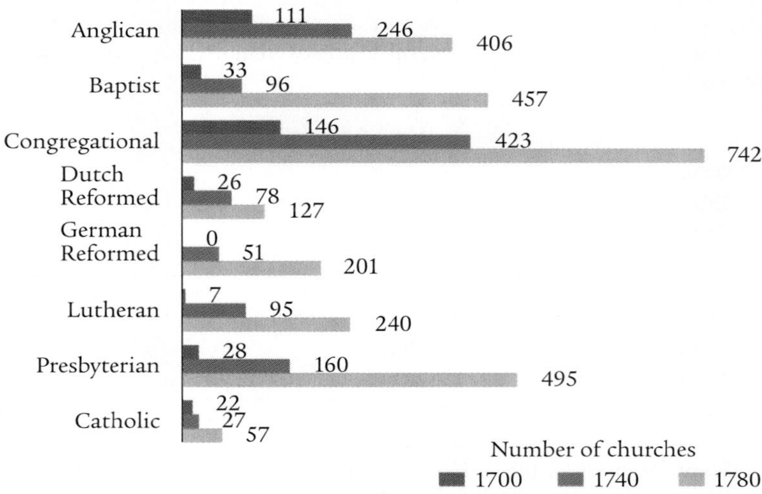

Source: James A. Henretta et al., *America's History.* New York: Worth, 1997. 119.

LINE GRAPH

Figure 3
Productivity and Wages, 1982 – 1995

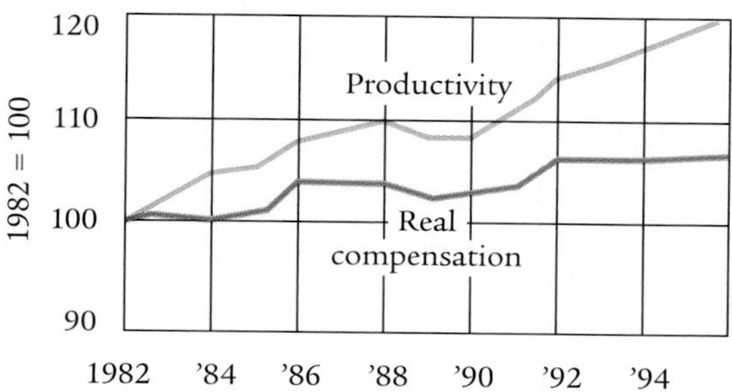

Source: New York Times, January 2, 1996, C20. Copyright © 1996 by The New York Times Co. Reprinted by permission.

DIAGRAM

Figure 4
Spanish-English Bilingualism and the Language Shift Process

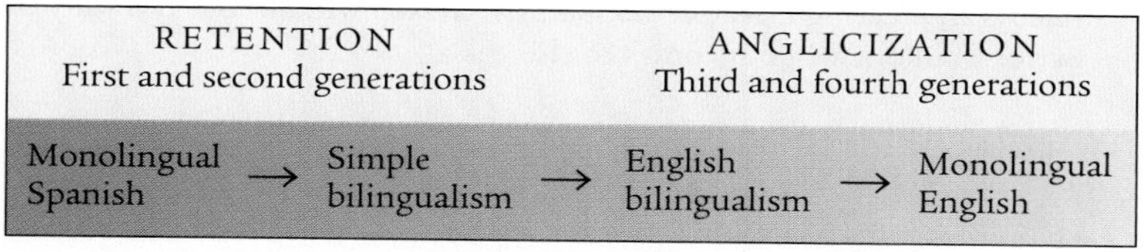

RETENTION First and second generations		ANGLICIZATION Third and fourth generations	
Monolingual Spanish →	Simple bilingualism →	English bilingualism →	Monolingual English

Source: D. Letticia Galindo. "Bilingualism and Language Variation." *Language Variation in North American English.* Ed. A. Wayne Glowka and Donald M. Lance. New York: MLA, 1993. 166.

→ Try drafting your visuals before drafting the document they accompany. Preparing visuals in this way can be an important part of your process of inventing and planning for the complete document.
→ Be sure to refer to the visual in your text before the visual itself appears, explaining the main point it makes or what it exemplifies. Say, for example, *As Table 1 demonstrates, the cost of a college education has risen dramatically in the last decade.*
→ Tell readers explicitly what the visual demonstrates, especially if the visual presents complex information. Don't assume that readers will necessarily infer from it what you want them to infer.
→ Number and title your visuals.
→ If you did not create the visual yourself, credit your source fully.
→ Use decorative touches sparingly if at all. Computer clip art is so easy to generate that you may be tempted to fancy up your visuals, but do so only if it enhances and clarifies your text.
→ Do a "test run" printout of your visuals to make sure your printer is adequate for the job.
→ Get responses to your visuals in an early draft. If readers can't follow them or are distracted by them, revise accordingly.
→ If you are working on a collaborative project, use every team member's talents in creating effective visuals. Two heads will almost certainly be better than one when it comes to this task.

51e Sample documents

www •

http://vera.inforamp.net/~poynton/notes/typesetting/

Ten Common Typesetting Mistakes. *This explanation of common typesetting mistakes made by those who use word processors gives a good thumbnail guide to document planning and desktop publishing.*

Interested in creating a flyer advertising your services as a tutor? Want to put together a newsletter for a campus group you belong to? Need to design a portfolio, including an eye-catching cover, for a course you are taking? Today, thanks to computer technology, such documents are easier to design and create than ever before. As a result, more and more college classes encourage (or require) you to respond to assignments in ways that go beyond the traditional essay or lab report. What follows is a catalog of documents we've collected from college students and others, along with annotations intended to guide you in creating similar documents for yourself.

1"

Zakiyyah Shabazz

Prof. Jerrideth Merrin

English 398 Paper 3

11-13-97

Putting "me" Back into America

Two hundred years ago, writers like William Wordsworth thought that language should be useful, should be able to tell or teach people something. More than a hundred years later, along came Langston Hughes, who set out to do just that. Many of his poems relate to the loss of dreams--the things that give us hopes and goals to reach--and to the unfair treatment of the African American people. In "Let America Be America Again" and "The Ballad of the Landlord," Hughes discusses the unfair conditions and treatment that "ethnic" people have been subjected to in the United States. He uses these poems to . . .

Name, name of instructor, title of course and assignment, and date are all at the left margin, double-spaced.

Double space between heading and title

Title centered

Paragraphs indent five spaces

Double space between title and first line of text

Sponsoring organization identified

Title prominently displayed in brightest color and distinctive typeface, with graphic border

Three colors — tan, brown, and black — used effectively together

Italics and color used for photo caption and byline

Graphic overlay with map of Africa appropriate to sponsoring organization but makes text hard to read

Double columns make text easier to read

The Frank W. Hale, Jr. Black Cultural Center

BARAZA

Annual

Toward a New Direction

Larry Williamson, Jr.

The Frank W. Hale, Jr. Black Cultural Center has been in existence for more than three years at The Ohio State University. As we look forward to a new direction, I feel compelled to thank many people who have helped shape and continue to influence our future. Although the names of people and organizations are far too numerous to mention in this issue, I will start by paying homage to a few.

First I would like to thank the "Original 34" OSU African American students. These young men and women stood up, took a stand, and planted the seed for cultural enrichment at The Ohio State University in their quest for a Black Cultural Center. Their dedication to our campus and community was great and should be emulated and documented for the future.

Second I would like to thank many administrators and faculty members for their support. I would like to express particular gratitude to Professor Charles Ross, Dr. Richard Kelsey, Mrs. Cynthia Zachery-Smith, Mrs. Ruth Gresham, Dr. William E. Nelson, Jr., Dr. Anne Pruitt, Dr. James Upton, Dr. Ike Newsum, Mrs. Rose Wilson-Hill, Dr. Ruth Russell, Mr. Lee Jones, Ms. Joyce Vaughn, Mrs. Tina Love, Dr. Vesta Daniel, Mrs. Lenora Barnes-Wright, Mrs. Pat Williams, Professor David Williams II, and without a doubt Dr. Frank W. Hale, Jr. for serving as a constant reminder of the struggles to obtain the Hale Center.

Third, I can not ignore the collective efforts of the Office of Minority Affairs, the Department of Black Studies, and African American Student Services. Their assistance and support has been greatly appreciated and remains continuous.

Fourth, I would like to thank the many staff members, civil service workers, student organizations, graduate and undergraduate students, community leaders and individuals. Your commitment has demonstrated the importance of African American heritage and helped to make the dream of the Center a reality.

Fifth, I would be remiss if I did not mention the major contributions of Samella Lewis, Beverly Turner, Pheoris West, Robert Stull, J.D. Jackson, Sam Gilliam, Queen Brooks, Kojo Kamau, Benjamin Crumpler, Smoky, Richard and LaVerne Brown, Kwame Clay, Larry Collins, Barbara Chavous, Bill Harris, Bill Agnew, Robert Farmer, E. Okechukwu Odita, Charles Hollingsworth, Ralph Bell, Ed Colston, Walt Neil, Sharon Farmer and many other talented artists who, via artwork, donated their legacies to the center.

Sixth, our list of supporters would not be complete if I did not mention those directly involved with the Center's advancement. People such as Joseph Russell, Linda Jackson, Greg Carr, Kellie Kirksey, Angela Small, Sunny Ekpo, Janice Rowley and especially, former Director, Teresa Drummond whose contributions still impact the Center today. In addition, our new Vice Provost, David Williams, II continues to be very instrumental in offering new ideas and initives for the Center's future.

Last, as we move forward into the twenty-first century we still have many people and organizations which have assisted and helped the Center move toward a positive future. Such organizations as Afrikans Committed to Improving Our Nation (A.C.T.I.O.N.), the Cultural Programming Advisory Board (C.P.A.B.), South Area Black Student Association (S.A.B.S.A.), the Black Graduate and Professional Student Caucus, Alpha Kappa Mu, just to name a few, will be depended upon heavily to assist and generate ideas for our future growth and development. Individuals such as Lee Smith, Bill Batson, Lori Waite, Menelik Fombi, and our work-study students will carry out the daily operations of the Center and serve as a link to the campus and community.

As Assistant Director of the Frank W. Hale, Jr. Black Cultural Center, I will always be aware of the dedication and commitment of numerous people whose contributions still heavily impact the Center today. When I look at Cultural Centers in general and link (through artistic expression) the struggles of our African and African American ancestors together, I realize that I cannot state anything here more profound than our ancestors have historically articulated.

by Larry Williamson
Assistant Director

Cover

Ample space around title and illustration

Informative title in large, eye-catching type

Appropriate illustration in central spot

Source of brochure identified

Interior Page

What Other Services Does The Writing Center offer?

Question used to organize information

In addition to individual consultation sessions, The Writing Center is able to offer a number of other services to members of the university community and beyond.

✎ Faculty / GTA Consultations

One answer to organizing question presented. Graphic image echoes the image on the cover and substitutes for a bullet

Through our Writing-Across-the-Curriculum Program (WAC), we provide consultations and conduct group seminars for faculty and departments who would like to incorporate more writing into their courses. Consultations and seminars are designed around the need of the individual teacher, course, or department and may take place during a single meeting, over several meetings, or over the course of the term. If you would like to know more about these services, please contact the WAC Consultants at The Writing Center.

Information presented in brief paragraphs.

✎ Peer Consulting

A second answer presented

The Writing Center offers peer consulting internships for selected undergraduates who have completed the first-year writing requirement. Peer consultants typically work in writing groups with first-year writers and attend weekly discussions and seminars. Peer consultants work under the supervision of the Peer Consulting Director and receive course credit for their work. Interested students should be encouraged to contact The Writing Center for more information.

Plenty of "white space" used

Name in boldface and larger type size

Position being sought

Details of educational background

Significant academic information

Work experience relevant to position being sought

Significant volunteer work

ANGELA SANTANA

CURRENT ADDRESS	PERMANENT ADDRESS
75 West Fourth Avenue	549 Tyler Street
Columbus, Ohio 43201	Anoka, Minnesota 54268
Phone: (614) 555-8926	Phone: (612) 555-1146
E-mail: SANTANA.324@OSU.EDU	

CAREER OBJECTIVE — Position on editorial staff of a journal or publishing firm

EDUCATION

B.A. in English, with Writing Emphasis, The Ohio State University, Columbus, Ohio, June 1998.
Senior thesis, "Literacy and Community Service"

Core courses: Literary Publishing, Poetry Writing Workshop, Writing and Learning Seminar, Rhetoric and Community Service, History and Theories of Writing

AWARDS — Foster Award for Outstanding Undergraduate Essay, 1997

EXPERIENCE

1995 – 1998 *Mosaic: The Ohio State University Undergraduate Art and Literature Magazine*
Editor-in-Chief, 1997 – 1998

- Oversaw work of editorial assistants; served as liaison to faculty advisor and to Chair of English Department; drafted annual budget and grant proposals with business manager and faculty advisor; used Quark XPress, PageMaker, and ClarisWorks to design and assemble layout

Associate Literature Editor, 1995 – 1997

- Read submissions; selected poetry, fiction, and nonfiction; copy-edited manuscripts; did public relations; solicited manuscripts and artwork

1997 Max M. Fisher College of Business
(The Ohio State University)
Summer Intern, Public Relations

- Designed and copy-edited brochures and promotional material; edited and proofread faculty biographical entries for 1997 – 1998 *Bulletin*

LEADERSHIP AND VOLUNTEER ACTIVITIES

Treasurer, Phi Beta Kappa, 1997 – 1998
President, Alpha Chi Omega Sorority, 1996 – 1998
Workshop Organizer for Developmentally Disabled Children, The Ohio State University Hospitals, 1994 – present
Tutor, Godman Guild Literacy Center, 1994 – present

REFERENCES — Available upon request

Facsimile

To: The Law School, The University of Chicago
Fax #: 773/702-9484
Re: Application for Admission
Date: 11/24/97
Pages: 4, including this cover sheet

Address block of fax follows regular memo conventions

Dear members of the Admissions Committee:

Salutation

Thank you for accepting me to your law school. I was very excited to see that you have offered me a full scholarship, and I have enclosed my income tax statements for the past year as you requested.

Body of fax follows regular business letter conventions

Double spacing between salutation and message and between message and closing phrase

Thanks again.

Jeffrey Robert Loew

Jeffrey R. Loew

From the desk of . . .

Jeffrey R. Loew
Department of English
Ohio State University
164 West 17th Avenue
Columbus, OH 43210

614-649-2843
Fax: 614-649-6513
Email: loew.6@osu.edu

Return address block provides address of sender, including relevant phone and fax numbers and email address.

Subject line provides specific information

Writer has included the part of an earlier posting she is responding to, which helps other list members follow the conversation

Double space indicates a new paragraph

Three-paragraph body of posting responds to query raised by another member and then calls for further comments. Tone is engaged, friendly, and polite.

Writer gives only first name and initial because this is a closed listserv for class members.

```
To: alenglh167@lists.acs.ohio-state.edu
From: Kristen Convery <convery.8@osu.edu>
Subject: Re: class discussion of "self"
Cc:
Bcc:

At 03:48 PM 11/17/97 -0500, Kate wrote:

>Has anyone had any interesting or pertinent discussions
>of the "self" in other classes this term?

I'm taking psychology this quarter and have found some
information that pertains to our discussion on the self.

Carl Rogers studied the self and self-concept, theorizing
that people do things in line with their concept of them-
selves in order to avoid having to rework that self-
concept.  For instance, if I think of myself as an artist
and not as a musician and I want to go to a concert, I
will go to the art museum just so that I do not have to
rethink and maybe change the way I view myself.

Comments from other class members?  It strikes me as
interesting that we seem to feel as if we must fit one
mold, and that that mold nullifies all other concepts of
the self.  Why can't we be both artists and musicians?
But it's true--especially when I look at families.  How
many families do you guys know where the parents proudly
introduce members as "the scientist (writer/artist/
musician/thinker) of the family"? And how does this
inhibit other siblings who might also want to be scien-
tists, writers, artists, musicians, thinkers, but fear
taking over someone else's place?

Just a few thoughts . . .

Kristen C.
```

H167 Writing Portfolio
Presented by Maia Gonzalez

Table of Contents

- Cover Letter
- Argumentative Essay
- Stylistic Analysis
- Imitation/Parody
- Exploratory Essay
- Final Examination

"Even if any given terminology is a *reflection* of reality, by its very nature as a terminology it must be a *selection* of reality; and to this extent it must function also as a *deflection* of reality."

--Kenneth Burke, "Terministic Screens"

Honors English 167
First-Year Reading and Writing in the Humanities
Professor Brenda Brueggemann
November 24, 1997

"Until I take pride in my language, I cannot take pride in myself."
-Gloria Anzaldúa, "How to Tame a Wild Tongue"

Colorful graphic encloses title and name of author

Bulleted list gives overview of portfolio's contents

Relevant and memorable quotations get readers' attention

Course information and date

MEMO

Initials of sender

Reason for memo and initial request presented

Double space between paragraphs

Details of request presented

Closing paragraph shows concern for employees

```
Date:    December 10, 1998
To:      Members of the Shipping Department
From:    Willie Smith, Supervisor  WS
Subject: Scheduling holiday time
```

With orders running 25% higher than average this season, I can give everyone an opportunity to work overtime and still enjoy the company's traditional half day off for holiday shopping. The schedule must be completed by tomorrow at 5:00 p.m., however; so let me know your preferences.

Please fill out the attached form with the days and hours you can work overtime and your first, second, and third choices for time off. Return it to me before you leave today.

I will try to accommodate everybody's preferences, relying on seniority in case of conflicts. If we work together, December should be good for all of us--on and off the job.

```
To: techsoup@indirect.com
From: Andrea Lunsford <lunsford.2@osu.edu>
Subject: help finding a correct address
Cc:
Bcc:

Dear Techsoup:

I am trying to send a message to Irene Whitney at Pacific
Synergies, which is headquartered in Whistler, B.C.  The
email address she gave me is pacsyn@direct.net -- which
is obviously not right since you returned it as undeliv-
erable.  Perhaps I should have tried adding "com" at the
end?  If you have an address for Pacific Synergies, I
would be very grateful to receive it.

Andrea Lunsford, Department of English
Ohio State University
164 W. 17th Street
Columbus, OH 43214
(614) 292-6065 (o)
(614) 292-5824 (f)
```

Precise email address of recipient

Sender's name and email address

Subject line provides accurate and specific information

Salutation

Double spacing between salutation and message

Message kept as succinct and direct as possible

Double spacing between end of message and signature line

Signature line gives name of sender and .sig file

CONSIDERING MEDIA

Sample Documents

THINKING CRITICALLY ABOUT YOUR FINAL DOCUMENT

Take a look at some writing you have recently finished. Using the guidelines in this section, assess the use of visual structure and page design, the consistent use of conventions for guiding readers through the work, and the use of headings and visuals for emphasis.

www

http://www.windweaver.com/email.htm

How to Fight Fair Online. *This guide combines practical advice grounded in sound rhetorical and psychological principles on how to conduct online discussions and disputes; see item 5 on the list.*

52 Working with Hypertext and Multimedia

Thanks to the electronic revolution — and especially to the forms it has taken in the last two decades — ordinary writers are increasingly able to mix the media of communication in new and exciting ways in everyday situations in school and on the job. In any one week, for example, you might find yourself using the World Wide Web to design a Web site for yourself or a group you belong to; to conduct research for a work-related task; to visit retail sites to do some comparison shopping; or to post an assignment to a class site. In that same week, you might use other kinds of multimedia to give a poster presentation for a class project, perhaps, or a PowerPoint presentation to potential customers. In all of these situations, you will be drawing on a mixture of oral, print, and other media, including the electronic form known as hypertext. And as you work with hypertext and multimedia, you may well find yourself thinking (and reading and writing) in some new ways as well. ■

52a Using hypertext

You might think of a **hypertext** as a series of electronic "pages," the first of which is the **homepage** that introduces the site. Each page contains highlighted words or images that serve as **links** to take you to other parts of the site or, if the site is part of the World Wide Web, to other sites as well. Clicking on these links allows you to navigate the site in your own way and at your own speed, going back and forth between pages to pursue your own interests.

As more and more people begin to work, play, shop, even go to school online, the uses of hypertext will no doubt expand. Already, we can identify three major ways in which you may find yourself using it. In college (or on the job), you may be called on to read, understand, and analyze hypertext documents: some textbooks already exist in hypertext form, and you may be assigned to read hypertext essays or articles as part of your work for a course. You also may need to create hypertexts for your course assignments and projects. A psychology instructor, for example, might ask you to prepare a hypertext that includes graphs and other images as well as links to both primary sources (original research reports, government documents, and so on) and secondary sources (such as the American Psychological Association Web site) that provided background information for your project. Or a biology assignment might require you to produce a hypertext that links a particular molecular model you've created to other models on the Web.

In addition, you may have occasion to use or to create hypertexts for clubs or groups you belong to – a homepage for the fencing team, for example, or for the undergraduate history majors club. One student we know recently created a hypertext for her biography reading group – and invited all members to add to it.

Finally, you may want to use and create hypertexts for yourself, your family, or your friends. You might decide to create a homepage or hypertext journal for friends to read, for example, or a hypertext family tree that all members of the family can contribute to. In short, your uses of hypertext may be limited only by your ability to imagine them.

1 Planning hypertexts

The ways you think through and plan a hypertext are similar to the ways you prepare to create any text. Begin by thinking about the purpose(s) for your hypertext, which should guide not only your overall format but also the nature and number of links you create. If you are trying to explain a concept to your audience, for example, you will want to provide links that will enhance the explanation. If you are trying to convince them of something, you will need to provide links to evidence.

You will also want to identify as clearly as possible the audience for your hypertext. If it is your instructor and classmates or other people you know, you can make certain assumptions about their background knowledge and how they will respond to your hypertext. If your audience is largely unknown to you, however, you can't make such assumptions.

Consider too how clearly and concisely you can state the topic of your hypertext. If it is too vague or broad – such as "World War II" – you would have to include far too many links to make the hypertext manageable for you and usable by others. In such cases, you will have to narrow and focus the topic and to clarify the angle you are taking on it. In addition, think about the stance you want to take toward your topic and audience. Are you presenting yourself as an expert on the topic, or as a novice who is seeking information from audience members?

Other important considerations relate to physical issues. What overall sensory impression do you intend to create with this text? If you can articulate this impression clearly, you will be more likely to achieve it, since it can guide your decisions about use of images, color, sound clips, and so on. Finally, think about the logistics involved not only in creating the hypertext but in reading it. How much memory will your hypertext occupy? How long will it take readers to download – and will they be able to access everything you may want to include, such as images and sound?

2 Designing hypertexts

www •
http://info.med.yale.edu/caim/manual/pages/page_design.html
Advice on Web page design from the Yale C/AIM Web Style Guide, one of the most comprehensive guides of its kind.

Before you begin working with hypertext, make sure that you have the necessary software. You'll probably need text-editing (NotePad, SimpleText) as well as word-processing software. Some software – such as Microsoft Word – allows you to save text in the **Hypertext Markup Language (HTML)** necessary for hypertext. (Otherwise, you will need to save text in **ASCII.**) HTML allows you to mark links within your document and to include images, text, sound, and so on. Although you can learn HTML code in a few hours of concentrated study and practice, the latest programs suggest that our computers may soon perform much of this task for us. In addition, you'll need a Web browser (Internet Explorer, Netscape Navigator) in order to "see" the hypertext you are creating.

You will be wise to take the advice offered by the Yale Center for Advanced Instructional Media: stick to a few basic principles of design with every page and link you create. In particular, *always include the title, author, and date; and give one link back to the homepage.*

www •
http://english.ttu.edu/kairos/2.2/news/youcanuse/craig/page0.html
Anatomy of a Web Page *offers basic design information specifically directed to students.*

The first or "home" page of any hypertext document is extremely important, for it introduces the subject and sets out the various paths readers can use to explore the entire document. Although the conventions for designing homepages are still evolving, it's pretty clear what *doesn't* work well. The Yale Center uses the term *clown's pants pages* to refer to the kind of haphazard use of color and clip art and fonts characteristic of many hypertexts. Fortunately, a little planning and attention to some simple design principles can help you produce effective pages:

- At the top of the homepage, put a *title* (and subtitle, if necessary) along with an eye-catching and easy-to-process *graphic or statement* that makes clear to readers what the document is about. Below this include an *overview* of what is on the document.
- In the middle of the page, list the links that readers can use to access other parts of the document or other sites.
- At the bottom of the page, include a logo, if appropriate, along with your name and contact information (such as your email address) and the date you

created the document. (You can later add dates on which you revise it.) You may also wish to add a button that users can click on to "return to top of page."

- Use graphics that are small enough to be loaded and downloaded without too much trouble.
- Use bullets, numbered lists, headings, and so on to serve as signposts for readers.
- If you use different fonts and typesizes for emphasis and variety, make sure that they really add to the effectiveness of the page. Some fonts are very hard to read, for example, so you should pass them up.
- Use color carefully and consistently. In general, use lighter colors for background so that the text will stand out, and use colors to help guide readers – one color to signal headings, for example, and another to signal subheadings.
- Ask some readers to respond to your pages, especially to the homepage. How understandable are the pages? How easy are they to navigate? How effective is the use of color and type?

3 Adding links

The success of any hypertext is tied to the effectiveness of the **links** within it. It may help to think of such links as the elements that add depth and texture to the hypertext: the opening page(s) provide an overview and announce the general aim of the document, but the links bring this aim to life, providing a level of detail not possible in the homepage. Here is the place, for example, for complex explanations, lists of supporting statistics, bibliographies, additional readings, or relevant URLs.

Especially as you begin working with hypertext, be fairly conservative in the number of links you plan. Although it can be tempting to add numerous links to a page – just as it might be tempting to add many footnotes to a page of text – too many links can overwhelm both you and readers. In particular, make sure that links to graphics or sound and video clips are closely related to your purpose(s). Readers have quickly tired of clichéd clip art, for example. And if you wish to use images created by others, remember that you may need to ask for permission to download and use these images in your own hypertext.

For an example of a request for such permission, see p. 433.

To signal a link, you may use underlining, **highlighting,** or labeling (*for additional readings on contemporary cultural taboos, click here*). In any event, make sure readers will know what the purpose of the link is and who created it. Indeed, you may create much of the text for links – again, just as you would create the text in a footnote to add information or explain a concept. But you may also add links to documents, images, and other material created by others – pertinent data from another Web site, for example, or a passage from a pertinent online book. In such cases, be sure to identify the source of the material clearly. And if you intend to post your hypertext on the Web, ask for permission to use the material you want to link to.

Finally, remember to add internal links so that readers can return from any link to the homepage, for example, or back to a previous page.

4 An opening page of a hypertext

For an English class, a group of students worked to create an effective opening page to which they planned to link a series of individual and collaborative projects. The homepage they created appears on the following two pages.

52b Making multimedia presentations

As you learn to create Web pages and hypertexts, you will probably wish to incorporate some of their qualities into your presentations for college classes as well as for work or community-related projects. Among the most popular forms of multimedia presentation are those that use programs like PowerPoint, those that use overhead transparencies, and those that use posters.

1 PowerPoint and similar programs

You can use PowerPoint and similar programs to add images and sound to your own voice (another oral medium) in order to create a memorable multimedia presentation. These programs allow you to prepare slides you want to display and even to enhance the images with sound. If you are using such a program to design presentation slides, keep some simple principles in mind:

- For captions or any other print text, use fonts for emphasis, and make sure your audience can read them: 44- to 50-point type for titles, for example, or 30- to 34-point type for subheads.
- For slides that contain print text, use bulleted or numbered points rather than running text. Keep these items as concise as possible, and use clear lan-

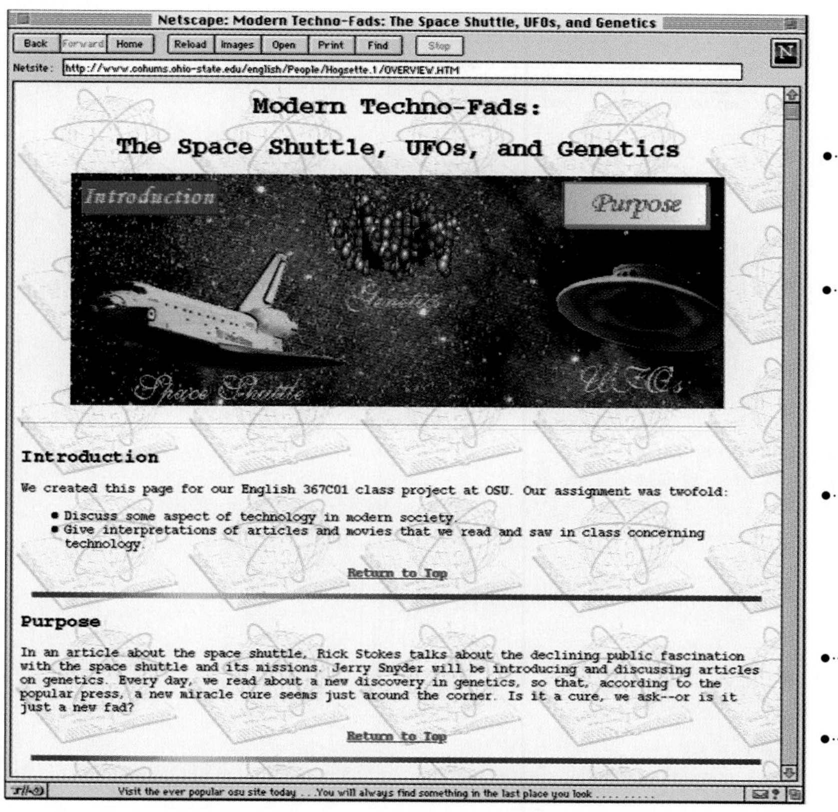

Title clearly announces subject of site

Eye-catching graphics reinforce subject matter

Introduction provides overview of site, with bulleted items delineating subtopics

Authors of page identified

Buttons provided for return to top of pages

guage. If you are using the points to guide your own discussion, include only three to five of them on each slide so that your audience doesn't have to look at one slide for too long.

- Create a clear contrast between the print text and the background. As a general rule, light backgrounds work better in a darkened room; dark backgrounds in a lighted one.

Underlining indicates links to related sites

Last update indicated

Name and email address of contact provided

Assistance acknowledged

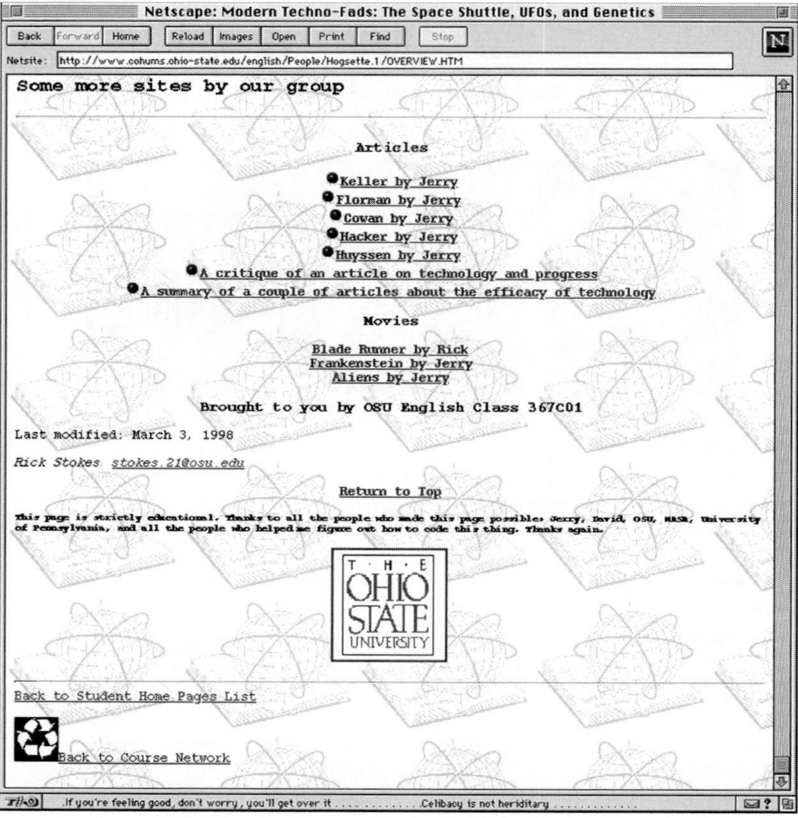

- Choose images – such as photographs, paintings, and so on – that will reproduce sharply, and make sure they are large enough to be clearly visible.
- If you are adding sound or video clips, make sure that they are clearly audible and that they relate clearly to the topic of the presentation. Especially if sound is to be used as background, make sure that it does not in any way distract from or drown out what you are trying to say.

The first two slides of a PowerPoint presentation on ancient Rome, prepared by two college students for a history class, appear on the following page.

ROME

Presented by

Mike Dangler

Adam Trimeloni

Dec. 1, 1997

CONSIDERING MEDIA

Making Multimedia Presentations

- *Title in large, easily readable type*
- *Creators of presentation identified*
- *Clear contrast between light-colored background and dark type*
- *Appropriate image used to illustrate first slide and raise interest in what is to come*

Rome:

★ The very name sounds of power, majesty, and grandeur. But Rome's beginnings were anything but grand and majestic.

★ Here is the miracle of Rome: that a small, insignificant city-state on the Italian Peninsula could become the center of a world-spanning empire

★ But how did this happen?

Rome, City Center

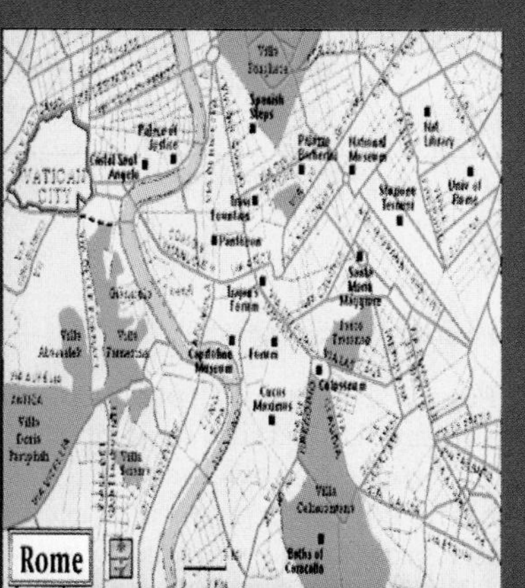

- *Title of presentation repeated*
- *Number of bulleted points limited to three, each of which clearly announces a subtopic*
- *Clear color contrast between background and type; last bulleted point a different color to emphasize importance of question it asks*
- *Graphic of torch creates three-dimensional effect*
- *Map is marked "copyright"; students can use this slide for class presentation but could not post this image to a site on the Web without obtaining permission from the copyright holder to do so*

2 Presentations using an overhead projector

Even if you do not yet have access to programs like PowerPoint, you have probably already used an overhead projector in making a class- or work-related presentation. Although less technologically complex, preparing transparencies for such a presentation involves the same kind of design effort that goes into a PowerPoint or other multimedia presentation. Most important, you want the material on the transparencies to augment what you are saying, not to distract from it. In addition, you want your transparencies to help guide you in your speaking and to help guide audience members in following what you say. Overhead transparencies, then, need to be kept sweet and simple: a clear title and a few bulleted items or key phrases, all in easily readable type sizes and fonts. As with PowerPoint, color should be easy on the eyes and should enhance rather than obscure the text. Here is an example of a transparency created for a presentation about the World Wide Web.

TRANSPARENCY FOR A PRESENTATION

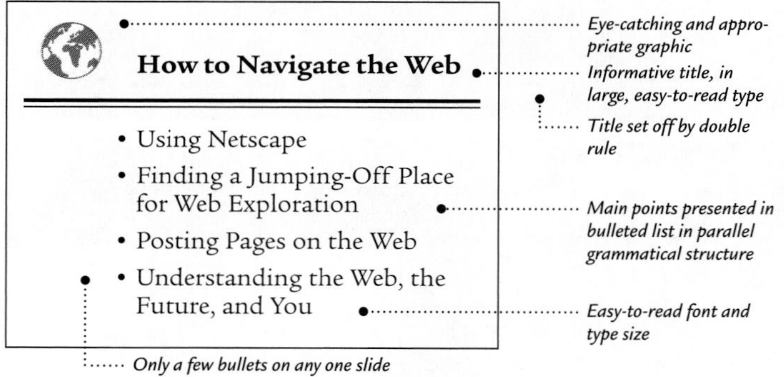

3 Poster presentations

For Shannan Palma's research essay, see 44d.

Page 681 shows the poster prepared by Shannan Palma, a student at Ohio State University, for a presentation based on the research essay she had written on movie heroes.

Many college courses and conferences now call on students to make poster presentations. In general, such presentations use a poster board, usually about 50″ × 40″, that displays major points or findings, a model or diagram, or a drawing. During the class or conference session, the

Hollywood and the Hero: Solving A Case of Mistaken Identity

- What happened when heroes made the transition from literature and legend to movie screen?
- Why did audiences begin to "mistake" the movie actor for the hero--and with what effects?
- If the hero is not now dead, what will our future heroes be like?

Cyborg Heroes?? OR Damaged Heroes??

Shannan Palma
Twelfth National Conference
on Undergraduate Research

April 23-25, 1998
Salisbury State University
Salisbury, Maryland

Title set off by large font and use of color background.

Photograph draws attention and adds emphasis.

List of bulleted questions provides talking points to lead audience through presentation.

White space is used effectively to highlight text and photo.

Two hypotheses elaborated on in conclusion are highlighted as questions in colored ovals.

Name of presenter, conference, place, and date are identified.

presenter uses this board as background while he or she talks through the presentation and answers questions. Although guidelines for poster presentations vary, if you are preparing one:

- create a board that can be read from at least three feet away
- include a clear title (at least two inches high) at the top of the board
- include your name and other appropriate information (course title and number, name of instructor, conference title or session, and so on) under the title or at the bottom of the poster
- use a series of bullets or boxes to identify the major points of the presentation
- include an arresting image or an important table or figure if it illustrates your points in a clear and memorable way
- consider using a provocative question toward the bottom of the poster to focus attention and anticipate your conclusion
- remember that simple, uncluttered posters are usually easier to follow and therefore more effective than overly complex ones.

PART 11

FOR MULTILINGUAL WRITERS: MASTERING THE NUANCES OF ENGLISH

documentation
writing/editing
hypertext
message
www.bedfordstmartins.com/nsmhandbook
thinking & collaborating

FAQ ·······→

FAQ: Multilingual Writers Online

What online resources are particularly helpful for multilingual writers?

The Virtual English Language Center provides an "idiom of the week," a "fable of the month," sound clips for pronunciation, online tests for comprehension and vocabulary, EMAIL, pen-pal programs, and more:

http://www.comenius.com

Dave's ESL Cafe offers games, activities, and — best of all — daily updates:

http://www.eslcafe.com/

English for Internet offers live CHATS, placement tests, and free English classes (which fill up quickly):

http://www.study.com

Grammar Safari allows you to learn grammar in context, with hundreds and sometimes thousands of examples of particular English words shown in the context of real-life communication:

http://deil.lang.uiuc.edu/web.pages/grammarsafari.html

schMOOzeU is a MOO devoted to practicing conversation:

http://schmooze.hunter.cuny.edu:8888/

WordWatch focuses on English vocabulary, with a new entry every day:

http://www.wordsmith.org/awad/index.html

Understanding Nouns and Noun Phrases

53

If you spoke another language when you first started learning English, you may have felt sometimes as though you were repeating the struggles of early childhood in trying to make yourself understood. Nevertheless, since all human languages are built on the same foundation, there is a great deal in your first language that you will encounter once again as you progress in English. For example, no matter what your first language is, you are familiar with the way sentences are built up out of two primary components — nouns and verbs.

English nouns differ from those in some other languages in various ways, however, including their division into count and noncount nouns and the use of plural forms and of articles and other modifiers. This chapter discusses these distinctive features of English nouns. ■

53a Distinguishing count and noncount nouns

Look at the following sentences:

The hill was covered with trees.

The hill was covered with grass.

Trees is a count noun, and *grass,* a noncount noun. **Count nouns** refer to separate individuals or things: *a doctor, a book, a tree; doctors, books, trees.* **Noncount nouns** refer to masses or collections without distinctly separate parts: *milk, ice, clay, blood, grass.* These terms do not mean that grass cannot be counted but only that English grammar requires that if we count grass, we express it indirectly: *one blade of grass, two blades of grass,* not *one grass, two grasses.*

Count nouns usually have singular and plural forms: *tree, trees.* Noncount nouns usually have only a singular form: *grass.*

COUNT	NONCOUNT
people (plural of *person*)	humanity
tables, chairs, beds	furniture
letters	mail
pebbles	gravel
beans	rice
facts	information
words	advice

Some nouns can be either count or noncount, depending on meaning.

COUNT Before there were video games, children played with *marbles.*

NONCOUNT The floor of the palace was made of *marble.*

When you learn a noun in English, you need to learn whether it is count, noncount, or both. Two dictionaries that supply this information are the *Oxford Advanced Learner's Dictionary* and the *Longman Dictionary of American English.*

53b Stating plural forms explicitly

Look at this sentence from a traffic report:

> All four bridges into the city are crowded with cars right now.

This sentence has three count nouns; one is singular (*city*), and two are plural (*bridges, cars*). If you speak a language with nouns that generally have no distinct plural forms (for example, Chinese, Japanese, or Korean), you might argue that no information would be lost if the sentence were *All four bridge into the city are crowded with car right now.* After all, *four* indicates that *bridge* is plural, and obviously there would have to be more than one car if the bridges are crowded. But English requires that every time you use a count noun, you ask yourself whether you are talking about one item or more than one, and that you choose a singular or a plural form accordingly.

Since noncount nouns have no plural forms, they can be quantified only with a preceding phrase: *one quart of milk, three pounds of rice, several bits of information.* The noun in question remains singular.

53c Using determiners appropriately

A noun together with all its modifiers constitutes a **noun phrase,** and the noun around which the modifiers cluster is called the **head.** For example, in *My adventurous sister is leaving for New Zealand tomorrow,* the noun phrase *my adventurous sister* consists of two modifiers (*my* and *adventurous*) and the head *sister.*

Words like *my, our,* and *this* are **determiners,** which are common and important words in the English language. Determiners identify or quantify the noun head.

COMMON DETERMINERS

- *a/an, the*
- *this, these, that, those*
- *my, our, your, his, her, its, their*
- possessive nouns and noun phrases (*Sheila's, my friend's*)
- *whose, which, what*
- *all, both, each, every, some, any, either, no, neither, many, much, (a) few, (a) little, several,* and *enough*
- the numerals *one, two,* etc.

Using determiners with singular count nouns

Every noun phrase with a singular count-noun head must begin with a determiner.

▶ **^adventurous sister** (inserted: *my*)

▶ **^big, bad wolf** (inserted: *the*)

▶ **^old neighborhood** (inserted: *that*)

If there is no reason to use a more specific determiner, use *a* or *an: a big, bad wolf; an old neighborhood.*

Notice that every noun phrase need not begin with a determiner, only those whose head is a singular count noun. Noncount and plural count nouns sometimes have determiners, sometimes not: *This grass is green* and *Grass is green* are both acceptable, though different in meaning.

Remembering which determiners go with which types of noun

- *This* and *that* go with singular count or noncount nouns: *this book, that milk.*
- *These, (a) few, many, both,* and *several* go with plural count nouns: *these books, those plans, a few ideas, many students, both hands, several trees.*
- *(A) little* and *much* go with noncount nouns: *a little milk, much affection.*
- *Some* and *enough* go with noncount or plural count nouns: *some milk, some books; enough trouble, enough problems.*
- *A, an, every,* and *each* go with singular count nouns: *a book, every child, each word.*

53d Choosing articles appropriately

The definite article *the* and the indefinite articles *a* and *an* are challenging to multilingual speakers. Many languages have nothing directly comparable to them, and languages that do have articles differ from English in the details of their use.

Using the

Use the definite article *the* with nouns whose identity is known or is about to be made known to readers. The necessary information for identification can come from the noun phrase itself, from elsewhere in the text, from context, from general knowledge, or from a superlative.

► **Let's meet at ^*the* fountain in front of Dwinelle Hall.**

The phrase *in front of Dwinelle Hall* identifies the specific fountain.

► **Last Saturday, a fire that started in a restaurant spread to a neighboring dry-goods store. ^*The store* ~~Store~~ was saved, although it suffered water damage.**

The word *store* is preceded by *the,* which directs our attention to the information in the previous sentence, where the store is identified.

► **Professor to student in her office: "Please shut ^*the* door when you leave."**

The professor expects the student to understand that she is referring to the door in her office.

► **^*The pope* ~~Pope~~ is expected to visit Africa in October.**

There is only one living pope, and so his identity is clear.

► **Willie is now ^*the* best singer in the choir.**

The superlative *best* identifies the noun *singer.*

Using a *or* an

Use *a* before a consonant sound: *a car.* Use *an* before a vowel sound: *an uncle.* Pay attention to sounds rather than to spelling: *a house, an hour.*

A or *an* tells readers they do not have enough information to identify what the noun refers to. The writer may or may not have a particular thing in mind but in either case will use *a* or *an* if the reader lacks the information necessary for identification. Compare these sentences:

I need *a* new *parka* for the winter.

I saw *a parka* that I liked at Dayton's, but it wasn't heavy enough.

The parka in the first sentence is hypothetical rather than actual. Since it is indefinite to the writer, it clearly is indefinite to the reader and is used with *a,* not *the.* The second sentence refers to a very specific actual parka, but since the writer cannot expect the reader to know which one it is, it is used with *a* rather than *the.*

If you want to speak of an indefinite quantity, rather than just one indefinite thing, use *some* with a noncount noun or a plural count noun.

This stew needs *some* more *salt.*

I saw *some plates* that I liked at Gump's.

Using no article

To make generalizations, you can use noncount and plural count nouns with no article or other determiner: *cheese, hot tea, crackers, ripe apples* (but not *cracker* or *ripe apple*).

In this world nothing is certain but *death* and *taxes.* – BENJAMIN FRANKLIN

The lack of an article indicates that Franklin refers not to a particular death or specific taxes but to death and taxes in general.

Here English differs from many other languages – Greek or Spanish or German, for example – that would use the definite article to make generalizations. In English, a sentence like *The snakes are dangerous* can refer only to particular, identifiable snakes, not to snakes in general.

You can also sometimes make general statements with *the* or *a/an* and singular count nouns.

First-year college students are confronted with many new experiences.

A first-year student is confronted with many new experiences.

The first-year student is confronted with many new experiences.

These sentences all make the same general statement, but the last two are more vivid than the first. The second focuses on a hypothetical

www •

http://www.edunet.com/english/practice/test-ces.html

Test Your English *is an 80-item test for those learning English as a second language. Post your answers and you'll receive the results via email.*

student taken at random, and the third sentence, which is characteristic of formal written style, projects the image of a typical student as representative of the whole class.

53e Arranging modifiers

Some modifiers precede the noun head, and others follow, and you need to learn both the required and the preferred positions for modifiers in order to know what can go where.

- Phrases or clauses follow the noun head: *the tiles on the wall, the tiles that we bought in Brazil.*
- Determiners go at the very beginning of the noun phrase: *these old-fashioned tiles. All* or *both* precedes any other determiners: *all these tiles.* Numbers follow any other determiners: *these six tiles.*
- Noun modifiers go directly before the noun head: *these kitchen tiles.*
- All other adjectives go between determiners and noun modifiers: *these old-fashioned kitchen tiles.* If there are two or more of these adjectives, their order is variable, but there are strong preferences, described below.
- Subjective adjectives (those that show the writer's attitude) go before objective adjectives (those that merely describe): *these beautiful old-fashioned kitchen tiles.*
- Adjectives of size generally come early: *these beautiful large old-fashioned kitchen tiles.*
- Adjectives of color generally come late: *these beautiful large old-fashioned blue kitchen tiles.*
- Adjectives derived from proper nouns or from nouns that refer to materials generally come after color terms and right before noun modifiers: *these beautiful large old-fashioned blue Portuguese ceramic kitchen tiles.*
- All other objective adjectives go in the middle, and adjectives for which a preferred order does not exist are separated by commas: *these beautiful large decorative, heat-resistant, old-fashioned blue Portuguese ceramic kitchen tiles.*

It goes without saying that the interminable noun phrase presented as an illustration in the last bulleted item is a monstrosity that would be out of place in almost any conceivable kind of writing. You should always budget your use of adjectives.

EXERCISE 53.1

Each of the following sentences contains an error. Rewrite each sentence correctly.

1. At an end of the eighteenth century, England and France were at war.
2. Napoleon, the French ruler, invaded Egypt with much soldiers.
3. His ultimate goal was India, which England had conquered many year before.
4. At Rosetta, near the Nile, some French soldiers were building fort.
5. They found a black large stone — the Rosetta Stone.

EXERCISE 53.2

Insert articles as necessary in the following passage from *The Silent Language,* by Edward T. Hall.

> Hollywood is famous for hiring _______ various experts to teach _______ people technically what most of us learn informally. _______ case in point is _______ story about _______ children of one movie couple who noticed _______ new child in _______ neighborhood climbing _______ tree. _______ children immediately wanted to be given _______ name of his instructor in _______ tree climbing.

54 Understanding Verbs and Verb Phrases

Verbs can be called the heartbeat of prose in every language, but in English the metaphor is especially meaningful. With rare exceptions, you cannot deprive an English sentence of its verb without killing it. If you speak Russian or Arabic, you might wonder what is wrong with a sentence like *My teacher very intelligent.* But unlike those and many other languages, English requires that sentences have a verb (for example, *My teacher impresses me as very intelligent*), and if no other verb is chosen, a form of the verb *be* must be used: *My teacher is very intelligent.*

English also differs from some other languages in its use of verb phrases, including perfect tenses, progressive forms, and modals. This chapter discusses some of the distinctive features of English verbs. ■

54a Forming verb phrases

Verb phrases can be built up out of a main verb (MV) and one or more auxiliaries. (See 9a.)

My cat *drinks* milk.

My cat *is drinking* milk.

My cat *has been drinking* milk.

My cat *may have been drinking* milk.

Verb phrases have strict rules of order. If you try to rearrange the words in any of these sentences, you will find that most alternatives are impossible. You cannot say *My cat drinking is milk* or *My cat have may been drinking milk.* The only permissible rearrangement is to move the first auxiliary to the beginning of the sentence in order to form a question: *Has my cat been drinking milk?*

Auxiliary and main verbs

In *My cat may have been drinking milk,* the main verb *drinking* is preceded by three auxiliaries: *may, have,* and *been.*

- *May* is a modal, which must be followed by the base form (*have*).
- *Have* indicates that the tense is perfect, and it must be followed by a past participle (*been*).

- *Been* (or any other form of *be*), when it is followed by a present participle (such as *drinking*), indicates that the tense is progressive.
- When a form of *be* is followed by a past participle, as in *My cat may have been bitten by a dog,* it indicates passive voice.

Auxiliaries must be in the following order: modal + perfect *have* + progressive *be* + passive *be.*

PERF PASS MV
Sonya *has been invited* to stay with a family in Prague.

PERF PROG MV
She *has been taking* an intensive course in Czech.

MOD PROG MV
She *must be looking* forward to her trip eagerly.

Only one modal is permitted in a verb phrase.

will be able to speak
▶ **She ~~will can speak~~ Czech much better soon.**

Every time you use an auxiliary, you should be careful to put the next word in the appropriate form.

Modal + base form

Use the base form of a verb after *can, could, will, would, shall, should, may, might,* and *must.*

Alice *can read* Latin.

Paul *should have* studied.

They *must be* going to a fine school.

In many other languages, modals such as *can* or *must* are followed by an infinitive (*to* + base form). In English, use only the base form.

▶ **Alice can ~~to~~ read Latin.**

www •

http://www.hiway.co.uk/~ei/intro.html

Click on modal auxiliary verbs for many examples of these verb forms.

Perfect **have** *+ past participle*

To form the perfect tenses, use *have, has,* or *had* with a past participle.

Everyone *has gone* home.

They *have been* working all day.

Progressive be + present participle

A progressive form of a verb is signaled by two elements, a form of the auxiliary *be* (*am, is, are, was, were, be,* or *been*) and the *-ing* form of the next word: *The children are studying.* Be sure to include both elements.

▶ **The children ^are studying in school.**

▶ **The children are ~~study~~ ^studying in school.**

Some verbs are rarely used in progressive forms. These are verbs that express unchanging conditions or mental states rather than deliberate actions: *believe, belong, hate, know, like, love, need, own, resemble, understand.*

Passive be + past participle

Use *am, is, are, was, were, being, be,* or *been* with a past participle to form the passive voice.

Tagalog *is spoken* in the Philippines.

Notice that with the progressive *be* the following word (the present participle) ends in *-ing,* but with the passive *be* the following word (the past participle) never ends in *-ing.*

Meredith *is* studying music.

Natasha *was* taught by a famous violinist.

If the first auxiliary in a verb phrase is *be* or *have,* it must show either present or past tense, and it must agree with the subject: *Meredith has played in an orchestra.*

Although a modal auxiliary may also show present or past tense (for example, *can* or *could*), it never changes form to agree with the subject.

▶ **Michiko ~~cans~~ ^can play two instruments.**

www •

http://www.hiway.co.uk/~ei/intro.html

Go here for downloadable help sheets, including several on verbs.

54b Using present and past tenses

Every English sentence must have at least one verb or verb phrase that is not an infinitive, a gerund, or a participle without any auxiliaries. Furthermore, every such verb or verb phrase must have a tense.

In some languages, such as Chinese and Vietnamese, the verb form never changes regardless of when the action of a verb takes place, and the time of the action is simply indicated by other expressions such as *yesterday, last year,* and *next week.* In English, the time of the action must be clearly indicated by the tense form of each and every verb, even if the time is obvious or indicated elsewhere in the sentence.

▶ **During the Cultural Revolution, millions of young people ~~cannot~~** *could not* **go to school and ~~are~~** *were* **sent to the countryside.**

If you speak Spanish

In some languages (Spanish, for example), words end in either a vowel sound or a single consonant sound, not in one consonant sound followed by another. If you speak such a language, remember to add the *-s* of the present-tense third-person singular and the *-ed* of the past tense.

▶ **Last night I ~~call~~** *called* **my aunt who ~~live~~** *lives* **in Santo Domingo.**

54c Understanding perfect and progressive verb phrases

The perfect and progressive auxiliaries combine with the present or past tense, or with modals, to form complex verb phrases with special meanings. In particular, you should learn to recognize sentences in which the perfect or progressive rather than a simple tense must be used.

Distinguishing the simple present and the present perfect

My sister *drives* a bus.

The simple present (*drives*) merely tells us about the sister's current occupation. But if you were to add the phrase *for three years,* it would be incorrect to say *My sister drives a bus for three years.* Instead, you need to set up a time frame that encompasses both the past and the present, and therefore you should use the present perfect or the present perfect progressive.

My sister *has driven* a bus for three years.

My sister *has been driving* a bus for three years.

Distinguishing the simple past and the present perfect

Since she started working, she *has bought* a new car and a VCR.

The clause introduced by *since* sets up a time frame that runs from past to present and requires the present perfect (*has bought*) in the subsequent clause. Furthermore, the sentence does not say exactly when she bought the car or the VCR, and that indefiniteness also calls for the perfect. It would be less correct to say *Since she started working, she bought a new car and a VCR.* But what if you should go on to say when she bought the car?

She *bought* the car two years ago.

It would be incorrect to say *She has bought the car two years ago* because the perfect is incompatible with definite expressions of time. In this case, use the simple past (*bought*).

Distinguishing the simple present and the present progressive

When an action is in progress at the present moment, use the present progressive. Use the simple present for actions that frequently occur during a period of time that might include the present moment (though such an assertion makes no claim that the action is taking place now).

My sister *drives* a bus, but she *is taking* a vacation now.

My sister *drives* a bus, but she *takes* a vacation every year.

Many languages, such as French and German, use the simple present (*drives, takes*) for both types of sentence. In English, however, it would be incorrect to say *But she takes a vacation now.*

Distinguishing the simple past and the past progressive

Sally *spent* the summer in Italy.

You might be tempted to use the past progressive (*was spending*) here instead of the simple past, since spending the summer involves a continuous stretch of time of some duration, and duration and continuousness are typically associated with the progressive. But English speakers use the past progressive infrequently and would be unlikely to use it in this case except to convey actions that are simultaneous with other past actions. For example:

Sally *was spending* the summer in Italy when she *met* her future husband.

Use the past progressive to focus on duration, continuousness, and simultaneousness, and especially to call attention to past action that went on at the same time as something else.

54d Using modals appropriately

The nine basic modal auxiliaries are *can, could, will, would, shall, should, may, might,* and *must.* There are a few others as well, in particular *ought to,* which is close in meaning to *should.* Occasionally *need* can be a modal rather than a main verb.

The nine basic modals fall into the pairs *can/could, will/would, shall/should, may/might,* and the loner *must.* In earlier English, the second member of each pair was the past tense of the first. To a limited degree, the second form still functions as a past tense, especially in the case of *could.*

Ingrid *can* ski.

Ingrid *could* ski when she was five.

But for the most part, in present-day English, all nine modals typically refer to present or future time. When you want to use a modal to refer to the past, you follow the modal with a perfect auxiliary.

If you have a fever, you *should* see a doctor.

If you had a fever, you *should have seen* a doctor.

In the case of *must,* refer to the past by using *had to.*

You *must* renew your visa by the end of this week.

You *had to* renew your visa by the end of last week.

Using modals to make requests or to give instructions

Modals are often used in requests and instructions. Imagine making the following request of a flight attendant:

Will you bring me a pillow?

You have expressed your request in a demanding manner, and the flight attendant might resent it. A more polite request acknowledges that fulfilling the request may not be possible.

Can you bring me a pillow?

Another way of softening the request is to use the past form of *will,* and the most discreet choice is the past form of *can.*

Would you bring me a pillow?

Could you bring me a pillow?

Using the past of modals is considered more polite than using their present forms because it makes any statement or question less assertive.

Now consider each of the following instructions:

1. You *can* submit your report on disc.
2. You *may* submit your report on disc.
3. You *should* submit your report on disc.
4. You *must* submit your report on disc.
5. You *will* submit your report on disc.

Instructions 1 and 2 give permission to submit the paper on disk but do not require it; of these, 2 is more formal. Instruction 3 adds a strong recommendation; 4 allows no alternative; and 5 implies, "Don't even think of doing otherwise."

Using modals to indicate doubt and certainty

Modals can also indicate how confident the writer is about the likelihood that what is being asserted is true. Look at the following set of examples, which starts with a tentative suggestion and ends with full assurance:

Please sit down; you *might* be tired.

Please sit down; you *may* be tired.

Please sit down; you *must* be tired.

54e Using participial adjectives appropriately

Many verbs refer to feelings – for example, *bore, confuse, excite, fascinate, frighten, interest.* The present and past participles of such verbs can be used as ordinary adjectives. Use the past participle to describe a person having the feeling.

The *frightened* boy started to cry.

Use the present participle to describe the thing (or person) causing the feeling.

The *frightening* dinosaur display gave him nightmares.

Be careful not to confuse the two types of adjectives.

▶ **I am ~~interesting~~** *interested* **in African literature.**

▶ **African literature seems ~~interested~~** *interesting*.

EXERCISE 54.1

Each of the following sentences contains an error. Rewrite each sentence correctly.

1. The Rosetta Stone was cover with inscriptions in two ancient languages, Greek and Egyptian.
2. Ancient Egyptian writing called hieroglyphics.
3. In the eighteenth century no one can read hieroglyphics.
4. Very soon after its discovery, the French have made copies of the stone.
5. They sent these copies to scholars who were interesting in hieroglyphics.

EXERCISE 54.2

Rewrite the following passage, adapted from "In a Jumbled Drawer" by Stephen Jay Gould, adding appropriate auxiliaries and verb endings where necessary.

As my son ____grow____, I ____monitor____ the changing fashions in kiddie culture for words expressing deep admiration — what I ____call____ "cool" in my day, and my father ____designate____ "swell." The half-life ____seem____ to be about six months, as "excellent" (with curious lingering emphasis on the first syllable) ____give____ way to "bad" (extended, like a sheep bleat, long enough to turn into its opposite), to "wicked," to "rad" (short for radical). The latest incumbent — "awesome" — ____possess____ more staying power, and ____reign____ for at least two years.

55 Understanding Prepositions and Prepositional Phrases

If you were traveling by rail and asked for directions, it would not be helpful to be told to "take the Chicago train." You would need to know whether to take the train *to* Chicago or the one *from* Chicago. Words such as *to* and *from,* which show the relations between other words, are prepositions. Not all languages use prepositions to show such relations, and English differs from other languages in the way prepositions are used. This chapter will help you in deciding which preposition to use for your intended meaning and in using verbs that include prepositions, such as *take off, pick up,* and *put up with.* ■

55a Using prepositions idiomatically

Even if you usually know where to use prepositions, you may have difficulty from time to time knowing which preposition to use. Each of the most common prepositions, whether in English or in other languages, has a wide range of different applications, and this range never coincides exactly from one language to another. See, for example, how English speakers use *in* and *on.*

The peaches are *in* the refrigerator.

The peaches are *on* the table.

Is that a diamond ring *on* your finger?

If you speak Spanish

The Spanish translations of these sentences all use the same preposition (*en*), a fact that might lead you astray in English.

▶ **Is that a ruby ring ~~in~~ *on* your finger?**

There is no easy solution to the challenge of using English prepositions idiomatically, but the following strategies can make it less formidable:

1. Keep in mind typical examples of each preposition.

   IN **The peaches are *in* the refrigerator.**

   There are still some pickles *in* the jar.

   Here the object of the preposition *in* is a container that encloses something.

   ON **The peaches are *on* the table.**

   The book you are looking for is *on* the top shelf.

   Here the object of the preposition *on* is a horizontal surface that supports something with which it is in direct contact.

2. Learn other examples that show some similarities and some differences in meaning.

   IN **You shouldn't drive *in* a snowstorm.**

   Here there is no container, but like a container, the falling snow surrounds and seems to enclose the driver.

   ON **Is that a diamond ring *on* your finger?**

   A finger is not a horizontal surface, but like such a surface it can support a ring with which it is in contact.

3. Use your imagination to create mental images that can help you remember figurative uses of prepositions.

   IN **Michael is *in* love.**

   Imagine a warm bath in which Michael is immersed (or a raging torrent, if you prefer to visualize love that way).

   ON **I've just read a book *on* computer science.**

   Imagine a shelf labeled COMPUTER SCIENCE on which the book you have read is located.

4. Try to learn prepositions not in isolation but as part of a system. For example, in identifying the location of a place or an event, the three prepositions *in, on,* and *at* can be used.

   At specifies the exact point in space or time.

   AT **There will be a meeting tomorrow *at* 9:30 A.M. *at* 160 Main Street.**

(Continued on page 702)

www •

http://vweb.1.hiway.co.uk/ei/sect9.html

Go here for many examples of idiomatic use of in, on, at, *and other prepositions.*

(Continued from page 701)

Expanses of space or time within which a place is located or an event takes place might be seen as containers and so require *in.*

IN **I arrived *in* the United States *in* January.**

On must be used in two cases: with the names of streets (but not the exact address) and with days of the week or month.

ON **The airline's office is *on* Fifth Avenue.**

I'll be moving to my new apartment *on* September 30.

55b Using two-word verbs idiomatically

www • http://www.eslcafe.com/pv/
Go here for an alphabetically arranged list of phrasal verbs along with definitions and examples.

Some words that look like prepositions do not always function as prepositions. Consider the following two sentences:

The balloon rose *off* the ground.

The plane took *off* without difficulty.

In the first sentence, *off* is a preposition that introduces the prepositional phrase *off the ground.* In the second sentence, *off* neither functions as a preposition nor introduces a prepositional phrase. Instead, it combines with *took* to form a two-word verb with its own meaning. Such a verb is called a **phrasal verb,** and the word *off,* when used in this way, is called an **adverbial particle.** Many prepositions can function as particles to form phrasal verbs.

The verb + particle combination that makes up a phrasal verb is a tightly knit entity that usually cannot be torn apart.

The plane *took off* without difficulty. [not *took* without difficulty *off*]

The exceptions are the many phrasal verbs that are transitive, meaning that they take a direct object. Some transitive phrasal verbs have particles that may be separated from the verb by the object.

For more about transitive verbs, see 7c2.

I *picked up my baggage* at the terminal.

I *picked my baggage up* at the terminal.

If a personal pronoun is used as the direct object, it *must* separate the verb from its particle.

I *picked it up* at the terminal.

Some idiomatic two-word verbs, however, do not operate like phrasal verbs.

We *ran into* our neighbor on the train.

In such verbs, the second word *is* a preposition, which cannot be separated from the verb: *We ran our neighbor into on the train* would be unacceptable. *Ran into* seems to consist of the verb *ran* followed by the preposition *into,* which introduces the prepositional phrase *into our neighbor.* Yet *to run into our neighbor* is different from a normal verb + prepositional phrase, such as *to run into the room.* If you know the typical meanings of *run* and *into,* you can interpret *to run into the room.* Not so with *to run into our neighbor;* the combination *run* + *into* has a special meaning ("find by chance") that could not be determined from the typical meanings of *run* and *into.* Therefore *run into* must be considered a two-word verb, but one that has much more in common with verbs followed by prepositions than with phrasal verbs. Such verbs as *run into* are called **prepositional verbs.**

Prepositional verbs include such idiomatic two-word verbs as *take after,* meaning "resemble" (usually a parent or other older relative), *get over,* meaning "recover from," and *count on,* meaning "trust." They also include verb + preposition combinations in which the meaning is predictable, but the specific preposition that is required is less predictable and must be learned together with the verb (for example, *depend on, look at, listen to, approve of*). There are also **phrasal-prepositional verbs,** which are verb + adverbial particle + preposition sequences (for example, *put up with, look forward to, give up on, get away with*).

Every comprehensive dictionary includes information about the various adverbial particles and prepositions that a verb can combine with, but only some dictionaries distinguish verb + particle from verb + preposition. The *Longman Dictionary of American English* is one that does.

EXERCISE 55.1

Each of the following sentences contains a two-word verb. In some, the verb is used correctly; in some, incorrectly. Identify each two-word verb, indicate whether it is a phrasal or prepositional verb, and rewrite any incorrect sentences correctly.

1. Shortly after the French invasion of Egypt, the British struck at Napoleon back.
2. By 1801, the French forces in Egypt were compelled to give up.
3. As part of the treaty of surrender, the French were required to turn the Rosetta Stone over to the British.
4. The British took back it to England.
5. The Rosetta Stone is now in the British Museum, where millions of visitors have looked at it.

56 Forming Clauses and Sentences

Sound bites surround us, from Nike's "Just do it" to Avis's "We try harder." These short simple sentences may be memorable, but they don't tell us very much. Ordinarily, we need more complex sentences to convey meaning. The sentences of everyday discourse are not formed in the same way in every language, however, and English has its own rules for doing so. Among the features of English sentences that give multilingual writers the most trouble are the need to express subjects and objects explicitly, word order, noun clauses, infinitives and gerunds, adjective clauses, and conditional sentences. This chapter will offer some guidance in dealing with these issues. ■

56a Expressing subjects and objects explicitly

English sentences consist of a subject and a predicate. This simple statement defines a gulf separating English from many other languages that leave out the subject when it can easily be inferred. With few exceptions, English demands that an explicit subject accompany an explicit predicate in every sentence. Though you might write *Went from Yokohama to Nagoya* on a postcard to a friend, in most varieties of spoken and written English, the extra effort of explicitly stating who went is not simply an option but an obligation.

In fact, every dependent clause must have an explicit subject.

it
▶ **They flew to London on the Concorde because ^ was fast.**

English even requires a kind of "dummy" subject to fill the subject position in certain kinds of sentences. Consider the following sentences:

It is raining.

There is a strong wind.

Transitive verbs typically require that objects also be explicitly stated, and in some cases even other items of information as well. (See 7c2). For example, it is not enough to tell someone *Give!* even if it is clear what is to be given to whom. You must say *Give it to me* or *Give her the passport* or some other such sentence. Similarly, saying *Put!* or *Put it!* is insufficient when you mean *Put it on the table.*

If you speak Spanish

Speakers of Spanish might be inclined to leave out dummy subjects. In English, however, *it* and *there* are indispensable.

It is
▶ ~~Is~~ ^ **raining.**

There is
▶ ~~Has~~ ^ **a strong wind.**

56b Using English word order

In general, you should not move subjects, verbs, or objects out of their normal positions in a sentence. In the following sentence, each element is in an appropriate place:

SUBJECT	VERB	OBJECT	ADVERB
Omar	reads	books	voraciously.

www •

http://vweb1.hiway.co.uk/ei/sect1.html

Go here for examples of idiomatic English word order.

This sentence would also be acceptable if written as *Omar voraciously reads books* or as *Voraciously Omar reads books,* but note that only the adverb can be moved. The three key elements of subject, verb, and object should be moved out of their normal order only to create special effects.

•·······*For more about changing word order for special effects, see 23c3 .*

If you speak Turkish, Korean, or Japanese

In these languages, the verb must come last. You may have to make a special effort never to write such a sentence as *Omar books voraciously reads,* which is not acceptable in English.

If you speak Russian

Because Russian permits a great deal of freedom in word order, you must remember never to interchange the position of subject and object (*Books reads Omar voraciously* is not acceptable English). In general, also avoid separating the verb from its object (*Omar reads voraciously books*).

•·······*For more on subjects and objects, see 7c1 and 7c2; for more on disruptive modifiers, see 17b .*

56c Using noun clauses appropriately

Examine the following sentence:

> In my last year in high school, my advisor urged that I apply to several colleges.

This is built up out of two sentences, one of them (B) embedded in the other (A):

> A. In my last year in high school, my advisor urged B.
>
> B. I (should) apply to several colleges.

When these are combined as in the original sentence, sentence B becomes a **noun clause** introduced by *that* and takes on the role of object of the verb *urged* in sentence A. Now look at the following sentence:

> It made a big difference that she wrote a strong letter of recommendation.

Here the two component sentences are C and D:

> C. D made a big difference.
>
> D. She wrote a strong letter of recommendation.

In this case, the noun clause formed from sentence D functions as the subject of sentence C, so that the combination reads as follows:

> That she wrote a strong letter of recommendation made a big difference.

This is an acceptable sentence but somewhat top-heavy. Usually when a lengthy noun clause is the subject of the sentence, it is moved to the end. When that is done, the result is *Made a big difference that she wrote a strong letter of recommendation.* If you speak Italian, Spanish, or Portuguese, you might see nothing wrong with such a sentence. In English, however, the subject must be stated. The dummy element *it* comes to the rescue.

It made
▶ **~~Made~~ ^ a big difference that she wrote a strong letter of recommendation.**

56d Choosing between infinitives and gerunds

Knowing whether to use an infinitive or a gerund in a particular sentence may be a challenge to multilingual writers. Though there is no simple explanation that will make it an easy task, some hints will help you.

My advisor urged me *to apply* to several colleges.

Her *writing* a strong letter of recommendation made a big difference.

Why was an infinitive chosen for the first and a gerund for the second? In general, **infinitives** tend to represent intentions, desires, or expectations, and **gerunds** tend to represent facts. The gerund in the second sentence calls attention to the fact that a letter was actually written; the infinitive in the first sentence conveys the message that the act of applying was something desired, not an accomplished fact.

Using gerunds to state facts

Jerzy *enjoys going* to the theater.

We *resumed working* after our coffee break.

Kim *appreciated getting* candy from Sean.

In all of these cases, the second verb form is a gerund, and the gerund indicates that the action or event that it expresses has actually happened. Verbs like *enjoy, resume,* and *appreciate* can be followed only by gerunds, not by infinitives. In fact, even when these verbs do not convey clear facts, the verb form that follows must still be a gerund.

Kim *would appreciate getting* candy from Sean, but he hardly knows her.

Using infinitives to state intentions

Kumar *expected to get* a good job after graduation.

Last year, Fatima *decided to become* a math major.

The strikers have *agreed to go* back to work.

Here it is irrelevant whether the actions or events referred to by the infinitives did or did not materialize; at the moment indicated by the verbs *expect, decide,* and *agree,* those actions or events were merely intentions. These three verbs, as well as many others that specify intentions (or negative intentions, like *refuse*), must always be followed by an infinitive, never by a gerund.

Understanding other rules and guidelines

A few verbs can be followed by either an infinitive or a gerund. With some, such as *begin* or *continue,* the choice makes little difference in meaning. With others, however, the difference in meaning is striking.

Carlos was working as a medical technician, but he *stopped to study* English.

The infinitive indicates that Carlos intended to study English when he left his job. We are not told whether he actually did study English.

Carlos *stopped studying* English when he left the United States.

The gerund indicates that Carlos actually did study English, but later stopped.

The distinction between fact and intention is not a rule but only a tendency, and it can be superseded by other rules. Use a gerund — never an infinitive — directly following a preposition.

▶ **This fruit is safe for ~~to eat.~~** *eating.*

▶ **This fruit is safe ~~for~~ to eat.**

▶ **This fruit is safe for** *us* **to eat.**

A full list of verbs that can be followed by an infinitive and verbs that can be followed by a gerund can be found in the *Index to Modern English*, by Thomas Lee Crowell Jr. (McGraw-Hill, 1964).

56e Using adjective clauses carefully

Adjective clauses can be a challenge to multilingual writers. Look at the following sentence, and then see what can go wrong:

The company *Yossi's uncle invested in* went bankrupt.

The subject is a noun phrase in which the noun *company* is modified by the article *the* and the adjective clause *Yossi's uncle invested in.* The sentence as a whole says that a certain company went bankrupt, and the adjective clause identifies the company more specifically by saying that Yossi's uncle had invested in it.

One way of seeing how the adjective clause fits into the sentence is to rewrite it like this: *The company (Yossi's uncle had invested in it) went bankrupt.* This is not a normal English sentence, but it helps demonstrate a process that leads to the sentence we started with. Note the following steps:

1. Change the personal pronoun *it* to the relative pronoun *which: The company (Yossi's uncle had invested in which) went bankrupt.* That still is not acceptable English.
2. Move either the whole prepositional phrase *in which* to the beginning of the adjective clause, or move just the relative pronoun: *The company in which Yossi's uncle had invested went bankrupt* or *The company which Yossi's uncle had invested in went bankrupt.* Both of these are good English sentences, the former somewhat more formal than the latter.
3. If no preposition precedes, substitute *that* for *which* or leave out the relative pronoun entirely. *The company that Yossi's uncle had invested in went bankrupt* or *The company Yossi's uncle had invested in went bankrupt.* Both of these are good English sentences, not highly formal, but still acceptable in much formal writing.

Speakers of some languages find adjective clauses difficult in different ways. Following are some guidelines that might help:

If you speak Korean, Japanese, or Chinese

If you speak Korean, Japanese, or Chinese, the fact that the adjective clause does not precede the noun that it modifies may be disconcerting, both because that is the position of such clauses in the East Asian languages and because other modifiers, such as determiners and adjectives, do precede the noun in English.

If you speak Farsi, Arabic, or Hebrew

If you speak Farsi, Arabic, or Hebrew, you may expect the adjective clause to follow the noun as it does in English, but you might need to remind yourself to change the personal pronoun (*it*) to a relative pronoun (*which* or *that*) and then to move the relative pronoun to the beginning of the clause. You may put a relative pronoun at the beginning but mistakenly keep the personal pronoun, thus producing incorrect sentences such as *The company that Yossi's uncle invested in it went bankrupt.*

If you speak a European or Latin American language

If you are a speaker of some European or Latin American languages, you are probably acquainted with adjective clauses very much like those of English, but you may have difficulty accepting the possibility that a relative pronoun that is the object of a preposition can be moved to the beginning of a clause while leaving the preposition stranded. You might, therefore, move the preposition as well even when the relative pronoun is *that,* or you might drop the preposition altogether, generating such incorrect sentences as *The company in that Yossi's uncle invested went bankrupt* or *The company that Yossi's uncle invested went bankrupt.*

Finally, the fact that the relative pronoun can sometimes be omitted may lead to the mistaken notion that it can be omitted in all cases. Remember that you cannot omit a relative pronoun that is the subject of a verb.

▶ **Everyone ^*who* invested in that company lost a great deal.**

56f Understanding conditional sentences

English pays special attention to whether or not something is a fact, or to the degree of confidence we have in the truth or likelihood of an assertion. Therefore English distinguishes among many different types of **conditional sentences,** that is, sentences that focus on questions of truth and that are introduced by *if* or its equivalent. The following examples illustrate a range of different conditional sentences. Each of these sentences makes different assumptions about the likelihood that what is stated in the *if* clause is true, and then draws the corresponding conclusion in the main clause.

> If you *practice* (or *have practiced*) writing frequently, you *know* (or *have learned*) what your chief problems are.

This sentence assumes that what is stated in the *if* clause may very well be true; the alternatives in parentheses indicate that any tense that is appropriate in a simple sentence may be used in both the *if* clause and the main clause.

> If you *practice* writing for the rest of this term, you *will* (or *may*) *get* a firmer grasp of the process.

This sentence makes a prediction about the future and again assumes that what is stated may very well turn out to be true. Only the main clause uses the future tense (*will get*) or some other modal that can indicate future time (*may get*). The *if* clause must use the present tense, even though it too refers to the future.

If you *practiced* (or *were to practice*) writing every single day, it *would* eventually *seem* much easier to you.

This sentence casts some doubt on the likelihood that what is stated will be put into effect. In the *if* clause, the verb is either past – actually, past subjunctive – or *were to* + the base form, though it refers to future time. (See 9h.) The main clause has *would* + the base form of the main verb.

If you *practiced* writing on Mars, you *would find* no one to show your work to.

This sentence contemplates an impossibility at present or in the foreseeable future. As with the preceding sentence, the past subjunctive is used in the *if* clause, although past time is not being referred to, and *would* + the base form is used in the main clause.

If you *had practiced* writing in ancient Egypt, you *would have used* hieroglyphics.

This sentence shifts the impossibility back to the past; obviously you are not going to find yourself in ancient Egypt. But since past forms have already been used in the preceding two sentences, this one demands a form that is "more past": the past perfect in the *if* clause, and *would* + the perfect form of the main verb in the main clause.

EXERCISE 56.1

Revise the following sentences as necessary. Not all sentences contain an error.

1. The scholar who deciphered finally hieroglyphics was Jean François Champollion.
2. Champollion enjoyed to study the languages of the Middle East.
3. By comparing the Greek and Egyptian inscriptions on the Rosetta Stone, he made a great deal of progress in understanding hieroglyphics.
4. Was of great importance that he knew Coptic, a later form of the Egyptian language.
5. In 1822 Champollion wrote a paper which he presented his decipherment of hieroglyphics in it.
6. If the Rosetta Stone was not discovered, it would have been much more difficult to decipher hieroglyphics.

Glossary of Grammatical and Computer Terms

absolute phrase See *phrase.*

acronym a word, usually a noun, formed from the first letter(s) of several words, such as FAQ for *frequently asked questions.*

active voice See *voice.*

adjective a word that modifies, quantifies, identifies, or describes a noun or a word or words acting as a noun. Most adjectives precede the noun or other word(s) they modify (*a good book*), but a **predicate adjective** follows the noun or pronoun it modifies (*the book is good*).

adjective clause See *clause.*

adjective forms changes in an adjective from the **positive degree** (*tall, good*) to the **comparative** (comparing two – *taller, better*) or the **superlative** (comparing more than two – *tallest, best*). Short regular adjectives (*tall*) add *-er* and *-est,* but most adjectives of two syllables or more form the comparative by adding *more* (*more beautiful*) and the superlative by adding *most* (*most beautiful*). A few adjectives have irregular forms (*good, better, best*), and some adjectives (*only, forty*) do not change form.

adverb a word that qualifies, modifies, limits, or defines a verb, an adjective, another adverb, or a clause, frequently answering the questions *where? when? how? why? to what extent?* or *under what conditions?* Adverbs derived from adjectives and nouns commonly end in the suffix *-ly. She will soon travel south and will probably visit her very favorite sister.* See also *conjunction.*

adverb clause See *clause.*

adverb forms changes in an adverb from the **positive degree** (*eagerly*) to the **comparative** (comparing two – *more eagerly*) or the **superlative** (comparing more than two –*most eagerly*). Most adverbs add *more* to form the comparative and *most* to form the superlative, but a few add *-er* and *-est* or have irregular forms (*fast, faster, fastest; little, less, least*).

agreement the correspondence of a pronoun with its antecedent in person, number, and gender or of a verb with its subject in person and number. See also *antecedent, gender, number, person.*

< > **angle brackets** an Internet convention (sometimes called "right and left arrows") meaning that all characters within the brackets must be treated as a single unit, with no spaces between parts. Example: <http://www.mapquest.com>. Angle brackets are used to enclose email addresses or Web site locations within other text.

antecedent the specific noun that a pronoun replaces and to which it refers. A pronoun and its antecedent must agree in person, number, and gender. *Ginger Rogers moved her feet as no one else has.*

appositive a noun or noun phrase that identifies or adds identifying information to a preceding noun. *Michael Jordan, the best player in the NBA, scored thirty-one points. My sister Janet has twin boys.*

Archie an early Internet tool for discovering and retrieving files from linked computers.

archive a collection of electronic files stored on a computer.

article *a, an,* or *the,* the most common adjectives. *A* and *an* are **indefinite;** they do not specifically identify the nouns they modify. *I bought an apple and a peach. The* is **definite** or specific. *The peach was not ripe.*

ASCII American Standard Code for Information Interchange, the most basic format allowing for transfer of text files between different computers and programs.

asynchronous ("asynch") communication online communication, such as email, involving a delay between the time a message is posted and the time it is received.

@ (the "at" sign) the part of every email address that occurs between the username and the domain name, indicating that someone is "at" a particular electronic address. For example, <jrobinson@osu.edu> indicates that Jane Robinson gets email at OSU, an educational institution.

auxiliary verb a verb that combines with the base form or with the present or past participle of a main verb to form a verb phrase. The primary auxiliaries are forms of *do, have,* and *be. Did he arrive? We have eaten. She is writing.* **Modal** auxiliaries such as *can, may, shall, will, could, might, should, would,* and *ought* [*to*] have only one form and show possibility, necessity, obligation, and so on. Also called **helping verb.**

\ (the backslash) the backward slash mark used mainly in DOS directory paths, as in <C:\windows\desktop\pcfile\survey>.

bandwidth a measure of the speed at which a given amount of electronic data can be transmitted. Fiber-optic data lines on computer networks allow for much greater bandwidth than do telephone lines.

base form the form of a verb that is listed in dictionaries, such as *go* or *listen.* For all verbs except *be,* it is the same as the first-person singular form in the present tense.

BBS (bulletin board service or **bulletin board system)** a local computer system that functions as an information clearinghouse for users, allowing people with common interests to post and receive messages.

bookmark a Web site listed in a bookmark list.

bookmark list a pulldown menu in Netscape or Explorer browsers that allows a user to save the addresses of favorite Web sites so they can easily be revisited.

Boolean term a word like *and* or *or* that allows for computer database searches using multiple words. Example: *Kahlo, Frida and American Literature.*

browser a World Wide Web program for negotiating the Internet. Browsers display Web sites and homepages and allow users to click on hyperlinks to move among sites. Netscape Navigator and Microsoft Explorer are the two most commonly used. Some browsers display text but not graphics; Lynx is the most popular of these.

bulletin board service See *BBS.*

bulletin board system See *BBS.*

case the form of a noun or pronoun that reflects its grammatical role in a sentence. Nouns and indefinite pronouns can be **subjective, possessive,** or **objective,** but they change form only in the possessive case. *The dog* (subjective) *barked. The dog's* (possessive) *tail wagged. The mail carrier called the dog* (objective). The personal pronouns *I, he, she, we,* and *they,* as well as the relative or interrogative pronoun *who,* have different forms for all three cases. *We* (subjective) *took the train to Chicago. Our* (possessive) *trip lasted a week. Maria met us* (objective) *at the station.* See also *person, pronoun.*

chat rooms See *IRC.*

clause a group of words containing a subject and a predicate. An **independent clause** can stand alone as a sentence. *The car hit the tree.* A **dependent clause,** as the name suggests, is grammatically subordinate to an independent clause, linked to it by a subordinating conjunction or a relative pronoun. A dependent clause can function as an adjective, an adverb, or a noun. *The car hit the tree that stood at the edge of the road* **(adjective clause).** *The car hit the tree when it went out of control* **(adverb clause).** *The car hit what grew at the side of the road* **(noun clause).** See also *nonrestrictive element, restrictive element.*

collective noun See *noun.*

comma splice an error resulting from joining two independent clauses with only a comma.

common noun See *noun.*

comparative degree See *adjective forms, adverb forms.*

complement a word or group of words completing the predicate in a sentence. A **subject complement** follows a linking verb and renames or describes the subject. It can be a **predicate noun** (*Anorexia is an illness*) or a **predicate adjective** (*Karen Carpenter was anorexic*). An **object complement** renames or describes a direct object (*We considered her a prodigy and her behavior extraordinary*).

complete predicate See *predicate.*

complete subject See *subject.*

complex sentence See *sentence.*

compound adjective a combination of words that functions as a single adjective (*blue-green sea, ten-story building, get-tough policy, high school outing, north-by-northwest journey*). Most, but not all, compound adjectives need hyphens to separate their individual elements.

compound-complex sentence See *sentence.*

compound noun a combination of words that functions as a single noun (*go-getter, in-law, Johnny-on-the-spot, oil well, southeast*).

compound sentence See *sentence.*

compound subject See *subject.*

conjunction a word or words that join words, phrases, clauses, or sentences. **Coordinating conjunctions** (such as *and, but, or,* or *yet*) join grammatically equivalent elements (*Marx and Engels* [two nouns]; *Marx wrote one essay, but Engels wrote the other* [two independent clauses]). **Correlative conjunctions** (such as *both, and; either, or;* or *not only, but also*) are used in pairs to connect grammatically equivalent elements (*neither Marx nor Engels; Marx not only studied the *world but also changed it*). A **subordinating conjunction** (such as *although, because, if, that,* or *when*) introduces a dependent clause and connects it to an independent clause. *Marx moved to London, where he did most of his work. Marx argued that religion was an "opiate."* A **conjunctive adverb** (such as *consequently, moreover,* or *nevertheless*) modifies an independent clause following another independent clause. A conjunctive adverb generally follows a semicolon and is followed by a comma. *Thoreau lived simply at Walden; however, he regularly joined his aunt for tea in Concord.*

coordinating conjunction See *conjunction.*

correlative conjunction See *conjunction.*

count noun See *noun.*

cyber- a prefix overused to mean anything created or existing electronically or online, as in *cybernovel, cyberkitchen, cybergeek.*

cyberspace originally a term describing a complex melding of mind and computer in William Gibson's science-fiction novel *Neuromancer;* now generalized to mean simply the Internet or the World Wide Web.

dangling modifier a word, phrase, or clause that does not logically modify any element in the sentence to which it is attached. *Studying Freud, the meaning of my dreams became clear* is incorrect because *the meaning* could not have been studying Freud. *Studying Freud, I began to understand the meaning of my dreams* is correct because now *I* was doing the studying.

declarative sentence See *sentence.*

degree See *adjective forms, adverb forms.*

dependent clause See *clause.*

descriptor a keyword used in a Web or Net search.

digital From its specific original meaning of "composed of binary on-off pulses," this term has come to mean simply "electronic" or "wired."

direct address construction that uses a noun or pronoun to name the person or thing being spoken to. *Hey, Jack. You, get moving.*

direct discourse a quotation that reproduces a speaker's exact words, marked with quotation marks.

direct object a noun or pronoun receiving the action of a transitive verb. *McKellan recited Shakespearean soliloquies.* See also *indirect object.*

directory a list or group of computer files that are somehow related; also called a folder. A directory can contain other directories, which are then called subdirectories.

directory path a listing of the order of directories and subdirectories a user must open to find a particular computer file in DOS and Windows applications. Directory paths are delineated by slash marks. For example, <C:\wp52\memos\walter.1> indicates that the file <walter.1> is in the directory <wp52>, subdirectory <memos>, on the hard disk drive designated <C:>.

domain name the characters and symbols identifying elements within a computer server on the Internet. Usually designating Web sites or email addresses, domain names have at least two parts, separated by dots. The first part designates the organization or server, and the final part identifies the type of organization operating the server, such as *.com* (commercial), *.edu* (educational), *.gov* (government), *.mil* (military), *.net* (network management), and *.org* (noncommercial/nonprofit). Domains outside the United States often identify the country in which a server is located, such as *.uk* for Great Britain and *.fi* for Finland.

. (the dot) the period symbol called "dot" when used to separate parts of email addresses, URLs, and newsgroup names, as in <bgm2 @umnvm1.umn.edu>.

download to move data electronically, usually from a server or mainframe to a microcomputer or PC.

email (electronic mail) sending or receiving electronic messages by means of various programs that allow asynchronous communication over a network.

email address the string of characters identifying a location for sending or receiving email. An email address contains a username, the @ symbol, and the domain name, as in <gbowe @hopper.unh.edu>.

emoticons combinations of ASCII characters used in online writing to indicate moods or facial expressions. (Look at them sideways.) Common emoticons include :-) (smile), :-((frown), ;-/ (skeptical), and :-o (surprised).

exclamatory sentence See *sentence.*

expletive a construction that introduces a sentence with *there* or *it,* usually followed by a form of *be.* *There are four candidates for this job. It was a dark and stormy night.*

FAQ (frequently asked questions) a file containing common questions about an online program or service (such as a listserv or newsgroup) and their answers.

file name the last part of a URL, indicating the specific computer file for which the URL is the address.

first person See *person.*

flaming personal attacks in email or other electronic communication. Considered bad manners.

FTP (file transfer protocol) the electronic commands used to transfer files between computers on the Internet.

fused sentence a sentence in which two independent clauses are run together without a conjunction or punctuation between them. Also called **run-on sentence.**

future tense See *tense.*

gender the classification of a noun or pronoun as masculine (*god, he*), feminine (*goddess, she*), or neuter (*godliness, it*).

gerund a verbal form ending in *-ing* and functioning as a noun. *Swimming is good exercise.*

gopher a set of programs for accessing information on the Internet through a series of hierarchically arranged menus. Gopher underlies the search capabilities of Web browsers, but it is usually used to seek out text-based files.

hard copy a version of an electronic document or file that is printed out onto paper.

header the subject line of a listserv or newsgroup posting. By looking at the index of headers, users can determine the different threads of a discussion.

helping verb See *auxiliary verb.*

hit an electronic connection on the World Wide Web. A hit can be either a match with a keyword a user is searching for with a search engine (as in *HOTBOT's search for* firewalking *turned up thirty hits*) or the accessing of a Web site by a remote browser (as in *The Beanie Babies page received two thousand hits today*).

homepage the introductory page users see when they access a Web site, which controls access to other links the site offers.

hotlink See *hyperlink.*

HTML (Hypertext Markup Language) an electronic coding system for creating World Wide Web pages, which indicates how browsers should display text and graphic images onscreen.

hyperlink a connection between two points on the World Wide Web that may be in the same or different sites. Hyperlinks are indicated in Web text by the use of different-colored letters and/or underlining. Also called "hotlink."

hypertext a document coded in HTML that contains hyperlinks, or a collection of such documents.

imperative mood the form of a verb used to express a command or a request. An imperative uses the base form of the verb and may or may not have a stated subject. *Leave. You be quiet. Let's go.* See also *mood.*

imperative sentence See *sentence.*

indefinite pronoun See *pronoun.*

independent clause See *clause.*

indicative mood the form of a verb used to state a fact or opinion or to ask a question. *Washington crossed the Delaware. Did he defeat the Hessians?* See also *mood.*

indirect discourse a paraphrased quotation that does not repeat another's exact words and hence is not enclosed in quotation marks. *Coolidge said that if nominated he would not run.*

indirect object a noun or pronoun identifying to whom or to what or for whom or for what a transitive verb's action is performed. The indirect object almost always precedes the direct object. *I handed the dean my application and told her that I needed financial aid.* See also *direct object.*

indirect question a sentence pattern in which a question is the basis of a subordinate clause. An indirect question should end with a period, not a question mark. *Everyone wonders why young people continue to take up smoking.* (The question, phrased directly, is "Why do young people continue to take up smoking?")

infinitive the base form of a verb preceded by *to* (*to go, to run, to hit*). An infinitive can serve as a noun, an adverb, or an adjective. *To go would be unthinkable* (noun). *We stopped to rest* (adverb). *The company needs space to grow* (adjective). An infinitive can be in either the active (*to hit*) or passive (*to be hit*) voice and in either the present (*to* [*be*] *hit*) or perfect (*to have* [*been*] *hit*) tense. An **infinitive phrase** consists of an infinitive together with its modifiers, objects, or complements. See *phrase.*

intensifier a modifier that increases the emphasis of the word or words it modifies. *I would very much like to go. I'm so happy.* Despite their name, intensifiers are stylistically weak; they are best avoided in academic writing.

interjection a grammatically independent word or group of words that is usually an exclamation of surprise, shock, dismay, or the like. *Ouch! For heaven's sake, what do you think you're doing?*

Internet originally a network of academic and military mainframe computers; now a worldwide "network of networks," linking computers of all sizes and types and providing access to the World Wide Web, among other services.

Internet service provider (ISP) an individual or group that provides access to the Internet, such as America Online or CompuServe.

interrogative sentence See *sentence.*

intransitive verb a verb that does not need a direct object to complete its meaning. *The children laughed.*

IRC (Internet relay chat) an Internet service that allows synchronous online communication (like telephone conference calls) with others; sometimes called "chat rooms."

irregular verb a verb whose past tense and past participle are not formed by adding *-ed* or *-d* to the base form, such as *see, saw, seen.*

keyword a word or phrase used to search a computer database. In a World Wide Web or Internet search, it is typed into the search engine's dialog box.

linkage data information about a hypertext document's links to other documents.

linking verb a verb that joins a subject with a subject complement or complements. Common linking verbs are *appear, be, become, feel,* and *seem. The argument appeared sound. It was actually a trick.* See also *verb.*

listserv the central server that controls an ongoing email discussion group about a particular topic. Participants subscribe to a listserv by sending a "subscribe" command to the server.

main clause an independent clause. See *clause.*

main verb the verb that carries the central meaning in a verb phrase, such as *given* in the phrase *could be given.*

misplaced modifier a word, phrase, or clause positioned so that it appears to modify a word other than the one the writer intended. *With a credit card, the traveler paid for the motel room and opened the door.* Unless the writer intended to indicate that the traveler used the credit card to open the door, *with a credit card* should follow *room.*

modal See *auxiliary verb.*

modem an electronic device connecting a computer to a telephone line or another line that allows it to communicate with other computers.

modifier a word, phrase, or clause that acts as an adjective or an adverb and qualifies the meaning of another word, phrase, or clause. See also *adjective, adverb, clause, phrase.*

MOO (multi-user domain, object-oriented) an online service that enables many people to communicate synchronously at prearranged times, usually to discuss a particular topic.

mood the form of a verb that indicates the writer's or speaker's attitude toward the idea expressed by the verb. Different moods are used to state a fact or opinion or to ask a question (indicative); to give a command or request (imperative); and to express a wish, a suggestion, a request or requirement, or a condition that does not exist (subjunctive). *The sea is turbulent* (indicative). *Stay out of the water* (imperative). *I wish the water were calm enough for swimming* (subjunctive). See also *imperative mood, indicative mood, subjunctive mood.*

mouse a handheld device, with two buttons and a cord at one end, used to enter commands into a computer.

MUD (multi-user domain) an online service for synchronous communication, usually in the form of role-playing games.

netiquette a set of standards for behavior on a computer network or the Internet.

newsgroup an arrangement made by a group of people with a particular interest to maintain a space for postings about the topic on the Usenet network.

noncount noun See *noun.*

nonrestrictive element a word, phrase, or clause that modifies but does not change the essential meaning of a sentence element. A nonrestrictive element is set off from the rest of the sentence with commas, dashes, or parentheses. *Quantum physics, a difficult subject, is fascinating.* See also *restrictive element.*

noun a word that names a person, place, object, concept, action, or the like. Nouns serve as subjects, objects, complements, and appositives. Most nouns form the plural with the addition of *-s* or *-es* and the possessive with the addition of *'s* (see *number, case*). **Common nouns** (*president, state, month*) name classes or general groups. **Proper nouns** (*Hillary Clinton, Florida, July*) name particular persons or things and are capitalized. **Collective nouns** (*family, committee, jury*) refer to a group of related elements. **Count nouns** (*woman, trees*) refer to things that can be directly counted. **Noncount nouns** (*sand, rain, violence*) refer to collections of things or to ideas that cannot be directly counted.

noun clause See *clause.*

noun phrase See *phrase.*

number the form of a noun or pronoun that indicates whether it is singular (*book, I, he, her, it*) or plural (*books, we, they, them, their*).

object a word or words, usually a noun or pronoun, influenced by a transitive verb, a verbal, or a preposition. See also *direct object, indirect object, object of a preposition.*

object complement See *complement.*

objective case See *case.*

object of a preposition a noun or pronoun connected to a sentence by a preposition. The preposition, the object, and any modifiers make up a **prepositional phrase.** *I went to the party without her.*

offlist sent to an individual member of a listserv or other online group but not to the entire group.

online connected to a network; on the Internet or the World Wide Web.

participial phrase See *phrase.*

participle a verbal with properties of both an adjective and a verb. Like an adjective, a participle can modify a noun or pronoun; like a verb, it has present and past forms and can take an object. The **present participle** of a verb always ends in *-ing* (*going, being*). The **past participle** usually ends in *-ed* (*ruined, injured*), but many verbs have irregular forms (*gone, been, brought*). Present participles are used with the auxiliary verb *be* to form the **progressive tenses** (*I am making, I will be making, I have been making*). Past participles are used with the auxiliary verb *have* to form the **perfect tenses** (*I have made, I had made, I will have made*) and with *be* to form the passive voice (*I am seen, I was seen*). These combinations of auxiliary verbs and participles are known as **verb phrases.** See also *adjective, phrase, tense, verbal, voice.*

parts of speech the eight grammatical categories into which words can be grouped depending on how they function in a sentence. Many words act as different parts of speech in different sentences. The parts of speech are *adjectives, adverbs, conjunctions, interjections, nouns, prepositions, pronouns,* and *verbs.*

passive voice See *voice.*

password a personal code used to access a computer account.

past participle See *participle.*

past perfect tense See *tense.*

past tense See *tense.*

perfect tenses See *participle, tense, verb.*

person the relation between a subject and its verb, indicating whether the subject is speaking about itself (**first person** – *I* or *we*), being spoken to (**second person** – *you*), or being spoken about (**third person** – *he, she, it,* or *they*). *Be* has several forms depending on the person (*am, is,* and *are* in the present tense and *was* and *were* in the past tense). Other verbs change form only in the present tense with a third-person singular subject (*I fall, you fall, she falls, we fall, they fall*).

personal pronoun See *pronoun.*

phrase a group of words that functions as a single unit but lacks a subject, verb, or both. An **absolute phrase** modifies an entire sentence. It usually includes a noun or pronoun followed by a participle (sometimes implied) or participial phrase. *The party (being) over, everyone left.* A **gerund phrase** includes a gerund and its objects, complements, and modifiers. It functions as a noun, acting as a subject, a complement, or an object. *Exercising regularly and sensibly is a key to good health* (subject). An **infinitive phrase** includes an infinitive and its objects, complements, and modifiers. It functions as an adjective, an adverb, or a noun. *The Pacific Coast is the place to be* (adjective). *She went to pay her taxes* (adverb). *To be young again is all I want* (noun). A **noun phrase** includes a noun and its modifiers. *A long, rough road crossed the barren desert.* A **participial phrase** includes a present or past participle and its objects, complements, or modifiers. It functions as an adjective. *Absentmindedly climbing the stairs, he stumbled. They bought a house built in 1895.* A **prepositional phrase** is introduced by a preposition and ends with a noun or pronoun, called the object of the preposition. It functions as an adjective, an adverb, or a noun. *The gas in the laboratory was leaking* (adjective). *The firefighters went to the lab to check* (adverb). *The smell came from inside a wall* (noun). A **verb phrase** is composed of a main verb and one or more auxiliaries, acting as a single verb in the sentence predicate. *I should have come to the review session.*

plural the form of a noun, pronoun, or adjective that refers to more than one person or thing, such as *books, we,* or *those.*

positive degree See *adjective forms, adverb forms.*

possessive case See *case.*

post to send a message, or posting, to an electronic correspondent, a listserv, or a newsgroup.

predicate the verb and related words in a clause or sentence. The predicate expresses what the subject does, experiences, or is. The **simple predicate** is the verb or verb phrase. *For years the YMHA has been a cultural center in New York City.* The **complete predicate** includes the simple predicate and any modifiers, objects, or complements. *John gave Sarah an engagement ring.* A **compound predicate** has more than one simple predicate. *The athletes swam in a relay and ran in a marathon.*

predicate adjective See *complement.*

predicate noun See *complement.*

prefix an addition to the beginning of a word to alter its meaning (*anti-French, undress*).

preposition a word or group of words that indicates the relationship of a noun or pronoun, called the object of the preposition, to another part of the sentence. *He was on top of the ladder* *before the other contestants had climbed to the fourth rung.* See *phrase.*

present participle See *participle.*

present perfect See *participle, tense, verb, verbal.*

present progressive See *participle, tense, verb, verbal.*

present tense See *tense, verb.*

progressive tenses See *participle, tense, verb.*

pronoun a word used in place of a noun, usually called the antecedent of the pronoun. **Indefinite pronouns** do not refer to specific nouns and include *any, each, everybody, some,* and similar words. *Many are called, but few are chosen.* **Personal pronouns** (*I, you, he, she, it, we, you,* and *they*) refer to particular people or things. They have different forms (*I, me, my, mine*) depending on their case. (See also *case.*) **Relative pronouns** (*who, whom, whose, which, that, what, whoever, whomever, whichever,* and *whatever*) connect a dependent clause to a sentence. *I wonder who will win the prize.*

proper noun See *noun.*

protocol the agreed command set used by many different kinds of computers to allow data exchange. Examples include FTP, telnet, and gopher.

real-time communication See *synchronous communication.*

regular verb a verb whose past tense and past participle are formed by adding *-d* or *-ed* to the base form (*care, cared, cared; look, looked, looked*). See also *irregular verb.*

relative pronoun See *pronoun.*

restrictive element a word, phrase, or clause that limits the essential meaning of the sentence element it modifies or provides necessary identifying information about it. A restrictive element is not set off from the rest of the sentence with commas, dashes, or parentheses. *The tree that I hit was an oak.* See also *nonrestrictive element.*

run-on sentence See *comma splice, fused sentence.*

search engine one of a variety of programs on the World Wide Web that allows users to search for information by keyword. When a keyword is typed into a search engine, the program seeks out all Web sites containing that keyword and displays them in a list of "hits." Examples: Alta Vista, Lycos, Yahoo!, Excite.

second person See *person.*

sentence a group of words containing a subject and a predicate and expressing a complete thought. In writing, a sentence begins with a capital letter and ends with a period, a question mark, or an exclamation point. A sentence may be **declarative** and make a statement (*The sun rose*), **interrogative** and ask a question (*Did the sun rise?*), **exclamatory** and indicate surprise or other strong emotion (*How beautiful the dawn is!*), or **imperative** and express a command (*Get up earlier tomorrow*). Besides having these functions, sentences are classified grammatically. A **simple sentence** is a single independent clause without dependent clauses. *I left the house.* Its subject, predicate, or both may be compound. *Sears and Roebuck founded a mail-order house and a chain of stores.* A **compound sentence** contains two or more independent clauses linked with a coordinating conjunction, a correlative conjunction, or a semicolon. *I did not wish to go, but she did.* A **complex sentence** contains an independent clause and one or more dependent clauses. *After he had* *cleaned up the kitchen, Tom fell asleep in front of the television.* A **compound-complex sentence** contains at least two independent clauses and one or more dependent clauses. *We had hoped to go climbing, but the trip was postponed because she sprained her ankle.* See also *clause.*

sentence fragment a group of words that is not a grammatically complete sentence but is punctuated as one. Usually a fragment lacks a subject, verb, or both or is a dependent clause that is not attached to an independent clause. In academic writing, fragments should usually be revised to be complete sentences.

server a computer that provides services, such as email or file transfer, in response to requests from other computers; often still called a "mainframe."

.sig file identifying information that many writers attach to the end of their electronic messages, such as their name, title, address, and phone and fax numbers.

simple predicate See *predicate.*

simple sentence See *sentence.*

simple subject See *subject.*

singular the form of a noun, pronoun, or adjective that refers to one person or thing, such as *book, it,* or *this.*

/ (the slash) the forward slash mark, called just "slash" when used to separate parts of email addresses, URLs, and newsgroup names, as in <http://quinine.lists/quinine.html>.

snailmail mail delivered in hard-copy form through the postal service, so called because it takes so much longer than email.

split infinitive the often awkward intrusion of an adverb between *to* and the base form of the verb in an infinitive (*to better serve* rather than *to serve better*).

squinting modifier a misplaced word, phrase, or clause that could refer equally, but with different meanings, to words either preceding or following it. For example, in *Playing poker often is dangerous,* the position of *often* fails to indicate whether the writer meant that frequent poker playing is dangerous or that poker playing is often dangerous.

subject the noun or pronoun and related words that indicate who or what a sentence is about. The **simple subject** is the noun or pronoun. The **complete subject** is the simple subject and its modifiers. In *The timid gray mouse fled from the owl, mouse* is the simple subject; *The timid gray mouse* is the complete subject. A **compound subject** includes two or more simple subjects. *The mouse and the owl heard the fox.*

subject complement See *complement.*

subject directory a hyperlinked list of sites, classified by subject, that results from a World Wide Web search.

subjective case See *case.*

subjunctive mood the form of a verb used to express a wish, a suggestion, a request or requirement, or a condition that does not exist. The present subjunctive uses the base form of the verb. *I asked that he be present. Long live the Queen!* The past subjunctive uses the same verb form as the past tense except for the verb *be,* which uses *were* for all subjects. *If I were president, I would change things.* See also *mood.*

subordinate clause a dependent clause. See *clause.*

subordinating conjunction See *conjunction.*

suffix an addition to the end of a word that alters the word's meaning or part of speech, as in *migrate* (verb) and *migration* (noun) or *late* (adjective or adverb) and *lateness* (noun).

superlative degree See *adjective forms, adverb forms.*

synchronous communication online communication in which messages are sent and received as they are being typed, with no delay, as in IRCs, MOOs, and MUDs; also called **real-time communication.**

syntax the arrangement of words in a sentence in order to reveal the relation of each to the whole sentence and to one another.

telnet a program that allows use of one computer from another computer.

tense the form of a verb that indicates the time at which an action takes place or a condition exists. The times expressed by tense are basically **present, past,** and **future.** Each tense has **simple** (*I love*), **perfect** (*I have loved*), **progressive** (*I am loving*), and **perfect progressive** (*I have been loving*) forms.

third person See *person.*

thread a series of postings to a listserv or newsgroup about a particular topic.

transitive verb a verb that takes a direct object, which receives the action expressed by the verb. A transitive verb may be in the active or passive voice. *The artist drew the sketch. The sketch was drawn by the artist.* See also *verb.*

URL (uniform resource locator) a series of characters identifying the address of a homepage or a whole Web site. The URL for the *New St. Martin's Handbook* Web site is <www.bedfordstmartins.com/nsmhandbook>.

Usenet a network within the Internet that provides access to newsgroups. Access to Usenet requires a newsreader program on a computer's local server.

username a series of characters that identifies a computer user and, together with a password, provides access to the user's computer account. Email addresses usually begin with a username.

verb a word or group of words, essential to a sentence, that expresses what action a subject takes or receives or what the subject's state of being is. *Edison invented the incandescent bulb. Gas lighting was becoming obsolete.* Verbs change form to show tense, number, voice, and mood. See also *auxiliary verb, intransitive verb, irregular verb, linking verb, mood, person, regular verb, tense, transitive verb, verbal, voice.*

verbal a verb form that functions as a noun, an adjective, or an adverb. The three kinds of verbals are gerunds, infinitives, and participles. See also *gerund, infinitive, participle.*

verbal phrase a phrase using a gerund, a participle, or an infinitive. See *phrase.*

verb phrase See *phrase.*

virtual existing only in electronic form; having no physical reality.

voice the form of a transitive verb that indicates whether the subject is acting or being acted on. When a verb is in the **active voice,** the subject performs the action. *Parker played the saxophone fantastically.* When a verb is in the **passive voice,** the subject receives the action. *The saxophone was played by Parker.* The passive voice is formed with the appropriate tense of the verb *be* and the past participle of the transitive verb. See also *verb.*

WAIS (Wide Area Information Server) a program that searches Internet databases for keywords. Usually found at central sites like libraries, it is often a service that must be purchased.

Web See *World Wide Web*.

Web site any World Wide Web location.

wired electronic; online.

World Wide Web (WWW) a graphically based international service connecting hypertext data on the Internet.

Glossary of Usage

Conventions of usage might be called the "good manners" of discourse. And just as our notions of good manners vary from culture to culture and time to time, so do conventions of usage. The word *ain't,* for instance, now considered inappropriate in academic and professional discourse, was once widely used by the most proper British speakers and is still commonly used in some spoken U.S. dialects. In short, matters of usage, like other language choices you must make, depend on what your purpose is and on what is appropriate for a particular audience at a particular time. This glossary provides usage guidelines for some commonly confused or otherwise problematic words and phrases. For fuller discussion of these issues, you may want to consult one of the references listed in 25c.

a, an Use *a* with a word that begins with a consonant (*a book*), a consonant sound such as "y" or "w" (*a euphoric moment, a one-sided match*), or a sounded *h* (*a hemisphere*). Use *an* with a word that begins with a vowel (*an umbrella*), a vowel sound (*an X-ray*), or a silent *h* (*an honor*).

accept, except The verb *accept* means "receive" or "agree to." *Except* is usually a preposition that means "aside from" or "excluding." *All the plaintiffs except Mr. Kim decided to accept the settlement.*

advice, advise The noun *advice* means "opinion" or "suggestion"; the verb *advise* means "offer advice." *Charlotte's mother advised her to dress warmly, but Charlotte ignored the advice.*

affect, effect As a verb, *affect* means "influence" or "move the emotions of"; as a noun used by psychologists, it means "emotions." *Effect* is a noun meaning "result"; less commonly, it is a verb meaning "bring about." *The storm affected a large area. Its effects included widespread power failures. The drug effected a major change in the patient's affect.*

aggravate The formal meaning is "make worse." *Having another mouth to feed aggravated their poverty.* In academic writing, avoid using *aggravate* to mean "irritate" or "annoy."

all ready, already *All ready* means "fully prepared." *Already* means "previously." *We were all ready for Lucy's party when we learned that she had already left.*

all right Avoid the spelling *alright.*

all together, altogether *All together* means "all in a group" or "gathered in one place." *Altogether* means "completely" or "everything considered." *When the board members were all together, their mutual distrust was altogether obvious.*

allude, elude *Allude* means "refer indirectly." *Elude* means "avoid" or "escape from." *The candidate did not even allude to her opponent. The suspect eluded the police for several days.*

allusion, illusion An *allusion* is an indirect reference. An *illusion* is a false or misleading appearance. *The speaker's allusion to the Bible created an illusion of piety.*

already See *all ready, already.*

alright See *all right.*

altogether See *all together, altogether.*

among, between In referring to two things or people, use *between.* In referring to three or more, use *among. The relationship between the twins is different from that among the other three children.*

amount, number Use *amount* with quantities you cannot count; use *number* for quantities you can count. *A small number of volunteers cleared a large amount of brush.*

an See *a, an.*

and/or Avoid this term except in business or legal writing. Instead of *fat and/or protein,* write *fat, protein, or both.*

any body, anybody, any one, anyone *Anybody* and *anyone* are pronouns meaning "any person." *Anyone* [or *anybody*] *would enjoy this film. Any body* is an adjective modifying a noun. *Any body of water has its own ecology. Any one* is two adjectives or a pronoun modified by an adjective. *Customers could buy only two sale items at any one time. The winner could choose any one of the prizes.*

anyplace In academic discourse, use *anywhere* instead.

anyway, anyways In writing, use *anyway,* not *anyways.*

apt, liable, likely *Likely to* means "probably will," and *apt to* means "inclines or tends to." In many instances they are interchangeable. *Liable* often carries a more negative sense and is also a legal term meaning "obligated" or "responsible."

as Avoid sentences in which it is not clear if *as* means "because" or means "when." For example, does *Carl left town as his father was arriving* mean "at the same time as his father was arriving" or "because his father was arriving"?

as, as if, like In academic writing, use *as* or *as if* instead of *like* to introduce a clause. *The dog howled as if* [not *like*] *it were in pain. She did as* [not *like*] *I suggested.*

assure, ensure, insure *Assure* means "convince" or "promise"; its direct object is usually a person or persons. *She assured voters she would not raise taxes. Ensure* and *insure* both mean "make certain," but *insure* usually refers specifically to protection against financial loss. *When the city rationed water to ensure that the supply would last, the Browns could no longer afford to insure their car-wash business.*

as to Do not use *as to* as a substitute for *about. Karen was unsure about* [not *as to*] *Bruce's intentions.*

at, where See *where.*

awful, awfully *Awful* and *awfully* mean "awe-inspiring" and "in an awe-inspiring way." In academic writing, avoid using *awful* to mean "bad" (*I had an awful day*) and *awfully* to mean "very" (*It was awfully cold*).

awhile, a while Always use *a while* after a preposition such as *for, in,* or *after. We drove awhile and then stopped for a while.*

bad, badly Use *bad* after a linking verb such as *be, feel,* or *seem.* Use *badly* to modify an action verb, an adjective, or another adverb. *The hostess felt bad because the dinner was badly prepared.*

because of, due to Use *due to* when the effect, stated as a noun, appears before the verb *be. His illness was due to malnutrition.* (*Illness,* a noun, is the effect.) Use *because of* when the effect is stated as a clause. *He was sick because of malnutrition.* (*He was sick,* a clause, is the effect.)

being as, being that In academic writing, use *because* or *since* instead of these expressions. *Because* [not *being as*] *Romeo killed Tybalt, he was banished to Padua.*

beside, besides *Beside* is a preposition meaning "next to." *Besides* can be a preposition meaning "other than" or an adverb meaning "in addition." *No one besides Francesca would sit beside him.*

between See *among, between.*

breath, breathe *Breath* is a noun; *breathe,* a verb. *"Breathe," said the nurse, so June took a deep breath.*

bring, take Use *bring* when an object is moved from a farther to a nearer place; use *take* when the opposite is true. *Take the box to the post office; bring back my mail.*

but, yet Do not use these words together. *He is strong but* [not *but yet*] *gentle.*

but that, but what Avoid using these as substitutes for *that* in expressions of doubt. *Hercule Poirot never doubted that* [not *but that*] *he would solve the case.*

can, may *Can* refers to ability and *may* to possibility or permission. *Since I can ski the slalom well, I may win the race.*

can't hardly *Hardly* has a negative meaning; therefore *can't hardly* is a double negative. This expression is commonly used in some varieties of English but is not used in standard academic English. *Tim can* [not *can't*] *hardly wait.*

can't help but This expression is redundant. Use the more formal *I cannot but go* or less formal *I can't help going* rather than *I can't help but go.*

censor, censure *Censor* means "remove that which is considered offensive." *Censure* means "formally reprimand." *The newspaper censored stories that offended advertisers. The legislature censured the official for misconduct.*

complement, compliment *Complement* means "go well with." *Compliment* means "praise." *Guests complimented her on how her earrings complemented her gown.*

comprise, compose *Comprise* means "contain" (*the whole comprises the parts*). *Compose* means "make up" (*the parts compose the whole*). *The class comprises twenty students. Twenty students compose the class.*

conscience, conscious *Conscience* means "a sense of right and wrong." *Conscious* means "awake" or "aware." *After lying, Lisa was conscious of a guilty conscience.*

consensus of opinion Use *consensus* instead of this redundant phrase. *The family consensus was to sell the old house.*

consequently, subsequently *Consequently* means "as a result"; *subsequently* means "then." *He quit, and subsequently his wife lost her job; consequently, they had to sell their house.*

continual, continuous *Continual* means "repeated at regular or frequent intervals." *Continuous* means "continuing or connected without a break." *The damage done by continuous erosion was increased by the continual storms.*

could of *Have,* not *of,* should follow *could, would, should,* or *might. We should have* [not *of*] *invited them.*

criteria, criterion *Criterion* means "standard of judgment" or "necessary qualification." *Criteria* is the plural form. *Image is the wrong criterion for choosing a president.*

data *Data* is the plural form of the Latin word *datum,* meaning "fact." Although *data* is used informally as either singular or plural, in academic writing, treat *data* as plural. *These data indicate that fewer people are smoking.*

different from, different than *Different from* is generally preferred in academic writing, although both phrases are used widely. *Her lab results were no different from* [not *than*] *his.*

discreet, discrete *Discreet* means "tactful" or "prudent." *Discrete* means "separate" or "distinct." *The leader's discreet efforts kept all the discrete factions unified.*

disinterested, uninterested *Disinterested* means "unbiased." *Uninterested* means "indifferent." *Finding disinterested jurors was difficult. She was uninterested in the verdict.*

distinct, distinctive *Distinct* means "separate" or "well defined." *Distinctive* means "characteristic." *Germany includes many distinct regions, each with a distinctive accent.*

doesn't, don't *Doesn't* is the contraction for *does not.* Use it with *he, she, it,* and singular nouns. *Don't* stands for *do not;* use it with *I, you, we, they,* and plural nouns.

due to See *because of, due to.*

each other, one another Use *each other* in sentences involving two subjects and *one another* in sentences involving more than two.

effect See *affect, effect.*

elicit, illicit The verb *elicit* means "draw out." The adjective *illicit* means "illegal." *The police elicited from the criminal the names of others involved in illicit activities.*

elude See *allude, elude.*

emigrate from, immigrate to *Emigrate from* means "move away from one's country." *Immigrate to* means "move to another country." *We emigrated from Norway in 1957. We immigrated to the United States.*

ensure See *assure, ensure, insure.*

enthused Use *enthusiastic* instead in academic writing.

equally as good Replace this redundant phrase with *equally good* or *as good.*

every day, everyday *Everyday* is an adjective meaning "ordinary." *Every day* is an adjective and a noun, meaning "each day." *I wore everyday clothes almost every day.*

every one, everyone *Everyone* is a pronoun. *Every one* is an adjective and a pronoun, referring to each member of a group. *Because he began after everyone else, David could not finish every one of the problems.*

except See *accept, except.*

explicit, implicit *Explicit* means "directly or openly expressed." *Implicit* means "indirectly expressed or implied." *The explicit message of the ad urged consumers to buy the product, while the implicit message promised popularity if they did so.*

farther, further *Farther* refers to physical distance. *How much farther is it to Munich? Further* refers to time or degree. *I want to avoid further delays.*

fewer, less Use *fewer* with nouns that can be counted. Use *less* with general amounts that you cannot count. *The world will be safer with fewer bombs and less hostility.*

finalize *Finalize* is a pretentious way of saying "end" or "make final." *We closed* [not *finalized*] *the deal.*

firstly, secondly, etc. *First, second,* etc., are more common in U.S. English.

flaunt, flout *Flaunt* means to "show off." *Flout* means to "mock" or "scorn." *The drug dealers flouted authority by flaunting their wealth.*

former, latter *Former* refers to the first and *latter* to the second of two things previously mentioned. *Kathy and Anna are athletes; the former plays tennis, and the latter runs.*

further See *farther, further.*

good, well *Good* is an adjective and should not be used as a substitute for the adverb *well. Gabriel is a good host who cooks well.*

good and *Good and* is colloquial for "very"; avoid it in academic writing.

hanged, hung *Hanged* refers to executions; *hung* is used for all other meanings.

hardly See *can't hardly.*

herself, himself, myself, yourself Do not use these reflexive pronouns as subjects or as objects unless they are necessary. *Jane and I* [not *myself*] *agree. They invited John and me* [not *myself*].

he/she, his/her Better solutions for avoiding sexist language are to write out *he or she,* to eliminate pronouns entirely, or to make the subject plural. Instead of writing *Everyone should carry his/her driver's license,* try *Drivers should carry their licenses* or *People should carry their driver's licenses.*

himself See *herself, himself, myself, yourself.*

hisself Use *himself* instead in academic writing.

hopefully *Hopefully* is often misused to mean "it is hoped," but its correct meaning is "with hope." *Sam watched the roulette wheel hopefully* [not *Hopefully, Sam will win*].

hung See *hanged, hung.*

illicit See *elicit, illicit.*

illusion See *allusion, illusion.*

immigrate to See *emigrate from, immigrate to.*

impact Avoid the colloquial use of *impact* or *impact on* as a verb meaning "affect." *Population control may reduce* [not *impact*] *world hunger.*

implicit See *explicit, implicit.*

imply, infer To *imply* is to suggest indirectly. To *infer* is to guess or conclude on the basis of an indirect suggestion. *The note implied they were planning a small wedding; we inferred we would not be invited.*

infer See *imply, infer.*

inside of, outside of Use *inside* and *outside* instead. *The class regularly met outside* [not *outside of*] *the building.*

insure See *assure, ensure, insure.*

interact, interface *Interact* is a vague word meaning "do something that somehow involves another person." *Interface* is computer jargon for "discuss" or "communicate." Avoid both words in academic writing.

irregardless, regardless *Irregardless* is a double negative. Use *regardless.*

is when, is where These vague expressions are often incorrectly used in definitions. *Schizophrenia is a psychological condition in which* [not *is when* or *is where*] *a person withdraws from reality.*

its, it's *Its* is the possessive form of *it. It's* is a contraction for *it is* or *it has. It's important to observe the rat before it eats its meal.*

kind, sort, type These singular nouns should be modified with *this* or *that,* not *these* or *those,* and followed by other singular nouns, not plural nouns. *Wear this kind of dress* [not *those kind of dresses*].

kind of, sort of Avoid these colloquialisms. *Amy was somewhat* [not *kind of*] *tired.*

later, latter *Later* means "after some time." *Latter* refers to the second of two items named. *Juan and Chad won all their early matches, but the latter was injured later in the season.*

latter See *former, latter* and *later, latter.*

lay, lie *Lay* means "place" or "put." Its main forms are *lay, laid, laid.* It generally has a direct object, specifying what has been placed. *She laid her books on the desk. Lie* means "recline" or "be positioned" and does not take a direct object. Its main forms are *lie, lay, lain. She lay awake until two.*

leave, let *Leave* means "go away." *Let* means "allow." *Leave alone* and *let alone* are interchangeable. *Let me leave now, and leave* [or *let*] *me alone from now on!*

lend, loan In academic writing, do not use *loan* as a verb; use *lend* instead. *Please lend me your pen so that I may fill out this application for a loan.*

less See *fewer, less.*

let See *leave, let.*

liable See *apt, liable, likely.*

lie See *lay, lie.*

like See *as, as if, like.*

likely See *apt, liable, likely.*

literally *Literally* means "actually" or "exactly as stated." Use it to stress the truth of a statement that might otherwise be understood as figurative. Do not use *literally* as an intensifier in a figurative statement. *Mirna was literally on the edge of her seat* may be accurate, but *Mirna is so hungry that she could literally eat a horse* is not.

loan See *lend, loan.*

loose, lose *Lose* is a verb meaning "misplace." *Loose* is an adjective that means "not securely attached." *Sew on that loose button before you lose it.*

lots, lots of Avoid these informal expressions meaning "much" or "many" in academic discourse.

man, mankind To refer to human beings in general, use *people, humans, humankind, men and women,* or similar wording instead of *man* or *mankind.*

may See *can, may.*

may be, maybe *May be* is a verb phrase. *Maybe* is an adverb that means "perhaps." *He may be the president today, but maybe he will lose the next election.*

media *Media* is the plural form of the noun *medium* and takes a plural verb. *The media are* [not *is*] *obsessed with scandals.*

might of See *could of.*

moral, morale A *moral* is a succinct lesson. *The moral of the story is that generosity is rewarded. Morale* means "spirit" or "mood." *Office morale was low.*

myself See *herself, himself, myself, yourself.*

nor, or Use *either* with *or* and *neither* with *nor.*

number See *amount, number.*

off of Use *off* without *of. The spaghetti slipped off* [not *off of*] *the plate.*

OK, O.K., okay All are acceptable spellings, but avoid the term in academic discourse.

on account of Use this substitute for *because of* sparingly or not at all.

one another See *each other, one another.*

or See *nor, or.*

outside of See *inside of, outside of.*

owing to the fact that Avoid this and other wordy expressions for *because.*

per Use the Latin *per* only in standard technical phrases such as *miles per hour.* Otherwise, find English equivalents. *As mentioned in* [not *As per*] *the latest report, the country's average food consumption each day* [not *per day*] *is only 2,000 calories.*

percent, percentage Use *percent* with a specific number; use *percentage* with an adjective such as *large* or *small. Last year, 80 percent of the members were female. A large percentage of the members are women.*

plenty *Plenty* means "enough" or "a great abundance." *They told us America was a land of plenty.* Colloquially, it is used to mean "very," a usage you should avoid in academic writing. *He was very* [not *plenty*] *tired.*

plus *Plus* means "in addition to." *Your salary plus mine will cover our expenses.* Do not use *plus* to mean "besides" or "moreover." *That dress does not fit me. Besides* [not *Plus*], *it is the wrong color.*

precede, proceed *Precede* means "come before"; *proceed* means "go forward." *Despite the storm that preceded the ceremony, it proceeded on schedule.*

pretty Avoid using *pretty* as a substitute for "rather," "somewhat," or "quite." *Bill was quite* [not *pretty*] *disagreeable.*

principal, principle As a noun, *principal* refers to a head official or an amount of money; as an adjective, it means "most significant." *Principle* means "fundamental law or belief." *Albert went to the principal and defended himself with the principle of free speech.*

proceed See *precede, proceed.*

quotation, quote *Quote* is a verb, and *quotation* is a noun. *He quoted the president, and the quotation* [not *quote*] *was preserved in history books.*

raise, rise *Raise* means "lift" or "move upward." (Referring to children, it means "bring up.") It takes a direct object; someone raises something. *The guests raised their glasses for a toast. Rise* means "go upward." It does not take a direct object; something rises by itself. *She saw the steam rise from the pan.*

rarely ever Use *rarely* by itself, or use *hardly ever. When we were poor, we rarely went to the movies.*

real, really *Real* is an adjective, and *really* is an adverb. Do not substitute *real* for *really.* In academic writing, do not use *real* or *really* to mean "very." *The old man walked very* [not *real* or *really*] *slowly.*

reason is because Use either *the reason is that* or *because* – not both. *The reason the copier stopped is that* [not *is because*] *the paper jammed.*

reason why This expression is redundant. *The reason* [not *reason why*] *this book is short is market demand.*

regardless See *irregardless, regardless.*

respectfully, respectively *Respectfully* means "with respect." *Respectively* means "in the order given." *Karen and David are, respectively, a juggler and an acrobat. The children treated their grandparents respectfully.*

rise See *raise, rise.*

set, sit *Set* usually means "put" or "place" and takes a direct object. *Sit* refers to taking a seat and does not take an object. *Set your cup on the table, and sit down.*

should of See *could of.*

since Be careful not to use *since* ambiguously. In *Since I broke my leg, I've stayed home, since* might be understood to mean either "because" or "ever since."

sit See *set, sit.*

so In academic writing, avoid using *so* alone to mean "very." Instead, follow *so* with *that* to show how the intensified condition leads to a result. *Aaron was so tired that he fell asleep at the wheel.*

someplace Use *somewhere* instead in academic writing.

some time, sometime, sometimes *Some time* refers to a length of time. *Please leave me some time to dress. Sometime* means "at some indefinite later time." *Sometime I will take you to London. Sometimes* means "occasionally." *Sometimes I eat sushi.*

sort See *kind, sort, type.*

sort of See *kind of, sort of.*

stationary, stationery *Stationary* means "standing still"; *stationery* means "writing paper." *When the bus was stationary, Pat took out stationery and wrote a note.*

subsequently See *consequently, subsequently.*

supposed to, used to Be careful to include the final *-d* in these expressions. *He is supposed to attend.*

sure, surely Avoid using *sure* as an intensifier. Instead use *surely* (or *certainly* or *without a doubt*). *I was surely glad to see you.*

take See *bring, take.*

than, then Use *than* in comparative statements. *The cat was bigger than the dog.* Use *then* when referring to a sequence of events. *I won, and then I cried.*

that, which A clause beginning with *that* singles out the item being described. *The book that is on the table is a good one* specifies the book on the table as opposed to some other book. A clause beginning with *which* may or may not single out the item, although some writers use *which* clauses only to add more information about an item being described. *The book, which is on the table, is a good one* contains a *which* clause between the commas. The clause simply adds extra, nonessential information about the book; it does not specify which book.

theirselves Use *themselves* instead in academic writing.

then See *than, then.*

to, too, two *To* generally shows direction. *Too* means "also." *Two* is the number. *We, too, are going to the meeting in two hours.* Avoid using *to* after *where. Where are you flying* [not *flying to*]?

two See *to, too, two.*

type See *kind, sort, type.*

uninterested See *disinterested, uninterested.*

unique *Unique* means "the one and only." Do not use it with adverbs that suggest degree, such as *very* or *most. Adora's paintings are unique* [not *very unique*].

used to See *supposed to, used to.*

very Avoid using *very* to intensify a weak adjective or adverb; instead, replace the adjective or adverb with a stronger, more precise, or more colorful word. Instead of *very nice,* for example, use *kind, warm, sensitive, endearing,* or *friendly.*

way, ways When referring to distance, use *way. Graduation was a long way* [not *ways*] *off.*

well See *good, well.*

where Use *where* alone, not with words such as *at* and *to. Where are you going?* [not *Where are you going to?*].

which See *that, which.*

who, whom In relative clauses, use *who* if the following clause begins with a verb. *Monica, who smokes incessantly, is my godmother.* (*Who* is followed by the verb *smokes.*) *Monica, who is my godmother, smokes incessantly.* (*Who* is followed by the verb *is.*) Use *whom* if the following clause begins with a noun or pronoun. *I have heard that Monica, whom I have not seen for ten years, wears only purple.* (*Whom* is followed by the pronoun *I.*) An exception occurs when a verbal phrase such as *I think* comes between *who* and the following clause. Ignore such a phrase as you decide which form to use. *Monica, who* [*I think*] *wears nothing but purple, is my godmother.* (Ignore *I think; who* is followed by the verb *wears.*)

who's, whose *Who's* is the contraction of *who is* or *who has. Who's the president of the club? Who's been using my computer? Whose* is a possessive form. *Whose coat is that on the chair?*

would of See *could of.*

yet See *but, yet.*

your, you're *Your* shows possession. *Bring your sleeping bag along. You're* is the contraction of *you* and *are. You're in the wrong sleeping bag.*

yourself See *herself, himself, myself, yourself.*

A Directory of Web Sites for Writers

This list is based on the work of Nick Carbone, of Colorado State University, who is widely known and respected as a teacher and scholar of online discourse. With so much useful information now available on the World Wide Web, we have designed *The New St. Martin's Handbook* to serve as a kind of atlas to useful Web sites for writers. All the sites listed here can be accessed via our own site at:

www.bedfordstmartins.com/nsmhandbook

The Writing Process

THE WRITERY
http://www.missouri.edu/~writery
A site from the University of Missouri offering writing advice via email as well as an open discussion list.

NETIQUETTE HOME PAGE
http://www.albion.com/netiquette/index.html
Provides links to a netiquette quiz and an online version of Virginia Shea's Netiquette, *with chapters on writing online, flaming, electronic style, and conventions of business and discussion group netiquette.*

THE PURDUE ONLINE WRITING LAB
http://www.owl@omni.cc.purdue.edu
Handouts on writing-related issues as well as an extensive list of other useful resources on the Web.

THE UNIVERSITY OF TEXAS WRITING CENTER
http://uwc.fac.utexas.edu
Resources on writing well in college, including handouts on specific issues such as revision and documentation. Includes many useful links to other helpful sites.

THE PARADIGM ONLINE WRITING ASSISTANT
http://www.spaceland.org/paradigm/whtfrms.htm
Advice and prompts to help you through all stages of the writing process.

THE ACADEMIC SKILLS PAGE
http://www.dartmouth.edu/admin/acskills/
Tips from Dartmouth College on reading and other study skills. Click on Learning Strategies Guides.

AMERICAN STORIES
http://www.wwcd.org/action/ampu/bray.html
A short essay on the importance of talking and listening to sustain a civil and culturally diverse society; author Rosemary Bray argues for the importance of shared stories and a kind ear.

THE COLLABORATOR
http://www.shout.net/~sigfried/
A site where you can post work for response.

TIPS ON WRITING ESSAY EXAMINATIONS
http://www.cohums.ohio-state.edu/history/essayexm.htm
Tips on writing essay exams, with useful — and downloadable — test-taking strategies.

THE WRITER A LA MODEM

http://www.levity.com/julian/alamodem.html
An essay by Julian Dibbell about how going online helped him as a writer.

DEJANEWS

http://www.dejanews.com/
Sometimes you can't find anyone who can talk with you about a topic. If so, try DejaNews, a tool for searching Usenet discussion groups.

INTRODUCTIONS AND THESIS STATEMENTS

http://www.hamilton.edu/academic/resource/wc/Intro_Thesis.html
This page by two students at Hamilton College provides useful advice and samples from student papers in many disciplines.

TEXAS A & M WRITING CENTER

http://www-english.tamu.edu/wcenter/journal.html
Questions to help you analyze an essay.

OCCASIONS FOR ARGUMENTATIVE ESSAYS

http://www.idbsu.edu/english/cguilfor/paradigm/argument.htm
An essay on argumentation with good definitions, examples, and charts — and links to many useful guidelines.

WHY AMERICANS CAN'T ARGUE

http://www.dartmouth.edu/alumni/almag/rhetoric1.html
Explores the need for civil discussion and fair argument in public debate.

GUIDE TO THE LOGICAL FALLACIES

http://calvin.assiniboinec.mb.ca/user/downes/fall/
Definitions and examples of fallacies from philosophy, rhetoric, and logic texts, with an excellent reference list.

WRITING PARAGRAPHS

http://aix1.uottawa.ca/academic/arts/writcent/hypergrammar/paragrph.html
A page providing an excellent overview and exercises, part of the University of Ottawa's HyperGrammar *site, a wonderful resource in itself.*

YALE C/AIM WEB STYLE GUIDE

http://info.med.yale.edu/caim/manual/pages/page_design.html
One of the most comprehensive guides to Web design.

Sentence Grammar

GRAMMAR AND STYLE NOTES

http://www.english.upenn.edu/~jlynch/Grammar/
Provides explanations of conventions of grammar, style, punctuation, and usage, broken into a file for each letter of the alphabet (for example: click on "a" for information on adjectives and adverbs).

THE LINGUA CENTER

http://deil.lang.uiuc.edu/web.pages/grammarsafari.html
Helps you get beyond the "safe confines of grammar books" to explore English on the Web. Want to hunt for adjective clauses in Little Women? *The* Grammar Safari *will show you how.*

THE WRITER'S COMPLEX

http://www.esc.edu/htmlpages/writer/workshop.htm
From Empire State College, this online writer's workshop offers good explanations and exercises. Click on Grammar Workout *for advice on structuring sentences.*

ASK A LINGUIST

http://linguistlist.org/~ask-ling/index.html
Not sure whether to use who or whom? *Go to this site, where a panel of linguists will answer questions about language.*

HOW TO MAKE SENTENCES CLEAR AND CONCISE
http://www.urich.edu/~writing/concise.htm
This downloadable reference sheet will help you identify and edit weak verbs.

HOW CAN I IDENTIFY WEAK VERBS?
http://www.io.com/~eighner/qa050152.html
This essay by Lars Eighner suggests a hierarchy for distinguishing weak from strong verbs.

HUNTER COLLEGE WRITING CENTER
http://myst.hunter.cuny.edu/~rwcenter/writing/on-line/sva.html
A downloadable exercise offering three ways to practice subject-verb agreement.

GRAMMAR AND WRITING
http://webster.commnet.edu/hp/pages/darling/grammar_original.htm
From Capital Community Technical College. Click on Quiz on Subject-Verb Agreement.

THE KING'S ENGLISH
http://www.columbia.edu/acis/bartleby/fowler
The 1908 version of H. W. Fowler's classic work.

WOMEN WHO DARED TO DISTURB THE LEXICON
http://vega.lib.vt.edu/ejournals/WILLA/fall94/h2-isele.html
An interview with two women who were among the first to question the generic use of he.

GEORGE ORWELL'S "POLITICS AND THE ENGLISH LANGUAGE"
http://english-www.hss.cmu.edu/langs/politics-english-language.txt
Download this classic essay for Orwell's advice on adjectives, and also as a text well worth examining. Read closely to see if Orwell follows his own advice.

SHAKESPEAREAN INSULTS
http://www.contrib.andrew.cmu.edu/user/bayer/humor/shakeinsult.html
Let thyself go: here you will find many inventive adjectives in a list of insults that sound Shakespearean.

WORDNET
http://www.cogsci.princeton.edu/~wn/
An online reference database of English nouns, verbs, adjectives, and adverbs that allows you to see words in many forms and to search for synonyms and antonyms (and much more).

Sentence Conventions

GUIDE TO GRAMMAR AND WRITING
http://webster.commnet.edu/hp/pages/darling/grammar/consistency.htm
A short page offering good examples of shifts in verb tense and "things we have to remember about pronoun reference" along with links to quizzes and other grammar resources.

EDITING AND PROOFREADING STRATEGIES FOR SENTENCE-LEVEL ERRORS
http://leo.stcloud.msus.edu/acadwrite/editing.html
Tips on how to proofread for comma splices, fragments, and other common errors.

MISPLACED MODIFIERS
http://www.engr.trinity.edu/~Review/1995/gallman24.html
This poem of longing and memory by Geoff Alman includes the lovely line "yet even misplaced modifiers reveal a propensity for intention," which is the reason we point you to it.

A COLLECTION OF AMBIGUOUS, INCONSISTENT, AND INCOMPLETE STATEMENTS
http://www.vuse.vanderbilt.edu/~jgray/funny.html
A treasure trove of inconsistent and incomplete statements from the real world (one favorite: the ad offering "dress shirts for men with 16 necks").

Sentence Style

THE ONLINE ELEMENTS OF STYLE
http://www.columbia.edu/acis/bartleby/strunk
Strunk and White's classic advice on usage and style.

WRITER'S WORKBENCH
http://www.emo.com/wwb/index.html
Information on stylistic issues with links to other programs on diction, spelling, punctuation, and so on.

WHAT IS A CONJUNCTION?
http://aix1.uottawa.ca/academic/arts/writcent/hypergrammar/conjunct.html co-ordinating conjunction
From the University of Ottawa's wonderful Hyper-Grammar *comes this clear and thorough advice on using coordinating and subordinating conjunctions.*

Effective Words

WEBSTER'S DICTIONARY ONLINE
http://c.gp.cs.cmu.edu:5103/prog/webster?
Search for definitions of any word in the dictionary.

THE NEW HACKER'S DICTIONARY
http://www.infowar.com/hacker/hack_042198f_j.shtml
Definitions of online jargon and discussions of such topics as "how jargon works," "hacker writing style," and so on.

WIRED STYLE
http://www.hotwired.com/hardwired/wiredstyle/
Advice on how to use the new language of the digital age.

MERRIAM WEBSTER'S DICTIONARY ON THE NET
http://www.m-w.com/netdict.htm
Wild card searches: if you recall how to spell only the beginning of carabiner *(an oblong, hinged metal ring used in climbing), you can enter* carab* *and choose* carabiner *from the list of words that begin with* cara.

A WEB OF ONLINE DICTIONARIES
http://www.bucknell.edu/~rbeard/diction.html
Links to 400 dictionaries in over 130 languages.

SYNONYMS DICTIONARY
http://vancouver-webpages.com/synonyms.html
Type in a word and this online dictionary will find its synonym.

WORD FOR WORD
http://peg.pegasus.oz.au/~toconnor/
Explores the history and origins of words and phrases.

ROGET'S THESAURUS OF ENGLISH WORDS AND PHRASES ON THE WEB
http://www.thesaurus.com/
A wonderful tool site offering hypertextual searches of the famed thesaurus.

THE USE OF CLICHÉS
http://www.nexus.edu.au/teachstud/dexed/docs/cliche.html
The account of an English teacher named Ms. English with an ax to grind who told her students to avoid clichés like the plague, this piece by Graeden Horsell says that sometimes clichés are needed, and that one should never say "never."

LANGUAGE POLICY WEB SITE AND EMPORIUM
http://ourworld.compuserve.com/homepages/JWCRAWFORD/home.htm
Links to articles and Web sites on many language policy issues, including the English Only movement, bilingual education, Ebonics, endangered languages, and language rights.

AFRICAN AMERICAN ENGLISH
http://www.cal.org/ebonics/
The Center for Applied Linguistics sponsors this page about African American vernacular English; it includes many useful links.

NONSEXIST LANGUAGE
http://www.stetson.edu/~history/nongenderlang.html

An essay exploring the origins of the practice of assigning masculine pronouns in gender-neutral or gender-inclusive situations and offering alternatives to the practice.

Punctuation

WWB STYLE PROGRAM
http://www.emo.com/wwb/index.html
A helpful program on punctuation.

THE MYSTERIOUS COMMA
http://www.fas.harvard.edu/~wricntr/comma.html
A handy page on "the mysterious comma" offering four tips for comma use.

A PUNCTUATION MISCELLANY
http://b11.edu.aca.mmu.ac.uk/Punct/Misc.html
Amusing, thought-provoking observations.

EMOTICONS AND SMILEYS
http://www.windweaver.com/emoticon.htm
This good list of emoticons is indexed by emotion: click on happy, trying to communicate, and so on.

Mechanics

INTERNET ACRONYMS DICTIONARY
http://home3.inet.tele.dk/hgaarde/Acronyms.html
Lists acronyms commonly used in email, Usenet, real-time discussions, and Web-based bulletin boards, including many acronyms that are used mostly by insiders. If you ever run into AWGTHTGTATA, *you'll know where to look it up.*

ONELOOK SITE
http://www.onelook.com/browse.shtml#all_acronym
This collection of acronyms dictionaries includes general interest, military, and Internet acronyms.

COUNTERPOINT
http://counterpoint.mit.edu/staff/writer/index.html
Guidelines for writers who submit text via email. Go there for sound advice on when to use italics as well as unique advice on how to indicate when italics should *be used.*

COMPUTER TIPS
http://www.computertips.com/
This site exists to help you find answers to computer-use problems. If you have trouble using the automatic hypenating function of your word processor, type in hyphenating as a search term to get help.

Research

ADVANCED SEARCHING: TRICKS OF THE TRADE
http://www.onlineinc.com/onlinemag/MayOL/zorn5.html
Advice on doing online research, from Peggy Zorn, Mary Emanoil, Luc Marshall, and Mary Panek.

WEB SITE EVALUATION
http://www.marlboro.edu/~nickc/research/evallist.html
Mary D. Been's list of Web site evaluation guides.

DOING RESEARCH ON THE WEB
http://www.cohums.ohio-state.edu/english/People/Locker.1/research.htm
Kitty Locker's step-by-step guidance to online research.

ONLINE! A REFERENCE GUIDE TO USING INTERNET SOURCES
http://www.smpcollege.com/online-4styles~help/toc.html
The electronic version of Andrew Harnack and Eugene Kleppinger's Online! *provides guidelines for documenting online sources using four different styles—MLA, APA, Chicago, and CBE.*

CITATIONS OF ELECTRONIC SOURCES
http://www.cas.usf.edu/english/walker/mla.html
Janice Walker provides this list.

CITATION GUIDES FOR ELECTRONIC DOCUMENTS
http://www.nlc-bnc.ca/ifla/I/training/citation/citing.htm
Eric Crump offers this list of style guides, online and off. One of the most comprehensive such lists, with lots of useful links.

INFO ZONE
http://www.mbnet.mb.ca/~mstimson/
This site clusters resources under steps in the research process, among them Wondering, Seeking, and Choosing. Even though it was designed for K – 12, many of the links will prove most useful for the college researcher as well.

STUDY SKILLS
http://www.csbsju.edu/advising/helplist.html
From the academic advising office of the College of St. Benedict/St. John's University comes this site full of study skills advice and with 21 links to tips on time management, taking an essay exam, effective reading and note-taking, and other academic skills.

A+ RESEARCH AND WRITING
http://www.ipl.org/teen/aplus/stepfirst.htm
From the Internet Public Library comes this site that offers a step-by-step approach to doing research. This page focuses on the beginning of research: preparing the assignment, discovering information, formulating a thesis, and gathering information. This site has many useful links.

THE DIRECTORY OF SCHOLARLY AND PROFESSIONAL E-CONFERENCES
http://www.n2h2.com/KOVACS/
This directory of e-conferences holds the best searchable data base of scholarly and professional discussions, covering both email lists and Usenet groups and offering a good forum for finding people interested and knowledgeable in your research area. Diane Kovacs updates the site regularly.

FINDING INFORMATION ON THE INTERNET: A TUTORIAL
http://www.lib.berkeley.edu/TeachingLib/Guides/Internet/FindInfo.html
From the library of the University of California at Berkeley, this site is consistently updated and keeps track of new trends in search engine protocols and browser developments, incorporating them into self-directed tutorials.

HOW TO SEARCH THE WEB: A GUIDE TO SEARCH TOOLS
http://daphne.palomar.edu/TGSEARCH/
Knowing how to use different search engines and how to phrase and punctuate your search terms will determine the quality of your WWW searches. This guide by Terry Gray offers expert advice on using 10 powerful search engines, as well as links to other resources for search advice.

THE INTERNET PUBLIC LIBRARY
http://www.ipl.org/
The American Library Association <www.ala.org> recommends this site, which organizes information according to subject categories, but more important, does a good job in choosing worthwhile sources (though you should still be independently critical), and of keeping links updated.

THE MOO CENTRAL HELP PAGE
http://139.182.93.107/jrgst7/MOOcentral.html
Written by Jeff Galin, this site offers links and leads on how to find and use educational MOOs and MUDs.

A STUDENT'S GUIDE TO RESEARCH WITH THE WWW
http://www.slu.edu/departments/english/research/
Designed by Craig Branham, this site offers tips for evaluating Web sources and reading a Web page, with discussion of different types of Web pages and a full tutorial on Web search strategies.

ONLINE OMBUDS NARRATIVE I
http://www.ombuds.org/narrative1.html
This narrative from the Online Ombudsman <www.ombuds.org> describes a case involving a person

whose Web site included summaries of a particular newspaper's articles. The debate provides a good example of how complex the issues of plagiarism and copyright can be in cyberspace.

WRITER'S CORNER DISCUSSION
http://www.researchpaper.com/forums/Writers_Corner/index.html
Discuss writing strategies and tips with other students and researchers who are working on their own research projects. Follow the URL back to <http://www.researchpaper.com/forums/> and you'll find links to research discussions organized by subject area.

TIPS FOR EFFECTIVE PROOFREADING
http://www.ualr.edu/~owl/proofrd.htm
Item 1 on this list of proofreading tips makes this short list worth consulting and printing out for later reference.

THE MODERN LANGUAGE ASSOCIATION SITE
http://www.mla.org/set_stl.htm
Go here for the MLA's most current style for citing electronic sources.

THE AMERICAN PSYCHOLOGICAL ASSOCIATION SITE
http://www.apa.org/journals/webref.html
This page gives the APA's most recent advice about using and citing Internet sources; check out its link to student FAQs on citing electronic sources.

THE COUNCIL OF BIOLOGY EDITORS STYLE
http://www.smpcollege.com/online-4styles~help
The CBE does not have guidelines for citing Internet sources on its own site, but Andrew Harnack and Eugene Kleppinger offer a way to do so following the principles in the 6th edition of The CBE Manual.

THE CHICAGO MANUAL OF STYLE FAQ (AND NOT SO FAQ)
http://www.press.uchicago.edu/Misc/Chicago/cmosfaq.html
Go here for the most current advice about Chicago *style, or submit your own questions about style.*

Academic Disciplines

INVENTION TECHNIQUES
http://myst.hunter.cuny.edu/~rwcenter/writing/on-line/invention.html
From Hunter College, this site offers questions and ways of thinking about topics that can be applied across disciplines and discourse communities.

SCHOLARLY JOURNALS DISTRIBUTED ON THE WEB
http://info.lib.uh.edu/wj/webjour.html
A directory with links to Web-based scholarly journals available free of charge. Maintained by the University of Houston.

ANALYZING AN ESSAY OR ARTICLE
http://www-english.tamu.edu/wcenter/journal.html
Provides a way to discern the academic conventions and styles of a discipline. Maintained by Texas A&M's writing center.

LITERARY RESOURCES
http://www.lib.lsu.edu/hum/lit.html
Excellent links for literary and literature resources.

LITERARY RESEARCH TOOLS ON THE NET
http://www.english.upenn.edu/~jlynch/Lit/
A searchable collection of links to sites dealing with American and English literature.

THE VOICE OF THE SHUTTLE
http://humanitas.ucsb.edu/
An especially rich Web site for humanities research, maintained by Alan Liu, the University of California at Santa Barbara.

ART

WWW VIRTUAL LIBRARY — ART
http://www.fisk.edu/vl/Literature/Overview.html
An excellent collection of links to both art and literature sites. Includes links to other virtual libraries.

HISTORY OF ART VIRTUAL LIBRARY
http://www.hart.bbk.ac.uk/VirtualLibrary.html
Includes links to art history sites, museums, galleries, art history organizations, and university art departments.

NATIONAL GALLERY OF ART
http://www.nga.gov/
Images from the collection and news about current displays and educational opportunities.

WORLD ART TREASURES
http://sgwww.epfl.ch/BERGER/index.html
In-depth links to selected artists' works and to areas of art, with good links to other sites.

VIRTUAL LIBRARY MUSEUMS PAGE
http://www.comlab.ox.ac.uk/archive/other/museums.html
A large number of links to recent and current exhibitions at many major museums, by country.

ART HISTORY RESOURCES ON THE WEB
http://witcombe.bcpw.sbc.edu/ARTHLinks.html
An extraordinarily detailed set of chronologically organized links to art history sources, from prehistoric through modern.

H-GIG ART HISTORY
http://www.ucr.edu/h-gig/horuslinks.html
Easy links to some of the best art history sources and directories, based in the large HORUS system at the University of California at Riverside. Smaller and more manageable than some of the full-service sites. Click on Art History.

BIOLOGY AND BIOSCIENCES

BIOSCIENCES INDEX
http://golgi.harvard.edu/htbin/biopages
Allows searching by keyword and provides an alphabetical list of links for specialties within the biosciences.

PASTEUR INSTITUTE
http://web.pasteur.fr/search/
Allows keyword searches of the Pasteur Institute's server and many other English-language-based bioscience servers.

WWW VIRTUAL LIBRARY — BIOSCIENCES
http://golgi.harvard.edu/biopages.html
Categorizes information by provider and subject. A good place to begin research, this site includes many links to journals, FTP sites, and subdisciplines.

HUMAN GENOME PROJECT
http://www.nhgri.nih.gov/index.html
The homepage for this important research project; situated at the National Institutes of Health.

NATIONAL SCIENCE FOUNDATION: BIOLOGY
http://www.nsf.gov/home/bio/start.htm
The site of the primary government agency funding scientific research. Allows a search of its Biology Directorate's sources and includes links to online documents, grants, and specific fields within biology.

INTERNET RESOURCES OF INTEREST
http://lib2.med.cornell.edu/Library/HTML/IntRes.html
From Cornell Medical School; provides constantly updated links to many medical and bioscience resources.

CENTERS FOR DISEASE CONTROL
http://ftp.cdc.gov/
The homepage of the famous virus hunters, with links to what they do, to search facilities, to other sites, and to a wide range of useful government data.

NATIONAL INSTITUTES OF HEALTH
http://www.nih.gov/
The central government organization dealing with health issues; site includes news, health information, grant descriptions, and links to scientific resources and to NIH suborganizations.

BUSINESS AND ECONOMICS

GALAXY BUSINESS GENERAL RESOURCES

http://www.einet.net/galaxy/Business-and-Commerce/Business-General-Resources.html

Links to a variety of resources for business; includes prices, statistics, trends, and general reading sources.

BUSINESS RESOURCE CENTER

http://www.morebusiness.com/

Specific links to advice about marketing, management, and financing. Also includes a search service.

SEC EDGAR DATABASE

http://www.sec.gov:80/edgarhp.htm

The Electronic Data Gathering, Analysis, and Retrieval system is the Securities and Exchange Commission's archive of business filings. Includes various search capabilities and a wide range of information.

INTERNATIONAL BUSINESS RESOURCES ON THE WWW

http://ciber.bus.msu.edu

Specializes in links to international business sites. Also offers keyword searches, browsing, and a variety of other links.

A BUSINESS RESEARCHER'S INTERESTS

http://www.brint.com/interest.html

Provides links to articles, papers, magazines, tools, and many other resources for "contemporary business, management, and information technology issues."

BUSINESS WEEK ONLINE

http://www.businessweek.com/

Offers online versions of some BW stories, quick news updates, stock and mutual-fund tracking data, and advertisements — some of which may, in fact, be useful.

BUSINESS AND ECONOMICS — SPECIAL FIELDS

http://bib10.sub.su.se/sam/sbspec.htm

An alphabetical list of links to many different resources, with an emphasis on economics and investment issues.

ECONOMICS WORKING PAPER ARCHIVE

http://econwpa.wustl.edu:80/Welcome.html

Working papers in economics, organized by subject areas, with many links to other sites and sources.

WEBEC

http://www.helsinki.fi/WebEc/

An award-winning site that attempts to categorize all the free information on economics available on the Web. Organized by area of economics, it is easily searchable and contains the valuable List of Economics Journals.

CHEMISTRY

BEGINNER'S GUIDE TO CHEMICAL ABSTRACTS

http://library.uwaterloo.ca/howto/howto12.html

Introduces users to the standard guide to chemical literature and shows how to do simple searches. A commercial site.

WWW VIRTUAL LIBRARY — CHEMISTRY

http://www.chem.ucla.edu/chempointers.html

Links to universities and organizations as well as to chemistry resources and other VLs. Especially useful are the links to gopher and FTP servers in chemistry.

CHEMCENTER

http://www.ChemCenter.org/

From the American Chemical Society; includes links to education, industry, publications, and searchable databases.

CIS-IU

http://www.indiana.edu/~cheminfo/cisindex.html

Chemical Information Sources from Indiana University is a guide to Internet and Web resources in chemistry; offers both alphabetical and keyword searches in a useful format.

MOLECULAR VISUALIZATION TOOLS AND SITES
http://www.indiana.edu/~cheminfo/mvts.html
Links to all the major Chime and RasMol sites as well as to various other free and commercial visualization sites.

THE ANALYTICAL CHEMISTRY SPRINGBOARD
http://www.anachem.umu.se/jumpstation.htm
Presents links to all the analytical chemistry resources on the Net, arranged by analytical techniques. Also includes lists of other Net and Web resources.

MANUAL AND COMPUTER-AIDED LITERATURE SEARCHING
http://www.brunel.ac.uk/depts/chem/ch361a/lect.htm
A long, detailed explanation of how to use the standard sources in chemical literature, by Dr. J. J. Gosper. Includes a section on Beilstein and full explication of CA and BIDS. Worth downloading.

ACSWEB
http://www.acs.org/
Provides searches of American Chemical Society resources as well as information on news, events, and publications.

BIOCHEMNET
http://schmidel.com/bionet.htm
Contains a directory and links to a variety of biology and chemistry sources, most of them oriented toward high school and college chemistry and education.

COMMUNICATION

ACA HOMEPAGE
http://www.americancomm.org/
The American Communication Association sponsors this full-coverage page, with links to the different subfields that make up communications, organized by field and by interest.

LINKS TO FRIENDLY COMMUNICATIONS HOMEPAGES
http://www.csufresno.edu/speechcomm/wscalink.htm
From the Western States Speech Association; provides easy access to many organizational homepages in communications.

APDA
http://www.mit.edu:8001/activities/debate/apdawww/pgone.html
The American Parliamentary Debate Association maintains this site for college and university debating, with links to members, officers, a newsletter, and other debating sites.

NATIONAL COMMUNICATION ASSOCIATION
http://www.natcom.org
Formerly the Speech Communication Association. The NCA site offers information on publications and conferences, links to sources, and related communication news and links.

CMU RHETORIC AND COMPOSITION
http://eserver.org/rhetoric/
A well-organized list of links to classical rhetoric, e-journals, writing centers, rhetoricians, and miscellaneous resources on the Net. An especially good collection of classical texts.

INVESTIGATIVE REPORTERS & EDITORS
http://www.ire.org
An organization dedicated to teaching the skills and issues of investigative journalism; the site's resource center includes a database of more than 11,000 abstracts of investigative articles.

LAUNCH PAD FOR JOURNALISTS
http://www.ccrc.wustl.edu/spj/resources.html
The Society of Professional Journalists produces this site.

COMMUNICATION STUDIES
http://www.lib.uiowa.edu/gw/comm/
From the University of Iowa; offers a wide range of links to listservs, journals, Web research, and electronic style guides, as well as to a broad range of fields from advertising through rhetoric.

ENGINEERING

IEEE SPECTRUM
http://www.spectrum.ieee.org/
Provides access to all major publications and resources of the Institute of Electrical and Electronics Engineers.

WWW VIRTUAL LIBRARY — ENGINEERING
http://arioch.gsfc.nasa.gov/wwwvl/engineering.html
Lists links to many relevant sources across engineering fields, including all the engineering VLs, from acoustic engineering to welding engineering. Includes information on standards, products, and institutions.

ICE — INTERNET CONNECTIONS FOR ENGINEERING
http://www.englib.cornell.edu/ice/ice-index.html
Links for all engineering disciplines; good for finding additional sources and bibliographic information.

WWW VIRTUAL LIBRARY — CHEMICAL ENGINEERING
http://www.che.ufl.edu/www-che/
Offers links to meetings, conferences, organizations, and information resources. Good specific subtopic list.

WWW VIRTUAL LIBRARY — CIVIL ENGINEERING
http://www.ce.gatech.edu/WWW-CE/home.html
Lists servers containing information on civil engineering, most of them from university programs.

ASCE'S CIVIL ENGINEERING DATABASE
http://www.pubs.asce.org/
Provides access to over 80,000 bibliographic and abstracted records in civil engineering since 1975.

WWW VIRTUAL LIBRARY — ELECTRICAL ENGINEERING
http://arioch.gsfc.nasa.gov/wwwvl/ee.html
A good place to start.

ELECTRONIC ENGINEERS' TOOLBOX
http://www.eetoolbox.com/ebox.htm
A search utility for specialized issues within electronics engineering. Provides links to both commercial and noncommercial resources.

INSTITUTE OF ELECTRICAL AND ELECTRONICS ENGINEERS
http://www.ieee.org/
Links to member services, related technical societies, search engines, databases, publications, and activities.

WWW VIRTUAL LIBRARY — MECHANICAL ENGINEERING
http://CDR.stanford.edu/html/WWW-ME/home.html
Provides good links to online services as well as the usual links to universities and societies.

HISTORY

HISTORICAL JOURNALS ONLINE
http://www.tntech.edu/www/acad/hist/journals.html
Links to many journals, book chapters, and reviews that can be accessed from the WWW. Not all journals are available online, but they can be sampled.

HISTORY SITES BY TIME PERIOD
http://www.tntech.edu/www/acad/hist/period.html
Provides access to many sites covering issues from ancient through contemporary history and links to other general sites.

HISTORY SITES BY SUBJECT
http://www.tntech.edu/www/acad/hist/subject.html
Offers links to subjects ranging from areas to methodologies.

HORUS'S WEB LINKS TO HISTORY RESOURCES
http://www.ucr.edu/h-gig/horuslinks.html
Provides a search engine for browsing databases.

THE HISTORY NET
http://www.theHistoryNet.com/
A project of the National Historical Society. Provides a historical magazine as well as a search service.

WWW VIRTUAL LIBRARY — HISTORY
http://history.cc.ukans.edu/history/WWW_specialized.html

Provides links to history servers by subject — General, Americas, Asia, Europe, Topics, and Organizations.

MODERN HISTORY
http://www.tntech.edu/www/acad/hist/modern.html
Texts, links, and documents on the period 1775 – 1945.

GATEWAY TO WORLD HISTORY
http://www.hartford-hwp.com/gateway/index.html
Supports searches for teachers and students of world history and allows links to more specific areas.

WORLD HISTORY ARCHIVES
http://www.hartford-hwp.com/archives/index.html
Offers access to actual versions of important texts in world history and many links to contemporary writings.

HISTORY — GEMS
http://galaxy.einet.net/GJ/history.html
Allows downloading of original archival documents from a variety of U.S. and world history sources.

EURODOCS
http://library.byu.edu/~rdh/eurodocs/homepage.html
Offers primary historical documents from western Europe; organized by country.

HISTORICAL TEXT ARCHIVE
http://www.msstate.edu/Archives/History/
Provides access to many world history texts; organized by both area and topic.

BEDFORD BOOKS HOME PAGE
http://www.bedfordstmartins.com
Provides an annotated list of links to history sites.

LITERATURE

IN OTHER WORDS: A LEXICON OF THE HUMANITIES
http://www.sil.org/humanities/index.html
Provides an interesting hyperlinked lexicon and glossary of major terms in literary criticism, rhetoric, and linguistics.

RESOURCES IN ENGLISH LANGUAGE AND LITERATURE
http://www.lib.cmich.edu/bibliographers/billmiles/english.htm
Offers many links to American studies, British literary studies, children's literature, and English literary studies in general. A useful place to begin research.

LITERARY RESOURCES ON THE NET
http://www.english.upenn.edu/~jlynch/Lit/
Allows you to search for literary materials on the Net, and provides a list of periodicals and genre-based categories to explore.

LITERARY RESOURCES — FEMINISM AND WOMEN'S LITERATURE
http://www.english.upenn.edu/~jlynch/Lit/women.html
Devoted entirely to women writers and feminist criticism.

PROJECT GUTENBERG MASTER INDEX
http://surf.germany.eu.net/bookland/classics/gutenberg/gutenberg.html
The best current index to PG texts, most of which are now in the public domain.

INTERNATIONAL GAY AND LESBIAN REVIEW
http://www.usc.edu/Library/oneigla/onepress/index.html
Provides abstracts and reviews of many books related to lesbian, gay, bisexual, and transgender studies.

AMERICAN STUDIES WEB
http://www.georgetown.edu/crossroads/asw/lit.html
Provides links to many elements of American studies, with an emphasis on literary texts, authors, approaches, genres, and associations.

ROMANCE LANGUAGES RESOURCE PAGE
http://humanities.uchicago.edu/romance/

Offers links to travel and study, research, university departments, and classroom help for those studying Romance languages.

FRENCH RESOURCES
http://blair.library.rhodes.edu/ForLanghtmls/french.html
Guide to French language, literature, and culture.

RESOURCES FOR RUSSIAN AND SLAVIC LANGUAGES AND LITERATURE
http://www.library.vanderbilt.edu/central/russian.html#russian
Links to Web sites, dictionaries, literary sites, e-journals, e-texts, departments, and professional organizations.

GERMAN RESOURCES
http://blair.library.rhodes.edu/ForLanghtmls/german.html
Links to sites, dictionaries, and texts in German.

MATHEMATICS

MATH ARCHIVES UNDERGRADS' PAGE
http://archives.math.utk.edu/undergraduates.html
Devoted to math issues of special interest to undergraduates. Includes societies, projects, research, competitions, and career issues.

MATH ARCHIVES BIBLIOGRAPHIES
http://archives.math.utk.edu/cgi-bin/bibliography.html
A list of bibliographies and subject links; supplements the Math Archives homepage.

THE MOST COMMON ERRORS IN UNDERGRADUATE MATHEMATICS
http://math.vanderbilt.edu/~schectex/commerrs/
From Eric Schecter at Vanderbilt University.

AMS MATHEMATICS ON THE WEB
http://www.ams.org/mathweb/
Offers literature guides and links both on- and off-line, references, topical guides, and links to individuals.

MATERIALS ORGANIZED BY MATHEMATICAL TOPICS
http://www.ams.org/mathweb/mi-mathbytopic.html
Links to specific issues in current mathematical work.

MATHSEARCH
http://www.maths.usyd.edu.au:8000/MathSearch.html
Searches over ninety thousand documents on English-language math and statistics servers, keying by phrase.

ERIC'S TREASURE TROVE OF MATHEMATICS
http://www.astro.virginia.edu/~eww6n/math/math.html
An alphabetical search list of important terms and concepts.

MUSIC

SIBELIUS ACADEMY MUSIC RESOURCES
http://www.siba.fi/Kulttuuripalvelut/music.html
Provides links to every aspect of music appreciation, production, and education.

UNIVERSITY OF MARYLAND MUSIC RESOURCES
http://www.lib.umd.edu/UMCP/MUSIC/LINKS.HTM
Provides electronic access to sources by composers, journals, indexes, libraries, and musicology and theory sites.

ONLINE RESOURCES IN MUSIC
http://www.ruf.rice.edu/~brownlib/music/music.html#hplibs
Links to databases, musicians, libraries, and publishers.

MUSIC SOURCES ON THE WEB
http://www.idbsu.edu/carol/music.htm
Organized by kinds of music.

WORLDWIDE INTERNET MUSIC RESOURCES
http://www.music.indiana.edu/music_resources/
A general list of links to musicians, composers, performance sites, genres, research, industry, and journals.

CLASSICAL MUSIC ON THE WEB
http://www.unc.edu/~baker/music.html
An "organized jumpstation" to the best classical music sites on the Web.

PHYSICS

PHYSICS NEWS
http://www.het.brown.edu/news/index.html
Lists latest work being done in physics, including NASA's Hot Topics *and the newsletter* The Scientist; *science news from wire services; and links to other journals and magazines.*

AIP PHYSICS INFORMATION
http://www.aip.org/
Links to societies, publications, career services, and databases from the American Institute of Physics.

HEPIC GLOBAL SEARCH
http://www.hep.net/search/global.html
Covers all the major electronic databases in physics, using a keyword search.

CONTEMPORARY PHYSICS EDUCATION PROJECT
http://pdg.lbl.gov/cpep.html
Provides links to several interactive explanations of fields in physics and lists of other sites.

THE NET ADVANCE OF PHYSICS
http://www.mit.edu/afs/athena.mit.edu/user/r/e/redingtn/www/netadv/welcome.html
Includes the Physicist's Encyclopedia, *a collection of review articles in physics arranged by subject.*

TIPTOP
http://www.tp.umu.se/TIPTOP/
Allows access to physics societies, databases, projects, news, and events.

AMERICAN PHYSICAL SOCIETY
http://www.aps.org/
Allows quick access to professional activities and databases.

WWW VIRTUAL LIBRARY — PHYSICS
http://www.fisk.edu/vl/Physics/Overview.html
Categorizes its links by subject.

US DEPARTMENT OF ENERGY
http://www.doe.gov/
Contains data on current research and developments in physics; subsidized by the Department of Energy.

THE NASA HOMEPAGE
http://www.nasa.gov/
Contains useful links to current NASA projects.

POLITICAL SCIENCE

POLITICAL SCIENCE VIRTUAL LIBRARY
http://spirit.lib.uconn.edu/PoliSci/polisci.htm
Links to departments, libraries, journals, government agencies, newsgroups and listservs, and related fields.

THOMAS: LEGISLATIVE INFORMATION ON THE INTERNET
http://thomas.loc.gov/
The homepage of the U.S. Congress, with links to current legislation, Congressional Record *archives, historical documents, and other government resources.*

THE WHITE HOUSE
http://www.whitehouse.gov/
The presidential site, with links to the president and vice-president, commonly requested federal services, news, a virtual library, and other executive-branch links.

FEDWORLD
http://www.fedworld.gov/
Links to government services and databases. Good search facilities and explanations, with information on how to order materials.

LEGAL INFORMATION INSTITUTE
http://www.law.cornell.edu/
A service of Cornell Law School. Access to recent and historic Supreme Court decisions and a hypertext version of all major federal laws. Good links to other central legal sites.

DEMOCRATIC PARTY ONLINE
http://www.democrats.org/
The homepage of the Democratic National Committee. Useful links to Democratic news, issues, and initiatives.

REPUBLICAN MAIN STREET
http://www.rnc.org/
The homepage of the Republican National Committee. Has many useful links, not all to party issues.

THE GALLUP ORGANIZATION
http:www.gallup.com/
The homepage of the organization, with short descriptions of some of its latest polls. No archive or search ability.

DTIC
http://www.dtic.mil
The Defense Technical Information Center is the U.S. military's own information service, with very detailed coverage of the Defense Technical Information Web and links to specific databases.

UNITED NATIONS
http://www.un.org/
A good general site, with links to many UN offices, policies, and activities. Also available in French and Spanish.

FOREIGN GOVERNMENT RESOURCES ON THE WEB
http://www.lib.umich.edu/libhome/Documents.center/foreign.html
Offers easy-to-find information about other countries and governments; organized by area or by governmental issue.

PSYCHOLOGY

AMERICAN PSYCHOLOGICAL ASSOCIATION
http://www.apa.org/
The APA homepage, with access to their PsychNet document site and information for students in psychology.

AMERICAN PSYCHOLOGICAL SOCIETY
http://psych.hanover.edu/APS/
Links to journals, departments, Net resources and discussion groups, and research information.

COGNITIVE AND PSYCHOLOGICAL SCIENCES ON THE NET
http://www-psych.stanford.edu/cogsci
Indexes resources on the Net that deal with research in cognition and psychology. Note that this site does not cover clinical psychology or mental health issues.

GALAXY PSYCHOLOGY PAGE
http://galaxy.einet.net/galaxy/Social-Sciences/Psychology.html
A large site divided into Clinical, Developmental, Educational, and Experimental lists. Also offers a search facility with links to academic organizations, collections, directories, and discussion groups.

FREUDNET: THE BRILL LIBRARY
http://plaza.interport.net/nypsan/
Psychoanalytic news, services, and links to electronic research.

NEUROPSYCHOLOGY CENTRAL
http://www.premier.net/~cogito/neuropsy.html
Links to almost any aspect of neuropsychology.

BEHAVIOR ANALYSIS RESOURCES
http://www.coedu.usf.edu/behavior/bares.htm
Links to resources in behavioral psychology.

INTERNET MENTAL HEALTH
http://www.mentalhealth.com/main.html
Links to the most common mental disorders and medications, news, diagnosis, and help.

SOCIOLOGY

SOCIAL SCIENCE SITES
http://www.tntech.edu/www/acad/hist/data.html
A historically weighted list of social sciences for general information.

SOCIAL WORK AND SOCIAL SERVICES WEB SITES
http://gwbweb.wustl.edu/
Information on abuse and violence, addiction, alternative medicine, emotional support, gender issues, and welfare.

SOCIOLOGICAL ABSTRACTS
http://www.socabs.org/
Provides links to other free sites in sociology.

WWW VIRTUAL LIBRARY — SOCIOLOGY
http://www.ixpres.com/lunatic/soc.html
Links to sites covering research centers, discussion groups, e-journals, organizations, and university departments.

ANNUAL REVIEWS SOCIOLOGY ON-LINE
http://www.annurev.org/soc/home.htm
Allows searches of twelve years' worth of databases for downloadable abstracts. Full articles can be ordered.

INTERNET/WEB RESOURCES FOR SOCIOLOGY
http://don.skidmore.edu/academics/sociology/soclinks.html
Offers links to sociology resources and areas of interest, including journals and listservs.

A SOCIOLOGICAL TOUR THROUGH CYBERSPACE
http://www.trinity.edu/~mkearl/index.html
Provides links within sociology, including theory, data, methods, paper-writing guides, and inquiry help.

THE SOCIOWEB
http://www.socioweb.com/~markbl/socioweb/
A general site of links and resources, including searches by topic.

ACA Rhetoric and Public Address Library

MEDIA
http://www.uark.edu/depts/comminfo/www/rhetoric.html
Maintained by the American Communication Association, this site links to speeches, literature, rhetoric, and guides to public speaking.

ARISTOTLE'S RHETORIC
gopher://gopher.vt.edu:10010/02/39/24
This text version of Aristotle's famous advice on how to properly present an argument explains why "some speakers succeed."

A BEGINNER'S GUIDE TO HTML
http://www.ncsa.uiuc.edu/General/Internet/WWW/HTMLPrimer.html
If you wish or need to learn the basics of HTML.

GRAPHION'S ONLINE TYPE MUSEUM
http://www.slip.net/~graphion/style.html
Good advice about indenting, using capitals, spacing, and leading. Hyperlinked definitions and examples round out the presentation.

A GLOSSARY OF TYPOGRAPHIC TERMS
http://www.slip.net/~graphion/gloss.html
A good starting point for anyone interested in design and layout in print and online venues.

A VISUAL THESAURUS
http://www.plumbdesign.com/thesaurus/
A strange and captivating site that gives a visual representation of synonyms; requires high-end computer with Java capability.

STATS EVERY WRITER SHOULD KNOW
http://nilesonline.com/stats/
This site describes writers' need for understanding and interpreting statistical data.

TEN COMMON TYPESETTING MISTAKES
http://vera.inforamp.net/~poynton/notes/typesetting/
This explanation of common typesetting mistakes made by those using word processors gives a good thumbnail guide to document planning and desktop publishing.

ADVICE ON WEB PAGE DESIGN
http://info.med.yale.edu/caim/manual/pages/page_design.html
Advice from the Yale C/AIM Web Style Guide, one of the most comprehensive guides of its kind.

THE BACKGROUND SAMPLER
http://www.fciencias.unam.mx/ejemplo/index_bkgr.html
Background patterns for Web sites.

THE ICON BROWSER
http://www.cli.di.unipi.it/iconbrowser/icons.html
Symbols and icons.

MULTIMEDIA AND CLIP ART
http://www.itec.sfsu.edu/multimedia/multimedia.html
Maintained at San Francisco State, this site features links to clip art, icons, and graphics.

WEBMUSEUM NETWORK
http://watt.emf.net/wm/net
Access to drawings and paintings from museums around the world.

YAHOO! GRAPHICS
http://www.yahoo.com/Computers_and_Internet/Graphics
Links to buttons, clip art, and other graphics.

For Multilingual Writers

THE VIRTUAL ENGLISH LANGUAGE CENTER
http://www.comenius.com
Provides an "idiom of the week," a "fable of the month," sound clips for pronunciation, online tests, pen-pal programs, and more.

DAVE'S ESL CAFÉ
http://www.eslcafe.com/
Games, activities, and — best of all — daily updates.

ENGLISH FOR THE INTERNET
http://www.study.com
Live chats, placement tests, and free English classes (which fill up quickly).

GRAMMAR SAFARI
http://deil.lang.uiuc.edu/web.pages/grammarsafari.html
Learn grammar in context, with thousands of examples of English words shown in the context of real-life communication.

SCHMOOZEU
http://schmooze.hunter.cuny.edu:8888/
A MOO devoted to practicing conversation.

WORDWATCH
http:www.wordsmith.org/awad/index.html
English vocabulary, with a new entry every day.

TEST YOUR ENGLISH
http://www.edunet.com/english/practice/test-ces.html
An 80-item test for those learning English. Post your answers and you'll receive the results via email.

AN ELEMENTARY GRAMMAR
http://www.hiway.co.uk/~ei/intro.html
Downloadable help sheets on verbs, prepositions, word order, and other important topics for multilingual writers.

Index

C

d

e

g

h

m

n

O

S

Y

Acknowledgments *(continued from copyright page)*

Citizens Trust. "Is Your Money Where Your Heart Is?" Mutual Fund ad. Courtesy of Citizens Trust, Portsmouth, NH 03801.
Craig R. Dean. Excerpt from "Legalize Gay Marriage." Originally published in *The New York Times.* Copyright ©1991 by The New York Times Company. Reprinted by permission of The New York Times.
Deja News. Website Newsgroups search page. Deja News™ is a registered trademark of Deja News Research Service, Inc. Copyright ©1995 - 98 Deja News, Inc. All rights reserved. Reproduced by permission of Deja News, Inc. Excite, Webcrawler, and the Webcrawler Logo are trademarks of Excite, Inc. and may be registered in various jurisdictions. Excite screen display copyright ©1995 - 1998 by Excite, Inc.
Emily Dickinson. Poems 435 and 1333 reprinted by permission of the publishers and the Trustees of Amherst College from *The Poems of Emily Dickinson,* Thomas H. Johnson, ed. Cambridge, MA: The Belknap Press of Harvard University Press. Copyright ©1951, 1955, 1979, 1983 by the President and Fellows of Harvard College.
Joan Didion. Excerpt from "Georgia O'Keeffe" in *The White Album* by Joan Didion. Copyright ©1979 by Joan Didion. Reprinted with the permission of Farrar, Straus & Giroux, Inc.
Robert Francis. "The Pitcher" from *The Orb Weaver* by Robert Francis. Copyright © 1960 by Robert Francis, Wesleyan University Press. Reprinted by permission of University Press of New England.
Robert Frost. "Fire and Ice" from *The Poetry of Robert Frost,* edited by Edward Connery Lathem. Copyright ©1951 by Robert Frost. Copyright ©1923, ©1969 by Henry Holt and Company, Inc. Reprinted by permission of Henry Holt and Company, Inc.
D. Letticia Galindo. Figure 4, "Spanish-English Bilingualism and the Language Shift Process" from p. 166 in *Language Variation in North American English,* ed. A. Wayne Glowka and Donald M. Lance. Copyright © 1993 by MLA.
Nikki Giovanni. Excerpt from *Racism 101* by Nikki Giovanni. Copyright ©1994 by Nikki Giovanni. Reprinted by permission of William Morrow & Company, Inc.
James A. Henretta et al. Figure 2: "Church Growth by Denomination, 1700 - 1780" from p. 119 in *America's History,* James A. Henretta et al., eds. Copyright ©1997 by Worth Publishers, Inc.
bell hooks. Excerpt from *Talking Back* by bell hooks. Copyright ©1989 by bell hooks. Reprinted by permission of South End Press.
A. E. Housman. "Loveliest of Trees" from *The Collected Poems of A. E. Housman* by A. E. Housman. Copyright 1939, 1940, 1965 by Henry Holt and Company, Inc., ©1967, 1968 by Robert E. Symons. Reprinted by permission of Henry Holt and Company, Inc.
Langston Hughes. "Theme for English B" from *Collected Poems* by Langston Hughes. Copyright ©1994 by the Estate of Langston Hughes. Reprinted by permission of Alfred A. Knopf, Inc.
Jeff Jarvis. "Monty" from *TV Guide,* February 5, 1994. ©News America Publications, Inc. Reprinted with permission from TV Guide.
June Jordan. Excerpt from "Aftermath" in *Naming Our Destiny* by June Jordan. Copyright © 1989 by June Jordan. Reprinted by permission of Thunder's Mouth Press.
Jewel Kilcher. From "Amen" by Jewel Kilcher. ©1995 WB Music Corp. (ASCAP) & Wiggly Tooth Music (ASCAP). All rights administered by WB Music Corp. All Rights Reserved. Used by permission of Warner Bros. Publications, U.S. Inc., Miami, FL 33014.
Martin Luther King Jr. Excerpt from "Our God Is Marching On" published in *Why We Can't Wait.* Copyright ©1963, 1964 by Martin Luther King Jr. Excerpt from "Letter from Birmingham Jail." Copyright ©1963 by Martin Luther King Jr., copyright renewed 1991 by Coretta Scott King. Reprinted by arrangement with The Heirs to the Estate of Martin Luther King Jr., c/o Writers House, Inc. as agent for the proprietor.
Mary McCarthy. From "A Tin Butterfly" (pp. 59 - 60) in *Memories of a Catholic Girlhood* by Mary McCarthy. Copyright 1951 and renewed 1979 by Mary McCarthy. Reprinted by permission of Harcourt Brace & Company.
Michael I. Miller. Table 1, "Word Choice by Race" from "How to Study Black Speech in Chicago" (p. 166) in *Language Variation in North American English,* ed. A. Wayne Glowka and Donald M. Lance. Copyright ©1993 by MLA. Reprinted by permission of the Modern Language Association of America.
Modern Language Association of America. "Film Hero" from *Modern Language Association's International Bibliography* on database. Reprinted by permission of the Modern Language Association of America.
Netsearch Web Page. Copyright ©1996 Netscape Communications Corp. Used with permission. All Rights Reserved. This electronic file or page may not be reprinted or copied without the express written permission of Netscape. Netscape Communications Corporation has not authorized, sponsored, endorsed, or approved this publication and is not responsible for

its content. Netscape and the Netscape Communications Corporate Logos are trademarks and trade names of Netscape Communications Corporation. All other product names and/or logos are trademarks of their respective owners.

The New York Times. "Productivity and Wages: 1982 - 1995" from *The New York Times,* January 2, 1996, C20. Copyright ©1996 by The New York Times Company. Reprinted by permission.

George Orwell. Excerpt from "Shooting an Elephant" in *Shooting an Elephant and Other Essays* by George Orwell. Copyright ©1950 by Sonia Brownell Orwell and renewed 1978 by Sonia Pitt-Rivers. Reprinted by permission of Harcourt Brace and Company. Copyright ©Mark Hamilton as the Literary Executor of the Estate of the late Sonia Brownell Orwell. By permission of Martin Secker & Warburg Ltd. and A. M. Heath & Co. Ltd.

PsycLIT Journal Articles 1991 – 6/97. Record 1 of 1. Reprinted with permission of the American Psychological Association, publisher of the PsychINFO® and PsycLIT® Databases. Copyright 1887 - 1998 by the American Psychological Association. All rights reserved. For more information contact <psychinfo@apa.org>.

Readers' Guide to Periodical Literature. "Heroes and Heroines in Motion Pictures." Copyright © The H. W. Wilson Company. Reprinted by permission of the publisher.

Richard Rodriguez. Excerpt from a postscript to *Aria: A Memoir of a Bilingual Childhood* by Richard Rodriguez. Copyright ©1980 by Richard Rodriguez. First published in *American Scholar.* Reprinted by permission of Georges Borchardt, Inc. for the author.

Carl Sagan. Excerpt from "The Nuclear Winter." Courtesy of the Estate of Carl Sagan.

Carl Sandburg. Excerpt from *Abraham Lincoln, The War Years,* Volume 1 by Carl Sandburg. Copyright ©1939 by Harcourt Brace & Company and renewed 1967 by Carl Sandburg. Reprinted by permission of the publisher.

Lewis Thomas. Excerpt from "The Attic of the Brain" from *Late Night on Listening to Mahler's Ninth* by Lewis Thomas. Copyright ©1980 by Lewis Thomas. Used by permission of Viking Penguin, a division of Penguin Putnam Inc.

Eudora Welty. Excerpt from *One Writer's Beginnings* by Eudora Welty. Copyright ©1983, 1984 by Eudora Welty. Reprinted by permission of Harvard University Press and Russell & Volkening as agents for the author.

Tom Wicker. Excerpt from article about J.F.K's assassination. *The New York Times,* November 22, 1963. Copyright ©1963 by The New York Times Company. Reprinted by permission.

Marie Winn. Excerpts from pp. 24, 141 in *The Plug-In Drug,* revised edition by Marie Winn. Copyright © 1977, 1985 by Marie Winn Miller. Used by permission of Viking Penguin, a division of Penguin Putnam Inc.

Richard Wright. Excerpt from *Black Boy* by Richard Wright. Copyright ©1937, 1942, 1944, 1945 by Richard Wright. Copyright renewed 1973 by Ellen Wright. Reprinted by permission of HarperCollins Publishers, Inc.

Yahoo! Screen prints from Yahoo! Web site. Copyright ©1994 - 1998 Yahoo! All Rights Reserved. This page may not be reprinted or copied without express written permission of Yahoo!

FAQs ABOUT ONLINE WRITING

Writing online has made communication faster and, in some ways, simpler than ever. But it has also raised a number of questions. You can find some of these questions — along with easy-to-understand answers — on the pages noted below.

PART II Mastering the Nuances of English

Chapter 53 Nouns and Noun Phrases

Chapter 54 Verbs and Verb Phrases

Chapter 55 Prepositions and Prepositional Phrases

Chapter 56 Clauses and Sentences

Notes in Other Sections of the Book

If You Speak . . .

ADVICE ABOUT KEY ASPECTS OF YOUR WRITING

REVISION SYMBOLS

abb	abbreviation *37*	**¶**	paragraph *6*
ad	adjective/adverb *12*	**/ /**	faulty parallelism *6d, 21*
agr	agreement *10, 11*	**para**	paraphrase *42c – e, 43d*
awk	awkward	**pass**	inappropriate passive *9, 23b*
cap	capitalization *36*	**ref**	unclear pronoun reference *13*
case	case *8*	**run-on**	run-on (fused) sentence *15*
cliché	cliché *27d*	**sexist**	sexist language *11d, 29a*
co	coordination *20a*	**shift**	shift *14*
coh	coherence *6d, 19a*	**slang**	slang *27a*
com	incomplete comparison *12d*	**sp**	spelling *24*
concl	weak conclusion *4f, 6d, 43c*	**sub**	subordination *20b*
cs	comma splice *15*	**sum**	summarize *42c – e*
d	diction *27*	**t**	tone *4g, 27a, 27d, 42b*
def	define *3d, 6e*	**trans**	transition *6d, 6f – h, 22b*
dev	development needed *6e*	**u**	unity *6c, 19a*
dm	dangling modifier *17c*	**verb**	verb form *9a – c*
doc	documentation *44, 45, 46, 47*	**vs**	verb sequence *9g*
emph	emphasis unclear *19a*	**vt**	verb tense *9d – h*
ex	example needed *3d, 6e*	**wv**	weak verb *23a*
frag	sentence fragment *16*	**wrdy**	wordy *19b*
fs	fused sentence *15*	**ww**	wrong word *4g, 27a – b*
hyph	hyphen *39*	**. ? !**	period, question mark, exclamation point *32*
inc	incomplete construction *18b – e*	**,**	comma *30*
intro	weak introduction *4f, 6f, 43c*	**;**	semicolon *31*
it	italics (or underlining) *38*	**’**	apostrophe *33*
jarg	jargon *27a*	**“ ”**	quotation marks *34*
lc	lowercase letter *36e*	**( ) [ ] —**	parentheses, brackets, dash *35*
log	logic *5g*	**: / ...**	colon, slash, ellipses *35*
lv	language variety *28*	**^**	insert
mix	mixed construction *18a*	**∼**	transpose
mm	misplaced modifier *17a*	**⌒⌣**	close up
ms	manuscript form *51*	**X**	obvious error
no ,	no comma *30j*		
num	number *37*		

Contents